THE ROUTLEDGE COMPANION TO MEDIA, SEX AND SEXUALITY

The Routledge Companion to Media, Sex and Sexuality is a vibrant and authoritative exploration of the ways in which sex and sexualities are mediated in modern media and everyday life.

The 40 chapters in this volume offer a snapshot of the remarkable diversification of approaches and research within the field, bringing together a diverse mix of scholars and researchers from around the world and from different disciplinary backgrounds, including cultural studies, education, history, media studies, sexuality studies and sociology.

The volume includes research from around the world to offer readers a broad array of global and transnational issues and intersectional perspectives, as authors address a series of important questions that have consequences for current and future thinking in the field. Topics explored include postfeminism, masculinities, media industries, queer identities, video games, media activism, music video, sexualization, celebrities, sport, sex-advice books, pornography and erotica and social and mobile media.

The Routledge Companion to Media, Sex and Sexuality is an essential guide to the central ideas, concepts and debates currently shaping research in mediated sexualities and the connections between conceptions of sexual identity, bodies and media technologies.

Clarissa Smith is Professor of Sexual Cultures at the University of Sunderland. A founding co-editor of the Routledge journal *Porn Studies*, Clarissa's research is focused on representations of sex and sexuality and their production and consumption. Publications include numerous articles and chapters exploring the specificities of pornographic imagery, forms of stardom, production and regulation.

Feona Attwood is Professor in Cultural Studies, Communication and Media at Middlesex University. Her research is in the area of sex in contemporary culture and, in particular, sexual cultures; new technologies, identity and the body; and controversial media. Her recent publications have focused on online sexual cultures, aesthetics, sex and the media and public engagement. She is currently writing a book entitled *Sex Media and Technology*. She is the co-editor of *Sexualities* journal and founding co-editor of the journal *Porn Studies*.

Brian McNair is Professor of Journalism, Media and Communication within the Creative Industries Faculty at Queensland University of Technology. His research and teaching interests include journalism, political communication and mediated sexuality. Brian is a regular media commentator across print, online and broadcast platforms. He has written more than 400 commentary articles for publications including *The Guardian*, *The Conversation*, *The Age*, *The Herald* and *Scotland on Sunday*.

Contributors: Kath Albury, Feona Attwood, Meg-John Barker, Rebecca Beirne, Ashley M. L. Brown, Kristina Busse, Paul Byron, Allison J. Carr, Karli June Cerankowski, Despina Chronaki, Frederik Dhaenens, Adrienne Evans, Maria San Filippo, Rosalind Gill, Kristina Gupta, Laura Harvey, Amy Adele Hasinoff, Neil Jackson, Steve Jones, Dion Kagan, Misha Kavka, Ummni Khan, Danielle J. Lindemann, Kate Lister, Gareth Longstaff, Alexis Lothian, Alan McKee, Brian McNair, Anna Madill, Giovanna Maina, John Mercer, Claire Moran, Sharif Mowlabocus, Gary Needham, Susanna Paasonen, Diane Railton, Barry Reay, Niall Richardson, Catherine M. Roach, Lauren Rosewarne, Clarissa Smith, Eliza Steinbock, Elizabeth Stephens, Holly Thorpe, Sofie Van Bauwel, Anne-Frances Watson, Angela Gabrielle White and Federico Zecca

THE ROUTLEDGE COMPANION TO MEDIA, SEX AND SEXUALITY

*Edited by Clarissa Smith and Feona Attwood
with Brian McNair*

LONDON AND NEW YORK

First published 2018
by Routledge
2 Park Square, Milton Park, Abingdon, Oxon OX14 4RN

and by Routledge
711 Third Avenue, New York, NY 10017

Routledge is an imprint of the Taylor & Francis Group, an informa business

© 2018 Clarissa Smith, Feona Attwood with Brian McNair

The right of Clarissa Smith, Feona Attwood with Brian McNair to be identified as the authors of the editorial material, and of the authors for their individual chapters, has been asserted in accordance with sections 77 and 78 of the Copyright, Designs and Patents Act 1988.

All rights reserved. No part of this book may be reprinted or reproduced or utilised in any form or by any electronic, mechanical, or other means, now known or hereafter invented, including photocopying and recording, or in any information storage or retrieval system, without permission in writing from the publishers.

Trademark notice: Product or corporate names may be trademarks or registered trademarks, and are used only for identification and explanation without intent to infringe.

British Library Cataloguing in Publication Data
A catalogue record for this book is available from the British Library

Library of Congress Cataloging in Publication Data
A catalog record for this title has been requested

ISBN: 978-1-138-77721-7 (hbk)
ISBN: 978-1-315-16830-2 (ebk)

Typeset in Goudy
by Sunrise Setting Ltd., Brixham, UK

Printed in the United Kingdom
by Henry Ling Limited

CONTENTS

List of figures and tables ix
List of contributors x

Introduction 1
Clarissa Smith and Feona Attwood

PART I
Representing sexualities 5

1 The normal body on display: public exhibitions of the Norma and Normman statues 7
  Elizabeth Stephens

2 Asexualities and media 19
  Kristina Gupta and Karli June Cerankowski

3 Representing trans sexualities 27
  Eliza Steinbock

4 Representing lesbians in film and television 38
  Rebecca Beirne

5 Representing gay sexualities 49
  Sharif Mowlabocus

6 Fifty shades of ambivalence: BDSM representation in pop culture 59
  Ummni Khan

7   The politics of fluidity: representing bisexualities in
    twenty-first-century screen media   70
    Maria San Filippo

8   Heterosexual casual sex: from free love to Tinder   81
    Kath Albury

9   Representing queer sexualities   91
    Dion Kagan

PART II
Sex genres   **105**

10 Erotica   107
    Catherine M. Roach

11 A history of slash sexualities: debating queer sex, gay politics
    and media fan cultures   117
    Kristina Busse and Alexis Lothian

12 Erotic manga: Boys' Love, *shonen-ai*, *yaoi* and (MxM) *shotacon*   130
    Anna Madill

13 Ways of showing it: feature and gonzo in mainstream
    pornography   141
    Federico Zecca

14 From the scene, for the scene! Alternative pornographies
    in contemporary US production   151
    Giovanna Maina

15 'Not on public display': the art/porn debate   163
    Gary Needham

16 User-generated pornography: amateurs and the ambiguity
    of authenticity   174
    Susanna Paasonen

17 Celebrity sex tapes   183
    Gareth Longstaff

18 The media panic about teen sexting   193
    Amy Adele Hasinoff

19	Sex advice books and self-help Meg-John Barker, Rosalind Gill and Laura Harvey	202
20	Social media platforms and sexual health Paul Byron	214
21	Young people, sexuality education and the media Anne-Frances Watson	223

PART III
Representing sex   237

22	Videogames and sex Ashley M. L. Brown	239
23	Sex and celebrity media Adrienne Evans	248
24	Sex and music video Diane Railton	259
25	Debating representations of sexuality in advertising Despina Chronaki	268
26	Media representations of women in action sports: more than 'sexy bad girls' on boards Holly Thorpe	279
27	Sex and horror Steve Jones	290
28	Sex in sitcoms: unravelling the discourses on sex in *Friends* Frederik Dhaenens and Sofie Van Bauwel	300
29	Sex and reality TV: the pornography of intimate exposure Misha Kavka	309
30	It's all about your sex appeal: deconstructing the sexual content in women's magazines Claire Moran	319

31	The Invisibles: disability, sexuality and new strategies of enfreakment Niall Richardson	328

PART IV
Deconstructing key figures — **341**

32	The metrosexual John Mercer and Feona Attwood	343
33	The sex addict Barry Reay	352
34	The stripper Alison J. Carr	362
35	The pen is mightier than the whore: Victorian newspapers and the sex-work saviour complex Kate Lister	371
36	The pornography consumer as Other Alan McKee	383
37	The porn performer Angela Gabrielle White	394
38	The dominatrix Danielle J. Lindemann	405
39	The pervert Lauren Rosewarne	416
40	The pornographer Neil Jackson	428
	Index	438

FIGURES AND TABLES

Figures

1.1 Dickinson and Belskie's Normman and Norma statues, 1945. Courtesy of the Warren Anatomical Museum in the Francis A. Countway Library of Medicine. Photograph by Samantha van Gerbig, Collection of Historical Scientific Instruments, Harvard University.   8
1.2 Search for Norma competition winner, Martha Skidmore, next to the Norma statue, 1945. Image courtesy of The Cleveland Museum of Natural History.   15
9.1 The Pansy: Peter Lorre as noir villain Joel Cairo in *The Maltese Falcon* (1941).   95
9.2 The femme: Eve Harrington (Anne Baxter) perversely imitates Margo Channing (Bette Davis) in *All About Eve* (1950).   96
9.3 Gothic butch: Mrs. Danvers (Judith Anderson) in *Rebecca* (1940).   97
9.4 Hitchcock's iconic demented queer: Norman Bates in *Psycho* (1960).   98
9.5 The (chaste) New Gay Man: Julia Roberts and Rupert Everett in *My Best Friend's Wedding* (1997).   100
9.6 Richie (Raúl Castillo) and Patrick (Jonathan Groff) being 'normal' and 'boring' in *Looking*.   101
25.1 Pamela Anderson leading a creative team meeting.   272
25.2 Close-ups of the girl-to-girl fantasy.   272
25.3 The advertisement for Kraft's Zesty sauce.   274
25.4 *Beauté* and *Cadeaux* front pages.   275
33.1 *Ricki Lake* (2004): female sex addicts.   356
33.2 *Sex Rehab with Dr. Drew* (2009): the money shot.   358
33.3 *Sex Rehab with Dr. Drew* (2009): the concerned doctor.   359
35.1 Nineteenth-century newspapers in circulation.   375
35.2 Use of synonyms for 'sex worker' in British newspapers.   376

Table

13.1 Feature pornography/gonzo pornography.   147

CONTRIBUTORS

Kath Albury is Associate Professor at the University of New South Wales, Sydney. Kath's work explores theoretical and applied understandings of mediated sexual self-representation, sexual sub-cultures and alternative sex practices, young people's mediated sexual cultures and the primary prevention of sexual violence. Her current research projects focus on young people's practices of digital self-representation and the role of user-generated media (including social networking platforms) in young people's formal and informal sexual learning.

Feona Attwood is Professor in Cultural Studies, Communication and Media at Middlesex University. Her research is in the area of sex in contemporary culture and, in particular, sexual cultures; new technologies, identity and the body; and controversial media. Her recent publications have focused on online sexual cultures, aesthetics, sex and the media and public engagement. She is writing a book entitled *Sex Media and Technology*. She is the co-editor of *Sexualities* journal and founding co-editor of the journal *Porn Studies*.

Meg-John Barker is a writer, therapist and activist-academic specialising in sex, gender and relationships. Meg-John is a senior lecturer in psychology at the Open University and a UKCP-accredited psychotherapist and has more than a decade of experience researching and publishing on her specialist topics, including the popular books *Rewriting the Rules*, *The Secrets of Enduring Love* and *Queer: A Graphic History*. Website: www.rewriting-the-rules.com. Twitter: @megjohnbarker.

Rebecca Beirne is a senior lecturer in film, television and cultural studies at the University of Western Sydney and has authored multiple essays discussing queer representation on television. She is also the author of *Lesbians in Television* and *Text after the Millennium* and its follow-up *Lesbians in World Cinema*.

Ashley M. L. Brown is Assistant Professor of Entertainment Arts and Engineering at the University of Utah. Her research interests are sex, sexuality and gaming. She is the author of *Sexuality in Role-Playing Games*.

Contributors

Kristina Busse has a PhD in English from Tulane University and is an active acafan. She is a co-editor of several fan-studies collections and author of the forthcoming *Fan Fiction as Literary and Social Practice*. Kristina is co-founder and editor of *Transformative Works and Culture* and on the Board of Directors for the Organization for Transformative Works.

Paul Byron (PhD) is a researcher at the University of Technology, Sydney, and teaches sociology/gender studies at Macquarie University. His research interests encompass young people's sexual health, digital intimacies, friendship and social-media practices of gender and sexuality diversities.

Alison J. Carr is an artist, writer, Iyengar yoga teacher and associate lecturer at Sheffield Hallam University. She has an MFA from the California Institute of the Arts and a PhD from Sheffield Hallam University. Her research interests include embodiment, showgirls, bodily display and pleasure. She is currently preparing a book for publication in 2017.

Karli June Cerankowski teaches in the Feminist, Gender, and Sexuality Studies Program at Stanford University. Karli is the co-editor of the volume *Asexualities: Feminist and Queer Perspectives* and has published articles in *Feminist Studies* and *WSQ* (*Women's Studies Quarterly*).

Despina Chronaki is a visiting lecturer at the faculty of Communication and Media Studies (National and Kapodistrian University of Athens). Her current interests involve children and the media, pornography, childhood and sexuality, sexuality, drag culture and audiences. She has published on children's experiences with sexual content, pornography consumption and production in Greece and drag culture (https://cut.academia.edu/DespinaChronaki).

Frederik Dhaenens is a member of CIMS (Centre for Cinema and Media Studies) and a post-doctoral researcher at Ghent University, Belgium. His research is situated within the field of critical media studies, cultural studies and gender studies, and focuses on popular media culture, LGBT representations and fan practices.

Adrienne Evans is Principal Lecturer in Media and Communications at Coventry University (UK). Her past research has explored sexiness; her current work develops accounts of digital culture, postfeminist masculinity and healthism. Her co-authored books include *Technologies of Sexiness: Sex, Identity and Consumer Culture* (2014) and *Postfeminism and Health* (forthcoming).

Maria San Filippo is Assistant Professor of Communication and Media Studies at Goucher College, and author of *The B Word: Bisexuality in Contemporary Film and Television* (2013), winner of a Lambda Literary Award. Her new book project examines sexual provocation in twenty-first-century screen media.

Rosalind Gill is Professor of Social and Cultural Analysis at City, University of London. She is the author or editor of several books, including *Gender and the Media* (2007), *Aesthetic Labour: Beauty Politics in Neoliberalism* (2017, with Ana Elias and Christina Scharff) and *Mediated Intimacy: Sex Advice in Media Culture* (2017, with Meg-John Barker and Laura Harvey).

Kristina Gupta is Assistant Professor in the Department of Women's, Gender, and Sexuality Studies at Wake Forest University. Her areas of interest include gender, science and medicine and contemporary asexual identities. Her work on asexuality has been published in *Signs*, the *Journal of Homosexuality* and the *Journal of Sex & Marital Therapy*, among others.

Laura Harvey is Lecturer in Sociology at the University of Brighton. Her interests include youth cultures, sexualities, everyday inequalities, research with young people, feminist methodologies and discourse analysis. She is particularly interested in the development of innovative qualitative methods for researching mundane, everyday experiences.

Amy Adele Hasinoff is Assistant Professor in the communication department at the University of Colorado Denver. Her book *Sexting Panic* (2015) is about the well-intentioned but problematic responses to sexting in mass media, law and education.

Neil Jackson is Lecturer in Film Studies at the University of Lincoln, UK. He is co-editor (with Shaun Kimber, Thomas Joseph Watson and Johnny Walker) of *Snuff: Real Death and Screen Media* (2016). His chapter on the 1981 film *Exhausted: John C. Holmes, the Real Story* appeared in *Grindhouse: Cultural Exchange on 42nd Street and Beyond* (2016) and he has contributed an article on the 1972 film *Forced Entry* to the journal *Porn Studies* (2017). He is currently working on a study of exploitation films and the Vietnam War, and researching the exhibition of global exploitation films in British cinemas.

Steve Jones is Senior Lecturer in Social Sciences at Northumbria University, England. His research principally focuses on sex, violence, ethics and selfhood within horror and pornography. His work has been published in *Feminist Media Studies*, *Porn Studies*, *Sexuality & Culture*, *Sexualities* and *Film-Philosophy*. For more information, please visit www.drstevejones.co.uk.

Dion Kagan is an early career researcher and lecturer at the School of Culture and Communication, University of Melbourne, working across Cultural, Screen and Gender Studies, with a particular research focus on media practices and sexuality. Dion has a doctorate in Cultural Studies. His book *Positive Images: Gay Men and the Culture of Post-Crisis* is to be published by I.B. Tauris. Dion also writes on film, TV, theatre, books, sexuality and popular culture for *Australian Book Review*, *The Big Issue*, *The Conversation*, *Metro* and *Kill Your Darlings*, as well as writing a regular queer column for *The Lifted Brow*. Dion is also a regular co-host on fortnightly Australian culture podcast *The Rereaders*.

Misha Kavka is Associate Professor of Media and Communication at the University of Auckland. She is the author of *Reality Television, Affect and Intimacy* (2008) and *Reality TV* (2012), and has published widely on affect in relation to film, television and media technologies.

Ummni Khan is an Associate Professor in Law, and Joint Chair in Women's Studies at Carleton University and the University of Ottawa. Her research addresses the construction of sexual deviancy in relation to gender, racialisation, class and disability, along with other axes of difference. Her book *Vicarious Kinks: SM in the Socio-Legal Imaginary* examines the regulation of BDSM in law, psychiatry, feminism and film.

Contributors

Danielle J. Lindemann is an Assistant Professor of Sociology at Lehigh University. Her research focuses on non-normative expressions of gender and sexuality, particularly as they relate to work and occupations. She is the author of *Dominatrix* (2012).

Kate Lister heads up a research team at Leeds Trinity University, researching sexual violence in contemporary culture. She has published in the fields of Victorian studies and gender studies, and has several publications in the field of gender and representations of sexual violence in historical dramas. Kate also curates the Twitter feed @WhoresofYore. The feed has been a significant success, gathering 68,000 followers to date.

Gareth Longstaff is a lecturer in media and cultural studies at Newcastle University. Both his teaching and his research interests are primarily concerned with queer sexuality, celebrity, discourses of self-representation, pornography and psychoanalysis. Gareth works at the intersection of how these are connected to other dimensions of queer, cultural, philosophical, mediated and social life, and in his upcoming monograph, *Bodies that Stutter: Celebrity, Pornography and the Psychoanalysis of Self Representation*, his approach to these issues engages and applies queer theory and Lacanian psychoanalysis to the impersonality of desire and the mediated screening of celebrity in self-representational photography, pornography/sexual representation and digital/networked media.

Alexis Lothian is Assistant Professor in the Department of Women's Studies and Core Faculty in the Design Cultures and Creativity Program at University of Maryland College Park. Her scholarship is situated at the intersection of queer studies, speculative fiction and social justice in digital culture. She is completing a book manuscript entitled *Old Futures: The Queer Cultural Politics of Speculative Fiction*, which will be published by NYU Press, and has published in venues that include *Poetics Today, International Journal of Cultural Studies, Cinema Journal, Camera Obscura, Social Text Periscope, Journal of Digital Humanities, Extrapolation* and *Ada: A Journal of Gender, New Media, and Technology*.

Alan McKee is an expert on entertainment and healthy sexual development. He has been awarded an ARC Discovery grant to bring together contradictory research data on pornography produced by different academic disciplines. He also holds an ARC Linkage with True (previously known as Family Planning Queensland) to investigate the use of vulgar comedy to reach young men with information about healthy sexual development, and he was co-editor of the *Girlfriend Guide to Life*. He has published on healthy sexual development, the effects of pornography on young people and entertainment education for healthy sexuality in journals including *Archives of Sexual Behavior*, the *International Journal of Sexual Health*, the *Journal of Sex Research* and *Sex Education*. He is Associate Dean (Research and Development) in the Faculty of Arts and Social Sciences at UTS.

Brian McNair is Professor of Journalism, Media & Communication within the Creative Industries Faculty at Queensland University of Technology. His research and teaching interests include journalism, political communication and mediated sexuality. Brian is a regular media commentator across print, online and broadcast platforms. He has written more than 400 commentary articles for publications including *The Guardian, The Conversation, The Age, The Herald* and *Scotland on Sunday*.

Anna Madill is Chair in Qualitative Inquiry, University of Leeds, UK. Anna is a Fellow of the British Psychological Society and of the Academy of Social Sciences. Her BL research is funded by the British Academy and her publications include 'Boys' Love manga for girls: paedophilic, satirical, queer readings and English law' in *Children, Sexuality and Sexualization* (2015).

Giovanna Maina is Research Fellow at the University of Sassari (Italy) and co-editor of *Porn Studies*. Her research interests are contemporary pornographies and Italian genre cinema. She co-edited *Porn After Porn* (2014, with Enrico Biasin and Federico Zecca) and coordinates the Porn Studies Section of the Gorizia Spring School (Italy).

John Mercer is Professor of Gender and Sexuality at Birmingham City University and is the author of *Gay Porn: Representations of Masculinity and Sexuality* (2017). He is co-editor of the *Journal of Gender Studies* and one of the editorial founders of *Porn Studies*. His research interests concern the politics of representation, in particular sexual representation, the connections between gay pornography and the making of a gay identity, the social and cultural construction of masculinities, performances of gender in the media and the wider culture and melodrama, emotion and affect in the media and their gendered modes of address.

Claire Moran has recently completed her PhD Health Psychology, with a focus on women's sexual health. She is currently an Honorary Research Fellow at the University of Queensland.

Sharif Mowlabocus is Senior Lecturer in Digital Media at the University of Sussex. His research explores sexual cultures in digital environments. His monograph *Gaydar Culture* was published by Ashgate in 2010. His recent research has focused on issues of sexual health, identity and representation in the context of digital media.

Gary Needham is Senior Lecturer in Film and Media at the University of Liverpool. He is the author of *Brokeback Mountain* (2010) and the co-editor of *Asian Cinemas* (2009), *Queer TV* (2009) and *Warhol in Ten Takes* (2013). He is currently working on a book about Andy Warhol and Edie Sedgwick.

Susanna Paasonen is Professor of Media Studies at University of Turku, Finland. Her work has revolved around internet research, affect theory and pornography for the past decade or more. Recently her interests have been shifting towards materiality, media and affect more generally, yet without abandoning porn altogether. She is currently working on the effect of technological failure, monster toon porn, theories of boredom and distraction connected to networked media, the films of Jan Soldat and the notion of sexual play, as well as preparing a book on the hashtag #NSFW together with Kylie Jarrett and Ben Light.

Diane Railton is Senior Lecturer in English Studies at Teesside University. Her research interests are in gender and popular culture, with a particular focus on music video. She co-authored *Music Video and the Politics of Representation* (2011) and is currently working on a paper on Beyoncé's album *Lemonade*.

Barry Reay holds the Keith Sinclair Chair in History at the University of Auckland, New Zealand. His books include *Sexualities in History: A Reader* (2001), *New York Hustlers:*

Masculinity and Sex in Modern America (2010), *Sex before Sexuality: A Premodern History* (2011) and *Sex Addiction: A Critical History* (2015).

Niall Richardson teaches film, media and cultural studies at the University of Sussex, where he is convenor of MA Gender and Media. He is the author of the monographs *The Queer Cinema of Derek Jarman* (2009) and *Transgressive Bodies: Representations in Film and Popular Culture* (2010).

Catherine M. Roach is Professor of Gender and Culture Studies in New College at The University of Alabama in Tuscaloosa, USA. She is the author of *Happily Ever After: The Romance Narrative in Popular Culture* (2016) and *Stripping, Sex, and Popular Culture* (2007). In 2013–14 she held the Fulbright Distinguished Chair in the Centre for Interdisciplinary Gender Studies at the University of Leeds (UK). She writes romance fiction under the pen name Catherine LaRoche; her first novel, *Master of Love*, was published in 2012, with *Knight of Love* following in 2014.

Lauren Rosewarne is Senior Lecturer at the University of Melbourne, Australia. She writes and teaches on gender, sexuality, politics and pop culture. Lauren has authored eight books, most recently *Intimacy on the Internet: Media Representations of Online Connections* (2016).

Clarissa Smith is Professor of Sexual Cultures at the University of Sunderland. A founding co-editor of the Routledge journal *Porn Studies*, Clarissa's research is focused on representations of sex and sexuality and their production and consumption. Publications include numerous articles and chapters exploring the specificities of pornographic imagery, forms of stardom, production and regulation. She is particularly interested in consumption of pornography and how different audiences engage with and make sense of sexual representations.

Eliza Steinbock (Assistant Professor Film and Literary Studies, Postdoctoral Fellow at Leiden University's Centre for the Arts in Society) publishes on trans* cultural production, porn/sexualities and contemporary mediascapes, including essays in the *Journal of Homosexuality*, *Photography and Culture*, *TSQ: Transgender Studies Quarterly*, *Spectator*, *Feminist Media Studies* and multiple edited volumes. www.elizasteinbock.com

Elizabeth Stephens is Associate Professor in Cultural Studies and Deputy Head of School (Research) in the School of Arts and Social Sciences at Southern Cross University. Her research focuses on philosophies and histories of the body, informed by gender studies, queer theory and French post-structuralism. Elizabeth is currently working on two monographs: *A Critical Genealogy of Normality* and *Twentieth-Century Sensorium: Bodily Technologies and the Training of the Senses* (funded by the ARC).

Holly Thorpe is Senior Lecturer and a researcher at the University of Waikato, New Zealand. Her areas of expertise include the sociology of youth culture, action sports, travel and tourism, gender and social theory.

Sofie Van Bauwel is Associate Professor in the Department of Communication Studies at Ghent University, where she teaches on cultural media studies, gender and media and television studies. She is part of the CIMS and her main field of interest is gender, media and film and television. She is involved in several projects with a focus on the media as signifying articulations in visual popular culture. She was vice-chair of the Gender and Communication section of the European Research and Communication Association (ECREA, 2006–12) and is part of the editorial board of the *Journal of Media Theory*. She is also co-editor of the working papers *Film and Television Studies* and publishes internationally and nationally on popular media culture, feminist theory and film.

Anne-Frances Watson is a lecturer in Media and Communication in the Creative Industries Faculty at Queensland University of Technology. Anne's research areas of interest are sex and sexuality, adolescent sexuality and sexuality education, with a particular interest in mediated sexuality and the media as a source of sexuality information.

Angela Gabrielle White is an AVN, XBIZ and XRCO award-winning adult performer, director and producer. She holds a degree with first-class honours in gender studies from the University of Melbourne, Australia. Now based in Los Angeles, White runs her own adult production company, AGW Entertainment. Her research interests include gender theory, queer theory and the qualitative study of performer experiences in the adult film industry.

Federico Zecca is Senior Lecturer at the University of Bari 'Aldo Moro' (Italy) and editor of *Cinergie*, *Cinéma & Cie* and *Bianco e Nero*. His main research interests are intermediality, contemporary pornographies, Italian popular cinema and media convergence. He coordinates the Porn Studies Section of the Gorizia Spring School (Italy). He recently co-edited a special section on gonzo pornography for *Porn Studies*.

INTRODUCTION

Clarissa Smith and Feona Attwood

Across the political spectrum, scholars and activists have noted the ways in which sex became the 'big story' of the twentieth century, and that importance shows no signs of abating into the new millennium. In this companion we explore representations of sex and sexuality in the media, recognising the various mediations of sex and sexuality across various platforms, and how some forms of media are themselves practices of sex. Explorations of sex and sexuality have always been complex, but as we see the spread of new media technologies, so too do we need more nuance and multifaceted understandings.

The Routledge Companion to Media, Sex and Sexuality identifies and engages with a series of issues, ideas and themes currently shaping the field of media and sexuality studies and activism from a broad range of conceptual and methodological approaches drawn from research around the world. It argues for the importance of fostering an international dialogue among media and sexuality researchers and activists so as to broaden and deepen our understanding of the many and varied relationships between media and sexuality in international, global and transnational terms. One of the central aims of this volume is to reinvigorate debates around media, sex and sexuality in order to draw on advances in studies of pornography and other sexually explicit media, online sexual cultures and the intersections between these and the spaces and places of media considered mainstream.

This is not to trace a history of movement from repression and displacement to full exposure and expression. Much progress has been made in widening media representations of sexualities. Fictional representations, especially films and television dramas, evidence growing interest in exploring sexual identifications and it is fair to say we see more lesbian- and gay-identified characters than ever before. Even so, such characters are still absolutely outnumbered by heterosexual roles, and almost always are greeted with a great deal of brouhaha which suggests we're still not entirely comfortable with 'alternative lifestyles' even as images. Reality television and documentaries have explored the complexities of sexual desire and sexual identification while there has been a notable increase in the availability of sexual material on the high street and on the internet, ranging from what some have termed the 'pornographication' of print media to the mainstreaming of sex aids and sex toys. In the past decade and a half, the film *Brokeback Mountain* (dir. Ang Lee: 2005), which portrays (relatively) explicit same-sex sexual activity between two men, attained recognition at the box office and won numerous Academy Awards, so it may seem as if we have moved into a new era that recognises sexual diversity and the freedom to explore sexual choices.

This companion is composed of 40 original chapters commissioned from both established authors and emerging scholars. Given our aim to reinvigorate current debates in relation to media, sex and sexuality research, we have sought authors whose innovative thinking reflects cutting-edge developments. The chapters are divided into four sections. Each chapter addresses a concrete set of issues in order to illuminate important aspects of the relationships between media, sex and sexuality. We feel this companion offers a unique and important contribution to the on-going theoretical, conceptual and methodological development of media, sex and sexuality research.

The chapters in Part I, 'Representing sexualities', provide a historical context to the issues, academic debates and political developments which have shaped the field of media and sexuality research. Our focus here is on the representation of particular sexual orientations or identities and how ideas of the 'normal' are contested even as they are often assumed to be culturally ubiquitous. In each of the chapters in this section, our authors open up questions around compulsory sexuality, heteronormativity, visibility and invisibility in order to offer new insights about media representations of hetero- and homo-sexualities, asexualities, transsexualities, BDSM and queerness. Recognising that non-normative sexualities have a history of invisibility in moving-image media, each chapter attempts to explore these sexualities' positive and resistant modes of expression and how they can continue to create more open spaces for expression and understanding.

In the second part, on 'Sex genres', the chapters address the range of media forms in which sex is the primary focus of representation. Our chapters here offer explorations of the ways in which sex genres from erotic fiction through to user-generated pornographies have developed, and how each of these represents sex and sexuality. Our authors take a variety of approaches to the individual genres, examining how particular structures, narratives and sensibilities invite particular forms of engagement from readers and viewers. Focusing first on 'sex media' – those forms, such as erotica and pornography, which have sex as their primary focus – the section then moves on to 'sexualised media', an admittedly very large category. Sexualisation of the media is generally described as ubiquitous, repetitive, normalised, everywhere, bombarding us; hence it is understandable that many may well feel there is an inappropriateness about pornographic imagery in public spaces. However, what we are seeing is not just liberalisation of the mores of the public sphere – as our chapters on selfies and other forms of self-presentation argue – it is a changing conception of what it means to represent the body as sexy.

The 'sexualisation' of mainstream media has become an intense focus of concern in policy and public debates in recent years, and the issues these concerns have raised are further explored in Part III, 'Representing sex'. The chapters in this section focus on particular formats, such as music video and lifestyle magazines, or genres, such as horror and reality television. The intention here is to highlight the diversity across media forms too often thought to be homogenous – not to parse good from bad representations but to recognise that there is more at stake in understanding how and why forms of sex sell.

In the final part, 'Deconstructing key figures', we demonstrate how certain figures, such as the sex worker or the porn user, have become both the locale(s) for contemporary media constructions of sex and sexuality and the focus of media fears. The chapters in this section unpick those constructions, exploring what each figure represents in contemporary culture, how they are constructed as victim or perpetrator, their historical antecedents and how sex and sexuality is vested, performed or negated within them. Taken together, the chapters in this section invite readers to investigate the changing place and significance of sex in contemporary society.

We have intentionally curated the chapters in the companion so that readers can profit from reading just one chapter or have a richer experience of engaging with a section or even the whole collection. We believe our chapters offer the kinds of close reading of individual and particular texts that makes clear their relations to other media genres and styles and broader traditions in fine-art practices or entertainment. We hope this companion enables further thinking about the contexts of particular genres and texts, and their links to groups and communities with particular tastes, values, practices and politics.

Putting together a body of essays of this size is, of course, a substantial and difficult undertaking. We would like to thank all our contributors for their contributions and, in some cases, for their patience through what has proved to be a very lengthy process. We also want to take the opportunity to thank Jamie Askew, Sheni Kruger and Natalie Foster at Routledge, who saw us through this process. Our thanks too to Danielle Egan, John Mercer, Valerie Reardon and Liam Wignall for their support in getting this project to completion.

Media

Brokeback Mountain (2005) Directed by A. Lee [Film]. USA: Focus Features.

PART I
Representing sexualities

1
THE NORMAL BODY ON DISPLAY
Public exhibitions of the Norma and Normman statues

Elizabeth Stephens

In June 1945, a pair of composite statues called Norma and Normman went on public display at the American Museum of Natural History in New York (see Figure 1.1).

The two statues had been modelled using the statistical averages of two very large anthropometric sets: Normman's dimensions were calculated from the anthropometric records of First World War soldiers collected by Albert G. Love and Charles Davenport, founder of the Eugenics Records Office;[1] Norma's were derived from the records of 15,000 'native white' American women collected by the Bureau of Home Economics in 1940, in an attempt to establish a system of standardised sizing for the ready-made clothing industry.[2] The statues were produced by the eminent gynaecologist and sexologist Robert Latou Dickinson, working in collaboration with the artist Abram Belskie. After a short but well-publicised exhibition at the American Museum of Natural History, reported in *Time* magazine, the statues were purchased with great fanfare by the Cleveland Museum of Health, where they were put on permanent exhibition in July 1945.[3] In September of that year, the local newspaper, the *Cleveland Plain Dealer*, announced a competition to find the living embodiment of Norma. The entry form, printed daily on the front page of the newspaper, was a detailed anthropometric chart, which applicants were required to fill out. Almost 4,000 women entered the contest, each recording over a dozen physical measurements. In the summer of 1945, the Norma and Normman statues (and especially Norma) provided a focal point for public debate about the new social and physical norms emergent in the immediate post-war period, and new expectations about gender, class and race. As such, Norma and Normman are a reminder of how culturally influential the space of public health exhibitions remained up until the middle of the previous century, constituting a key part of what Tony Bennett has termed the 'exhibitionary complex': that network of cultural institutions by which the disciplinary society produced docile, self-improving subjects (1995: 59–88). In 1945, public exhibitions were important sites of education and entertainment, serving much the same cultural function as would later popular media such as radio and television. Thus while, considered from a present perspective, composite statues might seem very marginal cultural objects, in their own day they had a significant impact on popular ideas and public discussion about gender, sexuality and race.

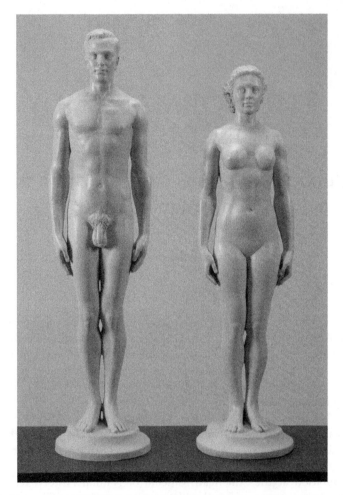

Figure 1.1 Dickinson and Belskie's Normman and Norma statues, 1945.

Source: Courtesy of the Warren Anatomical Museum in the Francis A. Countway Library of Medicine. Photograph by Samantha van Gerbig, Collection of Historical Scientific Instruments, Harvard University.

One of the most significant ways in which they did this, as their very names suggest, was by introducing the concepts of normal and normality to popular discourse. Prior to 1945, the word 'normal' was one rarely heard in everyday speech. Instead, it remained a term of medical and mathematic jargon, confined almost exclusively to professional discourses: in medicine, it had been used since the early 1800s to refer to the 'normal anatomy'; at the end of the nineteenth century it entered statistics through the term 'normal distribution'. But in 1945, the word remained in very limited circulation. The circumstances in which the normal first began to move into popular speech have been examined in two recent cultural histories of normality, both of which open with a detailed discussion of Norma and Normman: Anna Creadick's *Perfectly Average: The Pursuit of Normality in Postwar America* (2010) and Julian B. Carter's *The Heart of Whiteness: Normal Sexuality and Race in America, 1880–1940* (2007). For Carter, the statues are representative of the new formations of heterosexuality and whiteness emergent in the USA at the start of the twentieth century.

Carter argues that whereas in the late nineteenth century whiteness and heterosexuality had been often seen as precarious cultural formations, by the twentieth century they had become both institutionally and discursively entrenched, and disassociated from their disciplinary history, acquiring 'the appearance of blank emptiness and innocence' (Carter, 2007: 31). The history of the term 'normal' as a scientific and quantitative one further reinforced its epistemological neutrality (Carter, 2007). In the USA in the mid-century, Carter shows, the term normal gradually usurped the place of the earlier phrase 'native white American', erasing its racial specificity while further establishing its dominance. The concept of normality was hence embedded in a racial and corporeal specificity disguised as a neutral and universal standard. Like Carter, Anna Creadick argues that the cultural force and authority of normality as it emerged in the middle of the twentieth century derived in large part from its claims to mathematical rationalism and scientific objectivity. For Creadick, too, Norma and Normman are representative of the way in which what were seen as objective facts – statistical averages – were equally shaped by interpretive frameworks and evaluative judgements. Creadick, however, argues that even at its point of emergence, the concept of normality was the subject of contention rather than agreement, and that it fragmented as much as consolidated emergent ideas about gender, sexuality, race and embodiment. The post-war American culture of conformity so closely associated with the popular concept of normality was, even at its inception, an object of resistance and dissatisfaction and, as Creadick argues, perceived by some as stultifying and oppressive:

> Even as it was being employed at this time, however, normality was also being questioned and critiqued. The concept shifted from ... claiming the authoritative discourse of scientific rationality to voicing a contradictory discourse of popular psychology; from offering a source of security to being a metonym for conformity and danger to 'progress'.
>
> *(2010: 2)*

In the years following 1945, as the word moved into widespread circulation, its significance became much broader but also much vaguer and more difficult to define. The public exhibitions of Norma and Normman are thus both representative of and a significant catalyst for the cultural conditions in which the concept of normality came to be so pervasive and important in popular culture in the middle of the previous century. The Norma and Normman statues were thus produced at the very moment the word normal began to move into the popular sphere, and have much to tell us about the conditions in which it did so. In the years before televised media, these two statues were the very embodiment of new norms about gender and sexuality, and representative of the means by which these were widely disseminated.

The normal American: reimagining the statistically average American

Norma and Normman were the result of a previous successful collaboration between Dickinson and Belskie. This was a collection of obstetric models made for the 1939 New York World's Fair, and called the 'Birthing Series'. The models were designed to provide realistic yet respectable depictions of foetal development and childbirth, in a manner suitable to be seen by a broad audience. In this Dickinson and Belskie were very successful, and the exhibition proved enormously popular with visitors to the Fair. Afterwards,

Dickinson's correspondence reveals, he was inundated with requests from educational and community groups wanting to purchase photographic plates and reproductions of his models. Dickinson and Belskie published *The Birthing Atlas* in 1941, and began a follow-up volume, *Human Sex Anatomy: A Topographical Hand Atlas*, shortly afterwards. The idea for Norma and Normman developed during the preparation of that book, as visual representations of the normal ('native white' American) reproductive adult male and female.[4] Norma and Normman were thus 'normal' in the medical sense of the term: they were designed to make visible the 'normal anatomy' and 'normal state of health' of the average young white American, a project Dickinson argued (incorrectly) 'ha[d] never been undertaken before' (letter, 4 January 1945). They were also 'normal' in the statistical sense, because their dimensions had been calculated from the averaged anthropometrics measurements of (young white) American bodies.[5] Beyond this, however, Norma and Normman were also 'normal' in another, newer way, one whose meaning was much more general and difficult to articulate. They were conventionally, rather than exceptionally, fit and healthy; able-bodied and represented as a reproductive pair. As the word normal moved into more general circulation, its significance broadened and became more diffuse, disappearing into the cultural background even as it became conceptually more ubiquitous. The public exhibition of Norma and Normman, and its coverage in the popular media, thus allows us to see how new ideas of gender and sexuality coalesced around the semi-scientific understanding of normality at this time.

Norma and Normman first went on display at the American Museum of Natural History in New York, the location of the Second and Third International Congresses on Eugenics, in June 1945. A long article written by curator Harry L. Shapiro, entitled 'Portrait of the American People', appeared in the Museum's journal, *Natural History Magazine*, in the same month.[6] Shapiro argued that Norma and Normman were important scientific statues for two key reasons. First, they contributed to wider anthropological studies of the 'native white' American type, which he argued was a relatively recent area of research and a subject of contemporary fascination. Norma and Normman provided a rare and scientifically accurate portrait of this type.[7] Second, the statues prompted the viewer to reflect on what statistics had to tell us about that type, and the relation between the 'average' and the individual:

> Norma and Normman exhibit a harmony of proportion that seems far indeed from the usual or average. One might well look at a multitude of young men and women before finding an approximation to those normal standards. We have to do here then with apparent paradoxes. Let us state it in this way: the average American figure approaches a kind of perfection of bodily form and proportion; the average is excessively rare.
>
> Ordinarily, when we think of perfection ... we place it at one extreme of a curve of frequency, whose middle range or average is equivalent to mediocrity. Virtuosity, for example, is never at the middle range of a curve of frequency ... Why, then, should the average of our bodily proportions strike us as a form of perfection, and if it is average, why is it rare? I shall confine myself to statistical explanations. The extremes of any single physical character are generally statistically rare, whereas the average is frequent ... But the combination of many [individual] averages in one individual is rare and unusual.
>
> (Shapiro, 1945: 252–253)

How was it, Shapiro asked, that these models of the average American young man and woman seemed so much better than the actual average American? The answer, he explained, came from understanding the relationship between statistics and individuals. The 'perfectly average' bodies represented by Norma and Normman were 'excessively rare' because they embodied an anthropometric average in not just one part of their bodies but in every single aspect. Any individual body was statistically unlikely to coincide with so many averages.

After their short exhibition at the American Museum of Natural History, the statues were purchased by the Cleveland Museum of Health, where they went on display in July 1945. The Museum also bought the 'Birthing Series' at the same time, along with reproduction rights for photographic plates and plaster models for all Dickinson and Belskie's models.[8] The collection was exhibited together as 'The Wonders of Life'. The Director of the Museum, Bruno Gebhard, was already familiar with Dickinson and Belskie's work, having overseen the public health exhibitions at the 1939 World's Fair in New York. Gebhard had been the Curator of the Deutsches Hygiene Museum in Dresden from 1927 to 1935, and was well known for his eugenics exhibition at the Second International Hygiene Exhibition in Dresden. This was attended by a number of American health workers, including representatives of the American Public Health Association, who in 1934 arranged for the exhibition to be brought to the United States. Titled 'Eugenics in New Germany', it toured the US in 1934 before finding an eventual permanent home at the Buffalo Museum of Science.[9] Gebhard's role in public health education in the USA from the 1930s to 1960s is an important reminder both of how entrenched eugenics was to the exhibitory culture of this time and of how complex the field of eugenics was itself. Gebhard was both an enthusiastic supporter of eugenics and opposed to its uptake in Nazism: he was fired from his position at the Deutsches Hygiene Museum for refusing to join the Nazi party, and relocated to the United States shortly afterwards. None of the exhibitions he organised or curated in America were explicitly eugenicist; rather, they reinterpreted eugenic ideals of racial improvement within the American context of public education and self-improvement.

Dickinson had many close professional relationships with well-known eugenicists such as Gebhard. At the same time, however, he did not see the primary purpose of the Norma and Normman statues as a eugenic one, nor was he particularly interested in the anthropological questions that concerned Shapiro. Dickinson was a sexologist, and he saw the statues as a useful promotional tool by which to encourage more frank and open discussion about human sexuality. In the 1940s, Dickinson was well known as an energetic campaigner for public sex education who had published well-received books, such as *The Single Woman: a Medical Study in Sex Education* (1934), co-authored with Lura Beam and based on more than 5,000 case studies.[10] At an official luncheon to celebrate Cleveland Health Museum's purchase of the statues in July 1945, Dickinson congratulated the Museum for taking a bold and pioneering stance on this: 'No revolution is greater than the sex revolution that is in progress', he said in his address.

> To hide, to hush, to hurry past is giving place to directness of approach. But a vocabulary is needed and an anatomy to give language to the new attitude.... We have never studied sex behavior until now. Your museum has become a leader in this field.
>
> (Robertson, 1945e: 1)

That Norma and Normman were taken to be such important figures in three key areas of early-twentieth-century thinking – anthropology, eugenics and sexology – is representative of the cultural significance of these statues. That they could be taken to exemplify such different things in each of these areas attests to the increasingly wide and diverse range of the material and discursive networks in which the term 'normal' itself was beginning to circulate at this time, encouraged by the exhibition and media coverage of the statues.

The search for Norma: the living embodiment of the exceptionally unexceptional American woman

In September 1945, Gebhard announced that the Cleveland Museum of Health, in collaboration with the local newspaper, the *Cleveland Plain Dealer*, would hold a competition to find the living embodiment of Norma. There would be no parallel competition to find a Normman. The contest was scheduled to run for ten days, and a 'Norma editor', Josephine Robertson, was appointed and tasked with writing Norma-themed daily stories on topical issues, keeping the competition in the news. She announced the launch of the competition in a front-page article, headlined: 'Are you Norma, Typical Woman?' The article announced:

> A search for Norma, the typical American woman, will begin today in Ohio in order to discover whether there is actually a woman whose measurements coincide with those of an average computed from the measurements of 18 000 women all over the United States and represented by the statue Norma at the Cleveland Health Museum.
>
> *(Robertson, 9 September 1945b: 1)*

Robertson drew heavily on the Harry L. Shapiro article cited above to explain the significance of the Norma statue to the *Cleveland Plain Dealer* readership. Norma was described as the embodiment of an 'American type', that of the 'native white' young American female:

> Norma is the product of the American melting pot. In the beginning of this country's history, there was no truly typical American woman unless it was Pocahontas. Settlements were made largely according to European nationalities and there was not much intermingling. In the latter part of the 18th century, certain European scientists began to think of the Americans as a distinctive type, but as an inferior one due to what they termed an inferior environment ...
>
> It wasn't until after the American Revolution that inhabitants of this country began to think of themselves as one people and of being of a distinctive type. With the progressive intermarriage of the citizens of varied origins the American type began to emerge, and the American woman became easily recognizable wherever she travelled.
>
> However, statistics indicate that the typical American woman is still in the process of evolution, that Norma is growing taller and heavier and that her bust measurement is increasing. She exhibits 'a harmony of proportion that seems far indeed from the usual or the average', according to Harry L. Shapiro, curator of physical anthropology of the American Museum of Natural History in a recent article. He calls this average 'excessively rare'.
>
> *(Robertson, 9 September 1945b: 1, continued 8)*[11]

Here, what was still most commonly defined as the 'native white' American type is in the process of being transformed into the much more general category of the 'normal American'. The newspaper included an application form and detailed instructions on how to measure and record one's anthropometric data, which it reprinted daily for the duration of the competition. The caption for the photograph of the statue of Norma, pictured on the front page, was: 'The *Plain Dealer* Search for Norma seeks to learn if such a figure exists in life as well as statistics.'

For the next ten days, the *Cleveland Plain Dealer* ran front-page stories about the Norma competition. Robertson interviewed local prominent figures in medicine, health and education. Norma appeared in articles about fashion and sports, and in cartoons. The extensiveness and comprehensiveness of this media coverage is particularly remarkable if it is placed in its wider context. Norma first went on display in New York a month after the Second World War had ended in Britain, and the 'Search for Norma' competition was launched just a few weeks after the Second World War had come to an end for the USA, in the immediate aftermath of the two atomic bombs dropped on Nagasaki and Hiroshima. For ten days, the front page of the *Cleveland Plain Dealer* was occupied not by reportage of these epochal events but by daily updates on a local competition to find the physical embodiment of the 'perfectly average' woman. Yet this was perhaps not so surprising, since the competition was used as a means to consider the possible roles ahead for women, especially those who had been engaged as War Workers. It was precisely in such a volatile historical and cultural moment, perhaps, that questions about 'normal femininity' seemed so pressing. The Norma statue thus attests to the transformation and uncertainty about the normal at this time: that is, it was constitutive of the new ideas about the normal entering into the public sphere, rather than an illustration of an already established and familiar concept of normality.

Debate about the significance of Norma was again conducted primarily in the popular press and public sphere. This was reflected in the *Cleveland Plain Dealer*'s own coverage of the competition. For Robertson, Norma was a model of post-war American self-sufficiency and hard work, the new woman who had found a modern independence through her years as a War Worker:

> Norma is not attenuated like the ethereal women of Botticelli . . . but being nearer the earth she is more practical and useful in a work-a-day world . . . Her hands are strong and skilful from pounding the typewriter, milking the cow, playing the piano, stringing beans, washing dishes, operating the punch press, manipulating the forceps, employing the beaker and test tube, the mortar and pestle.
>
> The muscles of her arms and back are well developed from driving the car, the tractor, the jeep, swinging golf clubs, hoeing the corn, lifting the baby, rubbing the stains out of greasy overalls.
>
> No longer circumscribed by conservatism, she is free to choose her own work in the world. She is the physical expression of that new freedom. Perhaps she is also an expression of the political tendencies of the times which glorify the worker.
> (Robertson, 15 September 1945: 1, continued 10)

However, other references to Norma in the *Cleveland Plain Dealer* understood her significance in a very different way – as a representative figure for a generation of female War Workers happily returning to the domestic sphere, to resume their traditional roles as wife and mother. The 13 September edition of the *Cleveland Plain Dealer* included a cartoon of a woman identified as a 'War Worker' cooking in the kitchen, with the caption 'Gee Norma, We're Glad You're Home Again!' The different perspectives offered here by Robertson – for whom Norma was a model of the new woman, capable and independent – and the anonymous cartoonist – for whom she represented a welcome and reassuring return to domestic femininity – indicate an uncertainty about what 'normal' femininity might mean at the end of the exceptional conditions produced by the war. It is just this uncertainty that made both Norma and the new concept of normality she embodied so important. This uncertainty was what drove the search to find Norma's living embodiment, and it is the reason why the most exemplary figure of normality in the immediate post-war period is female.

However, finding a living embodiment of the statistically average body would prove elusive, as seen in the announcement of the winner of the 'Search for Norma' competition. When the contest closed on Wednesday 19 September, the *Cleveland Plain Dealer* reported that more than 3,700 women had sent in their measurements. On Friday 21 September, shortlisted finalists were invited to an Open House Day held at the local YWCA. Over a thousand people attended the open day, and several hundred finalists were measured by a panel of experts drawn from the YWCA, the Academy of Medicine of Cleveland, Flora Stone Mather College, the School of Medicine, Western Reserve University and the Cleveland Board of Education. The statue of Norma was also on display, and the eventual winner, Martha Skidmore, was photographed standing beside her (see Figure 1.2).

The article announcing the winner, 'Theatre Cashier, 23, Wins Title of "Norma", Besting 3,863 Entries', ran in the Sunday edition of the paper. Skidmore was described as 'a former war worker who now sells tickets at the Park Theatre' (Robertson, 23 September 1945d: 1). In occupation as well as physique, Skidmore was perfectly representative of 'native white' young women from Cleveland. In the interview celebrating her win, Skidmore 'indicated that she was an average woman in her tastes and that nothing out of the ordinary had ever happened to her until the Norma search came along' (Robertson, 23 September 1945d: 1). Ironically, the only exceptional thing that had ever happened to Skidmore, by her own account, was being identified as the most typical of her peers. Skidmore was exceptionally unexceptional: she was, as Shapiro had foreseen she would be, unusual in her very typicality. However, as Robertson noted, while Skidmore's measurements came closest to those of Norma: 'They did not coincide with those of the statue, however. After assessment of the measurements of 3,863 women who entered the search, Norma remained a hypothetical individual' (Robertson, 23 September 1945d: 1).

This space of non-identicality between Skidmore and Norma was highly consequential. In the first instance, the margin of difference between real bodies and statistical ideals was identified as a source of aspiration and potential (self-)improvement. For Gebhard, it reinforced the importance of cultivating one's body and health as a social as well as a personal responsibility:

> In this nation where we are so rich in all facilities, Dr Gebhard said: we haven't nearly realized our health needs nor that health is something that must be worked for. We cannot buy it from the druggist nor from the doctor. People must achieve physical fitness by their own efforts. The unfit are both bad producers and bad consumers. One of the outstanding needs in this country is more emphasis on physical fitness. And you can't make that statement too strong.
> (Robertson, 23 September 1945d: 1)

The normal body on display

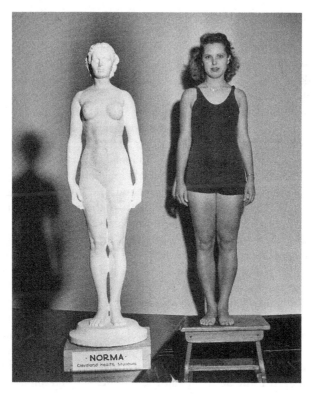

Figure 1.2 Search for Norma competition winner, Martha Skidmore, next to the Norma statue, 1945.

Source: Image courtesy of The Cleveland Museum of Natural History.

Here we see how a recognisably eugenic focus on un/fitness, by which Gebhard was certainly influenced, was reinscribed within mid-century discourses of public health education and self-improvement practices. The space between individual bodies and the new ideal of normality embodied by Norma was a gap to be narrowed, but one that could never be closed. In this way, Norma's average but aspirational anthropometric statistics provided a template for self-cultivation and an incitement to self-improvement, a quantitative chart to measure oneself against and try to live up to.

A second and related consequence of the non-identicality of Norma and Skidmore was that it encouraged new practices of measurement, in which not only medical but also mental and moral normality could be quantified and assessed. The Baptist minister Dr B. C. Clausen argued, during a sermon at the Euclid Avenue Baptist Church on the Sunday after the 'Search for Norma' competition had concluded, that anthropometric principles could be applied to spiritual life as well as physique. Clausen urged his congregation to:

> Measure yourself today... Where have you failed? What dimensions do you lack? Use the experience of prayer for daily measurement in comparison with your ideals. Then exercise, practice, restrict and discipline yourself, noting the improvement each day. Let your church serve as a constant incentive, as well as gymnasium, for your correction.
>
> (Robertson, 23 September 1945e: 1)

The context in which the Norma statue circulated was one of constant measurement and assessment, of vigilant self-scrutiny and cheerful self-improvement, but this was an endeavour in which falling short of one's goals was assumed to be inevitable ('Where have you failed? What dimensions do you lack?'). It is precisely this combination of the inspirational and the unachievable, of the evaluative and the quantitative, that would come to characterise the concept of the normal and the more general category of normality as these terms entered popular discourse and culture during the mid-century. The widespread coverage of the exhibition in the popular press is indicative of the cultural transformations of the period, in which earlier scientific concepts of the normal and earlier forms of public dissemination gave way to new popular ideas and media.

In this way, although they are not now widely remembered, the public exhibitions of the Norma and Normman statues played a pivotal role in popularising new ideas, and establishing new norms, about gender and sexuality in the middle of the previous century. They did this not through establishing consensus, as we have seen, but through encouraging public engagement and debate. Contemporary concepts of the normal retain something of this contested quality, even as it is often assumed to be culturally ubiquitous and unqualified in its cultural dominance. Yet the normal, at its point of popular emergence, signified not a static value but a dynamic property, something that required constant monitoring, measurement and cultivation. It is perhaps precisely for this reason that the term has proved so culturally enduring, and thus so central to recent fields of inquiry such as critical race and disability studies, as well as gender, sexuality and queer studies. This endurance derives in large part from the slippage between the average and the ideal that characterises the normal, and yet it is not the case that this slippage has gone unremarked. Rather, it is the debate about the significance and implications of this that drives its cultural ubiquity. In this way, this set of composite statues has much to tell us about the contemporary configurations of normative sex, gender and race, and the methods by which the white, heterosexual able-bodied youth became representative of the 'normal' American.

Notes

1 These records were publicly available: published first in *Defects Found in Drafted Men: Statistical Information Compiled from the Draft Records* (1919) and then in *Army Anthropology: Based on Observations Made on Draft Recruits, 1917–1918, and on Veterans at Demobilization, 1919* (1921). The data set used to model Normann was that of Robert Latou Dickinson, and augmented Love and Davenport's data with a number of smaller data sets: the records from an anthropometric laboratory Dickinson set up at the Chicago World's Fair in 1933 and insurance company data, as well as results from surveys of male college students undertaken by physical anthropologists, such as Earnest Hooton, who were working in university contexts (see Cogdell, 2004: 196; Creadick, 2010: 19).
2 In the 1930s, the Bureau of Home Economics was provided with a Federal Work Projects Administration grant to 'develop the measuring techniques and to train the measurers' (Department of Agriculture, 1941: 1). The programme thus served the secondary purpose of providing employment for large numbers of women during the Depression. The results were published in *Women's Measurements for Garment and Pattern Construction* (1941).
3 Contemporaneous copies of the original statues are on display at the Warren Museum of Anatomy, at Harvard.
4 A letter written by Dickinson to his publisher in early 1945 suggests that the statues were being made at the start of that year: 'Now [the book] has a noble opening – the perfect woman, the average American, in a Belskie sculpture in four aspects. . . . Over it will be a transparency of four outlines, front, back and side, with every measurement. . . . The man is as fine. I am urged to put

him in, also' (1945a). This helps date the manufacture of the statues to 1945 (dated to 1943 in Creadick).
5 The Bureau of Home Economics records, from which Norma was modelled, emphasise that what they have produced in the published version of this data consists of a normal distribution of these measurements, from which some data has been excluded in order to ensure the representationality of the results.
6 Shapiro, who had been Hooton's student at Harvard, was an associate curator during the eugenics congresses, and would later serve as the President of the American Eugenics Association (from 1956 to 1963).
7 This argument developed one of the central claims of Hooton's 1936 article 'What Is an American?'
8 The museum began to manufacture and sell copies of these pieces immediately, manufacturing them in a range of materials, at different price points.
9 The exhibition was re-curated in 1943, and all the displays relating to Nazi eugenic programmes were destroyed. A detailed account of this exhibition is provided in Rydell, Cogdell and Largent (2006: 359–384).
10 Dickinson used a method that combined physical examinations, anatomical illustrations (which he drew himself), psychological profiles and personal histories. Dickinson's technique, he explained, was to conduct 'pelvic examinations' of his patients as he questioned them, in order to stimulate 'free associations with the erotic life'. As a result, these 'associational elements are startled into expression' (Dickinson and Beam, 1934: 22).
11 Robertson's text is a direct summary of Shapiro's article, focusing on his discussion of the emergence of an American type.

Bibliography

Bennett, T. (1995) *The Birth of the Museum: History, Theory, Politics*. London and New York: Routledge.
Carter, J. B. (2007) *The Heart of Whiteness: Normal Sexuality and Race in America, 1880–1940*. Durham: Duke University Press.
Cogdell, C. (2004) *Eugenic Design: Streamlining America in the 1930s*. Philadelphia: University of Pennsylvania Press.
Creadick, A. (2010) *Perfectly Average: The Pursuit of Normality in Postwar America*. Amherst: University of Massachusetts Press.
Davenport, C. and Love, A. G. (1919) *Defects Found in Drafted Men: Statistical Information Compiled from Draft Records*. Washington, DC: War Department Government Printing Office.
Davenport, C. and Love, A. G. (1921) *Army Anthropology: Based on Observations Made on Draft Recruits, 1917–1918, and on Veterans at Demobilization, 1919*. Washington, DC: War Department Government Printing Office.
Department of Agriculture (1941) *Women's Measurements for Garment and Pattern Construction*. Miscellaneous Publication No. 454. Washington, DC: Government Printing Office.
Dickinson, R. L. (1945a) Letter to Richard Gill. 4 January. B MS c72. Francis A. Countway Library of Medicine, Harvard University.
Dickinson, R. L. (1945b) Letter to E. A. Hooton. 24 April. B MS c72. Francis A. Countway Library of Medicine, Harvard University.
Dickinson, R. L. and Beam, L. (1934) *The Single Woman: A Medical Study in Sex Education*. Baltimore: Williams & Wilkins.
Dickinson, R. L. and Belskie, A. (1940) *Birth Atlas*. Baltimore: Williams & Wilkins.
Dickinson, R. L. and Belskie, A. (1949) *Human Sex Anatomy: A Topographical Hand Atlas*. Baltimore: Williams & Wilkins.
Hooton, E. A. (1936) 'What Is an American?' *American Journal of Anthropology*. Volume 22(1): 1–26.
Robertson, J. (1945a) 'Health Museum's Sex Work Hailed'. 9 July. *Cleveland Plain Dealer*: 1.
Robertson, J. (1945b) 'Are You Norma, Typical Woman? Search to Reward Ohio Winners'. 9 September. *Cleveland Plain Dealer*: 1, 8.

Robertson, J. (1945c) 'Norma Is Appealing Model in Opinion of City's Artists'. 15 September. *Cleveland Plain Dealer*: 1, 10.

Robertson, J. (1945d) 'Theatre Cashier, 23, Wins Title of "Norma," Besting 3,863 Entries'. 23 September. *Cleveland Plain Dealer*: 1.

Robertson, J. (1945e) 'Dr. Clausen Finds Norma Devout, but Still Glamorous'. 23 September. *Cleveland Plain Dealer*: 1.

Rydell, R., Cogdell, C. and Largent, M. (2006) 'The Nazi Eugenics Exhibition in the United States, 1934–1943'. In *Popular Eugenics: National Efficiency and American Mass Culture in the 1930s*, edited by S. Currell and C. Cogdell. Athens: Ohio University Press.

Shapiro, H. L. (1945) 'Portrait of the American People'. *Natural History Magazine*. Volume 54: 246–255.

2
ASEXUALITIES AND MEDIA

Kristina Gupta and Karli June Cerankowski

What can we learn about asexualities from representations in the media? And what can a complex understanding of asexualities teach us about cultural representations of sex and sexuality? Wait – what do we even mean by asexualities? The Asexual Visibility and Education Network (AVEN), the largest and most visible online community for asexual-identified people and their allies, defines an asexual person as someone who experiences little or no sexual attraction to other people. Although many asexual-identified people agree on this common definition, there is significant diversity in terms of how asexual-identified people experience and even define their asexuality. For example, there is variance in levels of sexual attraction, types of interpersonal relationships sought and interest in different types of intimacy, physical and otherwise. Some people experience asexuality as a lifelong sexual orientation while others may inhabit their asexuality on a temporary basis, for a variety of reasons. Given this diversity of the 'asexual spectrum', we refer to asexualities in the plural sense to encompass all the different ways in which people identify with asexuality.

In this chapter, we specifically focus on asexualities and media in order to answer the questions with which we opened. We first describe two lenses of analysis that have been developed by activists and scholars in the field of asexuality studies – compulsory sexuality and asexual reading practices – and argue that these lenses yield new insights about media representations of asexuality, non-sexuality and sexuality more generally. We then offer a number of examples of media analysis that employ these two lenses to model critical asexual reading practices.

Compulsory sexuality

Activists and scholars in the field of asexuality studies have identified 'compulsory sexuality' as a system of social control different from 'compulsory heterosexuality' (Chasin, 2013; Emens, 2014; Gupta, 2015). Gupta (2015) defines 'compulsory sexuality' as including

> the assumption that all people are sexual, the norms and practices that compel people to experience themselves as desiring subjects, take up sexual identities, and engage in sexual activity, and the norms and practices that marginalise various

forms of non-sexuality (including a lack of interest in sex, a lack of sexual activity, or a dis-identification with sexuality).

(Gupta 2015: 134–135)

Other names have been used to describe this system, such as 'sexualnormativity' (Hinderliter, 2009; Chasin, 2011) and 'the sexual assumption' (Carrigan, 2011), but all of these terms perform similar work. As Gupta suggests (2015), compulsory sexuality regulates the behaviour of *all* people, not just people who identify as asexual, although the impact of compulsory sexuality on individuals will vary based on a number of factors, including race, class, gender and ability.

If we understand compulsory sexuality as a system that regulates the norms around sexual desire and practice, then how can we use this concept to better understand asexuality, low or no sexual desire/attraction and other forms of abstention from sex, whether temporary or lifelong? To begin with, compulsory sexuality can provide an analytic lens through which we can read and interpret various representations of sexuality in media. Using the lens of compulsory sexuality encourages us to ask questions such as: Does this portrayal of sexuality suggest that all people are motivated by sexual desire? Does this portrayal of sexuality suggest that sexual desire is necessary to human flourishing or an essential part of what makes us human? By asking these questions, we can also analyse various portrayals of 'non-sexuality', including explicit portrayals of asexuality, as well as portrayals of a lack of interest in sex or a lack of sexual activity that are not explicitly coded as instances of asexuality. The lens of compulsory sexuality can help us to recognise instances in which media representations of asexuality or non-sexuality serve to marginalise, stigmatise or pathologise various forms of non-sexuality. In addition to helping us recognise problematic representations of sexuality, asexuality and non-sexuality, the lens of compulsory sexuality can also help us recognise moments when asexuality or non-sexuality are represented in more nuanced ways or when sexuality is represented not as the only path to a good life but as one path among many.

Asexual reading practices

In addition to reading media representations of sexuality, asexuality and non-sexuality through the lens of compulsory sexuality, one may also adopt what we call an asexual reading practice, which shares some similarities with a reparative reading practice.[1] This practice of reading for asexuality or non-sexuality can be applied to literature, film, television, performance and other types of media and cultural production. Przybylo and Cooper refer to the practice of seeking out asexual moments as a 'queerly asexual reading method', in which asexuality can be understood 'outside of its current definitional parameters of unchangeability, inherentness, nonchoice, self-identification, heteronormativity, and maleness' (2014: 303). Further, they suggest that 'asexual resonances' help us 'search for asexuality in unexpected places' (2014: 4). In other words, rather than seeking out a biologically identifiable asexuality or one that is coded in the desires and actions of the body, we can read for moments in which non-sexual expression is meaningful.

The challenge in adopting such a reading method is in acknowledging the historical and persistent erasure of asexuality, even in queer reading practices. For example, Benjamin Kahan argues that 'queer theory tends to read "celibacy" as repression – referring to the celibate as a "latent", "closeted", or "unconscious" homosexual' (2013: 2). Much like celibacy, asexuality is often overlooked in favour of readings that suggest closeted homosexuality, pathology, or a combination of the two – pathologised closeted homosexuality. But the more we come to understand that sexual normativity is dictated not only by compulsory heterosexuality but also by compulsory sexuality, the more we might begin to recognise sexual 'absences' as being full of possibility for understanding sexuality, desire and intimacy in a more complex way. To read so-called absences in this way is to develop a mode of asexual reading that is attentive to the meanings that may be derived when sex is not at the centre of a relationship narrative, and when such absences are not meant to perform as a cover for 'unnarratable desires'.[2]

When compulsory sexuality dictates how we think about 'healthy' sexual lives, asexuality and non-sexual expression is then construed as a lack or as a failure to live up to the norm. Instead of construing the lack of sex as a failure to attain true intimacy, we can read with an attentiveness to asexuality that shifts the value of intimacy from one based on sexual contact to one based on affects, relations and expressions of love, connection and/or emotional bonding – moments that may otherwise be overlooked if there is no sexual payoff. We are then reading for affective and relational values that replace the sexual imperative dictated by the system of compulsory sexuality.

In the next section, we provide several examples of these kinds of reading practices. We do not necessarily attempt to define the characters' or personae's sexualities or attempt to otherwise identify them as asexual if not explicitly coded as such; doing so would be an impossible and futile project. Instead, we demonstrate how one might use asexual reading practices and compulsory sexuality as lenses for analysing and revising normative understandings of intimacy, relationships, kinship, desire and sex.

Examples of critical asexual reading practices

Now that we have a basic understanding of compulsory sexuality and asexual reading practices as lenses through which to analyse media representations of asexuality, non-sexuality and normative sexuality, let's apply them to some popular representations in film and television. As an example of a reading of a media representation of asexuality explicitly coded as such, we offer a reading of an episode of the American television show *House* that includes a subplot about asexuality (Gupta, 2012). The episode, titled 'Better Half' (2012), depicts a husband and wife who both identify as asexual at the start of the episode. The wife consults one of the main characters on the show, Dr Wilson, for a minor medical complaint. Upon learning about the couple, the title character, Dr House, sets out to prove that the wife's asexuality is caused by a medical condition. He lures her husband into the hospital and performs a number of tests on him, eventually discovering that the husband has a libido-depleting brain tumour. When Wilson tells the couple about House's finding, the wife admits that she had been pretending to be asexual for her husband's sake all along. The episode thus reflects many of the assumptions of compulsory sexuality – an asexual identity is represented as either a deception or a pathology. As depicted in the episode, the suggestion that asexuality is somehow not 'real', that it is rather a lie or a symptom of medical dis-ease, has implications beyond the fictional characters in the show. In fact, House makes such a message clear when he states: 'Lots of people don't have sex. The only people who don't want it are either sick, dead or lying.' To suggest that people who do not choose to engage in sex acts are sick and/or deceitful is to uphold the tenets of compulsory sexuality that deem sex as necessary to a healthy and honest human existence. By questioning House's statement, we can recognise how such an ideology has infiltrated popular media and continues to perpetuate false ideas about health and sexual expression.

Another example of a text in which asexuality is pitted against theories of pathology is the novel *The Bone People* (1986), written by Maori author Keri Hulme. The New Zealand-based novel has gained popularity in the asexual community for its representation of an adamantly asexual character named Kerewin Holmes, who bears a semi-autobiographical resemblance to the author, who has openly discussed her own asexual identification. The novel focuses on the life of Kerewin, a reclusive artist of part-Maori, part-Pakeha (European) descent who has won a small fortune in a lottery and lives alone in a tower on the seashore in New Zealand. She meets a young child named Simon Gillayley, or Haimona, when she catches him wandering around her property and attempting to climb through her window one night. Simon cannot speak, seemingly due to some past abuses and traumas that have left scars on his body. He lives with his abusive adoptive father, Joe Gillayley, a Maori man who found Simon washed up on shore after a shipwreck. Joe can only speculate as to who Simon's parents might have been and why it is that Simon is incapable of speech. Although Simon cannot speak, he can write and communicate through gesture. Joe lost his wife and young son to the flu and has been raising Simon on his own. Simon came to Joe with scars all over his body, but Joe adds to those marks with his continued abuse of the boy. Joe meets Kerewin when he receives a call to collect Simon at her property, and they quickly form a friendly bond as the three of them spend more time together. Joe becomes intent on building a family with Kerewin, noting that Simon does not get the 'woman's care' that he needs (1986: 50). Kerewin is resistant to Joe's advances, but nevertheless finds herself forming a sense of love and non-sexual intimacy with Joe and Simon. By the end of the novel, despite several fights, flights and rough patches, the three of them form what Jana Fedtke calls a 'patchwork family' (2014: 339).

The negotiation of the relationship between Kerewin and Joe reveals how compulsory sexuality operates in defining intimacy between two people, and asexual reading practices also help us recognise the ways in which Kerewin and Joe experience love, intimacy and kinship in meaningful yet non-sexual ways. For instance, Kerewin repeatedly reaffirms her aversion to and lack of interest in sex, and resists Joe's sexual advances. The narrative focalises on Joe's thoughts, as he ponders how Kerewin came to be the way she is: '... someone, sometime, must have hurt Kerewin' (Hulme, 1986: 174). Joe's first assumption is that Kerewin must have encountered pain or trauma in order to end up that way. Joe then asks Kerewin: '"I wondered, did anyone ever," shrug, "you know, hurt you so you don't like kissing? Love?"' Kerewin responds with a simple 'nope' and continues about her business in her library. Joe presses the issue: 'I thought maybe someone had been bad to you in the past and that was why you don't like people touching or holding you.' To this, Kerewin reacts with violent exasperation, saying 'Ah damn it to hell' as she slams a lamp down on a desk, and continues, 'I said no. I haven't been raped or jilted in any fashion. There's nothing in my background to explain the way I am' (1986: 265). Kerewin continues to explain that there was a time when she searched everything 'from the Kama Sutra and Kraft-Ebbing [sic] to a pile of know-yer-own body books' to find a cause for her disinterest in sex, only to conclude that there is no explanation, and although she is not 'normal', she is just 'one more variety in varied humanity' (1986: 266). When we analyse this exchange between Joe and Kerewin, we see how Joe's interrogation of Kerewin's sexuality replicates the sexual norms dictated by compulsory sexuality, but in the end, Joe comes to love and accept Kerewin just how she is. As Fedtke notes, Joe's contentedness with Kerewin is demonstrated in his resolution to accept what Kerewin has to offer asexually, rather than trying to bend her to his sexual whims (2014: 338). By understanding their relationship through an asexual lens, we can then see their relationship not as a failure or as Joe giving in or giving up on something, but instead as an expression of love and discovery of the intimacies possible outside of a sex-centred relationship.

In addition to recognising how compulsory sexuality operates in instances when asexuality is made explicit, we can explore media representations of non-sexuality that are not explicitly coded as asexual. Eunjung Kim's work on representations of disabled sexuality and Cynthia Barounis' analysis (2014) of the film *Shortbus* (2006, dir: John Cameron Mitchell) offer good examples. Kim explores how 'heterosexualising apparatuses' work in film to construct the disabled body as sexually broken and in need of fixing through access to heterosexual desire, arguing that in the films *Breaking the Waves* (1996, dir: Lars von Trier), *Born on the Fourth of July* (1989, dir: Oliver Stone) and *Breathing Lessons: The Life and Work of Mark O'Brien* (1996, dir: Jessica Yu), 'disabled men's sexuality is assisted and imagined through the terms of heterosexual normativity' (2010: 134). In other words, their disability not only asexualises these men but also emasculates them, as their perceived sexual ineptitude or undesirability is constructed as a failure of manhood. The only way these disabled men can recoup their manhood is through the heterosexual intimate attentions of (usually) non-disabled female sex workers. The humanness of these disabled characters is thus guaranteed by their participation in a universalised (hetero)sexuality, which aligns with the ideology of compulsory sexuality.

Similarly, in the South Korean film *Oasis* (2002, dir: Chang-dong Lee), Kim explores how the heterosexualising apparatus is employed on a female character with a disability. In this film, a young woman with cerebral palsy is raped by a man who is cast out from his family after spending time in prison for vehicular manslaughter. The man later returns to court the woman and she accepts his advances and engages in consensual sex with him. But when her brother discovers the sexual relationship, he assumes the man is raping his sister because he cannot imagine that she has any sexual agency, although he overlooks the time when she actually was raped. The audience is sympathetically wooed to the side of the rapist as the film creates a narrative of salvation, such that the man who abuses a disabled woman has rescued her from an unaffectionate, sexless life. And so again, the disabled body is characterised by an asexuality that needs to be overcome. When film and media utilise such heterosexualising apparatuses, they reinforce compulsory (hetero)sexuality on the disabled body, as they 'emphasize the desexualized status of disabled people, forging the imperative to bring disabled people into the normalized sexual realms in order for them to be humanized and recognized' (Kim, 2010: 154). So it would seem that all bodies, especially disabled bodies, must be circumscribed with sexual desire in order to become fully human.

In her essay 'Compulsory sexuality and asexual/crip resistance in John Cameron Mitchell's *Shortbus*', Barounis uses the lens of compulsory sexuality to rethink *Shortbus* (2006), a film that has been lauded as a celebration of queer and crip experience. The main character in the film, Sofia, is a couples counsellor who is unable to experience orgasm (a type of non-sexuality), and, according to Barounis, the film ultimately presents an unconventional retelling of a familiar sex-normative narrative, as Sofia engages in a number of practices to 'fix' her non-orgasmic body. According to Barounis, Sofia's cure (her ability to achieve orgasm at the end of the film) reinforces compulsory sexuality by suggesting that this 'rehabilitation' (via queer sex) has led Sofia to a new state of psychological health and physical wholeness. However, Barounis also employs an asexual reading practice by refusing the orgasmic endpoint to the narrative and instead seeking out other asexual resonances in the film. She argues that one character, Severin, offers a site of asexual or autoerotic resistance in the film, as she is presented as 'constantly turning away from the various forms of sexual relationality she is presented with' (2014: 191). Thus, rather than settling on a reading that provides a 'cure' to the non-orgasmic body, Barounis reads for other asexual moments that are full of active resistance to the sexual imperatives that drive orgasmic scripts.

Now that we've demonstrated how we might read media for explicit and inexplicit representations of asexualities, we can also apply our lenses of analysis to cultural rhetoric around sexuality writ broad. In Gupta's (2011) analysis of the 'sex for health' discourse in media articles and Gupta and Cacchioni's (2013) analysis of contemporary sex manuals, the lens of compulsory sexuality is used to help us understand the prescriptive production of 'healthy' sexuality. Gupta (2011) analyses a spate of recent media articles that describe the 'health benefits' of sexual activity. Drawing loosely on recently published scientific studies, these articles, published via outlets such as CNN and *Men's Journal*, argue that engaging in sexual activity can increase lifespan, reduce the risk of heart attack, lower blood pressure, reduce the risk of certain types of cancer, provide pain relief, strengthen immune function and promote weight loss, among other things. According to Gupta, this 'sex for health discourse' is, in some ways, a counter-hegemonic discourse, challenging sex-negative attitudes and using the social authority of science and medicine to legitimise sexual activity. However, when viewed through the lens of compulsory sexuality, it is also clear that these articles have the potential to create new sexual expectations and burdens. Gupta writes that 'popular press stories encourage individuals to engage in regular sex, monitor their sexual activity, and seek medical treatment when levels of sexual activity do not meet socially-structured expectations' (2011: 136), suggesting that, yet again, popular media relegate asexual expression to the realm of pathology.

Expanding on this research, Gupta and Cacchioni (2013) analyse a representative set of contemporary sex manuals. These sex manuals are diverse in many ways, ranging from Christian-themed advice manuals for married heterosexual couples to bio-medically informed advice for heterosexual adults to feminist- and queer-inspired manuals for a sexually diverse readership. When read through the lens of compulsory sexuality, it is clear that nearly all the manuals, from Christian to queer, share a common assumption about the importance of sexual interaction and pleasure to personal, interpersonal, physical and emotional happiness and fulfilment. According to Gupta and Cacchioni, the manuals offer three main justifications for the importance of sex. First, sex is presented as a human need and as necessary for maintaining intimate relationships, although in many of the manuals, men and women are expected to experience this need in stereotypically gendered ways. Second, some of the manuals present sex as an avenue for women's empowerment. Finally, as in the media articles discussed above, the sex manuals present sexual activity as necessary to maintain health and as a way to improve health. In addition, because almost all of the manuals position sex as fundamentally important to human well-being, almost all enjoin readers to engage in various practices to 'improve' their sex lives. Particularly relevant to the discussion here is the finding that a minority of manuals encourage their readers (both men and women) to have sex for the sake of a partner if they themselves do not want sex. Although the manuals address these messages to both male and female readers, Gupta and Cacchioni argue that women, in particular, are encouraged to engage in sexual improvement work. Gupta and Cacchioni write: '[in these manuals] sexual improvement is imbued with new urgency as sexual pleasure is constructed as if her humanity, empowerment, and now, even health depends on it' (Gupta and Cacchioni, 2013: 455). By applying a critical lens of analysis that engages understandings of compulsory sexuality and asexual expression, Gupta and Cacchioni are able to reveal the ways in which these texts continue to dictate 'normal' and 'healthy' sexuality at the exclusion of asexual and celibate practices.

Conclusions

In this chapter, we have discussed some of the intersections between asexualities and media, demonstrating that adopting asexual reading practices and utilising the lens of compulsory sexuality can provide insight into media representations of asexuality, non-sexuality and sexuality more broadly. Such analytical practices can reveal the ways in which the ideology of sex as healthy and necessary is reiterated time and again in popular discourse, but we can also increase our awareness of how this ideology operates and instead recognise positive and resistant modes of expressing non-sexualities that can create more open spaces for asexual expression and understanding. Indeed, the work of examining media representations with attention to compulsory sexuality and asexual resonances has really only just begun, and we expect this work to produce fascinating insights into both new and existing texts. As the asexual movement grows and more people become aware of asexuality, we expect the prevalence of asexualities in media to increase, hopefully in nuanced ways. We are happy to predict that in a few years this writing will be woefully outdated, as representations of non-sexuality become as commonplace as any other representation of sexual expression.

Notes

1 Eve Kosofsky Sedgwick (1997) encourages the adoption of a 'reparative reading' practice that, unlike a 'paranoid reading' practice, seeks not to reveal ever more insidious forms of homophobia, but rather to find ameliorative meanings that can help to create a more livable world.
2 By 'unnarratable desires', we refer to a history of silence around the expression of homoerotic and homosexual desire in film and television. For example, Terry Castle (1993) argues that lesbianism has been 'ghosted', made 'apparitional' or, in a sense, closeted in modern Western literature and culture since the eighteenth century. Similarly, in his study *The Celluloid Closet*, Vito Russo (1987) demonstrates how homosexuality has been historically closeted in film. We do not deny that homosexuality was – and continues to be – a taboo topic that artists and writers cleverly work around, cover up and covertly hint at, but we are also suggesting that sometimes we run the risk of reading more into absence than is actually there.

Bibliography

Barounis, C. (2014) 'Compulsory sexuality and feminist/crip resistance in John Cameron Mitchell's *Shortbus*'. In K.J. Cerankowski and M. Milks (eds) *Asexualities: Feminist and Queer Perspectives*. New York: Routledge.
Carrigan, M. (2011) 'There's more to life than sex? Difference and commonality within the asexual community'. *Sexualities*. Volume 14 (4): 462–478.
Castle, T. (1993) *The Apparitional Lesbian: Female Homosexuality and Modern Culture*. New York: Columbia University Press.
Chasin, C.D. (2011) 'Theoretical issues in the study of asexuality'. *Archives of Sexual Behavior*. Volume 40 (4): 713–723.
Chasin, C.D. (2013) 'Reconsidering asexuality and its radical potential'. *Feminist Studies*. Volume 39 (2): 405–426.
Emens, E.F. (2014) 'Compulsory sexuality'. *Stanford Law Review*. Volume 66: 303–386.
Fedtke, J. (2014) '"What to call that sport, the neuter human …": asexual subjectivity in Keri Hulme's *The Bone People*'. In K.J. Cerankowski and M. Milks (eds) *Asexualities: Feminist and Queer Perspectives*. New York: Routledge.
Gupta, K. (2011) '"Screw health": representations of sex as a health-promoting activity in medical and popular literature'. *Journal of Medical Humanities*. Volume 32 (2): 127–140.

Gupta, K. (2012) 'Illness and deception? Asexuality on House, MD'. Kinsey Confidential Blog. Available at http://kinseyconfidential.org/illness-deception-asexuality-house-md/ (accessed 4 August 2015).

Gupta, K. (2015) 'Compulsory sexuality: evaluating an emerging concept'. *Signs: Journal of Women in Culture and Society*. Volume 41 (1): 131–154.

Gupta, K. and Cacchioni, T. (2013) 'Sexual improvement as if your health depends on it: an analysis of contemporary sex manuals'. *Feminism and Psychology*. Volume 23 (4): 442–458.

Hinderliter, A. (2009) 'Methodological issues for studying asexuality'. *Archives of Sexual Behavior*. Volume 38 (5): 619–621.

Hulme, K. (1986) *The Bone People: A Novel*. New York: Penguin Books.

Kahan, B. (2013) *Celibacies: American Modernism and Sexual Life*. Durham: Duke University Press.

Kim, E. (2010) '"A man, with the same feelings": disability, humanity, and heterosexual apparatus in Breaking the Waves, Born on the Fourth of July, Breathing Lessons, and Oasis'. In S. Chivers and N. Markotić (eds) *The Problem Body: Projecting Disability in Film*. Columbus: The Ohio State University Press.

Przybylo, E. and Cooper, D. (2014) 'Asexual resonances: tracing a queerly asexual archive'. *GLQ: The Journal of Gay and Lesbian Studies*. Volume 20 (3): 297–318.

Russo, V. (1987) *The Celluloid Closet: Homosexuality in the Movies*. Rvd edn. New York: Harper and Row.

Sedgwick, E.K. (1997) *Novel Gazing: Queer Readings in Fiction*. Durham: Duke University Press.

Media

Born on the Fourth of July (1989) Directed by O. Stone [Film]. USA: Xtian.

Breaking the Waves (1996) Directed by L. von Trier [Film]. Denmark: Argus Film Produktie.

Breathing Lessons: The Life and Work of Mark O'Brien (1996) Directed by J. Yu [Film]. USA: Inscrutable Films.

House (2012) 'Better Half'. Season 8, episode 9, Fox Television, 23 January.

Oasis (2002) Directed by C. Lee [Film]. South Korea: Dream Venture Capital.

Shortbus (2006) Directed by J. Cameron Mitchell [Film]. USA: THINKFilm.

3
REPRESENTING TRANS SEXUALITIES

Eliza Steinbock

This chapter disentangles the web of terms that knots together the medical naming of transsexualism, the mediatised practices of trans sex and what might today be recognised as the multiplicities of trans sexualities. Carla A. Pfeffer has named trans sexualities 'a lacuna' in theorisations of sexuality and desire (2014: 598). For a growing number of (trans) scholars, trans sexualities, sex and their mediatised representations are vital academic and political concerns. Trans sex and sexuality reveals the myriad ways in which gender and sexuality are interdependent and mutually constitutive, moving forward studies of gender and sexuality in practice, in policy and even philosophically. Close analysis of erotic (self-)representations brings to light the possibility of experiencing both sexual fluidity and stability, resolving a long-standing impasse in feminist and queer approaches to sexuality (Steinbock, 2011). In this chapter I will focus on two domains that provide insight into the cultural shifts around how trans sexualities are mediatised: transfeminine activism in queer pornography and, by way of conclusion, some notes on news coverage of how to talk about trans sex.

Framing trans representation politics

In this chapter I understand representation as including re-presenting the self through language and bodily expression, as well as through media technologies such as film, television and digital forums, in genres ranging from news reporting to pornography. In each case, the representation of trans sexualities involves the double projection of a singular subject and collective subjectivities. Issues such as making available new collective vocabularies for self-definition – such as the much-publicised addition of gender qualifiers on Facebook and dating site OkCupid (North, 2014; Weber, 2014) – have a real impact on trans lives. Whereas users previously had to identify their gender as male or female and their orientation as straight, gay or bisexual, Facebook now has 50-plus different gender options (for US users), such as trans man, trans woman, cis/cisgender, bigender, genderfluid, gender nonconforming, intersex, agender, androgynous and two spirit.

Genealogies of trans identities have sparked heated debates about how to understand the entanglements of gender and sexual diversity (Reid-Smith, 2013).[1] The early medical nomenclature of *transsexual* stresses how sexology imagined the deviant 'crossing' of a sexual border. The diagnostic category of Gender Identity Disorder (GID) in the American Psychiatric Association's *Diagnostic and Statistical Manual of Mental Disorders, Fifth Edition* (*DSM-5*) (2013) allows for convoluted and contested terms, such as 'autogynephilia', that reduce gender identity to attraction, a paraphilia for becoming sexually aroused by imagining or having a normative female body (Blanchard, 1989).[2] The current clinical nomenclatures of GID and gender dysphoria classify trans as a condition that is universal across cultures and experienced by a minute proportion of the population, identifiable according to a set of symptoms such as disgust at their own genitalia. The distress, social isolation and depression that many self-identified trans people report are attributed by psycho-sexual literature such as the *DSM-5* to a response to genital incongruence. However, trans activists and scholars argue that this results from a society that expects one to hold a gender identity that conforms to one's assigned sex at birth (cf. Nadal, Skolnik and Wong, 2012).

In cultures that organise gender and sexual norms in ways that afford bodily transformation, value a multiplicity of gender expressions and honour legal rights to self-determination, reported stress and suicide rates decrease dramatically (cf. Cabral and Viturro, 2006; Spade, 2011). Trans activism of the past decade has called for the de-pathologisation, de-criminalisation and legal recognition of trans identity/experience (cf. Balzer and Hutta, 2012). Integral to this is making accessible a range of practices for transforming one's gendered embodiment, from name change to hormone replacement therapy to surgeries and clothing choices. Regrettably, many popular representations of trans sexualities continue to hark back to the ways in which psychomedical approaches both hypersexualise and de-eroticise trans individuals (Davy and Steinbock, 2012). A recent example is the film *The Danish Girl* (2015, dir: Tom Hooper), based on an historical novel about Lili Elbe, one of the first people to physically transition from male to female (in the 1930s), with the support of her wife. The film, however, presents trans womanhood as a forced feminisation fantasy, like those prevalent in pornography, in which a dominant woman dresses a submissive male who gains sexual enjoyment from his feminised status.

On (not) fitting in: LGB+T

A central question raised by the genealogies of trans -sexual, -gender and GID is how in fact trans relates to being *a* sexuality. The term 'trans sexualities' seems to presuppose a set of discrete sexual identities *of* trans people, or even a sexual orientation *towards* trans people.[3] Like queer sexualities, must trans sexualities be situated in relation to gay, lesbian and bisexual identity markers in order to become readable? Or could representations of trans sexuality emphasise instead the generation of one's gendered bodily aesthetic through sexual desire and erotic encounters (Davy and Steinbock, 2012)? These questions are complicated by the ever-expanding acronym of LGBT (Lesbian-Gay-Bisexual-Transgender) to include Transsexual-Queer-Questioning-Intersex-Asexual and sometimes also 2Spirit-Allies (resulting in the alphabet soup LGBTTQQIA2SA). This history of international community formation and institution naming shows how trans*, transgender and transsexual have been tacked onto larger lesbian, gay and bisexual sexual identities, forming an uneasy alliance.

If trans refers foremost to a gender identity that cuts across these sexual identity monikers, then the 'T' does not belong, because it suggests erroneously that transgender is a sexual orientation with a coherent set of shared political interests (Murib, 2014). On the other hand, the binary homo–heterosexual only makes conceptual sense within a masculine–feminine gender binary, so LGB shares with T a politics of questioning gender normativity. As Susan Stryker explains, '[g]ender's absence renders sexuality largely incoherent, yet gender refuses to be the stable foundation on which a system of sexuality can be theorized' (2004: 212).

The umbrella identity term 'transgender' purports to gather into one aggregate all formations of sex/ual and gender-nonconforming identities and expression, sheltering them from discrimination (Singer, 2014: 259). Yet the popular uptake of transgender in political and educational arenas since the 1990s continues to erase local manifestations of gender variance, and to subsume important cultural and racial differences in the understanding of gender and sexuality concepts (Davidson, 2007). David Valentine's 2007 study of New York City's gender-variant subcultures interrogates the ways in which the category transgender emerges from within White middle- and upper-class versions of gender, eliding interlinkages with racialised sexual subcultures. Two key sites of study are stud (African American queer female-bodied masculinity) and *travesti* (South American queer male-bodied femininity) identity cultures (cf. Lewis, 2013; Kuper et al., 2014). The elimination of local erotic knowledge can also occur through colonialising impulses, particularly found in anthropological research on *hijra* and *waria* Southeast Asian identities.[4] Nominations such as third sex or third gender collapse cross-cultural figures into the same sort of transgender experience, overlaying Western sex/gender systems while simultaneously 'romancing the transgender native' (Towle and Morgan, 2006). The *TSQ: Transgender Studies Quarterly* special issue on 'Decolonizing the transgender imaginary' challenges 'transgender studies to look closely at its geography and historical location as the product of a largely North American settler culture' (2014: 308).

The domination of North American conceptualisations is repeated in cultural representations, which more often than not present trans people as sexual freaks with improbable anatomy, e.g. pregnant men and she males. In a recent zine, trans woman Mira Bellwether states (2013):

> In most media we're either cast as sexual predators who prey on unsuspecting men (hence 'trap', the disgusting slur that's given to those of us who mostly pass as cis women or are taken to be cis women), or we're looked down upon as objects of pity who do not and could not pass as women at all, who couldn't conceivably even HAVE a sex life.

To combat these prejudices, safer sex handbooks and guidebooks like *Trans Bodies, Trans Selves* (2014) address the self-esteem issues that trans people can suffer from, which have the potential to result in abusive partners, sexual violence and high-risk sex that can lead to contraction of HIV.[5]

Genital epistemologies and the visual reveal

With the horror of stigma also comes fascination, or desire for the other. Erotically infused spectacles like drag performance and beauty pageants, as well as sex workers or sexualised display in pornography, have long dominated mainstream trans representation. Most well-known fiction films in the trans cinema canon deal with the Western focus on genitals as the essential determinants of sex and sexual identity through a shock device known as 'the reveal'. Danielle M. Seid describes the reveal as 'a moment in a trans person's life when the trans person is subjected to the pressures of a pervasive gender/sex system that seeks to make public the "truth" of the trans person's gendered and sexed body' (2014: 176). In media representations, such as those of trans woman Dil in *The Crying Game* (1992, dir: Neil Jordan) or Brandon Teena in *Boys Don't Cry* (1999, dir: Kimberley Pierce), this plays a structuring role in the audience's knowledge of a transgender life. Whereas the trans child Ludo in *Ma vie en Rose* (1997, dir: Alain Berliner) manages to avoid this cinematic device of exposure, the film still works within the harmful stereotype of trans people as 'evil deceivers and make-believers' (Bettcher, 2007). Bettcher explains the double bind of a conflated gender presentation (appearance) and sexed body (reality) as locking in a trans person to invisiblity or visiblity as a pretender; either way, she states, 'we are fundamentally viewed as illusory' (2007: 50, 59). All trans (self-)representation faces the predicament of how to break out of this logic. Visual representations of trans people are always already coded as sexual due to the socio-cultural reduction of gender identity to the sexed status of genitals.

The case of the sexually ob-scene in queer porn

Gender regimes are central to the development of visual sexual cultures. There is a stark difference in the ways in which trans men and genderqueers, versus trans women, have become integrated into the ever-expanding genre of dyke and queer porn. Queer porn has included trans men and masculine genderqueers (for example Papi Coxxx or Jiz Lee in *The Crash Pad Series*, 2005–) but transfemininity has largely been excluded from dyke and queer porn projects. This differential treatment relates to trans women's struggles for erotic visibility off-screen in queer sexual cultures. Though a few trans women have featured in queer porn production in the US and Canada in the past three years, significant barriers remain that are anchored in long-standing transphobic suspicions regarding trans women's real sex and real desire. To disentangle one strand of gender and sexuality in the term 'trans sexualities', I offer an analysis of the relationship between the social conditions of lesbian/queer trans women and the production of queer sex culture, whether DIY, alt or for-profit.

Taking the demarcation of what is obscene as her starting point for understanding sexual cultures, Linda Williams (1999) detects a shift away from the simple repression of sex, keeping it locked up in secret museums or in the repositories of the powerful few. She suggests that sex and sexuality are instead being generated, mobilised and pushed out into the open in the cultural gesture of on/scenity (1999: 282), 'the gesture by which a culture brings on to the public scene the very organs, acts, "bodies and pleasures" that have heretofore been designated ob-off-scene, that is, as needing to be kept out of view' (ibid.). To become visible as a sexual subject, one needs to speak sex, to have it intelligibly speak you. For trans sex, the story of entering the public scene and becoming visible appears fraught. As in mainstream sexual cultures, queer subcultures have cohesive aesthetics in terms of which organs, acts, bodies and pleasures they bring on/scene. Despite the proliferation of queer porn, transfeminine sex within supposedly progressive sexual cultures continues to be rendered obscene.

Tobi Hill-Meyer, a trans woman of mixed race from Eugene, Oregon, and an award-winning director and talent, offers the following analysis:

> Trans women are often told we need to hate our bodies and our sexuality. Denial of medical care is threatened if we admit to liking sex before vaginoplasty. Alternatively, we are often expected to find validation through being sexually available to men. Again, medical care can be denied if we admit to not being

attracted to men. We deserve better than these options . . . We deserve sexuality on our own terms. And queer porn is one way I've found that delivers that.

(Hill-Meyer, 2011)

The hope is that queer porn will counter the sexual stigma attached to the gendered feminine term, 'tranny', that is very often found in the niche description 'tranny porn'.

The spring of 2012 saw an explosion in the American blogosphere, and in the transnational formats of Facebook and other social media, over the use of the slur term 'tranny', invoked by gay men as well as by trans men in the porn industry.[6] Neil Patrick Harris, Dan Savage and even RuPaul came under fire for potentially propagating trans-hate in their use of the word. Trans man Morty Diamond, the porn director of the early *TrannyFags* videos, Ken Rowe at *Trannywood Pictures*, Buck Angel and Kate Bornstein, among others, weighed in on how the term has either historically been reclaimed or even started as a intracommunity term of endearment – but for many it conjures up a figure of the trans woman as hypersexualised, always hard, lascivious, or de-eroticised and grotesquely ugly; a 'male' body in women's clothing.

In a response to Hill-Meyer (2009), 'A' notes that 'its uncool to be a shemale, but rad to be a trannyfag' (*The Bilerico Project*, comment 25 March 2009). Shemale porn is marked by the contrast of high-femme garb and the centrality of the penis – a skewed picture of what sex is like for most trans women, who undergo hormone replacement treatment that makes it harder to have an erection, and who may call their penises 'clits' or 'girlcocks'. This porn is never screened in queer contexts, and cross-over performances of shemale stars in queer porn are rare. Buck Angel, the first commercial trans man performer recognised by the Adult Video News (AVN) Awards and the Feminist Porn Awards in Toronto, was celebrated with the prize 'Boundary Breaker of the Year' in 2008 for his trans and genre crossover work. In 2007 he teamed up with the hugely successful Allanah Starr, a 'real American shemale pornstar', to create the first trans-on-trans sex scene produced by a major production company, Gia Darling Entertainment. Nominated for the 2007 AVN awards for 'Most Outrageous Sex Scene', it also caught the attention of British artist Marc Quinn, who cast a life-sized bronze version of their coupling.

Julia Serano, who coined the term trans-misogyny in her 2007 book *Whipping Girl: A Transsexual Woman on Sexism and the Scapegoating of Femininity*, identifies the medical and cultural sexualisation of trans women as a logic that reduces women to their sexual attractiveness to men. In short, '[t]rans-misogyny is steeped in the assumption that femaleness and femininity are inferior to, and exist primarily for the benefit of, maleness and masculinity' (2012: 1). Transitioning on the femininity continuum is considered to be a way of enabling your own sexual objectification rather than something done for personal, emotional or aesthetic reasons. With the exclusion of lesbian and bisexual trans women, or those who desire other trans folks, this logic closes down sexual expression to passing as heterosexual. Serano argues that '[p]erhaps the most visible example of trans-misogyny is the way in which trans women and others on the trans female/feminine spectrum are routinely sexualised in the media, within psychological, social science and feminist discourses, and in society at large' (ibid.).

In this environment, trans women who confront sexualisation by participating in porno do so at risk of being read through a trans-misogynist lens. The tender and moving embrace of shared trans desire in the early short by Barbara DeGenevieve, *Out of the Woods* (2002), featuring Tennetty and JJ Bitch was presented on Ssspread.com, the premier porn site for 'hot femmes, studly butches and lots of genderfuck', from January 2001 to February 2004.

Yet while many trans men followed in the footsteps of JJ, the video didn't usher more trans women into the queer porn world. For example, it was not until 2011 that Courtney Trouble's QueerPorn.TV site featured two trans women.

Clearly, trans women are not out of the woods yet. A major step forward came when Drew Deveaux, a model and porn actress, won the Feminist Porn Awards 'Heartthrob of 2011'. Deveaux, an androgynous trans woman from Toronto, writes that 'Through performing in porn, I've been able to take the world's fucked up notions about trans women and fuck them into blissful oblivion' (Deveaux, 2010). She nevertheless experienced feeling isolated in queer sex culture as a trans woman with a vagina. In 2012 she coined the term 'the cotton ceiling' to describe the feeling of being invisible as a sexual, queer woman. The cotton ceiling, like the glass ceiling for women in the workplace, is a barrier that limits access to power, recognition and respect. It refers literally to the panties of (cisgender) dykes, suggesting a social barrier to being recognised in queer sex cultures by cisdykes. As trans writer and activist Roz Kaveney sees it, this obstacle is present because, 'however theoretically accepting of trans people a lot of progressives may be, when it comes to actually having sex with us, they vote with their ... um ... feet' (2012).

Hill-Meyer's award-winning video *Doing It Ourselves: The Trans Women Porn Project* (2010) is a project by a group that has chosen to stop waiting for recognition and make its own sexual images, with the very narrative of the vignettes held together by the communal excitement in *doing it*. It begins with Tobi shouting, 'June, Lucretia, there is a new Trannywood video!' No one rushes into the living room, so she enjoys it herself. During the sweet after-glow of a solo masturbation scene with her girlcock in a strap-on holder, a Hitachi wand and a butt plug, Lucretia walks in on Tobi. They argue over whether *TrannyFags* is better than the Trannywood videos. June interrupts: 'Why are you watching fags having sex? Why aren't you watching dyke porn?' Tobi claims: 'There isn't much in the way of transdykes, and feminist porn', to which Lucretia replies, 'I'd give a lot to see porn like *this*, except with trans women'. Tobi grabs the camera and encourages June and Lucretia to make out, to make what they wish they could see themselves. The video then cuts to Tobi editing the footage and deciding to expand the project to include more trans and queer folks having sex with trans women.

The next scene, with Drew (Deveaux) and Daisy (Joss Blains), begins in much the same way as the first one, with a discussion of the sexual representation problem for trans women. They both say they want to be part of this project of producing trans women porn, because trans girls are hot too. Avoiding the issue of shemale pornography, they focus on their shared desire for dyke porn, but, as Drew puts it: 'Why are trans girls not in it? They're hot too.' Their scene becomes indisputable proof that trans girls have hot dyke sex too, complete with fisting, strap-on sex, inventive positions and powerplay. In the progression of each scene, one can feel a palpable building-up of the self-confidence and sexual excitement of the trans women involved. The video is edited to emphasise the DIY dynamic of a community project, by and for trans women; a clear example is in the aesthetic, rather than functional, integration of the handheld camera.

Nevertheless, the scenes are obviously rehearsed and staged for the camera, and the 'let's make our own porn!' set-up is clearly predetermined. As in many porn films, the acting can be described as wooden. The video stands as an instance of political discourse, not a pure index of reality. In Judith Butler's discussion of censorship, she admits the utility of realist aesthetics for some representational images: 'when we *point to something as real*, and in political discourse it is very often imperative to wield the ontological indicator in precisely that way, this is not the end but the beginning of the political problematic'

(2000: 489). The realist mode of porn, particularly in our on/scene sexual culture, is the defining means by which to point to someone, some desire, as real. The aesthetic elements in *Doing It Ourselves* all point to trans women's desire as real. At the same time, the privileged confession of sexual desire evinced by each and every performance points out the limits of a culture's sexual fantasy, points to the edge of obscenity. For Butler, 'fantasy is not equated with what is not real, but rather what is not yet real'; hence the introduction of trans women in queer porn evidences what is not real *just yet* in queer sex cultures (2000: 489).

When queer pornographer Courtney Trouble released the unprecedented two-and-a-half-hour-long film *Trans Grrrls: Revolution Porn Style Now!* (2012), the film sold more copies than any of her other titles, while scooping up various nominations and awards. In the Troublefilms network, alongside James Darling's FTMFucker website for trans male porn, Hill-Meyer's site doingitonline.com releases episodes of 'sex positive porn with a trans female focus'. Other notable upcoming directors include Lola Clavo, a Spanish trans woman based in London whose work was awarded the Berlin PorYes Award in 2013 for her contribution to the field.[7] The limits of the queer fantasy just keep getting pushed.

To conclude: proliferating print, digital and alternative sexualities

From the first Western press coverage of trans figures such as Lili Elbe in the 1930s, and the American Christine Jorgensen who transitioned in Denmark in the 1950s, trans was framed as the alluring spectacle of a powerful new medical science that can transform bodies. Increasingly, though, representations of trans lives are not primarily psychomedical: the presentation of television star and trans woman of colour Laverne Cox on *TIME* magazine's May 2014 cover signposted the tipping point in the generation of new narratives, faces and relationships to media.

While porn is in the leading position at the forefront of sexual activism, in close second are the game-changing conversations taking place through social media, news websites and online media watchdogs.[8] Organisations like the UK's Trans Media Watch successfully attack popular representations of trans characters, such as those on the show *Little Britain* (2003–2006), that are used to comic or tragic effect.[9] Inflammatory language, for example on RuPaul's show *Drag Race* (2009–), is regularly checked by GLAAD. When mainstream press reporter Katie Couric presented an episode on trans lives, she was challenged for her intrusive questions about her guests' genitals (or hormonal/surgical transitions). In the next episode she offered a heartfelt apology and corrected the mistake in a widely circulated 'learning moment' speech.[10] Social media-led movements also provide a space for partners of trans people to affirm their relationships, with Janet Mock's partner Aaron Tredwell's podcast 'The Missing Piece' being a prime example.

New televisual series, webcasts and independent cinema are breaking ground by showcasing trans actors in trans roles while introducing narratives that engage trans lives beyond their transition. Jami Clayton as Nomi Marks in the Wachowskis' *Sense8* (2015–) may be a lesbian trans woman, but her primary concern is beating a shadowy enemy with her hacker skills, together with other sensates. *Tangerine* (2015, dir: Sean S. Baker) follows two trans women of colour sex workers over a day, but focuses on how, since one has been released from prison after a month inside, she needs to track down her cheating boyfriend, while her best friend spreads the word about her upcoming singing gig. Already attracting a large following online for its multi-racial casting, *Her Story* (2016, dir: Sydney Freehand), co-written by Laura Zak and Jen Richards, is about the sex lives of queer and trans women, told in short vignettes that tackle trans-misogyny and the cotton ceiling head-on. In the UK, *Boy Meets Girl* (2015–) is a BBC2 sitcom starring Rebecca Root in the role of a trans woman developing a relationship with a younger man, scripted by trans man Elliot Kerrigan, who was discovered as a winner of the Trans Comedy Award's (2013) search for trans-positive portrayals.

A major shift in how trans people dialogue with and in media forums is that finally a discussion around trans sexuality is addressing broader sexual dimensions than the status of one's genitals.[11] For instance, on the agenda are the disproportionate discrimination against trans sex workers, the media invisiblity of trans women and men of colour and the issues of trans people suffering sexual abuse, domestic violence and incarceration/prison rape (cf. Stanley and Smith, 2011). Discussions of trans sexualities, bodies and identities are now marked by trans people's refusal to be silenced and misrepresented by medical practitioners, academics and cisgender media-makers. The incredible upsurge of research in the field of transgender studies promises to deepen the specific contributions and insights provided by trans sexualities to include the study of not only gender and sexuality but also colonialisation, racialisation, biopolitics and transnational approaches to ending discrimination and hate-based violence.

Notes

1. Pink Therapy in London, UK has most famously propagated the term Gender and Sexual Diversities (GSD) as a replacement for what they see as an excessively narrow and exclusive LGBT umbrella (Reid-Smith, 2013).
2. The Standards of Care (SOC) for the Health of Transsexual, Transgender, and Gender Nonconforming People (version 7) written by the World Professional Association for Transgender Health take a more practical support to therapy, noting that clients may request assistance with their relationships and sexual health. For example, they may want to explore their 'sexuality and intimacy-related concerns' (2012: 30).
3. See Tompkins (2014) on the future of a sex-positive trans politics about how to deal with trans partners whose desire for trans people is considered fetishistic.
4. Many examples can be found in Gilbert Herdt's *Third Sex, Third Gender: Beyond Sexual Dimorphism in Culture and History*, which documents variations in gender roles and identities across the Balkans, Native American societies, India, Polynesia and New Guinea.
5. Today trans people, particularly women of colour, bear the brunt of the crisis (Centers for Disease Control and Prevention, 2016).
6. Since then, petitions to change the industry-standard category to 'trans porn' or 'trans feminine porn' from 'shemale' and 'tranny porn' have circulated widely; see, for example, Poe (2014). Something that is heartening is the change of name for the trans adult industry recognition body (hosted by Grooby Productions) from 'The Tranny Awards' (2008–) to 'Transgender Erotica Awards' in 2013, for its seventh edition.
7. Lola Clavo (personal website). Available at: http://lolaclavo.com (accessed 20 January 2016).
8. Leading the way in Europe is the transnational project sponsored by the GRUNDTVIG Learning Partnership, 'Page One', 'a collaboration of five European transgender equality organisations working together with the aim of exchanging knowledge and developing strategies to improve trans representation and visibility in the media'. Anyone can download a free media guide and trans guide. Available at: http://transandmedia.wordpress.com (accessed 20 January 2016).
9. Trans Media Watch. Available at: www.transmediawatch.org/ (accessed 20 January 2016).
10. The first episode can be watched on the Katie Couric site. Available at: http://katiecouric.com/videos/orange-is-the-new-black-laverne-cox/ (accessed 20 January 2016). Further discussion of the second episode, including the key clip, can be watched on the Advocate.com site. Available at: www.advocate.com/politics/transgender/2014/06/11/watch-laverne-cox-katie-couric-shows-power-education (accessed 20 January 2016).

11 A great example is trans activist and author Janet Mock responding to an intrusive interview with Piers Morgan by 'flipping the script' and interviewing a cisgender woman in the same manner to show how inappropriate questions about genitalia and personal memories about one's body are when posed to a trans woman. Available at: www.advocate.com/politics/media/2014/04/29/watch-janet-mock-flips-script-cisgender-host (accessed 20 January 2016).

Bibliography

American Psychiatric Association (2013) *Diagnostic and Statistical Manual of Mental Disorders: DSM V*. Arlington: American Psychiatric Association.

Balzer, C. and Hutta, J.S. (with Adrián, T., Hyndal, P. and Stryker, S.) (2012) *Volume 6: TRANS-RESPECT VERSUS TRANSPHOBIA WORLDWIDE—A Comparative Review of the Human-rights Situation of Gender-variant/Trans People, TGEU*. http://transrespect.org/wp-content/uploads/2015/08/TvT_research-report.pdf (accessed 11 September 2014).

Bellwether, M. (2013) 'Mira Bellwether and "Fucking Trans Women" Zine: The Autostraddle Interview By Kennedy'. 9 August. *Autostraddle.com*. www.autostraddle.com/mira-bellwether-author-and-illustrator-of-fucking-trans-women-zine-the-autostraddle-interview/ (accessed 20 January 2015).

Bettcher, T.M. (2007) 'Evil Deceivers and Make-Believers: On Transphobic Violence and the Politics of Illusion'. *Hypatia*. Volume 22 (3): 43–64.

Blanchard, R. (1989) 'The Classification and Labeling of Nonhomosexual Gender Dysphorias'. *Archives of Sexual Behavior*. Volume 18: 315–334.

Butler, J. (2000) 'The Force of Fantasy: Feminism, Mapplethorpe, and Discursive Excess', in D. Cornell (ed) *Feminism and Pornography*. Oxford: Oxford University Press.

Cabral, M. and Viturro (2006) '(Trans)Sexual Citizenship in Contemporary Argentina', in P. Currah, R.M. Juang and S. Price Minter (eds) *Transgender Rights*. Minneapolis: Minnesota University Press.

Centers for Disease Control and Prevention (2016) 'HIV Among Transgender People in the United States'. www.cdc.gov/hiv/group/gender/transgender/ (accessed 18 March 2017).

Davidson, M. (2007) 'Seeking Refuge Under the Umbrella: Inclusion, Exclusion, and Organizing within the Category *Transgender*'. *Sexuality Research and Social Policy*. Volume 4 (4): 60–80.

Davy, Z. and Steinbock, E. (2012) '"Sexing Up" Bodily Aesthetics: Notes Towards Theorizing Trans Sexuality', in S. Hines and Y. Taylor (eds) *Sexualities: Past Reflections, Future Directions*. New York: Palgrave Macmillan.

Deveaux, D. (2010) 'I Took It Good for Queer Porn TV and I Loved It'. 12 November. *QueerPorn.TV*. www.queerporn.tv/wp/drew-deveaux (accessed 20 January 2015).

Frank, C. (2014) 'The Tranny Awards Are Getting a Less Offensive Name'. 10 March. *Cosmopolitan*. www.cosmopolitan.com/entertainment/news/a21825/tranny-awards-becoming-transgender-erotica-awards/ (accessed 18 February 2017).

Herdt, G. (ed) (1993) *Third Sex, Third Gender: Beyond Sexual Dimorphism in Culture and History*. New York: Zone Books.

Hill-Meyer, T. (2009) 'What Transmisogyny Looks Like'. 25 March. *The Bilerico Project | Daily Experiments in LGBTQ*. www.bilerico.com/2009/03/what_transmisogyny_looks_like.php (accessed 20 January 2015).

Hill-Meyer, T. (2011) 'I Had a Titgasm for Queer Porn TV and I Loved It'. 7 February. *QueerPorn.TV*. www.queerporn.tv/wp/tobi (accessed 20 January 2015).

Kaveney, R. (2012) 'Some Thoughts on the Cotton Ceiling'. 26 March. *RozK.Livejournal.com*. www.rozk.livejournal.com/445853.html (accessed 20 January 2015).

Kuper, L., Wright, L. and Mustanski, B. (2014) 'Stud Identity among Female-Born Youth of Color: Joint Conceptualizations for Gender Variance and Same-Sex Sexuality'. *Journal of Homosexuality*. Volume 61 (5): 714–731.

Lewis, V. (2013) 'Thinking Figurations Otherwise: Reframing Dominant Knowledges of Sex and Gender Variance in Latin America', in S. Stryker and A. Aizura (eds) *The Transgender Studies Reader 2*. New York: Routledge.

Murib, Z. (2014) 'LGBT'. *TSQ: Transgender Studies Quarterly.* Volume 1 (1–2): 118–120.
Nadal, K.L., Skolnik, A. and Wong, Y. (2012) 'Interpersonal and Systemic Microaggressions towards Transgender People: Implications for Counseling'. *Journal of LGBT Issues in Counseling.* Volume 6 (1): 55–82.
North, A. (2014). 'How OKCupid Has Become More Inclusive on Gender and Sexuality'. 19 November. *NYtimes.com.* http://op-talk.blogs.nytimes.com/2014/11/19/how-okcupid-has-become-more-inclusive-on-gender-and-sexuality/?_r=0 (accessed 20 January 2016).
Pfeffer, C.A. (2014) 'Making Space for Trans Sexualities'. *Journal of Homosexuality.* Volume 61 (5): 597–604.
Poe, C. (2014) 'I Am a Pornstar Asking the Porn Industry to Stop Using the Name Shemale'. 8 December. *Xojane.com.* www.xojane.com/sex/chelsea-poe-shemale-slur-petition (accessed 20 January 2016).
Reid-Smith, T. (2013) 'Therapists Rename Gay, Bi, and Trans People as GSDs'. 21 February. *Gaystarnews.com.* www.gaystarnews.com/article/therapists-rename-gay-bi-and-trans-people-gsds210213 (accessed 20 January 2016).
Seid, D.M. (2014) 'Reveal'. *TSQ: Transgender Studies Quarterly.* Volume 1 (1–2): 176–178.
Serano, J. (2007) *Whipping Girl: A Transsexual Woman on Sexism and the Scapegoating of Femininity.* Berkeley: Seal Press.
Serano, J. (2012) 'Trans-Misogyny Primer'. 3 April. *Whipping Girl Blogspot.* http://juliaserano.blogspot.nl/2012/04/trans-misogyny-primer.html (accessed 19 January 2015).
Singer, T.B. (2014) 'Umbrella.' *TSQ: Transgender Studies Quarterly.* Volume 1 (1–2): 259–261.
Spade, D. (2011) *Normal Life: Administrative Violence, Critical Trans Politics and the Limits of Law.* Brooklyn: South End Press.
Stanley, E.A. and Smith, N. (eds) (2011) *Captive Genders: Trans Embodiment and the Prison Industrial Complex.* Oakland: AK Press.
Steinbock, E. (2011) 'Shimmering Images: On Transgender Embodiment and Cinematic Aesthetics'. Unpublished thesis. Amsterdam: University of Amsterdam.
Stryker, S. (2004) 'Transgender Studies: Queer Theory's Evil Twin'. *GLQ: A Journal of Lesbian and Gay Studies.* Volume 10 (2): 212–215.
Tompkins, A.B. (2014). '"There's no chasing involved": Cis/Trans Relationships, "Tranny Chasers" and the Future of a Sex-Positive Trans Politics'. *Journal of Homosexuality.* Volume 61 (5): 766–780.
Towle, E. and Morgan, L. (2006) 'Romancing the Transgender Native: Rethinking the Use of the "Third Gender" Concept', in S. Stryker and S. Whittle (eds) *The Transgender Studies Reader.* New York: Routledge.
Valentine, D. (2007) *Imagining Transgender: An Ethnography of a Category.* Durham: Duke University Press.
Weber, P. (2014) 'Confused by All the New Facebook Genders? Here's What They Mean'. 21 February. *Slate.com.* www.slate.com/blogs/lexicon_valley/2014/02/21/gender_facebook_now_has_56_categories_to_choose_from_including_cisgender.html (accessed 20 January 2016).
Williams, L. (1999) *Hard Core: Power, Pleasure, and the 'Frenzy of the Visible'.* Berkeley: California University Press.
World Professional Association for Transgender Health. (2012) *The Standards of Care (SOC) for the Health of Transsexual, Transgender, and Gender Nonconforming People (version 7).* https://s3.amazonaws.com/amo_hub_content/Association140/files/Standards%20of%20Care%20V7%20-%202011%20WPATH%20(2)(1).pdf (accessed 20 January 2016).

Media

Boy Meets Girl (2015–) [TV Series]. UK: BBC2.
Boys Don't Cry (1999) Directed by Kimberly Pierce [Film]. USA: Fox Searchlight Pictures.
Doing It Ourselves: The Trans Women Porn Project (2010) Directed by Tobi Hill-Meyer [Film]. USA: Handbasket Productions.

FTMFucker.com. Available at: http://ftmfucker.com/ (accessed 20 January 2016).
GLAAD. Available at: www.glaad.org/ (accessed 18 March 2017).
Her Story (2016) Directed by Sydney Freehand [Film/New Media]. USA: Katherine Fisher/Speed of Joy Productions. Available at: http://herstoryshow.com/ (accessed 20 January 2016).
Little Britain (2003–2006) [TV Series]. UK: BBC2.
Ma Vie en Rose (1997) Directed by Alain Berliner [Film]. France: Canal+.
Out of the Woods (2002) Directed by Barbara DeGenevieve [Video] No longer available at: www.ssspread.com (last accessible January 2001–February 2004).
RuPaul's Drag Race (2009–) [TV programme]. USA: LogoTV.
Sense8 (2015–) [TV programme]. USA: Netflix Originals.
Tangerine (2015) Directed by Sean S. Baker [Film]. USA: Duplass Brothers Productions.
The Crash Pad Series (2005–) Available at: http://crashpadseries.com/ (accessed 20 January 2016).
The Crying Game (1992) Directed by Neil Jordan [Film]. UK: Palace Pictures.
The Danish Girl (2015) Directed by Tom Hooper [Film]. UK: Working Title Films.
TrannyFags (2003) Directed by Morty Diamond [Film]. USA: Self-Produced.
Trans Grrrls: Revolution Porn Style Now! (2012) Directed by Courtney Trouble [Film]. USA: Trouble Films.
Tredwell, A. and Mock, J. (2011–2012) *The Missing Piece*. [Podcast] Available at: http://janetmock.com/missing-piece-podcast/ (accessed 20 January 2016).

4

REPRESENTING LESBIANS IN FILM AND TELEVISION

Rebecca Beirne

Mapping the key features of lesbian representation in the media is a difficult task. This is due to the frequent polarisation of lesbian representations, most notably when it comes to sex. Lesbian identity and sex are simultaneously fetishised and disavowed by the media and society at large, and this creates a problem when it comes to representational analysis. Visibility for lesbians in mainstream and alternative media is both desired and critiqued, with the same representations deemed positive or negative by different consumers. As a result, the complications of identifying the positions and boundaries of what defines lesbian representation are under constant negotiation. Thus, even if evaluating the authenticity of lesbian representation is broadly seen as important, how to achieve authenticity is more difficult to ascertain. The duality of lesbian representation is perhaps most clearly expressed in the complex representations of lesbian sex and sexuality in fiction film and television, marked as they are by a history of (sometimes concurrent) invisibility and fetishisation.

Lesbian sexuality has a history of invisibility in moving-image media. Strong sociocultural prohibitions against female same-sex desire and relationships, together with the structures and address of these media industries, have resulted in the relative absence of openly lesbian characters onscreen. Filmic representations of lesbianism have historically fallen within particular norms. Some of the most popular of these tropes have included lesbians as: villains, for example in *High Tension* (2003, dir: Alexandre Aja); victims, as seen in *The Children's Hour* (1961, dir: William Wyler) and *Lost and Delirious* (2001, dir: Léa Pool); or characters whose lesbian desires are narratively or visually structured in direct relation to male characters or audiences, such as in *Girlfriend* (2004, dir: Karan Razdan).

Lesbian representation in television series has also frequently followed similar themes. As a later form of moving-image media – one with different narrative structures, economic requirements and relationships to audiences – television has also built up a few tropes of its own. These include one-episode or mini-arc characters included to allow major (usually heterosexual) characters to come to terms with their prejudice or occasionally show how open-minded they are. There is also the character who is necessary to highlight aspects of the main character or perform narrative exposition but who enjoys almost no storyline, or at least no depiction of romantic and/or sexual relationships with other women. In *Friends* (1994–2004), for example, minor character Carol's relationship with another woman was not a story arc but instead the basis of jokes about ex-husband and major character Ross' masculinity and aptitude with women. Brief flirtations with lesbian desire by lead heterosexual female characters have also occurred, with such temporary heteroflexibility tending to coincide with ratings grabs (early Sweeps Week examples include *LA Law* (1991), *Picket Fences* (1993), *Party of Five* (1999) and *Ally McBeal* (1999)). Other series with major lesbian characters have had a double standard when it comes to the representation of their sexual relationships. Despite being celebrated for their lesbian representation, both *Buffy the Vampire Slayer* (1997–2003) and *South of Nowhere* (2005–8), for example, presented the relationships of their lesbian characters as less sexual than those of their heterosexual counterparts. The representation of lesbian characters in *Queer as Folk* (UK, 1999–2000; USA, 2000–5) was also insufficiently sexual.

Studying the representation of lesbian individuals and characters in moving-image media has helped us to understand the key tropes and characterisations that help define lesbians in the public imagination, debate the potential effects of these media forms and consider what kinds of media representations we would like to see going forward. Dominant scholarly approaches to lesbian representation in the media have included unearthing and documenting explicitly or subtextually lesbian characters (e.g. White, 1999; Gross, 2001; Capsuto, 2000; Tropiano, 2002; Walters, 2003; Benshoff and Griffin, 2005) and evaluating the discursive meanings of narratives, characters, celebrities or gendered representation (see, for example, Wilton, 1995; Cairns, 2006; Akass and McCabe, 2006; Beirne, 2008 and 2012; Heller, 2013). With mass media as the place 'where public life happens at this point in Western history' and 'where viewers learn about "others"' (Reed, 2005: 24), most scholars agree as to the importance of representation, even if they differ in their perspectives on what might constitute the best kind of lesbian visibility.

One of the potential outcomes of increased lesbian representation in the media is offering points of identification for lesbian and bisexual women. Sarah C. Gomillion and Traci A. Giuliano's 2011 study, for example, found that 'media role models serve as sources of pride, inspiration and comfort', with the potential to 'positively influence GLB identity' (2011: 330). In terms of how lesbian representation potentially impacts upon a more general viewership, Sue Jackson's study of 16–18 year olds indicated that particular kinds of lesbian representations in the media can result in viewers seeing lesbianism as 'hot' and 'experimental' (2012: 157–8). Observing that 'as yet we know little about the effect of these portrayals on the heterosexual majority with largely negative attitudes toward homosexuals' (Bonds-Raacke et al., 2007: 21), Bonds-Raacke and colleagues attempted to ascertain the recognition of positive or negative gay and lesbian characters within the media, and the effects they may have upon viewers' perception of homosexuality. While media-effects research can be contentious, it is essential within an area where much discussion of 'positive' textual representation relies upon an assumption that LGBT media images have the potential to educate potentially homophobic or misogynist viewers, even as they offer points of identification for LGBT viewers. Each of these studies is of course reliant on having a clear idea of what a good lesbian (or gay) character or representation should be like, yet establishing the characteristics of, and boundaries around, such an ideal is not at all straightforward.

Terminology and definition

Identifying and articulating definitional boundaries in lesbian and gay media studies is not quite as simple as it may initially seem, with associated terminology coming under fire where it is seen to exceed its relevance. Even using the term 'lesbian representation' is contentious. Writing about lesbian representation in the media, I frequently tie myself in knots debating whether to use 'same-sex desiring women', 'lesbians and bisexual women', 'female homosexuals' or multiple other formulations in order to describe a selection of characters that, while differing from each other in various ways, still express exclusive or primary desire for other women in dialogue, visually or narratively. In trying to find ways to categorise media texts focusing on lesbians, this becomes even more complicated; terms such as 'lesbian' or 'queer women', for example, are not necessarily appropriate when discussing the diversity of identities, and the representations thereof, among same-sex attracted women around the globe. For example, in mainland China some scholars have seen 'the appearance of lesbian films' to be 'closely tied to the infiltration of a global discourse on homosexuality' (Shi, 2012: 141). As Shi observes, however, 'the character of this cinema [is] no less shaped by the local environment' (ibid.), and just as there are differential understandings of lesbian desire and relationships around the world, national and regional cinemas, for example, can have their own trends and themes when it comes to the representation of female same-sex desire.

In the past, the limited cohort of screen representations of female same-sex desire has made national and regional trends difficult to identify, but steady growth in representation is making such studies more viable (see, for example, Cairns, 2006; Collins, 2007; Moss and Simić, 2011; Lewis, 2012; Shi, 2012). As global media products become ever more accessible through the internet, it is equally the case that most film and television creators are working in the context of the growing global group of screen texts representing female same-sexuality. Shi's use of terms such as 'lesbian cinema' and 'lesbian films', even in a cultural context where the very term 'lesbian' is contested, highlights that there are similarities between cultural depictions which focus on same-sex desiring female characters or lesbian relationships or sexuality, particularly when it comes to film.

As Bonds-Raacke et al. observe, 'we are now seeing gays and lesbians portrayed in the mass media with greater frequency than ever before' (2007: 21). The number of lesbian characters in film and television has certainly increased in the past two decades. Tricia Jenkins is correct that 'lesbian sexuality has become more explicitly manifest in mainstream film' (2005: 491), and in independent film from around the world, the number of representations have risen exponentially since the millennium. Television too has also come a long way, graduating (mostly) from the lesbian villains of the 1970s and the more sympathetic but desexualised characters of the 1990s (Moritz, 1994). Complexity of representation has also increased through the diversity of characters offered in lesbian-focused series such as *The L Word* (2004–9), *Sugar Rush* (2005–6), *Exes and Ohs* (2007, 2011), *Lip Service* (2010–11), *The Real L Word* (2010–12) and *Candy Bar Girls* (2011). These series offer power lesbians, a butch policewoman, desire-fuelled teenagers, an architect, lesbian lotharios, a filmmaker, lesbians with children and drug-taking lesbians. They may be neurotic or stable, coupled or single. The power of these series is that in offering more than one major lesbian character, the representational pressure on a single character or couple to signify lesbianism is relaxed, allowing for more representational diversity within the identity category.

Lesbian-identified characters and female same-sex relationships have also become more fully integrated in mainstream series with a broader address. This is most notably seen in television ensemble series, with their more extensive and complex narratives and the reduced signifying pressure on an individual 'lead'. Ensemble teen series, for example, such as *South of Nowhere* (2005–8), *Skins* (2007–13), *Glee* (2009–15) and *Pretty Little Liars* (2010–), have featured young lesbian and bisexual women among their major characters. In each of these cases a coming-out narrative is featured but, in keeping with the needs of serial narrative, the characters also have a number of other storylines, as a result of which the sexuality of a given character does not have to be their only or even their defining feature.

In the world of more adult television, perhaps the best example of a series that fully integrates its lesbian characters into a multiplicity of narratives and sexual relationships is the Netflix dramedy *Orange Is the New Black* (2013–). The series is particularly unique in its foregrounding of lesbian desire and sex in multiple characters of varying sexual orientations – including lesbian, bisexual and situational. Some of the diverse representations of lesbian sex seen in the series fit neatly into pre-existing representational economies of lesbian sex, especially in the pilot. Others are sad or comedic, erotic, prosaic or even a little gross. These scenes become less about the representation of lesbian sex as a whole and more about individual characterisation or the establishment of shifting power dynamics, as would also be expected of the representation of heterosexual sex on a television series. In *Orange Is the New Black*, lesbian sex becomes, through repetition, an ordinary part of the representational package. Such increasing visibility and variety in mainstream lesbian representation occurs in the context of a pre-existing, vibrant online subculture that produces and distributes its own lesbian-focused videos, ranging from fan production that assembles or shoots from, to and in between mainstream media, to original web series, short films and even low-budget feature-length films.

As lesbian characters and relationships in moving-image media slowly but steadily increase, the question remains as to how such visibility creates discursive constructs. What, for example, makes for a 'positive' character? For the purposes of their study, Bonds-Raacke and colleagues defined a positive character as one who is '[h]umorous, likeable, mentally stable, safe, honest, kind, responsible, and nonviolent' (Bonds-Raacke et al., 2007: 31). These character traits are clearly inspired by media histories of representing LGBT characters as violent, mentally ill and generally unlikeable. Yet Jack [from *Will and Grace*] and Ellen [DeGeneres] were commonly listed as 'both a negative portrayal and a positive portrayal, suggesting that different people evaluate the same characters very differently' (Bonds-Raacke et al., 2007: 30). This is in keeping with the sharply disparate scholarly and viewer response to lesbian-focused series such as *The L Word* (see Heller, 2013).

With the trend towards televisual anti-heroes in the late 2000s and early 2010s, Bonds-Raacke and colleagues' definition would exclude some of the most popular (heterosexual) television characters of our time. It would also eliminate a number of complex and interesting lesbian, gay and bisexual characters that have connected with audiences over the last decade, such as: Alex from *Orange Is the New Black* (dishonest and irresponsible); Bo from *Lost Girl* (2010–15) (violent); Ian and Mickey from the US version of *Shameless* (2011–) (mentally unstable, violent, dishonest and irresponsible); and pretty much every character in *Sugar Rush*, *The L Word* or *Queer as Folk*. To judge a heterosexual character by the same standards: Walter White (*Breaking Bad*, 2008–13) was certainly never a positive character, but he was without a doubt one of the most memorable of recent television history. Perhaps the definition of positive representation needs revision to take into consideration screen context as well as desired political outcomes.

While Bonds-Raacke et al. seek a sitcom-esque character for their idea of 'positive', the converse ideal is well represented in Vicki L. Eaklor's (2012) 'The Kids Are All Right But the Lesbians Aren't: The Illusion of Progress in Popular Film'. A good representation, according to Eaklor, is one that challenges the status quo. Eaklor asserts that 'visibility comes with a price: to seem as unthreatening as possible' and that 'mainstream and/or popular films remain in the ruts of the wagon road when it comes to queer images and themes, and that this is especially so when the topic is lesbians.' (2012: 167, 154). While Bonds-Raacke and colleagues saw non-threatening representations of lesbian and gay characters in a positive light, many critics, like Eaklor, would like to see lesbian representations that are, at least potentially, threatening to normative ideals of sexuality *and* gender.

The question of lesbian gender presentation in film and television has been of particular interest to scholars as a defining feature of whether a character should be considered a good – or 'authentic' – representation. As it is assumed by almost all scholars that male viewers will be more attracted to feminine-presenting actresses, casting is seen as a key attempt to make the subject matter and characters appeal to a male viewership. Discourse on femininity and lesbian representation has been readily reframed into discussion of the 'heterosexualization of lesbianism' (Jenkins, 2005: 500), with the potential to 'de-lesbianise' a same-sex attracted female character because of their presumed appeal to heterosexual male audiences. It is certainly the case that even non-mainstream films may come under pressure to accede to the standards of beauty prevalent in commercial culture in order to appeal to a broader audience.

An example thereof can be seen in independent Canadian film *Better Than Chocolate* (1999, dir: Anne Wheeler). The producer Sharon MacGowan revealed that some financers, 'who all have approval', disagreed with their casting choices on the basis of 'attractiveness' (according to standard ideals of feminine beauty), with the production almost losing its funding over this issue at one point (personal interview, 2008). To contend that feminine casting serves to 'de-lesbianise' this film, however, privileges costuming and gendered performance over dialogue and visual representations of lesbian desire and sex. To consider the mid-sex wars, trans-friendly 'lesbian utopia' (Stuart, 2006) portrayed in this film as de-lesbianised is way too simplistic, if not absurd.[1] It also discounts the fact that almost all female characters in film and television are feminine, with female masculinity rarely visually represented, even if it is suggested by dialogue. Lesbians are not immune from the limitations on how the media can imagine women.

The gaze, creators and authenticity

Feminist film theory's intensive focus upon the gaze has resulted in much scrutiny as to the extent to which lesbian sexual representation caters to the heterosexual male gaze. This is problematic considering more recent and better understandings of the diversity of audience response (that does not rest solely on gender), as well as consideration of the lesbian gaze. It is, however, understandable, and born of a desire to complicate and flesh out lesbian representations that have long been dominated by limited and simplistic tropes and norms. In both film and television, for example, many representations did, and still do, portray narratives of heterosexual conversion or lesbians who sleep with men. Even where male characters are absent, by inviting the male viewer in, female-exclusive sexuality is seen to be compromised. Equally, desexualised representations can be seen as removing the threat of lesbian sex. In order to be seen as above suspicion of pandering to the male gaze, lesbian sexual representation generally requires at least an air of authenticity.

What, however, *is* authenticity when it comes to lesbian representations in the media? And how exactly are we to establish what authenticity looks like within the conventions of screen media texts? At the simplest level, and in the context of a society that assumes heterosexuality until proven otherwise, a lesbian character on film or television is established onscreen either through:

1 Dialogue: a statement of lesbian identity or attraction to one or more women (in more subtextual contexts this may be more subtly framed through expressing a lack of desire for men).
2 Performance: visual representations of lesbian desire (looks, kisses, touches, sex).

3   Costuming/production design: clothing or cultural products stereotypically associated with lesbianism (particularly in the form of female masculinity or lesbian iconography).

Costume and production design are the most tenuous and culturally dependent of these means of representation. This is due to a reliance on cultural norms aligning lesbianism with female masculinity or feminism – neither of which are particularly apparent in any film or television context. The curious disjunction between the absence of visualised female masculinity onscreen and the dialogue suggesting it (see Beirne, 2008: 90–2) continues to this day, even when it is used to misread lesbianism in heterosexual characters. As the closest approximation to 'coming out' that a fictional character can have, dialogic statements seem the most reliable for establishing an 'authentic' lesbian character. The *performance* of lesbian desire is in contrast perhaps the most common defining moment of representation, but as it is more clearly subject to viewerly interpretation, it is also potentially contentious. How are we to read subtle or suggested representations of lesbian desire? Is a lesbian sex scene to be understood as denoting lesbian or bisexual identity, or might it just be a one-off, perhaps to attract audience attention?

These ways of 'showing' lesbianism onscreen (dialogue, performance, costume) are particularly complicated when it comes to considering lesbian sexuality in terms of audience address and authorship. As Linda Williams points out, the critical response to the sexual content of lesbian-focused film *Blue Is the Warmest Color* (2013, dir: Abdellatif Kechiche) was quite different to the response to similarly explicit films featuring gay male and heterosexual protagonists, reflecting a 'triple standard':

> ... lesbian love and obsession (*amour fou*) receives divided reviews depending on whether one believes heterosexual men are getting off on it – while the nature of its sexual representations are endlessly discussed; gay male love and obsession (*amour fou* again) receives enthusiastic reviews but is placed within its own hermetic world ... while no one worries much if heterosexual or homosexual viewers are also 'getting off' on the sex; finally heterosexual obsession ... is coyly presented in the guise of bogus feminism – and critics don't care about specific positions or acts except as they contribute to clichés about the auteur's filmography.
>
> (2014: 23)

Similarly, initial responses to lesbian sexual representation in *The L Word* were very concerned about the (heterosexual) male gaze. The heterosexual male gaze was seen as having the power to 'de-lesbianise' the depictions of sex between women. In anticipation and response to such charges, the paratexts of *The L Word* prominently featured the sexuality of creator ('auteur' equivalent) Ilene Chaiken, together with a genesis story regarding the series being based on Chaiken's circle of friends, in order to establish authenticity. Critics used the series' lack of diversity and preponderance of heterosexual sex scenes to argue that it was 'playing to straight viewers' (Moore, 2013: 193).

The authenticity of the lesbian characters in *The L Word* was also paratextually presented in terms of spectatorship. Accounts of positive identifications made by lesbian viewers were used to distance the series from an appeal to voyeurism and to prove its lesbian credentials. Such anxiety over authentic representation has its roots in a history of misrepresenting lesbian relationships and sex in film and television, and, perhaps most strikingly, through 'girl-on-girl' sex in pornographic video. In the context of lesbian-produced pornography, for example, producers go to some effort to emphasise the 'realness' of both producers and performers in order to demarcate these productions as different from girl-on-girl sex presumably oriented to a male audience. For example, promotional materials purport 'real' lesbian sex that is '100% dyke produced' (Rhyne, 2007: 42).

The entry for 'Pornographic film and video: lesbian' in online encyclopaedia *glbtq.com* likewise sees 'differences between lesbian-made and male-produced movies', characterising lesbian-made texts as 'non-commercial', with 'makeshift sets' and 'amateur actors' that also include 'women of different sizes, shapes, colors, and gender identities', many of whom have 'short nails, short hair, and modifications such as tattoos and body or facial piercings' (Theophano, 2002). Theophano further argues that the representations of lesbians in girl-on-girl pornography are 'generally so inaccurate, and so geared toward a straight male audience, that very few could truly be considered lesbian'. So what is necessary to be considered an 'accurate', truly lesbian sexual representation? I would be hard pressed to disagree with there being something *off* about most mainstream-produced 'girl-on-girl' pornography. What is interesting here is that lesbian representation in lesbian-authored texts is seen as differing from 'male' representations via politics (the inclusiveness of having diverse performers), fashion (though short nails are more a question of logistics) and the low-budget nature of production. The actual performance and stylisation of lesbian sex seems unimportant. When lesbian sex becomes almost invisible even in an encyclopedia entry about lesbian pornography, the most explicit of sexual representations, it shows the extent to which the discussion of lesbian sexual representation has become mired in discussions of authenticity, gender and politics.

Linda Williams has interrogated the critical response to *Blue Is the Warmest Color*, and whether or not the film is pornographic. A Palme d'Or-winning art film about young love between two women, the film is identifiable as a lesbian-themed film based on its content. However, there has been significant criticism as to 'whether the film's depiction of sex is "authentically" lesbian' (2014: 15). Williams contends that 'there is no such thing as authentic sex whether in art films, R-rated films, or pornography', instead arguing that '[t]he real point is not any actual accuracy of representation so much as the fact that there is a continuous history of different stylisations of sex acts, each trying to differentiate itself from previous inauthentic "norms"' (ibid.: 15). Feminist critical discontent was expressed regarding *Blue Is the Warmest Color*'s depictions of so-called 'scissoring' (ibid.: 10), a sexual position that sees two women engage in a form of genital-to-genital stimulation through the dual triangulation of legs. Such critique rests not only on the anatomically difficult, uncomfortable and orgasmically improbable nature of this position but also on the very specific discursive stylisation of lesbian sex it offers. Within a much less explicit context, characters in a lesbian relationship in teen musical comedy series *Glee* also refer to their sexual activities as scissoring, and this has become a popular suggestion of lesbian sex acts within popular culture – despite being received with hilarity by many lesbian viewers, as it is generally considered to be a lesbian sexual position favoured by pornography intended for a heterosexual male viewership.

Williams considers the criticism of scissoring representations in *Blue* inappropriate, since representing these kinds of non-penetrative lesbian sex positions (though they are not the only ones in the film) can be seen as expunging men, and potential identification with men, from the scene. Within this logic, *Blue*'s male authorship and, potentially, male spectatorship can be forgiven as the *text* is entirely lesbian (though one of the protagonists still does have sex with a man). Although this potential arises through imagining sex as non-phallocentric, the positions chosen seem based more on their ease to photograph/film in a way that provides maximum exposure of both female bodies, as well as an inability to imagine, or depict within heterosexual representational norms, fulfilling sex *without* direct genital-on-genital contact.

Explicit female same-sexual representation, even of the 'decorative' kind (Williams, 2014: 10), is still not, however, particularly common. There are plenty of examples in television texts, for example, where romantic interactions between two women are represented far more chastely than those of their heterosexual counterparts. And yet, mainstream representations of lesbians, even when portrayed without any particularly sexual representation at all, carry with them the *suggestion* of sex. This is perhaps most clearly visualised in teen cinema (as discussed by Jenkins, 2005) or in jokes in situation comedies, with even a misunderstanding of female same-sex desire resulting in the arousal of male characters. The equation 'lesbian representation = sex' has had a more negative impact in other contexts, famously in the case of the Australian children's TV show, *Play School*, which featured a segment depicting a lesbian family (2004). With the only reference to lesbianism being a young girl's statement that 'My mums are taking me and my friend Merryn to an amusement park', the resulting conservative outcry focused on the idea that the even the suggestion of a female same-sex couple was not suitable for children, with the quiet dismissal of the segment's (lesbian) producer occurring some months later. This indicates the extent to which even the barest hint of a lesbian relationship suggests sex within a mainstream culture that is paradoxically unable to imagine what lesbian sex might be, while simultaneously unable to *not* imagine sex when faced with lesbianism.

If heterosexual women are defined by the body in popular culture, then lesbians are defined by sex *as well as* the absence of (at least traditional understandings of) sex. As a result, there is a particular investment in the kinds of stylisations of lesbian sex occurring in film and television. Just as increasing societal acceptance of lesbians and gay men has increased the amount of representation of lesbian relationships and sex in Western television, the dominant culture's weird lack of understanding of, yet fascination with, what lesbians do, and can do, sexually has resulted in a situation in which lesbian sex seems a representational problem in and of itself: erotic yet usually vague; hypersexualised but with the surprising addition of heterosexual sex; or featuring sexless characters in a context where the very existence of lesbianism is suggestive of sex. Too deviant to be Madonna, yet too chaste, through the lack of heterosexual intercourse ('real sex'), to be whore.

In terms of the films with lesbian lead characters that have made it through to semi-mainstream success in recent years, lesbian sex has certainly been troubled. In *The Kids Are All Right* (2010, dir: Lisa Cholodenko) the lesbian characters have no sex life to speak of, and one of them is revealed to be a 'lesbian-identified bisexual' (Olson, 2010) when she has an affair with her children's sperm donor. Given writer and director Lisa Cholodenko's desire that the film perform the role of 'reaching out to the male population' (again a question of intent, but one that translates narratively in this case), it is unclear how much of a role this tailoring had in gaining enough mainstream respect to earn an Oscar nomination. The latest crossover film that offers representation of lesbian protagonists, *Carol* (2015, dir: Todd Haynes), is an adaptation of Patricia Highsmith's iconic 1952 novel *The Price of Salt*. In this erotically charged period drama with minimal explicit sexual representation, it takes a full 75 minutes of longing glances and lingering touches for the sexual tension between the protagonists to escalate into a kiss. The two subsequent sex scenes are highly stylised: the first offers two and a half minutes of beautifully choreographed and shot kisses, stroking and suggested, but not shown, stimulation, before cutting to black; the second consists of around 40 seconds of passionate but closed-mouth kissing before cutting to a shot of the women asleep and undressed under a sheet. When the first sex scene is revealed to have been recorded by a private detective, even this encounter is narratively mediated by the male gaze and homophobic legal structures.

Carol's mainstream success is no accident. By producing a film drama set during a time in which lesbianism was hinted at but generally ignored, *Carol*'s critique of institutional and social homophobia is authorised, as it sits safely in the past. Although the film is about desire, and drenched in eroticism, the representational problem of lesbian sex is solved by making it narratively taboo. Other films taking desire as a theme feature significantly more explicit sexual content than *Carol*, but the taint of lesbianism renders the film irredeemably sexual in the public discourse. This was perhaps most clearly seen in the hosting of the 88th Academy Awards, where *Carol*'s lead actors, Cate Blanchett and Rooney Mara, were both nominated for their performances: host Chris Rock stated that 'Of all the girl-on-girl movies I've watched this year, I'd say *Carol* was about the third best'. There is no reason to align a film as nuanced, as *polite*, as *Carol* with pornography other than that the desire represented is between two women.

This specific dismissal of *Carol* at the film world's most prominent event demonstrates an inability to classify texts featuring lesbian characters as serious features, making them fundamentally different to 'heterosexual' contemporaries. That films with lesbian lead characters, like *Carol* and *The Kids Are Alright*, have found establishment recognition and crossover success indicates that lesbian filmic representation can exist outside a minority discourse. Significant strides have been taken towards more diverse lesbian characterisation in both film and television. In terms of both quantity and quality, lesbian representation is better than ever, particularly in television. Films with lesbian lead characters are also no longer completely separate – but, as Rock's casual dismissal indicates, they are certainly not yet equal.

Note

1 Please note that due to limited space I have not specifically addressed the representation of transgender lesbians in this chapter.

Bibliography

Akass, K. and McCabe, J. (2006) *Reading the L Word: Outing Contemporary Television*. London: I.B. Tauris.

Beirne, R. (2008) *Lesbians in Television and Text after the Millennium*. New York: Palgrave Macmillan.

Beirne, R. (ed) (2012) *Televising Queer Women: A Reader*. New York: Palgrave Macmillan.

Benshoff, H.M. and Griffin, S. (2005) *Queer Images: A History of Gay and Lesbian Film in America*. Lanham: Rowman and Littlefield.

Bonds-Raacke, J.M., Cady, E.T., Schlegel, R., Harris, R.J. and Firebaugh, L. (2007) 'Remembering Gay/Lesbian Media Characters: Can Ellen and Will Improve Attitudes toward Homosexuals?' *Journal of Homosexuality*. Volume 53(3): 19–34.

Cairns, L. (2006) *Sapphism on Screen: Lesbian Desire in French and Francophone Cinema*. Edinburgh: Edinburgh University Press.

Capsuto, S. (2000) *Alternate Channels: The Uncensored Story of Gay and Lesbian Images on Radio and Television: 1930s to the Present*. New York: Ballantine Books.

Ciasullo, A. (2008) 'Containing "Deviant" Desire: Lesbianism, Heterosexuality, and the Women-in-Prison Narrative'. *The Journal of Popular Culture*. Volume 41(2): 195–223.

Collins, J. (2007) 'Challenging the Rhetorical Oxymoron: Lesbian Motherhood in Contemporary European Cinema'. *Studies in European Cinema*. Volume 4(2): 149–59.

Eaklor, V.L. (2012) 'The Kids Are All Right But the Lesbians Aren't: The Illusion of Progress in Popular Film'. *Historical Reflections*. Volume 38(3): 153–70.
Gomillion, S.C. and Giuliano, T.A. (2011) 'The Influence of Media Role Models on Gay, Lesbian, and Bisexual Identity'. *Journal of Homosexuality*. Volume 58(3): 330–54.
Gross, L.P. (2001) *Up from Invisibility: Lesbians, Gay Men, and the Media in America*. New York: Columbia University Press.
Heller, D. (ed) (2013) *Loving The L Word: The Complete Series in Focus*. London: I.B. Tauris.
Highsmith, P. (1952) *The Price of Salt*. New York: Coward-McCann.
Jackson, S. (2012) '(Un)recognizable Lesbians: Young People Reading "Hot Lesbians" through a Reality Lens'. In R. Beirne (ed) *Televising Queer Women: A Reader*. New York: Palgrave Macmillan.
Jenkins, T. (2005) '"Potential lesbians at two o'clock": The Heterosexualization of Lesbianism in the Recent Teen Film'. *The Journal of Popular Culture*. Volume 38(3): 491–504.
Lewis, R. (2012) 'Towards a Transnational Lesbian Cinema'. *Journal of Lesbian Studies*. Volume 16(3): 273–90.
Moore, C. (2013) 'The D Word'. In D. Heller (ed) *Loving 'The L Word'*. London: I.B. Tauris.
Moritz, M. (1994) 'Old Strategies for New Texts: How American Television Is Creating and Treating Lesbian Characters'. In J. Ringer (ed) *Queer Words, Queer Images: Communication and the Construction of Homosexuality*. New York: New York University Press.
Moss, K. and Simić, M. (2011) 'Post-Communist Lavender Menace: Lesbians in Mainstream East European Film'. *Journal of Lesbian Studies*. Volume 15(3): 271–83.
Olson, J. (2010) '"The Kids Are All Right" and the Grown-Ups are Bisexual'. 15 July. *Afterellen.com*. www.afterellen.com/general-news/76648-the-kids-are-all-right-and-the-grown-ups-are-bisexual (accessed 7 March 2016).
Reed, J. (2005) 'Ellen DeGeneres'. *Feminist Media Studies*. Volume 5(1): 23–36.
Rhyne, R. (2007) 'Hard-Core Shopping: Educating Consumption in SIR Video Production's Lesbian Porn'. *The Velvet Light Trap*. Volume 59(1): 42–50.
Shi, L. (2012) 'Contextualizing Chinese Lesbian Cinema: Global Queerness and Independent Films'. *New Cinemas: Journal of Contemporary Film*. Volume 10(2): 127–43.
Stuart, J. (2006) 'In Another Bracket: Trans Acceptance in Lesbian Utopia'. *Journal of Lesbian Studies*. Volume 10(1–2): 215–29.
Theophano, T. (2002) 'Pornographic Film and Video: Lesbian'. No date. *glbtq.com*. www.glbtqarchive.com/arts/porn_lesbian_A.pdf (accessed 18 March 2017).
Tropiano, S. (2002) *The Prime Time Closet: A History of Gays and Lesbians on TV*. New York: Hal Leonard Corporation.
Walters, S.D. (2003) *All the Rage: The Story of Gay Visibility in America*. Chicago: University of Chicago Press.
Weiss, A. (1993) *Vampires and Violets: Lesbians in Film*. New York: Penguin Books.
White, P. (1999) *Uninvited: Classical Hollywood Cinema and Lesbian Representability*. Bloomington: Indiana University Press.
Williams, L. (2014) 'Cinema's SexActs'. *Film Quarterly*. Volume 67(4): 9–25.
Wilton, T. (1995) *Immortal, Invisible: Lesbians and the Moving Image*. London: Routledge.

Media

Ally McBeal (1997–2002) [TV Series]. USA: Fox.
Better than Chocolate (1999) Directed by A. Wheeler. [Film]. Canada: British Columbia Film.
Blue Is the Warmest Color (2013) Directed by A. Kechiche. [Film]. France: Quat'sous Films.
Breaking Bad (2008–13) [TV Series]. USA: AMC.
Buffy the Vampire Slayer (1997–2003) [TV Series]. USA: The WB/UPN.
Candy Bar Girls (2011) [TV Series]. UK: Channel 5.
Carol (2015) Directed by T. Haynes. [Film]. UK: Number 9 Films.
The Children's Hour (1961) Directed by W. Wyler. [Film]. USA: Mirisch Corporation.

Ellen (1994–98) [TV Series]. USA: ABC.
Exes and Ohs (2007, 2011) [TV Series]. USA/Canada: Logo.
The Fosters (2013–) [TV Series]. USA: ABC Family.
Friends (1994–2004) [TV Series]. USA: NBC.
Girlfriend (2004) Directed by Karan Razdan [Film]. India: T-Series.
Glee (2009–15) [TV Series]. USA: Fox.
High Tension (2003) Directed by A. Aja. [Film]. USA: Alexandre Films.
The Kids Are All Right (2010) Directed by L. Cholodenko. [Film]. USA: Focus.
The L Word (2004–9) [TV Series]. USA: Showtime.
LA Law (1986–1994) [TV Series]. USA: NBC.
Lip Service (2010–12) [TV Series]. UK: BBC3.
Lost and Delirious (2001) Directed by Léa Pool. [Film]. Canada: Cite-Amerique.
Lost Girl (2010–15) [TV Series]. USA: Showcase.
Orange Is the New Black (2013–) [TV Series]. USA: Netflix.
Party of Five (1994–2000) [TV Series]. USA: Fox.
Picket Fences (1992–6) [TV Series]. USA: CBS.
Play School (2004) [TV Series]. Australia: ABC.
Pretty Little Liars (2010–) [TV Series]. USA: ABC Family.
Queer as Folk (1999–2000) [TV Series]. UK: Channel 4.
Queer as Folk (2000–5) [TV Series]. USA/Canada: Showcase (Canada/Showtime Networks).
The Real L Word (2010–12) [TV Series]. USA: Showtime.
Shameless (2011–) [TV Series]. USA: Showtime.
Skins (2007–13) [TV Series]. UK: E4.
South of Nowhere (2005–8) [TV Series]. USA: The N.
Sugar Rush (2005–6) [TV Series]. UK: Channel 4.
Will and Grace (1998–2006) [TV Series]. USA: NBC.

5

REPRESENTING GAY SEXUALITIES

Sharif Mowlabocus

Between 1994 and 2010, the United States government adopted a specific policy when dealing with LGBT staff serving, or wishing to serve, in the armed forces. Known as 'Don't Ask, Don't Tell' (DADT), this policy allowed lesbians, gay men and bisexual people to serve in the US military providing they were not open or explicit about their sexual identity. This was the result of a conflict between the election promises of President Clinton and the beliefs of US military leaders, who claimed that serving homosexuals would be detrimental to the morale of the Armed Forces.[1] To appease his supporters, Clinton prohibited the harassment of homosexual and bisexual service personnel by their peers and commanding officers. To appease the military hawks, he created a piece of legislation that allowed the military to get rid of anyone who *openly* expressed their homo- or bisexuality.

I begin my chapter with this piece of obsolete legislation because it helps us to identify the unique position that queer people often find themselves in, both in everyday life and in terms of representation. Imagine that it was not sexuality but race or gender that was the subject of DADT. Such a policy could not conceivably work in these instances because the idea of *needing* to ask someone's gender, or of *needing* to reveal one's racial identity, seems ridiculous. Race and gender are not so easily hidden as sexuality.

By contrast, the theme of invisibility pervades the life histories of queer people,[2] and for many it remains a double-edged sword. On the one hand, it allows us to 'pass' and live in environments where being non-heterosexual can be a criminal offence or might result in verbal abuse, bullying, violent assault, even murder. The invisibility of our queerness has been a cloak that has protected us and allowed us to survive. Hollywood has also historically been a homophobic industry and, for a long time, playing a 'gay role' was often considered career suicide. Yet, as evidenced by Rock Hudson, Dirk Bogarde, Alec Guinness and Montgomery Clift, Hollywood has always been filled with queer people.

At the same time, this invisibility has provoked violent acts of identification and persecution. It has meant that those who fear non-heterosexual people have become obsessed with revealing the 'hidden queer'. Under the Nazi regime, anyone identified as a 'sexual deviant' in the concentration camps was made to wear a pink triangle. On the other side of the Atlantic, McCarthy's witch-hunts of the 1950s were, in part, focused on rooting out homosexuality from public office. In what has been dubbed the 'Lavender Scare',[3] queer people were considered *invisible* security risks to the United States, and discovering those risks became an obsession. In times when homophobia has been in the ascendant, identifying non-heterosexual people has been a key tool in the persecutor's arsenal.

Since the era of Nazism and the Lavender Scare, processes of (self-)identification have been recuperated by queer folk, becoming an integral aspect of many LGBT rights movements across the world. In the 1970s (and shortly after homosexuality was decriminalised in the USA and the UK), the Gay Liberation Front took to the streets of New York, San Francisco and London inviting LGB people to 'come out!'. This political fight for rights and recognition was based upon the belief that being visible as lesbian or gay or bisexual was central to being accepted by the wider population.

Later, in the 1980s, this 'coming out' strategy was invoked again, as activists 'came out' as HIV positive, as PWA,[4] as survivors of the virus or as relatives of an 'AIDS victim'. HIV, like homosexuality, is invisible. Through creative forms of activism (including 'die-ins', marches, quilting and red ribbons), the virus (and often sexuality) was rendered spectacularly visible (see Shepherd, 2010). This spectacularisation of queer sexuality can also be found in the marches in England in the late 1980s, aimed at blocking a law (Section 28) that prohibited public funding for any activity that 'promoted homosexuality'. In relation to this, Ian McKellen (now Sir Ian) publicly came out as gay. He did so because, in his own words:

> I learnt that coming-out was crucial to self esteem [and] that people who thrived in society's mainstream and had access to the media, could, by telling the truth, help others in the backwaters, whose views were never sought and whom society either ignored or abused.
>
> (McKellen: 1988)

As McKellen suggests, sometimes it is only through the mainstream media that gay people can find their views reflected and see themselves represented. Representing queer sexualities over the past hundred years has often involved a discussion of identificatory power – of a *politics of representation* (Hall, 1996: 444). One of the central political struggles within twentieth-century LGBT representation was the issue of *who gets to represent queer people*: who is represented, who does the representing and what are the motivations and meanings of those representations?

Semantically speaking, 'gay' people did not exist before the 1960s (see Cage, 2003), and the idea that you might define and organise your identity around your primary sexual attractions is a nineteenth-century invention (see Foucault, 1976). Yet one of the projects of queer scholars has been to demonstrate that '*we* have *always* been everywhere'. Ancient Greek society, for instance, recognised and even condoned certain forms of male same-sex desire. Dover (1989) notes that same-sex love was often organised around intergenerational intimacy, with a younger man being the student and lover of his older teacher. This culture is some 2500 years old and it is through *representations* of that culture that we have learned how Ancient Greece treated homosexuality. Poetry and plays provide one source of representation. The decorations of ceramic ware provide another (see DeVries, 1997).

Prior to colonisation, Native American cultures included 'two-spirit' identities; while these identities were organised according to gender performance, as opposed to sexuality, 'queer' sexual relationships did exist, and were accepted (see Lang, 1997). In classical Indian poetry we find stories of same-sex lovers and transgender deities (see Vanita and Kidwai, 2000), providing evidence of indigenous queer people on the Indian sub-continent. Colonialism served to (re)frame these practices and identities as both homosexual and deviant (see Sinha, 1995; Aldrich, 2003, for discussion). Modern India continues to struggle with this colonial legacy and the colonial law statute known as Penal Code 377, effectively criminalising homosexuality, remains on the statute book at the time of writing. Ironically, defenders of the code claim that homosexual activity is 'not Indian' and is in fact a Western import (see Bhaskaran, 2002).

Today, Uganda, Nigeria and Zimbabwe are engaged in witch-hunts against queer people. Claiming that homosexuality is 'un-African', state-sponsored homophobia has been fuelled by a rise in a particular brand of (North American) evangelical Christianity. Their rhetoric fails to account for the many examples of queer sexual practice and queer identity that can be found in the literature, poetry and art of the African continent. Epprecht (2004: 5) provides numerous examples of male homosexuality throughout the history of Southern Africa, drawing upon linguistics but also representations (including photography) to prove that 'history, culture and humanity in Africa are assuredly as complex and diverse as in other regions of the world'.

Whatever shape or form queer sexualities took in the past, it is through textual and visual representations that we come to learn of them. These help us to realise the non-linear narrative of homosexuality and homosexual representation over the centuries. The development of media technologies (from the printing press through to photography, film, telephony and, latterly, networked ICTs), twinned with an increasingly connected world of remote access and mobile media, has changed the landscape in which queer representations are produced, disseminated and consumed. In what follows, I narrow my focus to the history of gay male representation in Britain in the twentieth and twenty-first centuries in order to highlight some of the challenges and opportunities that such representations – and those who produce and consume them – face and continue to face.

Twentieth-century representations of male homosexuality in Britain: censorship, closets and camping it up

Britain has a long and ignominious history of censorship. Until 1968, the Lord Chamberlain oversaw the regulation of British theatre and homosexuality was banished from the 'respectable' stage, a taboo subject not to be discussed in public settings (Sinfield, 1999). Cinema fared somewhat better: while the British Board of Film Classification worked closely with government (particularly during periods of war), it has remained independent and, therefore, more responsive to changes in the social, political and cultural climate of the nation (see BBFC, n.d.). Nevertheless, explicit discussions of homosexuality remained off-limits for British cinema until the release of the suspense-filled *Victim* (1961, dir: Basil Dearden). Widely credited as including the first use of the word 'homosexual' in British cinema (Burton, 2010), *Victim* raised controversy upon its release and has come to stand as a historical landmark, not just for British queer cinema but for queer British history and the British queer academy (see Medhurst, 1984). Mapping the contours of British attitudes at the time, Dearden's tragic story of blackmail and jealousy might not resonate with contemporary understandings of 'gay pride',[5] but its thinly veiled call to decriminalise homosexuality was nevertheless groundbreaking. That this was a mainstream film starring a matinée idol (Dirk Bogarde) only adds to its impact.

Films such as *Victim*, *Serious Charge* (1959: dir: Terence Young), *Oscar Wilde* (1960, dir: Gregory Ratoff) and *The Trials of Oscar Wilde* (1960, dir: Ken Hughes) addressed the 'issue' of homosexuality, but were the exception rather than the rule. Material that included homosexual themes regularly fell foul of Victorian obscenity laws, which continued to hold sway in matters of literary representation well into the twentieth century. Classic twentieth-century works of fiction including *The Well of Loneliness* (Hall, 1928) and *Last Exit to Brooklyn* (Selby, 1964) were banned by British censors for their homosexual content. Meanwhile, self-censorship prevented the publication of E. M. Forster's sensitive (and semi-autobiographical) coming-out novel, *Maurice* (1971), until after the author's death.

Yet sex – of any kind – has long been a headline-grabber in the newspaper business. The trial of playwright Oscar Wilde in 1895 is one example of how the British news media spoke about homosexuality. Half a century later, the arrest of actor John Gielgud (in 1953) for 'cottaging'[6] and the prosecution of Conservative politician Lord Edward Montagu for homosexual sex also stirred up passions via newspaper front pages. Through such reporting, homosexuality was represented – and debated.[7] Indeed, the publicity these trials and prosecutions received through the press helped to change public perceptions of homosexuality. Newspaper coverage of the time reveals far less consensus around the 'love that dare not speak its name' than one might imagine, and the mainstream press became a key site for ongoing debate about homosexuality and its criminal status (see Bengry, 2012).

Other traces of homosexuality can be found in British (and American) cinema, which is littered with characters who, while never being identified as 'gay', play to particular stereotypes that allow audiences to 'read' the character as queer. The 'sissy' is one such character (Russo, 1981), most commonly found playing comedic roles. Dyer's (1977) discussion of film noir details how certain character traits within this genre serve to connote queerness. In his landmark history of queer cinema, Russo notes:

> *Symbols* of masculinity were defended by the use of *symbols* of homosexuality. The fact that most early movie sissies were homosexual only if one chose to see them as being homosexual was simply a reflection of the fact that the existence of homosexuals in society was acknowledged only when society chose to do so.
> (Russo, 1981: 32)

Queer representation in the pre-liberation era of Anglo-American film was something to be discovered; something available to audiences 'in the know', but which had to be searched for, discovered and *identified*. It is perhaps unsurprising that, just as the history of queer people has been shaped by invisibility, so invisibility has been a defining factor in the history of queer representation.

Sometimes those clues were obvious; at other times they relied on sub-cultural knowledge. Just as queer audiences had to go and search out representations of queer people, so a level of reward was bestowed upon those who succeeded in being 'in the know'. For example, the popular BBC radio comedy 'Round the Horne' (1965–1969) featured the wonderfully arch and hysterically camp Julian and Sandy (played by Kenneth Williams and Hugh Paddick). British audiences tuned in on Sunday afternoons to hear about the latest commercial venture dreamed up by the two 'friends'. More than just innuendo, the scripts were littered with references that only those who had experience of queer sub-cultures would fully understand (see Baker, 2002a). References to Sandy's piano skills – being 'a master on the cottage upright' – might have passed the censor's ears, but anyone acquainted with queer culture at the time was well aware of the double meaning of the word 'cottage'. In this instance, this slang term was sufficiently well known that non-gay audiences also understood the joke. Williams's delivery of the line in his unmistakable voice, scaling octaves in a single breath, only served to underscore the invitation extended to listeners to read between the lines. On other occasions, the comedy went so far as to adopt gay sub-cultural language in its scripts: words such as 'bona' and 'lallies' and 'palone' – this was Polari[8] being spoken on the BBC.

In spite of censorship, legal constraints and social proscription, thinly veiled representations of gay effeminacy pervaded twentieth-century British media culture. Indeed, the unacknowledged queerness of Julian and Sandy was part of what made 'Round the Horne' so popular. While gay audiences played detective in order to read queerness into 'straight' texts, mainstream audiences have long enjoyed the camp antics of the swishy queen. Audiences, whether gay or straight, have understood what a limp wrist, a fondness for fashion and flower arranging, a love for one's mother and a soft (or indeed shrill) voice means. Larry Grayson, the comedian, drag act and game-show host, never 'came out' as a gay man, but his entire career was based on the audience understanding that he was homosexual. Likewise, the success of John Inman's Mr Humphries, in the BBC's *Are You Being Served?* (1972–1985), relied upon the audience acknowledging the character's unspoken sexual identity.

I mention the performances of Grayson and Humphries because these were the representations of male homosexuality I grew up with in the 1970s and 1980s. In the suburban, lower-middle-class world of heterosexuality that I grew up in, these *were* the only gay men I knew. Of course, such representations have been decried as dangerously out of touch with the real lives of gay men, and the stereotype of the 'swishy' queen was regularly the target of gay political activism in the 1970s and 1980s. At issue was not the representation per se, but who had control of that representation. To paraphrase Hall (1996), queer people have long been the object of representation, but rarely the subject of it. There *is* a great difference between a gay man taking to the street in full drag to march in a political rally (or, more recently, the less political parades that accompany Gay Pride celebrations) and a television producer instructing the writers of a sitcom to include a 'pansy' character (such as Marigold in *In Sickness and in Health*, 1985–1992) to provide comic fodder.

Coming of age at the end of the 1980s, I heard a great deal of protest over 'negative representations' of gay people. Of course, in demanding that representations of effeminate queens should be replaced by more 'realistic' images of gay men who embodied a 'regular' masculinity, this particular brand of gay politics only served to (re-)stigmatise gay men who related to a gender identity considered more 'feminine' than the hegemonic ideal. At the same time, this normalising rhetoric served to uphold hetero-patriarchal understandings of masculinity that always prioritised 'real' heterosexual men over 'queer' imposters. Replacing 'bad' stereotypes of effeminate queens with 'positive' gay role models only served to pigeonhole gay representations once more. By substituting 'bad queens' for 'good gays', the politics of assimilation that took hold in Britain in the 1980s and 1990s only served to bolster masculine supremacy and gender inequality.[9]

Self-representation

Recently, the boundaries between production, distribution and consumption have shifted dramatically, and the politics of representation have similarly been extended. Within the digital landscape of networked communication systems, LGBT people are able to both produce and consume representations, of themselves and of each other. In this final section, I explore how the advent of digital platforms and digital methods of (self-)representation have changed understandings of gay male representation and consider their power dynamics.

Gay male culture developed a particularly intense relationship with forms of digital representation as far back as the late 1990s. Pornography has been a common feature of gay male culture since before decriminalisation (Clarke, 2011), and gay porn became available online (usually at libido-crushing download speeds) via newsgroups, forums and thumbnail galleries around 1997. Alongside (and sometimes doubling as) sexually explicit representations, a digital dating/cruising culture developed, allowing men to meet online for a variety of purposes, including casual sex. By 1999, when mainstream culture still attached a social stigma to online dating services, gay men in the UK and elsewhere had already normalised the practice of meeting new sexual partners via the internet (Mowlabocus, 2010). A key reason for this early adoption is the invisibility of homosexuality in daily life. While visibility did increase in the period between 1967 and 1999, homosexuality still has to be revealed. It is not visible in the same way that gender or race is. Gay men developed an online presence in order to become 'visible' to other men, precisely because they were invisible offline.

Through the creation of user profiles, online photo galleries, video uploads and forum postings, gay men engaged in acts of digital self-representation, leading Thomas Foster (2001: 540) to assert that digital platforms provide opportunity to perform a 'spectacularised gayness'. Via the immaterial world of the web, gay men were materialising themselves; writing themselves into being as they engaged in *performative* acts of representation. There had been 'experiments' with forms of self-representation prior to the internet: gay magazines regularly carried contact adverts, allowing gay men to advertise themselves and attract new sexual partners and friends (see Thorne and Coupland, 1998). However, these were comparatively expensive and offered little space to describe one's self. Images were even rarer. The web changed this 'contact ad' culture and offered gay men a unique opportunity to render themselves visible. In many ways, since the 1990s, gay men have been engaged in a project not just of coming out online but of 'being' online, with their identities residing in digital as well as physical space and time.

Such acts of 'becoming', like all forms of representation, are not without their politics, and codes and conventions were soon developed for writing user profiles, displaying one's body and 'talking through' that body to communicate with others (Mowlabocus 2007, 2010). They include the central role that the 'face-pic' played in the first generation of dating websites. Showing your face online quickly became a form of representational 'currency' among gay men in Britain: a face-pic 'proved' that you were genuine, that you were a real person and that you were willing to be seen as gay. Not showing your face online is considered a social faux pas, suggesting that you have something to hide, or indeed that you are hiding – that you are in the closet. Thus, the way in which gay men represent themselves online determines how others approach and evaluate them.

More recently, the advent of mobile social media services such as Grindr, Scruff and Growlr (all utilise a similar profile and quick-message system and marry this to geo-locative technologies common in smartphones such as Apple's iPhone series) has seen the further development of this 'representational vernacular'. The term 'selfie' (a self-portrait taken on a mobile phone angled above the subject) became popularised in 2014 following the success of a dance track of the same name (produced by DJ duo The Chainsmokers), but within gay male culture 'selfies' have been a central strategy of self-representation for well over a decade. In 2003, the Labour MP Chris Bryant was (literally) caught with his trousers down when a tabloid newspaper published images he had taken of himself for a gay dating site, posing in his underwear in a bathroom. This type of semi-naked image, often taken in a bathroom, bedroom, locker room or gym, is so common in gay men's digital culture as to render it banal. Alongside these self-portraits, it is not uncommon for Grindr profiles to feature one specific body part – face, arms, abdomen, chest. Such self-representations provide the viewer with an idea of what the man in question values most about his body and how he wants to be seen by others.

This level of self-exposure and self-representation can be considered liberating. Given the ongoing stereotyping that can be found in the mainstream media today, the opportunity to represent one's sexuality on one's own terms is surely appealing. Taking back the means of production – becoming the *subject* and not just the *object* of representation – must surely be a positive political manoeuvre.

However, these self-representations are not neutral. Some (Batiste, 2013; Lorimer et al., 2013) have raised concerns regarding the intensely visual dimension of services such as Grindr, and I have argued elsewhere that such forms of identification are creating new representational challenges for gay men (Mowlabocus, 2010). Instead of the limp-wristed queen of the 1970s sitcom, we are now expected to be tanned, toned gym bunnies, with rippling abs and bulging pecs – the personification of an ideal masculinity, not that different from the (avowedly heterosexual – and homophobic) 1980s action hero of Hollywood cinema. Body fascism is not a new concept within gay male culture but, as demonstrated by the Tumblr blog 'Douchebags of Grindr',[10] these methods of self-representation take such discrimination to a new level. We may now be facing a situation in which the most strident forms of gay stereotyping and 'negative' representation do not occur on the big screens of our cinemas or the domestic screens of our televisions but on the small screens of our mobile phones, via the apps and sites that gay men use to meet one another. It is very easy to look back on the history of queer representation and see it as an unbroken path towards progress – from the 'bad old days' of repression and censorship towards a brighter future yet to come – but it remains imperative that we understand the political contexts in which representations are produced and the political investments that different people, at different times, have made in representations.

Notes

1 See Bérubé (1990) for a superb history of gay men and the US military.
2 In this chapter, I use the terms 'queer', 'homosexual' and 'gay', but not interchangeably. I use the reclaimed term 'queer' to signpost and speak on behalf of a broad range of identities, non-identities, practices and cultures that are not aligned with heteronormativity. I use the term 'homosexual' to discuss same-sex desiring men (and less often women) within the context of Europe and North America prior to 1967. I use the term 'gay' to refer to same-sex desiring men in a 'post-Stonewall' context.
3 David Johnson's (2004) book *Lavender Scare* is a useful reference point for those interested in this period of intense homophobia in the USA.
4 PWA – person or people living with AIDS.
5 A term that did not exist in 1961.
6 'Cottaging' is the British slang term for procuring sex in a public toilet. 'Tearoom' is used in the USA. In Australia, a 'beat' refers to a similar form of cruising.
7 The prosecution of 'respectable' figures, such as John Gielgud, became the impetus for a Departmental Committee on homosexual offences and prostitution. Set up in 1954, the committee (headed by Sir John Wolfenden) sought to examine whether engaging in homosexual acts should remain a criminal offence in the UK. In 1957, the committee's report recommended 'homosexual behaviour between consenting adults in private should no longer be a criminal offence' and that the age of consent be set at 21. In 1967 homosexual sex between consenting adults over the age of 21 and in a private setting was decriminalised in England and Wales. Scotland decriminalised homosexuality in 1980 and Northern Ireland followed suit in 1982.
8 Polari is a form of queer slang that was used among (some) queer people during the twentieth century. Paul Baker's (2002b) investigation of Polari is the most exhaustive analysis of this now sadly dead language.
9 For more on LGBT media studies see Bourne's (1996) collection, *Brief Encounters*, investigating the roles and representations of gay men and lesbians in twentieth-century British cinema; work by

Richard Dyer (1977, 1978, 2002) and Andy Medhurst (1984, 1991a, 1991b, 1992, 2002); and collections such as Gever et al. (1993), Davis and Needham (2009) and Griffiths (2006).

10 'Douchebags of Grindr' is a popular Tumblr blog cataloguing instances of racism, effeminaphobia and other forms of discrimination found in Grindr profiles.

Bibliography

Aldrich, R. (2003) *Colonialism and Homosexuality*. London: Routledge.
Baker, P. (2002a) 'Construction of Gay Identity via Polari in the Julian and Sandy Radio Sketches'. *Lesbian and Gay Review*. Volume 3 (3): 75–83.
Baker, P. (2002b) *Polari: The Lost Language of Gay Men*. London: Routledge.
Batiste, D. P. (2013) '"0 Feet Away": The Queer Cartography of French Gay Men's Geo-social Media Use'. *Anthropological Journal of European Cultures*. Volume 22 (2): 111–132.
BBFC (No date) *The History of the British Board of Film Classification*. www.bbfc.co.uk/education-resources/student-guide/bbfc-history (accessed 27 August 2014).
Bengry, J. (2012) 'Queer Profits: Homosexual Scandal and the Origins of British Legal Reform in Britain'. In H. Bauer and M. Cook (eds) *Queer 1950s: Rethinking Sexuality in the Post-War Years*. Basingstoke: Palgrave Macmillan.
Bérubé, A. (1990) *Coming Out under Fire: The History of Gay Men and Women in World War Two*. New York: Penguin.
Bhaskaran, S. (2002) 'The Politics of Penetration: Section 377 and the Indian Penal Code'. In R. Vanita (ed) *Queering India: Same Sex Love and Eroticism in Indian Culture and Society*. London: Routledge.
Bourne, S. (1996) *Brief Encounters – Lesbians and Gays in British Cinema 1930–1971*. London: Cassell.
Burton, A. (2010) 'Victim (1961): Text and Context'. *AAA – Arbeiten aus Anglistik und Amerikanistik*. Volume 35 (1). periodicals.narr.de/index.php/aaa/article/download/931/745 (accessed 20 August 2014).
Cage, K. (2003) *Gayle: The Language of Kinks and Queens: A History and Dictionary of Gay Language in South Africa*. Houghton: Jacana Media.
Clarke, K. (2011) *Porn – From Warhol to X-Tube*. Berlin: Bruno Gmünder Verlag.
Clinton, W. J. (1994) 'President's News Conference'. *Public Papers of the Presidents of the United States*. http://quod.lib.umich.edu/p/ppotpus/4733049.1993.001?view=toc (accessed 27 August 2014).
Committee on Homosexual Offences and Prostitution (1957) *Report of the Committee on Homosexual Offences and Prostitution*. London: Her Majesty's Stationery Office.
Davis, G. and Needham, G. (eds) (2009) *Queer TV*. London: Routledge.
DeVries, K. (1997) 'The "Frigid Eromenoi" and Their Wooers Revisited: A Closer Look at Greek Homosexuality in Vase Painting'. In M. Duberman (ed) *Queer Representation: Reading Lives, Reading Cultures*. New York: NYU Press.
Dover, K. J. (1978 [1989]) *Greek Homosexuality*. Cambridge: Harvard University Press.
Dyer, R. (1977) 'Homosexuality in Film Noir'. *Jump Cut*. Volume 16: 18–21.
Dyer, R. (1978) 'Gays in Film'. *Jump Cut*. Volume 18: 15–16.
Dyer, R. (2002) *Now You See It: Studies in Lesbian and Gay Film*. London: Routledge.
Epprecht, M. (2004 [2006]) *Hungochani: The History of a Dissident Sexuality in Southern Africa*. Montreal: McGill-Queen's University Press.
Forster, E. M. (1971) *Maurice*. London: Hodder Arnold.
Foster, T. (2001) 'Trapped by the Body? Telepresence Technologies and Transgendered Performance in Feminist and Lesbian Rewriting of Cyberpunk Fiction'. In D. Bell and B. M. Kennedy (eds) *The Cybercultures Reader*. London: Routledge.
Foucault, M. (1976 [1990]) *The History of Sexuality: Volume 1 – An Introduction* (trans. R. Hurley). London: Penguin.

Gever, M., Parmar, P. and Greyson, J. (eds) (1993) *Queer Looks: Perspectives on Lesbian and Gay Film and Video*. London: Routledge.

GLF London (1971) *Gay Liberation Manifesto*. http://sourcebooks.fordham.edu/pwh/glf-london.asp (accessed 18 March 2017).

Griffiths, R. (ed) (2006) *British Queer Cinema*. London: Routledge.

Hall, R. (1928) *The Well of Loneliness*. London: Jonathan Cape.

Hall, S. (1973) *Encoding and Decoding in the Television Discourse*. Birmingham: Centre for Cultural Studies, University of Birmingham.

Hall, S. (1996) 'New Ethnicities'. In D. Morley and K. H. Chen (eds) *Stuart Hall: Critical Dialogues in Cultural Studies*. Abingdon: Routledge.

Houlbrook, M. (2005) *Queer London: Perils and Pleasures in the Sexual Metropolis*. London: Chicago University Press.

Johnson, D. (2004) *The Lavender Scare: The Cold War Persecution of Gays and Lesbians in the Federal Government*. Chicago: Chicago University Press.

Lang, S. (1997) 'Various Kinds of Two-Spirit People: Gender Variance and Homosexuality in Native American Communities'. In S. Jacobs, W. Thomas and S. Lang (eds) *Two-Spirit People: Native American Gender Identity, Sexuality and Spirituality*. Chicago: University of Illinois Press.

Lorimer, K., Oakland, J., Frankis, J., Davis, M. and Flowers, P. (2013) *Social Media, Lanarkshire Men Who Have Sex with Men and Sexual Health: An Experiential Qualitative Analysis*. www.sexualhealthnetwork.org.uk/wp-content/uploads/2014/05/SMMaSH-Qualitative-Report-Final-For-Circulation1.pdf (accessed 27 August 2014).

McKellen, I. (1988) 'Coming Out'. *Capital Gay*. www.mckellen.com/activism/activism_coming_out.htm (accessed 21 August 2014).

Medhurst, A. (1984) '"Victim": Text as Context'. *Screen*. Volume 25 (4–5): 22–35.

Medhurst, A. (1991a) 'That Special Thrill: Brief Encounter, Homosexuality and Authorship'. *Screen*. Volume 32 (2): 197–208.

Medhurst, A. (1991b) 'Batman, Deviance and Camp'. In R. Pearson and W. Uricchio (eds) *The Many Lives of the Batman: Critical Approaches to a Superhero and his Media*. London: Routledge.

Medhurst, A. (1992) 'Carry On Camp'. *Sight and Sound*. Volume 2 (4): 16–19.

Medhurst, A. (2002) 'Tracing Desires: Sexuality in Media Texts'. In A. Briggs and P. Cobley (eds) *The Media: An Introduction*. London: Pearson.

Mowlabocus, S. (2007) 'Gaydar: Gay Men and the Pornification of Everyday Life'. In S. Paasonen, K. Nikunen and L. Saarenmaa (eds) *Pornification: Sex and Sexuality in Media Culture*. Oxford: Berg.

Mowlabocus, S. (2010) *Gaydar Culture: Gay Men, Technology and Embodiment in the Digital Age*. Farnham: Ashgate.

Murray, S. O. and Roscoe, W. (1998) 'Preface: "All very confusing"'. In S. O. Murray and W. Roscoe (eds) *Boy-Wives and Female Husbands: Studies of African Homosexualities*. New York: St. Martin's Press.

Norton, R. (1992) *Mother Clap's Molly House: Gay Subculture in England, 1700–1830*. London: Gay Men's Press.

Percy, W. A. (2013) 'Reconsiderations about Greek Homosexualities'. In B. C. Verstraete and V. Provencal (eds) *Same-Sex Desire and Love in Greco-Roman Antiquity and in the Classical Tradition of the West*. London: Routledge.

Russo, V. (1981) *The Celluloid Closet: Homosexuality in the Closet*. New York: Harper & Row.

Selby, H. (1964) *Last Exit to Brooklyn*. New York: Grove Press.

Shepherd, B. (2010) *Queer Political Performance and Protest*. Abingdon: Routledge.

Sinfield, A. (1999) *Out on Stage: Lesbian and Gay Theatre in the Twentieth Century*. London: Yale University Press.

Sinha, M. (1995) *Colonial Masculinity: The 'Manly Englishman' and the 'Effeminate Bengali' in the Late Nineteenth Century*. Manchester: Manchester University Press.

Thorne, A. and Coupland, J. (1998) 'Articulations of Same-Sex Desire: Lesbian and Gay Male Dating Advertisements'. *Journal of Sociolinguistics*. Volume 2 (2): 233–257.

Vanita, R. and Kidwai, S. (2000) *Same Sex Love in India: Readings from Literature and History*. New Delhi: Macmillan.

Media

Are You Being Served? (1972–1985) [TV Series]. UK: BBC.
'Douchebags of Grindr' (No date) Available at: www.tumblr.com/tagged/douchebags-of-grindr (accessed 17 November 2016).
In Sickness and in Health (1985–1992) [TV Series]. UK: BBC.
Oscar Wilde (1960) Directed by G. Ratoff [Film]. UK: Vantage Films.
Round the Horne (1965–1969) [Radio Series]. UK: BBC.
Serious Charge (1959) Directed by T. Young [Film]. UK: Alva Films.
The Trials of Oscar Wilde (1960) Directed by K. Hughes [Film]. UK: Viceroy Films.
Victim (1961) Directed by B. Dearden [Film]. UK: Allied Film Makers.

6
FIFTY SHADES OF AMBIVALENCE
BDSM representation in pop culture

Ummni Khan

In a 2015 interview with Nadia Neophytou, E.L. James explains that the genesis of her *Fifty Shades* trilogy lies in two wildly different literatures (Newman, 2012).[1] Many are aware that the love story started as fan fiction of Stephanie Meyer's (2006) teen-vampire series, *Twilight*, but the kink inspiration comes from Patrick Califia's (1988) anthology of lesbian BDSM erotica, *Macho Sluts* (De Kosnik, 2015: 116). This juxtaposition of a mainstream runaway bestseller and a subcultural queer text gestures towards the ambivalence that characterises the representation of BDSM (bondage/discipline/sadomasochism) in pop culture more broadly.

There are many different shades of this ambivalence. Stories of BDSM can portray kink as sexy, sublime, a slippery slope, comical, pathological, therapeutic, abusive, addictive, destructive, deviant or a pathway to normalcy. Significant factors that shape which tropes will dominate in a particular story include the genre of the text and the gender of the dominant and submissive partners, as well as their sexual orientation, race and class. Often, contrasting tropes will be contained in the same narrative. For example, in the *Fifty Shades* trilogy, female dominance is deviantised, while male dominance is romanticised. This chapter will use the *Fifty Shades* book series, composed of *Fifty Shades of Grey* (James, 2011a), *Fifty Shades Darker* (James, 2011b) and *Fifty Shades Freed* (James, 2012), along with the film adaptation of the first instalment (2015), as a portal through which to survey the landscape of popular BDSM representation.

Fifty Shades has been a phenomenal commercial success. The series has sold more than 100 million copies and joined the list of the top ten bestsellers of all time (Russon, 2014). The film adaptation of the first book became Universal Pictures' highest-grossing R-rated international release (Lang, 2015); the adaptation of the second book was released in early 2017, and that of book three is slated for release in 2018 (Stedman, 2015). Given its unprecedented popularity, the *Fifty Shades* series stands as an apposite cultural artefact to think through BDSM mainstream representation. Through a comparative analysis, this chapter takes a meandering journey through *Fifty Shades* to see how the story stacks up in relation to some of the dominant themes and ideologies found in an array of popular BDSM films, and, in so doing, will provide an overview of that body of work. I begin by summarising the plot of the trilogy, highlighting features that I later pick up in my analysis. I then turn to considering the two main genre categories that feature BDSM themes – the romantic drama and the erotic thriller – and discuss how *Fifty Shades* incorporates both, conforming to some conventions and defying others. After this, I consider the way in which stories with sympathetic BDSM characters, such as *Fifty Shades*, often displace stigma and abjection onto other identities and practices, using narratives of childhood trauma and pathology and reinscribing gender and sexual normativity, albeit with a tolerance towards mild heterosexual kink. By way of conclusion, I offer a brief summary of the analysis and then consider the progress made in humanising BDSM subjectivity.

Fifty Shades follows the relationship between Anastasia Steele ('Ana'), a virginal college grad, and Christian Grey, a billionaire businessman and sexual dominant whose intimate life has been confined to contractual BDSM relationships – until, of course, he meets Ana. The first instalment revolves around the conflict between Ana's desire for a conventional 'hearts and flowers' relationship and Christian's insistence on a consensual power-exchange agreement, which includes top/bottom sex play, consensual 'punishments' and stipulations regarding non-sexual aspects of Ana's life, such as frequency of exercise (James, 2011a). Christian introduces Ana to some kinky play, such as spanking, which she thoroughly enjoys, but she resists becoming his official submissive, and does not sign a BDSM contract. The first book ends with Ana allowing Christian to flog her with a belt in order for her to see 'how bad it can be' to engage in more hardcore activity (James, 2011a: 355). She hates the experience, calls Christian 'one fucked-up son of a bitch', determines they are fundamentally incompatible and breaks it off, much to the heartbreak of both (James, 2011a: 351). At the beginning of book two, they reconcile, with Christian agreeing to a 'regular vanilla relationship' with a dash of 'kinky fuckery', i.e. mild BDSM activities (James, 2011b: 29). The main challenges faced by the pair in books two and three revolve around other people, including Elena Lincoln, the older woman who introduced Christian to BDSM when he was a teen; Leila, Christian's ex-submissive, who is now stalking Ana; and Jack Hyde, Ana's sexually harassing boss. After navigating the dangers posed by these characters and working through Grey's 'dark' past, the two protagonists get married, and *Fifty Shades Freed* ends with Ana expecting their second child (James, 2012).

To decode the story, and to situate it within the broader array of BDSM pop-cultural representations, it is helpful to consider how genre shapes the storyline. *Fifty Shades* is, first and foremost, a classic love story. Boy meets girl, they clash (on how hardcore their kink should be), they resolve conflict (finding a happy medium), they get married and they have children. Like many Harlequin romances, the hero is an over-the-top alpha male: controlling, superlatively wealthy and sexy, but also wary of commitment. The heroine is both sexually inexperienced and feisty. She transforms the hero with the power of true love so that he overcomes his trust issues, allowing them to live happily and normatively ever after. The initial BDSM incompatibility operates – in many ways – as a suitable plot device for creating conflicts and erotic energy that conform comfortably with the romance genre. As Deller and Smith (2013: 947) argue, the series blends 'familiar romance tropes of emotional intimacy with graphic scenes of kinky sex which appear to defy standard conceptions of "feminine" sexual interests' and fits within the broader politics and pleasures of reading romance novels, as analysed by Radway (1983) more than 30 years ago. Indeed, despite the explicit discussion of consent and safewords, the BDSM eroticism can be read as a simple normalisation of the male dominant/female submissive sexual dynamic that characterises traditional 'bodice-ripper' romances. While books two and three feature romantic moments, lovers' spats and sex scenes, they also introduce elements of the thriller, as an ex-lover and an ex-boss threaten and terrorise the couple (James, 2011b; James, 2012). The multiple elements that make up *Fifty Shades* – love, kink and danger – thus resonate with two common types of BDSM stories in pop culture: the romantic drama and the erotic thriller.

In the romantic drama category, one of the most popular early BDSM films, *9½ Weeks* (1986, dir: Adrian Lyne), bears some striking similarities to *Fifty Shades of Grey*. For example, *9½ Weeks* features a controlling tycoon who initiates his lover into BDSM, which she initially enjoys but then resists, as he pressures her into kinkier activities that she finds repulsive. As with *Fifty Shades of Grey*, *9½ Weeks* ends with the heroine tearfully leaving her lover when desire is overcome by disgust with the dominant's perceived deviance. If the *Fifty Shades* story had concluded after book one, the ideological message would be the same: that BDSM eroticism is supremely arousing, but ultimately unsustainable – a slippery slope that leads to unwanted degradation. This idea echoes across genres, and in both low and high culture. For example, in the erotic thriller *Killing Me Softly* (2002, dir: Chen Kaige), the couple eventually separates. In a voice narration, the heroine implies in the last scene that she still thinks about her ex-dominant husband daily, but could not handle the intensity of their BDSM relationship. Interestingly, art cinema that engages with male-top/female-bottom BDSM also perpetuates this idea of unsustainability, suggesting a near-inevitable escalation towards violence. For example, in the celebrated Austrian–French film *The Piano Teacher* (2001, dir: Michael Haneke), a masochistic middle-aged woman convinces her music student to join her in BDSM activity. The film concludes with a violent interlude that blurs the line between BDSM and rape, suggesting that kink will lead to, and is contiguous with, assault. The student leaves for good and the heroine stabs herself.

In book two, *Fifty Shades* allows Ana and Christian to reconcile, thus refusing the narrative formula that dictates passionate BDSM relationships must always be short-lived or violent (James, 2011b). In this way, it echoes the highly acclaimed film *Secretary* (2002, dir: Steven Shainberg), contributing to the trend of tolerance found in more recent pop narratives that situate BDSM within certain normative strictures. In *Secretary*, a dominant boss initiates a BDSM relationship with his secretary. While the hero initially breaks it off because he is convinced that his desires are 'disgusting', the heroine convinces him that they can have both BDSM and long-term love. Interestingly, the final explicit sex scene in *Secretary* depicts the couple tenderly making love. This integration of vanilla with kink is also characteristic of the couple's sex life in *Fifty Shades*, and seems to be a key narrative strategy for rendering BDSM love stories more accessible to mainstream audiences. The other significant overlap is that in both stories, the couples end up getting married. Many critics of these two stories, including myself, argue that this marital resolution undercuts the transgressive potential of the BDSM elements (Cossman, 2004; Downing, 2013; Khan, 2009). Nonetheless, given the history of BDSM representation as unsustainable and destructive, this conventional happy ending does make gains within the social imaginary for not just the intelligibility but also the desirability of BDSM subjects who are otherwise normative. Ambivalence is thus resolved by normalising BDSM players who adhere to hegemonic markers of acceptability including heterosexuality, marital status, middle- or upper-class status, whiteness, conventional attractiveness and non-disabledness.

The thriller aspects of *Fifty Shades* also convey ambivalence, suggesting that danger accompanies the sexual thrills of BDSM courtship. In particular, the characters of Leila Williams, Christian's former submissive, and Jack Hyde, Ana's first employer, pose deadly threats to the couple. Ana's infatuated friend José, the only racialised character in the story, also represents the threat of sexual violence. Williams is pathologically jealous of Ana, so she begins to terrorise her by, for example, slashing her tires, and then threatening her with a gun. Hyde is not officially identified in relation to BDSM, but we learn that he does like 'rough sex' and also has a history of sexually harassing his employees, including Ana, whom he assaults. He is terribly jealous of Christian and attempts to kill him; when this fails, he kidnaps Christian's sister. José is Ana's friend from college, and at the beginning of the first novel he forces an embrace and a kiss on Ana while she struggles and pleads 'no'. Fortunately, Christian arrives before it goes any further, and Ana eventually forgives her friend. The threat to life and the danger of sexual assault that these three antagonists represent to the couple have contrasting connections to BDSM. Williams represents female masochism that goes awry when it becomes too extreme and has not been modulated by requited love. Hyde represents sexual dominance that is not modulated by love or consent, but rather driven by anger and the desire to violate. To a lesser extent, José also represents a dominant masculine subject who disregards consent. While some of Hyde's badness is explained by his rough childhood, José's assaultive behaviour seems to be narratively linked to his racialisation as a young Latino man. At the moment that he begins to sexually assault Ana, he uses the Spanish endearment 'cariño' as he begs her to submit (James, 2011b). *Fifty Shades* thus negotiates BDSM stigma by creating three foils who represent toxic versions of submission and dominance, and who thus render Ana and Christian pure and healthy by comparison.

Although *Fifty Shades* makes use of thriller tropes to signify sexual danger, it also differs from other BDSM thrillers in two key ways. First, the thriller elements are subordinate to the love story. In most BDSM thrillers, mystery and criminality form a core part of the story. In contrast, Williams, Hyde and José in *Fifty Shades* operate as secondary plot devices to increase tension in the narrative, and as outside subjects who attest to the obsession-inducing desirability of the main characters. The second difference is that, with *Fifty Shades*, the threat comes from outside the couple as opposed to within. In most BDSM thrillers, the dominant constitutes a real or perceived danger, and up to the end, the audience is kept wondering: do this person's sexual desires extend into murderous impulses? For example, in the blockbuster *Basic Instinct* (1992, dir: Paul Verhoeven), the female dominant (Sharon Stone) signifies a femme fatale who is both hyper-sexual and a suspected killer. Likewise, the courtroom thriller *Body of Evidence* (1993, dir: Uli Edel) has the audience guessing until the very end as to whether its female dominant (Madonna) is guilty of murder. In *Killing Me Softly*, although the male dominant has a violent streak and engages in abusive practices, we eventually learn that it was his sister who was the 'crazed killer'. Turning to the few representations of queer BDSM in thriller narratives, both *Cruising* (1980, dir: William Friedkin) and *Pulp Fiction* (1994, dir: Quentin Tarantino) conflate gay male dominance with non-consensual sadism and murder. And, if we take a brief detour through television land, we can find a more contemporary example of the logic that links consensual dominance with killer instincts. The 2015 *Criminal Minds* episode 'Breath Play' involves women who are sexually inspired by an erotic book called *Bare Reflections* (a veiled stand-in for *Fifty Shades*). Through a cheating website, they are lured by the 'unsub' who promises to fulfil their kinky submissive fantasies, but who then turns erotic asphyxiation into murderous strangulation.

It can thus be seen that many erotic thrillers capitalise on the sexiness of BDSM by allowing vicarious access, while continuing to perpetuate the slippery-slope moralism that casts most dominants as non-consensual sadists and murderers, and often punishes submissives for straying outside of normative sexuality. For all its hegemonic faults, *Fifty Shades* bucks this trend. However, as we are about to explore, it often does this at the expense of stigmatising other identities and practices.

For example, one of the key ways in which pop culture recuperates BDSM protagonists is to create origin stories of early childhood trauma and to deflect stigma onto bad parental figures. *Fifty Shades* adheres faithfully to this trend. As Leistner and Mark (2016: 15) state, 'One of the primary BDSM messages in the Fifty Shades series was that BDSM identities or preferences are induced by trauma and therefore, are not natural, healthy identities or behaviors'. The backstory to Christian's kink begins with his biological mother, a sex worker with addiction issues, who died of an overdose when he was four. Before her death, Christian was severely neglected, and this included her abusive 'pimp' extinguishing cigarettes on his chest. This early experience is used to rationalise Christian's sexuality and explain his problems with intimacy. As he states to his mostly vanilla lover, 'I'm a sadist, Ana. I like to whip little brown-haired girls like you because you all look like the crack whore – my birth mother' (James, 2012: 329). Interestingly, while Christian's history of hardcore male dominance is traced to a trauma narrative, Ana's pleasure in softcore submissiveness never requires an explanation; the story implies that women are naturally turned on by this dynamic.

The second part of Christian's trauma backstory involves Elena Lincoln, a married friend of his adopted mother, whom he met when he was a teen and spiralling down a self-destructive path. Elena initiated him into BDSM as his Domme, and in book one, Christian maintains that this secret affair was entirely healing for him and probably saved his life. Ana is both jealous and morally outraged. She calls Elena names such as 'Mrs Robinson', 'bitch troll' and 'the evil one' and describes her as a 'pedo'. At the conclusion of the story, Christian ends up agreeing with Ana; as he anticipates his impending role as a parent, he has an epiphany that it was wrong for an older married woman to lure a troubled teenager into kink. This is a notable moment of ideological repronormativity, whereby having a child seems to realign Christian's moral compass, so that he has now rewritten the script of this teenage affair as molestation (James, 2012).

The ideological trope that associates hardcore BDSM desire with a bad childhood is oft repeated in pop culture. In *Secretary*, Lee's alcoholic father and overprotective mother are narratively connected to her masochism, although BDSM is also credited for helping her sublimate her destructive self-cutting impulses into productive sexual fulfilment. The more recent film *A Dangerous Method* (2011, dir: David Cronenberg) also posits that the etiology of kinky desires is rooted in traumatic childhood experiences. In this biopic on the history of psychoanalysis, Jung assists a patient in confronting an early memory of being beaten by her father, which has spawned her desire for a lover's spanking. In the *Piano Teacher*, Erika's sexual submission is formed by her incestuous relationship with her domineering mother, with whom she still shares a bed despite being in her forties. In *Killing Me Softly*, incest is also entangled with kinkiness. We learn by the end that Adam and his sister had some sexual interactions when they were 'kids', and this is linked both to the sister's homicidal obsessions and to Adam's sexual dominance.

The bad-childhood account given for Christian's dominant inclinations in *Fifty Shades* can further be unpacked by considering how the story capitalises on the hegemonic disparagement of sex work and female sexual dominance. In particular, the series' construction of his mother, and Christian's use of the hateful epithet 'the crack whore', project abjection onto sex workers who do struggle with trauma, poverty and substance use, and pander to the stereotypes that all sex workers are drug addicts and all 'pimps' violent monsters. It further perpetuates the myth that sex-working mothers will necessarily be neglectful and unloving failures who warp their children. As Bromwich and DeJong (2015: 6) write, 'the social categories of the (virtuous/Madonna) mother and (fallen/Magdalene) prostitute are traditionally seen as ideologically separate and even constructed as binary opposites', and thus their intersection in one person creates an acutely contaminated identity in the social imaginary. *Fifty Shades* builds on a long history of pop-cultural stories that figure the children of sex-working mothers as mentally unstable and/or violent, including the film based on Alan Moore's graphic-novel series *Watchmen* (2009), Hitchcock's *Marnie* (1964) and Mangold's *Identity* (2003).

We can contrast Christian's biological mother to his adopted mother, who is rich, married and works as a physician, and whose 'goodness' is established, in part, by her class, sexual and marital privilege (Trevenen, 2014). Interestingly, we can also contrast Christian's mother to Ana herself. The notion of 'sex work' and the concept of being a 'whore' haunt the protagonist as she embarks on a relationship with this rich and generous man. Four times in the first book, Ana censures herself for being a 'ho'. For example, during an argument over whether Ana will accept a multi-thousand-dollar gift, Christian states:

'I will buy you lots of things, Anastasia. Get used to it. I can afford it. I'm a very wealthy man.' He leans down and plants a swift, chaste kiss on my lips. 'Please.' He releases me.

'*Ho*' my subconscious mouths at me.

'It makes me feel cheap,' I murmur.

(James, 2011a: 252)

In such conversations, Ana's 'subconscious' (more accurately, her superego) voices the social anxiety regarding conventional heterosexual courtship's resemblance to sex work. Yet her subconscious is in conflict with what she terms her 'inner goddess' (more accurately her id), who revels in the opulence that Christian bestows (gogreen1414, 2014). As Dymock (2013: 890) argues, 'In *Fifty Shades Darker* and *Fifty Shades Freed*, Anastasia's "inner goddess" is awoken not by Christian Grey's sexual transgressions, but primarily by the lure of consumerism'. By showing Ana both relishing and resenting Christian's authoritative gift-giving, the narrative alleviates reader guilt. If Ana protests, and Christian has to 'force' her to accept the luxury goods, then it's not really her fault, and she's not really a 'ho'. Just as a rape fantasy can operate to mask female guilt over sexual desire, the fantasy of forced luxury can mask female guilt over consumer desire. In both cases, ambivalence over deviant bad-girl desires can be resolved because 'he made me do it!'

The bad-girl figure of the female Domme in *Fifty Shades*, however, gets no such reprieve. In the story, Elena's deviancy is linked to her adultery and her participation in intergenerational sexuality. Her villainy in *Fifty Shades* reveals the significance of gender in determining whether sexual dominance will be portrayed as ultimately good or bad. While there are many examples of good male dominants alongside the bad ones, female dominants are more frequently characterised as hyper-sexual and deadly. Perhaps most infamously, *Basic Instinct* features a femme-fatale figure who likes to tie men up during sex play. By the end of the film, we also learn that she enjoyed stabbing her bound lover with an ice-pick at the moment of climax. Killing and kinkiness are also linked in the *Body of Evidence* (1993). Here the female dominant uses BDSM to get her rich lover into a vulnerable position in order to induce a heart attack. Although the motive for the murder is not sex but greed, her penchant for dominance is presented as an extension of her devious and homicidal actions.

But it should be noted that not all films demonise female dominants, particularly when the film is not an erotic thriller. For example, the erotic comedy *Exit to Eden* (1994, dir: Garry Marshall) takes place at a recreational BDSM resort and features two notable dominants, one good, one bad. The main sympathetic female Domme is presented as emotionally shut down and fearful of losing control. But through true (heterosexual) love, she opens up and enters into a normative committed relationship – although she does not give up her job as a professional Domme at the resort (making the story quite a bit more radical than *Fifty Shades*). The other Domme character, played by Iman, conforms more to the femme-fatale stereotype. She is one of the 'bad guys', who cares little for consent, and is also a killer. Notably, while almost all of the other characters are white, she is racialised. Thus, part of her badness relies on racist notions of Black women as sexually deviant and dangerous. The British film *Preaching to the Perverted* (1998, dir: Stuart Urban) also takes place within a BDSM community. The female protagonist is another white Domme who grapples with a fear of emotional vulnerability, but is transformed by the love and devotion of a sweet young man who – like Ana – is a virgin and newcomer to BDSM. By the end of the film, they are together and have a baby. These positive characters reveal that in pop culture, regardless of gender, sympathetic dominants are almost always shown as traumatised white individuals who compensate by exercising hyper-control in sex and in life. In *Exit to Eden*, *Preaching to the Perverted* and *Fifty Shades*, the dominants' healing and maturation are thus narratively signalled by their desire and willingness to integrate vanilla into their sex lives and enter into romantic reproductive relationships.

If sexual dominance is treated as both sexy and symptomatic of trauma in *Fifty Shades*, and mild female sexual submission is naturalised and eroticised, male sexual submission is more consistently denigrated. As stated, Christian's introduction to BDSM was as a submissive. While he initially claims this was a positive intervention in his life, the experience is ultimately deemed to have been abusive. There is, however, one interesting moment in the story when he reverts to submission with Ana. They have just had a fraught conversation, and he appears terrified that she will leave him. Suddenly he falls to his knees and assumes a submissive stance. Ana is horrified. This gender-transgressive moment is neither sexy nor appealing to her, and the narrative positions this act as stemming from fear of abandonment, not desire. She drops to her own knees to negate his inferior position, assures him she will never leave and then begs him to return to his old domineering self. He soon does, and a few moments later, he proposes marriage. In this way, one might argue that ultimately he submits to Ana in a more substantive way. He forsakes his lifestyle and identity as a Dom for a conventional romance that eventually leads to marriage and children.

Male submissives who never regain a position of sexual dominance in Hollywood films are often punished for their gender transgression. For example, in the crime comedy *One Night at McCool's* (2001, dir: Harald Zwart), the male submissive character is portrayed as an object of ridicule, with the film's last punchline having him killed by a freak accident. When men submit to dominant females in BDSM thrillers, they are often portrayed as heading down a self-destructive path. In *Basic Instinct*, the female dominant's first lover is killed after he allows himself to be tied up, and the male protagonist (played by Michael Douglas) sabotages his career and health as he succumbs to the pleasures of male submission. In the little-known sequel, *Basic Instinct 2* (2006, dir: Michael Caton-Jones), the man who falls under the seductive Domme's spell ends up institutionalised in a psychiatric hospital. Some alternative films, however, portray male submission and masochism in more complex ways. The Canadian film *Walk All Over Me* (2008, dir: Robert Cuffley) features an array of male submissives, some of whom are played for laughs, but all of whom are still sympathetic and sweet. One of the most interesting portrayals of male submission is found in Roman Polanski's *Venus in Fur* (2013), based on the play by David Ives. The entire film takes place in an empty theatre, where Thomas, a film director, auditions an actress for a play based on Sacher-Masoch's novel *Venus in Furs* (1977 [1870]). The story is far too nuanced to make any definitive statements about its meaning or ideology. However, one of its fascinating aspects is that it begins with a film director who is in control, but who seems, by the end, to be yearning for submission. The film closes with him turned on, tied up and transfixed by the actress, who has transformed into a kind of archetypal goddess-figure of dominance. In this alternative story, we thus see the switching goes in the opposite direction than is the case for Christian, with Thomas finding pleasure and liberation by discovering his submissive side.

Conclusion

The representation of BDSM in pop culture has evolved to allow for the intelligibility, likability and/or desirability of some kinky subjects. In most erotic BDSM thrillers, dominants are portrayed as sexy and alluring, even as their desires represent deadly threats, in particular with regard to femme-fatale characters. In romantic dramas, sympathetic portrayals of BDSM characters still effectively deviantise the identity and practice in numerous ways, dramatising an ambivalence towards kink. First, hardcore BDSM interest almost always requires an origin story in which some traumatic event has interrupted 'normal' (as in, vanilla) psycho-sexual development. As discussed above, in *Fifty Shades*, parental neglect, and corruption at the hands of an older female Domme, lie at the root of Christian's 'dark' (as in, sadistic) sexual impulses. Pop culture has also traditionally represented the trajectory of BDSM relationships as a slippery slope to degradation, criminality and sometimes murder. *Exit to Eden*, *Preaching to the Perverted*, *Secretary* and, more recently, *Fifty Shades* buck this trend. The latter two films are particularly noteworthy because their wide audience appeal seems to signal a shift in the social imaginary. However, it should also be pointed out that these positive inroads are confined to white, marital, male-top/female-bottom couples who practise mild kink. And in the case of *Fifty Shades*, the couple's reproductive activity is another brick in the wall of heteronormative assimilation. Furthermore, in BDSM films that have leading roles for practitioners, acceptability is often bought through abjection transference. Secondary characters who more seriously depart from normative sexual identity or practice take on the burden of deviancy and social rejection. In *Fifty Shades*, there are a number of striking Others, from Williams (who is too extreme in her sexual submissiveness) to Lincoln (who transgresses gender norms in her penchant for sexual dominance). Bad male characters, such as Hyde or José, reflect sexual dominance that is not regulated by consent. Stepping outside of the BDSM paradigm, Christian's mother is deviantised through her identity as a sex worker and her construction as a neglectful addict. Yet *Fifty Shades* also negotiates the resemblance of heterosexual courtship to sex work by staging an inner debate between Ana's superego (which disdains being a 'ho') and her id (which luxuriates in the gifts that Christian bestows). Finally, while female sexual submission is naturalised so long as it is not too hardcore, outside of alternative independent films such as *Walk All Over Me* and *Venus in Fur*, male sexual submission tends to be portrayed as either comical or pathetic. Yet one could argue that in the case of *Fifty Shades*, Christian's capitulation to a 'hearts and flowers' relationship shows that Ana is really the one on top.

So how far has pop culture really gone in challenging the deviantisation and dehumanisation of BDSM? If we return to the queer inspiration for *Fifty Shades*, Califia may have some insight. In his introduction to *Macho Sluts*, Califia ponders his choices as a writer and a sadomasochist, stating:

> I could become an apologist and seek to persuade the tyrannical majority that sadomasochism is not violent or self-destructive. But that would require telling many little, white lies – watering down the descriptions of frightening acts, softening the dialogue, emphasising what S/M has in common with vanilla rather than where they part company.
>
> (Califia, 1988: 10)

From this perspective, *Fifty Shades* does seem to water down BDSM, not only emphasising its commonality with vanilla, but ultimately conflating the two. One might argue that – ironically, given the influence of Califia's book on E.L. James – only 'apologist' BDSM stories have penetrated the mainstream consciousness. On the other hand, there is a documented '*Fifty Shades* effect' that has catapulted sales of mild kink products and seen high attendance at *Fifty Shades*-inspired workshops (Donnelly, 2015). While I grant Martin's (2013: 983) point that the *Fifty Shades* effect only advances 'a particular brand of BDSM that is presented as female friendly, fashionable, exciting and safe as opposed to extreme, marginalised and dangerous', we can take heart that on some marginal level, erotic imaginations and lives are shifting materially under the influence of pop culture.

Note

1 Some of this analysis is derived from earlier arguments made in Khan, U. (2014) *Vicarious Kinks: S/M in the Socio-Legal Imaginary*. Toronto: University of Toronto Press.

Bibliography

Bosman, J. (2014) 'For "Fifty Shades of Grey", More Than 100 Million Sold'. *The New York Times*. 26 February. www.nytimes.com/2014/02/27/business/media/for-fifty-shades-of-grey-more-than-100-million-sold.html (accessed 24 May 2016).

Bromwich, R. and DeJong, M.M. (2015) *Mothers, Mothering and Sex Work*. Bradford: Demeter Press.

Califia, P. (1988) *Macho Sluts: Erotic Fiction*. Boston: Alyson Publications.

Cossman, B. (2004) 'Sexuality, Queer Theory, and "Feminism After": Reading and Rereading the Sexual Subject'. *McGill Law Journal*. Volume 49 (4): 847–876.

De Kosnik, A. (2015) 'Fifty Shades and the Archive of Women's Culture'. *Cinema Journal*. Volume 54 (3): 116–125.

Deller, R. and Smith, C. (2013) 'Reading the BDSM Romance: Reader Responses to Fifty Shades'. *Sexualities*. Volume 16 (8): 932–950.

Donnelly, M. (2015) '"Fifty Shades" Effect: Famed Sex Shops Report Record Sales for Handcuffs, Collars, BDSM Toys'. 19 February. *TheWrap*. www.thewrap.com/fifty-shades-of-grey-effect-famed-sex-shops-report-record-sales-boosts-for-handcuffs-collars-bdsm-toys/ (accessed 24 May 2016).

Downing, L. (2013) 'Safewording! Kinkphobia and Gender Normativity in Fifty Shades of Grey'. *Psychology and Sexuality*. Volume 4 (1): 92–102.

Dymock, A. (2013) 'Flogging Sexual Transgression: Interrogating the Costs of the "Fifty Shades Effect"'. *Sexualities*. Volume 16 (8): 880–895.

gogreen1414 (2014) 'The Female Conscious and Unconscious'. 10 October. *Sex and Society*. https://wgs160.wordpress.com/2014/10/10/the-female-conscious-and-unconscious/ (accessed 24 May 2016).

James, E.L. (2011a) *Fifty Shades of Grey*. London: Vintage Books.
James, E.L. (2011b) *Fifty Shades Darker*. London: Vintage Books.
James, E.L. (2012) *Fifty Shades Freed*. London: Vintage Books.
Khan, U. (2009) 'A Woman's Right to Be Spanked: Testing the Limits of Tolerance of SM in the Socio-Legal Imaginary'. *Law & Sexuality*. Volume 18: 79–119.
Lang, B. (2015) '"Fifty Shades" Becomes Universal's Highest-Grossing R-Rated International Release'. 1 March. *Variety*. http://variety.com/2015/film/news/fifty-shades-of-grey-box-office-highest-grossing-r-rated-film-universal-1201444071/ (accessed 24 May 2016).
Leistner, C.E. and Mark, K.P. (2016) 'Fifty Shades of Sexual Health and BDSM Identity Messaging: A Thematic Analysis of the Fifty Shades Series'. *Sexuality & Culture*. Volume 20 (3): 464–485.
Martin, A. (2013) 'Fifty Shades of Sex Shop: Sexual Fantasy for Sale'. *Sexualities*. Volume 16 (8): 980–984.
Meyer, S. (2006) *Twilight*. New York: Little, Brown Books for Young Readers.
Neophytou, N. (director). (2015) 'Interview: Fifty Shades of Grey'. 12 February. www.youtube.com/watch?v=4wiz-IU-wvM&feature=youtu.be (accessed 24 May 2016).
Newman, R. (2012). 'Mommy Porn? How Dare Men Put Down Women's Sexual Fantasies'. 7 December. www.telegraph.co.uk/culture/books/9729588/Mommy-Porn-How-dare-men-put-down-womens-sexual-fantasies.html (accessed 24 May 2016).
Radway, J.A. (1983) 'Women Read the Romance: The Interaction of Text and Context'. *Feminist Studies*. Volume 9 (1): 53–78.
Russon, M.-A. (2014) '50 Shades of Grey Joins Top 10 Bestselling Books: How Many Have You Read?' 27 February. *International Business Times*. www.ibtimes.co.uk/50-shades-grey-joins-top-10-bestselling-books-how-many-have-you-read-1438234 (accessed 24 May 2016).
Sacher-Masoch, L. (1977 [1870]) *Venus in Furs*. Trans. John Glassco. Burnaby: Blackfish.
Stedman, A. (2015) '"Fifty Shades" Sequels to Be Released February 2017, 2018'. 23 April. *Variety*. http://variety.com/2015/film/news/fifty-shades-sequels-release-dates-1201478775/ (accessed 25 May 2016).
Trevenen, C. (2014) 'Fifty Shades of "Mommy Porn": A Post-GFC Renegotiation of Paternal Law'. *Journal of Popular Romance Studies*. Volume 4 (1). http://jprstudies.org/2014/02/fifty-shades-of-mommy-porn-a-post-gfc-renegotiation-of-paternal-lawby-claire-trevenen/ (accessed 25 May 2016).

Media

9½ Weeks (1986) Directed by Adrian Lyne [Film]. USA: MGM/UA Entertainment Co.
A Dangerous Method (2011) Directed by David Cronenberg [Film]. UK: Sony Pictures Classics.
Basic Instinct (1992) Directed by Paul Verhoeven [Film]. France: Carolco Pictures.
Basic Instinct 2 (2006) Directed by Michael Caton-Jones [Film]. UK: Sony Pictures.
Body of Evidence (1993) Directed by Uli Edel [Film]. Germany: MGM.
Breath Play (2015) *Criminal Minds* [TV Episode]. CBS, 41 min.
Cruising (1980) Directed by William Friedkin [Film]. USA: United Artists.
Exit to Eden (1994) Directed by Garry Marshall [Film]. USA: Savoy Pictures.
Fifty Shades of Grey (2015) Directed by Sam Taylor-Johnson [Film]. USA: Universal
Identity (2003) Directed by James Mangold [Film]. USA: Columbia Pictures.
Killing Me Softly (2002) Directed by Chen Kaige [Film]. USA: Metro-Goldwyn-Mayer.
Marnie (1964) Directed by Alfred Hitchcock [Film]. USA: Universal Pictures.
One Night at McCool's (2001) Directed by Harald Zwart [Film]. USA: Universal Studios.
Preaching to the Perverted (1998) Directed by Stuart Urban [Film]. UK: Pathfinder Pictures.
Pulp Fiction (1994) Directed by Quentin Tarantino [Film]. USA: Miramax Films.

Secretary (2002) Directed by Steven Shainberg [Film]. USA: Lionsgate.
The Piano Teacher (2001) Directed by Michael Haneke [Film]. Austria: Kino International.
Venus in Fur (2013) Directed by Roman Polanski [Film]. France: Lionsgate.
Walk All Over Me (2008) Directed by Robert Cuffley [Film]. Canada: The Weinstein Company LLC.
Watchmen (1986–1987) Written by Alan Moore [Comic-Book Series]. USA: DC Comics.
Watchmen (2009) Directed by Zack Snyder [Film]. USA: Warner Bros. Pictures.

7

THE POLITICS OF FLUIDITY

Representing bisexualities in twenty-first-century screen media

Maria San Filippo

Ask audiences today what fictional character they most associate with bisexuality, and along with Alyssa (Joey Lauren Adams) of *Chasing Amy* (1997, dir: Kevin Smith) or Catherine Trammell (Sharon Stone) of *Basic Instinct* (1992, dir: Paul Verhoeven), they are likely to say goth-punk hacker Lisbeth Salander – also known as 'The Girl with the Dragon Tattoo', female lead of Stieg Larsson's Millennial trilogy (2008) and played by actors Noomi Rapace and Rooney Mara, respectively, in Swedish and US adaptations (2009, dir: Niels Arden Oplev; 2011, dir: David Fincher). In Larsson's books and their filmed versions, Salander's bisexuality is a defining character trait, established through her sexual engagements with women and male protagonist Mikael Blomkvist. Following the books' success and in anticipation of the films' release, cultural commentators touted Salander's bisexuality, which hardly deterred the mainstream Euro-American audience that kept Larsson's books on the best-seller list, made the Swedish-language trilogy a Netflix streaming favourite and turned out at the multiplex for the English-language film's release.[1]

In her visibility and alterity, Salander embodies a significant shift in the representational politics of bisexuality. Unlike most bisexual screen characters, Salander is not confined to art cinema in the way of the characters of *3* (2010, dir: Tom Tykwer) and *Vic + Flow Saw a Bear* (2013, dir: Denis Côté), but nor is she rendered in the hypersexualised, fantasised tones of Hollywood/Indiewood products such as *Basic Instinct* and *Vicky Cristina Barcelona* (2008, dir: Woody Allen). Though performed by conventionally feminine actresses, Salander's unapologetically queer appearance and behaviour disrupts the history of representing female bisexuality as gender-conforming and desirable for heteromasculine consumers. Yet the straight male protagonist affirms Salander's femininity and desirability through a seduction that renders her emotionally fixated on him – conforming to the representational pattern whereby bisexual female characters ultimately fall for men. Moreover, her punked-out self-presentation proves reassuring precisely because she appears safely Other in her exoticism. Yet as a complex character whose bisexuality is but one of her non-conformist traits, Salander humanises non-normative gender and fluid sexuality.

To determine whether Salander and the trilogy overall display a logic of identity and desire that views gender and sexuality expansively rather than restrictively surely requires looking beyond a character's appearance or the gender-of-object choice at the narrative's end. Yet these superficial, displaced and arbitrary ways of determining bisexuality's presence and politics within representation persist. So does the precept that bisexuality be explicitly named within the text, even as Salander's legibility as *specifically* bisexual (rather than lesbian, bi-curious or heteroflexible) was widely acknowledged and reproduced within critical and popular discourse despite the B-word's omission from books and films. But with more characterisations and narrative articulations of desire's complexity and contingency, the imperative to instrumentalise bisexual representation gives way to an ultimately more liberating recognition of sexual fluidity.

Braving the B-word

Bisexuality as identity formation, representational trope and theoretical concept has reemerged with renewed force in twenty-first-century cultural discourse. Yet even as we grasp that sexuality is contingent upon emotional and material realities and thus irreducible to binary ways of thinking, as a culture we remain mired in binary trouble – or *compulsory monosexuality*, that is, the positioning of *either* heterosexuality *or* homosexuality as the two options for a socially recognised sexuality that is perceived as mature and sustainable.[2] Bisexuality's cultural and representational '(in)visibility', its simultaneous ubiquity and spectrality, stems from the concurrent fascination and anxiety it provokes. Bisexuality as a concept is produced through this crisis of signification – the contradictions and omissions that binary constructions of gender and sexuality reinforce. Bisexual media studies demonstrates how bisexuality is already present, if obscured – hidden in plain sight – by modes of representation and reading confined within monosexual logic.[3] What we can single out as representationally bisexual spaces are those non-binary and/or contingent characterisations, character configurations and narrative articulations that appeal to fluid spectatorial identifications and desires, and thus have the potential to 'unthink' monosexuality.

Representations of bisexuality are effaced not only by the mandate to explicitly speak the B-word and by compulsory monosexuality but also by *compulsory monogamy*, the heteronormative *and* homonormative inducement to reproduce the privatised, domesticised couple. Maria Pramaggiore underscores the impact of compulsory monogamy on popular representation:

> The continued and frankly perplexing inability to see or to speak bisexual in films and television programs that devote themselves to plurality of all kinds seems to me to be the logical outcome of a compulsory cultural regime that understands the couple as the only type of sexual relationship, as the cornerstone that organises society, and perhaps, as the very emblem of personhood.
>
> (2011: 592)

Moreover, bisexuality, unlike heterosexuality and homosexuality, seems to rely on a temporal component for its actualisation; at any given moment a bisexual person or character might appear monosexual depending on his/her present gender-of-object choice, thus contributing to bisexual (in)visibility. To indicate these representational attempts to grapple with the monosexism of our culture's logic of desire, I turn now to explore bisexuality's treatment in music video, film and television of the past 15 years, wherein consistently deployed character types and narrative devices reinforce associations of bisexuality with bohemianism and hedonism, immaturity and experimentation, narcissism and envy, sociopathology and criminality, infidelity and duplicity, sex addiction and perversion, elitism and white privilege. Yet there are also important new images and voices emerging that challenge this representational history and so demonstrate the capacity of screen bisexualities to reveal ways of seeing past compulsory monosexuality and monogamy.

Commodity bisexuality

While Lisbeth Salander departs from conventional representations of female bisexuality as safely femme – symptomatic of the need to quell anxieties around fluid desire – she remains in her sensationalised iconicity an instrument for commercial profit, or 'commodity bisexuality'.[4] A more typically gender-conforming, heteronormative exploitation of female bisexuality-as-marketing strategy appears in the music video (dirs: Kyle Newman and Spencer Susser) for American pop chanteuse Lana Del Rey's 'Summertime Sadness' (2012), a track from her album *Born to Die*. Though the lyrics avoid explicitly mentioning same-sex desire, the video interprets the themes of forbidden love and teenage tragedy as a lesbian romance pairing Del Rey with actress Jaime King. While their suggested Sapphic suffering could reference cases of gay youth suicide around the time, its depiction is hardly politicised outright. Instead, the intention seems to be to add another layer of provocation to Del Rey's nymphet–siren image, wherein the viewer's knowledge of Del Rey's expressions of heterosexual desire elsewhere qualify this as a distinct instance of commodity bisexuality. Both women appear femme, alternately womanly and girlish in their styling first as 1940s femme fatales shooting longing looks across a convertible's bench seat, then as adolescent friends astride bikes. The doomed adolescent coupling, the titular references to the seasonal and bittersweet and the stylised lapses between light-suffused SoCal romanticism and colour-faded home-movie nostalgia all conjure non-normative desire as tragic and temporary. While response to the video was knowing and often sarcastic, its references to same-sex desire served their function: to associate Del Rey with an enticing whiff of bisexuality, and to attract the interest of queer critics and consumers without alienating her mainstream, heterosexual fan base.[5] 'Summertime Sadness' serves to re-brand Del Rey as sexually fluid, commodifying bisexuality as a means to expand her marketability through representations that are titillating, depoliticised and unthreateningly ephemeral.

Bisexuality as (pathological) mimicry

As in commodity advertising and music videos that exude homoerotic suggestiveness, cinematic bisexuality emerges out of the impulse to connote, yet disguise, same-sex desire behind the smokescreen of one woman's fantasy identification with another. Just as spectators may experience eroticised identification with characters onscreen, for certain characters the desire *to have* is often conflated with the desire *to be*. This narrative motif often features an adolescent female pair as 'unnaturally' close, with one woman obsessively fixated on the other's persona and lifestyle. In *My Summer of Love* (2004, dir: Pawel Pawlikowski), working-class teen Mona's (Natalie Press) enthrallment with posh Tamsin (Emily Blunt) is inextricably inspired by class envy and same-sex desire. For all the controversy over its depiction of lesbianism, *Blue Is the Warmest Color* (2013, dir: Abdellatif Kechiche) relies on a similar (con)fusion of sexual identity, fascination and aspiration with the pronounced class difference between Emma (Léa Seydoux) and Adèle (Adèle Exarchopoulos) acting as a structuring silence in their tempestuous relationship and in critical discourse around the film. In *Black Swan* (2010, dir: Darren Aronofsky), *Breathe* (2014, dir: Mélanie Laurent) and *Water Lilies* (2007, dir: Céline Sciamma), erotic desire is predicated on competitiveness, social acceptance and envy conflated with awakening bisexual curiosity. Still more exaggerated visual and thematic motifs portraying bisexuality as pathological mimicry reference mother–daughter surrogates, doubling and even split personality. In *Chloe* (2009, dir: Atom Egoyan), *Love Crime* (2010, dir: Alain Corneau) and its English-language remake *Passion* (2012, dir: Brian de Palma), and *Side Effects* (2013, dir: Steven Soderbergh), bisexuality operates as a spoil of wealth and privilege or as a leveraging device for socioeconomic empowerment, constructing a character dyad I name the *rich bitch* and *dependent double* (San Filippo, 2013: 96–114). Such representations rarely affirm their bi-suggestiveness (Olivier Assayas' 2014 film *Clouds of Sils Maria* is a notable exception), but nonetheless lay bare the unavoidable if underacknowledged relationship between profit, power and pleasure to illustrate how desire and sexuality are predicated as much on circumstances of privilege and need as on the gender-of-object choice.

Bisexuality as erotic perversion

Pathological mimicry and other associations of bisexuality with the perverse stem from psychoanalytic diagnoses of fluid desire, such as gender 'inversion', as psychically debilitating. Fittingly, then, bisexuality is conflated with another perversion so deemed for its threat to coupling and procreation – incest – in *The Dreamers* (2003, dir: Bernardo Bertolucci), *Mildred Pierce* (2011, dir: Todd Haynes) and *Savage Grace* (2007, dir: Tom Kalin). Also perceived as an erotic perversion, nymphomania or sex addiction offers a stronger rationale than does incest for associations with bisexuality – orgasms receiving preference over gender-of-object choice – despite its less frequent representation than the family romances referenced above. Consider Joe (Charlotte Gainsbourg), the titular protagonist of *Nymphomaniac: Vol. I and II* (2014, dir: Lars von Trier), who proclaims her sexual needs in terms uncontained by gender, yet across her admitted hundreds of lovers and four hours of screen time engages only one woman as a sexual partner. Joe's dynamic with P (Mia Goth) carries *rich bitch/dependent double* associations, as the older Joe stalks P at school and incrementally brings the orphaned, deformed girl into her employ and bed. That this seduction was conceived by Joe's boss L (Willem Dafoe) suggests that Joe acts in subjugation to a male fantasy of lesbian desire. When Joe's hope that P would cure her impotence fails to launch, theirs becomes a chaste mother–daughter bond that soon erupts in jealousy and betrayal as P usurps Joe's authority and seduces the one man to whom Joe feels emotionally tethered. For a film that shows women to be as actively and autonomously desiring as men, it is disappointing that Joe's same-sex experimentation is so fleeting and underexplored, and in keeping with representational imaginings of bisexuality as straight male-dictated, predatory, competitive and narcissistic.

In *Shame* (2011, dir: Steve McQueen), Michael Fassbender plays sex addict Brandon, whose condition, it is strongly hinted, stems from unresolved incestuous desire for sister Sissy (Carey Mulligan) alongside an abusive experience in foster care – thereby conflating multiple sexual perversions in association with bisexuality. Following a numbing stream of sexual encounters, Brandon, in desperation, descends into an infernal-looking gay hardcore club for a backroom tryst with a male stranger, cuing his and (it is the film's expectation) our repulsion while offering the glimmering possibility that, having hit bottom, salvation awaits. That explicit representations such as this are configured in such alarmist extremes suggests that male bisexuality provokes deep anxiety even within films that otherwise offer sympathetic portraits of desiring subjects. However troublingly compulsive these depictions of (bi)sexuality, *Nymphomaniac* and *Shame* engender identification and understanding through their revealing of sexual subjectivity tortured by social dictates.

Within the more mainstream, commercialised culture of hip-hop, sexually curious and libidinous women are presented as exotic and submissive to heteropatriarchal authority. Rap artist Usher's video for his track 'Lil Freak' (2010, dir: Taj Stansberry) features Trinidadian pop star Nicki Minaj as a lascivious club-goer who (the lyrics announce) is 'on duty' to procure a good-looking blonde for a ménage à trois. It remains unclear which of the two women is the designated 'freak', though the video suggests the term could be applied interchangeably. Though known for her outspoken, sexually liberated persona, here Minaj pimps under orders ('You go get some girls and bring them to me', Usher raps) and voices her desire only in subservience to his authority, chatting up the blonde with 'I really like your kitty kat/And if you let me touch her/I know you're not a bluffer/I'll take you to go see Usher'. Where Minaj is relegated to the role of predatory, exoticised woman of colour in servitude to Usher, the blonde becomes the easily seduced prey, whom Usher lauds with lyrics conflating the two women as malleable objects of, and for, straight male desire:

> You'll let her put her hands in your pants/Aye girl, I see you like that/You gettin' excited/And you rockin' like a pro wit' it girl/By the way, you got right on it/With the chick you wanted/And now you in the corner kissin' on a girl/I'm bout to have a ménage with these here ladies.

As with Del Rey's 'Summertime Sadness', here too we see evidence of the commercial potency that commodity bisexuality holds within a genre (hip-hop), industry (music) and medium (music videos) even better known for its sensationalist marketing and exploitative structure than is the movie industry.

Bisexuality as (in)convenient truth

Art cinema, more than other cinematic modes, yields bisexual representability on account of its penchant for ambiguity, nuance and sexual frankness. Yet demanding the B-word's explicit articulation in films made outside of Western Europe or North America, in cultures where bisexual formations are relatively nascent or discouraged, threatens to efface what is readably bisexual about, for example, the female intimacies of *Attenberg* (2010, dir: Athina Rachel Tsangari), *Beyond the Hills* (2012, dir: Cristian Mungiu) and *The World* (2003, dir: Jia Zhangke). Representations of fluid desire meeting with cultural resistance may not directly voice bisexuality, but rather evoke it by foregrounding how material circumstances and social dictates, alongside desire, shape sexuality. The married men at the centre of *His Secret Life* (2001, dir: Ferzan Özpetek) and *Undertow* (2010, dir: Javier Fuentes-León) struggle to reconcile their same-sex desire with their culture's stringent expectation of heteromasculinity, with the toll of their repressed/closeted desire shown to affect not only bisexual men but their wives and family as well.

Cinematic treatments of real or fictional figures with documented or readably bisexual orientations follow a gendered schema of eroticising female bisexuality and effacing male bisexuality. *Domino* (2005, dir: Tony Scott), *Frida* (2002, dir: Julie Taymor) and *Violette* (2013, dir: Martin Provost) – based on the lives of bounty hunter Domino Harvey, artist Frida Kahlo and writer Violette Leduc, respectively – conflate their subjects' outlaw/bohemian status with their bisexuality, playing up these twinned elements narratively and visually. The *Carmen*-inspired heroine played by Djeïnaba Diop Gaï in *Karmen Geï* (2001, dir: Joseph Gaï Ramaka) queers the legendary temptress tale by immediately seducing her female prison guard both out of carnal desire and as a means to escape back to her multiple male lovers. Yet where depictions of (real or fictional) erotically adventurous women amplify bisexuality, when it comes to male bisexuality, biographical details and their visualisation are muffled, if not silenced altogether. In Baz Luhrmann's 2013 adaptation of *The Great Gatsby*, the homosexuality that F. Scott Fitzgerald's novel pointedly gestures at in its characterisation of narrator Nick Carraway (Tobey Maguire) is reconfigured as bromantic bonding with Jay Gatsby (Leonardo DiCaprio), and reduced to some intense gazes exchanged between the pair. The Oscar-embraced success of *Dallas Buyers Club* (2013, dir: Jean-Marc Vallée) was unbothered by accounts that Ron Woodruff, on whom the hero-protagonist is based, was openly bisexual in real life, and bore little resemblance to the homophobic womaniser portrayed by Matthew McConaughey. Presumably the rationale dictating these omissions was to retain the (however illusory) public image of a cherished canonical work of American literature, in the case of *Gatsby*, and to shape a risk-averse plea for empathy and advocacy around HIV/AIDS, in the case of *DBC*. For the apprehension lingers that to 'taint' a film with even a whiff of non-heterosexuality would indelibly colour it as being 'a gay film' or 'a bisexual film', no matter the marketing campaign attempts to tout it as 'a universal love story' – just think of *Brokeback Mountain* (2005, dir: Ang Lee). Certainly this hesitancy to align films with the so-called gay ghetto disproportionately affects representations of *male* bisexuality, given our culture's greater comfort with same-sex desire between women; one has only to look at the bromance craze to note how urgent we find the navigation of homoeroticism to be. While the majority of such representations recuperate relations between men as safely platonic, US indies *Chuck & Buck* (2000, dir: Miguel Arteta), *The D Train* (2015, dirs: Andrew Mogel and Jarrad Paul), *Humpday* (2009, dir: Lynn Shelton), *Old Joy* (2006, dir: Kelly Reichert) and *The Overnight* (2015, dir: Patrick Brice) each attempt to varying degrees to articulate and explore that which goes unacknowledged between heterosexually identified men.

Bisexuality as (not) just a phase

In the steady spate of lesbian romantic comedies released globally in the twenty-first century, a much-employed narrative formula ranging from *Butterfly* (2004, dir: Yan Yan Mak) and *Spider Lilies* (2006, dir: Zero Chou), to *I Can't Think Straight* (2008, dir: Shamim Sarif) and *The World Unseen* (2007, dir: Shamim Sarif), to *Blue Is the Warmest Color* and *Imagine Me & You* (2005, dir: Ol Parker) has an initially heterosexual-identified woman fall for a self-assured lesbian and lay claim to lesbian identity herself. I remain sceptical about this formula's challenge to compulsory monosexuality, for often the narrative engineers movement to an ostensibly fixed sexuality that also embraces monogamy as both the default and the ideal. *Puccini for Beginners* (2006, dir: Maria Maggenti) offers a refreshing twist on romcom's monosexism even if it strays only slightly from formula – protagonist Allegra (Elizabeth Reaser) still reunites with her temporarily estranged love Samantha (Julianne Nicholson) in what promises to be a monogamous coupling, even if Allegra's earlier diatribe against the myth of soulmates and monogamy's oppressiveness still echoes. *Puccini* departs from the monosexist script by allowing Allegra a sexually and emotionally fulfilling affair with a straight man, Philip (Justin Kirk) – a rebound-turned-juggling act given that Allegra two-times Philip with his ex-girlfriend Grace (Gretchen Mol), whose relationship with

Allegra is her first with a woman. What reads as most perceptive about *Puccini*'s representation of desire is its irreducibility to gender-of-object choice: Allegra's chemistry with Philip is shown to be as potent as that which she shares with women, and their relationship has everyday potential that shakes but does not crumble her sense of herself as lesbian.

A similar, if more controversial, negotiation of bisexuality as behaviour versus identity is taken up by *The Kids Are All Right* (2010, dir: Lisa Cholodenko), after long-partnered mother Jules (Julianne Moore) is caught having a steamy affair with sperm donor Paul (Mark Ruffalo). When wife Nic (Annette Bening) asks, 'Are you straight now?', Jules responds with a defiant 'No! That has nothing to do with it', and later refuses Paul's plea to continue their relationship by telling him insistently, 'I'm gay!' While bisexuality goes unspoken, Jules' affirmation of her lesbian identity seems less an endorsement of monosexuality than a reclaiming of her uninterrupted impulse, and right, to so identify despite having enjoyed sex with a man. Paradoxically, Jules' unwavering lesbian self-identification testifies to the film's affirmation of sexual fluidity, wherein personal/political identity does not preclude erotic/emotional desire – valuably revealing how desire is often steered by circumstance and emotional need ('to be appreciated', as Jules tearfully tells Nic). Just as bisexual-oriented characters might be read in terms of lesbian or heterosexual representation, *Puccini* and *Kids* are valuable instances of bisexual representation even if the characters ultimately reaffirm their lesbian identity.

Bi every week

Serial television offers a promising site for bisexual representation because seriality permits bisexuality to emerge over time, which is necessary for the accumulation of experiences that renders bisexuality not conceptually *viable* – for any individual is potentially bisexual, no matter his or her behaviours to date – but rather representationally *legible*. Characters as diverse – though nearly all female – as Brittany (Heather Morris) on *Glee* (2009–15), Dr Eleanor O'Hara (Eve Best) on *Nurse Jackie* (2009–15) and Cosima (Tatiana Maslany) on *Orphan Black* (2013–) have established a televisual template for being 'bi every week', to paraphrase what Anna McCarthy terms 'everyday queerness', embedding queer characters and non-interruptive storylines within the textual fabric but without necessarily applying identity labels or normalising queerness into apolitical non-specificity (2001: 593–620). Setting a series within an historical (and mythical) era ostensibly more accommodating of fluid sexual behaviour permits the particularly elusive male bisexual such as Oberyn Martell (Pedro Pascal) in *Game of Thrones* (2011–) to indulge his expansive sexual appetites to an orgiastic degree, while a supernatural premise accommodates fluid sexual subjectivities such as that of succubus Bo (Anna Silk) on *Lost Girl* (2010–). While these fantasy-based texts offer a liberating space for desires and identities beyond monosexuality, such spaces skew utopian and sensationalist in their sexual imaginings.

Having formerly confined its bisexual representations to 'very special' episodic treatment (read: necessarily fleeting, thus exceptions *sans* narrative repercussion), US network television has caught on to something pointed out by a recent *Slate* piece titled 'Why Bisexual Women are TV's Hot New Thing': 'a bisexual character does seem to double a show's chances of building a fan base' (Thomas, 2012). The sexually ambiguous woman constitutes a renewed form of 'having it both ways', as a recurring character whose sexuality remains perennially unresolved while providing exotic titillation in every episode. Investigator Kalinda Sharma (Archie Panjabi) on *The Good Wife* (2009–16) is bisexually behaving, if not identifying; while her single status paradoxically allows for bisexual explicitness in giving her multiple opportunities for both male and female sexual partners, her professional motivations frame her every erotic encounter as a transactional exchange for information – making Kalinda another bisexual mercenary, for whom power and pleasure are conflated. Vying with Kalinda for the role of US network television's landmark recurring bisexual female to date is Dr Callie Torres (Sara Ramirez) on *Grey's Anatomy* (2005–), whose sporadic trysts with her male colleague/friend-with-benefits Dr Mark Sloan (Eric Dane) span several seasons *and* relationships (on both their parts) with women. The series avoids polarising Callie's drives along the conventional binary that aligns women's erotic desire with heterosexuality and emotional desire with lesbianism, even if Callie's eventual partnering with female paediatrician Dr Arizona Robbins (Jessica Capshaw) works to contain Callie's legibility, if not her legitimacy, as bisexual.

Having shrewdly branded itself as sexually progressive, the emergent realm of original television content distributed online has already produced two notable treatments of bisexual representation. When Piper Chapman (Taylor Schilling), the incarcerated protagonist of women's prison drama *Orange Is the New Black* (2013–), clarifies in the pilot that she was a lesbian 'at the time' of her drug-related crime, it is the first of many references within the series to the temporal and otherwise contingent specificity determining any utterance of identity. Despite Piper's resistance to naming herself bisexual (or ascribing to herself any sexual identity in the present tense), *OITNB* effectively names her and 'gay for the stay' co-inmate Lorna (Yael Stone) as such in characterising them with associations made between bisexuality and same-sex environment, criminality, infidelity and white privilege. But while *Orange Is the New Black* reappropriates the women's-prison trope of mercenary bisexuals, it more predominantly emphasises how all-female environments construct a 'safe space' for exploring how logics of sexual desire might be reconceived along a more fluid range.

Though hailed for its landmark transgender representation of transitioning septuagenarian Maura (Jeffrey Tambor), Amazon Originals series *Transparent* (2014–) is moreover exceptional in presenting its other ensemble leads, Maura's three children, as correspondingly queer – each in their highly individual, not easily categorisable way. Complex histories and repressed family secrets inform these characters' libidinal logic, signalling the contingency of sexuality alongside its insuppressibility. With daughters Sarah (Amy Landecker) and Ali (Gaby Hoffmann) grappling with their respective sexual and gender fluidity, queerness becomes the show's norm, while straightness is defamiliarised and heteromasculinity problematised through the (self-)destructive machismo and transphobia exhibited by the cis male leads, Maura's son Josh (Jay Duplass) and Sarah's husband Len (Rob Huebel). Just as *Transparent*'s nuanced individuation of Maura redefines trans-ness in terms of uniqueness rather than imitation, so is sexuality articulated as infinitely varied and only socially shackled to gender.

Queer bisexualities

Iranian-American Desiree Akhavan's debut feature *Appropriate Behavior* (2014) adds a much-needed voice from a bisexually identified woman of colour to the conversation on bisexual representation. Performing as alter ego Shirin, a Brooklynite not out to her conservative parents and recently jilted by her girlfriend, Akhavan speaks volumes about the distinctive (though not essential or universal) experience of bisexual alterity. That its *Annie Hall*-like non-linear narrative compulsively lapses into flashbacks showing the heartbroken Shirin's memories subsumes us within her subjectivity, offering insight into and empathy for the ways bisexuality contends with straight *and* gay phobias. That Shirin is forced to straddle a cultural divide between queerer-than-thou Brooklyn hipsters and the equally arbitrary norms of her family's Persian community, where women openly dance together but lesbianism is verboten, provides an intersectionalist sense of bisexuality's uniquely adaptive yet, as a result, maligned, invisible status.

Akhavan's specifically and explicitly bisexual voice is equally, though paradoxically, as valuable as that of other auteurs who eschew identity markers but have created bodies of work wherein sexual fluidity is representationally pervasive. While most contemporary auteurs still display compulsory monosexuality's pull in conceiving characters and narratives within a binary logic of desire, the *oeuvres* to date of Cholodenko, Québec's Xavier Dolan, France's François Ozon and Taiwan's Tsai Ming-liang conjure worlds and construct characters that resist sexual categorisation, and thus richly probe the fluidity of desire and complexities of identity.

What I hope to have demonstrated through my analyses is that bisexuality's disambiguation, or its explicit articulation, matters less than its enunciation through representations of desire that go beyond compulsory monosexuality and monogamy. One may leave the B-word silent without silencing bisexuality or condemning it as marginalised Other. Its non-utterance functions to cast sexuality as continually in flux, and its characters as no less irreducible to fixed subjectivities than real people. Responding to ongoing hand-wringing both in queer studies and popular discourse over the B-word, David Halperin offers the following:

> Another solution, or nonsolution, would be to treat the perpetual crisis of bisexual definition as a useful one for dramatizing the larger crisis in contemporary sexual definition, to see it as witness to a world in which we cannot make our sexual concepts do all the descriptive and analytic work we need them to do.
>
> (2009: 454)

As Halperin cannily observes, it is precisely bisexuality's ontological, epistemological and representational polysemy that generates its subversive potential to lay bare the mutability, contingency and inherent transgressiveness of desire. The complex, queer understanding of bisexuality which I use to analyse its representations construes the B-word as a pluralistic construct rather than as a totalising essence, but one which nonetheless possesses a historical lineage and idiomatic specificity that emphasises the importance of emotional and material determinants (as much if not more than gender-of-object choice) informing sexual desire, behaviour and identity. In this conceptualisation, the B-word re-emerges as a deft device with which to explore and question the contours of desire, and to map intersections among bisexuality and other sexuality and gender alternatives.

Notes

1 David Fincher's 2011 English-language remake of Larsson's initial volume ultimately proved disappointing at the box office, and follow-up films *The Girl Who Played with Fire* and *The Girl Who Kicked the Hornet's Nest* remain unproduced.
2 I am recalibrating Adrienne Rich's view of 'compulsory heterosexuality' as the ideological, institutionalised suppression of lesbianism (1993: 227–54).
3 Foundational works on bisexual representation include Doty (2000: 131–54) and Hall and Pramaggiore (1996), to which my book *The B Word* (2013) is indebted.

4 I am adapting 'commodity lesbianism', Danae Clark's term for the strategic use of lesbian suggestibility within mainstream advertising images; such a 'dual market approach', she argues, 'allows a space for lesbian identification, but must necessarily deny the representation of lesbian identity politics' (1993: 195).
5 As 'Kate', a reviewer for queer women's website *Autostraddle*, asked: 'I guess we are supposed to infer that smoke machines + gazing at each other and crying = lesbianism?'

Bibliography

Clark, D. (1993) 'Commodity Lesbianism'. In H. Abelove, M. A. Barale, and D. M. Halperin (eds) *The Lesbian and Gay Studies Reader*. New York: Routledge.
Doty, A. (2000) *Flaming Classics: Queering the Film Canon*. New York: Routledge.
Hall, D. E. and Pramaggiore, M. (eds) (1996) *RePresenting Bisexualities: Subjects and Cultures of Fluid Desire*. New York: NYU Press.
Halperin, D. (2009) 'Thirteen Ways of Looking at a Bisexual'. *Journal of Bisexuality*. Volume 9(3–4): 451–5.
Kate (2012) 'Lana Del Rey's "Summertime Sadness" Video Revealed, Features Lesbians Being Sad'. 20 July. *Autostraddle*. www.autostraddle.com/lana-del-reys-summertime-sadness-video-revealed-features-lesbians-being-sad-141790/ (accessed: 19 June 2014).
Larsson, S. (2008) The *Millennium* series (*The Girl with the Dragon Tattoo, The Girl Who Played with Fire, The Girl Who Kicked the Hornet's Nest*). Trans. R. Keeland. New York: Alfred A. Knopf.
McCarthy, A. (2001) '*Ellen*: Making Queer Television History'. *GLQ*. Volume 7(4): 593–620.
Pramaggiore, M. (2011) 'Kids, Rock and Couples: Screening the Elusive/Illusive Bisexual'. *Journal of Bisexuality*. Volume 11(4): 587–93.
Rich, A. (1993) 'Compulsory Heterosexuality and Lesbian Existence'. In H. Abelove, M. A. Barale and D. M. Halperin (eds) *The Lesbian and Gay Studies Reader*. New York: Routledge.
San Filippo, M. (2013) *The B Word: Bisexuality in Contemporary Film and Television*. Bloomington: Indiana University Press.
Thomas, J. (2012) 'Why Bisexual Women are TV's New Hot Thing'. 8 March. *Slate*. www.slate.com/blogs/browbeat/2012/03/08/bisexual_women_are_tv_s_hot_new_thing.html (accessed: 22 March 2012).

Media

3 (2010) Directed by T. Tykwer [Film]. Germany: X-Filme Creative Pool.
Appropriate Behavior (2014) Directed by D. Akhavan [Film]. USA: Parkville Pictures.
Attenberg (2010) Directed by A. R. Tsangari [Film]. Greece: Haos Film.
Basic Instinct (1992) Directed by P. Verhoeven [Film]. USA: Carolco Pictures.
Beyond the Hills (Dupa dealuri) (2012) Directed by C. Mungiu [Film]. Romania: Mobra Films.
Black Swan (2010) Directed by D. Aronofsky [Film]. USA: Fox Searchlight Pictures.
Blue Is the Warmest Color (La vie d'Adèle) (2013) Directed by A. Kechiche [Film]. France: Quat'sous Films.
Breathe (Respire) (2014) Directed by M. Laurent [Film]. France: Move Movie.
Brokeback Mountain (2005) Directed by A. Lee [Film]. USA: Focus Features.
Butterfly (Hu die) (2004) Directed by Y. Y. Mak [Film]. China: Paramount Pictures.
Chasing Amy (1997) Directed by K. Smith [Film]. USA: View Askew Productions.
Chloe (2009) Directed by A. Egoyan [Film]. Canada: StudioCanal.
Chuck & Buck (2000) Directed by M. Arteta [Film]. USA: Artisan Entertainment.
Clouds of Sils Maria (2014) Directed by O. Assayas [Film]. France: CG Cinéma.
The D Train (2015) Directed by A. Mogel and J. Paul [Film]. USA: Ealing Studios Entertainment.
Dallas Buyers Club (2013) Directed by J.-M. Vallée [Film]. USA: Truth Entertainment.
Domino (2005) Directed by T. Scott [Film]. USA: New Line Cinema.

The Dreamers (2003) Directed by B. Bertolucci [Film]. France: Recorded Picture Company.
Frida (2002) Directed by J. Taymor [Film]. USA: Handprint Entertainment.
Game of Thrones (2011–) [TV Series]. USA: HBO.
The Girl Who Kicked the Hornets' Nest (*Luftslottet som sprängdes*) (2009) Directed by D. Alfredson [Film]. Sweden: Yellow Bird.
The Girl Who Played with Fire (*Flickan som lekte med elden*) (2009) Directed by D. Alfredson [Film]. Sweden: Yellow Bird.
The Girl with the Dragon Tattoo (*Män som hatar kvinnor*) (2009) Directed by N. A. Oplev [Film]. Sweden: Yellow Bird.
The Girl with the Dragon Tattoo (2011) Directed by D. Fincher [Film]. USA: Columbia Pictures.
Glee (2009–15) [TV Series]. USA: Fox.
The Good Wife (2009–16) [TV Series]. USA: CBS.
The Great Gatsby (2013) Directed by Baz Luhrmann [Film]. USA: Warner Bros. Pictures.
Grey's Anatomy (2005–) [TV Series]. USA: ABC.
His Secret Life (*Le fate ignoranti*) (2001) Directed by F. Özpetek [Film]. Italy: R&C Produzioni.
Humpday (2009) Directed by L. Shelton [Film]. USA: Magnolia Pictures.
I Can't Think Straight (2008) Directed by S. Sarif [Film]. UK: Enlightenment Productions.
Imagine Me & You (2005) Directed by O. Parker [Film]. UK: BBC Films.
Karmen Geï (2001) Directed by J. G. Ramaka [Film]. Senegal: Arte France Cinéma.
The Kids Are All Right (2010) Directed by L. Cholodenko [Film]. USA: Focus Features.
'Lil Freak' (2010) Directed by T. Stansberry [Music Video]. USA.
Lost Girl (2010–15) [TV Series]. Canada: Showcase.
Love Crime (*Crime d'amour*) (2010) Directed by A. Corneau [Film]. France: SBS Films.
Mildred Pierce (2011) Directed by Todd Haynes [TV miniseries]. USA: HBO.
My Summer of Love (2004) Directed by P. Pawlikowski [Film]. UK: Apocalypso Pictures.
Nurse Jackie (2009–15) [TV Series]. USA: Showtime.
Nymphomaniac: Vol. I and II (2014) Directed by L. von Trier [Film]. Denmark: Zentropa Entertainments.
Old Joy (2006) Directed by K. Reichardt [Film]. USA: Film Science.
Orange Is the New Black (2013–) [TV Series]. USA: Netflix.
Orphan Black (2013–) [TV Series]. Canada: Space.
The Overnight (2015) Directed by P. Brice [Film]. USA: Duplass Brothers Production.
Passion (2012) Directed by B. De Palma [Film]. USA: SBS Productions.
Puccini for Beginners (2006) Directed by M. Maggenti [Film]. USA: Eden Wurmfeld Films.
Savage Grace (2007) Directed by T. Kalin [Film]. USA: Celluloid Dreams.
Shame (2011) Directed by S. McQueen [Film]. UK: See-Saw Films.
Side Effects (2013) Directed by S. Soderbergh [Film]. USA: Endgame Entertainment.
Spider Lilies (*Ci qing*) (2006) Directed by Z. Chou [Film]. China: 3rd Vision Films.
'Summertime Sadness' (2012) Directed by Kyle Newman and Spencer Susser [Music Video]. USA.
Transparent (2014–) [TV Series]. USA: Amazon Originals.
Undertow (*Contracorriente*) (2010) Directed by J. Fuentes-León [Film]. Peru: Elcalvo Films.
Vic + Flow Saw a Bear (*Vic + Flo ont vu un ours*) (2013) Directed by D. Côté [Film]. Canada: La Maison de Prod.
Vicky Cristina Barcelona (2008) Directed by W. Allen [Film]. USA: The Weinstein Company.
Violette (2013) Directed by M. Provost [Film]. France: TS Productions.
Water Lilies (*Naissance des pieuvres*) (2007) Directed by C. Sciamma [Film]. France: Balthazar Productions.
The World (*Shijie*) (2003) Directed by J. Zhangke [Film]. China: Office Kitano.
The World Unseen (2007) Directed by S. Sarif [Film]. South Africa/UK: Enlightenment Productions.

8
HETEROSEXUAL CASUAL SEX
From free love to Tinder

Kath Albury

Does the popularity of Tinder among young metropolitan, middle-class heterosexuals signal the end of marital commitment and the dawn of a 'dating apocalypse' (Riley, 2015)? What does 'casual sex' mean in the context of contemporary Anglo-American (and Antipodean) heterosexual cultures? As this chapter will demonstrate, casual sex between heterosexuals is not a recent innovation, nor is the 'gamification' of dating a purely digital phenomenon. Further, sex outside of marriage has (from the nineteenth century at least) been actively championed by feminist activists and other radicals in the United States, Europe and elsewhere as an expression of personal and collective struggles for freedom.

In her influential and still relevant article 'Thinking sex: notes for a radical theory of the politics of sexuality', feminist anthropologist Gayle Rubin proposed the model of a 'charmed circle' of appropriate sexual desire and expression, which relies on implicit normative assumptions of heterosexuality (Rubin, 1992). As Rubin observes, married, monogamous heterosexual couples' sex is rarely pathologised, provided that they only have sex in conditions of privacy and abstain from excessive kink and/or 'commodified' sexual practices such as porn production and or consumption (1992: 282). While unmarried heterosexuals are not as far beyond the boundaries of the 'charmed circle' as commercial sex workers and 'promiscuous' queers, they still occupy an ambiguous zone in Rubin's good/bad sex continuum. As Rubin puts it, 'heterosexual encounters may be sublime or disgusting, free or forced, healing or destructive, romantic or mercenary. As long as it does not violate other rules, heterosexuality is acknowledged to exhibit the full range of human expression' (1992: 282). What, then, are these 'other rules'? Rubin suggests that casual sex, particularly sex pursued in an explicitly 'no strings' context, has a very high potential to exceed the bounds of 'good' heterosexuality.

Like sex within marriage or long-term committed relationships, casual sex can be joyous, pleasurable and intimate. Like marital sex, it can also be disappointing, unwelcome and emotionally and/or physically painful. At the same time, casual sex has been widely condemned by both feminist and non-feminist critics as a practice that politically disadvantages women and/or undermines the 'healthy' formation of long-term relationships that conform more closely to Rubin's 'charmed' ideal. As metropolitan heterosexuals in the Global North increasingly delay marriage and childrearing in order to prioritise education and the establishment of careers, young adults – that is, university students and graduates in their late teens and twenties – have been the target of considerable concern regarding their participation (both actual and imagined) in casual sex and hook-up cultures (see Hamilton and Armstrong, 2009; Garcia et al., 2012).

Since 2013, this critique has shifted to centre on young adults' mediated practices of casual dating/hooking up, reflecting the contemporary intermingling of anxieties regarding new technologies (particularly mobile phones and social networking platforms) and anxieties regarding young people's sexual cultures (see Crawford and Goggin, 2008; Albury and Crawford, 2012). Unsurprisingly, the popularity of the smartphone dating app Tinder has attracted attention from popular media commentators in North America, the UK, Australia and elsewhere. Popular media coverage of Tinder as a 'cesspool of casual sex' (Marinos, 2014) suggests the Tinder app is not simply facilitating, but inciting, 'apocalyptic' levels of destructive promiscuity (Sales, 2015). While Tinder is not the only app used by young people in search of casual (or longer-term) sexual partners, the hyperbole it has attracted makes the 'Tinder Panic' genre of popular reporting particularly productive as the basis for a case study of changing attitudes and approaches to heterosexuality and casual sex.

What is Tinder?

Tinder is a 'location-based real-time dating' smartphone application that 'facilitates local, immediate social or sexual encounters' (Handel and Shklovski, 2012; Blackwell et al., 2015). While this style of app has been popular among gay men for several years, Tinder is notable for its popularity among heterosexuals (although it should be noted that it is also used by same-sex-attracted people). Tinder is only one of many such apps targeting heterosexual users, but is notable because its name has become a generic or shorthand term for digitally mediated heterosexual hook-ups. Tinder's Terms of Service commit users to 'non-commercial use' and requires that users are over 13 (in accordance with Facebook's Terms of Service) and are not felons or sex offenders (www.gotinder.com/terms). While teenagers can legitimately access the app, Tinder reports that only 7 per cent of all users worldwide in 2014 were under 18 (Doutre, 2014) and that under-18s are restricted from interacting with users aged over 18 (Bochenski, 2014). The connection to Facebook is crucial to Tinder's success, as users are able to install the app in under a minute once they have verified their identity using their Facebook login. This cross-platform connection allows key details such as pictures, interests and friendship networks to be seamlessly imported from the user's Facebook profile.

Once these details are imported, the new user is offered access to Discovery Settings, via a set of sliders that allow them to choose when they are visible by other users and select a search distance from 2km to 160km in which they can see (and be seen by) other users. Users can also set a preferred age range for potential matches. The default offering is typically 18–50 for a generic adult user (whose age has been 'verified' via their Facebook profile). At this point they can then view other user profiles (known as 'cards'), within their nominated age range and geographical specifications. Public information can be accessed via a tap on the user's card, which reveals up to six photos (imported from Facebook), biographical notes, interests, approximate geographical location and information on when (and if) the user was recently active on the app. If the two users have mutual Facebook friends, these are also visible. To express interest in a profile, the user swipes the card to the right. To dismiss the profile they swipe left. If two users right-swipe on each other's profile the app notifies them both that 'It's A Match', at which point (and not before) they are able to directly message one another. As Duguay observes, 'the normative qualities of its target audience as young, cisgender, high socioeconomic status, urban dwellers, as depicted in Tinder's promotional video, are reflected in the application's design choices' (2014: 17).

Tinder represents itself as a dating application, promoting its ability to match users who are seeking romantic/longer-term relationships, as opposed to casual sexual encounters (www.gotinder.com/about). Despite this, the app has gained a popular reputation for facilitating 'hook-ups' or casual and/or no-strings-attached encounters (see Garcia et al., 2012). This reputation is buoyed by the app's game-like interface, which, according to Tinder's critics, encourages users to 'match' primarily on the basis of physical attraction and geo-proximity, rather than forming a 'deeper' attraction. Significantly, users can only message one another once mutual attraction has been established – a feature that has been praised for promoting a sense of increased privacy and security for female users (Greenfield, 2013). Tinder has been in use since 2012, and has been widely discussed on popular social networking platforms, blogs and other user forums since its inception. The app began to attract mainstream media attention around 2013, when outlets such as *The Guardian* began to publish articles describing the app as a 'sex satnav' (Heawood, 2013). The byline-free 'explainer' article, 'Tinder: The app that helps you meet people for sex', observed that 'the average age of users is 27 and most are just looking for something casual' (*Guardian*, 2013). By 2014, *Forbes* was reporting an official Tinder statement that global users 'now swipe through 1.2 billion Tinder profiles a day, and that each day, Tinder makes more than 15 million matches' (Bertoni, 2014).

Tinder and the 'dating apocalypse'

As this chapter will outline, sexual interactions between unmarried heterosexuals can be variously defined as 'promiscuity', 'free love', 'casual sex' or 'hook-up culture', depending on the ideological and/or disciplinary environment in which they are discussed. There is substantial historical evidence of the existence of casual heterosexual intimacies, significantly pre-dating the introduction of smartphones and geo-locative apps. However, the features of hook-up/dating apps in general (and Tinder in particular) have been the focus of significant popular media anxiety in recent years, particularly in relation to the sexual conduct (and, to a lesser extent, the sexual health) of young, educated, cosmopolitan heterosexuals. While a range of global media outlets have reported on the rise of Tinder, in recent years, representatives of mainstream US legacy media have adopted an increasingly hyperbolic tone.

Anxiety around Tinder's impact on heterosexual conduct peaked in Autumn 2015, when Nancy Jo Sales' high-profile feature in the September issue of *Vanity Fair* framed Tinder as the harbinger of a 'dating apocalypse'. Sales damningly compared the Tinder experience to online shopping, and particularly condemned the seamless gaming feature of 'the swipe' as 'the free-market economy come to sex': 'The innovation of Tinder was the swipe – the flick of a finger on a picture, no more elaborate profiles necessary and no more fear of rejection; users only know whether they've been approved, never when they've been discarded' (Sales, 2015).

Indeed, Tinder makes a feature of this gaming quality within the app, describing users' profiles as 'cards', and offering users the opportunity to 'play again' when they don't match with a prospective partner. But, as I will outline below, heterosexual dating, hook-ups and 'courtship' have a long and documented history of gamification and reliance on what

Kane Race (in his 2015 discussion of gay hook-up apps) has termed 'speculative pragmatism' in relation to the marketplace(s) in which sex, love and marriage take place. Indeed, as Fay and colleagues observe, it can be argued that all dating sites, even those focused on romance and marriage, undertake 'sexual marketplace' functions (Fay et al., 2016: 196).

Sales' *Vanity Fair* article presents a somewhat selective picture of Tinder users, featuring interviews with several US college students and recent graduates. Her respondents present a tale of Tinder (and associated app) culture as a 'hit-it-and-quit-it' space, in which heterosexual men experience significant market advantages, including the benefits of proximity-based locative software (Sales, 2015). Conservative *New York Post* columnist Naomi Schafer Riley improvises on Sales' article to forecast a 'Tinder effect' on heterosexual coupling, which will undermine heterosexuals' desire for marriage and (to paraphrase her column's title) 'tear society apart' (Riley, 2015). The Tinder effect, Riley argues, will have a particular impact on heterosexual men, for whom a habituation to 'endless swiping' will mean they 'live in a perpetual adolescence and never find out what it means *to put effort* into a relationship' (emphasis added).

While the *Vanity Fair* narrative attributes Tinder as the central causal agent in young heterosexuals' dissatisfaction with casual sex/hook-ups, it invokes many pre-digital bad-news stories of heterosexual dating dynamics. Key elements highlighted by Sales include:

- the application of calculative rules and 'gaming' principles to sexual relationships;
- the labour-based nature of heterosexual relationships;
- heterosexual male boorishness/lack of sexual skill;
- heterosexual women gold-digging/exploiting men by exchanging sex for food/drinks;
- heterosexual men's inherent unwillingness to 'commit'; and
- the seeming absence of an acceptable mainstream heterosexual script for ethical engagement with multiple/concurrent sexual partners.

It should be noted that more youth-focused media commentary responded to Sales' and Riley's articles with an explicit move to historicise and contextualise the use of technology to facilitate casual sexual and social encounters. As Amanda Hess put it in her article 'The women! They're using gadgets and having sex!', many young women experience distinct advantages in using apps such as Tinder; she believes that 'panic over hook-up technology like Tinder is out of control' (Hess, 2015). As I will explore below, many of the elements that trouble Sales' and Riley's interviewees have precedent in historical accounts of relationships between unmarried heterosexuals.

Gaming heterosexuality

> When it comes to hooking up, they say, it's not as simple as just having sex. 'It's such a game, and you have to always be doing everything right, and if not, you risk losing whoever you're hooking up with,' says Fallon, the soft-spoken one. By 'doing everything right' she means 'not texting back too soon; never double texting; liking the right amount of his stuff,' on social media. 'And it reaches a point,' says Jane, 'where, if you receive a text message' from a guy, 'you forward the message to, like, seven different people: "What do I say back? Oh my God, he just texted me!" It becomes a surprise. "He *texted* me!" Which is really sad.' 'It is sad,' Amanda says.

'That one A.M. text becomes "Oh my God, he texted me!" No, he texted you at one A.M. – it's meaningless.'

(Sales, 2015)

Sales' article offers the exchange above as an example of Tinder's 'apocalyptic' impact on heterosexual dating culture. Here, sorority sisters Fallon, Jane and Amanda debrief on their experience of recent casual sexual encounters, which include, in Fallon's case, unethical (i.e. non-negotiated and unwanted) rough sex. While the young women's account of the unspoken rules of digitally mediated hook-ups may seem 'new', they also echo historical modes of heterosexual interaction that entered the vernacular (in the US at least) as 'the dating game'. Psychologist and researcher Lillian Rubin describes the prevailing middle-class heterosexual scripts of the US in the 1950s as a paradoxical game, in which 'girls were expected to be sexually alluring and virginal at one and the same time' in order to ensure 'popularity' (and marriageability) without provoking stigma (1990: 28). The 'game' took on a more antagonistic flavour when described as 'the battle of the sexes', in which, as feminist author Barbara Ehrenreich described it, 'women "held out" for as long as possible, until, by dint of persuasion, sexual frustration or sudden pregnancy, they "landed" a man' (1983: 1).

In a reinvention of 1950s conventions, authors Ellen Fein and Sherrie Schneider's bestselling series of 1990s dating guidebooks defined *The Rules* by which young heterosexual women could guarantee male commitment in the form of marriage. In keeping with contemporary ideals of companionate marriage, 'Rules Girls' were instructed to withhold sex not simply to land their man, but to ensure a prospective husband understood both his partner's market value and the 'work' he must do to gain (and keep) her affections. Not only do the authors strictly forbid casual sex, they also prescribe strict guidelines for communication (i.e. The Rules), including instruction on when a woman might initiate a conversation (rarely) and when she might respond positively to a request for a Saturday-night date (never after Wednesday).

In 2005, journalist Neil Strauss documented the social codes and gaming strategies of heterosexual male pick-up artists, or PUAs, in his book *The Game*. In the book, Strauss spends a year with PUAs who promise that if the rules of the pick-up game are followed and, as with the sorority women, the PUA 'does everything right', heterosexual women will respond to sexual overtures with enthusiasm. While these two examples do not in themselves represent a trend, they suggest that the novelty of the 'Tinder effect' is not so much the gamification of heterosexual interaction, but the *volume* of potential matches made available (or at least made visible) to Tinder users. Indeed, historians of sexuality have documented several centuries of heterosexual hook-ups, in a range of settings and contexts – although none that quite match the potential for scale encountered by the Tinder user based in a cosmopolitan city.

A brief (recent) history of heterosexual casual sex

In his history of heterosexuality, Jonathan Ned Katz tracks the coining and usage of the term 'heterosexual' as it gradually changed from a description of pathology and deviance (i.e. a desire for sexual pleasure without reproductive potential) to a norm (Katz, 1996). In doing so he maps a long-standing struggle between 'private' practices of sensuality and eroticism between men and women and the 'public' face of heterosexuality as it aligns with marriage and reproduction.

Like other historians of sexuality, Katz makes it clear that idealised models of heterosexual conduct are not (and have never been) universal, but are always contingent on other factors such as religious custom, race and class. Consequently, the boundaries between 'respectable' and 'dissolute' modes of heterosexual relationships are not always clear-cut. For example, US historian Kathy Piess offers an account from an early twentieth-century investigation of 'vice' among young working-class women frequenting a popular dance hall, noting that the majority of women were not sex workers but 'charity girls' who came to dances to 'smoke cigarettes, drink liquers, and dance dis.[orderly] dances, stay out late, and stay with any man, that pick them up first' [sic] (1984: 134). Piess documents the confusion with which middle-class moral reformers of the late nineteenth and early twentieth centuries responded to young working-class women's willingness to be picked up by men at dances, music halls and amusement parks while still reserving the right to reject 'dishonourable' behaviour (as defined by the young women themselves) (1984: 127–8).

It was not only working-class men and women who pursued sex outside of marriage in the pre-digital era. As Ellen Carol DuBois and Linda Gordon note, there is a considerable feminist history of 'sex-radicalism'. Notable nineteenth-century feminists such as Emma Goldman and Margaret Sanger were among those who 'slept with men without marrying ... took multiple lovers ... became single mothers ... [and] ... had explicitly sexual relationships with other women' (Dubois and Gordon, 1984: 41). British socialists and working-class 'agitators' also drew a connection 'between sexual monogamy and the acquisitive mentality fostered by private property' (Snitow, Stansell and Thompson, 1983: 6).

R.W. Connell (1997) outlines the popularity of leftist/progressive liberationist approaches to sexuality within European and North American intellectual communities from 1920s onwards, drawing on the work of modernist political theorists such as Reich, Marx and Freud. These 'modern' ideals of sexual freedom gained traction within bohemian, artistic and religious communities in Europe and North America that had long championed the theory and practice of free love (see Trimberger, 1983; Rubin, 1990; Nicholson, 2002). Notions of sexual freedom achieved more widespread popularity among student political movements of the 1960s (particularly for those living in what Connell terms 'metropolitan capitalist countries') (1997: 60). For 1960s radicals, sexual revolution or 'breaking down sexual inhibitions was felt to be part of the general project of overthrowing authority and disrupting social control' (1997: 60).

As the rise of the women's liberation and gay liberation movements provided a political impetus for these shifts, the technological innovation of the contraceptive pill also facilitated a mainstreaming of heterosexual experimentation with sexual pleasure with multiple partners. Female sexual agency was popularised in the non-fiction work of authors such as Helen Gurley Brown (as well as in *Cosmopolitan* magazine) (Luckett, 1999), and within popular fiction writing by best-selling authors such as Erica Jong and Marge Piercy (Altman, 2003). Luckett (1999) argues that in the 1960s and 1970s, prime-time US television programmes such as *Peyton Place* (1964–9), *That Girl* (1966–71) and *The Mary Tyler Moore Show* (1970–7) 'not only replaced traditional [heterosexual] home-maker heroines with swinging singles, they constructed new relationships among the female body, desire, and social space' (1999: 280). Other aspects of 1960s and 1970s popular culture (particularly popular music) reflected this emerging female sexual visibility. As Segal puts it, 'having sex with men and flaunting rather than hiding it was the single main way in which young women in the sixties rebelled against parental and middle-class norms' (1994: 7–8).

Drawing on four mass population surveys of heterosexual behaviour from the 1940s to the early 1990s, R.W. Connell observes at least two significant changes in reported behaviour over this period:

> One is a rising rate of sexual contact outside of marriage, most notably a greater number of partners in youth. The other is a gradual but far from complete erosion of the double standard, with women's patterns becoming more like those of men.
>
> *(1997: 66)*

Participants in studies specifically targeting heterosexual students also reported steadily increasing rates of 'heavy petting' (including oral–genital sex) and pre-marital intercourse from the 1960s onward (1997: 66–7).

Rubin notes that while the mainstreaming of the sexual liberation movements promised to free heterosexuals from the rigidity and game-playing of sexual morality, some participants (particularly heterosexual women) felt one set of rules had been replaced with another. As one of Rubin's interviewees put it:

> There was no context for this freedom; there were no models and no guidance for how it could be. So we had all this freedom and didn't know how to live with it ... All these women weren't supposed to say no anymore. Well, the men didn't know what to do with it either, so it became a new version of *the old male–female game*.
>
> *(Rubin, 1990: 94, emphasis added)*

For Rubin's interviewees, the sexual revolution was as 'paradoxical' as 1950s heteronormativity: 'On one hand, sex was trivialized, stripped of symbolic content and meaning, of emotion and relatedness. On the other, it was invested with enormous importance' (1990: 96). Some recall their hook-ups in 'meat rack' singles bars of the late 1970s and early 1980s as 'empty' and 'frantic' experiences in which heterosexual men and women 'traded sex for company' (1990: 99–100). Rubin notes explicitly, however, that participants in the 'singles bar' scene were unlikely to identify as feminists. She adds that other interviewees (particularly those with a political commitment to sexual freedom) described casual and 'one-night stand'-type experiences with friends and strangers as expressions of intimacy, solidarity, community or care.

It was not only disappointed singles-bar patrons who expressed dissatisfaction with mid-twentieth century manifestations of hook-up culture. From the 1960s onwards, political and religious conservatives (including the Christian Right) opposed heterosexuals' pursuit of casual sex. Journalistic accounts in magazines such as *Newsweek* represented STIs such as herpes (and later HIV) as 'punishment' for one-night stands and 'mindless promiscuity' (Rubin, 1990; Heidenry, 1997: 298–9). While 'free love' was broadly embraced within a range of counter-cultural movements (including feminism), some second-wave feminists rejected the culture of sexual liberation as counter to women's political interests. In her introduction to *Anticlimax*, her 1993 book-length critique of the sexual revolution, radical feminist Sheila Jeffreys writes:

> Sex as we know it under male supremacy is the eroticised power difference of heterosexuality. As a political system heterosexuality functions more perfectly than the oppressive systems such as aparteid [sic] or capitalism. In heterosexuality

what we have been accustomed to see as the wellsprings of our pleasure and happiness, love and sex, are finely tuned to depend on the maintenance of our oppression.

(1990: 3–4)

For radical feminists, heterosexual casual sex was no more 'free' than obligatory sex within marriage, since it had as much potential to reinforce unequal power between men and women.

Conclusion

This chapter's comparison of contemporary reportage on young people's use of Tinder with historical concerns regarding young heterosexuals' casual sexual and social practices is necessarily limited in scope. This preliminary exploration suggests, however, that contemporary critiques of the 'Tinder effect' on heterosexual relationships are not simply a direct response to the mediation and 'appification' of dating and sexual encounters. Given that heterosexual practices have been described via game-playing metaphors for many decades prior to the popular uptake of smartphones, it seems shortsighted to view Tinder's gaming quality as a uniquely modern 'problem'. Reading Sales' and Riley's articles against a broader historical picture, it would seem that Tinder is not so much the creator of the game (or marketplace) in which heterosexual relationships take place, but rather a facilitator of new rules for the 'game' of heterosexuality.

It is clear, too, that apps like Tinder have not, in themselves, rewritten the rules of casual sex. As Connell's 1997 research demonstrates, young unmarried heterosexuals have been increasingly sexually active since the 1940s. However, as Duguay (2014) has argued, hook-up apps are undoubtedly 'non-human agents' in the Latourian sense. Certainly the design and affordances of Tinder (and other apps) have the capacity to both reshape and reflect their users' expectations of sexual and social encounters. As essayists Alicia Eler and Eve Peyser put it:

> Tinder doesn't require all the extra self-defining work that OKCupid's algorithms depend on, that paid dating services such as Match.com or eHarmony require. There is no 'matchmaker, matchmaker, make me a match.' You are your own matchmaker.
>
> (Eler and Peyser, 2015)

Within both Sales' and Riley's critiques, these new affordances are rule-breakers. Tinder (and associated apps, such as Hinge) are condemned for changing the odds in unprecedented ways, making the game both 'too easy' (primarily for men) and 'too hard' (primarily for women). Yet as the (brief) history of casual sex outlined above demonstrates, while there is certainly a very limited range of 'ideal' relationship models for heterosexuals, this ideal has never been embraced by all heterosexual men and women. There is not just one game being played, but many. As Meg-John Barker suggests in their book of the same title, an understanding that sexual and romantic intimacy – even among heterosexuals – takes *many* forms requires a continual attention to micro-political change, and a commitment to 're-writing the rules' (Barker, 2012). This commitment invites us to move beyond agonistic models of heterosexual 'battles of the sexes' and engage generously with shifting social and sexual manners and the ethics of not only long-term relationships, but casual heterosex too.

Bibliography

Albury, K. and Crawford, K. (2012) 'Sexting, consent and young people's ethics: beyond Megan's Story'. *Continuum*. Volume 26(3): 463–73.

Altman, M. (2003) 'Beyond trashiness: the sexual language of 1970s feminist fiction'. *Journal of International Women's Studies*. Volume 4(2): 7–19.

Barker, M. (2012) *Rewriting the Rules: An Integrative Guide to Love, Sex and Relationships*. Hove: Routledge.

Bertoni, S. (2014) 'Tinder swipes right to revenue', 20 October. *Forbes*. Available at: www.forbes.com/sites/stevenbertoni/2014/10/20/tinder-swipes-right-to-revenue-will-add-premium-service-in-november/ (accessed 30 October 2014).

Blackwell, C., Birnholtz, J. and Abbott, C. (2015) 'Seeing and being seen: co-situation and impression formation using Grindr, a location-aware gay dating app'. *New Media & Society*. Volume 17(7): 1117–36.

Bochenski, N. (2014) 'Hook-up apps crash Schoolies'. 23 November. *Sun-Herald*. http://newsstore.fairfax.com.au/apps/viewDocument.ac;jsessionid=2A34DF9C22A353C1E5FF4BFF4C4506BB?sy=afr&pb=all_ffx&dt=selectRange&dr=1month&so=relevance&sf=text&sf=headline&rc=10&rm=200&sp=brs&cls=339&clsPage=1&docID=SHD1411238C6L27DHJG0: (accessed 30 October 2014).

Connell, R.W. (1997) 'Sexual revolution'. In L. Segal (ed) *New Sexual Agendas*. Houndsmills: Macmillan.

Crawford, K. and Goggin, G. (2008) 'Handsome devils: mobile imaginings of youth culture'. *Global Media Journal*, Australian edition. Volume 1(1): 1–12.

Doutre, T. (2014) 'Tinder teens out for sex with strangers'. 2 June. *The Sydney Morning Herald*. www.smh.com.au/digital-life/digital-life-news/tinder-teens-out-for-sex-with-strangers-20140601-zrumt.html (accessed 3 June 2014).

Dubois, E.C. and Gordon, L. (1984) 'Seeking ecstasy on the battlefield'. In C.S. Vance (ed) *Pleasure and Danger: Exploring Female Sexuality*. London: Pandora.

Duguay, S. (2014) 'Playing with fire on Tinder: examining digitally delegated authenticity claims on a dating application'. *Connected Life Conference, 12 June*. University of Oxford, Oxford.

Ehrenreich, B. (1983) *The Hearts of Men: American Dreams and the Flight from Commitment*. New York: Doubleday.

Eler, A. and Peyser, E. (2015) 'How to win Tinder'. 26 August. *The New Inquiry*. http://thenewinquiry.com/essays/how-to-win-tinder/ (accessed 3 September 2015).

Fay, D., Haddadi, H., Seto, M.C., Wang, H. and Kling, C. (2016) An exploration of fetish social networks and communities. In A. Wierzbicki, U. Brandes, F. Schweitzer and D. Pedreschi (eds) *Advances in Network Science: 12th International Conference and School, NetSci-X 2016, Wroclaw, Poland, January 11–13, 2016, Proceedings*. Cham: Springer International Publishing, pp. 195–204.

Fine, E. and Schneider, S. (1995) *The Rules: Time-Tested Secrets for Capturing the Heart of Mr. Right*. New York: Grand Central Publishing.

Garcia, J.R., Reiber, C., Massey, S.G. and Merriwether, A.M. (2012) 'Sexual hookup culture: a review'. *Review of General Psychology*. Volume 16(2): 161–76.

Greenfield, R. (2013) 'Tinder – a hook-up app women actually use'. 27 February. *The Atlantic*. www.theatlantic.com/national/archive/2013/02/tinder-hook-app-women-actually-use/317875/ (accessed 3 October 2014).

The Guardian (2013) 'Tinder: the app that helps you meet people for sex'. 16 August. www.theguardian.com/lifeandstyle/shortcuts/2013/aug/16/tinder-app-meet-people-sex-celebrities (accessed 2 July 2014).

Hamilton, L. and Armstrong, E.A. (2009) 'Gendered Sexuality in young adulthood: double binds and flawed options'. *Gender & Society*. Volume 23(5): 589–616.

Handel, M. and Shklovski, I. (2012) 'Disclosure, ambiguity & risk reduction in real-time dating sites'. *Proceedings of the ACM Conference on Group Work, Sanibel Island, Florida, 27–31 October*. New York: ACM Press, pp. 175–78.

Heawood, S. (2013) 'Tinder: what the sex satnav could do for the shy and British'. 18 August. *The Guardian*. www.theguardian.com/commentisfree/2013/aug/18/tinder-sexual-relationships-dating-apps (accessed 2 July 2014).

Heidenry, J. (1997) *What Wild Ecstasy: The Rise and Fall of the Sexual Revolution*. Kew: William Heinemann.

Hess, A. (2015) 'The women! They're using gadgets and having sex!' 18 August. *Slate*. www.slate.com/articles/technology/users/2015/08/tinder_and_the_moral_panic_over_women_using_technology_to_meet_men_and_have.html (accessed 3 September 2015).

Jeffreys, S. (1993) *Anticlimax: A Feminist Perspective on the Sexual Revolution*. London: Women's Press.

Katz, J. (1996) *The Invention of Heterosexuality*. Chicago: University of Chicago Press.

Luckett, M. (1999) 'Sensuous women and single girls'. In H. Radner (ed) *Swinging Single: Representing Sexuality in the 1960s*. Minneapolis: University of Minnesota Press.

Marinos, S. (2014) 'Tinder craze: a casual sex cesspool or a swipe right for true love?' 26 September. *Herald Sun*. www.heraldsun.com.au/news/victoria/tinder-craze-a-casual-sex-cesspool-or-a-swipe-right-for-true-love/news-story/4e86de281c31b6f7503eb91728ce5075 (accessed 3 September 2015).

Nicholson, V. (2002) *Among the Bohemians: Experiments in Living 1900–1939*. New York: Harper Collins.

Piess, K. (1983) '"Charity girls" and city pleasures: historical notes on working-class sexuality, 1880–1920'. In A. Snitow, C. Stansell and S. Thompson (eds) *Desire: The Politics of Sexuality*. London: Virago.

Race, K. (2015) 'Speculative pragmatism and intimate arrangements: online hook-up devices in gay life'. *Culture, Health & Sexuality*. Volume 17(4): 496–511.

Riley, N. (2015) 'Tinder is tearing society apart'. 16 August. *New York Post*. http://nypost.com/2015/08/16/tinder-is-tearing-apart-society/ (accessed 2 September 2015).

Rubin, G. (1992) 'Thinking sex: notes for a radical theory of the politics of sexuality'. In C.S. Vance (ed) *Pleasure and Danger: Exploring Female Sexuality*. London: Pandora.

Rubin, L. (1990) *Erotic Wars: What Happened to the Sexual Revolution?* New York: Harper Collins.

Sales, N.J. (2015) 'Tinder and the dawn of the "dating apocalypse"', September. *Vanity Fair*. www.vanityfair.com/culture/2015/08/tinder-hook-up-culture-end-of-dating (accessed 3 September 2015).

Segal, L. (1994) *Straight Sex: The Politics of Pleasure*. London: Virago.

Snitow, A., Stansell, C. and Thompson, S. (1983) 'Introduction'. In C.S. Vance (ed) *Pleasure and Danger: Exploring Female Sexuality*. London: Virago.

Strauss, N. (2005) *The Game: Penetrating the Secret Society of Pick-Up Artists*. New York: Harper Collins.

Trimberger, E.K. (1983) 'Feminism, men and modern love: Greenwich Village 1900–1925'. In C.S. Vance (ed) *Pleasure and Danger: Exploring Female Sexuality*. London: Virago.

Media

That Girl (1966–1971) [TV Series]. USA: ABC.
The Mary Tyler Moore Show (1970–1977) [TV Series]. USA: CBS.
Peyton Place (1964–1969) [TV Series]. USA: ABC.

9
REPRESENTING QUEER SEXUALITIES

Dion Kagan

The study of queer representation emerged as something of a niche interest in the 1970s, licensed and inspired by feminist criticism and the burgeoning gay liberation movement. Now, a rough half-century later, it has developed into a field in its own right, filling hundreds of books and dedicated journals. Debates about queer representation have also flourished beyond the academy, in magazines, in documentaries and online. What unites all these discussions is the shared assumption that *representation matters*. This is the notion that representations have implications for social life – that images and narratives, both fiction and non-fiction, offer the stories, symbols and myths through which we form a common culture, including what it means and how it feels to inhabit a sexed, gendered and sexually coded body.

The common account is that, until recently, queer representation was characterised by *invisibility*, which itself reflected silence, phobia, shame and the closet, reinforcing the marginality and negativity of queer experience. But this is only part of the story. This chapter provides an introduction to three contexts in which, for those who could detect them, queer sexualities appeared quite visibly in modern Western European and Anglophone representation. The first of these, nineteenth-century sexology, offered elaborate descriptions of persons we would today recognise as queer. Many of the most enduring characteristics of modern representations of queerness can be traced back to this historical moment. The second context, studio-era Hollywood from the 1920s to the 1960s, furnished those nineteenth-century ideas with an aural, visual and narrative language that vividly brought queerness to life, projected it onto the cinema screen and distributed it widely. In spite of the taboos and industrial prohibitions against the representation of 'sex perversion' during this period, Classical Hollywood, a chief myth manufacturer of the twentieth century, forged enduring stereotypes. These two 'pre-visibility' moments have been especially powerful influences not only on Western representations of queer sexualities, but across the globe. In the current 'post-closet' age of increased and diversified queer visibility, in which media production and consumption is dispersed, segmented and often transnational, the legacies of these earlier moments are nonetheless apparent. The closing section of this chapter provides some observations on contemporary representations of queer sexualities and concludes by reflecting on the question: where are we, now that we are so prolifically represented?

Sexual minorities have not always easily found their desires and cultures portrayed in mainstream media culture, or have found them characterised in partial, insufficient or negative ways. Studies of queer representation have hence been invested in the so-called 'politics of representation'. The politics of representation is an approach concerned with the ideological meanings of images and their material effects. It recognises that contests over images have been a key site through which minorities struggle for a presence in social and cultural life. Richard Dyer, a pioneering figure in queer media studies, famously wrote that 'how we are seen determines in part how we are treated; how we treat others is based on how we see them [and] such seeing comes from representation' (1993: 1).

Pre-history: the scientific invention of modern queerness

Although conventional wisdom suggests that queers were invisible in northern/Western media until recent decades, queer sexualities have in fact been a tremendous site of studious inquiry and anxious fascination in Anglo-European cultures throughout industrial modernity, especially since biomedicine first turned its attention to human sexuality in the nineteenth century. The nineteenth century witnessed accelerating efforts among medical and legal fraternities to displace the church as the official authority on the sexual behaviour of populations. Practices that once fell into the category of 'sin', such as sodomy, masturbation and cross-dressing, were increasingly defined as crimes or as inherited or acquired physical or mental abnormalities (Foucault, 1978). Sexual abnormalities were increasingly understood as congenital to the *essence* of a person – 'implanted' in the body. Under the lens of medicine, biology, psychiatry and the emerging social sciences of anthropology, criminology, sociology and later clinical psychoanalysis, human desires and intimate physical practices were commingled with ideas about character and physiognomy. These 'sexual sciences' scrutinised bodies and behaviours fastidiously: they imagined that objective knowledge could be obtained through forensic examination, and that universal standards of sexual functioning could be discerned through comparative, statistical population studies that categorised difference among bodies and measured distributive norms (Race, 2015).

In biomedicine and sexology, queer sexualities were a central obsession, although they had other names, such as 'perversion', 'degeneration', 'hysteria', 'fetishism', 'masochism' and 'sadism'. Michel Foucault's *The History of Sexuality* (1976; English translation 1978) describes the birth of 'an entire sub-race' of person-types that included intriguing proto-queer categories like the hysterical woman and the masturbating child, 'zoophiles, zoo-erasts, auto-monosexualists, gynecomasts', 'precocious little girls, ambiguous schoolboys, dubious servants and educators, cruel of maniacal husbands, solitary collectors, ramblers with bizarre impulses' (Foucault, 1978: 40). What unified these myriad deviations was their divergence from procreative heterosexuality, the healthy sexual standard and emerging 'statistical norm'. The history of modern queer representation thus begins with this oppositional model: heterosexuality as the norm and queer sexualities as physical and psychological aberrations.

Though an encyclopaedic cast of sexual protagonists appeared in this literature, the emphasis on the *gender of object choice* introduced a very specific criterion for how to represent queer sexualities, bringing the homosexual/heterosexual binary to the centre of the modern system of sexual representation (see Sedgwick, 1985; 1990). 'Object choice' refers to the object – usually a person – upon which an individual's libidinous energy is concentrated. In a model based on two sexes, defining sexuality in these terms reduces it to two core species of sexual human: the homosexual and the heterosexual, both primarily categorised by the gender of their erotic investments. There is of course a third possible category in this paradigm, bisexuality, in whose case object choice crosses genders, but becomes harder to represent. Eve Sedgwick has marvelled at the 'rather amazing fact' that despite the many ways in which sexualities could be represented (according to 'certain acts, certain zones or sensations, certain physical types ... certain frequency ... relations of age or power'), gender of object choice emerged as the defining logic around which modern sexuality is organised (Sedgwick, 1990: 8–9).

Although sexology varied in its stories of sexual abnormality, by far the dominant account was of *inversion*, the precursor to modern homosexuality. The concept of inversion infused representations of same-sex desire with the idea of reversed or dysfunctional gender. In Krafft-Ebing's (1840–1902) work, for example, the sexuality of the invert was explained as a mysterious reversal of their inner 'nature' relative to the outward expression of gender.

The inversion model has had far-reaching consequences for the representation of queer sexualities, particularly homosexuality. As Mowlabocus argues in an earlier chapter of this volume, the homosexual's ability to pass as an 'ordinary' heterosexual has long been a potent source of social anxiety. The inversion model appeared to solve this problem: inverts became recognisable because they allegedly exhibited the gender characteristics of the 'soul' trapped within them. In *Sexual Inversion* (1897), Havelock Ellis (1859–1939) classified the female invert on a scale of inversion (effectively, how homosexual she was) that corresponded with her 'scale of masculinity' (how gender-inverted she was). Female inverts supposedly exhibited *physical signs* of masculinity, such as a masculine-appearing larynx; masculine *habits*, such as smoking and wearing men's clothing; and masculine *dispositions*, such as aggression and hypersexuality (Ellis, 1897: 154). Making homosexuality 'visible on the body' through some outward sign of gender dysfunction became the *sine qua non* of modern representations of homosexuality.

Although sexuality may not in fact be legible on the body, sexology borrowed from the visual signifying systems of gender (and also class and race) to *fix the pervert in the visual field* (see Somerville, 2000). In this anxious attempt to 'read' sexuality from the body, queers were viewed 'as bodies that might well bear a hallmark that could, and must, be read' (Edelman, 1994: 6). As we shall see, this strategy is echoed throughout the history of mass-mediated images of queers.

Sexology is only one among many discourses in which modern queer representation was 'invented'. Beyond the scientific world there is a large literary, legal and subcultural prehistory to the representation of modern queerness that itself could fill numerous volumes. To take a single but much discussed example: Oscar Wilde's nineteenth-century Decadent novel *The Picture of Dorian Gray* (1891) offered coded representations of queerness, and was especially prescient about the development of the modern, Western, urban male homosexual type. *Dorian Gray* popularised the stereotypical link between art, decadence and male homosexuality and other associations including narcissism, drug addiction, the divided self and the figures of the dandy and the aesthete (Cohen, 1993).

Modern queer representation has numerous historical genealogies. However, nineteenth-century scientific discourses gave birth not only to some of the most defining characteristics of queer sexualities but to the modern idea of *sexuality itself*. The way we understand sexuality today – as a core, organic property of the individual; a function of identity implanted in the body – emerged at this time. In sexology, sexuality became an essential, morphological function of the body, something innate that determines an individual's desires, disposition, moral character and social life trajectory. And, although the gender of object choice became the key indicator of a small, primary pool of modern sexual categories to which a person could belong (heterosexual, homosexual, bisexual), it co-existed alongside non-sexual qualities. As well as *physical abnormalities* (e.g. overdeveloped libido among prostitutes or impotence among masturbators), the representation of queers also involved *intellectual and emotional qualities* (e.g. heightened artistic sensibility in male inverts).

By looking back to this historical moment we can see that ideas about queer sexualities were produced in the same gestures of elaboration as they were represented. In other words, what sexology presented as an explanatory process – describing and categorising abnormalities that supposedly already existed – was actually a *constitutive* one. That representation does things to sexuality, including 'inventing' it (and therefore, potentially, *reinventing* it), has been a key motivating idea in queer media studies, lending further weight to the assertion that representation matters. In sexology's descriptions of the sexual, human representation comes to matter quite literally: sexology's capacity to make authoritative claims about the meaning of different varieties of human flesh imbued the matter of bodies with meanings that then fixed those bodies in hierarchical relations of medical, biological and juridical difference to other bodies in what have become enduring social, moral and political relations of inequality. The anxious cultural imperative to read the signs of sexual difference from anatomical and psychological characteristics and behaviours – to locate the sexual other in the visual field – became the defining logic underwriting twentieth-century representations of queers.

Screening the unspeakable

Much like the idea that sexuality was repressed during Victorian times, the conventional wisdom is that queers were absent from or invisible in Classical Hollywood. In fact, queer sexualities were represented prolifically from the early days of silent film, albeit in coded forms. During the Studio Era, when American film production and distribution was dominated by five major studios (MGM, Paramount, Warner Brothers, 20th Century Fox and RKO), cinema was the foremost Western entertainment system and Hollywood was its dominant player. Its products appealed across gender, age and, to some extent, race, class and national divisions. Throughout the twentieth century, Hollywood emerged as the most significant cultural institution for representing queer sexualities.

Long before activists and academics declared that 'representation matters', film industry insiders and government regulators recognised that mass-consumed images could shape social attitudes. This was the principal assumption underpinning the establishment of the Motion Pictures Producers and Distributors Association (MPPDA) Code. The Code set guidelines for a system of content self-regulation among the major studios from 1930 to 1968 that sought to protect social and moral norms surrounding sexual and intimate life. Its extensive catalogue of injunctions included scenes of lustful kissing, seduction, rape, adultery, white slavery, miscegenation, childhood sexuality and nudity. As for the portrayal of queerness, there was zero tolerance: 'Sex perversion or any inference to it is forbidden.' And yet, filmmakers found covert ways to include a bounty of queer images.

The prevailing means through which queerness materialised on screen were *connotation* and *implication*: iconographies, character-types and narrative subtexts that hinted at the presence of queer characters and desires without ever openly acknowledging that they existed. Film noir in its early cycles of the 1930s and 1940s, for example, was an especially capacious genre for the coded representation of sex perversion (see Dyer, 1977; 1993). These films expressed insecurities in American culture around shifting gender roles, the

Representing queer sexualities

post-war 'crisis of the housewife' and backlashes against the New Woman. Proximate to the breakdown in the romantic heterosexual couple were all manner of sex perverts, especially queer victims and villains, albeit represented in oblique and veiled ways.

Male noir villains often appeared within a luxury milieu (antiques, rich interiors, high culture) and acted in a gentlemanly manner, echoing the association of male homosexuality with aesthetes and aristocrats in Decadent literature. Their traits included bitchy wit, fastidious grooming and dress, art connoisseurship, jewellery and perfume (see Figure 9.1). This iconography was not necessarily identifiable as sexual per se, for it was forbidden to represent sex perversion explicitly. Queerness had to be indicated in other ways, through 'gestures, expressions, stances, clothing, and even environments that bespeak gayness', showing audiences what the 'person's person alone does not show' (Dyer, 1993: 19). Hollywood queers were also frequently villains, recalling the inverts of Victorian sexology – sterile, predatory and unnatural.

Certain queer stereotypes came to dominate in Hollywood representation. By the 1920s the 'pansy' had emerged as the mainstay of coded cinematic images of male homosexuality. The pansy was 'a flowery, fussy, effeminate soul given to limp wrists and mincing steps' (Benshoff and Griffin, 2006: 24), associated with 'feminine professions' like fashion design, hairdressing and floristry. The pansy reinforced the alleged femininity of male homosexuality, strengthening the gender-inversion model of representing queer sexualities.

Likewise, female queers in film noir were often distinguishable through 'manly' styles of dress, shortish hair, an aggressive 'hard' voice and macho styles of comportment (Dyer, 1993: 58). Implied lesbian relationships were often associated with tyranny and violence,

Figure 9.1 The Pansy: Peter Lorre as noir villain Joel Cairo in *The Maltese Falcon* (1941).

servitude and working-class femininities. Sometimes these figures were explicitly 'man haters' or expressed suffragette or proto-second-wave feminist attitudes. In most cases, sexology's inversion model applied: homosexualities were made visible through legible signifiers of gender dysfunction.

There were, however, representations that complicated the inversion model, particularly from the 1950s onwards. The publication of the Kinsey reports, *Sexual Behaviour in the Human Male* (1938) and *Sexual Behavior in the Human Female* (1953), suggested that homosexual experiences were far more prevalent than had been imagined. The implication of this – that human sexuality was a potentially more fluid continuum of desires, fantasies and behaviours rather than a straightforward homo/hetero binary – had unnerving implications for the representation of homosexuality on screen. For example, the 'femme', a feminine-acting woman who makes a lesbian object choice, became a figure of potent sexual anxiety during the Cold War (Corber, 2011). Unlike the butch, the femme was a particular kind of cultural menace because of her ability to pass as a 'normal' woman; her homosexuality was not legible through the signs of gender inversion. Cold War culture's unease and fascination with the femme is evident in *All About Eve* (1950, dir: Joseph L. Mankiewicz), in which Eve Harrington (Anne Baxter) is able to *perform* conventional femininity, masking a (lesbian) butchness that only reveals itself at certain moments in the film. *All About Eve* registers queer panic through the trope of imitation: Eve's usurpation of the theatrical fame of Margo Channing (Bette Davis) is a kind of pathological copying, 'a perverse form of reproduction' (Corber, 2011: 38; see Figure 9.2).

Sedgwick (1990) has traced the long history of the *unspeakability* of homosexuality as a means of representing queerness through silences, unspoken implications and literal absences. The representation of queerness through connotation in Code-era cinema reflects the functioning of the modern closet of queer desire more broadly. A good example is the

Figure 9.2 The femme: Eve Harrington (Anne Baxter) perversely imitates Margo Channing (Bette Davis) in *All About Eve* (1950).

Representing queer sexualities

Figure 9.3 Gothic butch: Mrs. Danvers (Judith Anderson) in *Rebecca* (1940).

insinuation of queer desire in characters that remained literally off screen. In *Rebecca* (1940, dir: Alfred Hitchcock), for example, the eponymous first wife haunts the film in physical traces and recollections that evoke her monstrous, unnatural sexuality. We discover that Rebecca was childless and an adulterer who 'despised all men', was wild and boisterous, and possibly had an affair with her maid, Mrs Danvers, a Gothic working-class butch 'dyke type' (see Figure 9.3). This is quite the catalogue of queer horrors: inversion, misandry, monstrosity, haunting, non-marital sex, excessive and unnatural (that is, non-reproductive) female sexuality; and yet, abiding by Production Code rules, sex perversion is never explicitly named.

For feminist and queer film critics, the most objectionable of Classic Hollywood's tendencies was its long history of signifying queer desire via the iconography of horror and murder, powerfully yoking queer sexualities to psychopathology, violence and monstrosity (see Wood 1995; 2002). Films featuring vampires had frequent undertones of lesbian and bisexual powers of seduction. Violent or psychotic characters often invoked androgyny or disorders of gender.

Hitchcock did perhaps more than any other director to strengthen this cinematic correlation between queer sexualities and homicidal psychopathy. *Psycho*'s (1960, dir: Alfred Hitchcock) Norman Bates (see Figure 9.4) infamously brought together transvestism and psychosis under the aegis of a pathological, melancholic over-identification with the mother: a pop-Freudian sexual disorder is revealed to be the source of the film's terrifying violence against women. The young murderers of *Rope* (1948, dir: Alfred Hitchcock), meanwhile, are a coded study in same-sex love and the perverse, violent implications of homosexual neurosis (Wood, 1995: 208).

First-wave feminist and queer-media scholars tended to view Hollywood's archive of negative images as queerphobic stereotypes that reinforced perceptions of queerness as

Figure 9.4 Hitchcock's iconic demented queer: Norman Bates in *Psycho* (1960).

pathological, criminal and abject. On the deplorable fate of queer sexualities, film endings were inevitably resolved: desire among men was melancholic, fleeting or would end violently; the sexually excessive femme fatale or inverted woman is frequently killed or kills herself. As figures of pity, ridicule or villainy, queers tended to be disposable; as Tom Waugh writes, they 'drop off like flies, with clockwork predictability, at the service of dramatic expediency and the sexual anxiety of the dominant culture' (2000: 19).

However, these same images have also been a source of pleasure, excitement and identification for some viewers. Historically, queer audiences have had to activate creative forms of identification and interpretation, including the re-appropriation of themes, characters, narratives and biographies, in ways that read between or beyond the lines of preferred heteronormative meanings or search for reparative meanings in unhappy resolutions. For example, the female vampire is monstrous, but, like the femme fatale, she is beguiling 'precisely', as Barbara Creed argues, because she threatens 'to undermine the formal and highly symbolic relations of men and women essential to the continuation of patriarchal society' (1993: 60). Although the pansy is a potentially misogynist and homophobic figure, he has also been celebrated as an acknowledgment that homosexuality existed and as an alternative to the monolithic construction of normative masculinity as 'straight-acting'. Many of the most grotesque queer stereotypes have enjoyed an afterlife well into the era of visibility in affectionate and camp reincarnations that have sought to reframe 'negative images' for their critical and pleasurable meanings (Hanson, 1999).

The era of queer visibility

The story of the coming-out of queer representation is another complex narrative too long and meandering to enumerate here in detail (see Gross, 2001), but we can identify some key developments. The 'rise to visibility' is neither a straightforward narrative of progress, nor does it apply evenly across different constituencies of queers. Moreover, with increased visibility comes the potential for enhanced surveillance, and trends in contemporary representation tend to favour what have been called 'homonormative' visions of queer sexualities and lives, perhaps at the expense of other, potentially *queerer*, possibilities.

The Code began to wane in the 1960s and was amended in 1961 so that certain sexual aberrations could be openly acknowledged but had to be handled with discretion. Films could be open about homosexuals, but narratives tended to depict them as cases of pity and self-loathing. In *The Children's Hour* (1961, dir: William Wyler), *The Killing of Sister George* (1968, dir: Robert Aldrich) and *The Boys in the Band* (1970, dir: William Friedkin), for example, same-sex desires and queer characters were central to the plot, but were portrayed as a 'social problem'.

Influential waves of scholarship from the 1970s onwards, including Dyer's *Gays and Film* (1977) and Vitto Russo's *The Celluloid Closet* (1981), charged mainstream cinema with a history of homophobia, calling for 'greater accuracy' in the representation of lesbians and gays. These emerged alongside 1970s affirmation politics, which sought to replace shame with pride and a demand for *positive images* to replace the history of negative ones. The positive-images agenda has since become a criterion informing the entire cultural enterprise of producing and consuming images of queers: Are they positive or negative? Are they accurate representations or stereotypes? The term 'positive images', as Dyer explains, implies presence, positivity and accuracy: 'thereness, insisting on the fact of our existence; goodness, asserting our worth and that of our life-styles; and realness, showing what we were in fact like' (1990: 274–275). 'Thereness' and 'goodness', however, are often at odds with 'realness' because shame, turmoil and marginalisation are still part of many queer lives. Moreover, 'positive images' has tended to translate to representations of white gay men and lesbians. Queers of colour, trans* and intersex people, kink and BDSM communities, bisexuals and polyamorists remained excluded from mainstream representation.

It was during the 1990s that positive images of queers really began to proliferate in Western popular culture. The 1980s had witnessed a backlash accompanying the sex panics associated with HIV/AIDS. And yet, paradoxically, HIV/AIDS ushered in new waves of queer visibility, especially in terms of images of gay men. Increasingly during the 1990s, uncloseted gay male characters began appearing in box-office hits such as *Philadelphia* (1993, dir: Jonathan Demme) and *The Birdcage* (1996, dir: Mike Nichols), and Hollywood manufactured the gay man/straight woman 'buddy' sub-genre of romantic comedy in films like *My Best Friend's Wedding* (1997, dir: P.J. Hogan; see Figure 9.5) and *The Object of My Affection* (1998, dir: Nicholas Hytner). The 1990s also saw the emergence of the 'New Queer Cinema', an underground movement that drew energy from queer politics, theory and activism, and which offered alternatives to mainstream gay and lesbian representation (see Rich, 1992). In popular film and TV, however, the post-AIDS rebranding of queerness was dominated by simplistically envisioned, positive images of 'the good gay man' and 'the good lesbian parent'. These dignified queers distracted audiences from the threat of bisexual fluidity (e.g. *Basic Instinct*, 1992, dir: Paul Verhoeven), the hedonism and promiscuity of gay male subcultures (e.g. *Cruising* 1980, dir: William Friedkin), HIV/AIDS and the gender trouble posed by trans identities, butch lesbians and drag queens (*Boys Don't Cry*, 1999,

Figure 9.5 The (chaste) New Gay Man: Julia Roberts and Rupert Everett in *My Best Friend's Wedding* (1997).

dir: Kimberley Pierce). Across mainstream entertainment cultures in the 1990s, queerness became something of a fashionable pop-culture trend; however, it was circumscribed, commercially manufactured and dominated by friendly, white, gay men.

Gay and lesbian characters populating the Hollywood and primetime landscape tended to be chastely single or in monogamous but sexually tepid relationships. Although queer characters became a staple of American dramas and situation comedies in shows such as *NYPD Blue* (1993–2005), *Chicago Hope* (1994–2000), *Roseanne* (1988–1997) and *Friends* (1994–2004), and were central protagonists in *Ellen* (1994–1998) and *Dawson's Creek* (1998–2003), queer sex was rarely depicted. Advertisers, production executives and audiences remained cagey about queer sex, particularly on broadcast television, the medium widely fetishised as the ultimate conferrer of visibility. Queer characters on TV tended to be nestled within the narrative and stylistic contexts of aspirational bourgeois culture, high-end consumer lifestyle practices, cultural, financial and taste capital and the sexual dignity amassed through proximities to monogamy, family, whiteness and material acquisition (see Sender, 2003). More than 50 per cent of American TV's queer characters in the 1990s were white (Becker, 2006: 180).

What has become increasingly clear is that the history of queer representation has a long and productive relationship with the commercial imperatives of media producers. Even as far back as 1920s Hollywood, films featuring mannish women and pansies alongside underworld violence and prostitution drew on a frisson of sexual transgression that titillated viewers. The more recent boom in queer representation was influenced by the mainstreaming of GLBTQ rights and multiculturalism; however, *commercial imperatives* have been a robust driving factor. In the highly competitive landscape of digital TV production in the new millennium, 'edgy' or 'groundbreaking' queer content has proven extremely marketable to both hip, educated audiences and the smaller but no less prized upscale lesbian and gay 'pink' market. Cable TV companies in particular have offered more detailed, explicit portrayals of queer life, partly because the aura of titillation and risqué sex that surrounds queer sexualities is highly marketable. So, while TV productions such as the iterations of *Queer as Folk* (1999; 2000–2005) presented by Channel 4 (UK) and Showtime (US) and Showtime's *The L Word* (2004–2009) have broken new representational ground,

Representing queer sexualities

they have also cashed in on queerness as a commodity, part of a global market in queer aesthetics and storytelling.

This imbrication of queer representation and market forces reached its apotheosis in lifestyle makeover show *Queer Eye for the Straight Guy* (Bravo, 2003–2007), where queers are represented as ideal figures of neoliberal, consumer citizenship. The lifestyle specialists of *Queer Eye* are avatars of design, lifestyle and consumer knowledge and know-how. Their cultural and aesthetic knowledge is put to work in the self-fashioning of heterosexual men and the micro-management of heterosexual romance. Like their nineteenth-century and Classical Hollywood counterparts, the homosexuality of these figures is articulated through (and partially veiled by) an appreciation of aesthetic forms. The intersection of cultural capital and queerness makes these gays intelligible and a source of value in the world of neoliberal economics. However, queer desire is reduced to taste and style. In other words: no sex.

The production and reception of sexual difference in mainstream popular culture is one that now appears to swing, paradoxically, between moments of transgression and banal normality. Ron Becker calls this ambivalence 'straight panic'. This, he explains, 'describes what happens when heterosexual men and women, still insecure about the boundary between gay and straight, confront an increasingly accepted homosexuality' (2006: 23). As a concept, straight panic helps to explain the mixed reception of images of queerness in contemporary popular culture. In this climate, images of homosexuality can be either or both scandalous sexual spectacles and mundane artefacts of commodity culture; both menacingly queer and practically normal at the same time.

These paradoxes of the current 'post-closet' moment of queer visibility are evident in the critical response to HBO's recent series *Looking* (2014–2015) (see Figure 9.6). Rich Juzwiak (2014) wrote that 'in *Looking*, gay men get to be boring on TV at last. They get to look for love in barely different ways than straight people'. Some consider this a progressive representation for its *un*remarkableness – its normality. On the other hand, Brian Lowder called *Looking* 'a PSA for how the mainstream increasingly expects gayness to look – butch enough, politically apathetic, generally boring'. Here, mainstream images are potentially bland, abandoning diversity and the radical destabilisation of normative categories of sexuality that queer representation has the potential to pose.

Figure 9.6 Richie (Raúl Castillo) and Patrick (Jonathan Groff) being 'normal' and 'boring' in *Looking*.

If queer sexualities have consistently posed problems for representation, it seems as if the contemporary solution to those problems is the bourgeois marriage plot. The same-sex marriage movements that have swept through parts of the globe over the past decade reflect a trend that has been unfolding on popular screens for some time now: neoliberalism and marriage have offered comfortable space to assuage the anxieties surrounding queer representation. And yet, while certain queer sexualities now enjoy widespread, positive-image representation, others continue to remain marginal or subcultural – dangerous, anachronistic, unhappy pathologies or near-invisibilities.

Bibliography

Becker, R. (2006) *Gay TV and Straight America*. New Jersey: Rutgers University Press.
Benshoff, H. (2004) 'The Monster and the Homosexual'. In H.M. Benshoff and S. Griffin (eds) *Queer Cinema, The Film Reader*. New York: Routledge.
Benshoff, H.M. and Griffin, S. (2006) *Queer Images: A History of Gay and Lesbian Film in America*. New York: Rowman and Littlefield Publishers.
Bersani, L. (1995) *Homos*. Cambridge and London: Harvard University Press.
Cohen, E. (1993) *Talk on the Wilde Side: Toward a Genealogy of a Discourse on Male Sexualities*. New York: Routledge.
Corber, R. (2011) *Cold War Femme: Lesbianism, National Identity, and Hollywood Cinema*. Durham: Duke University Press.
Creed, B. (1993) *The Monstrous Feminine*. London: Routledge.
Dyer, R. (1977) *Gays and Film*. London: British Film Institute.
Dyer, R. (1990) *Now You See It: Historical Studies on Lesbian and Gay Film*. London: Routledge.
Dyer, R. (1993) *The Matter of Images: Essays on Representation*. London and New York: Routledge.
Edelman, L. (1994) *Homographesis: Essays in Gay Literary and Cultural Studies*. New York and London: Routledge.
Ellis, H. and Symonds, J.A. (1897) *Sexual Inversion*. London: Wilson and Macmillan.
Foucault, M. (1978) *The History of Sexuality: Volume 1*. Trans. R. Hurley. London: Penguin.
Gross, L. (2001) *Up From Visibility: Lesbians, Gay Men, and the Media in America*. New York: Columbia University Press.
Hanson, E. (1999) 'OutTakes'. In E. Hanson (ed) *Outtakes: Essays on Queer Theory and Film*. Durham: Duke University Press.
Juzwiak, R. (2014) '*Looking?* Mmmmm, Maybe Another Time'. 16 January. *Gawker*. http://gawker.com/looking-mmmmm-maybe-another-time-1502622759 (accessed 12 September 2016).
Kinsey, A., Pomeroy, W., Martin, C. and Gebhard, P. (1953) *Sexual Behavior in the Human Female*. Philadelphia: Saunders.
Lewis, T. (2007) 'He Needs to Face His Fears with These Five Queers!' *Television & New Media*. Volume 8 (4): 285–311.
Lowder, J.B. (2014) 'Why Is *Looking* So Boring?' 21 January. *Slate*. www.slate.com/blogs/outward/2014/01/21/looking_hbo_s_gay_show_is_boring_and_bad_for_gays_straights.html (accessed 12 September 2016).
Race, K. (2015) 'Biomedical Discourses of Sexuality'. In P. Whelehan and A. Bolin (eds), *The International Encyclopedia of Human Sexuality*. 1st edition. Malden: John Wiley.
Rich, B.R. (1992) 'The New Queer Cinema'. *Sight and Sound*. Volume 2 (5): 31–34.
Russo, V. (1981) *The Celluloid Closet: Homosexuality in the Movies*. New York: Harper & Row.
Sedgwick, E.K. (1985) *Between Men: English Literature and Male Homosocial Desire*. New York: Columbia University Press.
Sedgwick, E.K. (1990) *Epistemology of the Closet*. Berkeley and Los Angeles: University of California Press.

Seitler, D. (2004) 'Queer Physiognomies: Or, How Many Ways Can We Do the History of Sexuality?' *Criticism*. Volume 46 (1): 71–102.
Sender, K. (2003) 'Sex Sells: Sex, Class, and Taste in Commercial Gay and Lesbian Media'. *GLQ*. Volume 9 (3): 331–365.
Somerville, S. (2000) *Queering the Color Line*. Durham: Duke University Press.
Waugh, T. (2000) *The Fruit Machine: Twenty Years of Writing on Queer Cinema*. Durham and London: Duke University Press.
Wilde, O. (1891) *The Picture of Dorian Gray*. London: Ward Lock and Co.
Wood, R. (1995) 'The Murderous Gays: Hitchcock's Homophobia'. In C. Creekmur and A. Doty (eds) *Out in Culture: Gay, Lesbian and Queer Essays on Popular Culture*. Durham and London: Duke University Press.
Wood, R. (2002) *Hitchcock's Films Revisited*. New York: Columbia University Press.

Media

All About Eve (1950) Directed by J.L. Mankiewicz [Film]. USA: Twentieth Century Fox Film.
Basic Instinct (1992) Directed by P. Verhoeven. [Film]. USA: Carolco Pictures.
The Birdcage (1996) Directed by M. Nichols [Film]. USA: United Artists.
Boys Don't Cry (1999) Directed by K. Pierce [Film]. USA: Fox Searchlight Pictures.
The Boys in the Band (1970) Directed by W. Friedkin [Film]. USA: Cinema Center Films.
Chicago Hope (1994–2000) [TV Series]. USA: CBS.
The Children's Hour (1961) Directed by W. Wyler [Film]. USA: Mirisch Corporation.
Cruising (1980) Directed by W. Friedkin [Film]. USA: CiP – Europaische Treuhand AG.
Dawson's Creek (1998–2003) [TV Series]. USA: The WB.
Ellen (1994–1998) [TV Series]. USA: ABC.
Friends (1994–2004) [TV Series]. USA: NBC.
The Killing of Sister George (1968) Directed by R. Aldrich [Film]. USA: Palomar Pictures.
The L Word (2004–2009) [TV Series]. USA: Showtime.
Looking (2014–2015) [TV Series]. USA: HBO.
The Maltese Falcon (1941) Directed by J. Huston [Film]. USA: Warner Bros.
My Best Friend's Wedding (1997) Directed by P. J. Hogan [Film]. USA: TriStar Pictures.
NYPD Blue (1993–2005) [TV Series]. USA: Fox Television Network.
Object of My Affection (1998) Directed by N. Hytner [Film]. USA: Twentieth Century Fox Film.
Philadelphia (1993) Directed by J. Demme [Film]. USA: TriStar Pictures.
Psycho (1960) Directed by A. Hitchcock [Film]. USA: Shamley Productions.
Queer as Folk (1999–2000) [TV Series]. UK: Channel 4.
Queer as Folk (2000–2005) [TV Series]. USA/Canada: Showcase (Canada/Showtime Networks).
Queer Eye for the Straight Guy (2003–2007) [TV Series]. USA: Bravo TV.
Rebecca (1940) Directed by A. Hitchcock [Film]. USA: Selznick International Pictures.
Rope (1948) Directed by A. Hitchcock [Film]. USA: Warner Brothers.
Roseanne (1998–1997) [TV Series]. USA: Wind Dancer Productions.

PART II

Sex genres

10
EROTICA

Catherine M. Roach

Introduction

Let's start with definition, since that's where the controversy begins. *Erotica* is a form of media representation that involves literature or visual art focused on sexuality. Often, and in a usage that I will follow, the term 'erotica' is used for forms of writing – novels, novellas, short stories – that take sexual activity as a central subject of their narratives. Here, then, is our simplest description: in the genre of erotica, writers tell stories about sex. Although erotica is in this sense very focused – offering explicit and detailed representations of sexuality that may leave room for little else in the narrative – it is at the same time very broad, offering the widest imaginable representation of sexual activity and desire (adult breast-feeding scenarios, werewolf shape-shifter ménage romance, etc.) In erotica, sexuality and sexual activity are presented in stories that range from the mildly suggestive, through the sexually explicit, all the way to the kinkiest of hardcore; from amateur online short stories to professionally published bestselling novels; from the mainstream to the alternative; and from the heterosexual to minority positions of sexual and gender expression across the LGBTQ+ spectrum. In this chapter, I focus on sexual narratives written in the Anglosphere in order to allow for a transnational approach while providing delimitation to a vast topic.

We can begin to complicate this preliminary definition of erotica and open up the controversy by asking how *erotica* differs from *pornography*. The second-wave feminist Gloria Steinem made much of this difference in her influential essay 'Erotica vs. pornography'. To Steinem, porn is bad, based on 'an imbalance of power that allows and requires sex to be used as a form of aggression', even violence; erotica, by contrast, 'rescue[s] sexual pleasure' with the inclusion of 'love and mutuality, positive choice, and the yearning for a particular person' (1977: 241). *Erotica* benefits from the ennobling power of love or deep emotional engagement and enjoys connotations of art and the highbrow. *Pornography*, for its part – or, even worse, its gruffer truncation, *porn* – carries more than a whiff of the crassly commercial, the unimpressively lowbrow and the downright tawdry.

Another perspective, however, sees in this desire to differentiate erotica from pornography less a real distinction of content or intent and more a politics of naming. In one famous illustration, D.H. Lawrence's *Lady Chatterley's Lover* was banned and censored for decades after its publication in 1928 and became the subject of major international obscenity trials; today, however, it is part of the literary canon, safely deemed *erotic* but not *pornographic*. John Preston, a prolific and successful American author of gay erotica from the 1970s and 1980s, said in his introduction to the anthology *Flesh and the Word* that 'pornography and erotica are the same thing. The only difference is that erotica is the stuff bought by rich people; pornography is what the rest of us buy' (1992: 11). In this reading, the term *erotica* represents class hypocrisy and self-deception played out along socioeconomic lines. Similarly, some third-wave sex-positive feminists, partly in reaction against anti-porn feminists, see the linguistic move from *pornography* to *erotica* as euphemistic, as a little precious and apologetic, in not fully acknowledging the force of women's sexual agency and desire.

Whatever one chooses to call this material, the feminist approach to erotica/porn highlights the gendered double standard at work around stories of sex. Because of traditional gender norms, when a woman reads or writes such sex narratives she risks greater social censure; she risks the label of 'dirty slut'. The annual Canadian Feminist Porn Awards and Porn Film Festival Berlin, as well as academic texts such as *One for the Girls!* (Smith, 2007) and *The Feminist Porn Book* (edited by Taormino *et al.*, 2013), all tend to avoid the cleaned-up literary term *erotica* in favour of loaded language such as *porn* and *smut* precisely in order to challenge stereotypes about sexuality as dirty, degraded and unladylike. The growth of feminist porn and queer porn (by sex workers, porn producers and porn scholars) makes the point that the production and study of sexually explicit material can be a political and progressive act that seeks to 'contest and complicate dominant representations' of sexuality and gender (Taormino *et al.*, 2013: 9).

A further delineation of erotica comes through its comparison with popular romance fiction, that behemoth of the publishing world with multibillion-dollar sales, mostly written in the Anglosphere but translated worldwide and with a devoted, mainly female, readership (Regis, 2003; Roach, 2016). Romance novels (where central protagonists are typically referred to as heroines and heroes) fall on a spectrum from sweet (no on-page sex) to moderately spicy (a few scenes of lovemaking) to full-blown erotic romance (more frequent and kinkier sex). Erotica and romance fiction overlap in this category of erotic romance. In *erotica* the characters come together in couplings that don't necessarily end with monogamous pair-bonding; in *erotic romance* or *romance erotica* such love-bonding does occur in at least a happy-for-now, if not a happily-ever-after, ending.

This overlap raises a question: what is the role of the loving relationship in erotica? The question is particularly pertinent because of another definition of erotica as that which is about *Eros*. Whatever erotica is or has become, its etymology is firmly rooted in understandings of this ancient Greek deity who is god of both love and sexual desire. In this word history, *love* is not merely a pretty euphemism for *sex*. According to Hesiod, the earliest author to make mention of Eros when he wrote the *Theogony* around 700 BCE, Eros is one of the primordial gods, involved in the origin of the cosmos and able through his unifying power of love to bring order and harmony to the original chaos. In this reading, union, creativity and relationship are all central to the deepest meanings of erotica. This link between love and sex remains crucial in contemporary romance publishing, resulting in erotic scenes and stories that, while starting out hot and steamy, tend to resolve as emotional, committed and tender.

For some, the controversy around erotica erupts at exactly this moment when sex is divorced from love. Stories of erotica told without love and commitment can seem dehumanising, draining human sexuality of its power to bond us to others and transform us for the better. From a religious point of view, such erotica may be deemed immoral or shameful. (In one example, the Catholic Church in the 1940s condemned Kathleen Winsor's historical romance *Forever Amber* for indecency and 14 American states banned it as pornography; it became the highest-selling US novel of the decade.) Others see the opposite problem as differentiating erotica from romance fiction: stories of love and commitment – at least as told in traditionally heterosexual, patriarchal and reproductive forms – limit sexuality. Here, it is precisely the intensity of pornography and sexuality, their raw and radical ability to disrupt boundary and convention, that can liberate and transform us in positive ways (Snitow, 1979; McNair, 2013). From this perspective, the power of erotica lies in its authors' refusal to hedge and hem sexuality within polite norms of romantic love. This debate about the role of love in erotica and its overlap with romance fiction is partly aesthetic: is sexuality sexier, its narration more compelling, when the curtain closes before the final act? If too much is told, does erotica risk devolving into the merely anatomical and the mechanical: 'Tab A fitting into Slot B' storytelling? The problem becomes one of too much: a narrative of excessive disclosure that loses its art, that numbs instead of frees.

This 'too much' problem is related to a final point of definition: we write and read erotica as individuals, but we consume it as a culture. Erotica can become controversial because of its entrance – its forceful, nonconsensual intrusion? – into the public sphere, because of a sense that the culture is oversexed and in perpetual rut. As the culture has undergone a 'pornification', erotica itself has gone mainstream (Nikunen, Paasonen and Saarenmaa, 2007; Attwood, 2009; McNair, 2013; Phillips, 2015). With ads for retailers such as Victoria's Secret and Abercrombie & Fitch taking their cues from soft porn, with high-school girls in stripperesque platform shoes at the mall, popular culture is awash in the look and feel of erotica. It is hard to avoid. Who hasn't heard of the blockbuster *Fifty Shades of Grey* (James, 2012), whether or not they've ever read the books or viewed the movies? The *Shades* publishing phenomenon, along with the privacy and anonymity afforded by the meteoric rise of e-readers and digital books, helped to inaugurate a new mainstream genre of erotica, sometimes dubbed 'mommy porn', quasi-respectable precisely because of its omnipresence.

One recent cultural history reframes the sexual revolution of the 1960s and 1970s as a mass sexualisation of the media; the revolution, in other words, was actually one of media, with stories of sex gaining new and more open circulation (Schaefer, 2014). Simon and Gagnon's (2003) influential notion of sexual scripts helps us to conceptualise the effect of broad social narratives that shape how people understand their sex lives. To think in terms of sexual scripts is to see erotica everywhere, whether or not it is explicit in the mass media: the culture writes this erotica for us. Cultural sexual scripts tell us how, where and when to have sex with whom. The culture provides romance and erotica scripts – dominant discourses about sexuality circulated in and through the media – that function, for better or worse, as templates for individuals' lived experience.

If erotica is all this – existing in these binaries of suggestive/explicit, artistic/commercial, highbrow/lowbrow, emotional/physical, empowering/exploitative, public/private, individual/sociocultural – what then to make of it? What is its significance? Here's the answer I want to argue for: we should think about erotica because it can help us imagine our way to a better sexual future. I move from definition to thesis in order to critically evaluate this liberating potential of erotica. The potential is real and powerful but often muffled or missed. Erotica can serve to endlessly reproduce tired old stereotypes and false master narratives, but the new wave of mainstream erotica and of feminist and queer pornography proves that erotica *can* also be a radical imaginative space that works towards sexual justice for women, sexual minorities and heterosexual men too long confined to narrow masculine roles. Erotica can – or could – function as a descriptive and prescriptive narrative for how sexuality can be lived for justice and joy. Sex-positive erotica takes the culture's existing sexual scripts and plays with them, defining new norms for the sexual scripts of the twenty-first century.

For example, the growing audience for same-sex erotica – with its significant female heterosexual readership of gay romance stories, and supported by the rise of boutique publishers such as the lesbian-themed Bold Strokes Books and the queer-positive Riptide Publishing – helps to normalise same-sex relationships. Erotica can also challenge gendered double standards about sexuality that are oppressive to both men and women. As one erotica heroine points out in the novel *Getting Some*, 'This is the twenty-first century, honey. It's high time we women embrace our sexuality and bury the shame. We have needs, the same as men do. Why do we feel so friggin' bad about going after what we want?' (Perrin, 2007: 133). Here, woman-centred erotica addresses cultural fears about female sexuality that can erupt in slut-shaming and sexual violence. By its very nature, erotica makes the point that sexuality is central to the human condition – for woman, man and transgender person alike. (The budding emergence of an asexual romance subgenre nuances this point in important ways: perhaps it is central to the human condition, but it is not central for all humans.) By, then, portraying the widest imaginable range of consensual fetish, kink and fantasy scenarios, erotica makes the further point that human sexuality manifests in dizzying diversity. Such variety in erotic storytelling lessens stigma for people whose desire delights along a different path. Here, erotica opens up dominant discourses that impose a one-size-fits-all vision of sexuality and gender. It instead offers wider alternatives and explores freer possibilities of sexuality lived for partners' mutual pleasure, support and emancipation. It creates new spaces of possibility for us all. In all these ways, educative and entertaining, erotica can ask and answer questions about what sort of sex is worth having. It becomes a powerful form of media for influencing positive expressions of sexuality in the culture. Indeed, how many other genres can boast of being named after a god?

Hold on, objects the critic: this all seems rather grandiose and naïve, even disingenuous. Surely the point of erotica is simply to titillate: to arouse desire and to help speed its gratification. (Back to definition: another synonym for erotica is 'stroke literature', referring to the action of the hand not occupied with holding the book.) But why, I ask, must erotica be either titillating *or* political? Viewing erotica as liberating is only disingenuous if we adhere to this either/or binary. What if erotica is titillating *and* political, at the same time? What if titillation *is* political? Such is exactly the argument of recent feminist and queer porn scholarship: erotica can transgress norms that keep sexuality tamed, boxed and in its place and norms that perform this same policing action for women and sexual minorities (Smith, 2007; McNair, 2013; Taormino et al., 2013; Phillips, 2015). Such is exactly the argument put into practice by the writers, actors and directors of the erotica/pornography celebrated through the Feminist Porn Awards and the Porn Film Festival Berlin. *Erotica can let sexuality out of that box.* How, then, can erotica reach this full potential for sexual storytelling that is sex-positive, feminist, queer-friendly, liberating – as well as hot and sexy? What might such erotica look like?

The concept of *imagination* is central to this discussion, as is the related notion of *fantasy*. As a genre of writing, erotica is not easily or necessarily categorised into the traditional prose divide of fiction versus nonfiction. The stories told in erotica do not necessarily bear any factual relation to reality and can, of course, be entirely made up. But whether the erotica is true or not – whether it is fiction or nonfiction – is beside the point. What is important is that erotica is *narrative*. Erotica inhabits the realm of imagination, of exaggeration, of archetype, of fantasy. It explores and plays with possibility, with 'what if?' scenarios. Herein lies the real freedom offered by erotica, the deep source of its liberating potential. In the story world of erotica we get to think about the quandaries and complications of desire, to play out the potential disasters and oppressions of sex, in a safe imaginative space and to see if we can write and read our way into a better future.

In order to realise this full potential, erotica needs to grapple with two things: *consent* and *climax*. In the storylines of erotica, partners agree to engage in sexual activity (consent) and they enjoy such activity (climax). In consent, rape is the problem. In climax, the problem is an overemphasis on penetration and the phallus. These problems stem from the fact that sexuality is one of the messiest aspects of human embodiment. It is complicated, asymmetrical and dangerous. Sexuality raises a host of psychosocial issues and anxieties: worry over losing control, fear of relationality and the vulnerability of opening oneself to another, male anxiety about women's sexuality rooted in childhood fear of the mother, the instability of male gender and sexual identity in mother-reared patriarchal societies, women's fear of men's assault – and men's fear of such assault – in a world that bears witness to the willingness of so many to use rape to humiliate and control, and the ability of desire to derail reason. Perhaps Hesiod said it first, in his description of Eros as 'fairest among the deathless gods, who unnerves the limbs and overcomes the mind and wise counsels of all gods and all men within them' (lines 120–2). This 'unnerving' and 'overcoming' central to the experience of sexuality, its sheer chaotic power, supplies erotica with endless subject material. Like a magic trick, erotica makes these problems and anxieties of sexuality disappear. But it is a tough trick to pull off well. To do so, erotica needs to deal with consent and to get beyond master narratives centred on penetrative, genital, orgasmic sexuality in order to develop a fuller literacy – a *cliteracy* – about human sexuality and, in particular, about women's sexuality. By doing so, erotica can play a key role as a cultural site for thinking through problems of sex and for imagining ourselves towards sexual justice.

The problem of consent: the fantasy of desire

Part of the appeal of erotica is how *easy* it makes sex out to be. In the imaginative world of erotica, the fantasy is that sex is easily had and easily enjoyed. While the story may require some plot development to get to these steamy parts (or it may require very little), readers know that in erotica sexual partners will be available, willing, desirous, and panting all over the page. Consent is always, magically, already there. In contrast, real-life good sex is often hard to find. Sex can – and too often does – play out as less than perfect: physically disappointing, emotionally unfulfilling, traumatically forced or tragically heartbreaking. As Leo Bersani famously said, 'There is a big secret about sex: most people don't like it' (1987: 197). In the stories of erotica, however, sex is good, plentiful, hot and easy. This is a seductive fantasy, indeed.

In the early twenty-first century, consent has become the sex talk of the moment. The press and popular culture are consumed by stories of sexual assault on college campuses and domestic violence in professional sports. Sexual health curricula teach consent in language that can come across as very legalistic, such as the need for partners to obtain clear affirmative consent before engaging in any sexual activity. In romance erotica, the point about consent can be summarised as the problem of the 'bodice ripper'. Romance novels from the 1970s and 80s earned this label for their popular subgenre of tales of forced seductions or rapes between characters who eventually end up happily mated and married.

(I thrilled to them as a teenager, even as my budding feminist consciousness made me question whether I should.) Much discussion about romance fiction has viewed scenes of nonconsensual sex between main characters destined for true love as problematic (Wendell and Tan, 2009; Toscano, 2012). In other words, someone worthy of being called hero should not 'rip the bodice of' or otherwise sexually assault the heroine. While romance erotica has generally moved away from storylines of nonconsensual sex, such storytelling has not entirely disappeared. Anna Campbell's historical erotic romance *Claiming the Courtesan* (2007) revived controversy about women's fiction as problematic bodice-rippers by staging repeated scenes of forced seduction, although the narrative function of this 'rape of possession' is as a story tool whereby the hero learns self-knowledge and true love and respect for the heroine (Toscano, 2012).

One place where authors of erotica play with the look or feel of nonconsensual sex is in BDSM stories. *Fifty Shades of Grey* is famously all about consent and sexual legalisms, with a BDSM contract that functions as a central plot device (and that, depending on your reading of the text, is also about coercion and lack of real consent). BDSM, of course, is not rape. Ideally, BDSM is about trust, power exchange and mutual pleasure in a relationship where partners negotiate consent and work out boundaries in advance. Consensual BDSM is not the same as nonconsensual sex but with its scenes of force, physical restraint, punishment and master–slave language it is not entirely different, either. The look of the two, as I said, can be similar. From this perspective, BDSM erotica represents a current politically correct framework for revelling in bodice-ripping, porn-y, rough sex that may address the concern about legalistic negotiations during sex not being sexy. In her academic book on *Fifty Shades*, Eva Illouz summarises this concern thus: 'Just fucking fuck me, already!' (2014: 59).

There is another place where issues of nonconsent are even more central to erotica. It is a standard story trope that romance-novel partners fight against falling in love in order to protect their hearts or to maintain a dull but safe status quo. In erotica that is not romance-oriented, partners may similarly fight their lust; they may find themselves oddly attracted to a person or sexual practice they'd never previously found appealing. Alexis Hall's *Glitterland*, finalist for the 2014 Lambda Literary Award, is one great example of mismatched lovers finding happiness: a British 'posho' with a working-class lover, separated by a vast gulf of education and social status. Lovers may fight these passions tooth and nail, but they will fail. Desire flares, nether parts melt, soul-mate destiny kicks in. The lovers can't resist the sexy allure of a partner, the pull of a wayward heart, the power of a budding love and – above all – the irresistible drive of lust. Erotic partners are forced to surrender and submit. The arrow of Cupid – what our Greek god Eros becomes in Roman and later iconography – conquers all resistance. Love or desire itself is forcible in its seduction, in its refusal to seek or respect consent.

All these storylines about consenting and not consenting and sort of consenting to love and to sex represent a root power of erotica. Erotica creates a safe imaginative space to work through these complicated problems of consent, will, agency and desire and to try to come to grips with them. Erotica may need the latitude of staging darker and dangerous 'what ifs' involving various forms of force and violence as a way to grapple with the problem of rape and the meaning of consent in people's lives. This latitude may be particularly true for women and sexual minorities whose social positioning means they lack the privileges of gender, class, heterosexuality and other identity markers that confer a degree of protection against assault, and who live with a keener daily knowledge of their vulnerability within rape culture. But when these readers are castigated for enjoying the stories – for example, women for revelling in their bodice-rippers – the dynamic veers close to that of blaming the victim in sexual assault ('She was asking for it with a skirt that short'; 'If she wants to read stories like *that*, she must like being oppressed'). Nobody wants to be raped, but people – women, primarily – are raped, every day. Reading erotica in which consent is violated does not mean you are participating in your own oppression. But it can serve as a means to work through the horror of our lived knowledge of oppression.

I don't believe erotica has to always stage perfect and politically correct scenes of consent. At the same time, however, I do think that erotica offers a superb cultural space to show what consent looks like, how consent can be sexy and why it is key to all forms of healthy sexual relationship in real life. *No consent* (adult, informed, safe, sane, sober, free of coercion), *no sex*. We need more cultural discourse about this foundational point. More sex-positive erotica certainly won't end the problem of assault or convince rapists of the error of their ways. But erotica shows what enthused consent looks like: *yes, more, there, oh God, yes!* It is precisely this enthusiasm of consent and abundance of desire in erotica that can make us think about the importance of consent in real life, where desire can be so fraught and fragile.

The problem of climax: re-writing the money shot

The second problem for erotica to engage in order to participate fully in a sex-positive project of sexual justice is that of climax. This problem can be summarised, to borrow a term from Wendell and Tan's tongue-in-cheek guide to romance fiction, as that of the 'Heroic Wang of Mighty Lovin' (2009, 83–7). In short, women do not climax from heterosexual intercourse in real life as easily and as often, with such earth-shattering pleasure and life-changing consequences, as they do in the pages of erotica and erotic romance. As I've noted, erotica is a genre of fantasy. It does not aspire to social realism. The sex on offer in its pages is fantasy sex, by which I intend dual senses of 'really great' and 'unrealistic'. Women, in particular, experience incredible sex in erotica. In heterosexual romance erotica, for example, romance heroines enjoy guaranteed orgasms, often through penis-in-vagina intercourse, with heroes who are masterfully sensitive and skilled lovers in complete control over their own sexual response. These male characters delight in pleasuring their women and are willing to postpone or even forgo their own climax for hers.

Now, how, you might ask, is this a problem? Earth-shattering orgasms sound pretty good. Why shouldn't the women characters of erotic storytelling enjoy such at the drop of a hat? Why shouldn't their desire and climax come easy (so to speak)? Why, for their part, shouldn't the men get to delight in their Mighty Wangs with nary a worry about premature ejaculation or erectile dysfunction? There is clearly an appeal to the compensatory or escapist play of an imagined romp wherein sex is easy and good. Unlike the sad truth set out in the iconic line in the movie *Tootsie* (1982, dir. Sidney Pollack) whereby actress Teri Garr accepts ownership of her sexual knowledge – 'I'm responsible for my own orgasms!' – in erotica women need not bear this responsibility. The genre sees to it for them, thank you very much, through a partner who knows the ropes and through the fantastically responsive sexual physiology with which nature (or the author) endows the heroine.

The problem lies in the extent to which this fantasy belies reality. The fantasy covers up a cultural fear and a lack of knowledge about women's sexuality. Female sexual pleasure is one of the most challenging yet potentially transformative aspects of erotica for the culture. This challenge becomes more acute, and the controversy around erotica intensifies, when women become the producers and consumers of this erotica. Groundbreaking publishers such as Black Lace (UK-based, founded in 1993 as the first publisher of erotic fiction by women, for women, with top authors such as international bestseller Portia Da Costa) and Ellora's Cave (US-based, launched in 2000 as the first ever erotic romance imprint) market themselves as offering female-authored stories to female readers. In these stories, women *like* sex. The story world is feminist and sex-positive in that women's desire is taken as a good – not a shameful – thing, and women's sexual pleasure is depicted on page and guaranteed. This element of delight in women's climax is missing in conventional male-oriented visual pornography, with its hackneyed focus on the money shot of male orgasm and ejaculation. Stories that revel in women's sexual pleasure provoke anxiety in a culture more comfortable with narratives of male arousal and satisfaction than with their female counterparts. Although the recent sexualisation of Western culture means that women can and do write and read erotica more commonly and openly than before, dynamics of shaming and closeting remain common as well (Smith, 2007; Phillips, 2015). Even today, many women writers of erotica use pseudonyms and hide their identities from family or employers for fear of exactly such reactions.

Addressing this pernicious cultural blind spot head-on is a new term gaining currency: *cliteracy*, as in literacy about the clitoris or knowledge about female sexuality. As explained by American conceptual artist Sophia Wallace in her art exhibition by this name, cliteracy 'explores a paradox: the global obsession with sexualizing female bodies in a world that is maddeningly illiterate when it comes to female sexuality' (Wallace, 2012; see also Stiritz, 2008). Erotica shares in the project of cliteracy (see, e.g., the online UK erotica and sex education magazine *Cliterati*, launched in 2001), but the genre as a whole, it must be said, could be more cliterate. According to various science-based sex studies, only about 25 per cent of women reliably reach orgasm from vaginal penetration alone; more than 90 per cent of women who masturbate do so with little or no vaginal penetration, concentrating on clitoral stimulation instead (Lloyd, 2006; Nagoski, 2015). And yet penetrative intercourse remains the norm – the definitive and climactic sex act – in much heterosexual erotica (and even, with phallic substitutes, in lesbian erotica). Indeed, it functions as more or less the standard cultural definition of sex: PIVMO, a friend of mine called it, for 'penis-in-vagina-male-orgasm' sex. Sex-positive erotica can queer – it can question and transform – this penetrative norm as the be-all-and-end-all of sex by offering alternatives and by being more cliterate. It can explore more diverse depictions of what gives most women more pleasure: clitoral stimulation, with or without penetration; the solo joys of masturbation; and a wide range of body pleasures, in a safe and supportive context.

Moving outside the world of fantasy

The challenge, then, for erotica with regard to these problems of consent and climax is that it must wrestle with its own fantasy world. How to inhabit the pleasurable realm of the imaginary wherein sex is easy because consent and climax are guaranteed, but also, at the same time, to do the political work of sexual justice to ensure real consent and climax outside the world of fantasy? How to be hot and politically correct at the same time? If the sex-positive potential of erotica lies in thinking through the complexities of sex and imagining our way into a better sexual future, then erotica, ironically, could be more sex-positive. Not in the sense of getting more sex on the page but in terms of bolder and more interesting sex. Sex that is hot and consensual or, if not fully consensual, that shows the cost when consent is lacking. Sex that celebrates healthy diversity. Sex that makes it clear that not everyone has to be sexually active – that sex is a choice. Sex that eschews shame and guilt. Sex that revels in pleasure for everyone. Sex that honours sexuality as a pathway for self-discovery, creativity and connection. My definition of good erotica is that which explores and supports a sex-positive, feminist, queer-friendly vision of sexuality – in a spice palette ranging from the coyly discreet to the full-on throbbing explicit.

Write on!

Bibliography

Attwood, F. (ed) (2009) *Mainstreaming Sex: The Sexualization of Western Culture*. London: I.B. Tauris.
Bersani, L. (1987) 'Is the rectum a grave?' *October*. Volume 43: 197–222.
Campbell, A. (2007) *Claiming the Courtesan*. New York: Avon.
Hall, A. (2013) *Glitterland*. Hillsborough, NJ: Riptide Publishing.
Hesiod ([1914] 2008) 'Theogony', in *Hesiod, the Homeric Hymns, and Homerica*. Trans. H.G. Evelyn-White. Project Gutenberg ebook #348. www.gutenberg.org/files/348/348-h/348-h.htm (accessed 17 June 2015).
Illouz, E. (2014) *Hard-Core Romance: Fifty Shades of Grey, Best-Sellers, and Society*. Chicago: University of Chicago Press.
James, E.L. (2012) *Fifty Shades of Grey*. New York: Vintage Books.
Lawrence, D.H. ([1928] 1983) *Lady Chatterley's Lover*. New York: Penguin Books.
Lloyd, E.A. (2006) *The Case of the Female Orgasm: Bias in the Science of Evolution*. Cambridge: Harvard University Press.
McNair, B. (2013) *Porno? Chic! How Pornography Changed the World and Made It a Better Place*. New York: Routledge.
Nagoski, E. (2015) *Come as You Are: The Surprising New Science that Will Transform Your Sex Life*. New York: Simon & Schuster.
Nikunen, K., Paasonen, S. and Saarenmaa, L. (eds) (2007) *Pornification: Sex and Sexuality in Media Culture*. London: Bloomsbury.
Perrin, K. (2007) *Getting Some*. Don Mills, ON: Spice Books.
Phillips, K. (2015) *Women and Erotic Fiction: Critical Essays on Genres, Markets and Readers*. Jefferson, NC: McFarland.
Preston, J. (ed) (1992) *Flesh and the Word: An Anthology of Erotic Writing*. New York: Penguin.
Regis, P. (2003) *A Natural History of the Romance Novel*. Philadelphia: University of Pennsylvania Press.
Roach, C. (2016) *Happily Ever After: The Romance Story in Popular Culture*. Bloomington: Indiana University Press.
Schaefer, E. (ed) (2014) *Sex Scene: Media and the Sexual Revolution*. Durham, NC: Duke University Press.
Simon, W. and Gagnon, J.H. (2003) 'Sexual scripts: origins, influences and changes'. *Qualitative Sociology*. Volume 26 (4): 491–7.
Smith, C. (2007) *One for the Girls! The Pleasures and Practices of Reading Women's Porn*. Bristol: Intellect Books.
Snitow, A. (1979) 'Mass market romance: pornography for women is different'. *Radical History Review*. Volume 20: 141–61.
Steinem, G. (1977; 2nd edn 1995) 'Erotica vs. pornography' in *Outrageous Acts and Everyday Rebellions*. New York: Henry Holt.
Stiritz, S.E. (2008) 'Cultural cliteracy: exposing the contexts of women's not coming'. *Berkeley Journal of Gender, Law & Justice*. Volume 23: 242–66.
Taormino, T., Penley, C., Parrenas Shimizu, C. and Miller-Young, M. (eds) (2013) *The Feminist Porn Book: The Politics of Producing Pleasure*. New York: The Feminist Press at the City University of New York.

Toscano, A.R. (2012) 'A parody of love: the narrative uses of rape in popular romance'. *Journal of Popular Romance Studies*. Volume 2 (2). http://jprstudies.org/2012/04/a-parody-of-love-the-narrative-uses-of-rape-in-popular-romance-by-angela-toscano/ (accessed 17 June 2015).

Wallace, S. (2012) *Cliteracy: 100 Natural Laws*. www.sophiawallace.com/cliteracy-100-natural-laws (accessed 18 June 2015).

Wendell, S. and Tan, C. (2009) *Beyond Heaving Bosoms: The Smart Bitches' Guide to Romance Novels*. New York: Fireside.

Winsor, K. (1944) *Forever Amber*. New York: Macmillan.

Media

Tootsie (1982) Directed by S. Pollack. [Film] USA: Columbia Pictures.

11
A HISTORY OF SLASH SEXUALITIES

Debating queer sex, gay politics and media fan cultures

Kristina Busse and Alexis Lothian

Introduction

The popularity of *Fifty Shades of Grey*'s reconfigured *Twilight* fan fiction has made heterosexual fan fiction a widely recognised cultural phenomenon. In contrast, slash stories about sexual and romantic relationships between same-sex fictional characters (or, frequently, real-world celebrities) have yet to achieve such commercial success. Both within academic fan studies and in popular culture, male/male slash's existence – from the Marvel Cinematic Universe to One Direction to the success of self-published erotic fiction ebooks – is widely acknowledged and discussed. One point that stands out in many discussions is that male/male fan fiction communities tend to be largely female, and thus distinct in history and membership from writers and readers of original gay male erotic fiction. (Slash about women characters, often called femslash, receives less attention, for reasons Julie Levin Russo (2010) examines in her work on femslash-specific communities and histories.) Though the majority of male/male slash writers have tended to be women who identify themselves as heterosexual, intra-community discussions suggest that there always have been many queer-identified writers, and that this number is increasing. In the absence of quantitative research, the gender and sexuality of slashers remain uncertain and open to debate. Is slash gay? Is it straight? Is it feminist? Is it political? Is it offensive? Is it romance? Is it porn? This chapter explores how male/male slash fan writers have transformed commercial characters and narratives into stories of gay romance, queer desire and even sexual activism.

While not all slash fan fiction is erotically explicit, news articles often focus on graphic homoerotic fan writings, and many academic essays follow suit. Thus fan fiction often gets reduced to its erotic aspects, whether for celebration or critique. Yet in 1985, in the first essay discussing slash, Joanna Russ argued that sexual fantasy is never just about the content of a fantasy, but is also about the structural position and social context of its writers and consumers. The erotics of slash have, over the past 30 years, served communities of readers and writers more diverse in their interests, concerns and identities than existing scholarship might lead us to believe.

Building on previous work on queer fan cultures, fans' community-building and transformative critique by the authors, this chapter historicises and explores the changing significance of sex and sexuality within slash communities in terms of politicised identities, self-presentation and the relationships between pleasure, subcultural community and media. With both fan culture and gay representations entering the mainstream in the past decade, the politics of sexual identity has become a central thematic concern within fan communities. The subcultural world of slash fan fiction writers can often seem highly removed from queer communities and practices, yet the shared romantic and erotic narrative pleasures of slash fan fiction are not necessarily distinct from issues of rights and representation. For some fan writers, political and social issues become as important to the production of erotic and romantic fan fiction as the engagement with source texts themselves. Accordingly, a range of critical analyses of the relationships among sex, capital, pleasure, gender, race and other axes of difference can be found in fan fiction as well as in queer scholarship and political movements. We work with slash stories to trace their engagement with multiple connected discourses: the content of the fan texts themselves; the context surrounding these texts in fan meta conversations; academic discussions; and the relationship between the texts and the readers and writers' own sexualities.

Beginning with a general overview of the historical roots of slash fan fiction and its theoretical interest to feminist and gender studies scholars, we posit three *waves* in the relationship between slash and queer culture:

1   Initial woman-centric slash that consciously used male protagonists and male bodies to envision ideal relationships and fantasise about sexual experimentation, often within deeply committed romantic relationships.
2   A politically self-aware movement towards realism that confronted these fantasy men not only with the realities of male bodies and sexualities but also with the cultural realities of gay lives.
3   Slash fiction that is deeply embedded within a self-defined queer space, neither fantastically creating nor idealising yet othering gay men, but rather writing multiple genders and sexualities as both reflections and fantasies of the complexly diverse community of readers and writers.

These stages are broadly chronological, yet it is important to note that they are also synchronic: as Elizabeth Freeman (2010)'s writing on temporal drag has shown, cultural formations that seem to have become old-fashioned and outmoded do not disappear as soon as academics have declared them to be so.

The first wave: like men, only better?

The term *fan fiction* describes works that employ settings and characters from established texts. While the term could be applied to all writing that takes on a transformative relationship to existing texts – from collective ancient storytelling to postmodern literature – fan fiction as a response to contemporary popular media became popular in the 1970s with *Star Trek* (CBS, 1966–9). Fans of television shows and other media created their own versions of the source texts, sharing them privately or via fanzines and APAs (Amateur Press Associations). Some stories retell the originating texts, while others comment critically on the sources; some stories focus on a particular moment that may not have been shown or shown sufficiently in the source text, while others create wide and sprawling new plots and universes for their protagonists. While there are many reasons for writing fan fiction, two primary motivations are clear: either to have more of the same story or to fulfil a desire for a different story, a different narrative or plot twist. From the outset, romantic relationships have been created alongside action and adventure stories, and most fan writers have been women (Verba, 1996). In the early 1970s, a subsection of women fan writers moved away from established canon pairings and imagined heteronormative romances and instead began to imagine romantic relationships between two male protagonists.

The term *slash* derives from the fanzine convention of declaring a story's central romantic pairing through initials, separated by a virgule. In 1974, the first homoerotic slash story was published by a *Star Trek* fan writer: Diana Marchant's 'A Fragment Out of Time'. The story doesn't contain any identifying names, yet clearly suggests that the Starship Enterprise's Captain James T. Kirk and its First Officer Commander Spock are in a sexual relationship.

For both fans and academics writing about slash in the 1980s and early 1990s, the central question was *why*: why would women, who seemed mostly to be straight and often married (though Russ identified as a lesbian and a slash fan and was certainly not the only writer to do so), choose to read and write homoerotic romances with often explicit sex scenes? Explanations mostly focus on the following points:

1 Many women enjoy the description and image of attractive men together in ways similar to heterosexual men enjoying images of women having sex.
2 Imagined homosexual relationships allow for equality between partners, especially when these partners are men and thus not subject to gender oppression as women are.
3 Gay erotica allows the woman reader to both have and be the male character, allowing for various fantasised subject positionings.

Theorists also acknowledge the value of an inclusive, primarily female community in which women whose lives were often very distant from queer cultural life could share erotic desires and fantasies with less fear of sexist repercussions.

This initial fannish and theoretical engagement with male same-sex eroticism was characterised by a seeming disengagement from gay politics and publics. Neither the slow legalisation of homosexual acts nor the increase in gay and lesbian visibility nor the outbreak of AIDS and its devastating effects are regularly reflected in slash fiction of the 1970s–90s. Instead, the emphasis in many slash stories remains on the individual or personal: on the sexual identity crises of the characters and the emotional turmoil the pairing may cause for the couple and their friends. For the world of *Star Trek*, set hundreds of years in the future, such a non-political take may make sense, but in slash written for non-science-fiction TV series set in the contemporary world, such as the US cop show *Starsky & Hutch* (ABC, 1975–9) or the British spy show *The Professionals* (ITV, 1978–83), gay identities and politics continue to be conspicuous by their absence.

Rather than reproaching these early slash stories for their lack of political awareness and LGBT consciousness, let's consider the meanings they held for the communities who wrote and read them. The purpose of these stories seems to have been not verisimilitude but rather an emotional self-engagement for readers and writers. In other words, a married, middle-aged, straight woman writing the *Professionals* pairing Bodie/Doyle was often writing more about her own desires and anxieties than about the realities of gay or bisexual men in the British military and secret service in the 1970s. In 2004, prolific and popular fan writer Speranza wrote about her longtime participation in the slash fan community that 'we're NOT writing about 'gay men' in any realistic/ mimetic way, just as I don't believe we're writing about real cops or sex in a realistic or mimetic way' (2004a). Invoking gay identity as a historical and politically contingent term, she emphasises the primarily female readership of slash and their particular needs and desires: 'the "best" stories are not the ones which gay men would find most recognizable, but the ones that give the female slash audience the most recognition and pleasure' (Speranza, 2004a). This emphasis on female spaces and desires is indicative of the first wave of slash fiction, reflecting a feminism relatively unconcerned with gay experiences. In what some might identify as an essentialist feminist erotics, the stories of this wave consciously take over – one might even say colonise – male bodies for the sake of female pleasures.

Not every story from the 1970s–90s period avoids gay culture or queer community themes. In general, though, stories focus more often on the interpersonal, romance and identity questions, and, in police, spy or military settings, on chain-of-command and fraternisation rules. The relationship that these slash sexualities hold to gay male cultures – one of avoidance if not outright rejection – is well exemplified by the 'undercover in a gay bar' trope, which is pervasive enough to have its own entry in the fan wiki, Fanlore.org. Fairly self-explanatory, this genre of story posits that circumstances require two supposedly straight protagonists to go undercover as a gay couple and pass in a gay environment, most often a club or bar. Within this unfamiliar context, play-acted physical affection and couplehood makes them realise their ability to be physically intimate with their partner, and/or the fact that they already share a most intimate bond, and/or the fact that at least one, if not both, of them already has had sex with men. We might expect that this scenario would be one of celebration of gay community. But in practice what appears is a clear juxtaposition, where the slash couple is defined against rather than with their environment, often returning to an explicitly internal focus and to emotional turmoils regarding the way feelings and physical relations could affect the all-important work environment around which the show's story lines revolve. The undercover trope allows the author to confront the characters with post-Stonewall, pre-AIDS gay club culture – yet the protagonists are marked out clearly as not part of the subculture that they infiltrate.

Alexandra's 1996 *Professionals* story 'Dance While You Can' showcases the awkward relationship between slash and gay culture when agents Bodie and Doyle are sent to a gay club to trap a blackmailer. During their encounters there, they admit to their mutual desire but also love. In a moment that reproduces stereotyping responses to the sexual freedom of 1970s gay male culture, they place their relationship in direct contradiction to the men around them:

> Doyle waved idly at the crowd. 'Look at these blokes. All they're here for is to get off. Don't they ever think about love?'
>
> Bodie smiled. 'No. I meant what I said. This isn't everything. I want you in my bed, Ray. But mostly I want you close, always, no matter what we're doing. Okay?'

In Flamingo's 2007 *Starsky & Hutch* story 'Cheap Sunglasses', both are called gay by a suspect they arrest in Venice Beach. This raises questions in Hutch's mind about the depth of their partnership. Later, the two main characters discuss their partnership and the world around them, leading to their first kiss and declarations of love.

> [Hutch] shook his head wearily. 'What kind of a fucked up world is this, Starsk? Where people have to hide love? Where people kill love?'
>
> . . .
>
> Starsky gave him a sudden shake. 'Not ours, Hutch. 'Cause we're our world. No one else. Just you and me. All we've ever needed.'

Interestingly, in both cases, the couples define themselves against predominant gay culture, both good and bad. They feel as little a part of the gay dance club scene as they do of the homophobia so clearly expressed in the second story. As Starsky describes, they are their own world, a trope common in traditional buddy slash pairings. A closeted, closed relationship – where only the two protagonists know of their love and are happy to not interact with any outsiders – is the explicit romantic ideal of these stories.

The idea of a slashed couple existing in a world of their own is epitomised in the 2001 fan fiction challenge '101 Ways to End Up in a Canadian Shack', in which 30 writers wrote short pieces in 62 fandoms. The title references the B-52's 'Love Shack' and the hunting cabin owned by a character in *Due South*, which featured in many slash stories. The challenge's only requirement was that 'all fandoms ought to end up in a Canadian shack', implicitly celebrating absolute seclusion from any professional, familial or communal environment. The shack/closet image is a particularly resonant metaphor in *Due South* fandom because Fraser lives in his office at the Canadian embassy, yet his closet opens to fantastic Canadian landscapes that his dead father and other friends often inhabit. Canada, here, is not just an idealised fantastic space (Bury, 2004) – it literally exists in Fraser's closet, just as the actual Canadian cabin becomes their virtual closet.

One major pitfall of the decontextualised slash relation favoured by first-wave slash authors is its tendency to promote a return to traditional gender roles. The small quantity of fan fiction written for serial drama suggests that the initial appeal is clearly the action, excitement and professional situation that tends to be central in procedurals, for example. In addition, the appeal of slash for heterosexual women is often explained through its portrayal of equal relationships, an equality often seen as impossible for opposite-sex couples (Lamb and Veith, 1986). Ironically, fan fiction often domesticates these professional protagonists, be they cops, secret agents, military officers or starship fighters. In the shows, popular characters are often family-less and, as a result, their team, their partnership, becomes their family. Fan writers fill in the gaps left by the frequent absence of personal lives in television procedurals. Challenging the existing paradigm of slash's subversive resistance of the source text, Sara Gwenllian Jones (2002) critiques this domesticating aspect of slash, suggesting that the homosocial, nondomestic setting of many shows invited the very slash pairings that fan writers would then domesticate into traditional gender roles. Especially in first-wave slash, all too often, once the relationship gets established, the stories replicate heteronormative scenarios. Often indistinguishable from the binary gender norms that characterise both the culture that the author inhabits and the one the characters do, these stories thus reestablish the very norms slash fiction tried to complicate.

The second wave: slash fandom meets gay politics

Cultural change in the 1990s not only created explicitly gay, lesbian and (more rarely) bisexual characters within the TV shows around which fan communities clustered, but also fostered an environment within slash fandoms that valorised direct engagement with gay topics and an approach driven more by realism and less by fantasy. Nowhere might this be more obvious than in the introduction of sexually transmitted infections, including AIDS, as a threat and reality in protagonists' lives. The scenes of disavowal played out in the 'undercover in a gay bar' stories are replaced by a sense that the characters' choice of love object must by necessity bring them into contact with a community organised around gay men's specific experiences and needs. Concurrently, slash fan fiction began to circulate primarily through online communities (first mailing lists and then web-based journal sites like LiveJournal), separating it from the publishing networks of science fiction fandom and making it more possible that potential readers might find stories because of their interest in same-sex representation rather than their fascination with a particular show as such.

The confrontation between first and second waves of slash sexuality is played out interestingly in the fandom of *The Sentinel* (UPN, 1996–9), which pairs a hypermasculine Special Forces agent-turned-cop with a long-haired, Jewish graduate student in anthropology. In canon, both men are shown as only interested in women. While slash fans tend to retain a more traditionally masculine representation for police officer Jim Ellison, they assign a variety of queer identity markers to grad student Blair: he frequents gay clubs, is a member of gay–straight student alliances and is comfortable with his sexuality. Many stories play off this opposition:

> Patience running low, Blair put down the paper he was reading, 'I *actually* remarked that; "exploring the *whole* gay lifestyle might be beneficial to you" when we first got together, because you were a little upset that what we had was, in fact, a homosexual relationship. . . . I still recall you saying; "But goddamn it Chief, I am *not* a homosexual, I do *not* get off on guys . . . just you."'
>
> (K9, 1999)

Here, Jim plays the role of the earlier slash protagonist, with Blair a relaxed representative of a younger generation comfortable with a nonheterosexual identity – although Blair goes on to reassure Jim that 'We are just Jim and Blair and we love each other, end of story'.

With AIDS looming large, condom use is a frequent point of discussion in late 1990s/early 2000s slash fiction, signalling both the characters' and the authors' sense of commitment to gay men's health. In Basingstoke's 2000 *Sentinel* story 'Strawberry Pop Tarts', Blair refuses unprotected sex with Jim because 'I've never had sex without a condom. Ever. I don't think I can . . . The thought of a naked dick is utterly not appealing, okay?' Such scenes emphasise the role of fiction in a potentially pedagogic relation to reality: if unsafe sex is wrong, then fiction should not portray it. One of the more popular sites of the 1990s – 'Sex Tips for Slash Writers', by gay male slash fan Minotaur – offered information from research and personal experience so slashers could write anatomically and culturally realistic gay sex.

Beyond sex descriptions sometimes verging on public service announcements, second-wave stories also often contain more general awareness of social and political issues, such as Gay Pride marches, AIDS and homophobia. Yet individual romantic relationships continued to be foregrounded even if the external world had entered the protected space. In Speranza's *Due South* story 'Hanged Man' (2004b), police partners Ray Kowalski and Benton Fraser's relationship is threatened when they have to choose between their professional and sexual partnerships:

> 'I want you to answer the phone, Fraser', and fuck, he really, really does. 'I want either of us to be able to pick up the phone at any time and for that to be okay.

Most of all', Ray says, putting his hands on Fraser's shoulders, his voice shaking a little, 'I don't want us ever, ever to have to talk about who's going to answer the phone again'.

Ray never considers himself straight in this story, yet he is deeply closeted and justifies this as both a desire for privacy and a response to external homophobia. This small conversation about who gets to answer the phone, then, indicates a fundamental shift where Ray is willing to stand by his relationship and have it be seen by the world. Moreover, the story ends with the couple's move to Canada, an interesting double move that resonates with the escapist fantastical space of Canada and its self-contained shack, while referencing the very realistic option of Canadian domestic partnership.

The move from first- to second-wave slash narratives was accompanied by extensive discussions within fandom about the nature and purpose of slash, its function as feminist fantasy space, its homophobic colonisation of gay men, the necessity of realism and its relationship to the historical changes of queer rights and representations. So even as first-wave slashers continued to write, more and newer fans increasingly saw slash fiction as part of a critique of heterosexuality in media and as a form of queer representation created by a subversive subcultural community rather than a romantic and erotic hobby of heterosexual women.

Political and social changes fundamentally altered slash fiction's relationship to narratives of sexual identity. With every new country or US state that gained marriage equality, stories appeared that responded to the new laws: Sherlock Holmes and John Watson responding to UK legislation in 2013; Charles Xavier whisking away Erik Lehnsherr to a private ceremony in New York in 2011; Starsky and Hutch finally legalising their commitment to one another in 2015. Likewise, the removal of 'Don't Ask, Don't Tell', the military imperative to keep one's queer sexuality hidden, spawned numerous writing fests, as did the US Supreme Court's overturning of the Defense of Marriage Act. Marriage fits seamlessly into the romance tropes so well loved by slash fans, yet the social and cultural recognition of same-sex marriage also means that romance is no longer set in opposition to participation in gay identity and culture. This does not necessarily mean, however, that slash fans' representations, desires and debates have begun to align smoothly with those of queer communities or movements.

The show that most forcefully required a rethinking of slash fans' terminology – and that highlighted the fault lines between queer and slash fan cultures, despite many fans' understanding of slash as a subversion of heterosexuality – was Showtime's *Queer as Folk* (2000–5). The show unapologetically celebrated queer lives and communities, depicting explicit onscreen gay and lesbian sex. With a wider array of queer characters, the show could present different points of view and directly address its cultural context. Debates over marriage in queer communities, for example, are reflected in the contrast between the two main characters. While Michael Novotny gets married, adopts a teenager and moves to the suburbs, his best friend Brian Kinney rejects heteronormative values of monogamy and domesticity:

> Look, I don't believe in love. I believe in fucking. It's honest, it's efficient. You get in and out with a maximum of pleasure, and a minimum of bullshit. Love is something that straight people tell themselves they're in, so they can get laid.

(1.2)

Like Michael Warner's 1999 popularisation of radical queer values, *The Trouble with Normal*, Brian passionately opposes same-sex marriage and advocates for an ethics modelled on queer life and sexuality – one that resists shame, values diversity and is based on pleasure, respect and honesty.

With an entire cast of gay men and women, one would expect a wide range of queer fan fiction, yet the traditional romance plot dominates much of *Queer as Folk* slash. Kyra Hunting (2012) describes how 'the dominant trend in fan fiction has been to favor the "happily ever after" over the messy, sometimes unsatisfying queer politics of the *Queer as Folk* canon'. The fandom all but fetishises the very values that Brian so adamantly repudiates, celebrating true love via if not marriage then at least monogamy and its assumed capacity for barrier-free sex. While it is certainly problematic to envision same-sex narratives with primarily heteronormative values, it is even more so when fans aggressively reinscribe such conservative values onto a text whose characters are 'already queer – and potentially queerer than many of their rearticulations in fans' creative products' (Hunting 2012).

The third wave: queerer, kinkier worlds exploring desire, identity and power

However strong the pull of heteronormative romance may remain, slash fan fiction offers a variety of queer pleasures to its readers and writers. There exist no hard numbers about the amount of fan fiction devotees that self-identify across the queer spectrum, but fannish surveys repeatedly suggest that slash fandom veers much queerer than any representative cross-section of internet users. Many younger fans describe writing and reading slash fan fiction as enabling them to explore and come to terms with their own queer identifications. Slash fandom has been experienced as an empowering space of 'women stepping forward to describe their own erotics, because our culture silences female desire as effectively as it silences queer desire' (T., quoted in Lothian et al., 2007: 106), where 'sexual activities and proclivities on the fringes of ordinary acceptability are considered quite normal' (Cat, quoted in Lothian et al.: ibid.). The erotic imaginaries that fans create are not always politically radical or diverse, yet the desires that women (and, increasingly, nonbinary-identified individuals and both transgender and cisgender men) speak through slash fiction also incorporate a spectrum of gender identities, sexual desires and other interests beyond romantic love and gay sex – and these have slowly begun to be recognised within academic work on fandom too.

The designation of 'third-wave slash' signals not only an organic shift in the relationship between fandom and queer culture but also an active engagement with concerns that, while present throughout feminist history, are often associated with third-wave feminisms, including growing commitment to intersectionality and racial justice alongside matters of gender and sexuality (TWC Editor, 2009; Wanzo, 2015). In terms of sexual desires, identities and politics, our third wave is defined by writers' willingness to reimagine sexual and social structures as they explore boundaries in fiction and reality. The elaborate fannish framework surrounding the term 'kink' is one framework within which fans have engaged sexual experiences, fantasies and even politics. The Fanlore entry for 'kink' notes that the term 'usually refers to various non-normative sexual practices or desires, such as voyeurism, fetishism, and the many activities included under the BDSM umbrella' ('Kink', n.d.). Fans may also 'refer to other, non-sexual preferences as 'kinks', meaning particular imagery, story-tropes, or elements that they enjoy so much they are worth considerable effort to find and collect' ('Kink', n.d.). Within this frame, mpreg and domestic romance become 'kinks' whose preference ranks on the same order as a love for fiction featuring rope bondage, sexual slavery or watersports. Desires often deemed illegitimate, for whatever reason, can feel normal and accepted, even celebrated, within the fan community. At the same time, the focus on erotics of power exchange within the BDSM definition of kink opens up spaces in which stories can engage in complex negotiations regarding the politics of gender and desire.

The organisers of one fannish project – the long-running challenge of Kink Bingo, which encourages fans to write stories featuring uncommon sexual practices – explicitly describe their embrace of kink as a 'political project': 'Kink bingo attempts to redefine kink, to question the naturalness of our responses to certain kinks, to reclaim desires and pleasures that are marginalized, ignored, and maligned in the popular press' (eruthros, 2009). For the Kink Bingo creators, fannish kink is a worldmaking project: welcoming and celebrating fannish fantasy, desire and pleasure, refusing the norms that structure sex and gender representation and thus becoming an explicitly, politically queer project (Berlant and Warner, 1998).

Some of the most intense explorations of non-normative sexual practices in fan fiction take place within stories that construct alternate universes where traditional sexual binaries are replaced with or supplemented by power dynamics that are or appear to be biologically determined. As with the *Queer as Folk* slash, there is no shortage of problematic stories repeating gender stereotypes without any critique or even awareness of their own reductive tendencies. And yet, we conclude our overview of queer ideas within slash fandom with the way in which this trope is often used not to celebrate biological essentialism, but as a conceit through which to interrogate current norms and assumptions of sex and gender.

Helenish's 2006 *Stargate: Atlantis* (SciFi, 2004–9) story 'Take Clothes off as Directed' takes place in a world where BDSM roles of 'top' and 'sub' are understood to be hardwired into characters' biology. Other fans had used this premise previously, but Helenish's story questions the social components of such a clearly bifurcated universe and riffs off racist and sexist discrimination:

> Until 1941, subs hadn't been allowed in the military at all; temperamentally unsuited, everyone said, for fighting. Much better to keep them safe at home. Subs were excellent aides and secretaries, junior engineers, kindergarten teachers, nurses, assembly-line workers, mechanics, accountants – careful, rule-following, meticulous, obedient.

The story uses the idea of sub identity to create an analogical narrative that describes the role of women in patriarchal society. Helenish's story takes first-wave slash's mapping of gender inequality onto male/male relationships and imagines the ways in which it would operate on a societal level through the same mechanisms as real-world sexism. Characters may chafe against societal prejudices and may even challenge their expected roles in the bedroom, but ultimately the story perpetuates the fantasy of a sexual relationship that can somehow create equality in an unequal world.

The difficulties such a universe creates are further explored in Sassbandit's 2011 My Chemical Romance story 'Forget About the Dirty Looks' and Montrose's 2013 Blackhawk story 'Switch'. The stories star celebrities, shaping their public personas into fictional narratives (Busse, 2006a, 2006b; Hagen, 2015): My Chemical Romance were an all-male group with a sizeable slash community; the Chicago Blackhawks are a National Hockey League team (hockey is one of the bigger sports slash fandoms). In different ways, both stories explore questions of power, desire, gender and inequality in both sexual and social situations – drawing from real-world experiences of bisexual marginalisation, transphobia and the social dimensions of Dom/sub identification within BDSM communities.

Montrose's story 'Switch' (2013) announces its central theme in the summary: 'You're supposed to know if you're a top or a sub by the time you're twelve. Fourteen at the outside. It's biological, the researchers say. It's not a choice. But sometimes Jon thinks that for him, it really was.' Montrose creates a binary world in which top/sub clearly aligns with male/female – in the way that subs are excluded from public life, sexualised and seen as lesser all round – though the experiences of openly gay sports players are clearly also part of the analogy. Using hockey players Jonathan Toews and Patrick Kane of the Chicago Blackhawks, she shows the difficulties experienced by a sub player on a professional sports team. Point-of-view character Jon is a top, but when he becomes attracted to his team-mate Patrick, his desires run outside of what he is supposed to want:

> He's not thinking about Patrick cuffed demurely to his headboard, eager to do whatever he's told. Oh, no. He's thinking about Patrick talking back. Refusing to go down on his knees. Grabbing the cuffs from Jon and joking about which one of them is going to wear them. Making Jon work for it. Making Jon beg.

The romance plot triumphs, but the story takes its time in examining the negotiations and personal challenges both characters experience in getting there. Both characters must – like so many protagonists of slash fiction – come to see themselves differently from that which their society considers normal. Jon's narration follows the format of a coming-out story, as he slowly recognises his experiences do not align with expectations. His feelings for Patrick make him recognise his desire to be dominated, and he recoils from that as we might imagine (and might have read in many slash fictions) a man thinking himself straight might respond to overwhelming sexual desire for a colleague and team-mate. Patrick's love for Jon is known to everyone on the team but Jon himself, yet the story does not simply bring the lovers together or enable Jon to gratify his desires in secret. Instead, Jon must learn that he is not the only one to experience social expectations as restrictive.

Jon must develop a collective understanding of who he is as a 'switch' – he must also educate Patrick, whose initial response is one of fear and misunderstanding. In a depiction of a common experience described by bisexuals, Patrick assumes that Jon's switch identity means that he cannot be happy with a sub but will require multiple partners. By the end of the story, though, Jon and Patrick have discovered that they can effectively be both top and sub within their partnership. The story climaxes when Jon gives Patrick a collar, symbolic of permanent submission to one's top and analogous with marriage in the logic of the alternate universe, but immediately proclaims that he wants to wear it too – celebrating a reciprocal and fluid exchange of power that offers a queer version of romantic utopia.

If 'Switch' offers an individual romance of choice within a queer version of a BDSM universe, Sassbandit's 2011 'Forget About the Dirty Looks' focuses on power dynamics and decisions at a social and cultural level. Depicting the queer-positive band My Chemical Romance, the story challenges conventions of the story's D/s society by portraying the band as advocating for greater respect for sub fans and by depicting band members' top/sub provocations. A fictional newspaper article, for example, reads:

> **Daily Mail:** Emo danger: Kids at risk as bands blur line between tops and subs.
>
> Parents are frightened for their kids' safety, and they're blaming the dangerous messages sent by 'emo' bands such as My Chemical Romance, who are currently touring the UK.
>
> The band's lead singer Gerard Way, 29/top, regularly appears on stage with long hair, heavy makeup, and torn clothing. He tells fans, who cross-dress in outfits that mix top and sub, to defy their roles and 'be whoever they want'.

On tour, we see various acts of oppression towards the subs, as tops in other bands throw their socially supported power around. These function as analogies, since we can imagine women in rock bands having similar experiences with objectification and delegitimisation from a music press that treats them as 'eye candy', or queer figures being perceived as a 'danger' to the gender norms of teenage fans. The story also explores the power dynamics of BDSM itself, with the band's sub characters engaging in a variety of consensual relationships that demonstrate how tops can use their power responsibly as well as abusing it.

The romance plot explores non-normative identity when frontman Gerard Way, who publicly challenges top/sub identity expectations, falls for band manager Brian Schechter, who was wrongly identified in childhood as a sub and is now passing as a top. In a story analogous to the outing of a transgender celebrity, the media get hold of the story. Brian's explanation identifies top/sub identity as operating through the same mode as gender production in childhood, though 'tests' rather than simple visual presumptions separate people into the two categories:

> Look, they did all the tests, they said I was sub, and I was four fucking years old. What was I going to say to them? So I went to school and I did all that shit, you know, but I hated it. So I told them I'm not a sub, I'm a top, and they put me in remedial classes.
>
> (Sassbandit, 2011)

Gerard must now see if he can live up to the playful challenging of roles he offers onstage. He also learns that his performative declarations to fans that they can 'be whoever they want' will require some complex negotiations when confronted with the lived complexities of non-normative identity. When he finally has sex with Brian, he knows Brian won't sub and so he instead switches, letting go of the expectations associated with his official identity for the sake both of romantic love and of practising what he preaches. Afterwards, he says: 'I want – I want to try everything. Can you fucking believe it? I've been saying for so long that roles don't matter, and now I get to really, you know. Do it. For real.' Public politics and private sexual desires come together at the climax of this critical, intertextual story.

Conclusion

We have sketched three broad waves: from women-oriented romance fantasies written onto male bodies, to self-conscious engagement with gay representation in mainstream television, to multilayered and complex metaphorical discourses engaging queer formations of sex, gender and power. Yet even in our discussion, it is clear that these distinctions are only the beginning point for more elaborate discussions. The question remains as to whether politically and socially problematic issues can or should ever be used as sexual fantasies, and how to acknowledge their inherent problems. Simplistically, one view reads the tropes (whether of ideal male love, of the transcendence of gay identity or of elaborate alternate universes) as fantastical and defends, if not celebrates, the explicit articulation of (female) desires, while another reads them as mimetic and criticises the potential for reductiveness and essentialism.

We have traced a progression from the more conservative to the more radical, but stories whose narratives fit into all three waves are being written every day; the complex narratives we discuss in the last section are more exception than rule, and much of fan fiction reinforces rather than challenges stereotypes. Nevertheless, the culture surrounding fan fiction does not expect and accept gender or sexual stereotypes; depictions of biologically determinist fantasies are popular, yet also constantly questioned and debated; and even the cathexis of gay male bodies to fulfil women's wish fantasies and desires is frequently debated within the community. While slash fandom may not provide an idealisable queer space, it certainly continues to queer media worlds and everyday experiences.

References

'101 Ways to End Up in a Canadian Shack' (2001) www.trickster.org/speranza/ShackedUp.html (accessed 15 September 2016).
Alexandra (1996) 'Dance While You Can'. *The Circuit Archive*. www.thecircuitarchive.com/tca/archive/0/dancewhile.html (accessed 15 September 2016).
Basingstoke (2000) 'Strawberry Pop Tarts'. *Archive of Our Own*. http://archiveofourown.org/works/792271 (accessed 15 September 2016).
Berlant, L. and Warner, M. (1998) 'Sex in Public'. *Critical Inquiry*. Volume 24: 547–66.
Bury, R. (2004) 'Of Mounties and Gay Marriage: Canadian Television, American Fans, and the Virtual Heterotopia'. *Refractory*. Volume 6. http://refractory.unimelb.edu.au/2004/06/17/of-mounties-and-gay-marriage-canadian-television-american-fans-and-the-virtual-heterotopia-rhiannon-bury (accessed 15 September 2016).
Busse, K. (2006a) '"I'm jealous of the fake me": Postmodern Subjectivity and Identity Construction in Boy Band Fan Fiction'. In S. Holmes and S. Redmond (eds) *Framing Celebrity: New Directions in Celebrity Culture*. London: Routledge.
Busse, K. (2006b) 'My Life Is a WIP on My LJ: Slashing the Slasher and the Reality of Celebrity and Internet Performances'. In K. Hellekson and K. Busse (eds) *Fan Fiction and Fan Communities in the Age of the Internet*. Jefferson, NC: McFarland.
Eruthros (2009) 'Please Don't Take the Fanfiction Survey'. *Dreamwidth*. 31 August. http://eruthros.dreamwidth.org/273840.html (accessed 15 September 2016).
Flamingo (2007) 'Cheap Sunglasses'. *Starsky and Hutch Archive*. www.starskyhutcharchive.net/viewstory.php?sid=127 (accessed 15 September 2016).
Freeman, E. (2010) *Time Binds: Queer Histories, Queer Temporalities*. Durham: Duke University Press.
Hagen, R. (2015) 'The Collapse of the Fourth Wall in Online Fan Fiction'. *Popular Music and Society*. Volume 38 (1): 44–58.
Helenish (2006) 'Take Clothes Off as Directed'. *Talk on Corners*. http://helenish.talkoncorners.net/asdirected.html (accessed 15 September 2016).
Hunting, K. (2012) '*Queer as Folk* and the Trouble with Slash'. *Transformative Works and Cultures*. No. 11. dx.doi.org/10.3983/twc.2012.0415 (accessed 15 September 2016).
Jones, S.G. (2002) 'The Sex Lives of Cult Television Characters'. *Screen*. Volume 43 (1): 79–90.
K9 (1999) 'I Read It in a Magazine'. *Archive of Our Own*. http://archiveofourown.org/works/792888 (accessed 15 September 2016).

'Kink' (n.d.) *Fanlore*. http://fanlore.org/wiki/Kink (accessed 15 September 2016).

Lamb, P.F. and Veith, D. (1986) 'Romantic Myth, Transcendence, and *Star Trek* Zines'. In D. Palumbo (ed) *Erotic Universe: Sexuality and Fantastic Literature*. Westport, CT: Greenwood Press.

Lothian, A., Busse, K. and Reid, R.A. (2007) 'Yearning Void and Infinite Potential: Online Slash Fandom as Queer Female Space'. *ELN*. Volume 45 (2): 103–11.

Marchant, D. (1974) 'A Fragment Out of Time'. *Grup*. Volume 3: 47–8.

Minotaur (n.d.) 'Sex Tips for Slash Writers'. www.squidge.org/~minotaur/classic/intro.html (accessed 15 September 2016).

Montrose (2013) 'Switch'. *Archive of Our Own*. http://archiveofourown.org/works/893909 (accessed 29 March 2015).

Russ, J. (1985) 'Pornography by Women, for Women, with Love'. In *Magic Mommas, Trembling Sisters, Puritans and Perverts: Feminist Essays*. Trumansburg, NY: The Crossing Press.

Russo, J.L. (2010) 'Indiscrete Media: Television/Digital Convergence and Economies of Online Lesbian Fan Communities'. Unpublished PhD thesis. Rhode Island: Brown University.

Sassbandit (2011) 'Forget About the Dirty Looks'. *Archive of Our Own*. http://archiveofourown.org/works/251449 (accessed 15 September 2016).

Speranza (2004a) Comment, *LiveJournal*, 3 December. http://executrix.livejournal.com/132158.html (accessed 15 September 2016).

Speranza (2004b) 'Hanged Man'. *Archive of Our Own*. http://archiveofourown.org/works/246883 (accessed 15 September 2016).

TWC Editor (2009) 'Pattern Recognition: A Dialogue on Racism in Fan Communities'. *Transformative Works and Cultures*. No. 3. dx.doi.org/10.3983/twc.2009.0172 (accessed 15 September 2016).

Verba, J.M. (1996) *Boldly Writing: A Trekker Fan and Zine History, 1967–1987* (2nd ed.). Minnesota: FTL Publications.

Wanzo, R. (2015) 'African American Acafandom and Other Strangers: New Genealogies of Fan Studies'. *Transformative Works and Cultures*. No. 20. dx.doi.org/10.3983/twc.2015.0699 (accessed 15 September 2016).

Warner, M. (1999) *The Trouble with Normal: Sex, Politics, and the Ethics of Queer Life*. Cambridge: Harvard University Press.

12
EROTIC MANGA
Boys' Love, *shonen-ai, yaoi* and (MxM) *shotacon*

Anna Madill

North American comics and Japanese manga have influenced each other since at least the end of the Second World War. The centrality of manga in Japanese popular culture, however, can be hard to appreciate given the low status usually afforded comics in the West. Manga have a distinctive history in terms of content, style and marketing strategy, and a symbiotic relationship exists between manga, anime (Japanese animation), gaming, live-action film and off-shoot merchandising, such that narratives and characters successful in one medium are often repackaged and marketed in others. There is also a considerable amount of amateur manga – *dojinshi*[1] – produced by Japanese teenagers, young adults and even professional *mangaka* (artist-authors) that is sold, swapped or made freely available on the internet and at Comiket and other amateur comics markets. A significant proportion of *dojinshi* activity is the production and consumption of *yaoi*.

The following sections will describe and contextualise the female-oriented media portraying romantic and sexual relationships between, usually young, men that is variously known as Boys' Love, *shonen-ai, yaoi* and (male–male) *shotacon*, and often denoted as 'mxm' and 'm/m'. Global, particularly original English language, Boys' Love will also be outlined, as will legal issues with regard to these often controversial works.

Boys' Love

Boys' Love (BL) is an umbrella term for female-oriented media, predominantly commercial manga, anime and games (and, hence, usually of Japanese origin), which focus on erotic relationships between men. BL is the term currently preferred in Japan, while in other parts of the world the work is often marketed and referred to as *yaoi*. In mid-1990s Japan, Schodt (1996) was surprised to see hordes of young women at the Comiket day dedicated to BL, and more recent academic research substantiates its mostly female fan-base. For example, Ui, Fukutomi and Kamise (2008) surveyed a random sample of Japanese college students (*n*=481) and found that significantly more women (33.6 per cent) than men (15 per cent) had experience of BL. And two online questionnaires for BL fans in the West saw female response rates of 89 per cent and 82 per cent, respectively, in an English-language survey (Pagliassotti, 2008b, *n*=478) and an independent survey in

Italian (Castagno and Sabucco, 2006–2007, n=315, cited in Pagliassotti, 2008b). It is also well known that most BL *mangaka* and *dojinshi* creators are female (Mizoguchi, 2003).

Not only are the majority of BL fans female, they tend also to be teenagers or young adults. In the Western BL readership surveys just cited, 55 per cent (Pagliassotti, 2008b) and 54 per cent (Castagno and Sabucco, 2006–2007, cited in Pagliassotti, 2008b) and 62 per cent (Pagliassotti, 2008b) and 66 per cent (Castagno and Sabucco, 2006–2007, cited in Pagliassotti, 2008b), respectively, of respondents clustered in the 18–24 age bracket had started to read BL at 19 years old or less. Similarly, a smaller survey of female Chinese mainland BL fans (Li, 2009, n=32) found that 69 per cent had started to read BL before they were 19 years old, and an interview study with female BL fans in Taiwan (Zhou, 2009, n=17) suggested, again, that most had started to read BL in their early and mid-teens. This echoes what is known about BL readers in Japan.

It is thought that most female BL fans in Japan identify as heterosexual (Pagliassotti, 2008a); however, although 62 per cent of respondents (including men) in Castagno and Sabucco's Italian survey identified as heterosexual, other Western-based research suggests a 'queerer' audience. For example, only 46 per cent of women identified as heterosexual in Pagliassotti's (2008b) English-language survey and my own survey of the Anglophone BL fandom, with an interim of 2,124 completions, at the time of writing gives a figure of 41 per cent.[2] The percentage of heterosexual-identifying women is even lower in the 2013 census of m/m readers and creators on the Archive of Our Own internet site (which includes BL but also a related, but wider, 'slash' fan-base; see below), at 25–36 per cent (depending on definition[3]), with an impressive 10,000+ responses.[4] Hence, there is growing evidence that, at least in the West, there is a majority non-heterosexual-identifying female audience for BL (Wood, 2006). It is also likely that dichotomous gender categories are problematic for some BL fans; currently, 8 per cent of those participating in my Anglophone BL Fandom survey identify as non-binary/trans, while 78 per cent identify as female.

BL may not be incontrovertibly 'queer-friendly'. For example, in 1992, gay activist Satō Masaki catalysed a debate in the feminist magazine *Choisir* in an exchange now known as the 'Yaoi Ronsō', in which *yaoi* creators and readers were accused of disseminating an unhelpfully idealised version of gay men which did not engage with the harsh realities of homophobia (Lunsing, 2006). There is also dissatisfaction with regard to the lack of recognition accorded to the gay male audience and producers of mxm (Brennan, 2013). More generally, in Japan, the ardent female fans of BL, which Mizoguchi (2003) estimates to number 500,000, are known derogatorily as *fujoshi* ('rotten girls'[5]) for their interest in fictionalised homoerotica, although this term is, arguably, being used by some in fandom recuperatively as a positive self-identity.

The West has its own genres of male–male romance for women, including the work of commercial popular-fiction authors from Anne Rice to Anne Harris (Haggerty, 1998). However, female engagement with mxm is to be found most strongly in the amateur, now mostly online, genre of slash which developed from early fan fiction sexualising the relationship between the *Star Trek* characters Kirk and Spock (Penley, 1991; Russ, 1985). The main difference between BL and slash is that homoerotic relationships are canon in BL, while slash is a fan-created activity in which characters from popular culture, who provide an accessible homoerotic subtext in canon, are 'shipped' (placed in a relation*ship* with each other). Otherwise, BL and slash can be difficult to differentiate. BL tends to emphasise the visual text, but BL light novels may have only a few pictures, slash fiction can be illustrated and the visual genre of slash manips – photo manipulations – exists (Brennan, 2013). Moreover, *yaoi*, understood in its original Japanese sense as fan-created, parodic, mxm *dojinshi*, is very similar to slash, possibly differentiated only in terms of utilising original characters from Japanese, as opposed to Western, popular culture.

BL can seem formulaic and be seen as utilising a rather limited variety of settings (e.g. school, workplace, home), narrative trajectories (the threat to boy-getting-boy may vary only slightly) and character types, in particular the almost always central *uke* ('bottom') and *seme* ('top') pairing (see Sihombing, 2011). However, market forces encourage these kinds of set elements given that there is a powerful feedback loop in the industry between audience, publishers and *mangaka*, and the boy-gets-boy theme *is* played out over an impressive range of genre templates, including comedy, melodrama, crime and fantasy. Moreover, BL is under continual development and consistently pushes its own boundaries with, for example, some 'reversible' pairings; with more manly characterisation and body types; and with 'new wave' BL, such as *Men of Tattoos* (2008) by Yuiji Aniya, which attempts to (re)introduce more serious themes such as unglamorised sexual violence, financial exploitation and domestic drudgery.

BL is an umbrella term for the *shonen-ai*, *yaoi*, and (mxm) *shotacon* genres.

Shonen-ai

Shonen-ai – literally 'boy love' – is the name given to a genre of male–male romance developed in Japan by a small number of ground-breaking female *mangaka* during the 1970s. Prior to this, *shojo* – girls' – manga had been created by men. Born circa 1949 and hence known as the 'Year 24 Group',[6] these young women not only revolutionised *shojo* in terms of content but are also famous for developing an intricate and metaphorical visual style which included stylistic variation in panel size, with action and decoration breaking out from their borders. The Year 24 Group introduced manga about intense, eroticised friendships between *bishonen* – beautiful boys – which found an enthusiastic audience with their young, female peers and provided a foundation for the more sexually explicit works that were to come (Kilpatrick, 2012). Interestingly, slash developed independently in the US in the early 1970s, possibly in mutual resonance with the burgeoning of second-wave feminism (Tanaka, 1995).

The first work of *shonen-ai*, which is thought to contain the first male–male kiss in manga, was a short story set in Europe – 'In the Sun Room' (aka 'Snow and Stars and Angels') – by Keiko Takemiya, published in *Girls' Comic Extra* in 1970 (Welker, 2011). Takemiya went on to create the long-running serial *Song of the Wind and Trees* (1976–1984), enough for a 17-volume *tankobon* – omnibus edition – some of which is available in English scanlation[7] only. Set in a French boarding school in the late nineteenth century, the narrative follows the erotically inflected relationship between Serge and the beautiful, but damaged, Gilbert, who is shown to be homosexually promiscuous. In fact, the manga commences with a strikingly erotic, but (just) non-explicit, sequence in which the young-looking Gilbert is in bed with an older boy. After a significantly long delay, *Song of the Wind and Trees* was finally awarded a prestigious Shogakukan Manga Award in 1979 in recognition of the influence Takemiya had had on the genre.

In the early days of women's breakthrough as independent and original *mangaka*, Takemiya shared a Tokyo apartment with Moto Hagio. In 1971 Hagio, who remains one of the most loved *mangaka*, published a serial called *The November Gymnasium* featuring unrequited love between boys in a German boarding school. Hagio developed this theme in a longer serial, *The Heart of Thomas* (1973–1975), the only *shonen-ai* from this early era to be published commercially in English, although not until 2013 (Thorn, 2005). Finally of note,

Ryouko Yamagishi's 1983 Kodansha Manga Award-winning *Emperor of the Land of the Rising Sun* (1980–1984) took *shonen-ai* into the 1980s. Yamagishi's manga told the story of the revered historical figure, Prince Shoutoku, controversially depicting his unrequited love for another man as a major motivating force in the tale.

One significant example bridging the early *shonen-ai* of the 1970s and the development of the commercial, globally marketed *yaoi* of the late 1990s/early 2000s is *Banana Fish* by Akimi Yoshida (1985–1994, first released in English in 1999). *Banana Fish* is a 19-volume, fully English-licensed series set in the US which follows the development of a close friendship between the heroic but traumatised Ash and the young Japanese visitor Eiji as they resist destruction by a criminal underworld. A second important, slightly later, fully English-licensed *shonen-ai* is the 12-volume *Gravitation* by Maki Murakami (1996–2002, first released in English in 2003), which charts the sexually inflected relationship between pop singer Shuichi and the antagonistic romance fiction writer Yuki. As a later *shonen-ai*, *Gravitation* is unlike the earlier stories in that, rather than being a tragedy that takes place abroad and/or in the past, it is a romantic comedy set in contemporary Japan. However, it does share the genre's tendency for long and involved narratives.

Shonen-ai may be considered a dead genre, or at least one that has been superseded by BL and *yaoi*. However, the term '*shonen-ai*' retains some currency among fans for describing stories focused on intense friendships between young men which have an erotic, but non-actualised, dimension. In fact, reporting fan-assigned categorisation, the website Baka-Updates Manga shows there to be around only 160 manga-tagged '*shonen-ai*' (among other categories, including '*yaoi*') available commercially in the Anglophone market, with a further 1300 published but not licensed in English. These are very small numbers in terms of the mass production of manga in Japan. However, even though *shonen-ai* is a minor genre in terms of output, its historical importance in the development of women's erotic culture has yet to be fully appreciated.

Yaoi

In the 1980s, young women began to be more irreverent with regard to fictionalised, male–male sexuality, creating amateur parodies of existing, non-erotic works, which became known as '*yaoi*'. *Yaoi* is an acronym for the phrase '*yama nashi, ochi nashi, imi nashi*', which can be translated as 'no peak, no point, no meaning'. This originally referred, in a playfully self-derogatory manner, to the way in which *dojinshi* depicting *bishonen* in sexually explicit scenarios tended to be narratively challenged. However, in recognition of the sexually explicit nature of these works, it is sometimes joked that the acronym actually means '*yamete, oshiri ga itai*' – 'stop, my butt hurts!' It is thought that *yaoi* began with the creation of mxm fan parodies of *Captain Tsubasa* (1981), a *shonen* – boys' – manga about a school football team. *Dojinshi yaoi* is a huge phenomenon and has influenced the commercial development of more sexually explicit, upbeat, original mxm manga targeting a female audience.

Through the mid to late 1990s, illegally and commercially translated Japanese manga and illustrated light novels and games found a global market, at first particularly in East and South Asian countries (Chin and Morimoto, 2013), with the female-oriented, male–male erotica tending to be marketed in the West as *yaoi*. Although a niche within a niche, *yaoi* has found a stalwart global audience and the number of commercially available translations is steadily increasing. A relatively large number of scanlations and some fan-subbed anime and language patches for online games are also available on the internet, which, although infringing copyright, may increase demand for the original product. Two of the first *yaoi* series to be translated commercially for the Anglophone market were the 11-volume Yakuza (gangster) comedy-drama-romance *Kizuna* by Kazuma Kodaka (1992, first released in English in 1998) and the seven-volume *Fake* by Sanami Matoh (1994–2000, first released in English in 1999). Set in New York, *Fake* is a relatively complex narrative about the relationship between two cops, Dee and Ryo, the latter of whom is half-Japanese.

Two *mangaka* who have a strong global following for their *yaoi* are Youka Nitta and Ayano Yamane. Nitta is creator of the 14-volume *Embracing Love* (1999–2009, first released in English in 2004), which portrays the development of a true romantic attachment between two male porn stars. This series is under re-re-release but, demonstrating its popularity, a second-hand copy of volume 5 recently sold on Amazon for £80. Yamane is creator of the 8+ volume *Finder Series* (2001–ongoing, first released in English in 2002), about a cat-and-mouse relationship between a young journalist and a senior Yakuza, and the 5+ volume series *Crimson Spell* (2004–ongoing, first released in English in 2007), a fantasy genre story about a young prince accompanied on a quest by a wizard. Baka-Updates Manga shows there to be around 700 manga licensed in English which, among other tags (including 'shonen-ai'), are considered by fans to be '*yaoi*'. This compares to around 7000 such published manga currently not commercially available in English.

Facilitated immensely by the internet (McLelland, 2000), a global transnational BL/*yaoi* fandom has developed (Nagaike and Suganuma, 2013; Wood, 2013) alongside a small amount of home-grown *yaoi*, or Global BL (GloBL). For example, original English-language (OEL) *yaoi* includes the four-volume, multi-authored *Yaoi Hentai* (2005–) by US publisher Yaoi Press. However, OEL manga, in general, appears much less popular in Anglophone countries compared to translations (Tai, 2007). The challenge, maybe, is that Western *yaoi* fans are attracted to the narrative and aesthetic format of the Japanese product, whereas my own initial impression is that OEL *yaoi* can have a rather Western sensibility, emphasising titillation over romance, and tends to follow a Western comics panelling style (see Cohn, 2011).

Webcomics are another route through which talented authors and artists are developing a hybrid product which brings together elements of both Japanese and Western traditions. For example, *Teahouse* by 'Emirain' (two US-based female creators), set in a high-class brothel, includes many *yaoi* tropes, including the *seme/uke* dynamic. However, other '*yaoi*' webcomics, which are interesting in their own right, appear to have less Japanese influence: for example, *Artifice*, written by Alex Woolfson and drawn by Winona Nelson, involves a male/male, human/android pairing (Wheeler, 2012). Of particular note are the US-based Guilt|Pleasure writer–artist duo Kichiku Neko and Jo Chen, who produce self-published, illustrated light-novel series and associated products. Although they describe their work as BL/*yaoi dojinshi*, Guilt|Pleasure appear to be taking the genre to a new and sophisticated level in terms of both narrative and artwork (Chao, 2013). Guilt|Pleasure are causing quite a buzz in fandom, with copies of volume 1 of *In These Words*, which is currently out of print, priced at up to £277 on Amazon.

The length of these popular series belies the fact that much *yaoi* consist of short 'one-shot' (one-story) manga, or series of episodes which, in Japan, appear in large, throw-away magazines. The only example of this kind of *yaoi* that is commercially available in English is the collection brought together in *J-Boy by Biblos* (2006). Otherwise, *yaoi* licensed in English tend to be *tankobon* collections of the episodes of one series, or independent short stories by one *mangaka*, and traditional *yaoi dojinshi* characteristically consist of one-off, short scenarios focused on pornographically rendered interludes. However, although some *yaoi* may appear to be 'pornography', the genre tends to steer closely towards romance (Pagliassotti, 2008a), albeit that this may need to be sometimes qualified as 'explicit romance' (Madill, 2015).

One of the possibly surprising aspects of *yaoi* is its often risqué sexual content, over and above its homoerotic nature. Common risqué themes include rape/non-con (non-consensual sexual activity)/dub-con (dubiously consensual sexual activity), BDSM, incest and underage sex. Zanghellini (2009b) makes a strong case that such themes are the result of the genre's exploration of relationship angst, compounded by the visual stylistics of *kawaii* – cuteness – which is a mainstay of Japanese popular culture, exaggerating seeming vulnerability and youthfulness. Frennea (2011) also suggests that rape may function as an angsty plot device that can bring a couple together and that very youthful-looking protagonists may be designed to evoke maternal and nurturing feelings in the reader. She also draws attention to how, despite its often difficult sexual themes, most *yaoi* is actually humorous. In fact, parody and self-parody are almost inherent features of *yaoi*, and this is well understood and played up within fandom. These kinds of informed positions counter assumptions that controversial sexual themes are included in *yaoi* merely for purposes of titillation.

Frennea (2011) reported the results (updated as of 4 May 2012) of that author's English-language survey, which was posted on a global *yaoi* internet forum and provided 15 non-exclusive options to the question: 'How do you feel about rape and *shota* [very young protagonists] in *yaoi*?' Of 476 respondents, 24 per cent indicated that they liked rape but not *shota*, 11 per cent that rape is how the *seme* expresses love and 26 per cent that they were aroused by rape in *yaoi*, while 15 per cent agreed that rape in *yaoi* 'makes me feel uncomfortable'.

Contextualising this possibly surprisingly high tolerance of non-con, Frennea reports that additional free-form answers 'showed that fans could recognise the difference between the non-normative sex practices of rape and child pornography as crimes in reality and the fantasy, genre-driven rape and child pornography in yaoi' (2011: 497). Moreover, in my own ongoing content analysis of original Japanese *yaoi* available commercially in English ($n=234$), clearly non-consensual sex or rape (but not dub-con) appeared in only 13 per cent of stories, possibly belying the perception that rape is almost ubiquitous in BL/*yaoi*. Even so, the appearance of non-con and rape, as well as dub-con (which *is* a common trope in BL/*yaoi*), in an erotic romance genre largely for and by women raises interesting questions, such as if (and, if so, how) such representations of sexual violence function productively for women on an individual and political level.

(MxM) *shotacon*

Shotacon contains erotic material deliberately portraying young, often pre-pubescent, boys. Male–male *shotacon* targeting a female audience is sometimes, and controversially, considered a BL sub-genre. In this respect, it is important to clarify that *shotacon* can be subdivided into material which is male-oriented or female-oriented and that, as the very small amount of research available in English reports, while the former is more overtly pornographic, the latter differs little in theme from BL/*yaoi* (Saitō, 2007). Baka-Updates Manga suggests there are four manga licensed in English which, among other tags, are fan-categorised as '*shotacon*' (one of which is a heterosexual *shotacon*). This compares to around 1000 published manga categorised as '*shotacon*' (both male–female and male–male) not commercially available in the Anglophone market.

Of the male–male *shotacon* licensed in English, *Almost Crying* (2002, published in English 2006) by Mako Takahashi is the most readily available. This manga is a collection of gently romantic and erotically suggestive stories ranging from a grumpy relationship between a merman and a prince to the discovery of true love between adoptive brothers. However, other manga marketed in English as BL/*yaoi* have strong *shotacon* resonances in which, in terms of both context and visual age, some characters appear pubescent. For example, *mangaka* Haruka Minami is infamous for drawing young-looking *yaoi* protagonists, such as in *Love A La Carte!* (2003). Of particular note is the ongoing, extremely popular *shonen-ai* fantasy series *Loveless* by Yun Kouga (2002–, first published in English in 2006), which revolves around the highly eroticised relationship between the traumatised 12-year-old Ritsuka and the 20-year-old Soubi.

Publicised as the first *shotacon* anime, *Pico No Boku* ('My Pico') was produced by Natural High Studio in three approximately 30-minute episodes (2006, 2007, 2008). The anime shows the pre-pubescent-looking boy Pico in sexual relationships first with the young man Tamotsu, who has mistaken Pico for a girl, then with the younger boy Chico, and finally with Chico and a runaway boy they find called CoCo. A one-off manga by Aoi Madoka, Katsuyoshi Yatabe and Saigado (2007) and a computer game (2010) based on the anime are also available, although not commercially in English, probably due to legal issues. *Shotacon* elements are unwelcome for many in BL/*yaoi* fandom, as Frennea's (2011) survey of BL readers (*n*=476) demonstrates. She reports 27 per cent agreement with the statement that '*shota* in *yaoi* makes me feel uncomfortable' and a 43 per cent endorsement of liking 'teenage boys, but not kids in *yaoi*'. On the other hand, 14.5 per cent endorsed the option 'I am aroused by/love *shota* in *yaoi*', 3 per cent agreed that they 'will not read/watch a story without *shota*' and 5 per cent 'do not have a problem with *shota*/child pornography in real life'.

One of the predominant commentators on *otaku* (approximately translated as 'nerd') culture in Japan, the psychoanalyst Saitō (2007), has suggested sympathetically, in relation to male *otaku*, that the desire that is realised through *shotacon* (and *lolicon*[8]) is distinct from the desire experienced towards real people in real life. The implication is that he believes the vast majority of *otaku* readers of *shotacon* are not reading it out of paedophilic desire or, at least, paedophilic desire that would seek satiation outside the consumption of fictional texts. With regard to the predominantly female fandom of BL/*yaoi*, statistics would support this view, in that female sexual offences against children are negligible in number, tend to occur in chaotic circumstances and tend to be perpetrated by girls and women who are themselves often vulnerable and exploited (e.g. Cortoni, 2010). Currently there is no research in English on the appeal of *shotacon* for female consumers.

Legal issues

BL has a complex history and unique place in Japanese popular culture. However, it can incorporate material with inflammatory potential in relation to most contemporary societies (Sabucco, 2003) and erotic images involving young-looking protagonists; hence, in the West, *shotacon* and some BL may be suspicious texts under child pornography legislation.

The principle of freedom of speech may be a defence in the US,[9] and the Child Pornography Prevention Act 1996, which was problematic for manga and anime, was struck down by the Supreme Court in 2002 (Fischel, 2013). However, this legislation was resurrected in only slightly amended form in the 2003 PROTECT Act (Prosecutional Remedies and Other Tools to end the Exploitation of Children Today: Wood, 2013), meaning that BL consumers remain possible targets for prosecution. In Australia, the legal concept of 'child abuse material' is notoriously wide and makes vulnerable the country's large BL fandom (McLelland, 2012). However, recent proposals on mass internet filtering in Australia have recently been defeated, if only for pragmatic reasons. In the UK, the Coroners and Justice Act 2009 specifies that 'prohibited images of children' can include cartoons, manga and drawings. However, the criteria for non-photographic images of children – defined as personages appearing to be under 18 years old – to reach prohibited status are quite stringent. The images must be: (1) pornographic (with reference both to the image itself and to the context in which it appears); (2) grossly offensive, disgusting or otherwise of an obscene character (according to the ordinary dictionary definition of 'obscene'); and (3) focused on the child's genitals or anal region, or portraying any of a given list of acts (including sex acts in the presence of a child and/or involving a child).[10] As I have argued in detail elsewhere, most BL, as a romance genre, is unlikely to meet prohibitive status, but UK legislation is, in many ways, deeply problematic and has the potential to criminalise a demographic – young people – that it was designed to protect (Madill, 2015).

Sexually explicit manga and related products are not unproblematic in Japan itself. Paradoxically, up to the early 1990s, when the laws were relaxed, Japanese obscenity legislation had the effect of censoring mere nudity while allowing a wide range of explicitly sexual and sexually violent material to be shown (Allison, 2000). And – again paradoxically – in 2010 the Tokyo prefecture banned from general sale manga, anime and games likely to interfere with the healthy development of youth, while allegedly removing a passage from an earlier draft of the legislation articulating a duty not to possess photographic child pornography.[11]

Conclusion

Of all the manga/anime genres, BL/*yaoi* has attracted some of the most sustained academic interest. Unfortunately, little Japanese scholarship is available in English, but Anglophone publications do report research from across Europe (e.g. Kamm, 2012), Asia (e.g. Abraham, 2008) and Australia (e.g. King, 2013), as well as North America (e.g. Perper and Cornog, 2002). The scholarship on BL, while recognising controversies raised by the material, is strikingly positive about its affordances in terms of being one of the few forms of female-oriented erotica and an expression of queer (in the broadest terms) identity, and its ability to inspire creativity, for example through cosplay[12] (King, 2013), fan fiction and fan art (Noppe, 2010). Overwhelmingly, scholarship is also critical of increasing legal sanctions which may conflate clearly fictional images, such as in BL and related genres, with pornography involving real children (e.g. McLelland, 2012; Ost, 2010). The field now has two ground-breaking academic collections, *Boys' Love Manga: Essays on the Sexual Ambiguity and Cross-Cultural Fandom of the Genre* and *Boys Love Manga and Beyond: History, Culture, and Community in Japan*, and a special section was dedicated to BL in a recent edition of the *Journal of Graphic Novels and Comics* (edited by Pagliassotti, Nagaike and McHarry, 2013). That is not to say that BL does not have problematic content, but this is recognised and hotly debated within fandom itself (Zanghellini, 2009a). As I hope to have shown, BL has a unique history and is at the forefront of the development of women's erotic culture. We can hardly expect this culture to avoid exploring difficult themes such as incest, underage sex and rape – or for erotic material to always be politically correct.

Notes

1 *Dojinshi* may be amateur but can be extremely polished, and commercially successful *mangaka* often start out, and continue, in a *dojinshi* circle.
2 https://leeds.onlinesurveys.ac.uk/blfandomsurvey (accessed 17 November 2017).
3 Individuals identifying solely or partially as female, and solely or partially as heterosexual.
4 http://centrumlumina.tumblr.com/post/63112902720/heterosexual-female-slash-fans (accessed 17 November 2017).
5 腐女子 – a visual pun pronounced the same way as for the term 'girls and women', but where the first kanji – 'fu' – has been changed to that indicating 'rotten', so converting the meaning to 'rotten girls'.
6 Showa calendar.
7 'Scanned and translated': fan-produced translation uploaded to the internet without copyright approval.
8 Erotic manga and anime, etc. involving pubescent and/or pre-pubescent girls.
9 See the Comic Book Legal Defense Fund: http://cbldf.org/2011/09/join-cbldf/ (accessed 17 November 2017).
10 www.cps.gov.uk/legal/p_to_r/prohibited_images_of_children/index.html#an04) (accessed 17 November 2017).
11 www.bbc.co.uk/news/magazine-11998385 (accessed 17 November 2017).
12 Costume play in which fans dress up as manga and anime characters, often in self-made, fabulously crafted costumes designed to replicate specific artwork.

Bibliography

Abraham, Y. (2008) 'Boys' love thrives in conservative Indonesia'. In A. Levi, M. McHarry and D. Pagliassotti (eds), *Boys' Love Manga: Essays on the Sexual Ambiguity and Cross-Cultural Fandom of the Genre*. North Carolina: McFarland & Co. Inc., pp. 44–55.

Allison, A. (2000) *Permitted and Prohibited Desires: Mothers, Comics, and Censorship in Japan*. CA: University of California Press.

Brennan, J. (2013) 'Slash manips: remixing popular media with gay pornography'. M/C Journal. Volume 16 (4). http://journal.mediaculture.org.au/index.php/mcjournal/article/view/677 (accessed 26 January 2015).

Castagno, S. and Sabucco, V. (2006–2007). Indagine manga boy's love. Unpublished raw data cited in Pagliassotti, 2008b.

Chao, T. (2013) 'Features of hybridization in *In These Words*'. *Journal of Graphic Novels and Comics*. Volume 4 (1): 9–29.

Chin, B. and Morimoto, L. H. (2013) 'Towards a theory of transcultural fandom'. *Participations: Journal of Audience & Reception Studies*. Volume 10 (1): 92–108. www.participations.org/Volume%2010/Issue%201/7%20Chin%20&%20Morimoto%2010.1.pdf (accessed 13 September 2015).

Cohn, N. (2011) 'A different kind of cultural frame: an analysis of panels in American comics and Japanese manga'. *Image [&] Narrative*, Volume 12 (1). www.imageandnarrative.be/index.php/imagenarrative/article/view/128 (accessed 24 January 2015).

Cortoni, F. (2010) 'Female sexual offenders: a special sub-group'. In K. Harrison (ed), *Managing High-Risk Sex Offenders in the Community: Risk Management, Treatment and Social Responsibility*. London/New York: Routledge.

Fischel, J. J. (2013) *Pornographic Protections? Itineraries of Childhood Innocence*. Commentary essay prepared for WPSA Discourses on LGBT Politics, Yale University.

Frennea, M. (2011) 'The prevalence of rape and child pornography in yaoi'. *Proceedings of the National Conference on Undergraduate Research, Ithaca College*. New York, 31 March–2 April 2011.

Haggerty, G. E. (1998) 'Anne Rice and the queering of culture'. *NOVEL: A Forum on Fiction. Reading Gender after Feminism*. Volume 32 (1): 5–18.

Kamm, B. O. (2012) 'Rotten use patterns: what entertainment theories can do for the study of boys' love'. *Transformative Works and Cultures*. Volume 12. http://journal.transformativeworks.org/index.php/twc/article/view/427/391 (accessed 25 January 2015).

Kilpatrick, H. (2012) 'Envisioning the shojo aesthetic in Miyazawa Kenji's "The Twin Stars" and "Night of the Milky Way Railway"'. *Journal of Multidisciplinary International Studies*. Volume 9 (3): 1–26.

King, E. L. (2013) 'Girls who are boys who like girls to be boys: BL and the Australian cosplay community'. *Intersections: Gender, History and Culture in the Asian Context*. Volume 32: 1–3.

Levi, A., McHarry, M. and Pagliassotti, D. (eds) (2010) *Boys' Love Manga: Essays on the Sexual Ambiguity and Cross-Cultural Fandom of the Genre*. London: McFarland.

Li, Y. (2009) 'Japanese boy-love manga and the global fandom: a case study of Chinese female readers'. Unpublished MA thesis, Department of Communication Studies, Indiana University, USA.

Lunsing, W. (2006) 'Yaoi Ronsō: discussing depictions of male homosexuality in Japanese girls' comics, gay comics and gay pornography'. *Intersections: Gender, History and Culture in the Asian Context*. Issue 21: January. http://intersections.anu.edu.au/issue12/lunsing.html (accessed 22 January 2012).

McLelland, M. (2000) 'No climax, no point, no meaning? Japanese women's boy-love sites on the internet'. *Journal of Communication Inquiry*. Volume 24 (3): 274–291.

McLelland, M. (2012) 'Australia's "child-abuse material" legislation, internet regulation and the juridification of the imagination'. *International Journal of Cultural Studies*. Volume 15 (5): 467–483.

McLelland, M., Nagaike, K., Suganuma, K. and Welker, J. (2015). *Boys Love Manga and Beyond: History, Culture, and Community in Japan*. Jackson: University Press of Mississippi.

Madill, A. (2015) 'Boys' Love manga for girls: paedophilic, satirical, queer readings and English law'. In E. Renold, J. Ringrose and R. D. Egan (eds), *Children, Sexuality and 'Sexualisation': Beyond Spectacle and Sensationalism*. London: Palgrave Macmillan, pp. 273–288.

Mizoguchi, A. (2003) 'Male–male romance by and for women in Japan: a history and the subgenres of YAOI fictions'. *U.S.–Japan Women's Journal. English Supplement*. Volume 25: 49–75.

Nagaike, K. and Suganuma, K. (2013) 'Editorial: transnational boys' love fan studies'. *Transformative Works and Cultures*. Volume 12. http://journal.transformativeworks.org/index.php/twc/article/view/504/394 (accessed 15 April 2013).

Noppe, N. (2010) 'Dojinshi research as a site of opportunity for manga studies'. *Comics Worlds & the World of Comics: Towards Scholarship on a Global Scale*. Volume 1: 115–131.

Ost, S. (2010) 'Criminalising fabricated images of child pornography: a matter of harm or morality?' *Legal Studies*. Volume 30 (2): 230–256.

Pagliassotti, D. (2008a) 'Better than romance? Japanese BL manga and the subgenre of male/male romantic fiction'. In A. Levi, M. McHarry and D. Pagliassotti (eds) *Boys' Love Manga: Essays on the Sexual Ambiguity and Cross-Cultural Fandom of the Genre*. London: McFarland, pp. 59–83.

Pagliassotti, D. (2008b) 'Reading boys' love in the West'. *Particip@tions*, Volume 5 (2). www.participations.org/Volume%205/Issue%202/5_02_pagliassotti.htm (accessed 19 July 2010).

Pagliassotti, D., Nagaike, K. and McHarry, M. (2013) 'Editorial: Boys' Love manga special section'. *Journal of Graphic Novels and Comics*. Volume 4 (1): 1–8.

Penley, C. (1991) 'Brownian motion: women, tactics, and technology'. In C. Penley and A. Ross (eds), *Technoculture*. Minneapolis: University of Minnesota Press, pp. 135–161.

Perper, T. and Cornog, M. (2002) 'Eroticism for the masses: Japanese manga and their assimilation into the U.S.'. *Sexuality and Culture*. Volume 6 (1): 3–101.

Russ, J. (1985) 'Pornography by women for women, with love'. In *Magic Mommas, Trembling Sisters, Puritans and Perverts: Feminist Essays*. Berkeley, CA: Crossing Press, pp. 79–99.

Sabucco, V. (2003) 'Guided fan fiction: Western "readings" of Japanese homosexual-themed texts'. In C. Berry, F. Martin and A. Vue (eds), *Mobile Cultures: New Media in Queer Asia*. London: Duke University Press, pp. 70–86.

Saitō, T. (2007) 'Otaku sexuality'. In C. Bolton, I. Csicsery-Ronay Jr and T. Tatsumi (eds), *Robot Ghosts and Wired Dreams: Japanese Science Fiction from Origins to Anime*. Minneapolis: University of Minnesota Press, pp. 222–249.

Schodt, F. L. (1996) *Dreamland Japan: Writings on Modern Manga*. Berkeley, CA: Stone Bridge Press.

Sihombing, F. (2011) 'On the iconic difference between couple characters in Boys Love manga'. *Image [&] Narrative*, Volume 12 (1). www.imageandnarrative.be/index.php/imagenarrative/article/view/130 (accessed 24 January 2015).

Tai, E. (2007) 'Manga outside Japan'. 23 September. *The Star Online*. www.thestar.com.my/story/?file=%2f2007%2f9%2f23%2flifebookshelf%2f18898783&sec=lifebookshelf (accessed 25 January 2015).

Tanaka, K. (1995) 'The new feminist movement in Japan, 1970–1900'. In K. Fujimura-Fanselow and A. Kameda (eds), *Japanese Women: New Feminist Perspectives on the Past, Present, and Future*. New York: The Feminist Press, pp. 343–414.

Thorn, M. (2005) 'The Moto Hagio interview'. *The Comics Journal*. Issue 269. http://classic.tcj.com/history/the-moto-hagio-interview-conducted-by-matt-thorn-part-four-of-four/ (accessed 28 March 2017).

Ui, M., Fukutomi, M. and Kamise, Y. (2008) 'Attitudes of Japanese adolescents towards comic magazines 1: characteristics of "Boys' Love" ("shonen-ai", "m/m slash") readers'. *The 29th International Congress of Psychology*, 20–25 July 2008, Berlin, Germany.

Welker, J. (2011) 'Flower tribes and female desire: complicating early female consumption of male homosexuality in shojo manga'. *Mechademia*, Volume 6 (1): 211–228.

Wheeler, A. (2012) 'American yaoi: a look at three man-on-man webcomics for women'. *Comics Alliance*. 23 February. www.comicsalliance.com/2012/02/23/american-yaoi-webcomics/ (accessed 14 June 2012).

Wood, A. (2006) '"Straight" women, queer texts: boy-love manga and the rise of a global counterpublic'. *Women's Studies Quarterly*. Volume 34 (1/2): 394–414.

Wood, A. (2013) 'Boys' Love anime and queer desires in convergence culture: transnational fandom, censorship and resistance'. *Journal of Graphic Novels and Comics*. Volume 4 (1): 44–63.

Zanghellini, A. (2009a) '"Boys Love" in anime and manga: Japanese subcultural production and its end users'. *Continuum: Journal of Media & Cultural Studies*. Volume 23 (3): 279–294.

Zanghellini, A. (2009b) 'Underage sex and romance in Japanese homoerotic manga and anime'. *Social & Legal Studies*. Volume 18 (2): 159–177.

Zhou, N. F. (2009) 'YAOI phenomenon in Taiwan from interviews with female readers'. *Journal of Gender Studies Japan*. Volume 12: 41–55. Translated for Anna Madill by Mayumi Shinya, 2012.

13
WAYS OF SHOWING IT
Feature and gonzo in mainstream pornography

Federico Zecca

Two stylistic models

Fifteen years ago, Martin Amis (2001) stated that 'there are ... two types of mainstream American pornography: features and gonzo'. Amis described features as 'sex films with some sort of claim to the ordinary narrative: characterisation, storyline', and gonzo as a kind of porn that 'shows people fucking without concerning itself with why they're fucking' (ibid.). Since Amis wrote this article, many significant changes have occurred in the US adult business: the sharp decline of DVD sales and rentals, once the industry's biggest source of revenue; the rapid growth of Web 2.0 as the main delivery channel for porn materials; the emergence of a new generation of 'independent' porn professionals; the huge proliferation of alternative and sub-cultural pornographies; the implementation of new laws regulating porn production. Yet feature and gonzo *still* continue to be the two main types of mainstream American pornography, making up the largest part of the overall market and employed as categories by the industry to distinguish between the two principal lines of porn production.

However, feature and gonzo have not been subjected to close analysis. While there has been a considerable growth of scholarly work dealing with feminist, queer and amateur pornography (Jacobs *et al.*, 2007; Taormino *et al.*, 2013; Biasin *et al.*, 2014), mainstream/ 'corporate' pornography has suffered from academic neglect, with little interest in its specific distinctive features. The purpose of this chapter is to begin to explore this field, by identifying the textual properties and the discursive strategies that constitute feature and gonzo pornographies. To perform this analysis, I draw on theoretical tools and critical methodologies developed in continental film studies, and especially in French and Italian film semiotics.

According to the Review Guide in *AVN Magazine*, a feature is 'a story-based title with a beginning, middle and end tied together by more than just a connecting device' (86), while gonzo is 'a reality-based production in which the camera person's presence is acknowledged, often via interaction with those onscreen' (86). These definitions are a useful starting point, but their application has produced limited analytical outcomes so far. For instance, Chauntelle Anne Tibbals has described gonzo as a pornographic 'content production form' (2014: 128) based on a single characteristic: what she calls the 'talking camera' (ibid.).

While the acknowledgement of the camera's presence is a fundamental feature of gonzo porn, gonzo aesthetics are too complex to be reduced to a single element.

My proposal is to consider feature and gonzo as *stylistic models*. Drawing on some recent reflections on film style (Quaresima, 2007; Buccheri, 2010; Martin, 2014), I describe a stylistic model as a 'coherent system of technical, grammatical, narrative, and communicative options' which are 'historically and socially situated, that is in close connection with the historical, technological, industrial, economic, and cultural context in which the texts are produced and consumed' (Buccheri, 2010: 36–37). Defining feature and gonzo as stylistic models means I regard them as complex and multi-layered systems, within which different kinds of elements (technical, expressive, narrative, representative, enunciative, etc.) interact and connect with each other – elements that are, in turn, shaped by social and economic constraints. Another advantage that can be drawn from this perspective is to correct the misconception that feature and gonzo are simple 'genres' – as stated for instance by Gail Dines (2010: XI). Being stylistic models, feature and gonzo cut *across* genres (Quaresima, 2007: 537); or, in other words, genres represent specific articulations of the models themselves. For example, pornographic genres such as 'anal sex' or 'interracial' can be conveyed through both feature and gonzo styles, thus acquiring different semantic and syntactic properties (Altman, 1984: 10). Thus, feature and gonzo are not genres; rather, they *include* and *subsume* several genres, remodelling their properties in different ways.

Girl Meets Boy vs *Elastic Assholes 5*

Broadly speaking, feature pornography can be considered the natural 'heir' of the hard-core narrative production of the 1980s and 1990s – which in turn represents the 'video evolution' of the classic feature-length hard-core film of the 1970s. Like their video predecessors, contemporary features have a cinematic 'propensity' (Burch, 1981), with a developing storyline, fictional characters, etc. Gonzo pornography, meanwhile, emerged in the late 1980s as a direct evolution of so-called wall-to-wall pornography, which abandoned the cinematic form in order to exploit the expressive possibilities of video technology. From wall-to-wall, gonzo derives and develops all-sex content and an episodic structure. In other words, a feature aims at presenting itself as a 'movie', by re-enacting the forms and genres of conventional fictional cinema, while gonzo aims instead at presenting itself as a factual 'report', by imitating the forms and modes of documentary, reality television and home movies.

To investigate the distinctive traits of feature and gonzo, I focus on two specific movies as examples of the two stylistic models: the feature porn comedy *Girl Meets Boy* (2009), and the gonzo *Elastic Assholes 5* (2007). *Girl Meets Boy* is produced by Wicked Pictures, one of the main US players in the feature market, and shot by the feature director Jonathan Morgan. *Elastic Assholes 5* is produced and directed by the popular gonzo practitioner Mike John. Both *Girl Meets Boy* and *Elastic Assholes 5* are 'average' movies, whose distinctive traits can be easily extended and generalised to their respective models.

I start by making a few observations on the socio-economic dimension of these products. It is in the pre-production phase – which includes all the activities preceding the actual shooting (Kuhn and Westwell, 2012: 327) – that the main differences between the two products can be seen. *Girl Meets Boy* is based on the writing of a screenplay, on the design and construction of different settings, on the selection of a cast of characters, etc. – that is, on the same process that characterises any 'legitimate' feature film. *Elastic Assholes 5* requires neither a screenplay nor a particular cast of characters (since there are no 'actual' fictional characters in a gonzo and the performers are largely interchangeable) nor a setting specifically designed and built for the film. Furthermore, *Elastic Assholes 5* benefits from an economy of scale, being the fifth issue of a series (which had reached issue 12 as of 2014): sharing the same subject and structure with the other films in the series, this product cuts any possible additional cost related to the preliminary 'conception phase'.

The production and post-production phases – including shooting and editing (Kuhn and Westwell, 2012: 325, 328) – reveal marked differences too. *Girl Meets Boy* is produced like a 'normal' fiction film, employing a multiple-camera setup (at least two cameras: one fixed for the full shots, and one hand-held for the close-ups) and with a pre-defined arrangement of the pro-filmic space (starting from the precise placement of the actors on the set), repetition of takes (especially during the shooting of non-sexual scenes) and their selection during the editing process. *Elastic Assholes 5* employs a more 'lightweight' (and less expensive) production mode, consistent with its gonzo aesthetics. Based on the (pseudo-)documentary representation of the sexual intercourse, *Elastic Assholes 5* is characterised by three main features: the mise-en-scène is 'emancipated' from any cinematic requirements (traditional acting, settings, screenplay, etc.); the sexual performance is shot without interruptions (with just one hand-held camera, and without any retakes); there is almost no editing, and therefore post-production work is reduced to the minimum. As a consequence, the size of the crew for *Elastic Assholes 5* is ten units (performer included), against the 20 units of *Girl Meets Boy*. From the limited information available (Anon., 2008; Braun, 2014; Lim, 2006; Curry, 2014; Snow, 2014), it is possible to estimate *Elastic Assholes 5*'s budget at around $15,000–20,000 dollars, and *Girl Meets Boy*'s at around $60,000–70,000.

In addition, *Girl Meets Boy* and *Elastic Assholes 5* are marketed and promoted in very different fashions. *Elastic Assholes 5* is considered as a product 'for men only', praised for its display of hard fucking and rough sex (bono-ONE, 2007), while *Girl Meets Boy* is described as a 'nice couples movie', 'a sexy romantic comedy everyone can relate to' (Warrior, 2009), addressing an audience of both men *and* women. In other words, *Elastic Assholes 5* is conceived for the 'solitary' consumption of a male viewer whereas, while *Girl Meets Boy* might also titillate a solitary male viewer, it is also designed as a means of 'spicing things up' for a heterosexual couple.

Continuity and 'idealism'

Focusing now on the textual dimension of *Girl Meets Boy* and *Elastic Assholes 5*, the first difference between these two movies is in their semio-pragmatic articulation (Odin, 1995). *Girl Meets Boy* is composed of interrelated *narrative sequences* that cooperate in the development of an overarching storyline, while *Elastic Assholes 5* is composed of autonomous *monstrative episodes* – based on the act of presenting the events as they occur (Gaudreault, 2009). Consequently, while *Girl Meets Boy* produces a *diegetic space*, related to an 'alternative' (narrative) reality that viewers perceive 'in place and in lieu of the images on the screen' (Odin, 2000: 19), *Elastic Assholes 5* constructs a *spectacular space* – conceived more for presenting a performance than for narrating an event – which directly addresses viewers, as if it belonged to the same level of reality they inhabit. In what follows, I analyse the initial parts of the two texts, in particular *Girl Meets Boy*'s first three sequences (which constitute a cohesive narrative block) and *Elastic Assholes 5*'s first episode.

The first part of *Girl Meets Boy* is structured in three sequences respectively composed of 6, 25 and 15 shots (a total of 46 shots and an overall duration of about 15'41"). In the first sequence, two friends, Vanessa and Aly, arrive at a house party, where Vanessa hopes

Aly will find someone with whom to have sex, following her breakup with her boyfriend, Michael. The second sequence (a flashback) shows Michael cheating on Aly with a maid in a hotel room. In the third sequence Vanessa pushes Aly to have sex with a redneck, but Aly says she is not interested and goes away. Drawing on the three-act-structure screenwriting model that divides the narrative into three parts (Field, 1979), these sequences compose the first act of the narrative: the so-called 'setup' phase used to establish the setting and the main character of the story, and to provide essential background information (Aly is disillusioned and saddened because her boyfriend cheated on her).

The three sequences, however, carry out different narrative functions. The second sequence is of a strictly pornographic nature, being almost completely dedicated to the explicit representation of sex (which occupies about 11' of its total 13'42"). It has a fundamental role in the generic definition of *Girl Meets Boy*, representing one of the 'building blocks' (Altman, 1984) that clearly mark the movie as pornographic. The first and third sequences (which are much shorter than the second one) offer a sort of narrative framing of or 'anchorage' (Barthes, 1977) to the second sequence. They also show genuine comedic tendencies, especially embodied in the character of Vanessa, in her colourful language and manic movements.

It should be noted that the crossover between pornography and legitimate film (or television) genres – such as romantic comedy, in the case of *Girl Meets Boy* – constitutes one of the cornerstones of feature porn. Often, features consciously (and sometimes in modes of parody) reemploy the defining elements of particular legitimate genres (storylines, characters, attitudes) in order to articulate their own narratives. This gives rise to a wide array of porn comedies, porn thrillers, porn action films, and so on. Loosely drawing on Altman's reflections on film genre, feature pornography thus seems to exist in a constant 'adjectival state' (1998: 62–68), that is, in a constant state of trans-generic hybridisation.

The sexual intercourse between Michael and the hotel maid follows a specific syntactic structure, articulated in four principal phases: 'excitement', 'foreplay', 'penetration' and (male) 'orgasm', following a supposed 'natural' disposition that closely resembles the one codified in the 1960s by traditional sexology (Lowen, 1965; Masters and Johnson, 1966). First, they caress and kiss each other ('excitement' phase); then the maid performs fellatio upon Michael and, in turn, he performs cunnilingus on her ('foreplay' phase); afterwards, they copulate in a reverse cowgirl position and in a doggy-style position ('penetration' phase); finally, Michael ejaculates on the maid's face ('orgasm' phase). Therefore, the sexual intercourse between Michael and the maid is represented according to an 'ideal' (sexological) model, based on the linear progression of determined sexual acts. Moreover, the sexual acts performed can be described as 'vanilla sex', that is, 'conventional' and devoid of any twist or kinkiness (Rubin, 1993; Rosewarne, 2011).

Moreover, the sexual intercourse between Michael and the maid is structured according to the principles of continuity editing, so that its progression appears seamless. The continuity is produced by employing a number of editing matching techniques that aim at the 'maintenance of orderly spatial, rhythmic, graphical, and temporal relations from shot to shot' (Kuhn and Westwell, 2012: 94). For example, during the 'reverse cowgirl' position, the cut from the full shot of the couple to the detail of the vaginal penetration (the so-called 'meat shot') is achieved through a match on action (in the second shot, the maid is still moving as in the first one) and through a sound match (in the second shot, the maid is moaning as in the first one). Furthermore, on occasion the intercourse between Michael and the maid is interrupted by a dissolve, which is employed to smooth the gap between one sexual number and the other. This is what happens, for instance, in the transition from the reverse cowgirl position to the doggy-style position: the couple are still having sex in the reverse cowgirl position (the maid is sitting astride Michael in a medium shot) when the shot fades and is replaced by a full shot of the couple (already) engaging in penetration in the doggy-style position. In this sense, the dissolve signals the presence of a short ellipsis: the changing of sexual position is indeed conceived as 'dead time' in their intercourse, and is therefore removed from the final edit.

Immediacy and hyperbole

The first episode of *Elastic Assholes 5* is structured in two sequences respectively composed of two and six shots lasting 3'50" and 32'38". The first sequence shows Keeani Lei standing in a backyard, dressed in underwear and high heels. As the camera comes close to her, Keeani smiles and says 'hi'. The operator asks her what she is up to, and she answers 'no good'. While the camera meticulously explores her body, she undresses and begins to fondle herself. The second sequence shows her (completely naked except for the heels) in a living room, where the performer Steve Holmes immediately joins her. Wasting no time, Holmes starts to perform cunnilingus on Keeani, then takes out his penis and puts it in her mouth. Shortly after, they copulate in a variety of positions, engaging especially in extended sessions of anal sex, during which Holmes often pulls out his penis to show Keeani's dilated anus to the camera. The episode ends with Keeani on her knees, laughing and smiling at the camera after having swallowed Holmes's ejaculate.

There is no interest here in integrating the sexual action in a story world; on the contrary, the objective is to directly 'show' the sex as it is performed, without any narrative mediation. Compared with *Girl Meets Boy*, *Elastic Assholes 5* produces a *semantic intensification* of the representation, which is based both on the extension of the sexual action and on the nature of the sexual practices. Its sexual performance is much longer than *Girl Meets Boy*'s – in *Girl Meets Boy* the sexual intercourse lasts about 11' (about 73 per cent of the whole segment); in *Elastic Assholes 5* it takes almost 34' (about 94 per cent of the whole episode). *Elastic Assholes 5*'s performers also engage in broadly 'fetishistic' and more physically demanding sexual acts, such as 'throat fucking', 'ass-to-mouth' and 'anal gaping' (Biasin and Zecca, 2009: 143; Maddison, 2012), which are absent in *Girl Meets Boy*. In particular, the practice of 'anal gaping' – the dilation of the performer's anus after a prolonged session of anal sex – is pivotal in *Elastic Assholes 5*: it not only relates the movie to a specific sub-(sub-)genre, but it also explains its very title (and that of the whole series).

Second, *Elastic Assholes 5* presents a (partial) *syntactic deconstruction* of the sexual representation. Unlike *Girl Meets Boy*, *Elastic Assholes* does not construct sexual intercourse that follows the excitement–foreplay–penetration–orgasm pattern highlighted above. For example, the central part of the second sequence (composed of three shots, lasting in total 25') shows the following order of sexual acts being performed: cunnilingus/masturbation, fellatio ('deep throat'), vaginal penetration, cunnilingus, fellatio ('deep throat'), vaginal penetration, anal penetration, ass licking, anal penetration, fellatio ('ass-to-mouth'), vaginal penetration, anal penetration/masturbation, fellatio ('ass-to-mouth'), anal penetration, cunnilingus, ass licking, anal penetration. As this arrangement demonstrates, these practices are not subjected to a pre-determined sexological order of appearance (and of importance). In particular, oral sex is not *positioned* as foreplay: instead, especially in its 'ass-to-mouth' and 'ass-licking' versions, it 'punctuates' the whole duration of the sexual intercourse, being a moment of 'transition' between the different (vaginal or anal) penetration sessions.

Unlike *Girl Meets Boy*, therefore, *Elastic Assholes 5* does not represent sexual intercourse according to the cultural codes of 'conventional' sexual behaviour; on the contrary, it drives the representation towards 'transgression' (Kipnis, 1998) and 'hyperbolic excess' (Biasin and Zecca, 2009; Paasonen, 2011). The sexual performance becomes a sort of 'athletic tour de force', punctuated by fetish activities and tinged with kinkiness.

Furthermore, *Elastic Assholes 5* differs from *Girl Meets Boy* on the technical–expressive level. It does not rely on continuity editing (widely used in *Girl Meets Boy*), choosing instead the 'continuous filming' technique. *Elastic Assholes 5* reduces editing to a minimum: the sexual performance is filmed 'live' through a hand-held camera that captures its development almost without interruptions. For example, the intercourse between Keeani Lei and Steve Holmes is composed of only six long takes (lasting on average 5'50" each), while that between Michael and the maid in *Girl Meets Boy* is articulated in 13 shots (with an average duration of 50" each). Even the use of dissolves does not have any elliptical function in *Elastic Assholes 5*, only corresponding to a brief interruption of the sexual intercourse.

Moreover, in *Elastic Assholes 5* the abolition of editing is strictly related to the objective of showing (and 'proving') the authenticity of the sexual acts, in order to guarantee that they are being performed 'for real' – that is, without any filmic *trucages* (Metz, 1977). For example, the 'ass-to-mouth' practice is always rigorously shot in long take in order to 'document' the *immediate* continuity between anal sex and fellatio. This kind of 'liveness' to some extent enhances the 'realness' of the sexual acts, while at the same time bolstering a 'new' frenzy of the visible (Williams, 1989) related to specific sexual practices.

Elastic Assholes 5 also makes use of another technique that differentiates it from *Girl Meets Boy* at a deeper level: 'interpellation' (Casetti, 1998). In film semiotics, this term is used to describe a scene that is 'staged in order to recognize someone outside the text to whom the film makes a direct appeal, "hailing" this "you" in the form of on aside' (Branigan, 2006: 51). During sex, Keeani often looks at (and talks to) the camera, openly winking at the operator and – through him – the viewers. The maid in *Girl Meets Boy* acts instead *as if* she was not aware of the camera, and carefully avoids directing her gaze into the camera lens.

Continuous shooting and interpellation are the expressive and enunciative 'keystones' of the semio-pragmatic strategy of *Elastic Assholes 5*, since they encourage viewers to activate a 'documentary mode ... of production of meaning' (Odin, 2000: 128). According to Warren Buckland (2000: 99), the documentary mode drives viewers to interpret a text as a factual report rather than as a fiction. Through this strategy, therefore, *Elastic Assholes 5* aims at disguising the staged nature of 'what is part of the realm of fiction, making it seem real instead' (Jost, 2003: 97) – very much like some contemporary television genres, such as reality shows.

Comparing the differences

As I suggested, I believe that my observations upon these two 'average' movies can be largely generalised to their respective stylistic models: feature and gonzo. Table 13.1 systematises the main characteristics of the two models.

First of all, feature and gonzo employ different modalities to represent sexual performance. Feature pornography structures sexual intercourse according to an 'ideal' (sexological) model characterised (on the syntactic level) by the 'excitement–foreplay–penetration–orgasm' progression, and (on the semantic one) by a limited set of 'vanilla' sexual acts that are culturally related to 'conventional' sexual behaviour (mainly masturbation, oral sex and vaginal penetration; anal sex is far less frequent). Gonzo pornography challenges this model through a double operation. On the syntactic level, it 'disarticulates' the progression of

Table 13.1 Feature pornography/gonzo pornography.

Feature pornography	Gonzo pornography
Representative/performative dimension	
Conventional sex	Kinky/rough practices
(Pre)codified progression	Deconstructed disposition
'Ideal' representation	Hyperbolic spectacle
Semio-pragmatic dimension	
Narrative integration	Monstrative attraction
Diegetic space	Spectacular space
Fictional regime	(Pseudo)documentary regime
Enunciative/communicative dimension	
Referential communication	Identification communication
Objective view	Interpellation/point-of-view
Invisible witnesses	Acknowledged 'participants'
Technical–expressive dimension	
Multiple-camera setup	Single-camera setup
Fixed camera	Hand-held camera
Continuity editing	Continuous filming
Socio-economic dimension	
High(er) production values	Low production values
'Couples' pornography	'For men only' pornography

the sexual intercourse, which no longer follows the structure pre-codified by traditional sexology. On the semantic level, it stages some 'kinky' and 'rough' practices, of broadly 'fetishistic' origin, which are often related to anal and oral sub-sub-genres: 'ass-to-mouth', 'anal gaping', 'anal creampie', 'throat fucking', 'snowballing', 'bukkake', 'multiple swallow', etc. These processes turn sex into a sort of excessive and hyperbolic spectacle, not dissimilar to an 'extreme sport' (Smith, 2012), which aims at testing the physical resistance and stamina of the performers (especially the female ones).

Second, feature and gonzo adopt different semio-pragmatic regimes, respectively fictional and (pseudo-)documentary. Feature pornography establishes a 'fictive world' based on the narrative integration of the sequences into a diegetic space. Gonzo presents itself instead as a factual recording of sex, which is delivered to the spectator as a 'pure' performance within a spectacular space. These two semio-pragmatic regimes are related to specific expressive and enunciative modes. Feature employs modes of expression typical of fictional cinema, with the aim of building a 'transparent' world where the events seem to tell themselves (Genette, 1976). Gonzo employs modes of expression typical of video reporting, based on the liveness of the audio-visual recording and on the self-exhibition of the enunciative presence. These different modes of expression also entail different production structures: feature pornography requires high(er) production values, a large crew and a broad array of facilities (multiple-camera setup, designed setting, special effects, etc.), while gonzo is characterised by low production values, a small crew and limited technical equipment.

These two semio-pragmatic regimes are related to different 'communication strategies' – and therefore to different modes of involvement of the viewers. Feature pornography is based on 'referential communication', which implies an objective and 'anonymous' view that shows reality in a direct way (Casetti, 1998: 139). It allows viewers to 'hide' behind the fourth wall and voyeuristically observe the development of the sexual intercourse.

Gonzo pornography, instead, is based on 'identification communication', which is characterised by two types of shots: interpellation and point-of-view. In the first type, the female performer looks into the camera, directly addressing viewers during the sexual action. In the second type, the viewer's gaze corresponds to that of an observer *within* the scene. This observer is generally either the operator (who freely moves around the bodies to capture the action) or the male performer himself (who directly records the sexual intercourse through a hand-held camera). Viewers look at the scene through the eyes of the operator/performer, while at the same time being looked at by the female performer. As a consequence, viewers are brought 'within' the scene, as if they were 'participants' in the action. This communication strategy aims at enhancing the engagement of the viewers, by combining their usual scopic activity with a sort of (virtual) performative interaction (Biasin and Zecca, 2009: 145).

These differences also influence the ways in which feature and gonzo are positioned in the market of adult entertainment, as their promotional and critical paratexts clearly illustrate. Gonzo is often promoted as 'for men only', and its paratexts stress its hyper-masculinised imagery and hyperbolic performativity. Feature pornography is mostly distributed and promoted as a romantic, funny and spicy form of sexual entertainment suitable for women and couples.

Conclusion

To conclude, feature and gonzo can be considered as stylistic models that inform much of mainstream contemporary porn production. These models show two fundamental traits: they are complex, in that they originate from the intertwining of various (economic, social, semiotic) elements; and they are divergent, since they use contrasting modes of expression and representation, and cover different market segments. Obviously, feature and gonzo are not immutable and 'impermeable' systems; on the contrary, especially in the past few years they have developed a sort of 'mutual interaction', which has sometimes created some 'hybrid' forms. For instance, the sexual performance enacted by Sasha Grey in Digital Playground's feature *Nurses* (2009, dir. Robby D.) to some extent 'exceeds' and 'perverts' the standards of (sexual) representation adopted in the whole film. Thanks to her status as gonzo star, Grey is allowed to perform extreme and hyperbolic sex in a 'vanilla' context: the feature appropriates some performative elements of gonzo, without undermining its general semio-pragmatic and communicative structure. Further research needs to be done on these issues, exploring both the migration of repertoires and representations within these two stylistic models, and their own historical developments.

Bibliography

Adult Video News (2016) 'Review Guide'. magazine-files.avn.com/avnmay2016/ (accessed 4 June 2016).
Altman, R. (1984) 'A Semantic/Syntactic Approach To Film Genre'. *Cinema Journal* 23 (3): 6–18.
Altman, R. (1998) *Film/Genre*. London: BFI.
Amis, M. (2001) 'A Rough Trade'. *The Guardian*. 17 March. www.theguardian.com/books/2001/mar/17/society.martinamis1 (accessed 4 June 2015).
Anon. (2008) 'Mika Tan Discusses the Porn Industry, Racism & Prostitution'. *AdultFYI*. www.adultfyi.com/mika-tan-discusses-the-porn-industry-racism-prostitution/ (accessed 28 March 2017).
Barthes, R. (1977) *Image, Music, Text*. London: Fontana Press.
Biasin, E. and Zecca, F. (2009) 'Contemporary Audiovisual Pornography: Branding Strategy and Gonzo Film Style'. *Cinéma & Cie: International Film Studies Journal* 9 (12): 133–147.

Biasin, E., Maina, G. and Zecca, F. (eds) (2014) *Porn after Porn: Contemporary Alternative Pornographies*. Milano: Mimesis International.
bono-ONE (2007) 'Elastic Assholes 5'. *Adult DVD Talk*. www.adultdvdtalk.com/review/elastic-assholes-5 (accessed 4 June 2016).
Branigan, E. (2006) *Projecting a Camera Language-Games in Film Theory*. New York: Routledge.
Braun, A. (2014) Unpublished interview with Giovanna Maina and Federico Zecca, 17 November.
Buccheri, V. (2010) *Lo stile cinematografico*. Roma: Carocci.
Buckland, W. (2000) *The Cognitive Semiotics of Film*. Cambridge: Cambridge University Press.
Burch, N. (1981) *Theory of Film Practice*. Princeton: Princeton University Press.
Casetti, F. (1998) *Inside the Gaze: The Fiction Film and Its Spectator*. Bloomington: Indiana University Press.
Curry, A. (2014) Unpublished interview with Giovanna Maina and Federico Zecca, 5 November.
Dines, G. (2010) *Pornland: How Porn Has Hijacked Our Sexuality*. Boston: Beacon Press.
Field, S. (1979) *Screenplay: The Foundations of Screenwriting*. Surrey: Delta Publishing.
Gaudreault, A. (2009) *From Plato to Lumière: Narration and Monstration in Literature and Cinema*. Toronto: University of Toronto Press.
Genette, G. (1976) 'Boundaries of Narrative'. *New Literary History*. Volume 8 (1): 1–13.
Jacobs, K., Janssen, M. and Pasquinelli, M. (eds) (2007) *C'Lick Me: A Netporn Studies Reader*. Amsterdam: Institute of Network Cultures.
Jost, F. (2003) *La Télévision du quotidien: Entre réalité et fiction*. Bruxelles: De Boeck.
Kipnis, L. (1998) *Bound and Gagged: Pornography and the Politics of Fantasy in America*. Durham: Duke University Press.
Kuhn, A. and Westwell, G. (2012) *A Dictionary of Film Studies*. Oxford: Oxford University Press.
Lim, G. (2006) *In Lust We Trust: Adventures in Adult Cinema*. Singapore: Monsoon Books.
Lowen, A. (1965) *Love and Orgasm*. London: Macmillan.
Maddison, S. (2012) 'Is the Rectum Still a Grave? Anal Sex, Pornography and Transgression'. In T. Gournelos and D.J. Gunkel (eds), *Transgression 2.0: Media, Culture, and the Politics of a Digital Age*. London: Continuum.
Martin, A. (2014) *Mise en Scène and Film Style: From Classical Hollywood to New Media Art*. Basingstoke: Palgrave Macmillan.
Masters, W. and Johnson, V.E. (1966) *Human Sexual Response*. Philadelphia: Lippincott Williams & Wilkins.
Metz, C. (1977) 'Trucage and the Film'. *Critical Inquiry*. Volume 3 (4): 657–675.
Odin, R. (1995) 'A Semio-Pragmatic Approach to the Documentary Film'. In W. Buckland (ed), *The Film Spectator: From Sign to Mind*. Amsterdam: Amsterdam University Press.
Odin, R. (2000) *De la fiction*. Bruxelles: Editions De Boeck Université.
Paasonen, S. (2011) *Carnal Resonance: Affect and Online Pornography*. Cambridge, MA: The MIT Press.
Quaresima, L. (2007) 'Postfazione'. In E. Biasin, G. Bursi and L. Quaresima (eds), *Lo stile cinematografico/Film Style*. Udine: Forum.
Rosewarne, L. (2011) *Part-Time Perverts: Sex, Pop Culture, and Kink Management*. Santa Barbara: Preager.
Rubin, G. (1993) 'Thinking Sex: Notes for a Radical Theory of the Politics of Sexuality'. In A. Habelove, M.A. Barale and D. Halperin (eds), *Lesbian and Gay Studies Reader*. London: Routledge.
Smith, C. (2012) 'Reel Intercourse: Doing Sex on Camera'. In D. Kerr and C. Hines (eds), *Hard to Swallow: Hard-core Pornography on Screen*. New York: Wallflower Press.
Snow, A. (2014) Unpublished interview with Giovanna Maina and Federico Zecca, 28 November.
Taormino, T., Shimizu, C.P., Penley, C. and Miller-Young, M. (eds) (2013) *The Feminist Porn Book: The Politics of Producing Pleasure*. New York: Feminist Press at the City University of New York.
Tibbals, C.A. (2014) 'Gonzo, Trannys, and Teens: Current Trends in US Adult Content Production, Distribution, and Consumption'. *Porn Studies*. Volume 1 (1–2): 127–135.

Warrior, A. (2009) 'Girl Meets Boy', XCritic. www.xcritic.com/review/33964/alektra-blue-girl-meets-boy (accessed 4 June 2016).
Williams, L. (1989) *Hard Core: Power, Pleasure, and 'the Frenzy of the Visible'*. Berkeley: University of California Press.

Media

Elastic Assholes 5 (2009) Directed by M. John. [DVD]. USA: Jules Jordan Video.
Girl Meets Boy (2009) Directed by J. Morgan. [DVD]. USA: Wicked Pictures.
Nurses (2009) Directed by Robby D. [DVD]. USA: Digital Playground.

14
FROM THE SCENE, FOR THE SCENE!
Alternative pornographies in contemporary US production

Giovanna Maina

Pornography, technology and 'the alternative'

The relationship between pornography and alternative (sub)cultures has always been complex and multifaceted, even before the birth of a porn industry proper. During the 1960s 'postwar American avant-garde', for example, the work of experimental filmmakers such as Andy Warhol and Jack Smith, among others, 'camped at the borderlands between art and pornography', producing oeuvres that 'engaged the viewer both corporeally and cognitively' (Osterweil, 2004: 433).[1] The 1970s porno-chic wave was also characterised by non-standard production and distribution practices, experimental ambitions and transgressive political statements, not so different from those traditionally associated with independent and underground cinema (Adamo, 2004; Lewis, 2002); sometimes there was even a downright overlapping of styles, themes and practices between these two seemingly conflicting spheres (pornography and the avant-garde), as can be seen in the arty and imaginative cinema of the two gay-porn pioneers Wakefield Poole and Fred Halsted (Capino, 2005).

However, the acknowledged antagonism between a *mainstream* and an *alternative* within pornography dates back to the second half of the 1980s. During that era, the video revolution that was starting to upset the inner balances of the media system as a whole dramatically hit the adult business, forever changing the ways in which audio-visual pornography was produced, consumed and experienced. This process entailed the gradual (though relatively quick) shift from a mostly public form of porn consumption (in movie theatres and arcades) to the privacy of home video viewing[2] and the subsequent total and irreversible conversion to video on the part of the major porn companies, in the US as well as in other burgeoning Western production contexts (Kleinhans, 2006; Williams, 1999: 231, 300–315; Zecca, 2011: 49–54). However, this technological and social turning point did not just affect the industrial practices of the big players in the domain of porn production. The lower production costs allowed by video technologies, together with the simplification and 'domestication' of distribution, paved the way for a multiplication and differentiation of pornographic production 'in relation to different market niches'

(Zecca 2011: 54),³ enabling ever-increasing expansion of access to pornographic materials on the part of previously 'neglected' target audiences, specifically heterosexual and homosexual women (Juffer, 1998; Butler, 2004; Smith, 2007).

In such a diversified scenario, it is no surprise that the first deliberate attempts at creating an alternative to the most visible forms of pornographic production (mostly male-dominated and generally male-oriented) specifically targeted these particular audiences and their (supposed) needs. Independent endeavours such as Femme Productions (established in 1984 by former porn star Candida Royalle and essentially aimed at women and couples) and Fatale Video (created by legendary *On Our Backs* co-founder Nan Kinney in 1985 and explicitly catering to a lesbian audience) were characterised by a mixture of sex-positive feminist militancy, artistic ambitions and commercial purposes, their imperative goal being an authentic representation of women's sexuality and desires, as opposed to the (allegedly) stereotyped representations provided by the average pornographic products of the time.

Although these two experiences have now been historicised as the inception of what has been (in more recent years) canonised as a distinct subgenre of pornography known as *feminist porn* (Taormino et al., 2013; Maina, 2014a),⁴ their ideological premises and material outcomes already showed some of the main features of alternative pornography as it is currently understood and shaped by both scholarly research and public debate.

Another technological and cultural shift was needed, though, for the first examples of (self-defined) alternative pornography – or *alt porn*, as it is usually referred to in the contemporary mediasphere – to effectively sprout and thrive. The so-called 'digital revolution' of the 1990s and the subsequent development of a more interactive and collaborative (virtual) environment with the advent of the World Wide Web in the 2000s contributed to both an exceptional proliferation of pornographic niches and markets (Williams, 2004) and an unprecedented 'plural and mobile porno performativity' (Ciuffoli, 2011: 230) of multiple interconnected audiences willing to become 'active subjects in the production and diffusion of X-rated materials' (ibid.) through the creative use of personal media, sharing platforms and social networks.⁵

Within the broader context of netporn (Jacobs, 2007; Jacobs et al., 2007), then, a new breed of 'porn professionals', who were 'younger, paler, decidedly less straight' (Attwood, 2010) than the average (mainstream) porn producers and performers, started making their way into the adult business at the end of the 1990s.

'Porn they can relate to': the rise (and fall?) of alt porn

In a 2005 article in the adult industry's trade journal *Adult Video News*, Peter Stokes explained the relatively recent success of alt porn – already a well-established and recognisable subgenre at that time – primarily as a consequence of a change in the demographics and consumption habits of pornographic audiences. He stated:

> No matter what your personal taste in [alternative porn] is, it's supplying the ever-increasing demand of people aged 18 to 25 who want to watch Porn They Can Relate To. They also want porn they can purchase on-line (where that computer genus was born and raised), and porn they can see advertised and promoted in *their* publications. In *their* world. According to some, the mainstream porn world has yet to wake up to much of this.
>
> (Stokes, 2005, emphasis in original)

While addressing the need for the adult business to expand its market reach by explicitly targeting this promising consumer sector, AVN's then managing editor was actually describing some of the core features of this 'new wave' of porn production. In spite of their differences in style, content and social meaning, the products and practices that fall under the umbrella category of 'alternative' do, in fact, share some common traits, as they all directly appeal to youth (sub)cultures (Tomlin, 2002; Ziegler, 2003), exploit the possibilities offered by the digital environment (Ray, 2007; Van der Graf, 2004), include pornography consumption in a broader notion of lifestyle (Maina, 2010, 2011) and 'sex taste culture' (Attwood, 2007) and establish complex interrelations with 'the mainstream' (Smith, 2014) – being at the same time the nemesis of corporate porn and its 'research and development arm' (Cramer and Home, 2007: 165), through which the industry itself can 'test' new aesthetic and commercial solutions.

Originally launched in 1992 as a print 'counterculture erotica' magazine by DC residents Amelia G and Forrest Black, *Blue Blood* is the first and, to date, longest-running alternative porn endeavour showcasing 'the beauty and sensuality of the emerging eclectic underground populated by gothic, punk and pre-Internet cyberculture'.[6] Within a few years of launch the thriving business had moved online, with a cluster of hard-core websites – now gathered under *BlueBlood.com* (established in 2001) – such as *Gothic Sluts* and *Barely Evil* (both launched in 2000 and inspired by goth and punk fashion styles and ethos), the latex fetish site *Rubber Dollies* (2003) and *Erotic Fandom* (2006), featuring models 'in chainmail, Renaissance garb, steampunk finery, alien contacts, fairy wings, superhero capes, and supervillain masks'.[7]

In 1999 Scott Owens created *Raver Porn* (subsequently renamed *EroticBPM*) as 'a participatory forum for club culture erotica' (Osgerby, 2014: 40), again stressing the direct link between the aesthetic choices developed by the website and bottom-up communication strategies targeted to a specific subcultural community. During the first half of the 2000s, other web entrepreneurs started their own businesses explicitly speaking to music subcultures (especially goth, punk, rockabilly), non-heteronormative communities (LGBTQI, fetish, polyamorous) and other, more general, contemporary alternative lifestyles (new hippies, vegans, nerds, cosplayers), and ranging from ephemeral indie *solo* websites to more successful and long-lasting companies.

The simplest format chosen by alt producers, the small *solo* pro-am site – where the (female) model is also owner, photographer and webmaster – was particularly popular at the beginning of the alt porn boom, also becoming a very important vehicle for self-expression and self-entrepreneurship for women willing to re-negotiate the boundaries between public and private through explicit sexual representations. In fact, according to Danielle De Voss, 'through self-sponsored and self-published porn sites specifically, women [were] forcing their embodied sexualities and subjectivities into public light and attention' (2002: 85). De Voss considers these websites to be 'identity projects' (76), as spaces where the models 'own and control their bodies and sexualities [and] appropriate stereotypical notions of pornography [in order to] deliberately transgress expected norms of sexuality' (77). Furry Girl, for instance, was the owner of a cluster of alt amateur websites – the most important being *furrygirl.com*, established in 2002 – through which she presented the fierce and unapologetic image of a 'gal with a full bush, fuzzy legs, and hairy pits'[8] in complete control of her image and publicly enjoying her private and 'real' sexuality. With her website *NerdPr0n*, geek girl Anna Logue directly addressed the nerd community, constantly referencing its specific accoutrements, lifestyles and values in the presentation of her erotic self.

A similar ethos, coupled with the aforementioned subcultural references, characterises other alternative companies that started their activity in the same period. Although created by a single webmaster or by a group of friends, websites such as *Suicide Girls* (2001), *burningangel.com* (2002) and *NoFauxxx.com* (2002), or independent studios such as Pink and White Productions (2005),[9] have developed more articulated production features, communication strategies and representational styles, which I will discuss in the following sections of this chapter.

In the past few years, however, such experiences have been challenged by a general reorganisation of the whole adult business within the web 2.0 environment, due mostly to the success of free porn sites and the spread of piracy, as well as to specific diversification and 'inclusion' strategies employed by corporate porn studios in order to enrich their offer (and widen their market). Many *solo* paysites such as the above-mentioned *furrygirl.com* (still visible, but no longer updated) and *NerdPr0n* (now expired) have in fact been superseded by more accessible, visible and easy-to-manage profile pages on porn tubes and sex-cam websites, alt modelling having become one of the many nuances of amateur porn online.

Alt porn websites in general started to show signs of decreased popularity around 2012, when the adult industry crisis hit the entire sector – and especially its less established fringes – much harder than in previous years.[10] For an (albeit necessarily partial) overview of the 'rise and fall' of the commercial offer of alternative pornography, we can consider the shifts in the number of alt porn sites listed on *altporn.net*, probably the biggest blog/portal covering almost all the subgenres related to online subcultural erotica. Browsing through the snapshots provided by Internet Archive, we see that in June 2004, for instance, *altporn.net* listed 17 commercial sites, 15 communities, 3 free sites, 6 models and 7 photographers.[11] In May 2008, at the peak of alt porn's popularity, *altporn.net* featured on its home page links to 17 sites in the 'A list' of alt porn, 29 alt-related sites, 25 alt *solo* sites, 25 blogs, 9 communities, 13 free sites, 10 illustrators and artists, 25 models, 49 photographers and (what is even more interesting) a list of 20 already dead alt porn websites.[12] The last time I checked the site, the 'A list' had been reduced to 9 sites; links to 4 generalist cam services had been added; the list of alt-related sites totalled 22 items, which also included the 9 'A'-list sites; and the 20 *solo* sites were for the most part related to bigger sites and networks (and some of them were actually expired). A list of 21 fetish sites featuring alt talent had also been added, providing links to indie websites such as *crashpadseries.com* (owned by Pink and White Productions) as well as to the BDSM giant *Kink.com* and the Evil Angel network (that is, to 'the mainstream' par excellence); moreover, scrolling down the home page, we find a section dedicated to dead sites, which features a list of 68 items.[13]

In the context of the general crisis of the pornography industry, then, only a few enterprises have survived, whether thanks to their stronger ties with specific subcultural communities or to their ability in establishing more articulated connections with the industry as a whole.

What's the alternative? Alternative pornographies and the adult industry

In the introduction to his book *American Independent Cinema*, Geoff King gives a preliminary definition of independence in relation to US film production. For King, 'how "independence" is defined can vary in both form and degree' (2005: 1), according to 'the position of individual films, or filmmakers, in terms of [. . .] their industrial location, [. . .]

the kinds of formal/aesthetic strategies they adopt and [. . .] their relationship to the broader social, cultural, political or ideological landscape' (2). Borrowing these three variables and adapting them to contemporary US pornographic production, we can easily identify different forms and degrees of 'alternative'.

A website like *crashpadseries.com* (and its production company Pink and White), for instance, seems to 'operate at a distance from the mainstream in all three respects' (ibid.). First, they are a small business, located outside the big corporations – even geographically, as they are based in San Francisco and not in the San Fernando Valley – producing medium-to-low budget films. Second, their aesthetic and narrative choices differ from most of the average pornography (more emphasis on the performers' whole bodies and less on the genitals, and a rather developed self-reflexive attitude, for instance). Third, and moreover, a strong political drive (against heteronormativity and for inclusiveness) not only visibly influences their commercial strategies – as they adopt sustainable porn production practices (Blakovich, 2013) and a networked distribution channel, *pinklabel.tv*,[14] that supports other companies with a similar ethos – but also informs other important aspects of representation, such as the display of specific body types, gender orientations and sexual acts.

Other companies 'exist in a closer, sometimes symbiotic relationship with the [corporate porn] behemoth, offering a distinctive touch within more conventional frameworks' (King, 2005: 2). *Burningangel.com*, for instance, was created by 'alt queen' 'punk princess' Joanna Angel with her Rutgers University roommate as a 'very small experiment at first' (Love, 2013), and in 2013 it was still running, after 11 years in the industry, 'much like a startup' (ibid.). However, over time the site has developed a successful commercial strategy based on a careful balance of differentiation from and contiguity to so-called mainstream porn.

Burningangel.com overtly winks at specific subcultural tastes, primarily in the models' attire and physical features (dyed hair, tattoos, piercings, etc.) and through explicit (and honest) allusions to its identifying references and patterns: for instance, Angel's work as a director encompasses many horror-themed parodies and films inspired by the world of indie music and alternative lifestyles, one of which, *Band Sluts* (2013), also features a song by her own band, Joanna Angel and the Gigolos. A sense of community is conveyed by the free content offered by the site, which includes interviews with alternative bands, music and game reviews and personal writings by some of the site's models. At the same time, however, the sex displayed on the website seems to comply with some of the general standards of contemporary pornographic representation, and especially with the core features of sexual representation in gonzo production: maximum visibility, frequent use of POV, athletic and hyperbolic sexual acts with particular emphasis on anal and oral practices (double penetration, ass-to-mouth, gang bangs, deep throat, etc.) and external ejaculation (the so-called *money shot*, especially in the *Cum on My Tattoo* section).

In this way, a site like *burningangel.com* can be perfectly palatable for both subcultural aficionados and generalist porn consumers who do not dislike tattooed girls and boys. Thus it stands as an example of the hybridisation and migration practices between the galaxy of the alternative and the universe of the mainstream – or, as Cramer and Home (2007) would say, of the porn industry's ability to intercept promising trends and make the most of them in order to expand their audiences: more recently, in fact, *burningangel.com* has been acquired by porn conglomerate Gamma Entertainment (and its Netherlands-based subsidiary Chargepay B.V.), becoming part of a wider network that includes some of the most successful international websites and porn stars, such as Evil Angel, Rocco Siffredi, Girlsway, Girlfriends Films and Falcon Studios, among many others.

The acquisition of successful independent companies by big studio distributors has been a characteristic feature of the contemporary Hollywood industry since the early 1990s: in 1993, for instance, the Weinstein brothers sold Miramax to the Walt Disney Company for $60–80 million, while New Line was bought by Ted Turner for $500–600 million around the same time (King, 2005: 41). In other cases, the Hollywood majors themselves have created specific subsidiaries in order to enter the indie film market, for instance as happened when 20th Century Fox established Fox Searchlight in 1994. In a similar fashion, the porn colossus Vivid tried to jump on the alt wagon in 2006 by establishing its subsidiary Vivid Alt, for which it hired the 'bad boy art prankster' (Smith, 2014: 71) Eon McKai as a director and a 'figurehead' (72), thus capitalising on the success and critical acclaim of his first films distributed by porn company VCA (*Art School Sluts*, 2004 and *Kill Girl Kill 1–3*, 2005). With this alt division, a big pornographic studio was trying to diversify its branding strategy (Biasin and Zecca, 2009, 2010) by acquiring 'a very up-to-date persona' (Smith, 2014: 71) through the offer of 'edgier' content, once again creating a hybrid between corporate production practices and alternative themes and aesthetic choices.[15] Through this it also made 'evident the starkness of the inner distinctions in contemporary heteroporn' (Paasonen, 2014: 30).

Whatever their 'degree of distance' (King, 2005: 2) from the industrial articulation of corporate porn, US alt porn producers (even the most radical) are forced to share some production and distribution routines with (more) mainstream studios in order to survive in such a competitive and fast-developing market. *Indie Porn Revolution*, owned by queer icon Courtney Trouble, replaced *NoFauxxx.com* in 2012 and presents itself as the 'home to a true subcultural shift in sexuality',[16] whose 'ideas of authenticity [. . .] hold the adult industry hostage' (Trouble, 2012). The site's membership also grants access to two other websites, *queerporn.tv* and *Fat Girl Fantasies* (BBW star April Flores's *solo* site), thus adopting at a smaller scale one of the most common marketing strategies in commercial pornography – that is, the practice of attracting potential paying subscribers with the promise of exclusive and diversified content. Trouble Films (the company established by Trouble in 2011) also produces DVD and VOD films, presented in 'all sex' anthologies (as, for example, the *Fuck Styles* and the *Lesbian Curves* series), and films with a storyline (*Nostalgia*, *Bordello* and *Speakeasy*, 2009). This method of 'branching out' reproduces one of the main staples of commercial pornographic production, that is, the polarisation into two different styles – pseudo-documentary and all-sex gonzo vs plot-based narrative feature (see Federico Zecca's chapter in this volume).[17] Another example of alternative productions taking advantage of corporate practices can be observed in the structure of the previously mentioned website *crashpadseries.com*: based on the successful *The Crash Pad* (directed by Shine Louise Houston, 2005), it offers its members narrativised serialisation of the original film, with more than 160 episodes available in streaming VOD or included in numbered DVDs.

Subversive smut: identity politics and strategies of representations

Although related in many ways to the adult business and its industrial conventions, the pornographic materials ascribable to the niche of alternative pornography show some common distinctive traits that differentiate them from other pornographic forms (that are more generalist in their scope) – the most important of which is certainly their militant attitude. From Joanna Angel's public assertions of feminism (Angel, 2005) to the explicit political manifestos included on sites such as *queerporn.tv*, *doingitonline.com* or *pinklabel.tv*, the verbal and visual content of such pornographic enterprises associates hard-core sexual representation with other, more complex discourses concerning sexual identity and queer/feminist/subcultural visibility. In a context where most media marginalise (if not overtly misrepresent) non-conforming or radical sexualities and individuals, genderqueer porn star Jiz Lee observes, 'queer porn is one of the few mediums that can explicitly tell our stories' (2013: 275). In this sense, contemporary alternative pornographies take on an important social function, perpetuating the role traditionally played in the past by the circulation of 'low' erotic texts (such as lesbian pulp fiction or beefcake magazines) in the establishment of real and symbolic links between non-normative communities and individuals: 'in a society that has historically demanded silence and invisibility from sexually noncompliant persons, such "smut" has affirmed identities, promoted visibility, forged community, and combated imposed normativity' (Strub, 2015: 147).

Another much debated characteristic of alternative pornographies is their claims of 'realness' and 'authenticity' in the representation of both sexual pleasure and sexual/gender identities. For reasons of space, I will not discuss this aspect in detail, as it has also been already fully explored and problematised elsewhere (Attwood, 2012; Hardy, 2008; Maina, 2010, 2011; Van Doorn, 2010). I will just note *en passant* that, as Julie Levin Russo rightly states, the 'real' invoked (and produced) by alternative pornographies is not directly related to 'the innate sexuality of its producers' (2007: 249), being instead the result of the 'mobilization of recognizable markers of [a specific] subculture (e.g. butch bodies, tattoos and piercings, fetish attire)' (ibid.); in other words, it can be interpreted as a '*strategic real* that is meant to participate in the protean dynamics of community and identity building, not a pre-given real that appears transparently in the image' (ibid., emphasis added).

Moreover, as I have already mentioned, unlike many other generalist forms, alternative pornographies often show a marked self-reflexive attitude, apparent first of all in their easy-going and unconventional taste for 'citationality' (Lipton, 2012), genre play and comedic mash-up – as, for instance, in Pink and White's porn mockumentary about San Francisco lesbians, *The Wild Search* (dir. Houston, 2007), or Joanna Angel's self-parodic story about sex, tattoos and pizza, *LA Pink – A XXX Porn Parody* (2009). Perhaps Courtney Trouble's *Nostalgia* represents the most striking example of such citationality. In a detailed, almost scene-by-scene, gender-bending and queer remake of some Golden Age classics,[18] Trouble re-visits and re-writes the (pornography of the) past in a film-manifesto that tries to imagine a utopian (pornography of the) future. 'The viewer familiar with the earlier films super-imposes the queer imagery onto the original image in order to create a new "double exposure"' (Lipton, 2012: 202). In doing so, Trouble (perhaps accidentally) creates a sort of 'revisionist history' (ibid.) through the anachronistic (Rohy, 2006) re-appropriation of traditional hard-core pornography, which thereby becomes 'the direct antecedent to an affirming sex-positive movement, rather than the catalyst for decades of feminist political infighting' (Lipton, 2012: 202).[19]

Complementary to this strategy of self-reflexivity, two other representational 'tactics'[20] inform alternative porn's interrelation with specific gender and genre norms and constraints. In the short film *Biodildo* (dir. Christian Slaughter, 2012),[21] a perfect, (seemingly) heterosexual couple lives in a beautiful neighbourhood reminiscent of the suburban family home described by Paul B. Preciado ([2010] 2014) as the quintessential embodiment of monogamy. They start to perform what initially appears as heteronormative sex, but actually end up engaging in some 'innovative' sexual practices involving a 'surprising' vagina (the male performer Kay Garnellen being a FTM trans), a copious female ejaculation and a human penis used as a disembodied (bio)dildo. Paraphrasing (and partially 'poaching') Judith Butler, I have named this tactic 'parodic repetition': on several occasions, alternative pornographies dis-articulate heterosexual practices, symbols and visual repertoires, through a 'replication of heterosexual constructs in non-heterosexual frames' that ultimately 'brings into relief the utterly constructed status of the so-called heterosexual original' (Butler, 1990: 43).

Conclusion

In concluding, I will only briefly examine another representational practice (probably the most common) employed by alternative pornographies, which I call 'subversive re-appropriation'. Some of the (quite extreme) sexual practices represented in the hybrid queer-gonzo *Belladonna's Strapped Dykes* (dir. Belladonna, 2009)[22] could easily be interpreted, at a first glance, as strategies of 'grotesque degradation' (Langman, 2004) enacted on the body of the female performers, in a sort of compensatory fantasy for a male viewer enduring a socially generated crisis of masculinity. In the context of films such as *Strapped Dykes*, however, the self-conscious exaggeration, the paradoxical 'stretching' of the visual stereotypes and the absolute reciprocity – that is, the absence of fixed roles such as active/passive, penetrator/penetrated – create a 'subversion of enunciative positions' (Preciado [2000] 2002: 33) that totally changes the meaning of the pornographic display of bodies and acts. The gaping orifices, the fluids, the attire, the make-up, the (playful) violence: every aspect of the sexual scene is thus re-signified as an expression of enjoyment and empowerment rather than of degradation, in a continuous re-articulation of genre- (and gender-)imposed models.

Regardless of the differences in commercial positioning or aesthetic and political investment, the many and heterogeneous alternative pornographies manifest, through the specific features I have outlined in this chapter, a sort of 'overflowing' intensity compared to generalist pornography *tout court*, as it is perceived and constructed in current (academic and social) discourses. Borrowing André Bazin's notion of *sur-western*, Enrico Biasin, Federico Zecca and I have defined the microcosm of the alternative as *sur-porno* (2014: 16), that is, as a pornography that does not want 'to be just itself, and looks for some additional interest to justify its existence – an aesthetic, sociological, moral, psychological, political [...] interest, in short some quality extrinsic to the genre and which is supposed to enrich it' (Bazin [1957] 2005: 151) – a pornography that ultimately refuses to be 'just porn' and tries to find other meanings in a (sometimes straightforwardly oppositional) dialectics with something else, be it either 'the mainstream', or societal and cultural norms more generally.

Notes

1 See also Osterweil (2014).
2 José Capino (2011), though, suggests we should reconsider or, at least, problematise the dichotomy between 'golden age' porn as exclusively public and video/digital porn as totally private. See also Herzog (2008).
3 All translations from Italian are made by the author.
4 I am aware that the concept of 'subgenre' used to define feminist porn can be quite problematic (a similar problem concerns, *mutatis mutandis*, alternative porn, queer porn and other forms of pornography). According to Rick Altman's approach to genre, the *genrification* process (and, by extension, the establishment of a given subgenre) is defined by the cooperation of semantic ('common topics, shared plots, key scenes, character types, familiar objects or recognizable shots

and sounds' [Altman, 1999: 89]), syntactic ('plot structure, character relationships or image and sound montage' [ibid.]) and pragmatic elements (that is, different 'uses' of the genre, made by different users, such as audiences, critics, producers, etc.). While there seems to be a certain degree of agreement in the way in which locutions such as 'feminist porn' and 'alt porn' are employed by different media players and communities (industry, audiences, fans, cultural intermediaries), the variety of materials that can be, in one way or another, ascribed to these particular classes of products does not seem to share a sufficiently significant number of coherent semantic/syntactic elements to allow the use of the notion of subgenre without stretching a point. Unfortunately, at the moment there does not seem to be a better identifying term with which to refer to feminist or alt porn, as other notions (such as movement, style, market niche or discourse, for instance) fall short of its complexity in other (even more problematic) ways. Anyway, I think that the use of theoretical tools such as 'genre' and 'subgenre' as commonly accepted devices for the analysis of porn production needs to be further discussed.

5 See also Coopersmith (2008).
6 'BlueBlood background: get to know us', www.blueblood.com/about-us-blueblood.html (accessed 10 December 2015).
7 http://eroticfandom.com/fantasy-costumes.html (accessed 10 December 2015).
8 www.furrygirl.com/home.html (accessed 10 December 2015).
9 Many scholars and journalists have written about these and other similar companies and websites. For an extensive bibliography, see the two anthologies edited by Biasin et al. (2014) and Jacobs et al. (2007); see also Magnet (2007).
10 On the crisis of the adult industry, see, among others, Moye (2013); Rosen (2013); Theroux (2012).
11 https://web.archive.org/web/20040607002715/http://altporn.net/wp/ (accessed 10 December 2015).
12 https://web.archive.org/web/20080605003054/http://altporn.net/ (accessed 10 December 2015).
13 http://altporn.net (accessed 16 January 2016).
14 www.pinklabel.tv (accessed 10 December 2015).
15 A detailed account of Vivid Alt and Eon McKai is given in Smith (2014).
16 http://indiepornrevolution.com/indie-porn/ (accessed 10 December 2015).
17 On the opposition between gonzo and feature see Biasin and Zecca (2009) and Biasin and Zecca (2010).
18 *Behind the Green Door* (dir. Mitchell Brothers, 1972); *Deep Throat* (dir. Gerard Damiano, 1972); *The Devil in Miss Jones* (dir. Damiano, 1973); *Babylon Pink* (dir. Henri Pachard, 1979).
19 For a discussion of parodic imitation in *Nostalgia*, see also Schaschek (2014): 145–175.
20 I use the term 'tactic' here in the sense that Michel de Certeau has given to it, as 'an art of the weak' (1988 [1980]: 37) through which the non-powerful adapt (and resist) to rules and organisational strategies established at a 'superior' level.
21 Though produced in Germany, *Biodildo* can be considered as an example of transnational queer porn, as it is distributed by *pinklabel.tv* and stars US performer Jiz Lee.
22 For an extensive analysis of this film, see Maina (2014b).

Bibliography

Adamo, P. (2004) *Il porno di massa. Percorsi nell'hard contemporaneo*. Milan: Raffaello Cortina.
Altman, R. (1999) *Film/Genre*. London: BFI.
Angel, J. (2005) '. . . On being a feminist with a porn site'. In C. Milne (ed) *Naked Ambition: Women Who Are Changing Pornography*. New York: Carroll & Graf.
Attwood, F. (2007) 'No money shot? Commerce, pornography and new sex taste cultures'. *Sexualities*. Volume 10 (4): 441–456.
Attwood, F. (2010) '"Younger, paler, decidedly less straight": the new porn professionals'. In F. Attwood (ed) *porn.com: Making Sense of Online Pornography*. New York: Peter Lang.
Attwood, F. (2012) 'Art school sluts: authenticity and the aesthetics of alt porn'. In C. Hines and D. Kerr (eds) *Hard to Swallow: Hard-Core Pornography on Screen*. London: Wallflower Press.
Bazin, A. [1957] (2005) *What is Cinema? Volume 2*. Berkeley and London: University of California Press.

Biasin, E. and Zecca, F. (2009) 'Contemporary audiovisual pornography: branding strategy and gonzo film style'. *Cinéma & Cie: International Film Studies Journal*. Volume 10 (12): 139–145.

Biasin, E. and Zecca, F. (2010) 'Putting pornography in its place'. In P. Dubois, F. Monvoisin and E. Biserna (eds) *Extended Cinema. Le Cinéma gagne du terrain*. Udine: Campanotto.

Biasin, E., Maina, G. and Zecca, F. (2014) 'Introduction'. In E. Biasin, G. Maina and F. Zecca (eds) *Porn After Porn: Contemporary Alternative Pornographies*, Milan: Mimesis International.

Blakovich, S. (2013) 'Ethics and business: sustainable porn'. *Pinklabel.tv*. Online. www.pinklabel.tv/on-demand/ethics-business-sustainable-porn/ (accessed 10 December 2015).

Butler, H. (2004) 'What do you call a lesbian with long fingers? The development of lesbian and dyke pornography'. In L. Williams (ed) *Porn Studies*. Durham, NC: Duke University Press.

Butler, J. (1990) *Gender Trouble: Feminism and the Subversion of Identity*. New York: Routledge.

Capino, J. B. (2005) 'Seminal fantasies: Wakefield Poole, pornography, independent cinema and the avant-garde'. In C. Holmlund and J. Wyatt (eds) *Contemporary American Independent Film: From the Margins to the Mainstream*. London: Routledge.

Capino, J. B. (2011) 'Beyond porno chic'. *Jump Cut: A Review of Contemporary Media*, Volume 53. Online. www.ejumpcut.org/archive/jc53.2011/JBCapino/ (accessed 10 December 2015).

Ciuffoli, E. (2011) 'Sexercise yourself: porno *grassroots* e pratiche di *egocasting*'. In E. Biasin, G. Maina and F. Zecca (eds) *Il porno espanso. Dal cinema ai nuovi media*. Milan: Mimesis.

Coopersmith, J. (2008) 'Do-it-yourself pornography – the democratization of pornography'. In J. Grenzfurthner, G. Friesinger and D. Fabry (eds) *pr0nnovation? Pornography and Technological Innovation: monochrom's Arse Elektronika Anthology*. San Francisco: Re/Search.

Cramer, F. and Home, S. (2007) 'Pornographic coding'. In K. Jacobs, M. Janssen and M. Pasquinelli (eds) *C'Lick Me: A Netporn Studies Reader*. Amsterdam: Institute of Network Cultures.

de Certeau, M. [1980] (1988) *The Practice of Everyday Life*. Berkeley and London: University of California Press.

De Voss, D. (2002) 'Women's porn sites – spaces of fissure and eruption or "I'm a little bit of everything"'. *Sexuality & Culture*. Volume 6 (3): 75–94.

Hardy, Simon (2008) 'The pornography of reality'. *Sexualities*. Volume 11 (1–2): 60–64.

Herzog, A. (2008) 'In the flesh: space and embodiment in the pornographic peep show arcade'. *The Velvet Light Trap*. Volume 62: 29–43.

Jacobs, K. (2007) *Netporn: DIY Webculture and Sexual Politics*. Lanham: Rowman and Littlefield.

Jacobs, K., Janssen, M. and Pasquinelli, M. (eds) (2007) *C'Lick Me: A Netporn Studies Reader*. Amsterdam: Institute of Network Cultures.

Juffer, J. (1998) *At Home with Pornography: Women, Sex and Everyday Life*. New York: New York University Press.

King, G. (2005) *American Independent Cinema*. London and New York: I.B. Tauris.

Kleinhans, C. (2006) 'The change from film to video. Pornography: implications for analysis'. In P. Lehman (ed) *Pornography: Film and Culture*. New Brunswick: Rutgers University Press.

Langman, L. (2004) 'Grotesque degradation: globalization, carnivalization, and cyberporn'. In D. D. Waskul (ed) *net.seXXX. Readings on Sex, Pornography and the Internet*. New York: Peter Lang.

Lee, J. (2013) 'Uncategorized'. In T. Taormino, C. Parreñas Shimizu, C. Penley and M. Miller-Young (eds) (2013) *The Feminist Porn Book: The Politics of Producing Pleasure*. New York: The Feminist Press.

Levin Russo, J. (2007) '"The Real Thing": reframing queer pornography for virtual spaces'. In K. Jacobs, M. Janssen and M. Pasquinelli (eds) (2007) *C'Lick Me: A Netporn Studies Reader*. Amsterdam: Institute of Network Cultures.

Lewis, J. (2002) *Hollywood v. Hard Core: How the Struggle over Censorship Created the Modern Film Industry*. New York: New York University Press.

Lipton, S. (2012) 'Trouble ahead: pleasure, possibility and the future of queer porn'. *New Cinemas: Journal of Contemporary Film*. Volume 10 (2–3): 197–207.

Love, D. (2013) 'This Brooklyn-born woman is porn's most successful entrepreneur'. 22 September. *Business Insider*. Online. www.businessinsider.com/joanna-angel-burning-angel-2013-9?IR=T (accessed 10 December 2015).

Magnet, S. (2007) 'Feminist sexualities, race, and the Internet: an investigation of *SuicideGirls.com*'. *New Media & Society*. Volume 9 (4): 577–602.

Maina, G. (2010) 'When porn meets identity: self-representation, art and niche market in alternative porn'. In P. Dubois, F. Monvoisin and E. Biserna (eds) *Extended Cinema. Le Cinéma gagne du terrain*. Udine: Campanotto.

Maina, G. (2011) 'Piaceri identitari e (porno)subculture'. In E. Biasin, G. Maina and F. Zecca (eds) *Il porno espanso. Dal cinema ai nuovi media*. Milan: Mimesis.

Maina, G. (ed) (2014a) 'After *The Feminist Porn Book*: further questions about feminist porn'. Forum Special Issue, *Porn Studies*. Volume 1 (1–2): 182–205.

Maina, G. (2014b) 'Grotesque empowerment: *Belladonna's Strapped Dykes* between mainstream and queer'. In E. Biasin, G. Maina and F. Zecca (eds) *Porn After Porn: Contemporary Alternative Pornographies*. Milan: Mimesis International.

Moye, D. (2013) 'Porn industry in decline: insiders adapt to piracy, waning DVD sales'. 19 January. *Huffington Post*. Online. www.huffingtonpost.com/2013/01/19/porn-industry-in-decline_n_2460799.html (accessed 10 December 2015).

Osgerby, B. (2014) 'Porn to be wild: identity and the aesthetics of "Otherness" in subcultural erotica'. In E. Biasin, G. Maina and F. Zecca (eds) *Porn After Porn: Contemporary Alternative Pornographies*. Milan: Mimesis International.

Osterweil, A. (2004) 'Andy Warhol's *Blow Job*: toward the recognition of a pornographic avant-garde'. In L. Williams (ed) *Porn Studies*. Durham, NC: Duke University Press.

Osterweil, A. (2014) *Flesh Cinema: The Corporeal Turn in American Avant-Garde Film*. Manchester: Manchester University Press.

Paasonen, S. (2014) 'Things to do with the alternative: fragmentation and distinction in online porn'. In E. Biasin, G. Maina and F. Zecca (eds) *Porn After Porn: Contemporary Alternative Pornographies*. Milan: Mimesis International.

Preciado, B. [2000] (2002) *Manifesto contra-sessuale*. Milan: Il Dito e la Luna.

Preciado, B. [2010] (2014) *Pornotopia: An Essay on Playboy's Architecture and Biopolitics*. New York: Zone Books.

Ray, A. (2007) *Naked on the Internet: Hookups, Downloads, and Cashing in on Internet Sexploration*. Emeryville, CA: Seal Press.

Rohy, V. (2006) 'Ahistorical'. *GLQ: A Journal of Lesbian and Gay Studies*. Volume 12 (1): 61–83.

Rosen, D. (2013) 'Is the Internet killing the porn industry?' 30 May. *Salon*. Online. www.salon.com/2013/05/30/is_success_killing_the_porn_industry_partner/ (accessed 10 December 2015).

Schaschek, S. (2014) *Pornography and Seriality: The Culture of Producing Pleasure*. Basingstoke and New York: Palgrave.

Smith, C. (2007) *One for the Girls! The Pleasures and Practices of Reading Women's Porn*. Bristol: Intellect.

Smith, C. (2014) '"It's important that you don't smell a suit on this stuff": aesthetics and politics in alt porn'. In E. Biasin, G. Maina and F. Zecca (eds) *Porn After Porn: Contemporary Alternative Pornographies*. Milan: Mimesis International.

Stokes, P. (2005) '"We want our porn and we want it now!" The youth market: who is it, why is it, and what does it mean for retailers?' AVN. Online. http://web.archive.org/web/20051103012000/www.adultvideonews.com/cover/cover1105_01.html (accessed 10 December 2015).

Strub, W. (2015) 'Queer smut, queer rights'. In L. Comella and S. Tarrant (eds) *New Views on Pornography: Sexuality, Politics, and the Law*. Santa Barbara, Denver and Oxford: Praeger.

Taormino, T., Parreñas Shimizu, C., Penley, C. and Miller-Young, M. (eds) (2013) *The Feminist Porn Book: The Politics of Producing Pleasure*. New York: The Feminist Press.

Theroux, L. (2012) 'How the internet killed porn'. 5 June. *The Guardian*. Online. www.theguardian.com/culture/2012/jun/05/how-internet-killed-porn (accessed 10 December 2015).

Tomlin, A. (2002) 'Sex, dreads and rock'n'roll'. 15 December. *Bitch*. Online. http://bitchmagazine.org/article/suicide-girls (accessed 10 December 2015).

Trouble, C. (2012) 'NoFauxxx.com is now Indie Porn Revolution'. 23 October. *Indie Porn Revolution Blog*. Online. http://indiepornrevolution.com/indie-porn/nofauxxx-com-is-now-indie-porn-revolution/ (accessed 10 December 2015).

Van der Graf, S. (2004) 'Blogging business: SuicideGirls.com'. *M/C Journal*, Volume 7 (4). Online. http://journal.media-culture.org.au/0410/07_suicide.php (accessed 10 December 2015).

Van Doorn, N. (2010) 'Keeping it real: user-generated pornography, gender reification, and visual pleasure'. *Convergence*. Volume 16 (4): 411–430.

Williams, L. (1999) *Hard Core: Power, Pleasure, and the 'Frenzy of the Visible'*. Berkeley and London: University of California Press.

Williams, L. (2004) 'Porn studies: proliferating pornographies on/scene: an introduction'. In L. Williams (ed) *Porn Studies*. Durham: Duke University Press.

Zecca, F. (2011) 'Porn in transition. Per una storia della pornografia americana'. In E. Biasin, G. Maina and F. Zecca (eds) *Il porno espanso. Dal cinema ai nuovi media*, Milan: Mimesis.

Ziegler, C. (2003) 'Orgasm addict: punk porn gets off on the Internet'. 23 January. *OC Weekly*. Online. www.ocweekly.com/2003-01-30/features/orgasm-addict/ (accessed 10 December 2015).

15
'NOT ON PUBLIC DISPLAY'
The art/porn debate

Gary Needham

As someone who likes both art and pornography, I have never been troubled by the way that those categories are treated by others like oil and water, or like the abject contiguity of fluids in Andres Serrano's *Blood and Semen II* (1990). There is a good deal of either/or thinking, policing and regulating, disavowal, even outlawing, that keeps art and pornography at odds with one another. As a teenager in the dark decades of 1980s UK censorship, when hardcore pornography was still illegal and sexual representations heavily regulated (especially gay ones), I knew you could find sexually explicit content in art books. Much to my disappointment, someone had already ripped the good pages from one Robert Mapplethorpe book in Glasgow's public library, leaving me with nothing but flower stems, portraits and classical nudes. I recently purchased from London bookshop Foyles the visual culture magazine *Kaleidescope*'s 'Art & Sex Edition' (2015) – note, 'sex' rather than 'pornography' is used here – which offers a good survey of contemporary artists working in different media who take sex *and* pornography as their subject. On page 146, an image by photographer Jeff Burton called *Untitled #211 (Hand in Butt)* (2006) depicts a male gay porn actor with his arm twisted behind his back inserting his own fist inside his ass. In the UK, legislation on 'extreme pornography' has declared that if you or I – as lay people, not artists – produce, own or circulate an image of anal fisting, we could be in trouble with the law; fisting is effectively banned from pornographic magazines and films available from retail outlets. However, if we know where to look, *Kaleidescope* presents us with an 'extreme image' on the high street. What allows the reproduction of Jeff Burton's photograph in an art context when that image depicts an act that is otherwise illegal in pornography in the UK? This is a question that ebbs at the fragile boundary of what distinguishes, or in some cases refuses to distinguish, the legal, aesthetic and interpretative line between art and porn. This chapter is about 'the problem' with distinction and lack of resolve between definitions of art and pornography, and how various disciplines (art history, philosophy, the law) make sense of it.

Historical, contemporary, cultural, legal and moral battles are fought over art, its legitimacy, its funding – particularly when sex becomes the subject or when sex enters into relation with other subjects such as religion, death, children, politics. Definitions of art and pornography and art/porn find themselves caught in the ever-shifting climates of tolerance and politics so that it is possible to infer that pornography is what conservative states call art when they want to remove funding, censor or destroy work. One recent instance of this occurred in 2014 at London's Mall Gallery when Leena McCall's *Portrait of Ms Ruby Ray, Standing* was deemed to be pornographic because pubic hair was visible in the painting. This work, by a female artist, about female sexuality, and selected by the Society for Women Artists (SWA), was challenged by the gallery management, who removed the work and made the following statement:

> As an educational arts charity, the federation has a responsibility to its trustees and to the children and vulnerable adults who use its galleries and learning centre. After a number of complaints regarding the depiction of the subject and taking account of its location en route for children to our learning centre, we requested the painting was removed.[1]

This situation is not unusual. The first art-historical book to construct a dialogue between the terms 'art' and 'pornography' – when pornography was not yet *Deep Throat* (1972) – was Morse Peckham's *Art and Pornography*, from 1969. Peckham appears to defend both art and pornography in suggesting that there is compatibility between the two: his argument is built through examples from East Asian art and Japanese *Shunga*. Yet *Art and Pornography* has long been discredited – not for its accommodation of pornography, but for the lack of specificity around Peckham's definition of art.[2] More recently, Kelly Dennis' *Art/Porn* draws upon a range of historical and contemporary examples to get to the core of what defines the aesthetic and affective dimensions of art/porn: her subtitle *Seeing and Touching* indicates it might be located in sense and affect. Tracing a lineage from classical sculpture to contemporary installations and internet porn, Dennis proposes that haptic concepts of 'touch' are a key feature of art/porn works whose power is in the moving of 'our own flesh' and the dissolution of critical distance (2009: 1). Thus proximity and affect define an art/porn dynamic in which there is an erasure of the distance often assumed necessary to art objectivity. The potential in this ambitious approach, and what debates about pornography can learn from art, is that pornography need not be defined in relation to rigid models of objectification either.

Dennis' art-historical account is one of a number of ways in which scholars and critics from a wide range of disciplines have attempted to grapple with the difficulty arising from artistic representations, whether in sculpture, painting, photography or moving image, that are sexually explicit or directly invoke a relationship with pornography, transgression and obscenity. Within the art/porn frame, there are three main disciplinary approaches to the debate: the aesthetic, the philosophical and the legal.

1   The aesthetic debate tends to focus on issues of form and medium that supersede the content of the work. This often leads to arguments that take composition, brushstroke, materials, installation context, lighting, and so on as artistic defence against the accusation that the work is pornography. For example, the representation of anal fisting in Mapplethorpe's *Helmut and Brooks* (1978) is often discussed at the expense of the artist's agency as a gay man; thus Mapplethorpe's series of photographs of the art director 'Helmut' and his partner 'Brooks' (including *Fist Fuck* and *Double Fist Fuck*, both 1978) are reduced to matters of angle and composition, with Helmut's submerged arm 'read' like the stem of a calla lily – thereby disavowing the queer kinship and relationality of fist-fucking practices and communities of the 1970s.
2   The philosophical debate makes a case for art and pornography as mutually exclusive even when the representation is, in the case of Jeff Koons' *Made in Heaven* series, a

simulacrum of pornography. Philosophers would argue that *Made in Heaven* can't be both, because art and pornography ask for different responses, reducible to appreciation vis-à-vis sexual arousal.

3   The legal debate is the third and potentially most problematic, since there has been a shift from recognising offence to morals and sensibilities towards prosecution and criminalisation. Shifting legal definitions and the move from obscenity to harm seek to definitively distinguish art from pornography. The definition of art/porn moves to the realm of managers, committees, judges and police officers, rather than that of curators, moral guardians, art critics and philosophers. Art/porn is cast as a threat to social order; it may exemplify and test the fault line in representational and categorical boundaries.

The Origin of the World/the origin of pornography

A useful starting point for art/porn questions is the nineteenth-century work *L'Origine du monde/The Origin of the World* (1866). *L'Origine du monde* is an oil-on-canvas work by Gustave Courbet, fairly small in fact (18 in × 22 in), that depicts 'a reclining woman, her legs spread apart, her garment lifted to the level of her breasts and her luxuriant pubic thatch exposed to the viewer' (Danto 2001: 42). Can *L'Origine du monde* be both a work of art and a work of pornography? Can it satisfy both artistic and pornographic appreciations and desires? In Linda Nochlin's words, it represents 'the cunt – forbidden site of specularity and ultimate object of male desire' (1986: 76).[3]

A number of libidinous contexts orbit around Courbet's *L'Origine*. The mid-nineteenth century is knowingly both sex- and *sexe*-obsessed. The century sees the publication of the sex journal *My Secret Life* (1888), the emergence of the medical specialism of gynaecology, the 'invention' of pornography as a generic category of photography (Hunt, 1993) and the establishment of 'special sections' and 'secret archives' in libraries and museums (Kendrick, 1997), and the term pornography enters the OED in 1857. Photography's indexical nature, its 'excess of realism' (Williams 1995: 4), arrives in a timely fashion to counteract the possibility that paint and pigment accurately render hardcore – as Solomon-Godeau (1991) has argued, the photograph invents pornography as a new genre precisely because it does not ape the forms and conventions of representation in preceding art forms. Another way of not talking about Courbet as porn is in reference to his use of perspective, yet this is perhaps a crucial aspect that positions us at a moment of sexual action, inferring an ideal position for cunnilingus. Such down-below perspectives have not been lost on feminist art historians tracing Courbet back to precursors such as Durer's *Draughtsman Drawing a Nude* (1538); Haraway suggests this is 'the disciplining screen between art and pornography. . . paradigmatically erected' (1997: 30). Both Haraway and Dennis see Durer's lesson in perspective as foundational to representations of the female nude and argue that the female body figures 'prominently in accounts of the emergence of modern ways of seeing' (Haraway, 1997: 32).

Many artists, particularly women and feminists, have reimagined both Durer's perspectival grid and Courbet's *sexe* in order to investigate the proliferating meanings and responses in depicting women's genitalia. However, women artists who use vaginal or yonic imagery (Georgia O'Keefe, Judy Chicago, Hannah Wilke, Betty Tompkins, Zoe Leonard), or even speak of such things (performance artists Karen Finley and Kembra Pfhaler), are usually marginalised by art history. Censorship, withdrawal of funding, being overlooked by critics and lack of exhibition possibilities have all troubled women artists who dare to represent their own sex in relation to sexual explicitness, sometimes through abstraction, or bodily function (Judy Chicago's *Red Flag*, 1971), or in reference to the codes and conventions associated with pornography. Betty Tompkins, whose work often comprises close-ups of heterosexual vaginal penetration, is explicit in her historical reference to both Courbet's *L'Origine* and the 'meat shot' in her *Cunt Grid #13 (Courbet)* (2007) and *Cunt Painting #7 (Courbet)* (2007). Orlan references Courbet in *L'origine de la guerre/The Origin of War* (1989), maintaining the framing and position of the body but flipping its gender in representing a rather ordinary male body and his modest erect penis. In contrast to Courbet and the male artist's nineteenth-century privilege, the majority of twentieth-century art so concerned with the nether regions of women is more often the work of women than of men. An important lineage of vaginal art exploration can be traced from Georgia O'Keefe's floral imagery through to the most iconic of feminist art works of the late twentieth century, Judy Chicago's *The Dinner Party* (1979), and up to even more contemporary works like Tracey Emin's Duchamp-titled *A Cunt Is a Rose Is a Cunt* (2009) and her neon *My Cunt Is Wet With Fear* (1998). Furthermore, in *Origin of the Universe 2* (2012), Mickalene Thomas not only reclaims *L'Origine* but also intersects it with race. This *Origin* would seem to have no ending.

The formal argument

The *Musee D'Orsay* in Paris, home of *L'Origine du monde*, counters any suggestion that *L'Origine* is pornographic by foregrounding the painterly-ness of the work. Technique, form and materiality provide critical and moral defence; thus the spectre of pornography is 'surrounded with enough art history to neutralize it' (Danto, 2001: 44). Photography and the moving image have a tougher job in mounting such defences because of their indexical relation to reality, in that a penis *is* a penis and not a brushstroke; this is perhaps nowhere more true than in the case of Robert Mapplethorpe, whose photography has been at the heart of art/porn censorship debates. Mapplethorpe's work, as Danto writes,

> was the most controversial art in America, raising so many issues of the limits of art, of the obligations of institutions of patronage supported by tax money to the moral codes of taxpayers, of the relationship of beauty and content, that, just for starters, one could not think about his art without touching on expression, democracy, freedom, censorship, the right to exhibit, the right to see, the right to make art.
>
> *(Danto 2001: 2)*

Mapplethorpe has been the straw man in both the Left and Right positions on art and pornography: the former hold him up in relation to freedom of expression, whereas the latter use him to reinforce morally conservative approaches to funding and the acceptable limits of art. The Right latched on to Mapplethorpe's death from AIDS in stressing that the art, contagiously, inherently, was also sick. Mapplethorpe's career is also a history of censorship in the arts, with his 1978 exhibition of the *X Portfolio* held up as threshold and litmus test between definitions of art and pornography; the portfolio was only recently exhibited in full, at LACMA in 2012.[4] The *X Portfolio* is a work of 13 photographs that includes the previously mentioned *Helmut and Brooks*; the defiant *Self-Portrait* (1978), with a bullwhip in his ass; *Jim and Tom, Sausalito* (1977; the one in which Jim is pissing in Tom's mouth); *Lou,*

NYC (1978, Lou's own finger used as a urethral sound); and one photograph of a bloodied penis 'crucified' on a wooden board, taken from the longer series of images with super-masochist *Richard* (1978).

The brouhaha around the X *Portfolio* is interesting since, in addition to their status as representations of gay BDSM subculture – as kinship, community and queer relationality, which is how I read those images – Mapplethorpe clearly selected the 13 based on their formal qualities rather than their apparent ability to shock and upset those of normative, censorious and right-wing dispositions. The 'scat and piss' photographs from the *Dominic and Elliot* series from 1979 (which includes a widely reproduced portrait of the couple) are likely considered unexhibitable, as is the complete *Richard* series from 1978; that series includes the before (a nail being hammered through the head of Richard's penis) and after (blood dripping from Richard's urethra), *contra* the more formally obvious 'Catholic image' of Richard's crucified penis.

The art/porn Mapplethorpe scandal, and the assertion of steadfastly polarised positions regarding it, fully emerged around the posthumous exhibition *The Perfect Moment* – a controversy which came to define the US 'war of culture' (Dubin, 1992; Steiner, 1995). The 'scandal' of Mapplethorpe spread far and wide as offending pages were discreetly cut out (including at my own university), monographs of his work were quietly removed from public libraries and a collection of Mapplethorpe photographs with an introduction by Arthur C. Danto was not so quietly removed from the library of University of Central England.[5] The title of Arthur Danto's canonical *Playing with the Edge* borrows from Mapplethorpe's own description of his work as a 'play with the edge' (1995: 76). The 'edge' is that oblique between art/porn, its danger lying in the lack of separation between sexually explicit gay content (i.e. fisting) and the subversion of art-historical conventions (i.e. portraiture reconfigured through SM relations). Mapplethorpe was aware, before there even was an art/porn debate, that the edge was worth exploring, as he recounts:

> I think it could be pornography and still have redeeming social value. It can be both, which is my whole point in doing it – to have all the elements of pornography and yet have a structure of lighting that makes it go beyond what it is.
> *(Danto, 1995: 89–91)*

Before his ascendency in the world of art photography, Mapplethorpe had already appropriated images from gay pornography (*Black XXX*, 1970; *Red Bag*, 1971; *Green Bag*, 1971) as a dialogue in his work. In some sense fascinated by what he perceived as the often art-less nature of pornography, Mapplethorpe

> ... wanted people to see that even those extremes could be made into art. [I wanted to] take those pornographic images and make them somehow transcend the images [of pornography]. And I think the best of those pictures do that, again because of the composition. I think that is an accomplishment. It was a problem that I set out to solve.
> *(Mapplethorpe in Levas, 1999: 14)*

What Mapplethorpe also represents, and conservatives find particularly difficult to take, is the reification of the frank truth of gay sex, SM in particular – the materiality of the gay body *in extremis* and loving it, and all daring to be aligned with established conventions of form, classicism and portraiture. It is the doubling up of disciplines, the artist's and the sadomasochist's – what Douglas Crimp refers to as 'the line between the aesthetics of traditional museum culture and the prerogatives of a self-defining gay subculture' (1993: 7). Richard Meyer characterises this, alternatively, as a *'cross-coding'* between sadomasochism and pornography, as *'over-laying the visual codes* of sadomasochism and art photography' (1993: 364). Mapplethorpe's images are irrefutable in their gay specificity, in their SM specificity, in treating the men and their practices as one would a regal portrait or a still life. It is a celebration of both subculture and its transcendence through art, yet the images are not intended to transcend the sexual arousal that art criticism would like to disavow and disengage.

For the Right there is no issue here – these images are, by definition of their content, abject pornography, and thus precluded from any associations with art by content alone. For the Left, defending Mapplethorpe's freedom is a constitutional issue: the point is not to defend the images in terms of their gayness but rather in terms of their form, thus 'reducing them to abstractions, lines and forms, light and shadow' (Crimp 1993: 10). Accordingly, both positions actually seek to eradicate the gay specificity of the art/porn image through condemnation or disavowal. In the catalogue for *The Perfect Moment*, exhibition curator Janet Kardon, who defended Mapplethorpe in court, refers not to gay men but to 'models' and 'inhabitants', who are 'often depicted in uncommon sexual acts' and 'assume gestures governed by geometry . . . against minimal backgrounds' (1989: 10). The truths of gay life, of the subcultural kinship in SM and of Mapplethorpe's own sexuality and agency as shaping his practice are, alas, nowhere to be found in this avoidance of the gayness of the imagery. In terms of the art/porn debate, the point I am trying to raise here is that this defence of art against pornography may be no better than the Right's outright condemnation, as both positions seek to destroy the pleasures of art and its relationship to pornography and sexual specificity. If Mapplethorpe is reducible to 'just art' then it suggests that sexual explicitness is not a unique condition of pornography, that even the most sexually explicit or transgressive indexical representations, like fisting, can be art if executed by an artist. But this comes at the expense of identity, context and agency, which are necessary political conditions of both queer and feminist art practice.

The philosophical debate

A more recent debate on art and pornography has emerged in the context of philosophy, organised around the mutual exclusivity of definitions. In these dialectical models of argumentation, there is Art, which is to be appreciated because it is complex and sophisticated and engages one intellectually. Pornography, on the other hand, is crude and simplistic and 'something' to be consumed, not appreciated; 'something' because philosophers, in their otherwise complex understanding of Art, never seem able to provide any concept of pornography that isn't vague, homogenous, generalising or monolithic.

In the journal *Philosophy and Literature*, Jerrold Levinson instigated debate with an argument in relation to erotic art, which he champions, and pornography, which he understands as crude and valueless. This argument reduces art/porn to a matter of appreciation/consumption, with Levinson stating that the concept of 'pornographic art' is itself an oxymoron (2005: 229). Levinson outlines the 'appreciation problem' approach to art/porn, but in order to champion 'erotic art' or sexually explicit art, he defaults to reducing pornography to the 'morally objectionable' category (230). He states that 'there is an *appreciative problem* about pornographic art, which makes it impossible to appreciate an object as art and pornography at the same time because attention to its artistic aspect entails inattention to its pornographic aspect, and vice versa' (235–6). Christy Mag Uidhir (2009) responded to Levinson with a title that appeared to have already reached a conclusion – 'Why Pornography Can't Be Art' – and asserted that 'it is *impossible* for something to be both art and pornography' (emphasis added: 193). Though Uidhir challenges Levinson's moralising position, the argument still proceeds to make a case for mutual exclusivity. His argument is more nuanced in making reference to *Red Butt*, from Jeff Koons' *Made in Heaven* series (1991),[6] as evidence that some art can in fact be sexually arousing. Even so, the work of art's specificity *as art* is nonetheless not easily reduced to a set of shared experiences or features between art and pornography. It is unclear whether Uidhir is referring to *Red Butt (Distance)* or *Red Butt (Close Up)*, even though there are important differences between the two works – *Close Up* is a typical close-up 'meat shot' of anal sex between Koons and Staller and certainly reproduces the porn convention of the meat shot; in fact, Staller wears the same signature look as that in her Italian porn films. However, the 'fact' that *Red Butt (Close Up)* was created by an artist, featuring his penis, allows for its definition and contextualisation as art. *Red Butt (Close Up)* is 'appreciated' as postmodern, reflexive pastiche, regardless of the hardcore content that, in some of the series' photographs at least, would otherwise be indistinguishable from a page in *Hustler* in all but the size of the work (usually 122" × 96") and the context of display (the art gallery).

However, there are no examples from pornography to balance Uidhir's argument. This lack of references to works of pornography either by title, genre, media or textual example represents an impasse, possibly even a failure, in the philosophical discourses on art and pornography. Pornography remains, in these assessments, vague – a largely undefined and homogenous category against which a range of art examples can be designated as *better*. In demonstrating no knowledge or understanding of *actual* pornography, it is safe to assume that porn is simply another straw man in a dialectical argument in which the outcome is known in advance – that art can't be porn and porn can't be art. Furthermore, these arguments fail to address those artists whose work actively tests art/porn distinctions as their *raison d'être* (John Currin, Jeff Burton, Slavo Mogutin, Marc Garrett, Terry Richardson), who take pornography or explicit sex as the subject matter of their art (Fiona Banner, Monica Majoli, John Waters, Jason Salavon) and who have sometimes created pornography in conjunction with or alongside their art (Andy Warhol, Nobuyoshi Araki, Richard Kern).

The debates, arguments and advances in philosophy are important, but in their failure to address pornography itself (there are no examples of pornography cited, nor acknowledgement of the different forms that pornography takes), it is difficult to trust their conclusions. There are good examples of moving-image pornography that is art, such as Andy Warhol's *Couch* (1964), *Three* (1964) and *Blue Movie* (1968), in addition to examples aspiring to be art, such as *L.A. Plays Itself* (Fred Halsted, 1972) and *Café Flesh* (Stephen Sayadian, 1982). Pornography, in this line of philosophical argument, seemingly only exists to demonstrate the other side of a binary: of lack of aesthetic value, of moral purpose or of an inability to foster a sense of appreciation.

The legal argument

It is now common to find warnings, age limits and age verifications as a necessary condition to enter the public spaces of art (galleries and museums) or to gain public access to art via institutional online repositories. There is a fear around sex in art – that 'minors' encountering art may be intellectually unable to distinguish between art and pornography, that funding may be in jeopardy following public complaints, that art and porn, in the minds of some, are no different from one another. In the current climate of right-wing resurgence across Europe and elsewhere, galleries are playing it safe. The 2014 Mapplethorpe retrospective at the Grand Palais in Paris had an age limit of 16 for the main exhibition, which was further raised to 18 in 'special areas' of the exhibition. Patrons were warned before crossing the imaginary line – to step over indicated informed consent, and set up the Mapplethorpe exhibit as *a priori* inviting visitors to take a risk. The curatorial choices on display failed to deliver on that invitation. Perhaps the Grand Palais feared the vandalism that often befalls art works of this nature. In the same year in Paris, Paul McCarthy's cheeky *Christmas Tree* (2014) – in fact a giant inflatable green sculpture of a butt plug installed in Place Vendome – saw the artist physically attacked and the work serially vandalised.

Two new major exhibitions of Mapplethorpe's work in Los Angeles in 2016 – *The Perfect Medium*, at the Getty and LACMA – aimed to contextualise the culture wars around 1988's *The Perfect Moment*, but this ambition to include everything excludes the two 'controversial images' of naked children that were part of the original obscenity trial. According to LACMA curator Britt Slavesen, the photograph of the child *Jesse McBride* (1976) is 'not crucial to an understanding of Mapplethorpe as an artist'. Yet one could argue it is crucial to understanding how the aggressive and homophobic censorship of Mapplethorpe's work (as that of a gay man who died from AIDS) collapses into anxiety around the non-sexual nudity of minors (Harris, 2016). The problem here is the paranoid and unfounded contiguity between the different categories of Mapplethorpe's work as somehow related to one another.

Recently, pornography (and thus art/porn) has found itself at a crossroads in law, hence further complicating the 'edge', where it is entirely possible that Mapplethorpe's *Helmut and Brooks* could be caught under the legal category of 'extreme pornography'. The UK's Criminal Justice and Immigration Act spells out 'extreme pornography' as that which depicts in realistic fashion sexual acts which could result in damage to the breasts, genitals or anus; in addition, the Act effectively bans all depictions of bestiality and necrophilia. The photographs from X *Portfolio* might qualify as extreme under the legislation, as would Andres Serrano's *The History of Sex* (1997). *The History of Sex* contains all the 'extremes' (watersports, fisting, bestiality), yet was widely exhibited across Europe and North American between 1997 and 1998. Could *The History of Sex* be exhibited in the UK now, even with informed consent? Would Serrano and the curators be in the dock for the possession and public display of 'extreme pornography' as defined under English legislation? This 'problem' also reveals the contextual shifts and periodisation in which the definitions of works may change from art to porn, reclassified from one decade to another, or vice versa (for example, Tom of Finland has shifted from porn to art).

The representation of fisting in *Helmut and Brooks* and Serrano's *Pieta* image (blasphemous too) could otherwise be classified as 'extreme pornography', since the law interprets fisting as one of the many acts that 'threatens a person's life' and cannot be indexically represented lawfully. Art on the subject of fisting has not been tested in the UK courts since the legislation was passed in 2008. It is still to be determined whether the owning and publishing of art works by someone like Mapplethorpe would be protected by the aura of art rather than prosecuted as photographic documents of 'extreme' and 'injurious' acts against a person's body, even if the subjects consented to those acts and the works have been previously exhibited and published. Underpinning this are fears of the normalisation of 'extreme sexual acts' (Attwood and Smith, 2010), understood as a perceived threat to authority and social order. These fears hide behind loaded terms such as 'harm' and 'deviance', claiming intentions to protect children but circumventing important questions of consent and expression. The outcome effectively censors art work by feminists, queers and minorities through arbitrary application of what is extreme; worryingly, definitions are left to non-specialists whose deliberations are rarely open to scrutiny.

Conclusion

This era of curatorial self-censoring, state regulation and NSFW culture conforms to what Elizabeth Mansfield (2005) terms the 'new iconoclasm'. Mansfield is concerned with the contexts of new legislation in the US around child pornography and the consequences this has for art, since the distinctions between reality and representation collapse 'into a single policeable category' (2005: 24). This new iconoclasm is in alignment with the potential inability to see complexity and negotiation at work not just in art/porn but also in representation more generally. In that sense there is an emerging crisis in art's being defined as art, seen in the exclusion of the *Jesse McBride* portrait from the Mapplethorpe exhibition, but even more so when art touches sexual explicitness, pornography and extremity. Art may in fact be usefully contributing to what Attwood and Smith refer to as 'the crisis over the meaning of porn' (2010: 182), and one may take that further here in suggesting that the crisis in meaning in relation to both art and pornography is what now defines art/porn. Nonetheless, art and its circulation, distribution, critical–intellectual framing, gallery and exhibition context and sales in auction houses all operate in different modes and contexts from those of pornography. Questions such as what distinguishes art from pornography, what makes art and pornography indistinct and what characterises pornographic art and artistic pornography are questions like those centred on *media effects* – endlessly explored, yet never to be answered and always producing entrenched positions on either side. The bigger question here is: why does it even matter? Of course, it *will* matter when someone is arrested for having a folder containing Mapplethorpe images on their iPad.

Notes

1 http://leenamccall.com/news/2014/7/2/eroticcensorship-the-mall-galleries-responds (accessed 26 August 2016).
2 Peckham's definition of art includes a range of popular visual culture artefacts, such as comics, which would have drawn ire from art history and criticism not yet accommodating of the 'the popular'.
3 *L'Origine du monde* was once an art history 'mystery' – endlessly reproduced and copied, but Courbet's original painting itself was missing until the late 1980s. The multitude of poor-quality reproductions and copies of Courbet's original, according to Nochlin, makes *L'Origine* 'literally indistinguishable from standard, mass pornography' (Nochlin 1986: 84). The painting's status as a work of sexual interest was confirmed when it turned up in the collection of Jacques Lacan's family. Lacan was the owner of the painting from the 1950s – we should not lose the irony of his ownership being kept secret (surely *L'Origine* is the ultimate high-culture porn stash), thereby illustrating one of the key themes of psychoanalytic theory, castration anxiety.
4 The photographs also measure 19.5 × 19.5 which is near enough the same as Courbet's *L'Origine*, and, like the painting, the *X Portfolio* was originally for private ownership rather than public display. Both works shift in context and meaning, and reception, when placed in the gallery.
5 The book *Mapplethorpe*, by Robert Mapplethorpe with an introduction by Arthur C. Danto (1992), offers a definitive collection of Mapplethorpe's black-and-white photographs, from the early Polaroids to the self-portraits taken shortly before his death. In the UCE case, the West Midlands Police Paedophile and Pornography Squad removed the book from the university library in 1997 and threatened to imprison the Vice Chancellor unless he agreed to the destruction of the book.

A full account of this incident can be found at https://web.archive.org/web/20021112205909/http://www.uce.ac.uk/mapplethorpe/ (accessed 25 August 2016).

6 *Made in Heaven* is a series of large, wall-sized, photographs and glass sculptures of Koons and his then wife Illona Staller (the Italian politician and porn star whose professional name is La Cicciolina) engaging in various sexual positions and activities. The title *Made in Heaven* references sex as 'lovemaking', not simply a physical act (as an assumption in and about pornography), but the work is also a pastiche of romantic clichés and tropes, as well as American magazine pornography's conventions of layout, shot and *mise en scène*.

Bibliography

Attwood, F. and Smith, C. (2010) 'Extreme Concern: Regulating "Dangerous Pictures" in the United Kingdom'. *Journal of Law and Society*. Volume 37 (1): 171–188.

Celant, G. (2014) *Mapplethorpe: The Nymph Photography*. Milan: Skira.

Crimp, D. (1993) *On the Museum's Ruins*. Cambridge: MIT Press.

Danto, A.C. (1995) *Playing with the Edge: The Photographic Achievement of Robert Mapplethorpe*. Berkeley: University of California Press.

Danto, A.C. (2001) 'Vagina Monologue'. *The Nation*, 3 September: 42–47.

Dennis, K. (2009) *Art/Porn: A History of Seeing and Touching*. Oxford: Berg.

Dubin, S.C. (1992) *Arresting Images: Impolitic Art and Uncivil Actions*. New York: Routledge.

Haraway, D.J. (1997) 'The Virtual Speculum of the New World Order'. *Feminist Review*. Volume 55 (Spring): 22–72.

Harris, G. (2016) 'Understanding Robert Mapplethorpe'. *Financial Times*, 25 February. www.ft.com/content/79c3cd4a-cc2e-11e5-a8ef-ea66e967dd44 (accessed 28 March 2017).

Hunt, L. (1993) *The Invention of Pornography: Obscenity and the Origins of Modernity, 1500–1800*. New York: Zone Books.

Kaleidescope (2015) 'The Art & Sex Edition'. No. 25.

Kardon, J. (1989) *Robert Mapplethorpe: The Perfect Moment*. Philadelphia: Institute of Contemporary Art.

Kendrick, W. (1997) *The Secret Museum: Pornography in Contemporary Culture*. Berkeley: University of California Press.

Levas, D. (ed) (1999) *Pictures: Robert Mapplethorpe*. New York: Arena Editions.

Levinson, J. (2005) 'Erotic Art and Pornographic Pictures'. *Philosophy and Literature*. Volume 29 (1): 228–240.

Maes, H. (2011) 'Art or Porn: Clear Division or False Dilemma'. *Philosophy and Literature*. Volume 35 (1): 51–64.

Maes, H. (2015) 'Who Says Pornography Can't Be Art?' In H. Maes and J. Levinson (eds) *Art and Pornography: Philosophical Essays*. Oxford: Oxford University Press.

Maes, H. and Levinson, J. (eds) (2015) *Art and Pornography: Philosophical Essays*. Oxford: Oxford University Press.

Mansfield, L. (2005) 'The New Iconoclasm'. *Art Journal*. Volume 64 (1): 20–31.

Mapplethorpe, R. (1992) *Mapplethorpe*, with an introduction by A.C. Danto. London: Jonathan Cape.

Meyer, R. (1993) 'Robert Mapplethorpe and the Discipline of Photography'. In H. Abelove, M.A. Barale and D. Halperin (eds) *The Lesbian and Gay Studies Reader*. New York and Oxford: Routledge.

Nead, L. (1992) *The Female Nude: Art, Obscenity, and Sexuality*. London: Routledge.

Nochlin, L. (1986) 'Courbet's *L'origine du monde*: The Origin Without an Original'. *October*. Volume 37 (Summer): 76–86.

Peckham, M. (1969) *Art and Pornography: An Experiment in Explanation*. New York and London: Basic Books.

Solomon-Godeau, A. (1991) *Photography at the Dock: Essays on Photographic History, Institutions, and Practices*. Minneapolis: University of Minnesota Press.

Steiner, W. (1995) *The Scandal of Pleasure: Art in the Age of Fundamentalism*. Chicago: University of Chicago Press.

Uidhir, C.M. (2009) 'Why Pornography Can't Be Art'. *Philosophy and Literature*. Volume 33 (1): 193–203.

Williams, L. (1995) 'Corporealized Observers: Visual Pornographies and the "Carnal Density of Vision"'. In P. Petro (ed) *Fugitive Images: From Photography to Video*. Bloomington: Indiana University Press.

Williams, L. (1999) *Hard Core: Power, Pleasure, and the 'Frenzy of the Visible'*. Berkeley: University of California Press.

16
USER-GENERATED PORNOGRAPHY
Amateurs and the ambiguity of authenticity

Susanna Paasonen

Introduction

Focusing on pornographic content generated by amateurs begins, to a degree, to undo 'pornography' as a point of reference, object of common knowledge and topic of public debate, policy and regulation. Largely, albeit not completely, detached from the porn industry as a system of production and distribution, the developments and histories of amateur pornography remain ill documented. These cultural artefacts are notably absent from publicly available media archives, yet enough traces of images, films and texts have remained to suggest that amateur production was both lively and multi-medial well before the rise of digital production and distribution and so-called user-generated porn. While DIY content is often associated with the affordances and specificities of networked media (e.g. Jacobs, 2007; McNair, 2013: 29–30), such claims come with the risk of ahistorical generalisation.

This chapter accounts for both the historical roots of amateur porn production across different media and the complexities involved in the contemporary distribution of user-generated content. In order to chart some of the mundane histories and experiences connected to amateur practice, I draw on memory-work material on pornography that my research group collected together with the Folklore Archives of the Finnish Literature Society in 2012.[1] These recollections are helpful in mapping out both transformations and continuities in everyday encounters with pornography across decades as they have played out in one specific North European country in the course of drastic changes in media culture, technology and the public visibility and regulation of sexual cultures alike.

The appeal of amateur content

The Latin root of the word *amare*, 'to love', suggests that amateurs do what they do for the love of the practice rather than for the objective of monetary or other gain. This separates amateurs from professionals, who also stand apart in their mastery of professional technique and tools. Furthermore, 'while the professional conducts activities for work, an amateur labors away from work, in free time or leisure time' (Zimmermann, 1995: 1). This category of the amateur, in its contemporary uses, is a creation of the late nineteenth century, connected to the separation of work from leisure and hobbyism from professionalism. In the process, the amateur 'shifted from the older, aristocratic notion of the *lover*, to the newer middle-class notion of the hobbyist' (Armstrong, 2000: 102). Aristocratic amateurs wrote poetry, created architectural plans, composed music and excelled in watercolour painting, whereas the new articulation of the amateur was more closely tied in with consumer markets catering to leisure diversions for the middle class.

Amateur photography and film have, since their nineteenth-century beginnings, been focused on the private sphere of home, leisure, family and intimate others, and amateur porn is no exception to the rule. Amateur camera markets broadened from photography to 16 mm film in the 1920s, 8 mm the following decade and Super 8 in the 1960s (Slater, 1991; Zimmermann, 1995; Citron, 1999). Polaroid cameras, with their self-developing film, became a popular format for amateur porn in the 1960s, the same decade that witnessed the launch of the very first portable video cameras (McNair, 2002: 39). It was nevertheless not until the expansion of the mass market for video cameras and VCRs in the 1980s that 'millions of people bought their first home video camera and budding film-makers decided to make their own pornography' (Esch and Mayer, 2007: 101). These home-grown products were occasionally shared through swap-and-buy services, yet broader distribution remained an obvious challenge. Later digital-imaging technologies – including inexpensive scanners and easy-to-use, often free, image-manipulation and video-editing software – built on these developments while also expanding the possibilities of sharing and recycling materials generated by non-professionals.

Before the era of the World Wide Web, images of both amateur and professional origins were shared through Usenet newsgroups, Bulletin Board Systems (BBSs) and IRC (Internet Relay Chat), which allowed for exchanges between people with similar sexual interests, tastes and preferences (Slater, 1998; Dery, 2007). Such DIY activities developed in tandem with the more mainstream distribution forms of online pornography which have, since 2006, increasingly focused on easy-to-use and mostly free video-sharing sites modelled after YouTube (such as PornHub, YouPorn, Tube8 and RedTube). The current era of smartphones and ubiquitous connectivity has amplified these developments, and the past decade has witnessed a radical increase in the available volume and forms of online pornography, and in the cultural visibility of amateur productions in particular.

Amateur porn distributed in the self-organising online networks of sexual subcultures has been identified as a gift economy driven by the pleasure of seeing and being seen (Jacobs, 2004a; Dery, 2007), where 'deviance is the norm' (Halavais, 2005: 21). The appeal of non-professionally produced pornography is regularly, even routinely, associated with its unpolished aesthetics of directness, authenticity, domestic intimacy and rawness, as well as with its supposed ethical principles and conditions of production (e.g. Hardy, 2009; van Doorn, 2010; McNair, 2013; Hofer, 2014; cf. Chalfen, 2002). This was the case for six respondents to our memory-work project, who wrote about favouring amateur content precisely because it is more raw, relaxed and unpolished than commercially produced imagery: 'you see real people in it, no unnaturally built-up men, or women drowning in silicone' (male, born 1986). User-generated pornography has also more generally been seen as broadening the range of body shapes and styles, sexual tastes and practices available in the palette of online porn, beyond North American video porn and its 'permatanned, waxed, bleached, artificially enhanced with silicon' female performers (Härmä and Stolpe,

2010: 113; also Albury, 2003: 204; Rooke and Moreno Figueroa, 2010: 227), even if the performers in the most viewed and most highly rated amateur videos do not deviate far from culturally hegemonic beauty norms. Some of our respondents doubted the authenticity of the amateur content they have consumed; others considered ethical dilemmas potentially connected to its circulation:

> I've watched almost exclusively amateur porn online. I like it a lot since I think it's real. It depicts ordinary people in sexual acts and they're not as false as regular porn films. I believe that for other people, this falseness offers fantasies to be experienced but what I want for porn is a sense of real life. So perhaps I'm a 'voyeur'. But then again amateur porn also evokes conflicting feelings. One can't know if a video uploaded online has ended there intentionally or through dishonest means. I've heard of cases where a video intended to be private has been uploaded after a break-up out of vengeance and without the other party's knowledge. I can't know that as a viewer so perhaps it'd be best for me not to think about it.
>
> (male, born 1988)

> I haven't produced porn material myself but I'm scared that my former partner might add personal pictures of me on some web site. There's nothing pornographic, revealing material, in them . . . but someone may perceive even mundane pictures as such.
>
> (female, born 1989)

Contra to the idea of amateur porn being more ethical in its production practices, the respondents cited above commented on the controversies and concerns connected to revenge porn (to which numerous sites have been dedicated, and which has sparked legal action in several countries) and other forms of non-consensual circulation of personal media materials (see also Parvez, 2006: 627). For the male respondent, the uncertainty of consensual distribution is a source of unease that eats away at the titillation provided by the videos themselves, even if such hesitations do not necessarily drive him to turn away from the materials in question. Some, primarily male, respondents emphasised the pleasures of authenticity and creativity that amateur content offers. For others, however, realness itself translated as boring, dull and unexciting:

> Neither have I been any consumer of amateur porn – its appeal has been said to lie in its realer connection with 'real sex' but I've really never been interested in 'real sex' or realism in porn. Porn is about fantasy tales for the adult that aren't for me meant to be fully realistic. I'm bothered by the bad lighting and such of amateur porn (I'm a very visual person) so I've chosen to consume less of it. Of course the boundary is mercurial these days.
>
> (male, born 1975)

In his study of YouPorn amateur videos, Niels van Doorn (2010) explored the similarities between amateur and professional pornography in the acts, poses and routines that they document and depict. As van Doorn points out, amateur porn both approximates the generic conventions of studio porn and provides alternatives to it as scenarios that are presumably more authentic and less 'acted out'. One crucial factor in these distinctions involves monetary compensation, given that amateur pornographers largely share their content online for free, 'for the love of it', while professionals do it for the money (see also Jacobs, 2004b). At the same time, most platforms on which amateur content is shared are far from non-profit in their principles of operation. User-generated pornography involves particular forms of gift economy whereby users post their pictures and videos for free and hosting sites sell advertising space and premium membership fees while often holding the rights to distribute the user-generated content in any formats they see fit. Users may therefore have precariously little control over the content that they generate and that they willingly give the site to host. The situation is not altogether different from that of mainstream social media services, such as Facebook, which reserve the right to use the content posted by users for any purposes they consider appropriate. In most instances, users are unlikely to read through the terms and conditions.

At the same time, not all amateur content is representative of such a gift economy, and the divisions separating the amateur from the professional, or the non-commercial from the commercial, are neither binary nor fixed (Paasonen, 2010a). The amateur–professional boundary has in fact never been particularly clear in its contours in the context of online pornography, where some of the first entrepreneurs to gain fame and fortune around the mid-1990s were amateurs running their own web sites (Paasonen, 2011: 93–7). User-generated content travels across platforms both for free and for money and, given its popularity, it is far from being a marginal feature in the landscape of contemporary pornography. On sites such as *Sell Your Sex Tape*, amateurs are compensated for the content they upload. In her analysis of that site, Kristina Pia Hofer notes that the videos depict pornographic heterosexual domesticity void of squabble, friction or compulsory routines. At the same time, their gendered domestic scenarios, including household chores, are elaborately staged 'to gloss over the fact that producing a pornographic video is labour' (Hofer, 2014: 335, 343–4). The authenticity of amateur pornography can therefore also be conceptualised as a form of emotional labour, with the suppression and expression of feeling adding value to the products generated and detaching them from the more scripted, glossy and acted forms of pornography (see also Parvez, 2006).

DIY across media

The standard narrative of amateur pornography usually travels from still photography and 8 mm home movies, through Polaroid and video (necessitating no photochemical developing or outside involvement), to the qualitative and quantitative rupture caused by digital media technologies and online distribution platforms. Through this rupture, amateur pornographers have become understood as content generators whose productions can be circulated on web sites openly or behind member-only paywalls, shared one-on-one or kept privately for nobody else to see.

It is nevertheless noteworthy that this narrative, while in many senses apt in summing up the central transformations that have occurred in the possible forms of engaging with media technology, heavily privileges image and video. This emphasis is aligned with how public concerns over the increased visibility and perceived effects of pornography – or, more broadly still, concerns over the so-called sexualisation or pornification of culture (Smith, 2010) – focus on visual and audiovisual media culture as a site of contestation and intervention. This gives rise to notable blind spots concerning the field of pornography as one spanning the written word and visual culture. Pornographic literature, drawing, painting and graphic prints preceded the era of photographic and audiovisual pornography by centuries (e.g. Hunt, 1996), and they remain notably lively fields in the production of user-generated content.

The popular appeal of the written word is easily exemplified by the cultural phenomenon of the *Fifty Shades of Grey* trilogy (and E. L. James' continuing publishing efforts connected to the series), which grew from sexually explicit amateur *Twilight* fan fiction to one of the largest financial literary successes of the new millennium (Deller and Smith, 2013; Illouz, 2014). Less successful amateur literary efforts accumulate on seemingly endless online platforms, of which Literotica (est. 1998) alone hosts well over 300,000 submissions. While the themes and scenarios of amateur erotica are often more explicit and controversial than those of video porn – incest and non-consent, for example, are among the most popular Literotica story categories – they tend to garner little public attention outside their readership, which not only reads but also grades the stories and provides authors with feedback on their strengths and shortcomings (see Paasonen, 2010b).

The sociability of people engaged in the production and consumption of pornographic content is hardly a phenomenon specific to the online platforms of the 2000s, many of which incorporate social media features into their principles of operation. Online platforms have nevertheless rendered such sociability and exchange increasingly available and visible outside the closed circuits of specialist clubs and networks. The current range of publishing forums for amateur pornography in its multiple forms also shows how user-generated content has, in general, come to be seen as a resource and source of profit since the dot.com crash. And it speaks equally of the popular appeal of low-fi production and its claims to authenticity that have, in obvious ways, added to the diversification of online porn.

The division between users and producers is highly blurred on online platforms, with the volume and range of peer-to-peer exchanges, personal uploads and practices of tagging and sharing contributing to the erasure of dualisms separating the producers of online content from its consumers, performers from audience members – or, to appropriate the terminology of classic communication models, 'senders' from 'receivers' (see Attwood, 2002; Dijck, 2009). Such an opening up of categories which are often seen as mutually opposing allows for a reconsideration of the degree to which the consumers, or audiences, of porn, have also been its producers, as well as the degree to which the practices of porn consumption and production have tended to entangle (also Wood, 2015).

DIY has been part and parcel of the cultures of pornography from the outset. It is therefore not surprising that 16 contributors to the memory-work project wrote of having made porn themselves, in productions that were amateur, professional and somewhere in between – and in multiple roles, as authors, performers, directors and publishers alike.

> I have both read and written erotic stories, or perhaps I should call it porn in this context. First of all I read them but since I was interested in reading also in other ways, at some point I noticed judging erotic stories also as literary achievements. I often thought how much clumsy description and bad language there was. And that I could probably write better. My first stories were published before I had accumulated any practical knowledge of sex.
>
> *(male, born 1973)*

This respondent had contributed short stories to Finnish men's magazines for a decade, for money. While he described the pleasure of 'how at best the story began to unfold at its own speed, and how it felt to channel one's growing arousal to writing', he also stated his current unwillingness to share such stories online for free:

> I know I'm good at erotica writing but why on earth would I write for free so that some site host makes money off his advertisers, and I get nothing out of it but the joy of writing? There's enough professional pride in me that I didn't want to go back in the amateur league, that is, to produce porn for the use of others without monetary compensation.
>
> *(male, born 1973)*

In this instance, the difference between amateur and professional author was articulated as one of skill and money, as well as insight into the profit mechanisms of online platforms.

In addition to their textual achievements, contributors described drawing both singular images and comics:

> I drew kinds of comics with colour pencils in notebooks. Then I started drawing on Xerox paper and some thicker paper. For some drawings I used photos as models. I mostly drew a series of one to three images. They featured curvy women. I also drew on a computer but it was too hard since I couldn't use the mouse well enough. I only have left 199 A4 sheets of drawings from 1989 to 2002. The drawings are stapled into three books with a plastic sheet and cardboard with a cover image drawing and black carton as the back.
>
> *(male, born 1970)*

It is noteworthy that encounters with material perceived as pornographic that took place before or during the Second World War primarily involved drawings, raunchy jokes and song lyrics: in other words, materials that would currently be understood as user-generated.

> At the end of the Winter War I was a 12-year-old school kid. Our school was closed for [use as] a military hospital during the winter. As we returned back to school at the eve of spring, then at some point as I was sitting at the ring of the outhouse and looking for some sort of a tissue, my attention focused on some paper roll [. . . stuck between the inner wall]. I only managed digging it out for my reach with some effort. As I managed spreading out the roll, I was looking at an A4-sized pencil drawing. I understood it to be of a man and a woman in what I later understood to be the missionary act position. It was a very beautiful drawing having some artistic eye. The image revealed well the genitals of both. I showed it to my comrades and we laughed and snickered about the image.
>
> *(male, born 1928)*

Men's magazines only became available in Finland after the Second World War, and audiovisual material remained even scarcer for decades to come. Drawings came across in the memory-work material as a particularly common form of generating – and, in instances such as the one described above, encountering – pornographic material. This was also the sort of material that people, with some exceptions, did not describe sharing online with others. The privacy attached to drawings in particular – which respondents often describe destroying soon after completion and possible masturbation – speaks of the ephemerality of such practices in terms of media historiography. Not only are these images privately generated and stored but also they are often immediately discarded and hence unavailable other than as traces that people are willing to later recall. A similar sort of privacy, temporality and ephemerality seem to apply to self-made pornography more generally. Respondents also wrote of their unwillingness to share written porn with people other than intimate partners, for whom this may also have been especially composed:

> I've written one porn story, it was especially for my partner as a gift. The story is about five pages long and includes many things that we've done and what I'd like us to do for real. I actually gave it to her and she was delighted that I'd made a story for her that she featured in.
>
> (male, born 1986)

Both male and female respondents described taking photos of themselves in order to see how they might appear to others, shooting videos with their partners and drawing erotic pictures for sexual titillation: some of these products were immediately discarded, while others were kept for private use. Despite the obvious limitations of this memory-work material in terms of its cultural specificity and the limited number of respondents, it allows for selected glimpses at people's mundane engagements with amateur pornography across decades as both producers and consumers.

Ephemerality and longevity

Unlike the ephemerality of amateur porn across the previous decades, materials once uploaded online have considerable tenacity. Digital files are often associated with immateriality (as opposed to the tangibility of print photographs, film reels, paper magazines or video cassettes), but this is hardly accurate. Hosted on servers that eat up considerable energy resources, produced and viewed on smartphones, tablets and computers, user-generated porn is copied and circulated in ways and in directions impossible for those who originally uploaded them to control.

The boundaries of pornography have grown ephemeral as people engage in intimate webcam sessions or share images that are sexually suggestive or explicit on social media sites, dating apps and sites specialising in porn. The issue is therefore not only one of rethinking the notion of pornography – who makes it and how, who consumes it and why – but one concerning the mediated forms, spaces and functions of sexual depiction and expression more generally. Sexual imaging and writing is shared on online platforms, even if the majority of people may choose to keep such practices private. The expansion of sexual amateur content nevertheless means its availability for consumption and analysis alike. Rather than framing this in terms of social concern over the pornification of culture, the accumulation of user-generated porn, in its more or less kinky forms, with its broad range of performers and other creators, can be seen as affording insights into how sexualities, and the norms attached to them, are lived, enacted and re-imagined.

Note

1 The memory work material involves 14 female and 31 male respondents born between 1924 and 1994 and spans a total of 853 pages of text. For a more detailed discussion of the research methodology, analysis and findings, see Paasonen et al. (2015); Kyrölä and Paasonen (2016).

Bibliography

Albury, K. (2003) 'The ethics of porn on the Net'. In C. Lumby and E. Probyn (eds) *Remote Control: New Media, New Ethics*. Cambridge: Cambridge University Press.

Armstrong, C. (2000) 'From Clementina to Käsebier: the photographic attainment of the "lady amateur"'. *October*. Volume 91 (Winter): 101–39.

Attwood, F. (2002) 'Reading porn: the paradigmatic shift in pornography research'. *Sexualities*. Volume 5 (1): 91–105.

Chalfen, R. (2002) 'Snapshots "r" us: the evidentiary problematics of home media'. *Visual Studies*. Volume 17 (2): 141–9.

Citron, M. (1999) *Home Movies and Other Necessary Fictions*. Minneapolis: Minnesota University Press.

Deller, R. A. and Smith, C. (2013) 'Reading BDSM romance: reader responses to *Fifty Shades*'. *Sexualities*. Volume 16 (8): 932–50.

Dery, M. (2007) 'Naked lunch: talking realcore with Sergio Messina'. In K. Jacobs, M. Janssen and M. Pasquinelli (eds) *C'Lick Me: A Netporn Studies Reader*. Amsterdam: Institute of Network Cultures.

Dijck, J. van (2009) 'Users like you? Theorizing agency in user-generated content'. *Media, Culture & Society*. Volume 31 (1): 41–58.

Doorn, N. van (2010) 'Keeping it real: user-generated pornography, gender reification, and visual pleasure'. *Convergence*. Volume 18 (4): 411–30.

Esch, K. and Mayer, V. (2007) 'How unprofessional: the profitable partnership of amateur porn and celebrity culture'. In S. Paasonen, K. Nikunen and L. Saarenmaa (eds) *Pornification: Sex and Sexuality in Media Culture*. Oxford: Berg.

Halavais, A. (2005) 'Small pornographies'. *SIGGROUP Bulletin* Volume 25 (2): 19–22.

Hardy, S. (2009) 'The new pornographies: representation or reality?' In F. Attwood (ed) *Mainstreaming Sex: The Sexualization of Western Culture*. London: I.B. Tauris.

Härmä, S. and Stolpe, J. (2010) 'Behind the scenes of straight pleasures'. In F. Attwood (ed) *Porn.com: Making Sense of Online Pornography*. New York: Peter Lang.

Hofer, K. P. (2014) 'Pornographic domesticity: amateur couple porn, straight subjectivities, and sexual labour'. *Porn Studies*. Volume 1 (4): 334–45.

Hunt, L. (ed) (1996) *The Invention of Pornography: Obscenity and the Origins of Modernity, 1500–1800*. New York: Zone Books.

Illouz, E. (2014) *Hard-Core Romance: 'Fifty Shades of Grey,' Best-Sellers, and Society*. Chicago: University of Chicago Press.

Jacobs, K. (2004a) 'The new media schooling of the amateur pornographer: negotiating contracts and singing orgasm'. *The Spectator*. Volume 24 (1): 17–29.

Jacobs, K. (2004b) 'Pornography in small places and other places'. *Cultural Studies*. Volume 18 (1): 67–83.

Jacobs, K. (2007) *Netporn: DIY Web Culture and Sexual Politics*. Lanham, MD: Rowman & Littlefield.

Kyrölä, K. and Paasonen, S. (2016) 'Glimmers of the forbidden fruit: reminiscing pornography, conceptualizing the archive'. *International Journal of Cultural Studies*. Volume 19 (6): 595–610.

McNair, B. (2002) *Striptease Culture: Sex, Media and the Democratization of Desire*. New York: Routledge.

McNair, B. (2013) *Porno? Chic! How Pornography Changed the World and Made It a Better Place*. London: Routledge.

Paasonen, S. (2010a) 'Labors of love: netporn, Web 2.0, and the meanings of amateurism'. *New Media & Society*. Volume 12: 1297–312.

Paasonen, S. (2010b) 'Good amateurs: erotica writing and notions of quality'. In F. Attwood (ed) *Porn.com: Making Sense of Online Pornography*. New York: Peter Lang.

Paasonen, S. (2011) *Carnal Resonance: Affect and Online Pornography*. Cambridge: MIT Press.

Paasonen, S., Kyrölä, K., Nikunen, K. and Saarenmaa, L. (2015) '"We hid porn magazines in the woods": memory-work and pornography consumption in Finland'. *Sexualities*. Volume 18 (4): 394–412.

Parvez, Z. F. (2006) 'The labor of pleasure: how perceptions of emotional labor impact women's enjoyment of pornography'. *Gender & Society*. Volume 20 (5): 605–31.

Rooke, A. and Moreno Figueroa, M. G. (2010) 'Beyond "key parties" and "wife swapping": the visual culture of online swinging'. In F. Attwood (ed) *Porn.com: Making Sense of Online Pornography*. New York: Peter Lang.

Slater, D. (1991) 'Consuming Kodak'. In J. Spence and P. Holland (eds) *Family Snaps: The Meanings of Domestic Photography*. London: Virago.

Slater, D. (1998) 'Trading sexpics on IRC: embodiment and authenticity on the Internet'. *Body & Society*. Volume 4 (4): 91–117.

Smith, C. (2010) 'Pornographication: a discourse for all seasons'. *International Journal of Media and Cultural Politics*. Volume 6 (1): 103–8.

Wood, R. (2015) 'Sexual consumption within sexual labour: producing and consuming erotic texts and sexual commodities'. *Porn Studies*. Volume 2 (3): 250–62.

Zimmermann, P. (1995) *Reel Families: A Social History of Amateur Film*. Bloomington: Indiana University Press.

17
CELEBRITY SEX TAPES

Gareth Longstaff

Introduction – private acts and public figures

On the morning of 12 May 1989, a 25-year-old male Hollywood movie star received a personal injury suit from J. Hue Henry, an Atlanta attorney. In the document the star was accused of using and exploiting 'his celebrity status as an inducement to females to engage in sexual intercourse, sodomy and multiple-partner sexual activity for his immediate sexual gratification, and for the purposes of making pornographic films of these activities' (Leviton and Dougherty, 1989). The star concerned was Rob Lowe and the indictment against him would go on to become perhaps the first instance of a celebrity sex scandal associated with the private production and public consumption of a celebrity sex tape.

The accusation against Lowe was related to events which began at Atlanta's Club Rio on the night of 17 July 1988. Lowe picked up two women – a 23-year-old named Tara Seburt and her friend Lena Jan Parsons, who was 16 at the time – and invited them back to his suite at the Atlanta Hilton & Towers hotel. A series of sexual activities between the movie star and two young women followed and were filmed on a video camera. After the sexual encounter ended, Parsons and Seburt stole and duplicated the videotape, thus transforming that night's sexual pleasures from a stimulating private scenario into an exhilarating public spectacle.

Interestingly, the night's transitions between a public space (the Rio club) and a private situation (the Hilton hotel suite) seem to be most lucidly captured in the March 1990 edition of American tabloid gossip magazine *People*:

> The setting is a louche [. . .] club where disaffected young moderns are sipping Stoli, watching an arty sex show and languidly cruising for a night's company. Actor Rob Lowe has his choice of astonishing-looking women; that night, he takes home not one bedmate, but two. After thrashing about with his brunette partner, he hops out of bed, naked, to saunter into the bathroom. The blond, reaching out to caress her companion, pipes, 'I'm next.'
>
> (Green, 1990)

However, this description did not refer to the incident in Atlanta, but to a key scene in Lowe's then 'up and coming' movie *Bad Influence* (1990, dir: Curtis Hanson). In the space of a few months, Lowe's identity as a celebrity had become so closely associated and defined by the sex tape that it was necessary to promote and contextualise his new movie by making reference to it. In this way, Lowe as a celebrity commodity and the sex tape as a mediated or technological tool converge to produce what Fredric Jameson recognises as a postmodern 'language of [. . .] texts and textuality' (1991: 77). Lowe's celebrity identity, the sex tape and the Hollywood movie do not exist in isolation; rather, they are 'superimposed on each other by way of the various intertextualities [and] successions of fragments' that fortify postmodern 'textual production or textualisation' (ibid.).

Move forward more than 25 years to 2014 and this intertextualisation of Lowe and the 1988 sex tape is even more apparent in the movie *Sex Tape* (2014, dir: Jake Kasdan). Here Lowe makes a cameo appearance as Hank Rosenbaum, the boss of a woman, Annie Hargrove (played by Cameron Diaz), whose private sex videos have been unintentionally synchronised by her husband to iCloud and are now being shared through social and networked media as well as online sites such as YouPorn.com. Lowe's self-referential and self-deprecating role serves not only to locate the original 1988 sex tape as a text that can now be sardonically referred back to but also to frame it as something that is retroactively understood as a combination of '(1) personal sex video production (as an intimate practice not intended for broader circulation); (2) amateur porn production (material produced for circulation either for limited exchange with other amateur producers and/or for broader circulation); and (3) mainstream porn production' (Hayward and Rahn, 2015: 49–50). Thus, the original sex tape and the surrounding incident involving Lowe, and its intertextual allegiance to both *Bad Influence* and *Sex Tape*, seem to articulate something about how we have come to understand and interpret celebrity sex tapes as cultural objects embedded in discourses of media, sex and sexuality.

Both the original 1988 sex tape and *Sex Tape* the movie rely upon personal, amateur and mainstream texts and representations in which the private sex act and the public personality of the celebrity intersect. Yet it is perhaps the materiality of the sex tape/video itself which captures what the postmodern celebrity sex tape might constitute. It is the amateurish production of the sex tape/video that has the power to 'transform the [celebrity] subject into an apparatus for registering the "machine time" of the object and the technological apparatus' (Bignell, 2000: 49), which 'distinguishes it from the illusory time of film' (ibid.) and, in Lowe's case, from the identity both *of* and *as* film star. Additionally, if the celebrity as an identity and the celebrity sex tape as a point of identification overlap, they could be read as a postmodern 'text' through the mediated specificity of the 'videotext' (Jameson, 1991: 67–97) itself. Through its mediation as a videotape, the sex tape reifies a situation in which the accepted codes of celebrity and sexual identity as private and/or distant overlay and, in so doing, allow 'reference and reality [to] disappear altogether, [. . . so that] even meaning – the signified – is problematized' (96). In this way the celebrity sex tape functions as an archetypal postmodern form through a series of fragmented, disposable, immersive, perceptible and ephemeral modes of production, identification and consumption.

Types and characteristics of sex tapes

Using this intertextual complexity, Hayward and Rahn (2015) identify some key types and also characteristics of sex tapes. In their work, the sex tape is aligned to several key discourses which connect to the way in which celebrity is related to the production and circulation of meaning in a capitalist/consumerist context. While the discourses allied to celebrity sex tapes are contingently formed through 'expose/extortion attempts; revenge porn; single participant exploitation; negotiated release; self-exposure; and celebrity look-alike videos' (52), it is the fundamental intersection between 'personal sex video production, amateur porn production and mainstream porn production' (ibid.) that informs the celebrity sex tape and its meaning. Hayward and Rahn recognise that while 'a particular form of intimate pornography, purposed to provide pleasure supplementary to the live experience of the sexual acts recorded' (50) is key, it is the five crucial markers of 'consent', 'risk', 'regulation', 'pleasure' and 'consequence' that prevail as discursive and representational features of the celebrity sex tape. All five are always interrelated, yet also unique to the cultural context of the celebrity sex tape concerned. Consent is connected to processes of knowing (and, perhaps more so, not knowing) if you are being filmed, in that the 'thin line between the thrill of being open to being discovered and the consequences of actually being discovered' (50) is negotiated. In turn, discourses of risk, regulation and pleasure are all interwoven to the extent that 'risk may also be a significant element of pleasure' (ibid.), which transgresses the regulatory boundaries of how celebrities are perceived. Here the issue of consequence and the fantasy of the sexual encounter as potentially 'consequence-free' also aligns itself to the visually pornographic nature of the sex tape and its steer towards a mode of representation that connects to 'pleasures to be anticipated and experiences in being discovered, in being watched and/or in being identified as the participant in represented sexual congress' (ibid.). In this way the interchanges between personal, amateur and mainstream porn inform the ways in which the recognisability, fascination and acceptability of celebrity, sex and audio-visual media are positioned and interpreted.

Moreover, Kavka and West suggest that sex tapes are associated with a 'present-ist temporality' (2004: 136) which synchronises with the experience of watching reality TV. Here production and consumption are connected to an 'intimacy (emotional closeness) through immediacy (temporal closeness) coupling the proximity of the "here" with the urgency of "now"' (137). The celebrity sex tape operates in a similar way: intimacy and immediacy work in partnership through the video-text and its power to proliferate a 'zone of liveness' (140) in which temporal immediacy allows the audience to participate in the affective illusion of 'live' intimacy. The level of emotional intimacy that the viewer may feel also emphasises that the relationship between sexual representation and technology entrenched in the celebrity sex tape is one in which 'the visible becomes an extension of the physical body [. . .] as a *mediated* image of undeniable *immediacy*' (Melendez, 2004: 403). The intimate and amateur aesthetic of the sex tape also permits the viewer to temporally 'be there' with the celebrity. Here the sex tape's symbolic and aesthetic 'convulsions come to signify both the throes of sexual pleasure and the impossibility of its representation' (404). It is as if the potential of immediacy and intimacy that the 'video-textuality' of the celebrity sex tape provides also fosters a way to consider how the public and private paradigms of celebrity and audience intersperse through the features of real time or reality, authenticity, and amateurism and its mediated representation as sexually explicit.

In her analysis of the reality TV show *Big Brother*, Su Holmes suggests that participants in the show are involved in 'a complex dialectic between [their] on- and off- screen persona' (2004: 124) in which personal forms of reality, disclosure and intimacy are all central features of the text. The celebrity sex tape is similar in that it hones in on these features, changing the ordinary viewer's perception of the star as 'extraordinary' (117–120) towards a mode of identification that seems to be more authentic and genuine. In a sex tape, the celebrity and/or star does not seem to have been manipulated and edited as they are in a film and, because it presents a public figure engaging in an act that was intended for private consumption, it connects to a way of seeing that fascinates and resonates in terms of the tension between the on- and off-screen identities of the celebrity. The celebrity as a simultaneously private and public figure has long been associated with 'intimacy at a distance' (Horton and Wohl, 1956: 215–229) and an audience's desire to consume and 'see' aspects of a celebrity's 'unseen' and 'off-screen' life. The celebrity sex tape permits the sexual identity of a celebrity to be viewed as transiently proximate, personal, explicit and experimental because of the way it is constructed through a combination of authentic and amateurish tropes.

Feona Attwood suggests (drawing on Ruth Barcan's 2000 work) that this means of identification is allied to 'a broad postmodern taste for "authentica" which includes webcam culture, celebrity nudity, amateur porn and reality TV, and which focuses on new public displays of "the ordinary" which often make use of images of naked bodies' (2007: 448). The celebrity sex tape is an integral part of this trajectory and facilitates a setting in which the authenticity of the celebrity occurs in place of the conventional and regulated modes of production and consumption we see in mainstream media. Through its amateur aesthetic, the celebrity sex tape points towards modes of production, representation and consumption that permit the public to see a private and seemingly more 'authentic' identity beyond the confines of conventional media constructions of celebrity. As well as this, the evolution of amateur video production, and also amateur pornography, that is closely connected to the video revolution of the 1980s aligns the celebrity sex tape to a mode of production that has 'home-grown roots [. . .] outside of the larger media production centres' (Esch and Mayer, 2007: 101) and has now 'brought the business of amateur [sex and thus porn] into line with other media businesses' (104). In this way the celebrity sex tape captures and amplifies the commodification and mainstreaming of the ways in which amateur aesthetics inform the video production of all sex tapes and videos.

Celebrity, sex and sex tapes

The celebrity sex tape is also something that actively strengthens and paradoxically undermines the structured star-systems associated with earlier forms of fame and the ideological assurance that a movie star acted identically in both their 'real' and 'reel' lives (Klaprat, 1985; Gamson, 1994). Sean Redmond suggests that contemporary celebrity 'embodies the condition of liquid modernity – it presents us with figures to identify with but asks us to see or experience these embodied ties as loose, free-floating' (2014: 23–24). Graeme Turner's concept of the 'demotic turn' as 'a means of referring to the increasing visibility of the "ordinary person" as they turn themselves into media content through celebrity culture' (2006: 154) is allied to the politics of how the everyday has been transformed into a series of stimulating and excessive 'pseudo-events' (Boorstin, 1992). In this landscape, the celebrity sex tape forms an aspect of the way in which public identities and identifications are staged and visualised through mass media to shock and stimulate.

Accounting for this, we might also surmise that the celebrity sex tape can be understood in two further ways. First, the experimental and/or amateurish nature of the tape is indicative of its visual content as a sexually stimulating and simultaneously shameful cultural text, allied to a celebrity, that is leaked or exposed. Second, this tension between the sex tape as shameful and stimulating is one that has the capacity to transform celebrities into profitable commodities through tropes of sexual self-objectification and self-representation. Since the leaking of the Rob Lowe tape, the celebrity sex tape has been produced and consumed in a number of ways. The remediation of the format, from a unique VHS tape to a duplicated copy, a commercially available DVD version and now a digital file which can be uploaded, shared, deleted and reinstated elsewhere, reflects its ephemeral and ubiquitous nature, but also its centrality in neoliberal systems of niche and consumer-led capitalism (Hennessy, 2000).

There is a growing body of scholarly work that examines the specific features of the celebrity sex tape and its shifting visual, cultural and technological value in consumer capitalism. Hillyer claims that historically the celebrity sex tape has moved on a trajectory 'between the safe and the video store, the home movie and the porno, or the private and the public' (2004: 69). The rhetoric of the celebrity sex tape and its transformation into a pornographic text builds on the contradictions between the ordinary/extraordinary, public/private, inauthentic/authentic dynamics of sexual activity and revelation. In perhaps the most famous celebrity sex tape, *Pam and Tommy Lee: Hardcore and Uncensored* (IEG, 1997), the discourses of the everyday, the pornographic and the celebrity are displaced and superimposed through a 'curious mixture of boredom and titillation' (Hillyer, 2004: 52) and through an aesthetic which appears to be purposefully amateurish. This aesthetic becomes a constituent part of amateur sex tapes, mainstream pornographic representation and the technical devices employed in reality TV and increasingly in film. Here 'a promise of authenticity' alongside 'the impression of amateurism' (Lehman, 1999: 363) links to the notion that the celebrity sex tape has the capacity to draw us closer to not only the truth and authenticity of its celebrity subject but also that of sexual desire itself.

These 'authenticating' techniques can also be linked to documentary genre or the hybridised techniques employed in much of reality TV which strategically frame sexual acts and bodies as 'real'. Just like documentary and reality TV, the celebrity sex tape 'provides a certain guarantee of authenticity [. . . so] that this authenticity becomes a process of self-expression, self-realisation, and self-validation' (Andrejevic, 2002: 265). As well as the globally notorious example of Pamela Anderson and Tommy Lee, there is a wide-ranging archive of other celebrity sex tapes. In the West, and particularly in a North American/European context, a discourse of the celebrity sex tape has emerged and evolved in relation to major celebrities such as Paris Hilton (2004), Fred Durst (2005), Kim Kardashian (2007), Gene Simmons (2008) and Usher (2010). There has also, contrastingly, been a proliferation of sex tapes within more localised spaces, where identities that may be allied to Turner's 'demotic turn' exist in niche markets: for example, in the UK, sex tapes linked to tabloid star Katie Price/Jordan (1999), TV presenter John Leslie (2000), pop star Tulisa (2012) and the reality TV star Lauren Goodger (2014) have been produced and circulated in comparable ways to those of Rob Lowe and Pamela and Tommy. In a global context this is affirmed through incidents such as the online disclosure and distribution of sexually explicit photographs of the Hong Kong actor Edison Chen, in which the paradigms of scandal, shame and also 'revenge porn' (Hayward and Rahn, 2015: 53–54) are apparent and the celebrity sex tape functions as something that will 'cause humiliation to that individual' (ibid.).

Self-representation, social media and the sex tape

In addition to the conventional celebrity sex tape, the rise of social networks and digital media has ensured both technological and representational shifts towards forms of celebrity and sexual revelation/scandal that are now fully mediated or remediated online. This change from the materiality of the sex tape to the sexual image as a blog post, file or meme is connected to issues of 'proximity and identification [. . . and] the *corporeality* of the encounter with pornography as well as the corporeality of the encounter with the computer' (Patterson, 2004: 105). Here the 'physical apparatus' of the computer and the embodied and affective nuances of viewing the celebrity as part of a sexually explicit image have transformed the corporeal and subjective relationship previously experienced by the viewer of celebrity sex tapes as pornographic 'video-texts' (in line with Rob Lowe/Pamela and Tommy). In this new setting, the sex tape is 'attached to new and perpetually renewed computer technology' (120) that has the power to transform the nature of both 'what is private and what is public' (ibid.) through the convergence and intensification of live, amateur, authentic and representationally 'real' modes of identification.

These practices also capture and amplify how 'the boundaries between public and private are implicated in and changed by digital media' (Baym, 2015: 5). In turn, they steer the celebrity sex tape away from processes of simply 'taping sex' towards a far more complex way of digitally networking it. The celebrity sex selfie and/or the sexually explicit images we see of celebrities on platforms such as Instagram, tumblr and Snapchat indicate that when the celebrity self-captures their own sexual image, this becomes 'both a political and a cultural matter because of the range of associations that we make' (Thumin, 2012: 3). This is perhaps most obviously performed through the sexually explicit selfie and its ubiquity online (Albury, 2015; Senft and Baym, 2015). Definitions and interpretations of the selfie suggest that they are primarily 'photographic *object[s]* that initiate the transmission of human feeling in the form of a relationship' (Senft and Baym, 2015: 1589), while also being 'a practice – a gesture that can send (and is often intended to send) different messages to different individuals, communities and audiences' (ibid.). For instance, the practice of sexting that has been associated with users of social media under the age of 18 is defined by Tim Gregory as both a resilient and subversive practice that adolescents might use to reposition 'the production and transmission of sexually explicit or suggestive photographs by mobile technologies' (2015: 342). Sexting relies upon 'a rupture caused by the invisible being made visible' (ibid.) and, in similar ways to the celebrity sex tape, the sext and the adolescent sexter 'rupture established boundaries of pornographic imagery' (345).

In contrast, Alice Marwick discusses Instagram as a platform that has fostered 'a specific type of visual self-presentation strategy' (2015: 139) and which has given rise to a new type of micro-celebrity known as the 'Instafamous'. These individuals, who use Instagram to self-represent and self-promote, facilitate 'a mania for digital documentation, the proliferation of celebrity and microcelebrity culture, and conspicuous consumption' (ibid.). Here the selfie is the dominant mode of representation and the desire to 'emulate the tropes and symbols of traditional celebrity culture' (ibid.) is central to how the ideological and visual markers of celebrity are assimilated and imitated. Often on sites such as Instagram the discourses of the conventional celebrity sex tape are exploited by the 'Instafamous', who are skilled at using a visual lexicon that is informed by celebrity and which converges around tropes of the personal, amateur, pornographic and self-representational. Here the intersections between celebrity culture, the selfie and social media move the established celebrity sex tape into a new and more publicly accessible sphere. In this way the micro-celebrity (and the platform they use) both incorporate and imitate the sexually desirable celebrities they admire and aspire to act, look and be like.

In late August 2014, some of these issues allied to pornography, self-representation and celebrity were captured in an event that was widely referred to as the 'Fappening', when online hackers of Apple's iCloud leaked sexually explicit images and videos to the website/image board 4Chan.org. Movie star Jennifer Lawrence was the most high-profile of the more than 400 celebrities who were targeted. Lawrence subsequently confirmed that the images, which were immediately circulated and shared on social networks such as Twitter, Reddit and tumblr, were real and were of her. The index of amateurism was once again a key visual marker in these images. Here the recognisability of a shaky, grainy, badly lit and instantaneously explicit and homespun sexual aesthetic enables the 'articulation of a certain proximity to the life of the spectator' (Patterson, 2004: 111) in conjunction with a far more accessible and proximate way of seeing and interpreting the discourse of celebrity. The assimilation of amateur sexual representation to celebrity identity redefines not only how that celebrity is interpreted but also, perhaps more pertinently, how 'the opportunities for "interaction" and "self-production" offered by the Internet' (110) allow the viewer as 'user' to produce and consume sexual desire in almost identical ways.

More problematically, the 'Fappening', and how it was exchanged and discussed on social media, could also be positioned as an example of what Adrienne Massanari refers to as symptomatic of 'toxic technocultures' (2015: 5): the online networks of exchange 'enabled by and propagated through sociotechnical networks such as Reddit, 4chan, Twitter, and online gaming' that 'often rely heavily on implicit or explicit harassment of others' (ibid.). In this way, the 'Fappening' and its alliance to the sexual self-representation of celebrity femininity (Lawrence) did little to further perceptions of celebrity and sexuality; rather, it was both underpinned and undermined by 'retrograde ideas of gender, sexual identity, sexuality, and race' (8) and demonstrated that 'users of social media sites such as Reddit had no trouble victimizing a person [Lawrence] that at least a portion of the community had previously idolized' (ibid.).

The sexually explicit images we now interpret through contemporary instances such as sexts, Instagram and events such as the 'Fappening' have a problematic relationship with the celebrity sex tape. In this way, and through the practices of photographing, posting, sharing, and re-blogging potentially limitless clips and selfies, the non-celebrity and celebrity subject are permanently fractured. Here we see that pornography, celebrity and sexuality are compounded to become indicative of a much broader trend often referred to as 'pornification'. This 'involves pornographic styles, gestures and aesthetics [. . .] as commodities purchased and consumed as individual self-representations and independent porn productions' (Nikunen, Paasonen and Saarenmaa, 2007: 1), whereby 'everyday people "pornify" their personalities – displaying themselves on webcams, appearing nude in public venues' (Esch and Mayer, 2007: 111). A notable example of pornifying practice may be seen in the personality of UK reality TV star Gaz Beadle, known for his participation in the show *Geordie Shore* (2011–present). When his fellow housemate Charlotte Crosby favourably compared his penis to a parsnip and a remote control, the producers (as well as Beadle himself) immediately endorsed this metonymic novelty, offering shots of Beadle coming out of the shower, showing off in a thong and waking up with an erection. Images of his penis have also emerged through social and digital media, including a self-filmed webcam video and stills of Beadle masturbating (leaked from Skype), as well as a selfie posing with a parsnip covering his penis as part of the unofficial Cancer Research UK '#cockinasock campaign'. Beadle is indicative of a new crop of minor celebrities who utilise the amateurish and salacious verisimilitudes that the celebrity sex tape has instilled. A huge range of evolving contexts such as the reality TV show *Love Island* and websites such as Cam4.com and faketaxi1.com offer further examples in which discourses of reality TV, web camming, amateur porn and self-representation are crucial to the visual index of sexual identification.

Conclusion

The discourse of the selfie and the expanse of celebrity and non-celebrity sex videos online now indicate that through reality and social media, the contingency of live, amateur, authentic and representationally 'real' images allows user and subject to imagine they are the same. The process of making and viewing the celebrity sex tape is pulled through into new forms of interaction and participation, which suggests that

> physical habits of pointing and clicking, of pushing the refresh button on a webcam, of the delays and frustrations of opening and closing windows [push] the viewer into a particular kind of interaction with the internet, one that not only reflects but also inscribes social relations.
>
> (Patterson, 2004: 108)

Alongside this, the repetitive modes of desire that have proliferated in relation to the sex tape and the sexualised selfie provide evidence that users who capture, crop, edit, post and share do so in light of such images' power to mark out desire through self-objectification and self-promotion as advantageously personal. Celebrities seeking to out themselves as gay or lesbian have increasingly constructed their own narratives through self-representational and self-defined techniques. When the UK sports star Tom Daley used social media to come out as gay in December 2013, he appeared through the conventions of the grainy, hand-held and thus personalised aesthetic of the amateur. Daley's account of his desire to be accepted as a young gay man was amplified and affectively constructed through the same paradigms of 'immediacy, actuality, and intimacy' (Kavka and West, 2004: 141) which inflect the sex tape.

Online location, a repetitive and assimilatory nature and an attempt at capturing the personality of the subject are evident in the transition of the sex tape to the selfie. Digital, mobile and online media have facilitated the intersections between public and private forms of sexual representation so that they are increasingly difficult to define. In this way the transformation of the audience from viewer into user and/or 'producer–consumer', initially embedded in home video use, has been refined into the more sophisticated processes of sexualised assimilation and pornified reproduction derived from celebrity sex tapes and celebrity culture itself.

Bibliography

Albury, K. (2015) 'Selfies, sexts and sneaky hats: young people's understandings of gendered practices of self-representation'. *International Journal of Communication*. Volume 9: 1734–1735.

Andrejevic, M. (2002) 'The kinder, gentler gaze of Big Brother: reality TV in the era of digital capitalism'. *New Media and Society*. Volume 4 (2): 251–270.

Attwood, F. (2007) 'No money shot? Commerce, pornography and new taste sex cultures'. *Sexualities*. Volume 10 (4): 441–456.

Barcan, R. (2000) 'Home on the Rage: nudity, celebrity, and ordinariness in the Home Girls/Blokes pages'. *Continuum: Journal of Media and Cultural Studies*. Volume 14 (2): 145–158.

Baym, N.K. (2015) *Personal Connections in the Digital Age*. Malden, MA: Polity Press.

Bignell, J. (2000) *Postmodern Media Culture*. Edinburgh: Edinburgh University Press.

Boorstin, D. (1992) *The Image: A Guide to Pseudo-Events in America*. New York: Vintage Books.

Esch, K. and Mayer, V. (2007) 'How unprofessional: the profitable partnership of amateur porn and celebrity culture'. In K. Nikunen, S. Paasonen and L. Saarenmaa (eds) *Pornification: Sex and Sexuality in Media Culture*. Oxford: Berg.

Gamson, J. (1994) *Claims to Fame: Celebrity in Contemporary America*. Berkeley: University of California Press.

Green, M. (1990) 'Rob Lowe's tale of the tape'. *People*. 19 March. Volume 33 (11). www.people.com/people/archive/article/0,,20117104,00.html (accessed 26 January 2015).

Gregory, T. (2015) 'Sexting and the politics of the image: when the invisible becomes visible in a consensus democracy'. *Porn Studies*. Volume 2 (4): 342–355.

Hayward, P. and Rahn, A. (2015) 'Opening Pandora's Box: pleasure, consent and consequence in the production and circulation of celebrity sex videos'. *Porn Studies*. Volume 2 (1): 49–61.

Hennessy, R. (2000) *Profit and Pleasure: Sexual Identities in Late Capitalism*. London and New York: Routledge.

Hillyer, M. (2004) 'Sex in the suburban: porn, home movies, and the live action performance in "Pam and Tommy Lee: Hardcore and uncensored"'. In L. Williams (ed) *Porn Studies*. Durham and London: Duke University Press.

Holmes, S. (2004) '"All you've got to worry about is the task, having a cup of tea, and doing a bit of sunbathing": approaching celebrity in *Big Brother*'. In S. Holmes and D. Jermyn (eds) *Understanding Reality Television*. London and New York: Routledge.

Horton, D. and Richard Wohl, R. (1956) 'Mass communication and para-social interaction: observations on intimacy at a distance'. *Psychiatry*. Volume 19: 215–229.

Jameson, F. (1991) *Postmodernism, or, The Cultural Logic of Late Capitalism*. London: Verso.

Kavka, M. and West, A. (2004) 'Temporalities of the real: conceptualising time in reality TV'. In S. Holmes and D. Jermyn (eds) *Understanding Reality Television*. London and New York: Routledge.

Klaprat, C. (1985) 'The star as market strategy: Bette Davis in another light'. In T. Balio (ed) *The American Film Industry*. Madison: University of Wisconsin Press.

Lehman, P. (1999) 'Ed Powers and the fantasy of documenting sex'. In J. Elias (ed) *Porn 101: Eroticism, Pornography and the First Amendment*. New York: Prometheus.

Leviton, J. and Dougherty, S. (1989) 'A video romp in the buff gives heartbreaker Rob Lowe too much southern exposure'. *People*. 5 June. http://people.com/archive/a-video-romp-in-the-buff-gives-heartbreaker-rob-lowe-a-little-too-much-southern-exposure-vol-31-no-22/ (accessed 28 March 2017).

Marwick, A. (2015) 'Instafame: luxury selfies in the attention economy'. *Public Culture*. Volume 27 (1): 137–160.

Massanari, A. (2015) '#Gamergate and The Fappening: how Reddit's algorithm, governance, and culture support toxic technocultures'. *New Media and Society*. Published online 9 October 2015: doi:10.1177/1461444815608807.

Melendez, F. (2004) 'Video pornography, visual pleasure, and the return of the sublime'. In L. Williams (ed) *Porn Studies*. Durham and London: Duke University Press.

Nikunen, K., Paasonen, S. and Saarenmaa, L. (eds) (2007) *Pornification: Sex and Sexuality in Media Culture*. Oxford: Berg.

Patterson, Z. (2004) 'Going on-line: consuming pornography in the digital era'. In L. Williams (ed) *Porn Studies*. Durham and London: Duke University Press.

Redmond, S. (2013) *Celebrity and the Media*. Basingstoke: Palgrave Macmillan.

Senft, T.M. and Baym, N.K. (2015) 'What does the selfie say? Investigating a global phenomenon'. *International Journal of Communication*. Volume 9: 1588–1606.

Thumin, N. (2012) *Self-Representation and Digital Culture*. Basingstoke: Palgrave Macmillan.

Turner, G. (2006) 'The mass production of celebrity: "celetoids", reality TV and the "demotic turn"'. *International Journal of Cultural Studies*. Volume 9 (2): 153–165.

Media

Bad Influence (1990) Directed by C. Hansen [Film]. USA: Epic Productions.
Big Brother (2000–) [TV Series]. UK: Channel 4 and Channel 5.
Geordie Shore (2011–) [TV Series]. UK: MTV.
Love Island (2015–) [TV Series]. UK: ITV.
Pam and Tommy Lee: Hardcore and Uncensored (1997) [Film]. USA: IEG.
Sex Tape (2015) Directed by J. Kasdan [Film]. USA: Sony Pictures Entertainment.

18
THE MEDIA PANIC ABOUT TEEN SEXTING

Amy Adele Hasinoff

Around one-third of teens and up to half of young adults have sent a sexual image of themselves to someone else (Drouin *et al.*, 2013; Strassberg *et al.*, 2013). For many people, sexting is a normal part of their intimate relationships. In surveys, people report that they sext because it is a fun, pleasurable way to engage in sexual communication with their partners, and many see it as a form of foreplay (Albury and Crawford, 2012; Burkett, 2015; McDaniel and Drouin, 2015). Since many social interactions occur online, it should be no surprise that interpersonal sexual communication has been digitised as well. Indeed, if we view sexting as a continuation of phone sex and nude Polaroids, and even as a creative form of media production (Hasinoff, 2013), it becomes clear that the problem is not, as the media panic claims, the practice of sexting itself.

Yet, in many Western countries, including the US, UK, Canada and Australia, there has been an ongoing panic in the mass media about sexting since 2009 (Hasinoff, 2015b; Podlas, 2011). With adults, sexting is usually discussed in cases of celebrity infidelity and political scandal. Sexting teenagers garner far more negative attention. Media coverage of teen sexting often highlights the potential legal consequences, focuses on cases that have led to bullying and even suicide and discusses sexting in ways that are often victim-blaming and slut-shaming (Hasinoff, 2015b; Karaian, 2014; Draper, 2012; Albury *et al.*, 2013; Döring, 2014; Podlas, 2011). The key thing that is missing in most of these mainstream discourses is a clear distinction between consensual sexting and privacy violations. In this chapter, I discuss three ways in which consent is erased from the popular discussions about sexting: the criminalisation of sexting, gender disparities in discussions about sexting, and the promotion of sexting abstinence. I conclude with some recommendations regarding how we might talk about sexting in more nuanced and productive ways.

To contextualise these problems in mass media representations of sexting, it is important to remember that many Western cultures have a long history of media-driven moral panics about teen girls and sexuality. Such panics are predicated on a notion of a fragile white, middle-class girlhood of purity and virtue that is a constant source of worry and concern (Walkerdine, 1997; Egan, 2013). The figure of the vulnerable and sexually innocent girl has repeatedly been at the centre of moral panics over the past century, and threats to her safety and well-being are often invoked to legitimate attempts to control young people, especially girls (Cocca, 2004; Odem, 1995). Girls of colour, queer and trans girls and low-income girls are not presumed to be innocent and pure in quite the same way – instead, those girls are criminalised and punished at school at much higher rates than their more privileged counterparts (Dohrn, 2004; Chesney-Lind and Irwin, 2008). Thus, while the panics about dance halls, dime novels, online predators, and now sexting are centred on the figure of the presumably sexually innocent white girl (Karaian, 2014), the new laws that are passed and new forms of social control that are developed often disproportionately affect other people.

Such panics provide an occasion for hand-wringing and scolding, which is a common way of discussing sexuality in Western culture (Foucault, 1990). At the same time, media narratives about sexting often sexualise girls, through the detailed language used to describe their sexual behaviours and through the sexually suggestive photos that accompany the newspaper articles about sexting that denounce girls' sexuality. Many news stories about sexting include an image of a sexy, often partially obscured, pixelated, darkened or blurred image of a white teenage girl sexting. The hypocrisy is that adults are choosing sexualised images of teenage girls to accompany articles that harshly judge teenagers for sexting and condemn girls for sexualising themselves. Apparently it is only a moral problem when the girls create such images themselves. As I discuss later, this is because while we are comfortable looking at girls as sexual objects, there is often great concern when they seem to be acting as sexual subjects.

The panic about sexting is particularly amplified because it is also part of a long tradition of concern about new communication technologies. As Baym (2010) points out, it dates back at least to Socrates sounding the alarm about the negative impact of written language on memory and the oral tradition, and continues through the telegraph, the telephone, and now the internet and mobile phones. New communication technologies are often a focal point both for our greatest hopes about equality, democracy and mutual understanding and at the same time for our deepest fears about the potential breakdown of civilisation (Peters, 1999; Carey, 1989). The panic about youth and new communication technologies, and especially about youth and sexual media, has recurred frequently in the past century or so (Heins, 2001; Levine, 2002). For example, under an 1886 headline that could be used today – 'The dangers of wired love' – a newspaper reported the story of a young woman who met a married man over the telegraph lines and then eloped with him (Standage, 1998). Indeed, many panics about technology are at the same time a way of expressing anxiety about girls' sexual autonomy (Cassell and Cramer, 2008). Discourses about girls, in particular, seem to take on heightened emotional significance and resonance, as these conversations often discuss girls in order to express all sorts of anxieties, including about the economy and social change (Gonick, 2006; Harris, 2004; Projansky, 2007).

The sexting panic in mass media

Criminalisation

One of the reasons why sexting garners so much media attention is that it can be illegal. US federal laws on child pornography, which are similar in many other countries, define it as a depiction of a person under 18 years old involved in 'sexually explicit conduct'.[1] This means that if a 17-year-old merely creates a sexually explicit image of herself, this act technically constitutes the production and possession of child pornography. If her partner then distributes that image to someone else without her permission, this act technically constitutes the distribution and possession of child pornography. While many news stories about teen sexting acknowledge that child pornography charges are too harsh in this respect, most still express the view that sexting should remain illegal in some way for teens. For example, in praise of a new anti-sexting misdemeanour law, one commentator explains: 'Without question, sexting is crude, deplorable and juvenile. But it's up to adults to ensure that the punishment fits the offense' (O'Brien, 2009). The problem with this misdemeanour law, and nearly all of the laws that apply to teen sexting, is that they treat consensual sexting and sexual privacy violations as legally equivalent by criminalising them both. Consensual sexting is a common practice of media production and sexual interpersonal communication – and there is no evidence that consensual sexting is harmful in and of itself. However, the creation or distribution of a private sexual image without permission can be traumatic and devastating (Powell, 2010; Ringrose et al., 2012).

Though felony charges for teen sexting are not common, US researchers estimate that a few hundred consensual sexters were arrested on child pornography charges in 2009 (Wolak et al., 2012b; Wolak et al., 2012a). Many observers and legal scholars argue that it is unjust to criminalise consensual sexters and that, while privacy violations should be addressed, child pornography laws are far too harsh (Nunziato, 2012; Newton-Brown et al., 2013). A key problem with simply criminalising sexting for all involved regardless of consent is that it deters victims from reporting, since informing authorities about the incident means that victims of a privacy violation can be punished for their involvement by their school or by law enforcement. In general, both the media and the justice system have failed to adequately address sexual violence and routinely blame victims and demonise perpetrators, both of which are unproductive ways to address a complex social problem that is both broadly structural and often intertwined with intimate relationships (Smith et al., 2006; Spade, 2012). While legal scholars have argued for the decriminalisation of teen sexting (e.g. Nunziato, 2012; Wastler, 2010; Tallon et al., 2012), this position is politically unpopular – Vermont attempted it in 2009 but was met with a strong backlash in national US media (Hasinoff, 2015b).

The criminalisation of sexting also likely has a disproportionate impact on the same people who are already targeted by the criminal justice system because parents and law enforcement can decide which incidents to ignore and which to prosecute. For example, in one case, the mother of a 16-year-old, who did not approve of her daughter dating a 19-year-old woman, turned the girl's phone over to the police, who used images and text messages on the device to press charges against the older girlfriend (Slovic, 2010). Because this young woman is African American, her prosecution can be interpreted as an illustration of systematic biases in the criminal justice system, which disproportionately targets queer people (Sullivan, 1996; Spade, 2012; D'Emilio, 1989) and people of colour (Davis, 2005; Alexander, 2010). These same prejudices likely contributed to the fact that this particular case garnered no national media attention in the US.

Gender disparities

Much of the media coverage of teen sexting focuses on girls who produce images of themselves (e.g. Hasinoff, 2015b; Draper, 2012). Because boys' sexual expression is usually expected and tolerated, it seems less newsworthy when boys sext. Even though girls and boys report that they send sexual images at similar, though not identical, rates (Mitchell et al., 2012; Strassberg et al., 2013), nearly all the concern about the creation of sexual images is about girls. This reflects the longstanding double standard that girls' sexuality is dangerous and wrong and needs to be contained, while boys who engage in the same behaviours are seen as 'studs' or 'players'. The Texas School Safety educational programme about sexting, for example, notes that the negative consequences of sexting could include the possibility that 'Others may think of you as "easy" or sexually active' and 'Others may be embarrassed to be seen with you' (Texas School Safety Center, 2012). Unlike girls, teen boys are expected to be sexual, and their behaviour is often tolerated or praised.

A case in Seattle that garnered some of the earliest media attention to sexting further illustrates the gender biases in the reporting on teen sexting. In this case, two female cheerleaders were suspended for sexting, while the boys who distributed their private images without permission were not punished at all (Blanchard, 2008). School officials found that the girls' actions – sharing nude photos of themselves – violated the athletic code, but the boys' intrusions on their privacy by passing around the images among themselves did not. Responding to this case, CNN commentator Mike Galanos stated: 'It's the girls that are to blame, not the school!' and called it 'ridiculous' that the parents had tried to sue the school for treating their daughters unfairly by punishing only the girls and not the boys (Galanos, 2008). Because of the sexual double standard, it seems obvious to Galanos and many other observers that the girls in this case were the transgressors and the boys' behaviour was unremarkable; here, gender norms are so powerful that consensual sexual behaviour looks like the problem and is viewed as though it were as bad as or worse than malicious sexual privacy violations.

Media responses like these reflect the gender norm that women are generally expected to be passive sexual objects, whose role is to be looked at and acted upon, while men are often viewed as sexual subjects who do the acting and the looking. In Western culture, it is expected that women and girls will be depicted in oil paint, in print and on screens as passive sexual objects. Women and girls transgress these expectations by sexting, where they are choosing to be sexual objects and at the same time are acting as sexual subjects by doing the looking (at themselves) and creating sexual images. When girls choose to sext, many observers assume that these girls are victims of some external force causing them to do it. Angelides reports, in a UK study:

> Trading in popular, long-standing narratives of teenagers as foolish, rash, hormone-driven, and psychologically and emotionally immature, teenage sexters are represented as lacking the wherewithal both to engage in the practice maturely and to deal with any unforeseen consequences.
>
> *(2013: 682)*

Much of the media commentary about sexting offers explanations and excuses for why teen girls might sext, including low self-esteem, raging hormones, still-developing brain structures, sexualisation in mass media and pressure from peers (Hasinoff, 2015b). While any of these factors might have an influence on a person's sexual acts and expressions, these discourses reflect and reinforce the problematic erasure of girls' sexual agency and desires (Tolman, 1999; Fine and McClelland, 2006). Even though denying the sexual agency of girls who sext might seem like a sympathetic gesture, the problem with this pervasive discourse is that it shames and pathologises sexually active girls and fails to actually protect anyone from harm. If we are unwilling to recognise teen girls' desires for sexual pleasure and expression, we will continue to give them the bad (and heteronormative) advice that their agency lies solely in their ability to resist male sexual advances and sexualisation in mass media (Hasinoff, 2014).

Abstinence

The solution to sexting many schools and national public service announcements offer is abstinence. Public service announcements from the Australian Federal Police, National Society for the Prevention of Cruelty to Children (UK) and National Center for Missing and Exploited Children (US) all typically promote the same simple message: don't sext. These campaigns consistently stress abstinence, emphasise the risks and potential negative outcomes, and use scare tactics and often blame female victims (Döring, 2014). For example, the US *Think Before You Post* campaign aims to address online sexual exploitation by telling girls not to post or share images of themselves online. These ads do not instruct men or boys not to exploit or violate people, but rather put the responsibility on girls for preventing their own victimisation (Hasinoff, 2015b). Anti-sexting campaigns like this one offer reasons for teens to avoid the practice, and point out the risk that a peer might distribute a private image. While the intent of these messages is to protect teens from harm, the problems with abstinence-only education are the same for sexting as they are for abstinence messages about other kinds of sexual behaviours. Decades of research demonstrates that abstinence-only education at best only slightly delays sexual activity, and can have a negative effect on young people because it leaves them ill-equipped to take precautions when they do have sex, thus resulting in higher rates of sexually transmitted infections and unwanted pregnancies (Alford, 2007). Abstinence messages about sexting have similar problems – many teens will sext regardless, and an abstinence-only approach precludes vital discussions about safer-sexting strategies.

In addition to being ineffective, promoting sexting abstinence is particularly problematic because it blames consensual sexters and ignores privacy violators. Since the advice is simply to avoid sexting, this sends the message that those who do sext are to blame when their privacy is violated. This tells sexters who have experienced a privacy violation that they should have known better than to send the sext in the first place. For example, in a TV news interview, an attorney comments: 'Anytime you take a digitized image of yourself in an embarrassing or compromised position, you're asking for trouble' (Galanos 2009). Blaming the victims of a sexual privacy violation is similar to holding a woman who was out late or wore a short skirt responsible for rape. These assumptions about sexual assault and privacy violations turn attention away from perpetrators and back onto victims. For teen sexters who have experienced privacy violations, the usual legal and educational response to counsel abstinence and simply punish everyone involved, sends a clear message that consensually taking a photo and trusting the wrong person is as reprehensible as maliciously distributing a person's private sexual image. These biases against sexting are gendered, but they also reflect the common practice of judging sexual behaviours which are consensual but are outside the narrow confines of what is considered 'normal' as deviant, pathological or immoral (Rubin, 1993).

Alternative responses to sexting

Laws need to change in order to prevent the criminalisation of consensual sexters and to better address the harm that is created through privacy violations. While most new sexting misdemeanour laws in the US passed since 2009 provide prosecutors with an option to apply lesser penalties than felony child pornography changes, these laws continue to criminalise consensual sexting (Greenberg, 2012; Hasinoff, 2015b). A 2013 report from the Law Reform Committee of the Victoria Parliament in Australia points to a way forward and suggests a number of vital policy changes. The report criticises anti-sexting educational campaigns and curricula, and recommends that such efforts focus on privacy violators rather than consensual sexters (Newton-Brown et al., 2013). The report also suggests a number of reforms to child pornography laws: making it impossible to charge a teen who creates a photograph of herself with producing child pornography, decriminalising sexting between minors who are close in age and giving judges discretion to leave convicted sexters off the sex offender registry. These legal reforms are a radical departure from many US states' responses to the criminalisation of youth sexting, and would be a significant step forward if they were adopted.

The even more crucial shift is to change how we think about sexting. Instead of viewing it as an inherently dangerous or deviant practice, it would be more productive to view it as a form of creative, sexually expressive media production and communication (Hasinoff, 2013). While most educational campaigns about sexting to date have stressed abstinence and worst-case scenarios and have not offered any safer-sexting strategies (Döring, 2014; Hasinoff, 2015b), a 2015 campaign from a branch of the UK National Crime Agency offers a new model with significant improvements. This campaign focuses on telling parents not to panic about sexting, and to instead try to listen to their kids and understand why they do it (Child Exploitation and Online Protection Command, 2015). In the first video of the series, the adult narrator remembers how her parents disliked her outfits as a teen and suggests that sexting is similar – a way for teens to 'feel good about themselves', 'push boundaries' and 'experiment'. This PSA offers the crucial message that sexting is not is not a concern in and of itself, since teens often do it simply for pleasure, and includes the important point that forwarding a private photo without permission is a serious violation.

There are no simple solutions to the violation of sexual privacy or to sexual violence, but it is clear that abstinence and criminalisation are ineffective and actually exacerbate the harm of a violation. As many feminist anti-rape advocates argue, one way to address these forms of harm is to develop and promote social norms of engaging in dialogue and explicit discussions about sexual consent, a model also known as affirmative consent (e.g. Remick, 1993). Indeed, a study comparing sexting tips to general advice about sex online, found that it is possible that the asynchronicity of mobile phone communication and the lack of nonverbal cues might encourage people to be more explicit in their dialogues about sexual consent (Hasinoff, 2015a). As many researchers advocate, the affirmative consent model helps to disrupt the idea that men are entitled to access to women's bodies – which includes cat calls, groping, rape, and forwarding a picture without permission. As I argue elsewhere (Hasinoff, 2015b), we should extend the practice of dialogue about consent to the production and circulation of all private information.

Norms of privacy in digital interactions are still developing, but most people agree that distributing a sexual image without permission is a violation (Albury and Crawford, 2012; Hasinoff and Shepherd, 2014). Indeed, most sexts are never distributed widely (Mitchell et al., 2012), though rates are higher for images that were sent as a result of coercion or pressure (Englander, 2015). Our task moving forward is not to prohibit sexting but to focus on reducing these privacy violations.

Conclusion

The media panic about sexting demonstrates that the development of more effective responses will require paying critical attention to the pervasive stigmatisation of both female sexual agency and the use of new media technologies for sexual communication.

While it is easy to panic about a new way in which people can harm and humiliate one another, analysing the problematic biases in the responses to sexting can serve as a reminder of the importance of questioning our knee-jerk reactions. As is the case with all sexual behaviours, engaging in sexting without a dialogue of enthusiastic consent between partners is the problem we must focus on.

Note

1 The law defines 'sexually explicit conduct' as: (i) sexual intercourse, including genital–genital, oral–genital, anal–genital or oral–anal, whether between persons of the same or opposite sex; (ii) bestiality; (iii) masturbation; (iv) sadistic or masochistic abuse; or (v) lascivious exhibition of the genitals or pubic area of any person (18 USC § 2256).

Bibliography

Albury, K. and Crawford, K. (2012) 'Sexting, consent and young people's ethics: beyond Megan's story'. *Continuum*. Volume 26: 463–473.

Albury, K., Crawford, K., Byron, P. and Mathews, B. (2013) *Young People and Sexting in Australia: Ethics, Representation and the Law*. www.cci.edu.au/sites/default/files/Young_People_And_Sexting_Final.pdf (accessed 29 March 2017).

Alexander, M. (2010) *The New Jim Crow: Mass Incarceration in the Age of Colorblindness*. New York: The New Press.

Alford, S. (2007) *Abstinence-Only-Until-Marriage Programs: Ineffective, Unethical, and Poor Public Health*. www.advocatesforyouth.org/publications/publications-a-z/597-abstinence-only-until-marriage-programs-ineffective-unethical-and-poor-public-health (accessed 29 March 2017).

Angelides, S. (2013) '"Technology, hormones, and stupidity": the affective politics of teenage sexting'. *Sexualities*. Volume 16 (5/6): 665–689.

Baym, N.K. (2010) *Personal Connections in the Digital Age*. Malden, MA: Polity.

Blanchard, J. (2008) 'Cheerleaders' parents sue in nude photos incident: two were the only ones suspended'. *Seattle Post-Intelligencer*, 21 November. www.seattlepi.com/local/article/Cheerleaders-parents-sue-in-nude-photos-incident-1292294.php (accessed 29 March 2017).

Burkett, M. (2015) '(Sex)t Talk: a qualitative analysis of young adults' negotiations of the pleasures and perils of sexting'. *Sexuality & Culture*. Volume 19 (4): 835–863.

Carey, J.W. (1989) *Communication as Culture: Essays on Media and Society*. Boston: Unwin Hyman.

Cassell, J. and Cramer, M. (2008) 'High tech or high risk: moral panics about girls online'. In T. McPherson (ed) *Digital Youth, Innovation, and the Unexpected*. Cambridge, MA: The MIT Press.

Chesney-Lind, M. and Irwin, K. (2008) *Beyond Bad Girls: Gender, Violence and Hype*. New York: Routledge.

Child Exploitation and Online Protection Command (2015) *Nude Selfies: What Parents and Carers Need to Know*. www.pershore.worcs.sch.uk/media/1907/nude-selfies-help-for-parents-and-carers.pdf (accessed 28 March 2017).

Cocca, C.E. (2004) *Jailbait: The Politics of Statutory Rape Laws in the United States*. Albany, NY: State University of New York Press.

Cuklanz, L.M. (1996) *Rape on Trial: How the Mass Media Construct Legal Reform and Social Change*. Philadelphia: University of Pennsylvania Press.

D'Emilio, J. (1989) 'The homosexual menace: the politics of sexuality in Cold War America'. In K. Peiss and C. Simmons (eds) *Passion and Power: Sexuality in History*. Philadelphia: Temple University Press.

Davis, A.Y. (2005) *Abolition Democracy: Beyond Empire, Prisons, and Torture*. New York: Seven Stories Press.

Dohrn, B. (2004) 'All ellas: girls locked up'. *Feminist Studies*. Volume 30 (2): 302–324.

Döring, N. (2014) 'Consensual sexting among adolescents: risk prevention through abstinence education or safer sexting?' *Cyberpsychology: Journal of Psychosocial Research on Cyberspace.* Volume 8 (1). doi: 10.5817/CP2014-1-9

Draper, N. (2012) 'Is your teen at risk? Discourses of adolescent sexting in United States television news'. *Journal of Children and Media* Volume 6 (2): 221–236.

Drouin, M., Vogel, K.N., Surbey, A. and Stills, J.R. (2013) 'Let's talk about sexting, baby: computer-mediated sexual behaviors among young adults'. *Computers in Human Behavior.* Volume 29: A25–A30.

Egan, R.D. (2013) *Becoming Sexual: A Critical Appraisal of the Sexualization of Girls.* Malden, MA: Polity.

Englander, E. (2015) 'Coerced sexting and revenge porn among teens'. *Bullying, Teen Aggression & Social Media.* Volume 1 (2): 19–21.

Fine, M. and McClelland, S. (2006) 'Sexuality education and desire: still missing after all these years'. *Harvard Educational Review.* Volume 76 (3): 297–338.

Foucault, M. (1990) *The History of Sexuality.* New York: Vintage Books.

Galanos, M. (2008) 'Kicked off cheer squad for "sexting": girls' parents sue school over nude pics'. www.liveleak.com/view?i=932_1228594647&comments=1 (accessed 28 March 2017).

Galanos, M. (2009) 'Is "sexting" a teen's right?' http://edition.cnn.com/video/#/video/bestoftv/2009/03/30/pn.sexting.right.cnn (accessed 25 May 2016).

Gonick, M. (2006) 'Between "girl power" and "reviving Ophelia": constituting the neoliberal girl subject'. *NWSA Journal.* Volume 18 (2): 1–23.

Greenberg, P. (2012) *2012 Legislation Related to "Sexting".* http://firstamendmentlawyers.org/articles/2012_2_0222sexting.pdf (accessed 29 March 2017).

Harris, A. (2004) *Future Girl: Young Women in the Twenty-First Century.* New York: Routledge.

Hasinoff, A.A. (2013) 'Sexting as media production: rethinking social media and sexuality'. *New Media & Society.* Volume 15 (4): 449–465.

Hasinoff, A.A. (2014) 'Blaming sexualization for sexting'. *Girlhood Studies.* Volume 7 (1): 102–120.

Hasinoff, A.A. (2015a) 'How to have great sext: consent advice in online sexting tips'. *Communication and Critical/Cultural Studies.* Volume 13 (1): 58–74.

Hasinoff, A.A. (2015b) *Sexting Panic: Rethinking Criminalization, Privacy, and Consent.* Champaign, IL: University of Illinois Press.

Hasinoff, A.A. and Shepherd T. (2014) 'Sexting in context: privacy norms and expectations'. *International Journal of Communication.* Volume 8: 2932–2955.

Heins, M. (2001) *Not in Front of the Children: 'Indecency,' Censorship and the Innocence of Youth.* New York: Hill and Wang.

Karaian, L. (2014) 'Policing "sexting": responsibilization, respectability and sexual subjectivity in child protection/crime prevention responses to teenagers' digital sexual expression'. *Theoretical Criminology.* Volume 18 (3): 282–299.

Levine, J. (2002) *Harmful to Minors: The Perils of Protecting Children from Sex.* Minneapolis: University of Minnesota Press.

McDaniel, B.T. and Drouin, M. (2015) 'Sexting among married couples: who is doing it, and are they more satisfied?' *Cyberpsychology, Behavior, and Social Networking.* Volume 18 (11): 628–634.

Meiners, E.R. (2009) 'Never innocent: feminist trouble with sex offender registries and protection in a prison nation'. *Meridians: Feminism, Race, Transnationalism.* Volume 9 (2): 31–62.

Mitchell, K.J., Finkelhor, D., Jones, L.M. and Wolak, J. (2012) 'Prevalence and characteristics of youth sexting: a national study'. *Pediatrics.* Volume 129 (1): 1–8.

Newton-Brown, C., Garrett, J. and Carbines, A. (2013) *Report of the Law Reform Committee for the Inquiry into Sexting.* www.parliament.vic.gov.au/images/stories/committees/lawrefrom/isexting/LRC_Sexting_Final_Report.pdf (accessed 25 May 2016).

Nunziato, D.C. (2012) 'Romeo and Juliet online and in trouble: criminalizing depictions of teen sexuality (c u l8r: g2g 2 jail)'. *Northwestern Journal of Technology and Intellectual Property.* Volume 10 (3): 57–91.

O'Brien, B. (2009) 'To deal with "sexting," XXXtra discretion is advised'. http://usatoday30.usatoday.com/printedition/news/20090505/editorial05_st.art.htm (accessed 29 March 2017).

Odem, M.E. (1995) *Delinquent Daughters: Protecting and Policing Adolescent Female Sexuality in the United States, 1885–1920*. Chapel Hill: University of North Carolina Press.

Peters, J.D. (1999) *Speaking Into the Air: A History of the Idea of Communication*. Chicago: University of Chicago Press.

Podlas, K. (2011) 'The "legal epidemiology" of the teen sexting epidemic: how the media influenced a legislative outbreak'. *Pittsburgh Journal of Technology Law and Policy*. Volume 12 (1): 1–48.

Powell, A. (2010) 'Configuring consent: emerging technologies, unauthorised sexual images and sexual assault'. *The Australian and New Zealand Journal of Criminology*. Volume 43 (1): 76–90.

Projansky, S. (2007) 'Mass magazine cover girls: some reflections on postfeminist girls and postfeminism's daughters'. In D. Negra and Y. Tasker (eds) *Interrogating Postfeminism: Gender and the Politics of Popular Culture*. Durham, NC: Duke University Press.

Remick, L.A. (1993) 'Read her lips: an argument for a verbal consent standard in rape'. *University of Pennsylvania Law Review*. Volume 141 (3): 1103–1151.

Ringrose, J., Gill, R., Livingstone, S. and Harvey, L. (2012) *A Qualitative Study of Children, Young People and "Sexting": A Report Prepared for the NSPCC*. London: National Society for the Prevention of Cruelty to Children.

Rubin, G. (1993) 'Thinking sex: notes for a radical theory of the politics of sexuality'. In H. Abelove (ed) *The Lesbian and Gay Studies Reader*. New York: Routledge.

Slovic, B. (2010) 'Sext crimes: Oregon has a name for teens who take dirty photos with their cell phones: child pornographer'. www.wweek.com/portland/article-16544-sext-crimes.html (accessed 29 March 2017).

Smith, A., Richie, B.E. and Sudbury, J.U. (2006) *Color of Violence: The INCITE! Anthology*. Cambridge, MA: South End Press.

Spade, D. (2012) 'Their laws will never make us safer: an introduction'. In R. Conrad (ed) *Against Equality: Prisons Will Not Protect You*. Oakland, CA: AK Press.

Standage, T. (1998) *The Victorian Internet: The Remarkable Story of the Telegraph and the Nineteenth Centurys On-Line Pioneers*. New York: Walker and Co.

Strassberg, D., McKinnon, R., Sustaita, M. and Rullo, J. (2013) 'Sexting by high school students: an exploratory and descriptive study'. *Archives of Sexual Behavior*. Volume 42 (1): 15–21.

Sullivan, C.A. (1996) 'Kids, courts and queers: lesbian and gay youth in the juvenile justice and foster care systems'. *Law & Sexuality: A Review Of Lesbian, Gay, Bisexual, and Transgender Legal Issues*. Volume 6: 31–62.

Tallon, K., Choi, A., Keeley, M., et al. (2012) *New Voices/New Laws: School-Age Young People in New South Wales Speak Out about the Criminal Laws that Apply to Their Online Behaviour*. www.lawstuff.org.au/__data/assets/pdf_file/0009/15030/New-Voices-Law-Reform-Report.pdf (accessed 25 May 2016).

Texas School Safety Center (2012) *Before You Text…* http://beforeyoutext.com/ (accessed 25 August 2016).

Tolman, D.L. (1999) *Asking Some Unasked Questions*. www.wcwonline.org/Past-years/asking-some-unasked-questions (accessed 29 March 2017).

Walkerdine, V. (1997) *Daddy's Girl: Young Girls and Popular Culture*. Cambridge, MA: Harvard University Press.

Wartella, E. and Jennings, N. (2000) 'Children and computers: new technology – old concerns'. *The Future of Children*. Volume 10 (2): 31–43.

Wastler, S. (2010) 'The harm in "sexting"? Analyzing the constitutionality of child pornography statutes that prohibit the voluntary production, possession, and dissemination of sexually explicit images by teenagers'. *Harvard Journal of Law & Gender*. Volume 33: 687–702.

Wolak, J., Finkelhor, D. and Mitchell, K.J. (2012a) *Trends in Arrests for Child Pornography Possession: The Third National Juvenile Online Victimization Study (NJOV-3)*. www.unh.edu/ccrc/pdf/CV269_Child%20Porn%20Possession%20Bulletin_4-13-12.pdf (accessed 25 May 2016).

Wolak, J., Finkelhor, D. and Mitchell, K.J. (2012b) *Trends in Arrests for Child Pornography Production: The Third National Juvenile Online Victimization Study (NJOV-3)*. www.unh.edu/ccrc/pdf/CV270_Child%20Porn%20Production%20Bulletin_4-13-12.pdf (accessed 25 May 2016).

19
SEX ADVICE BOOKS AND SELF-HELP

Meg-John Barker, Rosalind Gill and Laura Harvey

Introduction

Sex advice is a rapidly growing media genre spanning newspaper problem pages, magazine articles, TV shows and a multiplicity of online forums, blogs and videos. In this chapter we examine the ways in which sex and sexuality are currently constructed and contested within one particular medium: sex advice books. After locating sex advice books within the wider context of self-help culture, sex therapy and sexual subjectification, we provide a brief history of the genre, and then draw together the existing literature with our own analysis of books published over the last two decades (Barker, Gill and Harvey, forthcoming).

As we will demonstrate, the basis on which sex advice books are sold is generally the perceived 'problem' of ensuring consistent levels of sex throughout a relationship. This 'problem' is grounded in assumptions: that sex is imperative, that it must take place within the context of monogamous coupledom and that it must follow a normative sexual script. Thus the 'solutions' proposed in the books generally limit themselves to varying, or 'spicing up', the normative sexual script in ways which erase the diversity of erotic possibilities and individualise what could be more accurately conceptualised as social struggles. However, as we will see, there are also pockets of resistance which exist, in both mainstream and 'alternative' sex advice books, to such constructions, as well as media other than written books which may offer potentials for more 'sex-critical' forms of sex advice (Downing, 2012).

Contextualising sex advice books

Sex advice books are part of the wider genre of self-help books, which focus, for example, upon confidence and assertiveness, planning a career, dieting or various other ways to become 'a new, improved you'. The multi-billion-dollar self-help industry and the therapeutic culture in which it is embedded have been criticised for individualising people's experiences in ways which exacerbate the very problems they claim to address (Illouz, 2008; Barker, 2013a). Solutions are located in the atomised individual, who is responsible for determining the future course of their life through taking on board the expert advice being offered (Vanderkam, 2012). Happiness and success are presented as equally available to all people, as long as they work hard enough at change.

Sex advice books can also be located within the wider arena of sexology and sex therapy, drawing on sexological classifications, research and therapeutic techniques (Barker, 2011; Barker and Richards, 2013). Just as therapeutic culture has been accused of contributing to the problems that it aims to address, so has sex therapy been implicated in 'disordering' people (Barker and Iantaffi, 2015). This occurs through the categorisation of those who deviate from the normative sexual script – of penis-in-vagina (PIV) intercourse leading to orgasm – as dysfunctional or paraphilic (Irvine, 2005), as well as through individualising sexual difficulties which are actually highly social (Tiefer, 1995) and providing universalising explanations for sexual experiences which have multiple meanings (Kleinplatz, 2012).

The distinct genre of sex advice books emerged in the early twentieth century in North America, Europe and other 'western' countries. Prior to this, such advice was contained within marriage manuals and generally focused purely on sex for procreation, presenting other forms of sex as dangerous (Gordon and Bernstein, 1970). In the early twentieth century, sex manuals presented sexual pleasure as vital for the happiness of middle-class marriage (Weeks, 2003). Sex advice became more focused on the importance of knowledge and skill, reflecting the growing scientific fields of sex research and sex therapy. Drawing upon psychoanalytic theory, emphasis was placed on women reaching orgasm through PIV intercourse, and inability to do this was frequently blamed on their perceived deficiencies (Neuhaus, 2000).

A further shift occurred in the 1960s and 70s, when sex advice books began to draw on more humanistic models of the self and to present sex as a means towards personal growth (Tiefer, 1995). Despite a move away from the reproductive focus, sex advice was still largely heteronormative, and only in the late 1970s did sex advice emerge which was aimed at lesbians or gay men (Klesse, 2007). Even today, as we will see, most books are clearly aimed at heterosexual audiences.

Following the HIV/AIDS pandemic in the 1980s, sex advice books put greater emphasis on safety and health; discourses of health remained key in the 1990s, as sex became (re)medicalised (Gupta and Cacchioni, 2013), alongside the shift towards 'treating' sexual dysfunctions with pharmaceuticals such as Viagra. Sex advice books increasingly drew on the medicalised language of function and dysfunction, as well as presenting sex as necessary for health (Gupta, 2011).

The recent turn towards a neoliberal, postfeminist sensibility has also meant a shift towards a lexicon of choice, empowerment, rights and pleasure, and a highly individualised turn which encourages people – particularly women – to work at sex through processes of self-transformation and consumption (Gill, 2009).

As we will see, aspects of all of these historical strands remain in current sex advice: sex for relationship success, sex for personal fulfilment, heteronormativity and rigid gender roles, medicalisation and 'healthicisation' (Gupta and Cacchioni, 2013) and neoliberal invocations to work at sex as a matter of personal choice and under the veneer of fun and pleasure.

Contemporary sex advice books

While there is a growing body of research on contemporary sex advice, much of this has focused on newspapers and women's magazines (e.g. Jackson and Scott, 1997;

Farvid and Braun, 2006; Gill, 2009; Moran and Lee, 2011). However, there is a burgeoning body of knowledge on books, including Potts's (1998, 2002) detailed examination of the still best-selling *Mars and Venus in the Bedroom* (Gray, 2003), Tyler's (2008) analysis of books recommended by sex therapists to their clients and Gupta and Cacchioni's (2013) analysis of 17 of the most popular sex manuals. We will weave their findings in here with our own analysis (Barker, Gill and Harvey, forthcoming), returning briefly to other forms of sex advice towards the end of the chapter.

For our analysis we obtained 65 sex advice books – those most popular on Amazon.com (and Amazon.co.uk) and those most frequently recommended by sex therapists and other professionals. We also endeavoured to obtain a selection of books recommended by 'sex-critical' professionals (educators, advisors and therapists), by asking for suggestions from colleagues in these areas. We obtained books which were recommended by other authors and those which were aimed at specific groups or dealt with specific sexual practices. For the final analysis we had 30 mainstream books, around half of which were aimed at couples and half specifically at female or male readers. The rest were either aimed at specific groups (e.g. lesbians, gay men or kink practitioners) or were explicitly presented as in some way 'alternative' or 'critical'.

The books contained many different styles. Perhaps most common was a conventional sex-manual format, but there were also several more explicitly therapeutic books (such as those addressing specific sexual problems), A–Z guides, books structured around busting various 'sex myths' and other formats. Taking a sex-critical approach to our analysis (Downing, 2012), we were mindful that sex advice is both a vehicle for pleasure and a purveyor of oppressive ideology (Ballaster, Beetham, Frazer and Hebron, 1991), and we recognised that the books were polysemic, contradictory and capable of being read in different ways by different audiences and at different times (Tasker, 1991). We attempted to attend to multiple possible meanings and to consider what was opened up and closed down, perpetuated and resisted, and included and excluded. We return specifically to points of resistance towards the end of the chapter, after presenting the general sense of the 'problem' constructed across the books and the most common proposed 'solutions' to it.

Positioning of the authors

The authors of the books are positioned in various ways as (s)experts in terms of both professional and personal (s)expertise (Potts, 2002). Several of the books emphasise the medical, psychological and/or counselling qualifications of their author/s, often referring to them with 'Dr' prefixes or letters after their names (e.g. Foley *et al.*, 2011; Berman, 2011). This implies that medicine and psychology are the appropriate realms for sex advice. Many books foreground the 'best-selling' nature of the author and their experience and expertise as a sex advisor (e.g. Berman, 2011; Corn, 2013). Several mention the personal expertise of the author in terms of the longevity and 'success' of their relationships, or their sexual prowess, reinforcing some of the assumptions inherent in the books about the importance of sex in relationships, and of techniques (e.g. Mintz, 2009; Gray, 2003). Authors are sometimes referred to in hyperbolic terms, such as 'sex guru' (Godson, 2002) or 'one of the world's foremost (and hottest) writers on sex' (Cox, 2011).

However, there are some authors who counter these claims to (s)expertise, such as de Botton (2012), a philosopher who challenges the assumption that the medical and psy disciplines are the appropriate realm for sex advice, and Hancock (2013) and similar sex-educator authors who position themselves as fellow travellers struggling with the complex world of sex and relationships.

The 'problem' set up by sex advice books: sex in intimate relationships

It is striking how similar sex advice books are in tone, structure and content. The vast majority rest on an assumed problem: that the reader is struggling, or will struggle, to maintain a sexual intimate relationship. A relationship without sex will inevitably end, so the reader requires the expertise of the author to provide them with 'solutions' to the problem if they put the necessary time and effort into learning and practicing these.

In order to construct sex and intimacy as a problem to be solved, books assume:

- The sexual imperative: that 'healthy' individuals and relationships must be sexual.
- Relationship normativity: that a 'relationship' means long-term heteromonogamous coupledom.
- The coital imperative: that 'sex' means the normative sexual script of 'foreplay' followed by PIV intercourse leading to orgasm.

The sexual imperative

The books reinforce the sexual imperative (Carrigan, Morrison and Gupta, 2013) by portraying sex as a basic human need analogous to eating and breathing (e.g. Litvinoff, 2008) and as an essential feature of personal identity (e.g. Berman, 2011). Sex is also presented as a vital way of achieving personal growth and improving individual health and well-being, and readers are exhorted to work at it in order to gain the greatest rewards to mind and body, for example through enhancing the quality of their sexual desire (e.g. Comfort and Quilliam, 2012), through engaging in more frequent sex (e.g. Mintz, 2009) and through learning techniques to improve sexual experience (e.g. Thomas and Thomas, 2010; see Gupta and Cacchioni, 2013).

Sex is also presented as necessary for relationships. Mintz writes that sex is the 'glue' that holds relationships together, and 'without sex, marriages can fall apart' (2009: 62). Readers are encouraged to aspire to 'great' sex (Gray, 2003; Corn, 2013).

Relationship normativity

While virtually all of the texts present the drive for sex as natural, universal and necessary to act upon, there are rigid limits around the contexts in which it is deemed acceptable to fulfil sexual desires. The books reproduce an ideology of sex in relationships which is mononormative and heteronormative. Books with a sex-manual format are often lavishly illustrated with photographs or drawings almost exclusively depicting male/female couples, and generally portray the same couple (e.g. Comfort and Quilliam, 2012; Page and Stanway, 2011) or set of couples (e.g. Berman, 2011; Thomas and Thomas). Open non-monogamy is rarely considered, and any form of group sex is presented as dangerous to the relationship (e.g. Banks, 2004), so readers are encouraged to try alternatives such as having sex in front of a mirror (e.g. Berman, 2011).

Men and women are presented as being naturally different yet 'complementary', and many books are sold to help readers understand where the 'opposite sex' is coming from (e.g. Gray, 2003; Corn, 2013; see Potts, 1998; 2002; Tyler, 2008). Many sex advice books simply ignore the fact that people could – presumably – find a better sexual match with somebody of the same gender, presenting heterosexuality as the only, natural and normal sexuality (e.g. Bake, 2010). Others present 'gay and lesbian' relationships in tokenistic sections (e.g. Page and Stanway, 2011), reassuring readers that same-sex attraction does not necessarily mean that they are gay (e.g. Mintz, 2009; Cox, 2011) and/or suggesting that people in same-sex relationships generally face distress and/or sexless relationships (e.g. Berman, 2011).

The coital imperative

The coital imperative – that 'sex' means PIV intercourse leading to orgasm – is constructed through the structure and content of the books. Many follow their introductory sections with sections on solo sex, foreplay and then 'sex' (mostly depicted as PIV), often with a final chapter on more 'spicy' forms of sex. Oral and manual sex are often relegated to the 'foreplay' sections, suggesting they are not 'real' sex (see Barker, Gill and Harvey, forthcoming). As Potts (2002) and Tyler (2008) point out, while the majority of women require external clitoral stimulation for orgasm, the modes of sex which are privileged are not those through which this is most easily achieved.

Solo sex is predominantly constructed as a means for the reader to tune into how their body works in order to enable a partner to give them an orgasm (e.g. Cox, 2011), or as a means to practice specific techniques to improve the sexual experience of a partner (e.g. Page and Stanway, 2011). Sections of books are devoted to sexual problems (e.g. Litvinoff, 2008; Berman, 2011), particularly those which interfere with the 'sexual response cycle' of desire, arousal, penetration and orgasm (see Barker, 2011).

So, through these three normativities the problem of sex in intimate relationships is set up. Relationships (and individuals) must be sexual, but within the confines of a heteromonogamous relationship and a specific form of sex. Books urge their readers to resist any drop-off in sexual activity over time. They present images of ideal kinds of sex and orgasms so that people can be ever striving for better, more health-giving, relationship-restoring sex. This is decontextualised from lives in which people are tired, stressed or worried about money, or have to do housework or look after children. Even when cultural pressures are considered (e.g. Comfort and Quilliam, 2012; Litvinoff, 2008), the solution is presented as an internal one. Couples must make time, work at sex, replace negative or distracted thoughts with positive or sexy ones and 'trick' their brains into 'stimulating the hot and wild sex chemicals throughout a relationship' (Kerner, 2013: 64). A happy sex life is presented as both the reader's choice and their responsibility (Berman, 2011; see Ahmed, 2010).

Most books do not consider many of the possible 'solutions' which could resolve the 'problem' of sex in intimate relationships (if, indeed, we consider it a problem). For example, they cannot countenance the possibility that it might be acceptable to be asexual or celibate, or that couples may have differing levels or types of desires and get some or all of these met alone (through solo sex and/or fantasy and/or porn) or outside of coupledom (e.g. through casual/friend sex or some other form of non-monogamy). And they cannot conceive of any radical departure from the normative sexual script, or expansion of what counts as sex (for example sex without orgasms, or that does not involve PIV).

We now turn our attention to the two dominant – almost hegemonic – 'solutions' which are put forward in sex advice books, before considering moments of resistance to these models that do occur.

'Solutions' proposed by sex advice books

Two potential 'solutions' to the 'problem' are proposed in sex advice books: varying elements surrounding the normative sexual script and 'spicing up' the standard script with tightly policed forays into sex toys, kink, fantasy, erotica or anal sex.

Variations

The main 'solution' proposed is to vary the positions for PIV intercourse. Bevan (2013: 32) states that the solution to 'growing stale' is mastering multiple positions. Thomas and Thomas (2010) provide 90 pages of photographs of positions for PIV. Elsewhere, 'sexpert' Tracey Cox (e.g. Cox, 2011), has 'golden rules' for avoiding a 'sex rut': always finish sex in a different position to that in which you started it, and never do the same position on two subsequent occasions (Gill, 2009: 360). Several books suggest altering costumes and locations for sex as a form of variation which keeps the normative sexual script intact (e.g. Page and Stanway, 2011; Mintz, 2009; Comfort and Quilliam, 2012).

Spicing it up

The notion of 'spicing up' your sex life with anything other than varied positions, costumes or locations creates a tension for sex advice books. While this is widely regarded as a key 'solution' to the 'problem' of sex in intimate relationships (e.g. Corn, 2013; Bevan, 2013; Mintz, 2009), some 'spicy' forms of sex lend themselves to being done alone (e.g. fantasy and porn/erotica), and some may involve something other than the normative sexual script (e.g. sex with toys, anal sex, kinky sex – involving light bondage, sensation play or power play, for example). Therefore books have to do a great deal of boundary work in order to encourage the reader to engage in spicy sex, without straying so far that 'something unspeakable will skitter across' (Rubin, 1984: 282).

Most books manage this with a declaration of openness or questioning of what counts as normal, while locating 'spicy sex' at the very end of the book, suggesting that it is of only minority interest. They also produce warnings about potential emotional or physical damage that are not present in relation to discussion of other forms of sex. Some present more 'extreme' practices in a sensationalist or ridiculing manner; Godson (2002), for example, states that 'there is no such thing as normal' (66), but later begins her 'sexploration' chapter with the words: 'Warning: This chapter contains strong words, violence and graphic descriptions of sometimes illegal sexual acts that you will most probably never choose to try' (156).

Boundary-drawing is a key feature of these books – not just between 'normal' and 'spicy' but also between sharing fantasies and acting on fantasies (e.g. Berman, 2011), between erotica and porn (e.g. Litvinoff, 2008) and between 'fun' kink (mostly adding light bondage or spanking to PIV intercourse) and 'real' BDSM (bondage and discipline, dominance and submission and sadomasochism) (e.g. Kingsley, 2011).

The 'solutions' of varying or 'spicing up' sex severely restrict erotic imaginations. The focus on individuals learning sexual skills and techniques and/or buying products and toys to enhance their sex lives (see Harvey and Gill, 2011a; 2011b) also locates the problem within the individual, rather than within the wider cultural messages which insist that people have a certain kind of sex at a consistent level (Barker and Iantaffi, 2015). As de Botton puts it:

> sex manuals ... have been united in locating the problems of sexuality in the physical sphere. Sex will go better – they variously assure us – when we master the lotus position, learn to use ice-cubes creatively or apply proven techniques for attaining synchronised orgasms.
>
> (2012: 6)

Such 'solutions' fail to recognise the role of sex advice media in constructing the very templates against which people judge themselves during sex, often preventing them from relaxing and from 'being present' and experiencing pleasure in the ways that the books advocate (see Barker, 2014).

Resistances

So far we have presented a fairly uniform, normative picture of sex advice books. However, like other media, sex advice books are polysemic and contradictory, and many tensions and paradoxes are present, such as those around presenting sex between the genders as difficult but same-sex relationships as no solution, and around both challenging and simultaneously policing the notion of 'normal' sex.

Certainly contemporary best-selling sex advice books reveal a cultural re-drawing of the dividing line between acceptable and unacceptable sex (Rubin, 1984), although they leave intact the idea that such a dividing line, or hierarchy of acceptability, exists. Same-sex attraction is rarely excluded completely; bodies which have previously been deemed inherently non-sexual are generally included, albeit tokenistically (e.g. older and disabled bodies); and kink practices find their way into the 'spicy' chapter of the book and occasionally escape into other areas (e.g. Zopol (2009), lists blindfolds alongside everyday kit for sex, and Banks (2004) includes the potential for asphyxiation in a general section on safer sex). Most books question the idea that sex means PIV intercourse, despite implicitly reinforcing that norm through their structure and imagery. There is both a doing and an undoing of what counts as 'normal' sex: an acknowledgement that there is more to it than PIV, yet a repeated reiteration of this elsewhere as what sex 'is'.

Similarly, it is not possible to simply divide sex advice books into those which are 'mainstream' and those which are 'critical' or 'alternative' because all books include moments of resistance, as well as reproductions of normative assumptions. However, it is useful to touch here on those books which explicitly position themselves as inclusive of diverse sexualities or as critical of conventional messages around sex.

Again, there are points of both construction and contestation in these books. For example, Godson (2002) includes lesbian, gay and bisexual people throughout her book and her illustrations of sexual positions are inclusive of PIV, anal sex and strap-on sex, demonstrating that it is possible to follow standard formats in ways that challenge norms. However, the book does some very clear boundary-policing around kinky sex. Similarly, some books which take an explicitly 'myth-busting' approach to sex, with titles like *The Sex Myth* (Magnanti, 2012) or *Everything You Know about Sex is Wrong* (Kick, 2006), may challenge some normativities (e.g. natural gender differences or the idea of sex addiction – Magnanti) while reproducing others as fact (e.g. the healthiness of sex – Kick). They also provide individualised 'solutions' in places (see Barker, Gill and Harvey, forthcoming) – a feature of most books aimed at kinky readers, which generally present sexual negotiation and consent as an agentic act between equal individuals, rather than as inevitably embedded within social structures which limit and constrain agency (see Barker, 2013c).

Books aimed at lesbian and gay readers contest heteronormativity and sometimes mononormativity, while buying into many normative assumptions – about the sexual imperative and sexual dysfunctions, for example. Klesse (2007) has demonstrated how such books construct a normative white, middle-class ideal of a successful same-sex partnership through a standard self-help narrative of individualisation and responsibilisation. Similarly, the one book which foregrounded disability (Kaufman, Silverberg and Odette, 2003), including diverse bodies and practices and considering sexual ethics and structural power dynamics, has been criticised by Sothern for reproducing the sexual imperative and for 'rendering the project of disabled sexual liberation as a personal project of self-governance' (2007: 144) rather than locating it within a disabling society.

Two books explicitly highlight the 'problem' set up by other sex advice books, and consider different 'solutions' to those generally proposed. De Botton writes that mainstream sex books are 'intolerably humiliating' and that they mock 'the sort of challenges we are usually faced with' (2012: 6), such as mutual resentments over childcare and finances, craving sex with people we do not love or having an affair and breaking a partner's heart. Perel's *Mating in Captivity* (2007) also recognises the problems that are set up by the cultural insistence on both the sexual imperative and on long-term monogamous relationships. While de Botton's 'solutions' mostly focus on changing the cultural mores around affairs, Perel considers open non-monogamy in addition to enhancing eroticism in monogamous relationships. Thus both present rather more of a radical/social challenge than other books.

Perhaps it is when we read *across* sex advice books that there is most scope for challenging normative assumptions. As Attwood (forthcoming) points out, reading across can enable us to see the diversity of practices that are considered under 'sex' and the diversity of contexts in which sex can take place, blurring the lines between sex and other activities such as play, leisure, spirituality, art and relaxation (Barker, 2013b). Such a reading-across also highlights the contradictory 'solutions' that are proposed, such as the arguments of Kingsley (2011) and Corn (2013) that men and women both really want men to be more dominant sexually, while Keesling (2011) and Kerner (2013) instead present female dominance, assertion and empowerment as the universal answer to the same problem. This disrupts the gender normativity that is present in any of the books taken alone, although most books still construct the responsibility for ensuring 'great sex' to maintain a relationship as more 'women's work' than it is men's (Potts, 1998; Tyler, 2008; Gupta and Cacchioni, 2013).

Conclusions

The construction of sex in sex advice books presented here is consistent with that in other forms of sex media that we have analysed, such as television documentaries (Harvey and Gill, 2011a; 2011b) and magazines (Gill, 2009). However, there may be scope in other forms of media to destabilise some of the normative assumptions we have described. For example, our analysis of newspaper problem pages revealed that aspects which are presented as solid and unimpeachable in sex advice books seem far more shaky and precarious in the former medium. The most common problems in these columns relate to infidelity and attraction to those of the 'same sex', suggesting that neither mononormativity nor heteronormativity are as stable as sex advice books suggest. The fact that men and women are represented equally in concerns around sexual problems suggests that sexual experience may be much less gendered than advice books portray it as (see Barker, Gill and Harvey, forthcoming). Barker (2013c) has also demonstrated that the format of online blogs opens up the possibility of considering sex as a highly social situation, where agency operates within multiple intersecting power dynamics.

While textual analyses are very helpful in this area, it is useful to supplement them with research on the ways in which audiences read sex advice books and negotiate their own understandings and experiences of sex in relation to these. Woodiwiss (2014) has conducted such research in relation to books specifically aimed at survivors of sexual abuse (analysing both the books and reader accounts), but we are not aware of any research doing the same with readers of more general sex advice books. However, van Hooff's (2013) research on heterosexual couples does open an important window onto everyday experiences of sex. Van Hooff's participants construct sex as an essential feature of long-term relationships, drawing upon discourses of the sexual imperative, the natural male sex drive, mononormativity and sex as women's work, much as they are presented in sex advice books (van Hooff, 2014).

We would like to see attempts towards more sex-critical sex advice books, and will be engaging in such possibilities ourselves in future (Barker and Hancock, 2017). Instead of being framed around a specific sexual script, these should be framed around consent and ethical treatment of self and others, as well as around mutual pleasure/fulfilment. Normative underlying assumptions would be replaced with the following:

- Sex can happen in diverse contexts, with none prioritised over others.
- Differences in amount and type of desires (in individuals over time, and between individuals) are inevitable and acceptable, not problems to be solved.
- There is benign variation of both bodies and sexual practices (Rubin, 1984).
- People are socially and culturally situated, making sex fundamentally a biopsychosocial experience.

It is debatable whether the self-help format can produce a sustained social challenge without lapsing into individualistic projects of self-transformation (see Barker, 2013b). One of the key tensions is how to address an individual reader in a way that situates sexual experience more socially. We hope that supplementing the book with other media (podcasts, online videos and discussions and workshop materials) will help with this, given the potential of multi-media approaches outlined above.

Bibliography

Ahmed, S. (2010). *The promise of happiness*. Durham, NC: Duke University Press.
Attwood, F. (forthcoming). *Media, sex and technology*. Edinburgh: Edinburgh University Press.
Bake, C. (2010). *The joy of mindful sex: Be in the moment and enrich your lovemaking*. Lewes: Ivy Press Ltd.
Ballaster, R., Beetham, M., Frazer, E. and Hebron, S. (1991). *Women's worlds: Ideology, femininity and women's magazines*. London: Palgrave Macmillan.

Banks, I. (2004). *Sex: 16 years onwards, all models, shapes, sizes and colours – the practical guide to sexual health and enjoyment (Haynes Owners Workshop Manual)*. London: Haynes Publishing.

Barker, M. (2011). 'Existential sex therapy'. *Sexual and Relationship Therapy*. 26 (1): 33–47.

Barker, M. (2013a). *Mindful counselling and psychotherapy: Practising mindfully across approaches and issues*. London: Sage.

Barker, M. (2013b). *Rewriting the rules: An integrative guide to love, sex and relationships*. London: Routledge.

Barker, M. (2013c). 'Consent is a grey area? A comparison of understandings of consent in 50 *Shades of Grey* and on the BDSM blogosphere'. *Sexualities*. Volume 16 (8): 896–914.

Barker, M. (2014). 'How social is your mindfulness? Towards a mindful sex and relationship therapy'. In M. Bazzano (ed) *After mindfulness*. Basingstoke: Palgrave Macmillan.

Barker, M. and Hancock, J. (2017). *Sex: A practical guide*. London: Icon Books.

Barker, M. and Iantaffi, A. (2015). 'Social models of disability and sex'. In H. Spandler, J. Anderson and B. Sapey (eds) *Distress or disability? Madness and the politics of disablement*. Bristol: Policy Press.

Barker, M. and Richards, C. (2013). Brief report: What does Bancroft's *Human Sexuality and Its Problems* tell us about current understandings of sexuality? *Feminism & Psychology*. Volume 23 (2): 243–251.

Barker, M., Gill, R. and Harvey, L. (forthcoming). *Mediated intimacy: Sex advice in media culture*. London: Polity.

Berman, L. (2011). *Loving sex: The book of joy and passion*. London: Dorling Kindersley.

Bevan, K. (2013). *Drive her wild: 100 sex tips for men: A red-hot guide to seduction, with techniques to thrill and exhilarate your partner*. London: Lorenz Books.

Carrigan, M., Morrison, T. and Gupta, K. (2013). 'Asexuality special theme issue'. *Psychology & Sexuality*. Volume 4 (2): 111–120.

Comfort, A. and Quilliam, S. (2012). *The joy of sex: The timeless guide to lovemaking*. London: Hachette.

Corn, L. (2013). *101 nights of great sex*. Los Angeles, CA: Park Avenue Publishers.

Cox, T. (2011). *Hot sex: How to do it*. London: Corgi Books.

de Botton, A. (2012). *How to think more about sex*. London: The School of Life.

Downing, L. (2012). 'What is "sex critical" and why should we care about it?' *Sex Critical*, 27 July 2012. http://sexcritical.blogspot.co.uk/2012/07/what-is-sex-critical-and-why-should-we.html (accessed on 22 October 2012).

Farvid, P. and Braun, V. (2006). '"Most of us guys are raring to go anytime, anyplace, anywhere": male and female sexuality in *Cleo* and *Cosmo*'. *Sex Roles*. Volume 55 (5–6): 295–310.

Foley, S., Kope, S. A. and Sugrue, D. P. (2011). *Sex matters for women*. New York: The Guilford Press.

Gill, R. (2009). 'Mediated intimacy and postfeminism: a discourse analytic examination of sex and relationships advice in a women's magazine'. *Discourse & Communication*. Volume 3 (4): 345–369.

Godson, S. (2002). *The sex book*. London: Cassell Illustrated.

Gordon, M. and Bernstein, M. C. (1970). 'Mate choice and domestic life in the nineteenth century marriage manual'. *Journal of Marriage and Family*. Volume 32 (4): 665–674.

Gray, J. (2003). *Mars and Venus in the Bedroom*. London: Vermillion.

Gupta, K. (2011). '"Screw health": Representations of sex as a health-promoting activity in medical and popular literature'. *Journal of Medical Humanities*. Volume 32 (2): 127–140.

Gupta, K. and Cacchioni, T. (2013). 'Sexual improvement as if your health depends on it: an analysis of contemporary sex manuals'. *Feminism & Psychology*, Volume 23 (4): 442–458.

Hancock, J. (2013). *Sex explained: A real and relevant guide to sex, relationships and you*. Self-published.

Harvey, L. and Gill, R. (2011a). 'Spicing it up: sexual entrepreneurs and the sex inspectors'. In R. Gill and C. Scharff (eds) *New femininities: Postfeminism, neoliberalism and subjectivity*. Basingstoke: Palgrave Macmillan.

Harvey, L. and Gill, R. (2011b). 'The sex inspectors: self-help, makeover and mediated sex'. In K. Ross (ed) *Handbook on gender, sexualities and media*. Oxford: Blackwell.

Illouz, E. (2008). *Saving the modern soul: Therapy, emotions, and the culture of self-help*. Berkeley: University of California Press.

Irvine, J. M. (2005). *Disorders of Desire*. Philadelphia: Temple University Press.

Jackson, S. and Scott, S. (1997). 'Gut reactions to matters of the heart: reflections on rationality, irrationality and sexuality'. *The Sociological Review*. Volume 45 (4): 551–575.

Kaufman, M., Silverberg, C. and Odette, F. (2003). *The ultimate guide to sex and disability: For all of us who live with disabilities, chronic pain or illness*. San Francisco, CA: Cleis Press.

Keesling, B. (2011). *The good girl's guide to bad sex*. London: Bantam Books.

Kerner, I. (2013). *Passionista: The empowered woman's guide to pleasuring a man*. New York: Harper-Collins.

Kick, R. (ed) (2006). *Everything you know about sex is wrong*. New York: The Disinformation Company.

Kingsley, E. (2011). *Just f*ck me! What women want men to know about taking control in the bedroom: A guide for couples*. Nashville, TN: Secret Life Publishing.

Kleinplatz, P. J. (ed) (2012). *New directions in sex therapy: Innovations and alternatives*. Routledge.

Klesse, C. (2007). '"How to be a happy homosexual?!" Non-monogamy and governmentality in relationship manuals for gay men in the 1980s and 1990s'. *The Sociological Review*. Volume 55 (3): 571–591.

Litvinoff, S. (2008). *The Relate guide to sex in loving relationships*. London: Vermillion.

Magnanti, B. (2012). *The sex myth: Why everything we're told is wrong*. London: Weidenfeld & Nicolson.

Mintz, L. (2009). *A tired woman's guide to passionate sex: Reclaim your desire and reignite your relationship*. Avon, MA: Adams Media.

Moran, C. and Lee, C. (2011). 'On his terms: representations of sexuality in women's magazines and the implications for negotiating safe sex'. *Psychology & Sexuality*. Volume 2 (2): 159–180.

Neuhaus, J. (2000) 'The importance of being orgasmic: Sexuality, gender, and marital sex manuals in the United States, 1920–1963'. *Journal of the History of Sexuality*. Volume 9 (4): 447–473.

Page, R. and Stanway, A. (2011). *The lover's guide laid bare: The art of better lovemaking*. Cambridge: Lifetime Vision Ltd.

Perel, E. (2007). *Mating in captivity: Sex, lies and domestic bliss*. London: HarperCollins.

Potts, A. (1998). 'The science/fiction of sex: John Gray's Mars and Venus in the bedroom'. *Sexualities*. Volume 1 (2): 153–173.

Potts, A. (2002). *The science/fiction of sex: Feminist deconstruction and the vocabularies of heterosex*. London: Routledge.

Rubin, G. (1984). 'Thinking sex: Notes for a radical theory on the politics of sexuality'. In C. Vance (ed) *Pleasure and danger: Exploring female sexuality*. London: Routledge.

Sothern, M. (2007). 'You could truly be yourself if you just weren't you: Sexuality, disabled body space, and the (neo) liberal politics of self-help'. *Environment and Planning D*. Volume 25 (1): 144–159.

Tasker, Y. (1991). 'Having it all: Feminism and the pleasures of the popular'. In C. Lury, S. Franklin and J. Stacey (eds) *Off-centre: Feminism and cultural studies*. London: Routledge.

Thomas, K. and Thomas, K. (2010). *The modern Kama Sutra: The ultimate guide to the secrets of London: Erotic pleasure*. London: HarperElement.

Tiefer, L. (1995). *Sex is not a natural act*. Boulder, CO: Westview Press.

Tyler, M. (2008). 'Sex self-help books: Hot secrets for great sex or promoting the sex of prostitution?' *Women's Studies International Forum*. Volume 31(5): 363–372.

Vanderkam, L. (2012). 'The paperback quest for joy: America's unique love affair with self-help books'. *City Journal*, Autumn. www.city-journal.org/2012/22_4_self-help-books.html (accessed 18 June 2014).

Van Hooff, J. (2013). *Modern couples? Continuity and change in heterosexual relationships*. Farnham: Ashgate.

Van Hooff, J. (2014). 'Doing it with the lights on: An exploration of the sexual lives of married and cohabiting heterosexual women'. Paper presented at *Gender, Equality and Intimacy: (Un)Comfortable Bedfellows?* Institute of Education, 7 April, London.

Weeks, J. (2003). *Sexuality*. London: Routledge.
Woodiwiss, J. (2014). 'Negotiating intimate and (a)sexual stories'. Paper presented at *Gender, Equality and Intimacy: (Un)Comfortable Bedfellows?* Institute of Education, 7 April, London.
Zopol, F. (2009). *Sex instruction manual: Essential information and techniques for optimum performance*. San Francisco, CA: Quirk Productions.

20
SOCIAL MEDIA PLATFORMS AND SEXUAL HEALTH

Paul Byron

This chapter considers the recent history and practices of promoting sexual health through social media. It considers dating/hook-up apps such as Grindr and Tinder, and common social media platforms like Facebook. In the past decade, public health researchers have entered these spaces to extend their reach to key populations, particularly the designated 'risk populations' of young people and men who have sex with men (MSM). Through its attention to new media, public health often expands its risk focus beyond the concept of sexual 'risk behaviours', to encompass digital media practices as risky, or as contributing to sexual health risks. This has generated claims that social media users (particularly users of geo-locative dating/hook-up apps) are more likely to engage in sex that puts them at risk of HIV/STI transmission. However, there is disagreement on these claims, and media studies and cultural studies approaches have offered more complex understandings of how risk and safeties are negotiated through digital and social media. This can be seen in accounts of the opportunities and affordances of these media. This chapter will trace some of these tensions within recent public health and cultural/media studies literature.

Public health use of social media for sexual health promotion

Public health professionals increasingly seek to reach target populations through social media (Capurro *et al.*, 2014). Studies considering the viability of promoting sexual health through social media have tended to focus on young people (Gold *et al.*, 2011), citing their high use of various platforms. Digital sexual health promotions also commonly target gay and other men who have sex with men, extending a legacy of online health strategies for HIV prevention. Reports of successful social media-based interventions are scarce (Capurro *et al.*, 2014), and to date, most literature regarding social media use for sexual health promotion is observational rather than interventional. For many practitioners, 'SNS [Social Networking Sites] are too important a communicative social venue to be completely neglected by health promoters' (Loss *et al.*, 2014: 169), and a common focus of health research is measuring the feasibility and acceptability of such interventions.

Considerations of the potential value of social media interventions extend upon an earlier discourse of eHealth, and a focus on social marketing approaches (Lefebvre, 2007; Thackeray *et al.*, 2008). Public health practitioners have increasingly engaged in social marketing to communicate health information to specific populations, often engaging with mobile technologies and social media (Lefebvre, 2009). In this work, digital media use is seen as an opportunity for public health professionals to expand their audiences, and to foster relationships with targeted populations. It has been highlighted that web 2.0 platforms are not simply new tools with which to do the same kinds of work, because they have changed the landscape of public health social marketing (Lefebvre, 2007). However, many social media interventions have not offered a new style of health promotion, nor have they engaged with the participatory and interactive communication cultures of these media (Byron, 2015).

Considering the HIV/STI prevention literature regarding social media, four main approaches can be ascertained. The first is the recruitment of study participants through social media outreach. The second uses social media for surveillance, utilising data collected from sites such as Grindr or Craigslist to consider the risk status of site users (see, for example, Delaney et al., 2014; Fries et al., 2014). The third considers the feasibility of using social media platforms for sexual health promotion (see, for example, Sun et al., 2015). The fourth reports on sexual health interventions that have taken place, including the development of new platform-specific content (see, for example, Bull et al., 2012; Pedrana et al., 2013).

When HIV/STI prevention research considers social media as an added 'risk' to a population's likelihood of infection, social and digital media are often presented as 'a challenge' to public health (Fries et al., 2014). This emphasis can overlook the opportunities that digital media provide for negotiating sexual safety (Pingel et al., 2013; Race, 2010). It also overlooks how sexual safety strategies can extend beyond STI/HIV-prevention practices, such as screening partners through in-app chatting, or arranging to meet in public places (Bauermeister et al., 2010). While they are neglected in many risk-focused studies of MSMs' use of dating/hook-up apps, these practices highlight active negotiations of safety and risk that are more expansive than public health agendas, but may accommodate these. According to Bauermeister et al. (2010), men who meet partners online often saw potential violence as the greatest risk. This fear can be read into numerous media articles about Grindr-assisted assaults and robberies published in recent years.

Often, established public health tools and health promotion methods that preceded the advent of social media are not adjusted for new media environments. For example, health interventions commonly employ a 'settings-based' approach in which target populations are reached through spaces they already occupy (Poland et al., 2009). Traditionally, a setting is a geographical locale with physical boundaries, but social media differ from common settings such as schools, workplaces or community groups on this basis (Loss et al., 2014). The porous boundaries of social media networks, and their overlap with offline communities and relationships, do not correlate with a settings-based approach. This is particularly pertinent when considering Facebook, and the diversity of relational ties in this space – many of which were forged through a range of offline environments (Ellison et al., 2007). On this basis, Facebook cannot be considered as a site housing certain populations or clusters of identity groups, but rather as always hosting a dispersed community of networks that include close and distant friendships, family members, colleagues and people with shared interests (Witzel et al., 2016). This makes Facebook an unlikely space for circulating sexual health content (Byron et al., 2013).

Young people, social media and sexual health

As digital ethnographers argue, new media participation is 'intertwined with young people's practices, learning, and identity formation' (Ito et al., 2010: 31). Social media spaces do not necessarily sit apart from schools, workplaces, bedrooms or family spaces, and for many young people, social media constitutes everyday communication across various channels, platforms and devices. For young people, sex and relationship information is enmeshed with media and friendship practices (Powell, 2008: 301). Such information is widely available both formally and informally and can include, but not necessarily prioritise, sexual health information.

That social media contributes 'new ideas and experiences of intimacy, friendship and identity' (Chambers, 2013: 1) further complicates public health attempts to infiltrate these sites. Young people's social media spaces do not offer a captive audience for health promoters. Young people interact across a range of spaces and media, and in ways that may erode boundaries between spaces for learning and socialising (Albury, 2013: 8). Typically, sexual health interventions have relied on such boundaries to reach specific populations. For young people, media and friendship practices integrate through digital communications, and this poses a significant challenge to sexual health promotion strategies.

Despite the claims of many adults, young people are concerned about their privacy and manage their social media practices accordingly (Livingstone, 2008; Marwick and boyd, 2014). The risk of sexuality disclosures within social media can be of concern, particularly for young same-sex-attracted people (Duguay, 2016; Rubin and McClelland, 2015). Cassidy's study of young gay men's 'technocultural entanglement' of Facebook and Gaydar use highlights the difficulties in managing one's gayness through social media (2013: 11). In this context, health interventions seeking to engage LGBTIQ young people through social media such as Facebook are likely to meet resistance. And where interventions are based on the stated identity of user profiles, these are unlikely to reach LGBTIQ populations who are not 'out' in these spaces.

The stigma of sexual health and HIV/STIs is a key barrier to the success of social media-based sexual health promotion (Evers et al., 2013; Witzel et al., 2016). The disclosure that posting and sharing HIV-prevention information can imply or suggest has limited the uptake of recent social media interventions (Witzel et al., 2016). Young people and MSM do discuss and share information about sexual health, but typically with close friends and in person, where there is greater privacy and less likelihood of this information being forwarded to others (Byron et al., 2013; Divecha et al., 2012).

In facing these issues, health researchers increasingly engage with cultural and ethnographic studies of social media practice. These highlight how social media are dynamic spaces in which users both consume and produce media, simultaneously interacting as authors, recipients and curators of information (Byron, 2015). Young people have noted that social media-based sexual health interventions are more likely to work if they are humorous, so as to avoid or reduce STI-related stigma and increase the likelihood of peer-to-peer sharing (Evers et al., 2013; Pfeiffer et al., 2014). Facebook advertising has also been noted as a potential avenue for health promoters to reach young people because it is more discreet, less 'identifying' and optional – that is, the user can access this information without it being visible to their networks (Byron et al., 2013).

Gay men and digital HIV prevention

Unlike those for young people, online HIV-prevention strategies for MSM precede and inform the current social media interventions for this population. This can be seen through two decades of research and health interventions engaging with men through websites such as Gaydar and Gay.com.[1] In part, this reflects a longer history in which gay men have been classified as a 'risk population' by public health and its policy and research agendas, as well as a history of practice in which gay men have actively disseminated sexual health information through peer and friendship networks.

Prior to the current social media landscape, HIV-prevention studies saw health professionals interact with gay men in the chat rooms of Gaydar and similar sites, as part of a 'community outreach' approach (Rhodes, 2004). For Mowlabocus and colleagues, community outreach involves 'taking information, resources and support systems out (of the clinic, the health centre, the hospital) into the spaces and places where people meet to socialize – and "hook up"'(2014: 6). While reflecting a 'settings-based' approach (Poland et al., 2009), much MSM outreach is also peer-led and administered, so has more in common with the peer-based interactions central to social media practice. Mowlabocus and colleagues argue that, given the extent of gay men's digital media practices, community outreach through these media is absolutely necessary (2014: 18), and allows for the streamlining of information to particular demographics in line with current discourses of personalised health care (ibid.). In a discussion of recruiting and training MSM to undertake HIV-prevention work through social media, Young et al. (2012) report that 'peer leaders' can be recruited as 'peer health educators' without the need for social media training, since they are already skilled in this practice.

Today, HIV-prevention interventions for MSM increasingly engage with Grindr – the most popular dating/hook-up app for men in Western countries. Globally, the Chinese app Blued is the most populated dating/hook-up app for MSM, yet health literature regarding this platform is just beginning to surface (Bien et al., 2015; Liu, 2016). Health studies of all such apps typically focus on the sexual health risks of users, measuring associations between risk practices and the use of specific media platforms (see, for example, Holloway et al., 2014). Such studies distinguish groups of MSM based on their media practices, as per reference to 'Grindr-Using MSM' (Goedel et al., 2016). Through such language, a discourse of media risk is developed and sustained, despite the opportunities these media can also provide for safer sexual negotiations (Race, 2010).

Despite decades of health studies measuring correlations between sexual risk-taking and the use of dating/hook-up sites, there is no agreement on whether or how these media influence risk-taking behaviours (Albury and Byron, 2016). While this risk emphasis prevails in public health accounts of MSM and social media practice, studies of gay men's sexual and media cultures question it. Such studies highlight how safety is negotiated in particular ways, such as through serosorting (Davis et al., 2006), and propose that Grindr use cannot neatly fit into a risk/opportunity assessment (Race, 2015). Rather, digital dating/hook-up negotiations can offer users new and surprising formations of intimacy (Race, 2015) that can challenge traditional understandings of gay men's sexual relations (Davis et al., 2006).

In a study of the website Manhunt, Race notes that this was the first dating site on which Sydney MSM were routinely asked to record and share their HIV status for sexual purposes (Race, 2010: 9) – a platform feature that reflects a culture of 'negotiated safety' (Kippax et al., 1993). Since this, other platforms have incorporated HIV and sexual health status features, including Hornet, where users can display the date of their last sexual health test (Cassidy, 2013: 203). These public statements are not the full extent of the sexual health information provided, however, since they say little of how private chat functions 'enable various forms of controlled and potentially anonymised disclosure prior to any sexual encounter' (Race, 2015: 503).

For many gay men, social media and sexual health practices integrate through the use of mobile phone apps, and can generate 'new distributions of intimacy' (Race, 2015).

Although the practice of finding sex through these media is common, different sites and apps offer different cultural formations (Léobon and Frigault, 2008). In taking a universal approach to a range of social media, HIV-prevention strategies overlook the specific cultures of a platform, and how these can represent, accommodate and produce different sexual practices, identities and communities. Previously, Gaydar was said to contribute to an ongoing typology of gayness (Payne, 2007), producing a 'cultural legibility' of gay (Mowlabocus, 2010b). Sites such as Grindr, Scruff, Blued, etc. might also be considered in relation to how these inform, produce and challenge cultural aspects of current and emerging communities and identities, such as the 'Scruff guy' (Roth, 2014).

Formal approaches to informal networks

A key problem with sexual health promoters using social media is their instrumental approach to these spaces (Lupton, 2015). This approach fails to engage with the diversity of media use, or the range of community and intimacy practices that stray beyond anticipated sex and relationship-seeking. Given the different relationships practised through hook-up apps and other social media platforms, including Facebook, 'safer sex' discussion among peers, partners and friends is likely to exist in communications taking place there, but it may not be visible to health professionals, one's networks or the platforms. Increasingly, public health organisations ask the platforms to provide explicit sexual health information for their users.

While social media, sexual relations and sexual health may be relatively integrated for many gay men, this may not be the case for young people negotiating sexual activity through apps such as Tinder. Concerns about Tinder's effect on young people's sexual health have emerged recently, and while as yet there is no published academic literature on the issue, correlations have been made in online media stories. These include coverage of billboard advertising by the Los Angeles-based AIDS Healthcare Foundation (AHF) in 2015, which associated STI increases with Tinder and Grindr (Brait, 2015). This resulted in Grindr removing all AHF advertising from the app, and Tinder publicly stating that the advertising could damage their reputation. Months later, Tinder introduced a 'health safety section' to the app, which was said to have been prompted by the AHF campaign (Schrimshaw, 2016).

Given the current popularity of dating/hook-up apps, and the continued emergence and renewal of platforms, media accounts of these platforms could offer more timely and useful descriptions of their use. Including the above example, there are many ongoing tensions between public health practice, social media platforms and the users of these platforms. In 2016, Grindr surveyed its users asking how they would feel about being able to search and filter users in relation to their HIV status, causing much concern among users and HIV activists (Rodriguez, 2016). This demonstrates the understanding that these platforms can influence gay men's sexual cultures, including discriminating behaviours towards HIV-positive men. Elsewhere, MSM have led changes to apps based on their in-app practices, including the display of sexual health information. For example, a user-initiated practice of declaring PrEP use has led to platforms (such as Scruff) adding this information to their user profile template.

Conclusion

This chapter traces some key arguments in the recent history of sexual health promotion in social media. As studies of media and sexualities suggest, today's communication environments offer a range of risks and opportunities for one's management of social and intimate relations. Traditional modes of formal health promotion do not align with these new media environments. While public health continues to support young people and MSM through providing health information and services, this work must also adapt to shifting communication cultures. An instrumental approach that sees social media as simply another venue for information dissemination (Lupton, 2015) overlooks ways in which social media networks, and/or the specificities of a platform and its user base, produce/ support specific relational codes and practices. As discussed, social media are more conducive to peer-led education and a lateral distribution of information, as found in some community-based health interventions for MSM.

Practices of meeting and hooking up through social media do not simply replicate 'offline practices', but broaden social repertoires of sex and intimacy (Mowlabocus, 2010a; Race, 2015). Social media practices and platforms not only communicate something about a user's identity, but can also contribute to the ways in which social and sexual identities are produced through one's digital networks. As discussed, these media are not neutral spaces where sexual health interventions can be inserted for easy uptake and circulation. Yet social media practitioners may, and sometimes do, foster new modes of doing sexual health and negotiations of safety. While health promoters do not control this environment, they could initiate and foster more collaboration with social media practitioners.

Note

1 This also reveals a North American bias to this research, where each of these sites are/were most common.

Bibliography

Albury, K. (2013) 'Young people, media and sexual learning: rethinking representation'. *Sex Education.* Volume 13 (1): 32–44.

Albury, K. and Byron, P. (2016) 'Safe on my phone? Same-sex-attracted young people's negotiations of intimacy, visibility and risk on digital hook-up apps'. *Social Media + Society.* Volume 2 (4).

Bauermeister, J.A., Giguere, R., Carballo-Diéguez, A., Ventuneac, A. and Eisenberg, A. (2010) 'Perceived risks and protective strategies employed by young men who have sex with men (YMSM) when seeking online sexual partners'. *Journal of Health Communication.* Volume 15 (6), 679–690.

Bien, C.H., Best, J.M., Muessig, K.E., Wei, C., Han, L. and Tucker, J.D. (2015) 'Gay apps for seeking sex partners in China: implications for MSM sexual health'. *AIDS and Behavior.* Volume 19 (6): 1–6.

Brait, E. (2015). 'Tinder and Grindr outraged over STD testing billboards that reference apps'. *Guardian*, 30 September. www.theguardian.com/technology/2015/sep/29/tinder-grindr-std-testing-aids-healthcare-foundation-billboards (accessed 12 September 2016).

Bull, S.S., Levine, D., Black, S.R., Schmiege, S.J. and Santelli, J. (2012) 'Social media–delivered sexual health intervention: a cluster randomized controlled trial'. *American Journal of Preventive Medicine.* Volume 43 (5): 467–474.

Byron, P. (2015) 'Troubling expertise: social media and young people's sexual health'. *Communication Research and Practice.* Volume 1 (4): 322–334.

Byron, P., Evers, C. and Albury, K. (2013) '"It would be weird to have that on Facebook": young people's use of social media and the risk of sharing sexual health information'. *Reproductive Health Matters.* Volume 21 (41): 35–44.

Capurro, D., Cole, K., Echavarría, M.I., Joe, J., Neogi, T. and Turner, A.M. (2014) 'The use of social networking sites for public health practice and research: a systematic review'. *Journal of Medical Internet Research*. Volume 16 (3): 79.

Cassidy, E.M. (2013) *Gay Men, Social Media and Self-Presentation: Managing Identities in Gaydar, Facebook and Beyond*. PhD, Queensland University of Technology.

Chambers, D. (2013) *Social Media and Personal Relationships: Online Intimacies and Networked Friendship*. New York: Palgrave Macmillan.

Davis, M., Hart, G., Bolding, G., Sherr, L. and Elford, J. (2006) 'Sex and the internet: gay men, risk reduction and serostatus'. *Culture, Health & Sexuality*. Volume 8 (2): 161–174.

Delaney, P.K., Kramer, R.M., Waller, A.L., Flanders, D.W. and Sullivan, S.P. (2014) 'Using a geolocation social networking application to calculate the population density of sex-seeking gay men for research and prevention services'. *Journal of Medical Internet Research*. Volume 16 (11): e249.

Divecha, Z., Divney, A., Ickovics, J. and Kershaw, T. (2012) 'Tweeting about testing: do low-income, parenting adolescents and young adults use new media technologies to communicate about sexual health?' *Perspectives on Sexual and Reproductive Health*. Volume 44 (3): 176–183.

Duguay, S. (2016) '"He has a way gayer Facebook than I do": investigating sexual identity disclosure and context collapse on a social networking site'. *New Media & Society*. Volume 18 (6): 891–907.

Ellison, N.B., Steinfield, C. and Lampe, C. (2007) 'The benefits of Facebook "friends:" social capital and college students' use of online social network sites'. *Journal of Computer-Mediated Communication*. Volume 12 (4): 1143–1168.

Evers, C.W., Albury, K., Byron, P. and Crawford, K. (2013) 'Young people, social media, social network sites and sexual health communication in Australia: "this is funny, you should watch it". *International Journal of Communication*. Volume 7: 263–280.

Fries, J.A., Polgreen, P.M. and Segre, A.M. (2014) 'Mining the demographics of Craigslist casual sex ads to inform public health policy'. In *2014 IEEE International Conference on Healthcare Informatics (ICHI)*. IEEE. www.researchgate.net/publication/275209790_Mining_the_Demographics_of_Craigslist_Casual_Sex_Ads_to_Inform_Public_Health_Policy (accessed 29 March 2017).

Goedel, W.C., Halkitis, P.N., Greene, R.E., Hickson, D.A. and Duncan, D.T. (2016) 'HIV risk behaviors, perceptions, and testing and pre-exposure prophylaxis (PrEP) awareness/use in Grindr-using Men who have sex with men in Atlanta, Georgia'. *Journal of the Association of Nurses in AIDS Care*. Volume 27 (2): 133–142.

Gold, J., Pedrana, A.E., Sacks-Davis, R., Hellard, M.E., Chang, S., Howard, S., Keogh, L., Hocking, J.S. and Stoove, M.A. (2011) 'A systematic examination of the use of online social networking sites for sexual health promotion'. *BMC Public Health*. Volume 11 (583): 1–9.

Holloway, I.W., Dunlap, S., del Pino, H.E., Hermanstyne, K., Pulsipher, C. and Landovitz, R.J. (2014) 'Online social networking, sexual risk and protective behaviors: considerations for clinicians and researchers'. *Current Addiction Reports*. Volume 1 (3): 220–228.

Ito, M., Baumer, S., Bittanti, M., Cody, R., Herr-Stephenson, B., Horst, H.A., Lange, P.G., Mahendran, D., Martínez, K.Z. and Pascoe, C. (2010) *Hanging Out, Messing Around, and Geeking Out: Kids Living and Learning with New Media*. Cambridge, MA: MIT Press.

Kippax, S., Connell, R.W., Dowsett, G. and Crawford, J. (1993) *Sustaining Safe Sex: Gay Communities Respond to AIDS*. London: Falmer Press.

Lefebvre, C. (2009) 'Integrating cell phones and mobile technologies into public health practice: a social marketing perspective'. *Health Promotion Practice*. Volume 10 (4): 490–494.

Lefebvre, R.C. (2007) 'The new technology: the consumer as participant rather than target audience'. *Social Marketing Quarterly*. Volume 13 (3): 31–42.

Léobon, A. and Frigault, L.-R. (2008) 'Frequent and systematic unprotected anal intercourse among men using the internet to meet other men for sexual purposes in France: results from the "Gay Net Barometer 2006" Survey'. *AIDS Care*. Volume 20 (4): 478–484.

Liu, T. (2016) 'Neoliberal ethos, state censorship and sexual culture: a Chinese dating/hook-up app'. *Continuum*. Volume 30 (5): 557–566.

Livingstone, S. (2008) 'Taking risky opportunities in youthful content creation: teenagers' use of social networking sites for intimacy, privacy and self-expression'. *New Media & Society*. Volume 10 (3): 393–411.

Loss, J., Lindacher, V. and Curbach, J. (2014) 'Online social networking sites – a novel setting for health promotion?' *Health & Place*. Volume 26: 161–170.

Lupton, D. (2015) 'Health promotion in the digital era: a critical commentary'. *Health Promotion International*. Volume 30 (1): 174–183.

Marwick, A.E. and boyd, d. (2014) 'Networked privacy: how teenagers negotiate context in social media'. *New Media & Society*. Volume 16 (7): 1051–1067.

Mowlabocus, S. (2010a) *Gaydar Culture: Gay Men, Technology and Embodiment in the Digital Age*. London: Ashgate Publishing Company.

Mowlabocus, S. (2010b) '"Look at me!" Images, validation, and cultural currency on Gaydar'. In C. Pullen and M. Cooper (eds) *LGBT Identity and Online New Media*. New York: Routledge.

Mowlabocus, S., Harbottle, J., Dasgupta, R. and Haslop, C. (2014) *Reaching Out Online: Digital Literacy and the Uses of Social Media in Health Promotion*. Brighton: Cultures and Communities Network + and University of Sussex.

Payne, R. (2007) '"Str8acting"'. *Social Semiotics*. Volume 17 (4): 525–538.

Pedrana, A., Hellard, M., Gold, J., Ata, N., Chang, S., Howard, S., Asselin, J., Ilic, O., Batrouney, C. and Stoove, M. (2013) 'Queer as f**k: reaching and engaging gay men in sexual health promotion through social networking sites'. *Journal of Medical Internet Research*. Volume 15 (2): e25.

Pfeiffer, C., Kleeb, M., Mbelwa, A. and Ahorlu, C. (2014) 'The use of social media among adolescents in Dar es Salaam and Mtwara, Tanzania'. *Reproductive Health Matters*. Volume 22 (43): 178–186.

Pingel, E.S., Bauermeister, J.A., Johns, M.M., Eisenberg, A. and Leslie-Santana, M. (2013) '"A safe way to explore": reframing risk on the internet amidst young gay men's search for identity'. *Journal of Adolescent Research*. Volume 28 (4): 453–478.

Poland, B., Krupa, G. and McCall, D. (2009) 'Settings for health promotion: an analytic framework to guide intervention design and implementation'. *Health Promotion Practice*. Volume 10 (4): 505–516.

Powell, E. (2008) 'Young people's use of friends and family for sex and relationships information and advice'. *Sex Education*. Volume 8 (3): 289–302.

Race, K. (2010) 'Click here for HIV status: shifting templates of sexual negotiation'. *Emotion, Space and Society*. Volume 3 (1): 7–14.

Race, K. (2015) 'Speculative pragmatism and intimate arrangements: online hook-up devices in gay life'. *Culture, Health & Sexuality*. Volume 17 (4): 496–511.

Rhodes, S.D. (2004) 'Hookups or health promotion? An exploratory study of a chat room-based HIV prevention intervention for men who have sex with men'. *AIDS Education and Prevention*. Volume 16 (4): 315–327.

Rodriguez, M. (2016). 'Grindr asked users about filtering matches out by HIV status and people are pissed'. *Mic*, 12 July. https://mic.com/articles/148457/grindr-asked-users-about-filtering-matches-out-by-hiv-status-and-people-are-pissed#.mvABhfb4I (accessed 25 August 2016).

Roth, Y. (2014) 'Locating the "Scruff Guy": theorizing body and space in gay geosocial media'. *International Journal of Communication*. Volume 8: 21.

Rubin, J.D. and McClelland, S.I. (2015) '"Even though it's a small checkbox, it's a big deal": stresses and strains of managing sexual identity(s) on Facebook'. *Culture, Health & Sexuality*. Volume 17 (4): 512–526.

Schrimshaw, E. (2016). 'Swipe right for sexual health '. Columbia University, Mailman School of Public Health. 9 February. www.mailman.columbia.edu/public-health-now/news/swipe-right-sexual-health (accessed 25 August 2016).

Sun, C.J., Stowers, J., Miller, C., Bachmann, L.H. and Rhodes, S.D. (2015) 'Acceptability and feasibility of using established geosocial and sexual networking mobile applications to promote HIV and STD testing among men who have sex with men'. *AIDS and Behavior*. Volume 19 (3): 543–552.

Thackeray, R., Neiger, B.L., Hanson, C.L. and McKenzie, J.F. (2008) 'Enhancing promotional strategies within social marketing programs: use of Web 2.0 social media'. *Health Promotion Practice*. Volume 9 (4): 338–343.

Witzel, T.C., Guise, A., Nutland, W. and Bourne, A. (2016) '"It starts with me": privacy concerns and stigma in the evaluation of a Facebook health promotion intervention'. *Sexual Health*. Volume 13 (3): 228–233.

Young, S.D., Harrell, L., Jaganath, D., Cohen, A.C. and Shoptaw, S. (2012) 'Feasibility of recruiting peer educators for an online social networking-based health intervention'. *Health Education Journal*. Volume 72 (3): 276–282.

21
YOUNG PEOPLE, SEXUALITY EDUCATION AND THE MEDIA

Anne-Frances Watson

Teaching children about sex without thinking of the real consequences is like teaching them to shoot firearms and kill. At 9 or 10 years, they can't possibly comprehend the more intricate mechanisms of a rifle, let alone the actual harm that it can do. And, just like the child soldiers of Congo, they can more easily be brain washed into thinking they can be invincible. It is the same with sexual education, the responsibility is upon us, as adults, to protect children, not to enable them to harm themselves and others. I remember one of my children when she was four or five, and came home from pre-school with a new word, 'vagina'. Shortly after we caught her trying to insert something in the cat's back-orifice!

(Ng, below-the-line comment in Walsh, 2012)

Recent public debate in Australia, the UK and US has seen increasing concern about young people, their sexual behaviour and knowledge levels (Agius *et al.*, 2010) and, in particular, the perceived 'sexualisation' of children. The comment that opened this chapter came from an article on the news and commentary site 'The Conversation' (Walsh, 2012) and illustrates the key concerns: uncertainty regarding the kinds of information young people should receive about sex; at what age this information should be provided; and whether providing information can have negative effects, encouraging young people to experiment sexually in ways they would not otherwise think to. This idea that young people need to be 'protected' from information about their changing bodies and developing sexualities is at the forefront of sexualisation debates (Faulkner, 2010), raising a number of questions, the most pressing of which is: can giving young people information about sex cause them harm?

Researchers agree that access to information about sex and sexuality is an important part of healthy sexual development (Allen, 2001; Halstead and Reiss, 2003; Carmody, 2009; McKee *et al.*, 2010). The societal ideal is that parents should be the primary educators for their children (Shtarkshall, Santelli and Hirsch, 2007; Elliott, 2010). This works well in countries such as the Netherlands, where there is less stigma and taboo around discussions of sex and sexuality (Weaver, Smith and Kippax, 2005). However, in Australia, the UK and the US, discussions of sex tend to be associated with embarrassment and discomfort; thus parents are less likely to have these conversations with their children (El-Shaieb and Wurtele, 2009; Wilson and Koo, 2010; Turnbull, van Wersch and van Schaik, 2011;

Dyson and Smith, 2012). Instead, parents often wait to broach the topic until they think their child is ready or will soon be engaging in sexual behaviours – with the lack of previous discussion increasing the discomfort felt by both parties.

The classroom can be a key site for learning about sexuality, but many teachers responsible for the delivery of such education have very little formal training in teaching sexuality (Eisenberg et al., 2010: 338). When teachers were asked to answer the question 'I learned about sex from. . .' (Klein and Breck, 2010: 4), four main sources of information emerged: parents, friends/peers, school and the media. When asked to evaluate their own sex education, 71 per cent of the teachers gave a negative appraisal of their experiences (ibid.: 6). Klein and Breck (2010: 7) found that teacher candidates were unlikely to have health education training, and even less likely to have specific sexuality education training. This lack of expert training, teamed with teachers' own poor sexuality education in childhood, perpetuates 'the cycle of inadequate sexuality education' (ibid.: 7).

If the primary focus of sexuality education in schools has often been on 'puberty, procreation, and penetration' (Sorenson and Brown, 2007: 34), with a particular focus on scientific information about the body, STIs and pregnancy (Carmody, 2009), then it has also been characterised by a distinct lack of information about the areas that young people are interested in – pleasure and relationships:

> When sexuality education fails to take young people's content suggestions and perceptions of their own sexuality seriously it risks their disengagement from its messages. Content that does not address the questions and issues young people deem important may be dismissed as irrelevant and unhelpful. Ultimately this means that young people are unlikely to act on the knowledge and messages offered by sexuality education.
>
> (Allen, 2008: 589–590)

A brief history of sexuality education

Some of the first forms of sexuality education for children and young people were provided by the social and sexual hygiene movement – in part a reaction to the outbreaks of post-war venereal diseases brought back by returning soldiers from the Anglo-Boer War (1899–1902) on into the First World War (1914–1918) (Nelson and Martin, 2004; Egan and Hawkes, 2010). As the focus shifted from viewing sex and sexuality as an 'individualistic, moral, and familial endeavor' (Egan and Hawkes, 2010: 52) to viewing it as a societal concern, activists and academics began to argue that sexuality education should not be left in the hands of parents, who were ill equipped to give the required information to their children, and indeed were 'a hindrance if they failed to draw on the capabilities of hygiene experts' (ibid.: 59).

Aside from hygiene, the focus of much early sexuality education was driven by a moralistic imperative to control 'the sex impulse' (Egan and Hawkes, 2010: 61) and keep children from external negative influences. Jumping forward to the 1980s, the concern over the HIV/AIDS epidemic, STIs and teen pregnancy in the US, Australia and the UK was a driving force in implementing sexuality education as we know it in schools (Kendall, 2012: 1). Although the need for sexuality education was recognised, the forms of its delivery were still hotly contested. The two main forms of sexuality education – abstinence-only versus comprehensive – are still being fought over to this day.

Aggleton and Campbell (2000) examined the dominant discourses surrounding young people and their sexual health, finding there were a number of factors influencing the view of young people as needing protection from themselves and others. The first of these is the term 'sexual health'. The World Health Organisation (WHO) has developed the following working definition of sexual health:

> Sexual health requires a positive and respectful approach to sexuality and sexual relationships, as well as the possibility of having pleasurable and safe sexual experiences, free of coercion, discrimination and violence. For sexual health to be attained and maintained, the sexual rights of all persons must be respected, protected and fulfilled.
>
> (Cook, 2012: 5)

However, when sexual health is discussed in practice – and particularly in relation to young people – the use of the term is often distant from, or even in direct opposition to, this definition. In practice, 'sexual health' is rarely spoken about in terms of the healthy aspects of sex and sexuality, and is instead 'linked (in the public health imagination at least) to infection and disease and, in the case of young people, to unintended pregnancy' (Aggleton and Campbell, 2000: 284; see also Bale, 2010). Coupled with this, policy-makers and researchers tend to view adolescents and young people 'as "problems" for adults – wayward individuals whose behaviour "needs to be brought into line"' (Aggleton and Campbell, 2000: 286), reflecting the traditionally adversarial nature of health promotion for young people, in which they are viewed as irrational people who need to be controlled and told what to do *for their own good*.

Somers and Surmann examined young people's sources of sexuality education and its timing, as well as the 'comparative contribution' (2005: 37) that this had to their sexual attitudes and behaviours. Their research lists 'desired outcomes' for young people's sexual attitudes and behaviours, which they define as 'less risk-taking and more conservative attitudes'; according to Somers and Paulson (in ibid.: 48), these relate to 'lowered pregnancy and STI rates'. One indicator of these 'desired outcomes' was derived from the survey topic asking where the respondents learned about 'whether premarital sex is right or wrong' (41). These researchers used the words 'impact', 'effect' and 'influence' when discussing the various sources of sex education. For young women in particular, the authors spoke about 'resisting sexual pressure instead of succumbing to it' (50), thus failing to address the possibility that young people may be sexual beings who have formed or are forming their own, differing ideas about their sexuality that are not tied to traditional ideals about sex before marriage.

The place of pleasure and desire in sexuality education

Currently young people are not being told about pleasure in school-based sexuality education. In particular, a 'missing discourse of desire' has been identified in adults' discussions of girls' sexuality (Fine, 1988: 35). This silence on the subject of desire does not cause teen pregnancy, but, as Martin observes, acknowledging adolescent female desire allows the young person to feel a sense of agency:

> Sexual subjectivity (the ability to feel confident in and in control of one's body and sexuality) shapes one's ability to be agentic (the ability to act, accomplish, and feel efficacious in other parts of one's life) and vice versa.
>
> (Martin, 1994: 50, cited in Welles, 2005: 35)

Fine's (1988) study centred on females, but with a positive and empowering incorporation of desire and pleasure in sexuality education:

> A discourse of erotics would involve the acknowledgement that all young people, whatever their gender and sexual identity . . . are sexual subjects who have a right to experience sexual pleasure and desire.
>
> (Allen, 2007: 582)

Using pleasure as a 'means of reframing sexuality education is based on it being central to life, adding meaning to who we are, what we feel and what we value' (ibid.). This is not an argument for a society in which young people are 'encouraged to engage in sexual activity' (Coleman, Kearns and Collins, 2010: 72). 'Young people's views, experiences and needs' in learning about sex and sexuality must be acknowledged (ibid.). Accepting young people as legitimate sexual beings in this way may assist in increasing the 'relevance and effectiveness of sexual health education' (ibid.) Teens with a positive view of sexuality are more likely to 'admit to themselves that they were sexually active and take all of the steps necessary to protect themselves, including communication with their partner and the acquisition and consistent use of contraception' (Fisher, 1990, cited in Fay, 2002: 14). Furthermore, 'Sexuality education informed by an ethics of pleasure may benefit young people beyond equipping them to successfully negotiate intimate relationships and help transcend normative sexual identities and practices' (Allen, 2004: 152).

Media as sexuality educator

Given the discussion above, it is difficult to imagine how schools could ever cover information about pleasure, desire, masturbation and non-coital sex. Parents face similar difficulties in talking to their children about sex and sexuality. In such a context, young people look to other sources for their information, and in particular the media.

Children and adolescents today are 'voracious consumers of mass media' (Steinberg and Monahan, 2011: 562) and have unprecedented access to it, with free-to-air and pay television, DVDs, smartphones, 'as well as the opportunity to be connected with friends (and family) virtually any time of the day or night' (Brown and Bobkowski, 2011: 95). Young people spend between 6 and 8 hours a day with their televisions, computers, video games consoles and various other devices (Pinkleton et al., 2008: 462; Strasburger, Jordan and Donnerstein, 2010: 757; Steinberg and Monahan, 2011: 562).

When using a variety of media concurrently – for example, using the computer while watching television – 6 to 8 hours can become as much as 10 hours and 45 minutes a day (Brown and Bobkowski, 2011: 95), longer than is spent at school, with their parents or sleeping. Clark (cited in ibid.) has called this the 'constant contact' generation. This level of contact and consumption has raised concerns among researchers and academics about the effects that the media are having on children and adolescents.

Media effects

Traditionally, the media have been seen to have effects on young people's sexual behaviours and attitudes, with some considering that the media encourages young people to engage in behaviours before they are ready (Escobar-Chaves et al., 2005) or going so far as to suggest a causal relationship between young people seeing sexual content in the media and becoming sexually active (Escobar-Chaves et al., 2005: 304). Differing approaches are premised on different models, for example, a model of the media consumer as active or passive in their consumption; a view of the mechanisms of causations as direct or indirect; a concern with the focus of effects – on either individuals or groups, behaviour, beliefs, attitudes or values.

Some researchers assert, for example, a positive correlation between early or increased sexual activity and media use. One of the largest such studies was a longitudinal research project conducted by Collins et al. (2004) which found associations between the amount of sexual content viewed on television and initiation of sexual behaviour in young people. It showed that predictors of earlier sexual activity were associated with variables that indicated lower socioeconomic backgrounds. This may be read against the context that, traditionally, the 'lower' classes are already greater consumers of media, and many of the young people in the study had previously exhibited sensation-seeking behaviours and had minimal supervision. These are factors that have previously been associated with sexual risk (Collins et al., 2011). Other studies of media effects (Steinberg and Monahan, 2011) show an emerging picture of more relaxed attitudes towards sexual behaviours and earlier sexual initiation that appears to be linked to the increase in consuming mediated sexual content.

According to Steele (1999), if a young person is already sexually curious, they will actively seek out media with more sexual content. In short, the relationship between media consumption and sexual behaviour is heavily contingent on other contextual factors. Most studies of media effects underplay the individual differences between the young people they are discussing, such as socioeconomic, cultural and ethnic variations. Bleakley et al. (2011: 538) examined the association between sexual content exposure and sexual initiation in African-American adolescents, who consume more media content than White youth (ibid.). They showed no hastening of sexual activity in relation to viewing habits, supporting the idea that context is important in understanding media effects.

Another difficulty of many studies is the approach taken to categorising sexual content in the media. A study conducted by Manganello et al. (2010) used the coding of sexual content previously conducted by Kunkel et al. (2005, in ibid.) and had adolescents code the same television programmes. They found differences between the ideas of what was sexual in the eyes of these young people and those of the experienced coders. Manganello et al. (2010: 371) found that intended viewers can and do interpret messages differently according to their 'age, sex, race or other characteristics'.

The positive effects of the media

An alternative approach to that of the effects-research tradition is to consider the positive effects of sexual content in the media. As noted previously, young people are not provided with all the information they need about sexuality from their formal schooling or parents. In this context, the media may be a rare site of education about sexual pleasure and desire. Very little academic work – with the exception of Pearce (2006), who speaks to the importance of films such as American Pie (1999, dir: Paul Weitz) in providing sexuality education – has looked at the possibility that mainstream sexualised media content may serve as a form of sexuality education. However, the media can play a significant part in providing information about sexuality and relationships to young people (Buckingham and Bragg, 2004; Epstein and Ward, 2008: 113; Brown and L'Engle, 2009: 147; Strasburger, Jordan and Donnerstein, 2010: 760; McKee, 2012; Mulholland, 2013). The media can also help in identity formation; characters on television may provide a range of models that may validate what young people are feeling, because of perceived similarities and shared problems (Ward, Day and Epstein, 2006: 62, 64; Brown and Bobkowski, 2011: 96). Adolescents are naturally curious about sex and sexuality, and the media often provides information that can be judgement-free or even positive, and is accessible in private (Brown and L'Engle, 2009: 129; Brown and Bobkowski, 2011: 100).

What do young people want, and need, to learn about sexuality?

Research shows that young people want to know about the pleasurable and emotional aspects of relationships (Allen, 2004, 2007). Young people have demonstrated a desire to 'learn about what love means to sex' and 'what love feels like' (Coleman, Kearns and Collins, 2010: 70). In an evaluation of New Zealand school-based sexuality education, most senior-school students wanted to know more about 'how to make sexual activity enjoyable for both partners' (Allen, 2005, cited in Allen, 2007: 584). Interest in pleasure is also evident in research in which young people show a greater interest in pleasure and erotics than in information about STIs (ibid.) These discussions stand in stark contrast to 'adult discourses of young people's sexuality' (Coleman, Kearns and Collins, 2010: 70).

Public concern exists about the sexualisation of children and young people, levelled at the media in particular. News media constantly reveal how sexual young people have 'become', pointing to entertainment media such as magazines, pornography, movies and television as sources of sexualisation. These concerns have sparked investigations in the US (American Psychological Association (APA), 2010), the UK (Papadopoulos, 2010; Bailey, 2011) and Australia (Rush and La Nauze, 2006). More recently, and particularly with the advent of internet-capable smartphones, concerns about 'sexualisation' have extended to two particular anxieties about young people and their sources of information about sexuality: social networking websites and the internet, and pornography.

The first, and most prevalent, concern is about young people watching or being 'exposed' to increasing amounts of pornography. The primary, and oft-quoted, concern here is that young people are seeing pornography everywhere, have easy access to it and will undoubtedly go on to mimic what they see there:

> The single defining characteristic of teenage sex in 2013 is porn. Graphic, hardcore sex, free for anyone with a smart phone to watch. It's so ubiquitous that the average age of first exposure to porn is now just 11 years old, warping kids' ideas of what normal sex is years before they are likely to try it themselves.
>
> 'When you put a smart phone in the hands of a teen or tween, you're basically giving them access to online porn,' says Liz Walker, the national director of Get a Grip Teenz education program. 'How do we equip kids to understand the difference between porn and real sex? A huge percentage of people who watch porn then want to try it.'
>
> (Marriner, 2013)

My research demonstrates that adults' concerns do not bear much relation to the issues with which young people are struggling. In focus-group discussions I conducted with teens, pornography was *not* considered a source of information. Young men I spoke to demonstrated significant media literacy and knew that pornography was not an accurate representation of how sex would be for them: 'but I know it's not like that because that's crazy' (6.M.1); 'yeah, that's obviously over-exaggerated when you watch it [sex] on that [pornography]' (6.M.2); 'My mate showed me this, umm, porn video and it's so stupid and it was so fake. She sounded kind of like a monkey when she was having sex and I was like, "aw that's stupid, that's stupid"' (19.M.3).

Nor did they consider pornography a source for learning:

4.M.5:	What do you want to know about the porn . . . like what we actually looked up?
Facilitator:	What you learn about sex from looking at it?
4.M.5:	Um, when I look at porn I don't do it to learn about sex, I just do it for the feeling at that moment.
4.M.3:	Well said.

Young women largely spoke about pornography as something that young men consumed:

10.F.2:	I went on my brother's computer once and I opened a new tab, one of the frequently visited was Redtube and I was like . . . my brother is 16, but, yeah, like it's sort of accepted when they do it because. . .
10.F.4:	It's a bit different for girls as well, like guys it's okay to watch porn, but girls. . .
10.F.2:	Because guys do it all the time.
10.F.1:	Yeah I don't understand that.

But it was also clear that young women were aware of the public discourses about pornography, and echoed them, while plainly being ambivalent:

Facilitator:	But really why do you think that – like do you think that it's okay for girls to watch porn?
10.F.4:	I think it is.
10.F.2:	Yeah.
10.F.3:	Yeah.
10.F.1:	It's alright, but everyone else is just – it's just not what society thinks we should do, like I don't know why but they just don't have a view of girls watching porn, it's more of a guy thing, I don't know, probably because it's guys exploiting the women.
Facilitator:	Do you think that it is guys ex. . .
10.F.2:	It's not exploitation but it is. . .
10.F.1:	I don't know, like more like it makes the guys have – like they think that they have a better body, do you know what I mean, like they expect girls to have a better body because they've been watching that.
10.F.4:	Yeah it does give them expectations.
10.F.1:	Yeah their expectations get a bit high, and then – yeah so I don't think it's. . .
Facilitator:	Have you seen any?
10.F.1:	No.

'Experts' and media commentators are also concerned that young people are using social networks and the internet to find out information about sex and sexuality: 'Using social media is a new trend. You hear they ask for tips and advice on social networks and also they read blogs so they might not necessarily be professional sites they are getting their information from' (Power and Lentini, 2012).

However, in my focus groups, young people did not speak about using social networks or blogs (in fact, blogs were not mentioned at all) in this way. Facebook – the most popular of the social networking sites at the time of my research – was mentioned as a communication tool, but not as a source of information about sex.

For young women, the wide range of magazines available to them, and in particular *Cosmo*, *Cleo*, *Girlfriend* and *Dolly*, are key sources of learning about pleasure and the possibility that sex can be good: 'they really go into depth about everything' (8.F.3). These magazines provided information about pleasure and the sexual topics in which these young women were interested, such as 'sex techniques types of pieces' (9.F.3). Young women also spoke about seeking out 'iPhone apps' (9.F.2) such as 'Sex Facts, Sex Positions' (9.F.4) and 'Sex Dice Game' (9.F.5), which they felt were important sources of information for learning about pleasure and good sex.

Young men had fewer sources of mediated information here, but also mentioned apps:

> I downloaded an iPod Touch app, like one of those sex position ones. For fun. Like just to see what it was . . . and, you know, they tell you all these different ones [positions] and how they do it. And they rate them like one to ten, whatever. And, you know, you can look through them as well I suppose.
>
> (3.M.1)

The media also provided information about the importance of sex being good for both parties:

> It could be good sex as in pleasing your partner. In, um, which case I think in media I've seen that the males can never go like far enough because they always climax before the girls and it's hard for them to keep going.
>
> (4.M.5)

A second area in which media provided information to young people that they did not receive from parents or schools was that of navigating relationships. Through the media, young people learned about all stages of relationships, from the beginning to the end, as follows.

- How and when to ask someone out: '*Girlfriend* and *Dolly* . . . has asking people out' (9.F.2); 'oh, well, like all the movies you see somebody ask somebody out' (18.M.3); 'stressing about asking people out' (18.M.4).
- Getting what you want and how to conduct yourself within that relationship: 'well, they [magazines] say that you should always know what you want in a relationship' (10.F.3) 'and you shouldn't let the other person . . . pressure you into things that you don't want to do' (10.F.3); 'those [magazines] are more like what you do in a relationship' (9.F.3); 'like *Dolly* magazine, they post a lot about dating and all that stuff about it' (2.F.4).
- How to deal with problems: 'the movies and the teenage drama shows' (15.F.4) such as '*Gossip Girl*, *OC*, any of those sort of dramas' (15.F.5) provided examples of things going wrong in relationships – 'you see the bad experiences from the dramatic programmes' (15.F.4).
- Ending the relationship: 'teen magazines in general have information on how to break up and that stuff' (9.F.1); 'be careful about it. Make sure you're doing the right thing'

(9.F.1); 'But if you're breaking up with them think about it a lot. Don't just get a feeling that you want to break up with them and then do it and then regret it later' (9.F.3); 'Um, I've seen one thing. But then it's just, ah like one of the comedy shows. Take them to a public place so they don't like get angry, because they don't want to look like idiots in front of a lot of people' (4.M.2).

This was information that the young people did not receive or that was in limited supply at school – 'no, they [school] don't talk about relationships, just sex and genitals and health' (9.F.5) – or from parents: 'You don't really talk about that sort of thing with your parents. Like your parents will sit you down and have the sex talk, but they don't really have a talk about like, going out with people' (2.F.2).

It was felt that schools and parents avoided discussion of how to navigate relationships for fear that being in a relationship would lead to sex, because 'touching makes babies' (7.F.3). Some parents made their feelings about teen relationships very clear:

> My parents, well, my dad in particular is not a fan for teenage relationships. He gets very angry and says lots of things. He told me, with my previous boyfriend, he's, like, 'Well, that's fine now you can go be a prostitute on the streets or something.'
>
> *(17.F.1)*

> Her [17.F.1] dad is like . . . he was just getting angry and telling me that . . . girls who are in relationships at high school are frowned upon by everyone. And how no one likes them. And how they're destined for bad lives . . . you're not going to have a nice life.
>
> *(17.F.3)*

This negative or missing information from parents and schools means that young people do need to look to the media to find out about key areas of their sexual development. However, unfortunately, the negative messages given by parents and schools often override or counteract any positive information or messages that young people may receive from the media.

My research took a culture-centred approach to exploring what young people learn about sex and how they learn about it, rather than starting with assumptions about the key elements of sexual learning. I did not assume that social media or pornography would be their most important sources of information. From data gathered in focus groups, parents, schools and friends all emerged as more important elements of young people's sexuality education than the media. In fact, the claim that the media did not represent their everyday 'real life' was a recurring theme in young people's discussions. Letting young people set the agenda on sex education, and listening to their perspectives, points us towards a number of issues that they see as key. The first is the relentlessly scientific – and therefore irrelevant – nature of school education about sex and sexuality: as discussed at the beginning of this chapter, Allen's research suggests that when sexuality education fails to address pleasure and the aspects of sexuality that young people want to hear about, they disengage from everything else (2008b: 589–590). The second is parental awkwardness in discussion about sex and, in most cases, parents' failure to present positive accounts of what sex and relationships should be like.

Little (or no) research has been undertaken that looks comprehensively at the place of sexualised content in the media, within the context of the wider sexuality education of young people. However, it is clear that the media has an important and undervalued part to play in the sexuality education of young people. Young people are receiving positive messages and information about sex and sexuality from the media in a number of key areas that are counter to the negative messages – or absence of any messages – that they are receiving from their two more formal sources: parents and schools. Pleasure is the first area for which young people are receiving or seeking out information and messages.

Conclusion

This essay opened with a comment by Dania Ng, posted in response to an article by Walsh (2012) on 'The Conversation', which equated educating young people about sex and sexuality with 'teaching them to shoot firearms and kill'. The article – and the subsequent comment – was penned as a response to the controversial public debate surrounding the Australian Curriculum, Assessment and Reporting Authority's (ACARA) development of a national curriculum to include sexuality education.

Comprehensive, age-appropriate sex education is a positive contribution to young people's healthy sexual development. Despite the worries expressed by Ng, there is no evidence that young people are scarred, damaged or sexualised by being given appropriate information about sex and sexuality as they grow up. However, the wider questions of what kinds of information should be supplied, and how that information should reach young people, are more difficult to answer.

When we take a culture-centred approach to understanding learning about sex – comparing what young people learn from schools, from parents, from media and from peers – we get a very different picture from that produced if we only look at one source at a time. Typically, media have been seen as a source of negative effects, such as lowering the age of sexual debut (Collins *et al.*, 2004). By contrast, parents and schools have been seen as providing a positive corrective to negative media messages. This is not the case in any simple way, and indeed, on some occasions, the media provide a positive corrective to the failings of schools and parents in providing sex education. The creation of a binary whereby the media can only provide negative information and parents and schools can only provide good information is so simplistic that you would think nobody would do it; however, this 'straw man' argument essentially demonstrates the way the media is viewed in relation to young people and their sexuality. Perhaps it is now time to consider how media might take their place in educating young people about sex, as researchers who adopt a culture-centred approach are doing (McKee, Watson and Dore, 2014; McKee, Bragg and Taormino, 2015).

Bibliography

Aggleton, P. and Campbell, C. (2000) 'Working with young people – towards an agenda for sexual health'. *Sexual and Relationship Therapy*, Volume 15 (3): 283–296.

Agius, P. A., Pitts, M. K., Smith, A. M. A. and Mitchell, A. (2010) 'Sexual behaviour and related knowledge among a representative sample of secondary school students between 1997 and 2008'. *Australian and New Zealand Journal of Public Health*, Volume 34 (5): 476–481.

Allen, L. (2001) 'Closing sex education's knowledge/practice gap: the reconceptualisation of young people's sexual knowledge'. *Sex Education*, Volume 1 (2): 109–122.

Allen, L. (2004) 'Beyond the birds and the bees: constituting a discourse of erotics in sexuality education'. *Gender & Education*, Volume 16 (2): 151–167.

Allen, L. (2005) *Sexual Subjects: Young People, Sexuality and Education*. New York: Palgrave Macmillan.

Allen, L. (2007) 'Doing "it" differently: relinquishing the disease and pregnancy prevention focus in sexuality education'. *British Journal of Sociology of Education*, Volume 28 (5): 575–588.

Allen, L. (2008) '"They think you shouldn't be having sex anyway": young people's suggestions for improving sexuality education content'. *Sexualities*, Volume 11 (5): 573–594.

American Psychological Association (APA), Task Force on the Sexualization of Girls (2010) *Report of the APA Task Force on the Sexualization of Girls*. Washington DC: American Psychological Association.

Bailey, R. (2011) *Letting Children Be Children: Report of an Independent Review of the Commercialisation and Sexualisation of Childhood*. London: Department of Education.

Bale, C. (2010) 'Sexualised culture and young people's sexual health: a cause for concern?' *Sociology Compass*, Volume 4 (10): 824–840.

Bleakley, A., Hennessy, M., Fishbein, M. and Jordan, A. (2011) 'Using the integrative model to explain how exposure to sexual media content influences adolescent sexual behavior'. *Health Education & Behavior*, Volume 38 (5): 530–540.

Brown, J. D. and Bobkowski, P. S. (2011) 'Older and newer media: patterns of use and effects on adolescents' health and well-being'. *Journal of Research on Adolescence*, Volume 21 (1): 95–113.

Brown, J. D. and L'Engle, K. L. (2009) 'X-rated: sexual attitudes and behaviors associated with U.S. early adolescents' exposure to sexually explicit media'. *Communication Research*, Volume 36 (1): 129–151.

Buckingham, D. and Bragg, S. (2004) *Young People, Sex and the Media*. New York: Palgrave Macmillan.

Carmody, M. (2009) *Sex and Ethics: Young People and Ethical Sex*. South Yarra: Palgrave Macmillan.

Clark, L. S. (2005) 'The constant contact generation: exploring teen friendship networks online'. In S. R. Mazzarella (ed), *Girl Side Web: Girls, the Internet, and the Negotiation of Identity*. New York: Peter Lang.

Coleman, T. M., Kearns, R. A. and Collins, D. C. A. (2010) '"Anywhere you can talk about how you feel is better": young people's experiences of sexual health messages'. *New Zealand Geographer*, Volume 66 (1): 61–73.

Collins, R. L., Elliott, M. N., Berry, S. H., Kanouse, D. E., Kunkel, D., Hunter, S. B. and Miu, A. (2004) 'Watching sex on television predicts adolescent initiation of sexual behavior'. *Pediatrics*, Volume 114 (3): e280–e289.

Collins, R. L., Martino, S. C., Elliott, M. N. and Miu, A. (2011) 'Relationships between adolescent sexual outcomes and exposure to sex in media: robustness to propensity-based analysis'. *Developmental Psychology*. Volume 47 (2): 585–591. doi: 10.1037/a0022563.

Cook, H. (2012) 'Getting "foolishly hot and bothered"? Parents and teachers and sex education in the 1940s'. *Sex Education*, Volume 12 (5): 555–567.

Dyson, S. and Smith, E. (2012) '"There are lots of different kinds of normal": families and sex education – styles, approaches and concerns'. *Sex Education*, Volume 12 (2): 219–229.

Egan, R. D. and Hawkes, G. (2010) *Theorizing the Sexual Child in Modernity*. New York: Palgrave Macmillan.

Eisenberg, M. E., Madsen, N., Oliphant, J. A., Sieving, R. E. and Resnick, M. (2010) '"Am I qualified? How do I know?" A qualitative study of sexuality educators' training experiences'. *American Journal of Health Education*, Volume 41 (6): 337–344.

Elliott, Sinikka (2010) '"If I could really say that and get away with it!" Accountability and ambivalence in American parents' sexuality lessons in the age of abstinence'. *Sex Education*, Volume 10 (3): 239–250.

El-Shaieb, M. and Wurtele, S. K. (2009) 'Parents' plans to discuss sexuality with their young children'. *American Journal of Sexuality Education*, Volume 4 (2): 103–115.

Epstein, M. and Ward, L. (2008) '"Always use protection": communication boys receive about sex from parents, peers, and the media'. *Journal of Youth and Adolescence*, Volume 37 (2): 113–126.

Escobar-Chaves, S. L., Tortolero, S. R., Markham, C. M., Low, B. J., Eitel, P. and Thickstun, P. (2005) 'Impact of the media on adolescent sexual attitudes and behaviors'. *Pediatrics*, Volume 116 (Supplement 1): 303–326.

Faulkner, J. (2010) 'The innocence fetish: the commodification and sexualisation of children in the media and popular culture'. *Media International Australia*, Volume 135: 106–117.

Fay, J. (2002) 'Teaching teens about sexual pleasure'. *SIECUS Report*, Volume 30 (4): 12–17.

Fine, M. (1988) 'Sexuality, schooling, and adolescent females: the missing discourse of desire'. *Harvard Educational Review*, Volume 58 (1): 29–54.

Halstead, M. J. and Reiss, M. J. (2003) *Values in Sex Education: From Principles to Practice*. London and New York: Routledge and Farmer.

Kendall, N. (2012) *The Sex Education Debates*. Chicago: University of Chicago Press.

Klein, N. A and Breck, S. E. (2010) '"I wish I had known the truth sooner": middle school teacher candidates' sexuality education experiences'. *RMLE Online: Research in Middle Level Education*, Volume 33 (6): 1–10.

Kunkel, D., Cope, K. M. and Biely, E. (1999) 'Sexual messages on television: comparing findings from three studies'. *Journal of Sex Research*, Volume 36 (3): 230–236.

Kunkel, D., Eyal, K., Finnerty, K., Biely, E. and Donnerstein, E. (2005). *Sex on TV 4: A Biennial Report of the Kaiser Family Foundation*. Menlo Park, CA: Kaiser Family Foundation. www.kff.org/entmedia/upload/Sex-on-TV-4-Full-Report.pdf (accessed 15 November 2016).

McKee, A. (2012) 'The importance of entertainment for sexuality education'. *Sex Education*, Volume 12 (5): 499–509.

McKee, A., Albury, K. Dunne, M. Grieshaber, S. Hartley, J., Lumby, C. and Mathews, B. (2010) 'Healthy sexual development: a multidisciplinary framework for research'. *International Journal of Sexual Health*, Volume 22 (1): 14–19.

McKee, A., Bragg, S. and Taormino, T. (2015) 'Editorial introduction: entertainment media's evolving role in sex education'. *Sex Education*, Volume 15 (5): 451–457.

McKee, A., Walsh, A. and Watson, A. F. (2014) 'Using digitally distributed vulgar comedy to reach young men with information about healthy sexual development'. *Media International Australia*, Volume 153 (1): 128–137.

McKee, A., Watson, A. F. and Dore, J. (2014) '"It's all scientific to me": focus group insights into why young people do not apply safe-sex knowledge'. *Sex Education*, Volume 14 (6): 652–665.

Manganello, J., Henderson, V., Jordan, A., Trentacoste, N., Martin, S., Hennessy, M. and Fishbein, M. (2010) 'Adolescent judgment of sexual content on television: implications for future content analysis research'. *Journal of Sex Research*, Volume 47 (4): 364–373.

Marriner, C. (2013) 'Sex in the schoolyard'. 29 September. *The Sydney Morning Herald*. www.smh.com.au/lifestyle/life/sex-in-the-schoolyard-20130924-2ubwi.html (accessed 13 October 2016).

Mulholland, M. (2013) *Young People and Pornography: Negotiating Pornification*. London: Springer.

Nelson, C. and Martin, M. H. (2004) *Sexual Pedagogies: Sex Education in Britain, Australia, and America, 1879–2000*. London: Palgrave Macmillan.

Papadopoulos, L. (2010) *Sexualisation of Young People Review*. London: Home Office.

Pearce, S. (2006) 'Sex and the cinema: what *American Pie* teaches the young'. *Sex Education*, Volume 6 (4): 367–376.

Pinkleton, B. E., Austin, E. W., Cohen, M., Chen, Y. and Fitzgerald, E. (2008) 'Effects of a peer-led media literacy curriculum on adolescents' knowledge and attitudes toward sexual behavior and media portrayals of sex'. *Health Communication*, Volume 23 (5): 462–472.

Power, L. and Lentini, R. (2012) 'Teens prefer blogs and Google over talking with parents about sex'. 9 July. *The Daily Telegraph*. www.dailytelegraph.com.au/teens-prefer-blogs-and-google-over-talking-with-parents-about-sex/story-e6freuy9-1226420448937 (accessed 13 October 2016).

Rush, E. and La Nauze, A. (2006) *Corporate Paedophilia: Sexualisation of Children in Australia*. Canberra: The Australia Institute.

Shtarkshall, R. A., Santelli, J. S. and Hirsch, J. S. (2007) 'Sex education and sexual socialization: roles for educators and parents'. *Perspectives on Sexual and Reproductive Health*, Volume 39 (2): 116–119.

Somers, C. L. and Surmann, A. T. (2004) 'Adolescents' preferences for source of sex education'. *Child Study Journal*, Volume 34 (1): 47–59.

Somers, C. L. and Surmann, A. T. (2005) 'Sources and timing of sex education: relations with American adolescent sexual attitudes and behavior'. *Educational Review*, Volume 57 (1): 37–54.

Sorenson, A. and Brown, G. (2007) *Report on the Sexual Health Education of Young People in WA*. Perth: W.A. Health.

Steele, J. R. (1999) 'Teenage sexuality and media practice: factoring in the influences of family, friends, and school'. *Journal of Sex Research*, Volume 36 (4): 331–341.

Steinberg, L. and Monahan, K. C. (2011) 'Adolescents' exposure to sexy media does not hasten the initiation of sexual intercourse'. *Developmental Psychology*, Volume 47 (2): 562–576.

Strasburger, V. C., Jordan, A. B. and Donnerstein, E. (2010) 'Health effects of media on children and adolescents'. *Pediatrics*, Volume 125 (4): 756–767.

Turnbull, T., van Wersch, A. and van Schaik, P. (2011) 'Parents as educators of sex and relationship education: the role for effective communication in British families'. *Health Education Journal*, Volume 70 (3): 240–248.

Walsh, J. (2012) 'Worried about the sexualisation of children? Teach sex ed earlier'. 26 October. *The Conversation*. http://theconversation.com/worried-about-the-sexualisation-of-children-teach-sex-ed-earlier-10311 (accessed 13 October 2016).

Ward, L. M., Day, K. M. and Epstein, M. (2006) 'Uncommonly good: exploring how mass media may be a positive influence on young women's sexual health and development'. *New Directions for Child and Adolescent Development*, Volume 112: 57–70.

Weaver, H., Smith, G. and Kippax, S. (2005) 'School-based sex education policies and indicators of sexual health among young people: a comparison of the Netherlands, France, Australia and the United States'. *Sex Education*, Volume 5 (2): 171–188.

Welles, C. (2005) 'Breaking the silence surrounding female adolescent sexual desire'. *Women & Therapy*, Volume 28 (2): 31–45.

Wilson, E. K. and Koo, H. P. (2010) 'Mothers, fathers, sons, and daughters: gender differences in factors associated with parent–child communication about sexual topics.' *Reproductive Health*, Volume 7: 31.

Media

American Pie (1999) Directed by P. Weitz [Film]. USA: Universal Pictures.

# PART III

Representing sex

22
VIDEOGAMES AND SEX

Ashley M. L. Brown

Introduction

The relationship between videogames and sexuality is complex and contested. From moral panic over representations of sexuality in games (Karlsen, 2014; Brathwaite, 2013) to discussions of the medium's immature treatment of sexual themes (Krzywinska, 2012; Gallagher, 2012) to the science fiction-esque blurring of technology and the body through teledildonics (Krzywinska, 2012; Brathwaite, 2013), sex occupies an uncomfortable space within the medium of videogames. Perhaps because of an association of games and play with childhood and an association of sex and sexualities with adulthood (Brown, 2015; Sjöblom, 2015), there is discomfort regarding the representation and treatment of sex as something playful. This persistent separation between sex and play continues despite a growing culture of adult play in other areas of daily life.

From the myriad boardgames found in lingerie shops which encourage couples to spend the weekend at home to relationship experts doling out playful advice for maintaining active sex lives (Betcher, 1987), the gamification of sex is hardly new or hard to find (Krzywinska, 2012). If we consider boardgames, cardgames and other types of freeform play, it is easy to see that some aspects of sexuality have been playful or game-like for some time. Games such as 'hide the thimble' (Sutton-Smith, 1997), spin the bottle, seven minutes in heaven and strip poker have both a playful and a sexual component to them. However, the purpose of this chapter is to focus specifically on sex and videogames. The term 'videogame' is used here to indicate any digital game which may be played on a computer, console, mobile or handheld device.

The chapter will cover three main areas of interest. The first concerns how games are different from other types of media. This section distinguishes videogames from other media through their interactive nature. This is not to say, of course, that books, films and television programmes are not interactive, but rather that videogames demand a temporally sensitive type of interaction (Dovey and Kennedy, 2006). The second section will consider the discussion of games as a specific medium and move on to look at how sex has been represented in games. The discussion of representation will begin by detailing how the burden of sexuality and sexualisation is more often than not placed on the virtual bodies of female avatars. Although not a representation of the sex act itself, the hypersexualisation of some avatars over others is useful for describing the political economy in which sex is represented in videogames (Dovey and Kennedy, 2006; Taylor, 2006; Pearce and Artemesia, 2009; MacCallum-Stewart and Parsler, 2008). A discussion about how sexual acts are represented will follow. More often than not, games avoid depictions of sexual activities on screen, preferring instead to use allusive tricks from cinema, such as fading to black, to imply sexual acts are taking place (Krzywinska, 2012). When the sexual act is depicted, it is usually done so under the mitigating aegis of humour (Gallagher, 2012). The second section of this chapter looks at specific games which explicitly include sex. Following a short revisiting of pre-digital games, the section will look at *Playboy: The Mansion* as an example. The section will conclude by looking at two more games, *Luxuria Superbia* (Tale of Tales, 2013) and *Fingle* (Game Oven Studios, 2011), both of which are centred on sexuality without actually depicting it. Both games, developed for tablets, involve simulating sexual intercourse through the interaction of fingers and a touch-sensitive tablet screen. The chapter will conclude with some reflection on how the interactive nature of games presents challenges for representation and design.

Games and other media

Before videogames and sexuality can be thoroughly discussed, the ways in which games are different from other types of media must first be established. Games' distinction as different to literature or film appears here not to reinforce disciplinary boundaries, but rather to highlight the tactile and interactive nature of the media. This is, of course, not to suggest that other media lack interaction or tactility, but rather to place emphasis on the temporal nature of videogame interaction.

Not only do books, television and film usually have some physical, tactile distribution format, but they also require some degree of interaction. More than just pressing a remote control or opening the cover of a book, traditional forms of media require thought and interpretation on the part of the reader or viewer. Exemplifying this thought and interpretation is fan culture. As Henry Jenkins writes, fans 'passionately embrace favoured texts and attempt to integrate media representations within their own social experience' (2006: 59). If definitions of interactivity are expanded to include the activities of the fan cultures which surround various media, then the distinctions between the first and second media ages become blurry at best.

Likewise, videogames often borrow form, structure and content from other media. The narrative structure of adventure games, for example, most often follows the narrative structure of adventure novels (Dovey and Kennedy, 2006). The content within the games themselves borrows themes and tropes established in other forms of media. The exploits of Lara Croft, for example, may feel familiar to audiences already familiar with the tomb-raiding exploits of Indiana Jones (Atkins, 2003). The application of similar themes across multiple media platforms likely occurs because games are created by people living within certain cultural perspectives, but also because, as a platform for storytelling, games usually follow a linear narrative.

Of course there are examples of games with more than one narrative path, such as *The Stanley Parable* (Galactic Café, 2013), but more often than not what seems like free choice afforded to players by the interactive format of videogames is little more than illusion. Indeed, although it may seem as though a player can direct a character to any number of actions or endings, the choices available to the player usually amount to little more than kill or be killed (Atkins, 2003). This is perhaps most clearly demonstrated by the restricted sexual actions made available to players in games such as *Playboy: The Mansion* (Cyberlore Studios, 2005) or the limited choice of sexual partners in games such as *Dragon Age: Origins* (Bioware, 2009). In videogames, players' actions are necessarily limited by the coded-in commands afforded to them by the developer. The pre-scripted nature of games means that not every sexual position is offered to the player and not every non-playable character can be seduced. Much of this restriction is due to the nature of the medium.

Although at first glance many gameworlds seem open and limitless, there are inaccessible areas and impossible actions that are cordoned off from players' experiences of the game. The limited availability of game content, sexual or otherwise, is due to constrictions in design. Specifically, underpinning most games is some form of economy. Economy might be the scoring of points, the collection of currency or any other numerical system which can be used as player feedback. A greater amount of points scored or objects collected usually means the player is doing well, with the opposite also holding true. This economic modelling of gameplay becomes a problem when attempts are made to apply it to sex. For example, in *Dragon Age II* (Bioware, 20011), players have friendship and rivalry bars which quantify their relationships to non-player companions. Dialogue options and the presentation of gifts can increase or decrease the relationship bar, and a series of flirty conversations will score the player enough points to have sex with the non-player character. This particular economy makes it seem as though 'sex is treated as a prize or award for playing the game correctly, rather than as another aspect to romance and love' (Kelly, 2015: 58). As may be evident, the problem with the medium's limitations is that 'romance and sexuality are nearly the opposite of a menu-based system or flipping a switch' (Ware, 2015: 227).

These design constraints are in addition to any social restraints that may be put in place by ratings boards such as the Entertainment Software Review Board (ESRB) or the Pan European Games Information system (PEGI). Without diminishing the importance, creativity or skill of players who modify or alter the code of a videogame to include nudity or sexual content unintended by the developer, sexual choice and freedom in games is often extraordinarily restricted. A false dichotomy predominates over discussions of games and sexual content: games are for children and sexual content is for adults. Perhaps because of this, few games explicitly engage with sexual content. The bulk of sexual content in games comes from player modifications, transformative play (Salen and Zimmerman, 2004) and emergent play (Sotamaa, 2007). Transformative play 'occurs when the free movement of play alters the more rigid structure in which it takes shape' (Salen and Zimmerman, 2004: 321). Similarly, emergent play describes player behaviour which was not anticipated by a game's designer, but rather emerges out of gameplay (Sotamaa, 2007). Both terms make reference to a way in which games are different to other media. Just as slash fiction or fan fiction might be created by fans of television, books and cinema who want to take a romantic narrative in a direction different to that which was planned by the director, transformative and emergent gameplay changes the structure and/or content of a game by using in-game and out-of-game resources.

Machinima, or videos which use a game's engine to create content, contain many examples of this type of play as it applies to sex. Machinima such as 'Not Just Another *World of Warcraft* Love Story' demonstrate players' ingenuity in the careful positioning of avatars to simulate sexual interaction (Lowood, 2011). Although in the teen-appropriate *World of Warcraft* (2012) there are no animations to signify any type of sexual activity, players in the example above and countless other Machinima figured out ways to position the camera angle and make best use of pre-coded avatar animations to create a type of emergent, transformative sexual play. Such actions can be thought of as emergent in that they were not pre-planned or coded by the developers but rather emerged out of player interactions. They can be thought of as transformative because they transform the narrative and mechanics of the game; whereas sexual animations were not previously possible, with player ingenuity they become so.

Representations of sex

While the previous section discussed the difference between games and other media, this section focuses specifically on the ways in which sex is represented in videogames and, in particular, the body politics of avatars. Similar to the 'real' world, in which women's bodies carry the burden of being unduly objectified and sexualised (Fredrickson and Roberts, 1997; Szymanski, Moffitt and Carr, 2011), much has been written about the sexualised bodies of female avatars.

A generalisation which perennially crops up in discussions of sexuality and videogames is the tendency towards hypersexualised female bodies. Although there have been public calls for diverse bodies in videogames (Sydell, 2014), and although there are of course exceptions, the default representation of the female form still includes tiny waists, rounded hips and large, exaggerated breasts complete with jiggle physics (Gray, 2015). Such heavily sexualised representations only apply to virtual women, with virtual men usually appearing fully clothed. Indeed, MacCallum-Stewart and Parsler note that in *World of Warcraft* 'it is common to find that a piece of clothing that fully covers the male figure is overly revealing on a woman' (2008: 231). They go on to give the example of the infamous Black Mageweave armour set, which on a male avatar appears as an unremarkable shirt and trousers but on female avatars appears as stockings, suspenders and a basque top. Placing female avatars in lingerie and male avatars in armour not only burdens the female body with the task of being the sole representation of sexuality in a game, but also affords titillation primarily for the heterosexual male gaze, at the expense of other forms of sexual interest or identifications.

This phenomenon is, of course, not unique to videogames and can be found in other media, as other chapters in this volume attest. However, as Dovey and Kennedy note,

> the visual imagery in many mainstream games seems to be entirely ignorant of the critiques that have been made of the stereotypes in other visual media and appear to import some of the worst examples in an entirely unreflexive and uncritical way.
> (2006: 93)

Videogame producers seem to have been reluctant to engage or reflect on their employment of digital women's bodies as vehicles to convey sexual meaning, even though research suggests that the heavy-handed sexualisation of female avatars has the potential to alienate some populations of players. Writing on *EverQuest* (Verant Interactive, 1999), T. L. Taylor noted 'that women in *EQ* often struggle with the conflicting meanings around their avatars ... when faced with the character-creation screen, it can feel as if one is choosing the best of the worst' (2006: 110).

Although videogames use the bodies of female avatars for their symbolic value, very few games have dared to actually represent the sexual act. Game scholar Tanya Krzywinska (2012) has compared the games industry's treatment of sexual themes to that of the film industry under the Production Code. The Production Code, which laid out moral guidelines for films developed in the United States from 1930 (Lewis, 2000), prevented frank depictions or discussions about sex and sexuality in cinema for more than 30 years – and, arguably, still to this day, through its successor, the Motion Picture Association of America (MPAA). The Production Code 'certainly produced a sublimation of sex into other charged images/themes, particularly in melodrama and screwball comedy, which often relied on innuendo to speak in code about sex to its audience' (Krzywinska, 2012: 157). For this reason, perhaps, many games take on an immature, almost coming-of-age-movie attitude towards representations of sexuality. Taken as a case study, Rob Gallagher's research (2012) on the use of the Wiimote to mimic male masturbation in the game *No More Heroes* (Grasshopper Manufacturer, 2007) exemplifies this.

The game's protagonist is a lonely young man by the name of Travis Touchdown who can be taken as an allegory for videogames' relationship to sex. Through answerphone messages from the videostore reminding Travis about his overdue porn rentals, the main character is humorously presented as someone who is lonely and desperate – so desperate, in fact, that the premise of the game is centred on Travis' attempts to impress, and sleep with, a beautiful assassin. The game is filled with innuendo and titillation from scantily clad background characters, 'but sex remains teasingly, embarrassingly out of *No More Heroes*' reach' (Gallagher, 2012: 401). The closest the game comes to representing sex is forcing the player to make back-and-forth hand gestures with the Wiimote to recharge their weapon in a way which suggests penile stimulation. Perhaps due to the previously noted limitations of the medium, or perhaps as its makers sought to avoid a media panic about sexual content in a game, *No More Heroes* itself 'seems agonizingly aware that the medium [of videogames] has, by and large, failed to mature to the point of successfully incorporating sex' (ibid.).

Although games have not been subjected to an equivalent of Hollywood's Production Code, they are still subjected to a review system. Much like the MPAA rates films according to content, the Entertainment Software Review Board (ESRB) in North America and the Pan European Games Information (PEGI) system in Europe rate games according to the age-appropriateness of their content. Depending on location, the ratings of games may or may not have legal enforcement, with accompanying penalties for failure to follow legislation. While the intention of games-rating systems is to allow consumers to make an informed choice about what they or their children might encounter in a game, there is a secondary and perhaps unintentional effect of censorship. In what game developer Brenda Brathwaite calls 'pseudo censorship' (2013: 216), games which explicitly feature sexual or even sensual content are given either a 'mature' or 'adults only' rating which severely limits where they may be bought or sold. As she observes, large North American retail chains such as Walmart, Best Buy and Target outright refuse to sell some 'mature' and all 'adults only' rated games. Therefore, if sex is represented in a game, it is done at the risk of limiting potential retail outlets for its sale. This is not to suggest, however, that some games don't take the risk, as shall be evidenced in the next section.

Games about sex

If we expand the definition of games to include the non-digital, then it suddenly becomes easier to think of games about sex. As I have already noted, spin the bottle, seven minutes in heaven, variations on *Twister* (Milton Bradley, 1964) and 'strip' versions of games such as poker can all be thought of as games that have sexuality at their heart. Rather than represent sex in a literal way, these games present a type of abstract sexuality.

Many videogames also represent sexuality in an abstract way. The masturbatory hand motions required to charge the weapon in *No More Heroes* can, as I outlined above, be thought of as a type of abstract representation for sex. By depicting masturbation in a humorous, slapstick way, the moral sensibilities of the presumed audience are not called into action. Ethnographic work studying role-playing games which deal with sexual or erotic content has shown that humour is a strategy or tool for mitigating discomfort when discussing or playing with potentially uncomfortable themes and topics (Brown, 2015). The deployment of humour allows for a distancing of the self from the potentially embarrassing or shameful action taking place. The very idea that sex is a shameful topic or one which shouldn't be engaged with in public settings comes from a cultural history much older than videogames (see Giddens, 1992, and various chapters in this collection).

While humour can likewise be found in games such as spin the bottle, it is not their primary theme, and actions undertaken during the game are not done for the sake of generating laughter. Flirtation, experimentation and even sensuality can be said to be the primary compulsions to play and to keep playing. In videogames the conveyance of flirtation, experimentation and sensuality becomes difficult to locate. The nuance required to simulate or articulate human sexuality seems at odds with the current capabilities of artificial intelligence and the ways in which we engage with the medium. *Playboy: The Mansion* can be taken as an example of this.

The game is based on the softcore magazine empire of the same name and allows players to assume the role of Hugh Hefner, with the goal of building the *Playboy* business from scratch. As a type of business simulator, the player must maintain relationships between Hugh Hefner and a range of playmates, celebrities, writers and photographers in order to create a successful magazine. The playmates pose topless during photo shoots and it is possible to have partially clothed simulated sex with various characters in the game. Because of its nudity and 'late-night television' types of sexual references, the game has a 'Mature' rating from the ESRB (Brathwaite, 2013). Despite the name of the game, and its associated franchise, its representations of sex are non-explicit and rely on pre-set animations and diegetic moaning to imply penetrative sex is occurring. Aside from choosing the necessary dialogue options to have sex, the player is not involved in the act. The animation happens on screen without the use of keyboard, mouse or controller input. Practically speaking, sex happens in the game as it does on late-night television – as something for the player to watch, but not to participate in.

Playboy: The Mansion is not alone in its representation of sex as a type of animation. Other games, such as *Grand Theft Auto III* (DMA Design, 2001), also use this strategy. While the player has input and control over dialogue options which lead up to sexual intercourse, they have no direct input during the act. There are, of course, notable exceptions to this rule. The 'Hot Coffee Mod' for *Grand Theft Auto: San Andreas* (Rockstar North, 2004), for example, allowed players to partake in clothed sex by using the controller to help the on-screen couple reach climax. However interactive this scene might be, the tactility found at the core of non-digital games is difficult to replicate with a controller. This lack of tactility is somewhat alleviated in the application and use of touch-screen tablets for gaming. *Luxuria Superbia* and *Fingle* are two examples of games which use touch-screen interfaces to inspire feelings of sensuality or emotional closeness.

In *Luxuria Superbia*, players travel to the centre of a flower, to an interactive yet minimalist soundtrack of soft sighs and thudding heartbeats. The player receives instructions in how to play by way of floating and fading text that details how to touch the walls of the flower. As the player taps, slides and flicks their finger across the screen, positive feedback is provided in the changing colour and features of the flower's internal landscape; the speed and complexity of the soundtrack also increases as encouragement/reward to the player. Upon completion of each level, the player is confronted with a white screen with fading textual commentary on their performance. The text, accompanied by soothing music, presumably replicates post-coital bliss.

As a game, *Luxuria Superbia* stands out not just for its abstract and artistic representation of intercourse but also for its use of the tablet medium. By making the player deploy their own fingers against the screen, the distance between player and game is shortened. It becomes the responsibility of the player to stroke the inner petals of a flower instead of just pushing buttons and moving a joystick on a control pad. The hand motions used in the game are not entirely different to those used to stimulate 'real-world' clitorises. Although there have been many attempts at developing teledildonic devices for all manner of gaming consoles, the simple contact of fingers on a screen breaks down barriers between human body and technology without the need for a peripheral device. The ways in which the game responds to the player's touch through auditory and graphical feedback are an abstract representation of the feelings and emotions associated with intercourse rather than just an on-screen representation of the physical act. In representing the rather abstract sensations of intimacy, pleasure and lust through graphical responses to player touch, *Luxuria Superbia* provides an example of the ways in which games can utilise specific forms of user/viewer interactions unique to videogames as a media to explore sexuality.

Likewise, *Fingle* also uses the full capabilities of the tablet platform to simulate and represent flirtation, intimacy and sexual intercourse. In a type of table-top *Twister*, the game is played by two players seated across from each other at a table, who use their hands and fingers to perform the feats of agility demanded by the screen. Each level of the game features two sets of colour-coded blocks – a set for player one and a set for player two. Each player is instructed to rest their fingers on the blocks and to never lose contact between their skin and the screen. In some levels, the blocks move and so the players' hands must follow, and in some levels only select blocks move, meaning players must move some fingers while keeping others stationary. Certain patterns appear during the game which demand the players move their hands perilously close to each other, with some levels requiring players' fingers to slide in between each other. In other contexts, the amount of skin-to-skin contact between players might seem as innocent as a handshake, but the game features a funk soundtrack with heavy use of guitars and 'wah-wah' pedals reminiscent of 1970s sexploitation or softcore films. Between levels, words such as 'groovy' flash across the screen, evaluating the couple's performance, and later levels get 'hotter' and require players to hold their hands closer and in increasingly suggestive positions for longer lengths of time. These individual elements combine to provide an overall aesthetic which feels flirtatious and sensual, even if it is tongue-in-cheek.

Similar to *Luxuria Superbia*, *Fingle* uses a tablet's tactile capability to get players to directly interact with and respond to technology in a way that feels both flirtatious and sensual. Rather than represent sexuality on screen through the use of cinematics or cutscenes, and rather than require a teledildonic peripheral attachment, *Fingle* allows players to use their bodies to interact with technology and each other. Although it has striking similarities to non-digital games, *Fingle* uses the medium of digital games and technology to represent sex and flirtation through the sliding of hands across a screen. In many ways, the game provides a prompt, if not an excuse, for players to flirt as they may do when playing *Twister* or spin the bottle.

Conclusions

This chapter discussed how games are different to other media, representations of sex and games and games about sex. It was established that videogames are different to traditional forms of media due to the temporal nature of their interactivity (Dovey and Kennedy, 2006). They demand feedback from players in ways different to traditional forms of media. In this demand for feedback, there is potential for digital games to play with sexuality in ways impossible for other media. As research on sex and games attests, however, there are problems with how sex is currently represented. From the overt sexualisation of female avatars to potential problems with moral codes and review boards, the representation of sex in videogames has been an area of contention. The resulting representations are often categorised as immature (Krzywinska, 2012; Gallagher, 2012) because when sex does appear in a game, it is often treated as the punchline to a joke. While part of this immaturity connects to larger discourses of sexuality-as-taboo (Giddens, 1992), part of it also has something to do with the utilisation of the medium of the videogame.

When considering videogames' treatment of sexuality as immature, the immaturity of the artform must also be acknowledged. As a medium, videogames are young. The nuance of designing sexuality in games as more than narrative, more than mechanical sets of movements and more than representation is in its infancy and still subject to a range of constraints. Although there are examples of games, such as *Luxuria Superbia* and *Fingle*, that have taken steps towards integrating the specific capabilities of digital platforms to develop the tactility of sexual play, they are exceptions which suggest future possibilities that other developers might build on. As future studies and future games test the capabilities of interactive digital media further, the creative application of new modes of interaction to represent or simulate sexual interaction will surely follow.

Bibliography

Atkins, B. (2003). *More than a Game: The Computer Game as Fictional Form*. Manchester: University of Manchester Press.
Betcher, W. (1987). *Intimate Play: Creating Romance in Everyday Life*. New York: Penguin Books.
Brathwaite, B. (2013). *Sex in Video Games*. Newton Centre, MA: Charles River Media.
Brown, A. (2015). *Sexuality and Role-Playing Games*. London: Routledge.
Dovey, J. and Kennedy, H. (2006). *Game Cultures: Computer Games as New Media*. New York: Open University Press.
Fredrickson, B. L. and Roberts, T. (1997). 'Objectification theory: toward understanding women's lived experiences and mental health risks'. *Psychology of Women Quarterly*, Volume 21: 173–206.
Gallagher, R. (2012). 'No sex please, we are finite state machines: on the melancholy sexlessness of the video game'. *Games and Culture*, Volume 7 (6): 399–418.
Giddens, A. (1992). *The Transformation of Intimacy: Sexuality, Love and Eroticism in Modern Societies*. Stanford, CA: Stanford University Press.
Gray, K. (2015). 'Let me get something off my chest about boob physics in video games'. *The Guardian*, 21 January. www.theguardian.com/technology/2015/jan/21/boobs-breasts-physics-video-game (accessed 13 March 2015).
Jenkins, H. (2006). *Fans, Bloggers, and Gamers: Exploring Participatory Culture*. London: New York University Press.
Karlsen, F. (2014). 'Analysing the history of game controversies', Proceedings of Digital Games Research Association Conference 2014. www.digra.org/wp-content/uploads/digital-library/digra2014_submission_97.pdf (accessed 24 February 2015).

Kelly, P. (2015). 'The digital courting process in *Dragon Age 2*'. In J. MacCallum-Stewart and E. Enevold (eds) *Game Love: Essays on Play and Affection*. London: McFarland.
Krzywinska, T. (2012). 'The strange case of the misappearance of sex in videogames'. In J. Fromme and A. Unger (eds) *Computer Games and New Media Cultures*. London: Springer.
Lewis, J. (2000). *Hollywood v. Hard Core: How the Struggle over Censorship Created the Modern Film Industry*. New York: New York University Press.
Lowood, H. (2011). 'Video capture: Machinima, documentation, and the history of virtual worlds'. In H. Lowood and M. Nitsche (eds) *The Machinima Reader*. London: MIT Press.
MacCallum-Stewart, E. and Parsler, J. (2008). 'Role-play vs. game play: the difficulties of playing a role in *World of Warcraft*'. In H. Corneliussen and J. Walker Rettberg (eds) *Digital Culture, Play, and Identity: A World of Warcraft Reader*. Massachusetts: MIT Press.
Pearce, C. and Artemesia (2009). *Communities of Play: Emergent Cultures in Multiplayer Games and Virtual Worlds*. Cambridge, MA: MIT Press.
Salen, K. and Zimmerman, E. (2004). *Rules of Play: Game Design Fundamentals*. Cambridge, MA: MIT Press.
Sjöblom, B. (2015). 'Killing digital children: design, discourse and player agency'. In T. Mortsen, J. Linderoth and A. Brown (eds) *The Dark Side of Game Play*. New York: Routledge.
Sotamaa, O. (2007). 'Let me take you to *the movies*: productive players, commodification and transformative play'. *Convergence: The International Journal of Research into New Media Technologies*, Volume 13 (4): 383–401.
Sutton-Smith, B. (1997). *The Ambiguity of Play*. Cambridge, MA: Harvard University Press.
Sydell, L. (2014). 'Critics renew calls for more diverse video game characters'. *National Public Radio All Tech Considered Blog*, 14 June. www.npr.org/blogs/alltechconsidered/2014/06/13/321673815/critics-renew-calls-for-more-diverse-video-game-characters (accessed 13 March 2015).
Szymanski, D., Moffitt, L. and Carr, E. (2011). 'Sexual objectification of women: advances to theory and research'. *The Counselling Psychologist*, Volume 39 (1): 6–38.
Taylor, T. L. (2006). *Play Between Worlds: Exploring Online Game Culture*. MIT Press: Cambridge, MA.
Ware, N. (2015). 'Iterative romance and button-mashing sex: gameplay design and videogames' Nice Guy Syndrome'. In E. Wysocki and M. Lauteria (eds) *Rated M for Mature*. London: Bloomsbury.

Media

Dragon Age: Origins (2009). [PC]. Redwood City, CA: Bioware/Electronic Arts.
Dragon Age II (2011). [PC]. Redwood City, CA: Bioware/Electronic Arts.
EverQuest (1999). [PC]. Los Angeles: Verant Interactive/Sony Online Entertainment.
Fingle (2011). [iPad]. Utrecht: Game Oven Studios.
Grand Theft Auto III (2001). [Playstation 2]. New York: DMA Design/Rockstar Games.
Grand Theft Auto: San Andreas (2004). [PC]. Edinburgh: Rockstar North.
Luxuria Superbia (2013). [iPad]. Brussels: Tale of Tales Games.
No More Heroes (2007). [Wii]. Montreal: Grasshopper Manufacture/Ubisoft.
Playboy: The Mansion (2005). [PC]. Montreal: Cyberlore/Ubisoft.
The Stanley Parable (2013). [PC]. Bellevue, CA: Galactic Café/Steam Greenlight.
Twister (1964). [Boardgame]. East Longmeadow, MA: Milton Bradley Company.
World of Warcraft: Cataclysm (2004/2010/2012). [PC]. Irving, CA: Blizzard Activision.

23
SEX AND CELEBRITY MEDIA

Adrienne Evans

Introduction: the intimate lives of public selves

I am extremely concerned for you that those around you have led you to believe, or encouraged you in your own belief, that it is in any way 'cool' to be naked and licking sledgehammers in your videos.
Sinead O'Connor, open letter to Miley Cyrus (2013)

In the late twentieth and early twenty-first centuries the concept of celebrity has undergone shifts in meanings, making celebrity seem at once more accessible, attainable and personable, but equally more invasible, and so fragmenting illusions of private life, including in terms of the celebrity's sexual and intimate relations. Although our categories of celebrity have always been about 'living in the spotlight', a 'demotic' or 'hypertrophic' turn in celebrity culture means the personal lives of the rich and famous are made much more fluid and flexible, suggesting not only that we can glean insight into the personal lives of celebrities but also that we may also live the life of one (Redmond, 2014; Turner, 2013).

Reality TV has been one of the most significant markers of the changing nature of celebrity culture, giving 'celebrity' the appearance of a democratic and attainable identity category. Happening at 'celebrity's border zone', the mechanisms through which the 'ordinary' person reaches celebrity status take place through a process of self-revelation, confession and the public documentation of private life (Couldry, 2001: 111; Littler, 2004). Meanwhile, new media technologies have produced their own 'micro' celebrities through online platforms, such as Twitter, Facebook and YouTube, that create new categories of 'DIY' celebrities and 'unintended' celebrities through practices of tagging, sharing, remixing and the meme (Attwood, 2006; Marwick and boyd, 2011; McNair, 2002; Turner, 2013).

Against the backdrop of a seemingly more democratic model of celebrity, and narrowing concepts of public and private lives, celebrity culture has itself become both more intimate and public. Lady Gaga, Justin Bieber, Taylor Swift and Miley Cyrus tweet the mundane details of their everyday lives to millions of fans. Intimate moments between celebrities have also become more visible. The sex tape, for example, has become a managed promotional tool: Kanye West's recent music video for *Bound 2* featured West and Kim Kardashian simulating sex on a bike, with images from the video alluding to climax and oral sex. With sex tapes no longer characterised by the grainy images of *1 Night in Paris* or the infamous Pamela Anderson and Tommy Lee recordings (see Hillyer, 2004, 2010 and Longstaff, in this volume), the highly stylish and stylised gyrations of *Bound 2* present a controlled and manufactured version of what sexual moments shared between West and Kardashian 'might' be like.

Alongside the visibility of the intimate lives of celebrities, we have also witnessed heightened examples of privacy invasion. In 2014, 'The Fappening' saw young female celebrities, including Jennifer Lawrence, having their personal devices hacked in order to access naked images of them (Sanghani, 2014). The act of hacking private accounts and posting such images online was explicitly misogynistic and sexually aggressive, not least in the naming of the event – the hacker's use of the slang term 'fap' as a synonym for masturbation suggesting that the public consumption of these images would likely be used for sexual pleasure. Lawrence, among others, called the hacking a 'sex crime', citing it as evidence of an increasingly prevalent 'rape culture' (see Ferreday, 2015 for further discussion of rape culture). Another infringement of celebrity privacy led to legal action being taken by the British royal family against French *Closer* magazine in 2012, after the magazine printed topless images of Kate Middleton on holiday. The images of Middleton, despite being banned in the UK, were able to proliferate through social media platforms.

Fuelled by new platforms, formats and contexts, the mediation of celebrity has altered dramatically over the past hundred years. What has changed very little, however, is the importance of celebrity 'sex' and 'sexiness'. Elvis' suggestive hip-swinging and Marilyn Monroe's pout and 'come hither' gaze of the 1950s and 60s were followed by the 'sexual revolution' of 1970s celebrity. Madonna's liberated and expressive 'sex bomb' femininity in the 1980s was echoed in Sharon Stone's seated seduction in the 1990s film *Basic Instinct*. Celebrity culture, as Dyer (2004) suggests, gives us opportunities to chart society's changing relationships to sex, sexuality and sexual appeal (see Mercer's 2013 special issue of *Celebrity Studies* on 'Sex and the Celebrity'). The celebrity sex symbol bears the symbolic weight of taboo-breaking and the changing moral codes around what we understand 'sexy' to mean.

This chapter presents dominant approaches to making sense of sex and celebrity media. I begin below by outlining approaches that suggest celebrity can be read as a representation of 'our times', and for its processes of production and consumption. Following this, the chapter then explores feminist approaches to celebrity culture, paying special attention to notions of the 'sexualisation of culture', postfeminist celebrity culture and the objectification of female celebrities. Case studies are drawn from analyses of the fetishisation of female celebrity 'bums' and the sexualised, gendered, classed and racialised representation of body parts. I finish the discussion by drawing attention to the selective but hyperbolic media discussion of and reaction to sexy and publicly intimate performances of celebrity culture with reference to Miley Cyrus, where the layering of commentary on top of commentary about Cyrus' sexiness reflects a cultural anxiety around intimate life, and concern for future sexual conduct.

Representing celebrity

Traditional approaches to celebrity studies are rooted in film studies and the analysis of 'stardom'. While not the first analysis of the celebrity, Richard Dyer's discussion of Paul Robeson, Marilyn Monroe and Judy Garland in *Heavenly Bodies* (originally published 1986, reprinted 2004) has been particularly important in shaping academic discussion of celebrity (see also Dyer's earlier influential book, *Stars*, published in 1979). Principally an analysis of representation, Dyer was interested in the 'ideological function' of the star and the way in which this comes to shape the available discourses for making sense of the self (Dyer 1979).ABer's (2004: 19) notion of 'discourse' refers to a set of 'media signs' that, far from being coherent, contain 'clusters of ideas, notions, feelings, images, attitudes and assumptions', meaning that the star image could be understood as a representation of wider social, political and cultural sense-making.

Dyer's (2004) analysis of Marilyn Monroe, for example, focuses on how Monroe came to represent sex during a historical period of shifting notions of what 'sex' meant. As the first centrefold of the *Playboy* franchise, and in the wake of the Kinsey reports (1948 and 1953) that reshaped notions of 'normal' sexual practice, Monroe's sexuality came to be filtered through ideas of the naturalness of sex and sexual innocence. Thus while her *Playboy* centrefold was controversial and challenged sexual attitudes of the time, her quip that 'It's not true I had nothing on. I had the radio on' plays with notions of the naturalness and normalcy of the naked body (Dyer, 2004; Scheibel, 2013). Alongside these shifting concepts of sexuality, Dyer (2004) also notes the growing significance of psychoanalytic language in the 1950s, and its view of inherent sexual difference. Here, Monroe represented 'ideal' femininity: vulnerable, dependent on men and visually desirable.

Dyer's analysis of the sexiness of Marilyn Monroe suggests that the meanings that were attached to her celebrity were permissible to mainstream America because of their associations with purity. Monroe's image is socially significant because she was able to act out American values: as a symbol of femininity, her whiteness and blondness meant that sex could function in society (and to her audience) in ways that did not present sex appeal as dangerous and sinful. Monroe's sex-symbol status allowed people to make sense of ideological conflict during a period of social anxiety about the meanings of sex.

Dyer's approach to understanding celebrity has been important because it was one of the first to recognise that the meaning of the celebrity had wider cultural significance. For Dyer (2004: ix–x) the study of stardom was able to open up questions of emotion, sexuality and everyday life, reflecting what kinds of people we are able to become in particular social and historical contexts. Accounts since have invariably drawn on Dyer's approach, but have also brought an understanding of media industries to bear on the significance of celebrity culture in contemporary society. Rojek (2012), for example, understands celebrity as something that is staged and carefully managed, produced through a supply–demand relationship between the celebrity and their audience, while Turner (2013) likens celebrity to a relationship of 'commercial property' that can mutually benefit both commodity and celebrity brand.

However, this supply–demand model is often highly unstable. For example, following revelations of Tiger Woods' infidelities in 2009 and 2010 he was dropped by several of his sponsors, and his exposure in the media arguably led to a decline in the profits of those brands that continued to support him – a loss that was subsequently passed onto shareholders (Rojek, 2012). The relationship between overexposure and market decline, however, does not always hold. For example, Rojek cites the release of 'soft-porn' images of Madonna, which were then used by her management in the run-up to the publication *Sex*. Although the publication of *Sex* provoked conservative backlash against Madonna, her overexposure worked in favour of her celebrity brand and sales, and more generally became a 'defining moment in the sexualization of mass culture' (McNair, 1996: 160). These kinds of outcomes in the patterns of overexposure have led Rojek to claim that 'the fame formula is a deeply flawed doctrine' (2012: 81).

There are two points I want to take forward in linking these previous approaches to the study of celebrity in feminist media studies. In terms of accounts of representation, Dyer's approach to understanding the celebrity has been useful for feminist media studies because it pays attention to representations of gender, race and sexuality. These issues have been undeniably important in feminist analyses of contemporary celebrity representations, as have accounts of celebrity-as-commodity. Here, the industry approach allows us to make sense of the 'exchange value' of female celebrity bodies. I discuss these below, paying particular attention to the celebrity 'bum'.

Sexy bums and body parts

Feminist approaches to celebrity have been important in making sense of the limited roles that women and female celebrities have played in the media and the ways in which their images are presented to us, especially through the intersections of class, race, sexuality and physical embodiment (Gill, 2007). This approach has been particularly important in making sense of the assumed democratisation of fame and celebrity and the associated promise of social mobility, alongside the denigration of particular groups of women through the celebrity system (Biressi and Nunn, 2004). While the 'celebrity' category becomes less rigid and seemingly more replicable through platforms such as reality TV, what counts as 'sexy' remains homogeneous and hierarchical: the white, slim, middle-class female body maintains desirability (Evans and Riley, 2013; Gill, 2007).

In the UK, a particular political and cultural moment has shaped notions of disgust in relation to class and gender; new forms of hate have been encouraged through the representation of poverty (e.g. *Benefit Street*), and reality TV celebrities who become glamour models are at one and the same time hyper-sexualised and denounced as trashy, slutty, vulgar and unclean (Tyler and Bennett, 2010). Race and ethnicity also play a part in shaping celebrity's democratisation; see, for example, the way that *My Big Fat Gypsy Wedding* worked to represent Roma, Gypsy and Traveller brides as antithetical to constructs of the sexy, modern, self-determined woman. While the existence of a particular sexiness within that community demonstrated a plurality of sexy aesthetics, the popular reception of *My Big Fat Gypsy Wedding* marked the 'Gypsy' bride as the tasteless white-other, with their sexuality often associated with the excessive, overly fleshy body that reaffirms associations between consumption, body weight and sexuality (Jensen and Ringrose, 2014; Tremlett, 2014; Tyler, 2013). Women who fall outside of celebrity's cultural constructs of 'sexy' are often violently denied and denigrated, despite celebrity's seeming accessibility.

Feminist media studies has been equally interested in how intersections of class, race, gender and sexuality come to frame how the celebrity body is imag(in)ed and how these intersections determine the commodity object of the female celebrity body. A key term in making sense of female celebrity has been 'objectification', wherein the selective process of turning the visual image of women's bodies into discrete parts constitutes a form of gender power. The objectification of female body parts is evident, for example, in the sexualisation of celebrities' legs, breasts, labia and buttocks. In a series of 'upskirting' shots taken by the paparazzi in 2007, for example, images of celebrity female labia worked to sexualise and class the female body. Where the upskirting of Paris Hilton was normalised as evidence of the celebrity's overexposure and attention-seeking, the intrusive images of Britney Spears held a different meaning: her postpartum caesarean scar and 'white trash' status branded her a bad mother and a dangerously excessive, pathologically (hetero)sexual subject (later cemented in her apparent 'breakdown') (Schwartz, 2008).

The visualisations of celebrities' labia are rendered intelligible through the camera's association with heterosexuality and its (implied) penetration, whereas the bum has been a mainstay of racialising representations of the sexy female celebrity, where 'black female sexuality is literally embodied in voluptuous black buttocks' (Railton and Watson, 2005: 56). In Beltran's (2007: 281) analysis of Jennifer Lopez's 'cross-over butt', for example, she suggests that the discussion surrounding the celebrity's backside during the late 1990s amounted to the 'exoticization and sexualisation of the non-white body' (similar arguments could be made about the more recent media treatment of Kim Kardashian's bum and its capacity to 'Break the Internet': see Evans, 2015). Lopez's 'cross-over butt' became an object of public obsession and fascination, alongside her repeated proclamation that she was happy with her curves. While the language of positive body image employed by Lopez suggests self-image control, agency and transgression, bringing new, non-white and Latina bodies into the public consciousness, it also poses questions about the viability of equality merely through becoming visible. Beltran's (2007) analysis demonstrates how Lopez's image was also used in ways that alluded to colonial discourses that shape how sex, sexiness and the sexualisation of non-white women come to be imagined. The intense public scrutiny of Lopez's posterior bears close resemblance to the treatment of black women's backsides during the colonial period, where they were treated as objects of scientific experimentation and public display because of the associations made between large buttocks and savage sexuality (McClintock, 1995). The representation of non-white women is not homogeneous. However, by locating non-white women as being closer to nature, or as 'dangerously' or 'excessively' sexual, non-white female sexuality is demarcated as animalistic and immoral, in contrast to white female sexuality, which becomes moral and civilised (Beltran, 2007; Railton and Watson, 2005; McClintock, 1995).

A useful contrast here is the media discussion of Pippa Middleton's backside during and after the wedding of her sister, Kate Middleton, to Prince William in 2012. The wedding itself was presented in the media as a moment of national pride and evidence of the meaningfulness of love and romance, but Pippa Middleton's backside was also the subject of a significant amount of media discussion. This was followed shortly after by the creation of the Facebook group 'Pippa Middleton ass appreciation society' and reported requests in cosmetic surgery consultations for the 'Pippa'[1] (see McCabe, 2011). In her 'buttermilk body-skimming gown', Kate Middleton's sister 'seductively embodie[d] a type of feminine empowerment that is completely digestible' (McCabe, 2011: 355–356).

In the context of a traditional, if highly mediated, 'white' wedding, the fetishisation, objectification and sexualisation of Pippa Middleton's 'sexy bum' was largely unremarkable: indeed, its location as a sexy object at the intersection of upper-middle-class whiteness remained invisible. It was not deemed necessary, for example, for Pippa to constantly extol her own pride in her body or her ethnicity; neither was it ever suggested that Pippa's curvy backside has any relationship to her sexual appetite. The differences in modes of representation are evidently presented in the music video format: for example, Lilly Allen's music video for *Hard Out Here*, which was arguably intended to highlight the sexism experienced by all women in the music industry, demonstrated a clear racial hierarchy whereby white women's demand for freedom came at the expense of black women, who were nominally visualised as hyper-sexual, voiceless backing dancers (Moore, 2013). A similar observation of celebrities' 'sexy bums' is suggested in Railton and Watson's (2005) analysis of Kylie Minogue's whiteness in music videos, which is only made visible through comparison to the representation of black female singers such as Beyoncé and Rihanna.

Railton and Watson (2005) suggest that Beyoncé's video for *Baby Boy* is exemplary of the representation of sexy black female celebrity through associations with an excessive and dangerous sexuality. Variously located in the jungle, by the sea, on the beach, her body is affected and moved by the environment, and her body, backside and hair are always shown in constant, often uncontrollable movement (Railton and Watson, 2005). In contrast, Minogue's video for *Can't Get You Out of My Head* is clinical, clean, light and white. Her sexiness is controlled through the use of slow-motion techniques that work to manage the body's movement: this body does not writhe, roll, crawl or get covered in sand or water in the same way that Beyoncé's does (Railton and Watson, 2005). Comparing the two celebrities' use of the body in performance allows for an analysis of the hyper-sexual and primitive sexuality represented by Beyoncé's music video, which makes visible the purity represented in the performance of Minogue (e.g. motionless hair and flawless, taut skin).

The status of celebrity sexiness in contemporary culture bears signs of classed, racialised and gendered inequalities that have a history which still carries weight today (see McClintock, 1995). While limited constructs of sexiness still shape the way we view female celebrities, what has changed is the media landscape and the technologies that we have available to produce, maintain, share and comment on these images. This takes place alongside an explosion of discussion about and representations of sex and sexiness throughout the media, referred to variously as 'pornification', 'raunch culture' and the 'sexualisation of culture' (Attwood, 2009; Evans and Riley, 2013; Gill, 2012; McNair, 2002). Below, I suggest that drawing together these accounts to analyse contemporary sexy celebrity has wider implications for understanding sexual identity. I do this by focusing on the recent media attention on Miley Cyrus.

Narratives of concern: what is 'sexy' celebrity?

The pop star Miley Cyrus is one of the most talked-about celebrities of recent years. Alongside her constant public performance of celebrity through social media, every act or public 'confession' seems worthy of scrutiny for what it represents of the body, sexuality, rumoured sexual practices, sexiness and femininity of Cyrus. Social commentary surrounding Cyrus has become all-pervasive, an intense media noise. Cyrus' most controversial moments to date have been the release of the video for *Wrecking Ball*, her performance at the VMAs with *Blurred Lines* singer Robin Thicke and her popularisation of 'twerking'. But even her small deviations from normative notions of good, white, innocent femininity have been controversial.

One example of the media hyperbole surrounding Cyrus occurred after a haircut in 2012. Cyrus posted images on Instagram of herself having her waist-length hair cut short, resulting in a backlash from her fans, who thought the cut both unfeminine and too sudden. Cyrus' long hair had represented an appropriate heterosexual femininity, whereas the short haircut located her as potentially 'boyish'. Even while Cyrus' image was just-about-heterosexy-enough, the apparent deviation from normative scripts of good girlhood also led to speculation about her sexuality (as potential lesbian or bisexual) that worked to fold gender, appearance and sexuality into a series of heterosexist binaries (McRobbie, 2009). But the haircut was also, we were told, part of her managed 'rebranding'.

Cyrus' association with provocation appeared, however, before the notorious haircut. In 2009, Cyrus' Teen Choice Awards performance of her single *Party in the U.S.A*, in which she briefly dipped against a stage-prop pole, became part of the narrative of sexualisation and evidence of the exploitation of contemporary young female stars by the celebrity industry: the 'sex sells' motto of modern capitalism. Online discussions of the performance questioned Cyrus' authenticity, agency and choice, suggesting that the idea for the dance was a product of her management (Lamb, Graling and Wheeler, 2013). Because of her location within the celebrity system and our current cultural preoccupation with neoliberal postfeminist notions of 'choice' and 'freedom', Cyrus' routine was deemed a manufactured performance of 'sexy' and therefore not representative of modern, sassy, self-knowing sexiness, because it lacked the authenticity of the neoliberal call to 'be who you really are' (Lamb, Graling and Wheeler, 2013; Banet-Weiser and Portwood-Stacer, 2006).

Sinead O'Connor later repeated these claims in her open letter to Cyrus. In 2013, Cyrus released a video for her song *Wrecking Ball*, in which she is seen swinging naked on the titular wrecking ball. The video also makes allusions to O'Connor's *Nothing Compares 2 U*, whereby Cyrus is shot in close up and in tears. The video proved highly controversial, provoking a series of social commentaries. In response to Cyrus' video, Connor stated:

> The music business doesn't give a shit about you, or any of us. They will prostitute you for all you are worth, and cleverly make you think its what YOU wanted . . . and when you end up in rehab as a result of being prostituted, 'they' will be sunning themselves on their yachts in Antigua, which they bought by selling your body and you will find yourself very alone.
>
> (O'Connor, 2013)

I am interested here in the public reactions to these mediated 'moments'. I am also interested in how we have made these moments 'public' through insisting that sex, sexuality and sexiness are visible and accountable (Foucault, 1998). This is not to say that we shouldn't have an emotional response to Cyrus, either finding her a worrying example of the exploitation of a young woman who grew up in the spotlight of the celebrity 'star' system or a playful symbol of sexual exuberance and healthy, youthful body confidence. Both responses are not only reasonable but necessary, given the current ways we have of making sense of sexy celebrity. But, following Dyer (2004), we could also turn our attention to the public response to the rise of Cyrus as 'sex symbol' as a reflection of current notions of what the 'sexy' female body means today; of our cultural values towards sexiness and 'sexualisation'.

If we take this approach, then it can be argued that cultural feelings around sexiness are the result of a deeply ambivalent anxiety about (youthful) female sexuality. The public reaction to Cyrus' *Wrecking Ball* video demonstrates a range of noisy and contradictory perspectives, including concern over the 'tarnishing' of good, clean, proper and pure femininity (with all its racial connotations), the imposition of Cyrus' perceived lack of agency over her own sexual representation and also evidence of our prior 'prudish' attitudes towards sexuality – a celebratory cheer for sexual liberation. The social commentaries around Cyrus' *Wrecking Ball* video, whether celebratory or concerned, were quick to place its cultural meanings within the realm of sex. Discussion of the video paid little attention to the fact that the lyrics of *Wrecking Ball* are not overly sexual. Commentary assumed that the young naked female body was in itself a sexual and sexualised object, not merely a naked body. Unlike Monroe's quip about having the radio on, which Dyer (2004) tells us reflects the normalcy of the naked body, Cyrus' rebuttal and appeal was to see the video through its emotional value:[2] this was a naked body that needed defending and taking seriously, and not one to take lightly.

Public reactions to Cyrus' various performances also need to be located in the context of her celebrity narrative. Having come from the successful Disney show *Hannah Montana*,

Cyrus is already located in a recognisable 'sexy' narrative. Britney Spears and Christina Aguilera, both of whom appeared as Disney stars, were also framed through media storytelling as having 'transformed themselves' into sex symbols during the transition into adulthood (and in ways that also included changes in hairstyle, whether shaven or braided). Our concern with their transitions into 'adult' sexuality is not only located in their image but also in their audience. Given that they have previously been consumed by a 'young', largely female audience, the narrative of concern that follows these celebrities is also wrapped up with their apparent 'role model' status and the 'effect' that this may have on young girls (even while young girls reproduce the same narratives of concern around celebrities like Cyrus: see Jackson, Vares and Gill, 2013).

The noise about Cyrus and other 'sex symbol' celebrities is therefore not a concern about the celebrities themselves, but a future-oriented concern for a new generation of women and their sexual behaviour. In a recent article in the *Daily Mail*, journalist Laura Cox (2013) reported on a study that found that sexy celebrities such as Cyrus 'affect women's confidence, education and even their employment prospects' because of the 'mixed messages' that these celebrities send out to 'impressionable' young girls. Nearly 350 comments follow the article, many of which lambast the recent sexualisation of women:

> The rise of so called feminism has damaged women so much, instead of being the sexually liberated sex they keep telling us they are, they have only become more and more exploited. Women are now meat products being exploited for a sex driven culture. Sad.
>
> (Lemonsorbet, Ireland)

In the article and nearly all the comments following it, the reaction to Cyrus (and others) demonstrates a concern that young women are going to be unable to take part in the continuation of middle-class self-betterment (education, employment) because of a sexualised media context that encourages them to be more sexual, thereby reducing the narrative of concern 'to a problem of sexual behaviours and sexuality rather than sexism' (Egan, 2013: 267). In addition, the article associates sexualisation with body issues, lack of confidence and poor self-esteem, taking place within a culture that demands that women 'love their bodies': a cultural discourse that extols women to already understand their bodies as a site of failure of confidence (Gill and Elias, 2014). The discussion takes place within a sentiment where young girls' 'confidence' has become an individual problem, not a societal issue perpetuated by the very same noise represented by the social commentary around celebrity sexiness (Evans and Riley, 2014). Where any societal blame lands, of course, is at the feet of feminism itself – as suggested in the comment above – for providing a framework for 'sexual liberation' in the first place! (See Ringrose, 2013 for a similar observation of how feminism becomes discredited in education discourses.)

Public reactions to Cyrus therefore suggest that intimacy, sexiness and sexual subjectivity have become sites of anxiety, with attendant concerns about the 'proper' sexual conduct of a future generation of women, who are expected to 'do' sexiness in particular ways. What is perhaps more intriguing about the mediated noise and anxiety surrounding Cyrus, whose 'sexiness' has become an issue of public concern, is where the noise doesn't follow. In 2013, Cyrus released the short film *Tongue Tied*. The film featured Cyrus against a white backdrop, wrapped in latex and covered in black paint, and variously drew on allusions to bondage, S&M and fetish fashion. It was perhaps best defined by the expression 'porno chic' (McNair, 2002, 2013). Yet there was little media discussion or contention surrounding this video.

And what seemed to differentiate this representation of Cyrus from others that year was its production: the video was produced by Quentin Jones, a photographic artist. The hyperbole around sexy celebrity is thus selective. We might therefore want to suggest that *Tongue Tied*'s comparatively 'high-brow', 'tasteful' and 'stylish' production placed it outside of the realms of concern, anxiety and regulation. Thus the apparently 'democratic' media-spheres in which we live today are only available to those few with the cultural capital to understand its codes and take up its calls to 'sexual liberation'.

Notes

1 The growth in 'butt augmentation' surgery has been estimated at 58 per cent, with many asking for the 'Brazilian' butt lift. Many commentators imply its popularity is related to the visibility of celebrities like Kim Kardashian: see, for example, www.fashiontimes.com/articles/17891/20150122/trending-plastic-surgery-kim-kardashian-instagram-game-twitter-brazilian-butt-lift-fat-transfer-breast-augmentation-tummy-tuck-surgery-most-popular-for-2015-north-west-mommy-makeover.htm (accessed 17 November 2016).
2 www.mtv.com/news/1713881/miley-cyrus-defends-wrecking-ball/ (accessed 17 November 2016).

Bibliography

Attwood, F. (2006) 'Sexed Up: Theorizing the Sexualization of Culture'. *Sexualities*. Volume 9 (1): 77–94.
Attwood, F. (ed) (2009) *Mainstreaming Sex: The Sexualization of Western Culture*. London: I.B. Tauris.
Banet-Weiser, S. and Portwood-Stacer, L. (2006) '"I Just Want to Be Me Again!" Beauty Pageants, Reality Television and Post-Feminism'. *Feminist Theory*. Volume 7 (2): 255–272.
Beltran, M.C. (2007) 'The Hollywood Latina Body as Site of Social Struggle: Media Constructions of Stardom and Jennifer Lopez's "Cross-Over Butt"'. In S. Redmond and S. Holmes (eds) *Stardom and Celebrity: A Reader*. London: Sage.
Biressi, A. and Nunn, H. (2004) 'The Especially Remarkable: Celebrity and Social Mobility in Reality TV'. *Mediactive*. Volume 2: 8–25.
Couldry, N. (2001) 'The Hidden Injuries of Media Power'. *Journal of Consumer Culture*. Volume 1 (2): 155–177.
Cox, L. (2013) 'Raunchy, Hyper-Sexualised Popstars like Miley Cyrus and Rihanna Damage Girls' Self-Esteem – and Could Harm Education and Job Prospects – Says Leading Academic'. *Daily Mail*. 13 September. www.dailymail.co.uk/femail/article-2419993/Miley-Cyrus-Rihanna-damage-girls-self-esteem--harm-education-job-prospects-says-academic.html#ixzz4K9jCNsLV (accessed 21 November 2015).
Dyer, R. (1979) *Stars*. London: BFI.
Dyer, R. (2004) *Heavenly Bodies*. London: Routledge.
Egan, D. (2013) 'Lost Objects: Feminism, Sexualisation and Melancholia'. *Feminist Theory*. Volume 14 (3): 265–274.
Evans, A. (2015) 'Diversity in Gender and Visual Representation: A Commentary'. Special Issue: Diversity in Gender and Visual Representation. *Journal of Gender Studies*. Volume 24 (4): 473–479.
Evans, A. and Riley S. (2013) 'Immaculate Consumption: Negotiating the Sex Symbol in Post-feminist Celebrity Culture'. *Journal of Gender Studies*. Volume 22 (3): 268–281.
Evans, A. and Riley, S. (2014) *Technologies of Sexiness: Sex, Identity and Consumer Culture*. Oxford and New York: Oxford University Press.
Ferreday, D. (2015) 'Game of Thrones, Rape Culture and Feminist Fandom'. *Australian Feminist Studies*. Volume 30 (83): 21–36.
Foucault, M. (1998) *The History of Sexuality: Volume 1*. London: Penguin Books.

Gill, R. (2007) *Gender and the Media*. London: Polity Press.
Gill, R. (2012) 'Media, Empowerment and the "Sexualization of Culture" Debates'. *Sex Roles*. Volume 66: 736–745.
Gill, R. and Elias, A.S. (2014) '"Awaken Your Incredible": Love Your Body Discourses and Postfeminist Contradictions'. *International Journal of Media and Cultural Politics*. Volume 10 (2): 179–188.
Hillyer, M. (2004) 'Sex in the Suburban: Porn, Home Movies, and the Live Action Performance of Love in Pam and Tommy Lee: Hardcore and Uncensored'. In L. Williams (ed) *Porn Studies*. Durham and London: Duke University Press.
Hillyer, M. (2010) 'Underexposed Overexposure: One Night in Paris'. *The Velvet Light Trap*. Volume 65: 20–21.
Jackson, S., Vares, T. and Gill, R. (2013) '"The Whole Playboy Mansion Image": Girls' Fashioning and Fashioned Selves within a Postfeminist Culture'. *Feminism and Psychology*. Volume 23 (2): 143–162.
Jensen, T. and Ringrose, J. (2014) 'Sluts that Choose vs Doormat Gypsies: Exploring Affect in the Postfeminist, Visual Moral Economy of *My Big Fat Gypsy Wedding*'. *Feminist Media Studies*. Volume 14 (3): 369–387.
Kinsey, A., Pomeroy, W. and Martin, C. (1948) *Sexual Behavior in the Human Male*. Philadelphia: W.B. Saunders.
Kinsey, A., Pomeroy, W., Martin, C. and Gebhard, P. (1953) *Sexual Behavior in the Human Female*. Philadelphia: W.B. Saunders.
Lamb, S., Graling, K. and Wheeler, E.E. (2013) '"Pole-arized" Discourse: An Analysis of Responses to Miley Cyrus's Teen Choice Awards Pole Dance'. *Feminism and Psychology*. Volume 23 (2): 163–183.
Littler, J. (2004) 'Making Fame Ordinary: Intimacy, Reflexivity and "Keeping It Real"'. *Mediactive*. Volume 2: 8–25.
McCabe, J. (2011) 'And Bringing Up the Rear: Pippa Middleton, Her Derriere and Celebrity as Feminine Ideal'. *Celebrity Studies*. Volume 2 (3): 355–357.
McClintock, A. (1995) *Imperial Leather: Race, Gender and Sexuality in the Colonial Contest*. London: Routledge.
McNair, B. (1996) *Mediated Sex: Pornography and Postmodern Culture*. London: Arnold.
McNair, B. (2002) *Striptease Culture: Sex, Media and the Democratization of Desire*. London: Routledge.
McNair, B. (2013) *Porno? Chic! How Pornography Changed the World and Made It a Better Place*. London: Routledge.
McRobbie, A. (2009) *The Aftermath of Feminism: Culture, Gender and Social Change*. London: Sage.
Marwick, A.E. and boyd, d. (2011) 'I Tweet Honestly, I Tweet Passionately: Twitter Users, Context Collapse, and the Imagined Audience'. *New Media and Society*. Volume 13 (1): 114–133.
Mercer, J. (ed) (2013) 'Special Issue: Sex and Celebrity'. *Celebrity Studies*. Volume 4 (1): 1–112.
Moore, S. (2013) 'Lily Allen Says Her Video for Hard Out Here Isn't to Do with Race. She Is Wrong'. *The Guardian*. 13 November. www.theguardian.com/commentisfree/2013/nov/13/lily-allen-hard-out-here-racism (accessed 21 December 2015).
O'Connor, S. (2013) 'Open Letter to Miley Cyrus'. *The Guardian*. 3 October. www.theguardian.com/music/2013/oct/03/sinead-o-connor-open-letter-miley-cyrus (accessed 15 November 2016).
Railton, D. and Watson, P. (2005) 'Naughty Girls and Red Blooded Women: Representations of Female Heterosexuality in Music Video'. *Feminist Media Studies*. Volume 5 (1): 51–63.
Redmond, S. (2014) *Celebrity and the Media*. Basingstoke: Palgrave Macmillan.
Ringrose, J. (2013) *Postfeminist Education? Girls and the Sexual Politics of Schooling*. London: Routledge.
Rojek, C. (2012) *Fame Attack: The Inflation of Celebrity and Its Consequences*. London: Bloomsbury.
Sanghani, R. (2014) 'Jennifer Lawrence Photo Leak: Let's Stop Calling This Hacking "The Fappening"'. *The Telegraph*. 2 September. www.telegraph.co.uk/women/womens-life/11069829/Jennifer-Lawrence-photo-leak-Lets-stop-calling-this-hacking-The-Fappening.html (accessed 21 November 2015).

Scheibel, W. (2013) 'Marilyn Monroe, "Sex Symbol": Film Performance, Gender Politics and 1950s Hollywood Celebrity'. *Celebrity Studies*, Volume 4 (1): 4–13.
Schwartz, M. (2008) 'The Horror of Something to See: Celebrity "Vaginas" as Prostheses'. *Genders*. Volume 48.
Tremlett, A. (2014) 'Demotic or Demonic? Race, Class and Gender in "Gypsy" Reality TV'. *The Sociological Review*. Volume 62: 316–334.
Turner, G. (2013) *Understanding Celebrity*. London: Sage.
Tyler, I. (2013) *Revolting Subjects: Social Abjection and Resistance in Neoliberal Britain*. London: Zed Books.
Tyler, I. and Bennett, B. (2010) 'Celebrity Chav: Fame, Femininity and Social Class'. *Cultural Studies*. Volume 13 (3): 375–393.

Media

1 Night in Paris (2004) [Film] USA: Red Light District.
Benefits Street (2014–) [Television Series] UK: Channel 4.
My Big Fat Gypsy Wedding (2010–) [Television Series] UK: Channel 4.
Pam and Tommy Lee: Hardcore and Uncensored (1997) [Film] USA: IEG.
Tongue Tied (2014) Directed by Q. Jones [Short] USA: Nowness.

24
SEX AND MUSIC VIDEO

Diane Railton

The terms 'sex' and 'music video' have become almost synonymous, in that it is difficult to talk about music videos without the subject of sex featuring in the conversation. This has long been the case both within academia and without. Whether we are considering the varied reactions to Madonna's controversial videos of the 1980s and 90s or Sheri Kathleen Cole's claim that 'the commodification of sexuality is central to the creation of most music videos' (1999), Imani Perry's analysis of the sexual exploitation of women in 1990s hip-hop videos (2003) or Meredith Levande's (2008) discussion relating the increased sexualisation of women in music video to changes in ownership of the companies distributing them, the subject of sex has been central to debates about what music video can and should do. Recent popular discussions about music video, both online and in the press, have tended to focus on the sexual nature of videos made by women artists and the potential impact of this on young girls. So, for example, while *The Guardian* reports that 'the former Spice Girl Melanie Chisholm has banned her daughter from watching Rihanna videos to protect her from the overtly sexual content' (14 October 2014), posts on the Netmums forum express concern about the public display of music videos by singers such as Rihanna and Nicki Minaj and argue for stricter control of music television (Netmums, no date). Indeed, the British Board of Film Classification (BBFC) reports that 'Music videos were identified [by parents] as a key source of sexual imagery believed to be potentially harmful to young girls' emotional wellbeing and social development' (Cooke, 2014: 116). Similarly, the American Psychological Association Task Force on the Sexualization of Girls argues that through exposure to sexualised media content (and they see music video as a key element of this), 'girls may be learning to prioritize certain rewards (male attention) over other rewards (academic accomplishment), thus limiting their future educational and occupational opportunities' (APA, 2010: 32). Academics from the University of South Australia have suggested that sexualised music videos shown on free-to-air TV at times when children are watching could have an impact on their socio-sexual development and cite instances of girls as young as five imitating music video performers in terms of both dress and behaviour (Ey and Cupit, 2013).

Such discussions link music video both with societal concerns about the potential adverse effects of early sexualisation on girls and with girls' own concerns with their bodily appearance. In this chapter, therefore, I will trace some of the ways in which music video has served as a means both of representing the female body as a sexual body and of defining what constitutes a sexually attractive female body.

Sex and popular music

Whether we take the development of MTV in the early 1980s as the starting point for a discussion of music video or prefer, as I do here, to begin the story with the Scopitone films and early promotional clips of the 1960s that prefigured it, we have to acknowledge that sex has been an integral part of the form since the very beginning. Indeed, links were made between sex and popular music long before the birth of music video. Parents suggested to the BBFC researchers mentioned above that 'adults have always been "shocked" by teenage music and queried whether music videos were fundamentally any different' (Cooke, 2014: 116).

Even before the birth of rock 'n' roll in the 1950s, there was concern that popular music might be instrumental in the sexualisation and exploitation of girls and young women. In 1945, for example, *The Guardian* published an article about 'an amiable young singer of popular songs' – Frank Sinatra – commenting that 'psychologists have written soberly about the hypnotic quality of his voice and the remarkable effect upon susceptible young women'. Richard T. Stanley, discussing the music of Elvis Presley in the 1950s, describes 'teenage girls everywhere' who 'swooned at the sound of his voice' (Stanley, 2012: 37), and for one West German commentator, 'the behavior of female rock 'n' roll fans illustrated the dangerous "sexualization of the 15-year-olds"' (Heigert, 1959, cited in Poiger, 1996: 577). Discussing fans of the Beatles in the early 1960s, Barbara Ehrenreich argues that 'for the girls who participated in Beatlemania, sex was an obvious part of the excitement' (1992: 90), and Paul Johnson, writing in *The New Statesman* in 1964, expressed concern about the 'young girls, hardly any more than 16' who were leaving a recording of a TV music programme wearing 'chain-store makeup' and 'broken stiletto heels', 'dressed as adults and already lined up as fodder for exploitation' (1964: 39).

The concern expressed here is that girls were being sexually aroused by the sight and sound of their male idols. As Ehrenreich argues, the 1950s and 60s were a time when 'teen and preteen girls were expected to be not only "good" and "pure" but to be the enforcers of purity within their teen society' (1992: 85). Contemporary concerns about popular music, by contrast, are very much about female idols' impacts on young girls. While discussions about sex in music still almost invariably relate to heterosex, they now most often focus on the display of the scantily clad female body and its influence on innocent and vulnerable girls. Today's concern is not so much that young girls become sexually aroused but rather that they may, albeit unwittingly, provoke that response in boys and men. Despite changes over time, therefore, the end result seems to be that girls and young women continue to be held responsible for the sexual behaviour of society, whether they are performers who are vilified for being 'bad role models' or young fans being 'protected' from sexually explicit images.

Women in popular music

In many ways, this shift in concern can be linked to the development of music video and the changing roles which this focus on the visual has mandated for women in the music industry. When girls and young women were screaming at a glimpse of Frank Sinatra or The Beatles the screaming was prompted, at least in part, by the fact that the opportunity to see such an idol in any form other than that of a picture pinned to a bedroom wall was rare indeed. Television programmes featured such bands but the technology did not exist in the home to save and replay that performance time and time again. The development of the home video recorder/player, and the growth in the number of homes with more than one television set, meant that the visual aspect of music and fandom became increasingly normalised, to the extent that it is now almost impossible to imagine a successful song that is not available in at least one video format. Not only did it become possible to record music being performed on television shows, but this technological advance enabled the development of performances designed to be watched as videos – something I have referred to elsewhere as 'staged-performance videos' (Railton and Watson, 2011: 58). These are videos that put on a display of the music that is often only possible in this format, utilising close-up camerawork, frequent costume changes, multiple settings, special effects and CGI. Importantly for what I want to discuss here, they often also feature complexly choreographed dance routines.

Simon Frith and Angela McRobbbie, writing in 1978, argued that 'female creative roles are limited and mediated through male notions of female ability' (1978: 373). Historically, the main role of women in popular music has been that of singer. Although there have always been women who have played instruments, they have often been seen as something of an oddity. As Julie Burchill put it, 'A girl in a dress with a guitar looks weird. Like a dog riding a bicycle. Very odd' (cited in Raphael 1995: xi). Lisa Lewis (1990) has argued, however, that with the advent of music video this limitation on women's roles could be turned to their advantage. The vocalist is often the star of the video and the main focus of the camera; they are often quite literally centre stage. The visualisation of music has, therefore, allowed women more space to perform without necessarily transgressing their familiar roles. They can get the public's attention, make a name for themselves and develop their image in a way that simply wasn't available in the past. The female singer can use the music video form to help construct an image of a strong woman; a woman with agency actively involved in the construction of her own image and performance.

However, the most common role for female music video performers is, and always has been, that of dancer. Indeed, Madonna's use of male dancers in the 1980s was seen as a radical and even feminist move. Women routinely act as backing dancers to both male and female artists. Male dancers do exist but they are a much less common sight. Women dancers perform choreographed routines often designed as sexual display, which eroticise their bodies and make them available to the viewer's gaze. Indeed, there is a history in popular music of men making the music while women performers function simply to be looked at and to titillate. However, female singers are now increasingly called on to dance as energetically and erotically as their backing dancers. As such, dancing women have come to symbolise not only the sexual attractiveness and sexual availability that has long been linked to the backing dancer but also the sexual agency and empowerment that video has made available to the singer.

Top of the Pops and choreographed dance performance

An important moment in the history of the visual in popular music, and of women's role in it, was the introduction of *Top of the Pops* to the BBC TV schedules in 1964. *Top of the Pops* was a weekly chart music programme broadcast between 1964 and 2006 and shown in the early evening as part of the family viewing slot. The mainstay of the programme was the 'live' performance of chart hits, but the programme also included short promotional films that we can understand as a form of proto-video and, interestingly, featured regular choreographed dance routines which can be seen as precursors of the type of performance common to many contemporary videos. There were a number of different dance troupes during the programme's existence and they were generally women-only. Their role was to provide a visual accompaniment to the music when the band did not appear in the studio.

Pan's People's 1970 dance accompanying the Creedence Clearwater Revival song 'Green River' provides a useful example of the type of performance considered appropriate in this context. The six women in the dance troupe are identically dressed in fringed white bikinis and silver knee-high boots. They perform on an empty stage with a mirrored background. Their dancing is vigorous and energetic: breasts and buttocks shake, and the shaking is emphasised by the movement of the fringes attached to the dancers' costumes. They all crouch and bend in a way that displays their crotches and buttocks to the audience. The performance is in no way motivated by the song lyrics or the band's 'southern rock' style. It is simply a group of young women enthusiastically displaying their bodies as they dance to the music. In other words, even before the onset of music video, the figure of the highly sexualised female dancer as the on-screen accompaniment to music was being established. And, indeed, with the regular dance performances on *Top of the Pops* the visual became the focus, an item in its own right, rather than simply a substitute for the appearance of the band.

Scopitone films and the sexualised female body

Scopitone jukeboxes (which played short 16mm films of the performance of popular songs and were popular in the 1960s primarily in France, where they originated, and in the USA) can also be seen as precursors to music video, or early examples of the 'staged-performance video', and they too feature a version of the highly eroticised female dance performance that is so familiar in today's videos. Indeed, Amy Herzog notes 'their shameless, clumsy reliance on sexploitative visual material, regardless of the subject matter or tempo of the song' (2007: 46). It is interesting to explore the Scopitone promotional clips of the 1960s to see how certain key signifiers of heterosexual attractiveness that were established in the proto-video era have been maintained and adapted over time.

Perhaps most common is the way in which women's bodies are put on display not only to the camera but also to the (usually) male singer of the song. For example, the Scopitone clip for Bobby Vee's 1963 song 'Pretty Girls Everywhere!' is based around the figure of Vee, wearing dark trousers and a rollneck sweater under a tailored jacket, strolling around the set and gazing appreciatively at women as he sings about the happy coincidence of seeing 'pretty girls everywhere' he goes. The women walk around the set wearing bathing suits and stiletto-heeled shoes, pose provocatively on a plush circular bed or stand, bikini-clad, in front of a waterfall. They dance in dresses that are transparent and reveal the body or that swing out to reveal a tantalising glimpse of their underwear. Vee's 1961 song 'Baby Face' similarly features young women's bodies on display, with the women on a beach, dressed in bikinis, accompanied by the singer dressed in knee-length shorts and a jacket zipped to the neck, his body hidden from view.

Another feature of these early proto-videos is the emphasis on particular parts of the female body – the buttocks, the breasts, the upper thigh – as sites of sexual attractiveness. In Bobby Vee's Scopitone for 'Baby Face', the first thing we see on the screen is a close-up of a woman's bottom, covered by green bikini pants and shaking vigorously. Moreover, embellishment of the buttocks to make them appear to be larger and to shake more vigorously is common in the Scopitone clips. In Gale Garnett's 'Small Potatoes', one of the dancers has a large feathery tail attached to her flesh-coloured body suit. In Nino Ferrer's 'Le Telefon', very short full skirts add breadth and movement to the dancer's bottoms as they undulate in front of the camera, and fringes and frills are common additions to bikini pants in any number of clips. And it is not just buttocks that get this treatment. Jane Morgan's 'C'est Si Bon' starts with the camera positioned to give a view up the skirts of the rather demurely dressed dancers, revealing stocking tops and the naked flesh above, and in Marilyn Maye's 'Cabaret' we are presented with a number of surprisingly close close-ups of the dancers' inner thighs as they kick their legs.

Plus ça change, plus c'est la même chose

There are clearly, then, a number of things that have remained the same since even before music videos, as such, were a commonplace aspect of the music industry. The primary role for women in music was, and still seems to be, to be looked at. Almost naked women, dressed to emphasise the shape of their bodies, are juxtaposed with men who are fully clothed, and clothed in such a way that the shape of the body is disguised. While Bobby Vee's 'Pretty Girls Everywhere!' or 'Baby Face' Scopitone films appear to be very different to, for example, Akon's 2008 video for the song 'I Wanna Love You', the underlying ethos is the same. The latter video features Akon and Snoop Dogg, who are fully (even over-)dressed in heavy coats worn over shirts, jumpers and baggy trousers as they rap, sing and dance in the studio. The anonymous women in the video, by contrast, dance provocatively, wearing underwear and cropped tops that reveal their breasts and buttocks and enable them to display their bodies erotically. Indeed, Snoop Dogg's line 'You can't see me but I can see you' seems particularly apt: the women dancers' bodies are very much on show; the singers' bodies are completely hidden.

There are, however, important differences between the Scopitone clips and this video. In the first instance, developments in technology have enabled more sophisticated ways of filming and editing today's videos and, thus, more complex ways of putting women's bodies on display. Split screens and fast editing allow us to see buttocks, breasts and legs from multiple angles and with close-up detail. Moreover, what was considered revealing 50 years ago is a lot more demure than what is considered revealing today. The bathing suits and bikinis in 'Pretty Girls Everywhere!' or 'Baby Face' may draw attention to the breasts and buttocks, but they are cut in such a way that these parts of the body are covered. The parts of the body that are on display – the midriff, the legs, the upper arms – are soft and fleshy. By contrast, in 'I Wanna Love You', firm breasts bulge out of skimpy bra tops, midriffs are taut and flat and briefs are small and tight. It is also noteworthy that the women in the Bobby Vee clips perform individually rather than as a team. Their clothing is not co-ordinated in any way and some never appear on the main set of the video. Indeed, many of the shots of women posing and dancing seem to have been shot for a different purpose and added to the video in post-production. Even when dancing together the choreography is very limited, and their movements are not synchronised but performed with differing levels of enthusiasm and energy. The women in 'I Wanna Love You', however, wear colour co-ordinated outfits and perform choreographed dance routines with precision. Even individual routines are often mirrored to give the impression of close co-ordination. The overall effect is to give the impression that the older clips are rather 'tame' and very amateur when compared to the sleek professionalism of the more recent one, yet in both we have women dancers who must present their bodies and display them not only for the audience but also for the very obvious appreciation of the male performers.

Music videos are now big-budget essentials in the promotion of any song or album. Indeed, it is fair to say that they are no longer always a promotional tool but can be important saleable artefacts in their own right. And as their importance has increased, so too have production values; the videos have become more professional and demand more of those taking part. The women's bodies in the Scopitones weren't toned or muscular, as we would expect from a dancer in music videos today. The performance of sexual attractiveness appears to be very mundane, requiring willingness but not technique. Today's videos, by contrast, present sexual attractiveness as requiring professional skill and effort rather than mere enthusiasm. The image portrayed of what the sexually attractive body looks like and what it can do could hardly be more different to the depiction of the women in the early Scopitones. Gone is the everyday, 'girl next door' body shaken in front of the camera with lots of enthusiasm but little skill. Instead we have a body that is sleek and polished, with well-rehearsed and carefully choreographed movements. On the one hand, this body is stronger and healthier than its predecessor. It is flexible and athletic, with thighs that are muscular and strong, toned by dancing and exercise. On the other hand, it is much less natural in appearance: not only honed and sculpted in the gym, but often augmented surgically to enhance the size of the breasts and buttocks. The sexually attractive female as represented in music video has changed, therefore, from a keen amateur to a consummate professional, from a 'Baby Face' to a 'Money Maker'.

And yet many of the ways of presenting the female body to the viewer persist. Women's bodies, or more precisely discrete parts of women's bodies, are still primarily to be looked at and lusted after. Beyoncé's 2013 video 'Yoncé', for example, begins with a view of a woman's buttocks showing under her skirt as she walks down the street, similar in content to the opening of 'Baby Face', and the objectification of the body continues as we see flashes of lips, hands, breasts and buttocks without ever being able to identify with any certainty which of the women in the video they belong to. The willing display of the body and the ability to make that body move in a way that draws attention to the breasts, buttocks and inner thighs are still central to very, very many music videos, from Ludacris's 'Money Maker' or NERD's 'Lapdance' to Little Mix's 'Salute'.

Another thing that remains constant is that the role of sexy and available woman is given to the dancers. In the early Scopitone films and, indeed, in the early *Top of the Pops* programmes, women singers often enjoyed the masculine privilege of performing while fully clothed. In the Scopitone clip for Jody Miller's 'The Race Is On', for example, Miller wears a knee-length, high-necked dress, holding binoculars and standing in front of a painted backdrop of a crowd at the races. The 'horses' being watched, however, are four female backing dancers, wearing skimpy bikinis with long, feathery 'horses' tails' attached to them. There are close-ups of their breasts bouncing as they dance; they shake their 'tails' and buttocks at the camera. Yet, in contrast to the Bobby Vee clips discussed earlier, Miller's watching of them is never sexualised. She is rarely in the same shot as the 'horses' and the obvious artificiality of the setting and its disjunction from the lyrics work to distance her performance from theirs.

Clothing often seems to remain a masculine privilege, with any number of videos that could be used as examples to demonstrate the juxtaposition of heavily clothed men to scantily clad women. In Robin Thicke's 'Blurred Lines' (2013), for example, women wearing only skimpy flesh-coloured thongs and shoes parade in front of men dressed in suits. Even without hearing the lyrics it is clear where power lies within the imagery of the video, whose body is to be looked at and who is enabled to look. In Sasha Dith's 'Russian Girls' (2005) a similar situation arises. Women 'soldiers' remove their camouflage uniforms to reveal camouflage briefs and then dance together while getting sprayed with water as they perform in front of their 'prisoner' who is dressed in trousers, shirt and greatcoat. His body is protected, hidden from view. The women soldiers are there only for his pleasure, for him to look at and become aroused by.

But changes *do* happen

There are, however, major differences in the representation of the sexy female dancing body in music video that can be pointed to over the 50 years since the Scopitones. Perhaps most significant is the fact that all of the dancers I have discussed from that time, whether appearing on *Top of the Pops* or in the Scopitone films, were white – in the Scopitones, black female singers appear to have been significantly outnumbered by white people. Given the contemporary status and influence of black women who sing and dance – Beyoncé and Nicki Minaj, for example – it comes as a shock to realise just how recent this phenomenon is.

Writing in 1992, bell hooks argued that contemporary representations of black women are strongly linked to representations from the past: the iconography of slavery and colonisation. Black women's bodies have long been put on display for the gratification of white men and their 'butts' have been used to signify an 'animalistic sexuality'. She cites Tina Turner as an artist who has appropriated 'the wild woman pornographic myth of black female sexuality created by men in a white supremacist patriarchy' (1992: 69) for economic gain and argues that: 'Representations of Black female bodies in contemporary popular culture rarely subvert or critique images of black female sexuality which were part of the apparatus of 19th Century racism and which still shape perceptions today' (ibid.: 62).

For many videos this argument undoubtedly still holds true, but what is significant about artists such as Beyoncé and Minaj is the way that they have used music videos to subvert and critique the images that hooks refers to. The visual imagery can work to either reinforce or overturn the message of the song and, by using this facility to the full, they can produce a critique that is effective. The lyrics of Nicki Minaj's 'Anaconda', for example, are a paean to commercial sex, detailing ways that the protagonist has traded sexual favours for luxury goods. The video, however, with its artificial jungle setting, its playful use of bananas and pineapples, Minaj's winks and grins to camera and its constant repetition of the sampled lyric 'Oh my gosh, look at her butt' – a phrase reiterated on the clothing of the dancers – not only mocks the fascination with black women's buttocks that hooks discusses but also, in its knowing artificiality, subverts racist views that have historically linked whiteness with civilisation and blackness with the primitive and the natural. The song alone undeniably does nothing to challenge 'old stereotypes which make the assertion of black female sexuality and prostitution synonymous' (hooks 1992: 69), but the video adds layers of humour that take the emphasis away from the lyrics and undermine them.

Beyoncé's eponymous 2013 album, which features more videos than audio tracks, enables her to develop a complex portrait of black womanhood that works to challenge any notion that black women can be reduced to their sexuality. By using the 17 videos to display different ways of being a black woman, she presents a self-portrait of a rounded and politically aware woman. From the critique of beauty ideals graphically expressed in 'Pretty Hurts', with its visual references to bulimia and anorexia; to the celebration of wantonness, albeit in a marital context, that is 'Drunk in Love'; to the acclamation of motherhood that is 'Blue' and the street-smart sexiness that is 'Yoncé', Beyoncé creates a complex, layered image of contemporary black femininity, and because this image is created through videos, it can be much more nuanced than is the case with simple audio tracks. Lyrics that are crude, simplistic or opaque become transformed into narratives of both confidence and vulnerability. Sex and the sexualised portrayal of the female body are certainly not absent from these videos, but this is only one component of an intricately woven fabric of personal history, family relationships, emotions, politics and artistic expression.

Music video and representations of heterosexual attractiveness have a long and often controversial history. The definition of sexual attractiveness presented in music video performance has changed significantly over time. It is interesting now to see the way in which artists such as Beyoncé and Nicki Minaj are bringing humour and politics into that definition.

Bibliography

American Psychological Association, Task Force on the Sexualization of Girls (2010). *Report of the APA Task Force on the Sexualization of Girls*. www.apa.org/pi/women/programs/girls/report-full.pdf (accessed 25 September 2015).

Beebe, R. and Middleton, J. (eds) (2007). *Medium Cool: Music Videos from Soundies to Cell Phones*. Durham, NC: Duke University Press.

Cole, S.K. (1999) '"I Am the Eye, You Are My Victim": The Pornographic Ideology of Music Video'. *Enculturation*. Volume 2 (2). http://enculturation.net/2_2/cole/ (accessed 25 September 2015).

Cooke, D. (2014) *BBFC Guidelines: Research Report*. www.bbfc.co.uk/sites/default/files/attachments/2014%20Guidelines%20Research.pdf (accessed 26 January 2015).

Ehrenreich, B., Hess, E. and Jacobs, G. (1992) 'Beatlemania: Girls Just Want to Have Fun'. In L. Lewis (ed.) *The Adoring Audience: Fan Culture and Popular Media*. London: Routledge.

Ey, L.-A. and Cupit, C.G. (2013) 'Primary School Children's Imitation of Sexualised Music Videos and Artists'. *Children Australia*. Volume 38 (3): 115–123.

Ey, L.-A. and McInnes, E. (2015) 'Sexualised Music Videos Broadcast on Australian Free-to-Air Television in Child-Friendly Time Periods'. *Children Australia*. Volume 40 (1): 58–68.

Frith, S. and McRobbie, A. (1978) 'Rock and Sexuality'. In S. Frith and A. Goodwin (eds) *On Record: Rock, Pop and the Written Word*. London: Routledge.

Frith, S. and Goodwin, A. (1990) *On Record: Rock, Pop and the Written Word*. London: Routledge.

The Guardian (1945) 'Frank Sinatra and the Bobby-Soxers'. www.theguardian.com/century/1940-1949/Story/0,,127764,00.html (accessed 26 January 2015).

The Guardian (2014) 'Mel C: Rihanna Is Too Raunchy for My Daughter'. www.theguardian.com/music/2014/oct/13/mel-c-rihanna-daughter (accessed 26 January 2015).

Heigert, H. (1959) 'Ein neuer Typ wird produziert: Der Teenager'. *Deutsche Jugend*. Volume 3: 117–121.

Johnson, P. (1964) 'The Menace of Beatlism'. In E. Thomson and D. Gutman (eds) *The Lennon Companion: Twenty-Five Years of Comment*. Boston, MA: Da Capo Press.

Herzog, A. (2007) 'Illustrating Music: The Impossible Embodiments of the Jukebox Film'. In R. Beebe and J. Middleton (eds) *Medium Cool: Music Videos from Soundies to Cell Phones*. Durham, NC: Duke University Press.

hooks, b. (1992) *Black Looks: Race and Representation*. Boston, MA: South End Press.

Levande, M. (2008) 'Women, Pop Music, and Pornography'. *Meridians*. Volume 8: 293–321.

Lewis, L. (ed) (1992) *The Adoring Audience: Fan Culture and Popular Media*. London: Routledge.

Lewis, L.A. (1990) 'Female Address on Music Television: Being Discovered'. *Jump Cut: A Review of Contemporary Media*. Volume 35: 2–15.

Netmums (no date) Chat, Thread: 'Why Can't We Stop? – Parents Launch Backlash Against "Porn Not Pop" Videos' www.netmums.com/coffeehouse/general-coffeehouse-chat-514/news-current-affairs-topical-discussion-12/1017213-why-can-t-we-stop-parents-launch-backlash-against-porn-not-pop-videos-all.html (accessed 25 January 2015).

Perry, I. (2003) '"Who(se) Am I?": The Identity and Image of Women in Hip-Hop'. In G. Dines and J.M. Humez (eds) *Gender, Race, and Class in The Media*, 2nd edition. London: Sage.

Poiger, U.B. (1996) 'Rock 'n' Roll, Female Sexuality, and the Cold War Battle over German Identities'. *The Journal of Modern History*. Volume 68: 577–616.

Railton, D. and Watson, P. (2011) *Music Video and the Politics of Representation*. Edinburgh: Edinburgh University Press.

Raphael, A. (1995) *Never Mind the Bollocks: Women Rewrite Rock*. London: Virago Press.

Stanley, R.T. (2012) *The Eisenhower Years: A Social History of The 1950's*. Bloomington, IN: iUniverse.

Thomson, E. and Gutman D. (eds) (1987) *The Lennon Companion: Twenty-Five Years of Comment*. Boston, MA: Da Capo Press.

Videography

Akon ft. Snoop Dogg, 'I Wanna Love You' available online www.youtube.com/watch?v=GJzF7H2e3Tw (accessed 25 January 2016)

Beyoncé, 'Blue' available online www.youtube.com/watch?v=gSsMhQv6KZ8 (accessed 25 January 2016)

Beyoncé, 'Drunk in Love' available online www.youtube.com/watch?v=p1JPKLa-Ofc (accessed 25 January 2016)

Beyoncé, 'Pretty Hurts' available online www.youtube.com/watch?v=LXXQLa-5n5w (accessed 25 January 2016)

Beyoncé, 'Yoncé' available online www.youtube.com/watch?v=jcF5HtGvX5I (accessed 25 January 2016)

Sasha Dith, 'Russian Girls' available online www.youtube.com/watch?v=0TQPPGl-W8c (accessed 25 January 2016)

Nino Ferrer, 'Le Telefon' available online www.youtube.com/watch?v=unjvxHtcpKQ (accessed 25 January 2016)

Gale Garnett, 'Small Potatoes' available online www.youtube.com/watch?v=-wSW_bwJXvo (accessed 25 January 2016)

Little Mix, 'Salute' available online www.youtube.com/watch?v=Kjpa0SMOug0 (accessed 25 January 2016)

Ludacris, 'Money Maker' available online www.youtube.com/watch?v=T9Op2YQ7yyU (accessed 25 January 2016)

Marilyn Maye, 'Cabaret' available online www.youtube.com/watch?v=tBS5CvcxoLc (accessed 25 January 2016)

Jody Miller, 'The Race Is On' available online www.youtube.com/watch?v=XW2SV8eyH_4 (accessed 25 January 2016)

Nicki Minaj, 'Anaconda' available online www.youtube.com/watch?v=LDZX4ooRsWs (accessed 25 January 2016)

Jane Morgan, 'C'est Si Bon' available online www.youtube.com/watch?v=y8Oshs1fWrY (accessed 25 January 2016)

Jane Morgan, 'Under Paris Skies' available online www.youtube.com/watch?v=rCl9Z8yUw0A (accessed 25 January 2016)

Pan's People performing 'Green River', available online www.youtube.com/watch?v=Kob-H7a6AWY (accessed 25 January 2016)

Robin Thicke, 'Blurred Lines' available online www.vevo.com/watch/robin-thicke/blurred-lines-(unrated-version)/USUV71300526 (accessed 25 January 2016)

Bobby Vee, 'Baby Face' available online www.youtube.com/watch?v=qmHfxUxHIWw (accessed 25 January 2016)

Bobby Vee, 'Pretty Girls Everywhere!' available online www.youtube.com/watch?v=co2ieQuLIHQ (accessed 29 March 2017)

25
DEBATING REPRESENTATIONS OF SEXUALITY IN ADVERTISING

Despina Chronaki

Introduction

Williams called advertising a 'magic system' (2000) with inordinate powers to persuade by tapping into our unconscious desires, promising us 'the good life' and all the things that go with it. As a genre, advertising is frequently discussed in negative terms both in public and academic discourses, and, given its commercial nature and objectives, it has rarely been considered as having any intrinsic value to audiences or having artistic or aesthetic value in its own right beyond giving meaning to the consumer items it sells (Gibbons, 2011). Many cultural studies and feminist scholars consider advertising media as 'locations for exploring "sexualisation" while also enabling broader expressions of sexuality' (Gill, 2009: 140). In this chapter I draw upon a conceptualisation of sex as a discursive technology and as a socially constructed idea, in the sense that meanings of sex and sexuality are produced within specific social, cultural, political and historical contexts (Burr, 1995), in order to explore the ways in which sex and sexuality are represented in advertising as reflections of sex within contemporary society (Foucault, 1986; Chronaki, 2014).

In what follows, I contextualise my discussion within the binary of private and public (Williams, 2004), before discussing two important and much debated aspects of the topic: representations of sexuality in advertisements and how recent debates position children within what has been decried as hyper-sexualised culture. Drawing on second-wave feminist perspectives on sexuality and gender (e.g. Wolf, 1990) and mainstream psychological perspectives about media effects (e.g. Jones, Stanaland and Gelb, 1998), some have argued that modern media portray sexuality in ways which undermine love, or which objectify women and men. Other feminist scholars have considered the matter through a conceptualisation of a new sexually and socially agentic female figure, forcing 'a reconsideration of earlier modes of representation' (Gill, 2008: 149). In line with broader concerns about children's sexual development and children's engagement with popular culture, concerns have been focused on the possible effects of an increasingly sexualised culture (including representations in advertising) on children's understandings, behaviour and attitudes towards sex and relationships (e.g. Levin and Kilbourne, 2008). Other research has emphasised children's agency in engaging with all forms of representation, even those which are sexual in nature (e.g. Gill and Scharff, 2011; Egan, 2013), arguing that the cultural construction of children as ideally without sexuality until they reach young adulthood generates the particular ways in which we understand the status of childhood in general, not least in relation to sexuality (e.g. Buckingham et al., 2010).

Illustrations of sex in advertising are by no means a recent marketing strategy. Kakoudaki (2004) notes that the visual genre of the pinup

> has its roots in *cartes postales* (postcards) of exotic places, art nudes, portraits of actresses of the burlesque theater, erotic photographs, "Little Egypt" and the hoochie-coochie dances of the Chicago Fair in 1893, cigarette cards, early movie posters, and the cancan.
>
> (2004: 344)

Soley and Kurzbard argued in 1986 that there had been an increase in sexually oriented advertisements in general interest magazines, that sexual illustrations had become more overt and that visual sexual elements outnumbered verbal ones (1986: 53). They also suggested that while there had been no significant increase between 1964 and 1984 in the percentage of advertisements featuring sexual content, representations of female models in suggestively clad or nude positions outnumbered males. This example indicates a long-standing interest in *how much* and *what kind of* sexual information is provided in advertisements, as well as an interest in identifying sexuality as something that could be potentially problematic for audiences.

Gill (2009: 140) has argued that there are three main stances towards the 'sexualisation of culture' and reflects upon them in her analysis of sexuality in advertising. They are: the 'public morals' position, in which sexualised media representations are considered as an indication of moral decline, while any judgements are related to appropriateness and decency (e.g. Hitchens, 2002); the 'democratising sex' position, which considers the increasing discursivity of sex in popular culture as a reason to celebrate a more open and less censorious approach to sexuality (e.g. McNair, 2002); and feminist approaches, which critique women's agentic and empowering role in representations in popular culture, and in advertising more specifically (e.g. McRobbie, 2004).

What is at stake when private becomes public?

Rossi (2007: 127) notes that 'advertising imagery plays a definite role in the sexualization of urban space' and that it is connected with soft-porn representations because of its visual patterning and fragmenting of the body 'by cropping and foregrounding the culturally eroticized parts of it'. As McNair (1996) notes, sex has been a frequently used 'weapon' in advertisers' 'armoury', and pornographic iconography has long been embedded in commercial products within popular culture. In fact, advertisements, especially since the late 1990s, have attracted media, public and research attention because of their increasingly explicit, transgressive and voyeuristic design (McNair, 1996). Advertising is understood to give meanings to goods and those meanings have values, which tap into hierarchies of taste and expressions of culture. A recurring discourse underlying analyses of representations in advertising draws attention to the very fact that through it sexuality is brought to public view, and in inappropriate forms. In this respect, it is important to consider how we think and talk about sex in general. Since the 1990s, sexuality and popular culture have been examined in the light of social constructionist, post-structuralist, post-feminist and psychoanalytic approaches. There have been theoretical discussions about sexuality (e.g. Attwood, 2006) and studies of sexual content as texts (e.g. Smith, 2007), the sex industry (e.g. McKee *et al.*, 2008) and that industry's audiences (see Chronaki, 2014 for a review). Even as popular culture has embraced sex (after all, 'sex sells'), and even if McNair is correct and we now live in a 'striptease culture', we should not assume that everyone has been happy about this. We do need to consider the extent to which the seeming proliferation of 'sexualised' advertising has contributed to broader public concerns about increasingly permissive attitudes to sex, moral decline and propriety. Certainly in the UK, advertising has come under particular fire for its permissiveness and, according to former Prime Minister David Cameron, its dumping of

> waste that is toxic on our children. Products and marketing that can warp their minds and their bodies and harm their future. That can take away their innocence, which I know most parents would agree is so precious and worth defending.
> (Cameron, 2010)

Cameron's complaints and his call for more propriety in advertising were underpinned by heteronormativity and threatened increased regulation and even censorship. His claim that

> More and more today, sexual-provocative images are invading public space – space shared by children. In the Tube station, at the bus stop, on the billboard – there's the creeping sense that we're sleepwalking to a place where 'porn is the norm'

offers an illustration of what some commentators have understood as the perils of 'pornification'. Across various media and policy platforms, the late 2000s and the subsequent decade have been characterised by what Linda Williams termed 'onscenity' – the paradoxical way in which formerly 'private' and/or 'obscene' discussions and representations of sex are brought into the public view, marking 'both the controversy and scandal of the increasingly public representations of diverse forms of sexuality *and* the fact that they have become increasing available to the public at large' (2004: 3). While many discussions about sexuality in advertising trace links between its iconographies and an increasingly 'pornified culture', also at stake are the ways in which femininity, masculinity, heterosexuality and homosexuality are appropriated in advertising. Heteronormativity remains a significant feature of advertising, its imagery often sexist and regressive, yet calls for regulation or even censorship are most often spurred by the very visibility of adverts featuring sexual themes – the loudest voices are raised to question the appropriateness of taking sex and sexuality out of the private space and into the public arena.

Representation of sexuality in advertising I: *Crazy Domains* advertisement

Cortese (2008: 29) argues that 'successful advertising is able to manifest rich, intimate, and astute cultural and sub-cultural messages and representations as well as universal biological desires'. He elaborates on how advertising reproduces a Darwinian approach to sexual selection and observes that men are presented in terms of their resources and power, while women are presented through their possession of beauty, youth and fertility (2008: 30). Earlier analytical work has focused on the visual illustration of such elements as beauty, sexiness, power or youth performed through particular expressions, postures or gestures

(Goffman, 1979). Contemporary discourses about dominant sexualities concern the ways in which gender relations, homosexuality and heterosexuality are constructed.

Simpson (1994) notes that the desire to be desired is now more often associated with men than women. Gill (2009: 144) also comments on the increasingly eroticised representation of male bodies since the 1990s, especially 'in fashion and fragrance advertising and the emerging market for male grooming products'. The male figure is now 'metrosexual' – slim, muscular, young and clean-shaven – and has facial characteristics that appeal both to men and women (Edwards, 1997). Social and political movements led to the rise of the 'new man' along 'more gentle, emotional and communicative lines' (Gill, 2009: 144).

The new man is subject to the gaze of the active and sexually agentic female (Moore, 1988), another new figure in advertising. She is young, white, heterosexual, attractive and sexually active (Gill, 2009); a 'fun fearless female' (Machin and Thornborrow, 2003) embodying confidence, power and sexiness (Arthurs, 2004). Gill (2009) calls this status *sexual subjectification*, as opposed to *objectification*. Women's portrayal in advertising has moved from a passive to an active presentation of femininity, and this has also opened up the possibility of representations of 'girl-to-girl' relationships, usually connoting an erotic, intimate or sexual relationship between women. These images could be read as connected to and reflective of pornographic illustrations of lesbian sex or fantasies, but they also may connote female friendship (e.g. Rossi, 2007). Such categories of representations can be understood at the same time in terms of dominant heteronormativity and/or homonormativity.

I discuss two advertisements within this conceptual framework so as to illustrate how representations of sexuality appear in advertising and what kinds of discourses might be underlying these representations. The first is the *Crazy Domains* advertisement featuring Pamela Anderson, as a CEO, starring in a fantasy with her secretary. The second is an advertisement for Kraft's salad sauce, *Zesty*, showing a masculine, semi-naked, well-built man adding Zesty dressing sauce to his salad.

The Crazy Domains advertisement seems to fit within what Gill (2009) calls the 'hot lesbians' figure in advertising, namely representations of women that appear in 'sexualised' girl-to-girl relations. The ad is set in a meeting room where a creative team is working on a new domain name under Pamela Anderson's management. Pamela Anderson is, of course, a celebrity and sex symbol associated with exhibitionism and public sex (see Longstaff, this volume); she can be described as stereotypically attractive, being slim, toned, blonde (although we should also note that that stereotype is a very specifically West Coast American one). She is also well known for having had breast implants and other forms of plastic surgery in order to conform to that particular beauty ideal. As Figure 25.1 shows, Anderson is dressed in a sexy version of the black suit and white shirt considered *de rigueur* in certain workplaces. Anderson stands at the head of the table; she leads the discussion and is positioned as 'the boss'. Her secretary, an equally attractive brunette dressed in a similar style to Anderson, appears in the meeting room to serve coffee. The creative team seated around the table consists of men – all attractive, clean-shaven and well built (Dyer, 1982), with the exception of the second man on the right-hand side of the table, who is less attractive. His unkempt eyebrows, floppy hair and slightly wonky facial features mark Adam as a bit of a loser. It is his fantasy to which we gain access. As Anderson barks her orders to the table, Adam zones out of the meeting to fantasise about her engaging in a bit of girl-on-girl gyration with her assistant.

This short ad (45 seconds) offers us a fairly standard yet popular narrative wherein we see the hopeless dreams of a 'less attractive' man whose only access to 'trophy' women, or sexually assertive women, is through fantasy (or via porn: McKee *et al.*, 2008). When her

Figure 25.1 Pamela Anderson leading a creative team meeting.

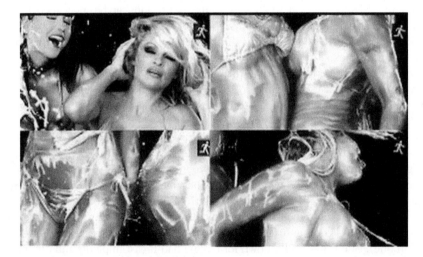

Figure 25.2 Close-ups of the girl-to-girl fantasy.

assistant asks Pamela if she wants cream in her coffee, Adam's fantasy begins; in his imagination the two women, dressed in gold swimwear and covered in cream, touch themselves as well as each other (Figure 25.2).

This representation seems to fulfil the conditions of the 'luscious lesbian' figure as discussed by Gill (2009), wherein attractive, conventionally feminine women engage in sexualised woman-to-woman relations for the gratification of a male viewer. These relations – although labelled as lesbian – take place in a heteronormative context, where women's heterosexuality is not lost but further asserted as a form of sexual agency. In addition, according to Garrity (2001), the very nature of such a lesbian sexually agentic activity makes the representation even 'hotter', and therefore even more pleasurable. The expression of girl-on-girl sexual activity is made more explicit here with the addition of the cream which covers the women's bodies, connoting semen and male ejaculation – imagery directly referencing pornographic tropes and emphasising the particularity and politics of this girl-on-girl moment as a product of Adam's fantasising. Heather Butler (2004: 168, 173) has argued that lesbian sex in heterosexual pornography is the 'lesbo-jelly in the heterodonut', in the sense that it functions as a form of foreplay: 'Typically, the "lesbian" number serves as a warm-up for the "real" thing, that is, sex with a penis that will eventually ejaculate.'

The fantasy comes to an end when Anderson's voice calls Adam back to reality: 'What are we going to do about the web address?' Adam shakes himself awake and hesitatingly suggests the 'crazydomains' site: his inspiration comes from the excitement of the fantasy, almost as if the sexy representation of 'lesbian' femininity has generated his (and by implication, men's in general) success.

Given that advertising in the UK context is highly structured and regulated (Gill, 2009: 139) and defined by codes of 'taste and decency' (Smith, 2007), this advertisement's censorship by Ofcom comes as no surprise. However, complaints did not centre on the re-establishment of familiar gendered power relations (Anderson's outfit and overt sexiness undermining any idea that she really has control of the meeting and Adam's fantasy absolutely undercutting her authority); rather, the advert was removed because of the proximity of its referents to pornography and the discomfort that closeness produces, demonstrating that negotiations of sex in public arenas remain difficult.

Representation of sexuality in advertising II: Kraft's *Zesty* advertisement

My second example is an advertisement for Kraft's salad sauce, *Zesty*. The campaign for Zesty sauce utilised television and print advertisements and attracted broad media and social media attention, especially through articles debating the advert's allegedly offensive character versus its reversals of the ways in which women's bodies have been used to sell products (Bahadur, 2013). The image (see Figure 25.3) shows a well-built, masculine, attractive and carefully groomed semi-naked man pouring sauce onto a large salad as he lies on a table, lit by candles.

The message at the top right-hand side of the picture makes the advert's sexual connotations clear: '*The only thing better than dressing is undressing. Let's get zesty.*' The model exudes a Latin sensuality, his dark hair, dark skin and quirked eyebrow hinting at the exotic (Nixon, 1996). The lit candles on the table signify not only a romantic dinner but also an 'artistic' sensibility – he poses as if a work of art, his pressed white shirt open and revealing his toned musculature. From one perspective, this is a stereotypically handsome man – a popular figure in advertising, according to Edwards (1997) – offered up to the postmodern agentic female gaze, inviting a sexually assertive response. He is presented as on offer as a sexual meal to the female audiences targeted by the product.

However, the Zesty campaign also offers insights into dominant discourses about sexuality. The way the model looks at the prospective female audience, his pose balanced between strength and tenderness, power and submission, reflects what has become an iconic perception of the modern man (Edwards, 1997). We should, however, look at how this advertisement leaves dominant constructions of man-to-woman relations undisturbed. This is to say that no matter the alleged sexual assertiveness to which the model is hypothetically subject, the romance implied by the lit candles reflects the normative heterosexual context within which the human erotic relationship is understood. The same goes for the idea that this man knows how to cook, or at least has a taste for good and healthy food – this conforms to the heteronormative idea of him being 'partner' or 'husband' material. Thus, even that

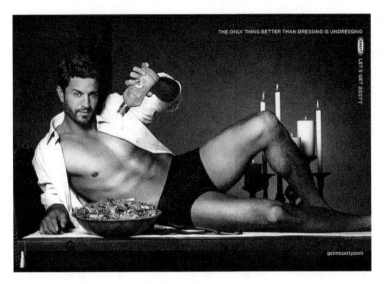

Figure 25.3 The advertisement for Kraft's Zesty sauce.

which seems to break boundaries or introduce different ways of interpreting sexualised content does not disturb well-established notions about how we understand and negotiate sexuality in the public space.

Childhood and sexualisation: the case of advertisements

In the ongoing debates about sexualisation, children have been the centre of concern and, as advertising is such a public format (available on street corners, at bus stops and in shopping centres, as well as on TV, in the cinema and in magazines), there is particular interest in how children's 'healthy' development might be at risk from casual or inadvertent 'exposure' to sexual representations of adults in advertising, or from sexualised representations of children themselves. The political context of work on the 'sexualisation of children' has been framed by four recent reports, in which advertising has been of particular interest. The Australian *Corporate Paedophilia* report (Rush and LaNauze, 2006) addresses the topic at a public policy level, while the *American Psychological Association Report* (American Psychological Association [APA], 2007) claims to offer evidence about the negative effects of sexualised culture on girls. Following these, the UK government commissioned celebrity psychologist Linda Papadopoulos to conduct a review of evidence in the UK, including the effects of sexualised advertising, which came to be known as the *Sexualisation of Young People Review* (2010). Finally, the *Bailey Review* (2011) reported on the commercialisation and sexualisation of childhood, with the focus on children as consumers of sexualised products.

Rush and LaNeuze (2006) argued that there has been an increase in images of the sexualised child in advertising, and that 'children's general sexual and emotional development is affected by exposure to advertising and marketing that is saturated with sexualised images and themes' (Rush and LaNeuze, 2006: 2). Papadopoulos (2010: 6) suggested that 'children are being portrayed in "adultified" ways and women are "infantilised"' in advertising, and claimed that this leads to 'a notion that children can be related to as sexual objects'. For Papadopoulos, advertising and other adult media lead to the 'hyper-sexualisation and objectification of girls on the one hand, and hyper-masculinisation of boys on the other' (2010: 3); citing 'inappropriate clothing and games for children' as key indicators of changed behaviours, she states:

> I want my little girl, indeed, all girls and boys, to grow up confident about who they are and about finding and expressing their individuality and sexuality, but not through imposed gender stereotypes or in a way that objectifies the body or commodifies their burgeoning sexuality.
>
> *(2010: 4)*

Here Papadopoulos is taking aim at images such as that shown in Figure 25.4, which she believes offer children hidden messages.

The *APA Report* and *Bailey Review* also took the line that advertising is a key component in the sexualisation of childhood. In these accounts, girls' sexuality is, by default, considered problematic – 'simultaneously present (and once catalysed, quite dangerous) and absent (that normal sexuality is something that will come much later)' (Egan and Hawkes, 2008: 309). When it comes to matters that have been classified as 'for adults only', and certainly where these matters relate to sex, there must be a clear line of separation between them and the figure of the child, or indeed the presence of actual children. According to these reports, the presence of the young girls on the *Beauté* and *Cadeaux* front pages make these pictures about the sexual availability of girls, if not actually incitement to child molestation. In these accounts, childhood is uniquely susceptible to risks associated with sexuality – sex and knowledge of sex are a kind of taint which inevitably changes the child; thus adult supervision and protection of children's innocence is needed. For the authors of these reports, for the policymakers who commission them and the media outlets which report on them, sexualisation is the 'pollution' of everyday life (Cameron, 2010). Childhood ought, they say, to be an innocent state of being, a time separate from adulthood; but it is 'bombarded', 'surrounded' by and 'under pressure' from inappropriate messages. The discomfort felt by many whenever questions of sex are raised is heightened in these accounts by the proximity of a child (even if that child is entirely notional). The 'unspeakable' topic of sex must never come close enough to infect the 'untouchable' child.

Figure 25.4 *Beauté* and *Cadeaux* front pages.

Scholars within cultural and feminist studies have offered rich critiques of the ways in which these reports (and others) offer the child figure as a passive victim of sexualising media messages (Smith and Attwood, 2011). Socio-psychoanalytical and feminist (e.g. Egan, 2013) and social constructionist and post-feminist accounts about childhood (Buckingham, 2013; Tsaliki, 2016) have sought to deconstruct these dominant discourses regarding sexualisation. For instance, Buckingham et al. (2010) did research with young people and found that teens understand themselves as active and knowledgeable consumers of sexualised goods advertised to them, and position themselves in opposition to adult discourses that construct them as passive victims of marketisation and sexualisation. They found that children 'saw themselves as using sexualised products in very particular ways (to have fun), rather than falling prey to risks, as implied in the concerns of adults who "make too much fuss" about sexualised goods' (2010: 60). Children and young people's interests in various products were, Buckingham and colleagues found, driven by a complex set of influences, not simply a result of 'media messages' or 'poison'.

In a special issue of *Sex Education*, editors McKee, Bragg and Taormino (2015) explored entertainment media's evolving role in sex education, rejecting the 'homogenising' and negative tendencies in accounts of sexualisation to instead stress the 'learning' element possible in children's encounters with media (including advertising). McKee and his fellow editors highlighted the ways in which critiques of media view 'pleasures . . . with suspicion; although a prime target is often the supposedly "unrealistic" nature of media representations' (2015: 451). In a broader context, critiquing the *Bailey Review*, Barker and Duschinsky (2012) commented upon its demonisation of (an undefined yet obvious form of) sexual content in media (including advertising) and its one-dimensional focus on girls as particularly at risk. Thus, they noted that the report conflates 'a concern for sexism with a concern about female and deviant sexualities [and this] serves to subsume, under a right-wing narrative, the feminist concerns about gender stereotyping which originally brought the issue of "sexualisation" to the public eye' (2012: 304). Last but not least, another point of critique concerns the obsessive interest in protectionist agendas, the focus of which is parents' role in keeping children away from almost any kind of sexual knowledge (Renold, 2005).

Conclusion

Advertising is just one more platform within popular culture where concerns about children and sexuality are conveniently projected and reflected. Certainly, the issue is complicated; children are indeed targeted as potential consumers and in ways which speak to sexual interests (often reinforcing reactionary sexual stereotypes), which sits uncomfortably alongside parents' concerns that their children should develop at their own pace, and with their guidance. Regulating what children can see and enabling them to work towards their own self-regulation is a challenging task for adults (parents, educators, researchers and policymakers); it is not helped by the current focus on risk or on accounts which discursively construct sexuality as appropriate or inappropriate, as healthy or problematic, as acceptable or as in need of control.

Bibliography

American Psychological Association (2007). *Report of the APA Task Force on the Sexualization of Girls*. Washington, DC: APA.

Arthurs, J. (2004). *Television and Sexuality: Regulation and the Politics of Taste*. Maidenhead: Open University Press.

Attwood, F. (2006). 'Sexed up: theorizing the sexualization of culture'. *Sexualities*. Volume 9 (1): 77–94.

Bahadur, N. (2013). 'Kraft Zesty ad offends "One million moms", sparks debate'. *Huffington Post*. 14 June. www.huffingtonpost.com/2013/06/14/kraft-zesty-dressing-ad_n_3441805.html (accessed 7 February 2016).

Bailey, R. (2011) *Letting Children Be Children: Report of an Independent Review of the Commercialisation and Sexualisation of Childhood*. London, UK: Department for Education, www.education.gov.uk/publications/eOrderingDownload/Bailey%20Review.pdf (accessed 2 March 2012).

Barker, M.J. and Duschinsky, R. (2012) 'Sexualisation's four faces: sexualisation and gender stereotyping in the Bailey Review'. *Gender and Education*. Volume 24 (3): 303–310.

Bragg, S. and Buckingham, D. (2013). 'Global concerns, local negotiations and moral selves: contemporary parenting and the "sexualisation of childhood" debate'. *Feminist Media Studies*. Volume 13 (4): 643–659.

Briggs, V. (2013) 'Child pornography and the sexualisation of children'. 28 November. https://shardsofsilence.wordpress.com/tag/sexualisation-of-children/ (accessed 7 February 2016).

Buckingham, D. (2013). 'Representing audiences: audience research, public knowledge, and policy'. *The Communication Review*. Volume 16 (1–2): 51–60.

Buckingham, D., Willett, R., Bragg, S. and Russell, R. (2010). *Sexualised Goods Aimed at Children: A Report to the Scottish Parliament Equal Opportunities Committee*. Edinburgh: Scottish Parliament Equal Opportunities Committee.

Burr, V. (1995). *An Introduction to Social Constructionism*. London: Routledge.

Butler, H. (2004). 'What do you call a lesbian with long fingers? The development of lesbian and dyke pornography'. In L. Williams (ed) *Porn Studies*. Durham and London: Duke University Press.

Cameron, D. (2010). 'Too much, too young'. *Daily Mail*. 19 February. www.dailymail.co.uk/debate/article-1252156/DAVID-CAMERON-Sexualisation-children-too-young.html (accessed 15 November 2015).

Chronaki, D. (2014). *Young People's Accounts of Experiences with Mediated Sexual Content during Childhood and Teenage Life*. PhD thesis, Loughborough University, UK.

Cortese, A.J. (2008). *Provocateur: Images of Women and Minorities in Advertising*. Lanham: Rowman & Littlefield Publishers Inc.

Dyer, R. (1982). 'Don't look now: the male pin-up'. *Screen*. Volume 23 (3–4): 61–73.

Eby, M. (2013). 'Pamela Anderson commercial banned in Britain for being "sexist and degrading to women"'. *nydailynews.com*. 5 June. www.nydailynews.com/entertainment/tv-movies/sexist-pamela-anderson-ad-banned-britain-article-1.1364044 (accessed 7 February 2016).

Edwards, T. (1997) *Men in the Mirror: Men's Fashion, Masculinity and Consumer Society*. London: Cassell.

Egan, R.D. (2013) *Becoming Sexual: A Critical Appraisal of the Sexualization of Girls*. Cambridge–Malden, MA: Polity Press.

Egan, R.D. and Hawkes, G.L. (2008) 'Girls, sexuality and the strange carnalities of advertisements'. *Australian Feminist Studies*. Volume 23 (57): 307–322.

Foucault, M. (1986) *The History of Sexuality, Volume 3: The Care of the Self*, translated by R. Hurley. Harmondsworth: Penguin.

Garrity, J. (2001) 'Mediating the taboo: the straight lesbian gaze'. In C. Thomas (ed.) *Straight with a Twist*. Urbana: University of Illinois.

Gianatasio, D. (2013) 'Hunkvertising: the objectification of men in advertising'. *Adweek.com*. 7 October. www.adweek.com/news/advertising-branding/hunkvertising-objectification-men-advertising-152925 (accessed 7 February 2016).

Gibbons, J. (2011) *Art and Advertising*. London: I.B. Tauris.

Gill, R.C. (2008) 'Empowerment/agency: figuring female sexual agency in contemporary advertising'. *Feminism and Psychology*. Volume 18 (1): 35–60.

Gill, R.C. (2009). 'Beyond the "sexualization of culture" thesis: an intersectional analysis of "six-packs", "midriffs" and "hot lesbians" in advertising'. *Sexualities*. Volume 12 (2): 137–160.

Gill, R. and Scharff, C. (eds) (2011). *New Femininities: Postfeminism, Neoliberalism and Subjectivity*. Basingstoke: Palgrave Macmillan.

Goffman, E. (1979). *Gender Advertisements*. London: Macmillan.

Hitchens, P. (2002). 'The failure of sex education'. In E. Lee (ed) *Teenage Sex: What Should Schools Teach Children?* London: Hodder and Stoughton.

Jones, M.Y., Stanaland, A.J.S. and Gelb, B.D. (1998). 'Beefcake and cheesecake: insights for advertisers'. *Journal of Advertising*. Volume 27: 33–52.

Kakoudaki, D. (2004). 'Pinup: the American secret weapon in World War II'. In L. Williams (ed) *Porn Studies*. Durham and London: Duke University Press.

Levin, D. and Kilbourne, J.E. (2008). *So Sexy, So Soon: The New Sexualized Childhood and What Parents Can Do to Protect Their Kids*. New York: Ballantine Books.

Machin, D. and Thornborrow, J. (2003). 'Branding and discourse: the case of Cosmopolitan'. *Discourse and Society*. Volume 14 (4): 453–471.

McKee, A., Albury, K. and Lumby, C. (2008). *The Porn Report*. Melbourne: Melbourne University Press.

McKee, A., Bragg, S. and Taormino, T. (2015). 'Editorial introduction: the entertainment media's evolving role in sex education'. *Sex Education*. Volume 15 (5): 451–457.

McNair, B. (1996). *Mediated Sex: Pornography and Postmodern Culture*. London: Edward Arnold.

McNair, B. (2002). *Striptease Culture: Sex, Media and the Democratization of Desire*. London: Routledge.

McRobbie, A. (2004). 'Post-feminism and popular culture'. *Feminist Media Studies*. Volume 4 (3): 255–264.

Moore, S. (1988). 'Here's looking at you, kid!' In L. Gamman and M. Marshment (eds) *The Female Gaze*. London: The Women's Press.

Nixon, S. (1996). *Hard Looks: Masculinities, Spectatorship and Contemporary Consumption*. London: UCL Press.

Papadopoulos, L. (2010). *Sexualisation of Young People Review*. http://webarchive.nationalarchives.gov.uk/20130128103514/http://homeoffice.gov.uk/documents/Sexualisation-young-people2835.pdf?view=Binary (accessed 29 March 2017).

Renold, E. (2005). *Girls, Boys and Junior Sexualities*. London: Routledge-Falmer.

Rossi, L.-M. (2007). 'Outdoor pornification: advertising heterosexuality in the streets'. In S. Paasonen, K. Nikunen and L. Saarenmaa (eds) *Pornification: Sex and Sexuality in Media Culture*. London: Berg.

Rush, E. and La Nauze, A. (2006). *Corporate Paedophilia: Sexualisation of Children in Australia*. Canberra: The Australia Institute.

Simpson, M. (1994). *Male Impersonators: Men Performing Masculinity*. London: Cassell.

Smith, C. (2007). *One for the Girls! The Pleasures and Practices of Reading Women's Porn*. Bristol: Intellect.

Smith, C. and Attwood, F. (2011). 'Lamenting sexualization: research, rhetoric and the story of young people's "sexualization" in the UK Home Office review'. *Sex Education*. Volume 11 (3): 327–337.

Soley, L. and Kurzbard, G. (1986). 'Sex in advertising: a comparison of 1964 and 1984 magazines advertisements'. *Journal of Advertising*. Volume 15 (3): 46–64.

Tsaliki, L. (2016) *Children, Pornography and the Politics of Sexuality*. London: Palgrave Macmillan.

Williams, L. (2004). 'Porn studies: proliferating pornographies on/scene: an introduction'. In L. Williams (ed) *Porn Studies*. Durham and London: Duke University Press.

Williams, R. (2000). 'Advertising: the magic system'. *Advertising & Society Review*. Volume 1 (1).

Wolf, N. (1990). *The Beauty Myth*. London: Chatto and Windus.

Media

'Crazydomains.com TV ad starring Pamela Anderson'. YouTube. 2009. www.youtube.com/watch?v=hNhSBhJHBls&oref=https%3A%2F%2Fwww.youtube.com%2Fwatch%3Fv%3DhNhSBhJHBls&has_verified=1 (accessed 7 February 2016).

26
MEDIA REPRESENTATIONS OF WOMEN IN ACTION SPORTS
More than 'sexy bad girls' on boards

Holly Thorpe

The female sporting body has long been a site of public discussion and debate. This is perhaps not surprising when we look to the history of sport and recall that men designed sports for men, often with the explicit purpose of teaching boys how to become a particular type of man (Aitchison, 2007; Burstyn, 1999). Thus, women's participation – particularly in those sports that celebrate traditionally defined masculine traits and values such as physical contact, aggression, dominance, courage, risk-taking and the acceptance (even glorification) of pain and injury – poses a serious threat to the long-held relationship between sport (especially male team sports) and masculinity. Over the past half-century, women have forged new spaces in sports, demonstrating exceptionally high levels of skill and commitment in an ever-growing list of sporting pursuits ranging from mountain climbing, to ice hockey, to boxing. Yet almost 40 years of research reveals various attempts by the media to undermine women's sporting participation, and thus maintain the supposedly 'natural' relationship between sport and masculinity (see Bruce, 2015).

Men have been the voices of 'authority' in sporting media, as commentators, journalists and editors, and, notwithstanding the growing number of female commentators on TV and other platforms, the mainstream sports media continues to assume a heterosexual male gaze. When women pose a serious threat to the maleness of sports (and the sports media per se), and particularly when they 'fail', or refuse, to perform an appropriate femininity (for the consumption of the male viewer), their sex, sexuality and sexual identities are called into question. The latest research suggests that, despite increased visibility of women's sports more broadly and more women holding positions of power in the sports media, very little has changed in terms of media representations of sportswomen. The media continues to marginalise and trivialise sportswomen via an array of evolving techniques ranging from exclusion to gender marking, infantilisation and hypersexualisation (Bruce, 2008, 2015; Cooky, Messner and Hextrum, 2013; Crouse, 2013; Hardin, 2013; Kane, 2013).

Inspired by Foucault's concept of panopticism, a number of sports scholars have examined the disciplining of the female sporting body into a docile body (e.g. Cole, 1998; Duncan, 1994; Markula, 1995). More specifically, they have explored how sports media practices act as technologies of domination that draw individuals 'into a discursive web of normalizing practices' (Markula, 2003: 88), and in so doing ultimately 'constrain female sport and exercise practices' (Pringle, 2005: 263). Observing this trend, Markula (2003) states that such studies have focused on the sport, fitness and health industries as discursively constructed disciplines that limit possibilities of existence and subsequently act as 'vehicle(s) of women's domination' (88). While these studies have contributed much to our understanding of the mass media as a technology of domination of sportswomen's sexual and athletic identities, some scholars express concern that research focusing on 'technologies of dominance' results in 'pessimistic representations of sport and exercise practices' (Markula and Pringle, 2006: 48). Gruneau (1993), for example, proclaims that such a focus 'can too easily deflect attention from analysing the creative possibilities, freedoms, ambiguities, and contradictions also found in sport' (cited in Markula and Pringle, 2006: 48). Moreover, such an approach overlooks the various forms of media (mass, social, niche) and their production and reproduction of multiple, and often conflicting, discourses of sportswomen's bodies. Furthermore, this top-down understanding of power ignores the dialectical relationship between the media and sporting cultures, and particularly women's interpretations, readings, responses and contributions to such media portrayals. Hence, rather than focusing on the media as a 'technology of discipline' (which is only one form of power discussed by Foucault), I have sought to draw more broadly upon Foucault's unique conceptualisation of power and, in so doing, facilitate a discussion of the media in newer, action sport cultures as not only repressive but also positive and productive. Ultimately, this chapter reveals signs of change in the media representations of (some) women in action sporting cultures, as well as ongoing structural and ideological constraints.

'Sexy bad girls' of action sports: representations of risk and sexuality

For many years, action sports, such as skateboarding, surfing and snowboarding, were considered the bastion of young, white, privileged males (Beal, 1996; Kusz, 2007; Wheaton, 2000). Early media coverage contributed to such perceptions via the celebration of youthful, hedonistic fratriarchal masculinities and the marginalisation of women and 'other' men in action sports (Kusz, 2007; Thorpe, 2013; Wheaton, 2000). Despite their absence from much of the early media, it is important to note that women have always been active participants in action sports cultures. While certainly fewer in number than men, women successfully negotiated space in these male-dominated sports via active participation and demonstrations of physical prowess and commitment (Beal, 1996; Thorpe, 2009; Wheaton and Tomlinson, 1998).

In the mid and late 1990s, however, a *select few* female action sports athletes gained mainstream visibility, particularly those who embodied a sexy 'bad girl' athletic identity (Gill, 2008; Owen, Stein and Vande Berg, 2007). According to Gill, the 'fun, fearless, young, attractive, heterosexual woman who knowingly and deliberately plays with her sexual power' became a striking feature of mass media advertising, film and television during this period (2008: 41). In the realm of action sports, professional US snowboarder Tara Dakides became the archetypal 'sexy bad girl' during the late 1990s and early 2000s. Embodying a unique combination of physicality, femininity and sexuality, Dakides captured the imagination of both the mass media and her peers, including editors of snowboarding magazines, journalists, photographers and film-makers, and thus garnered more media coverage than any female snowboarder before her. Dakides' exceptional physical prowess and a risk-taking attitude ('If it scares me then I just want to do it more') – combined with a distinctive clothing style (e.g. wearing low-riding, baggy pants, urban gangster-inspired bandanas, pink punk-inspired studded belts and tank-tops); an athletic physique; long, messy, multi-coloured hair; piercings; and extensive tattoos – appealed to many young female snowboarders seeking an 'alternative femininity', as well as many desiring heterosexual male snowboarders. One journalist described the commercial appeal of Tara Dakides' alternative femininity as 'a knockout combo of skill, swagger and sex appeal', adding: 'it helps that she's beautiful: deep green eyes and toothpaste-ad grin, a hyper-athletic body, biceps bulging and abs rippling ... pierced nostril and belly button, and an intriguing tattoo...' (Elliot, 2001). Dakides achieved broader celebrity status, featuring in *Rolling Stone*, *Sports Illustrated*, *Maxim*, *FHM* and *Sports Illustrated for Women*, the latter of which named her 'the coolest sports woman in 2001'. With such visibility, she became a valuable source of inspiration for many female boarders.

According to Gill (2008), however, we should be wary of 'too easy' celebrations of 'empowered sexual agency'. She argues that representations of young women such as Dakides, and other sorts of 'midriff advertising', are highly problematic because they operate within a 'resolutely hetero-normative economy, in which power, pleasure and subjectivity are all presented in relation to heterosexual relationships'; they are also 'profoundly racialized' as a white femininity, and they exclude 'older women, disabled women, fat women and any woman who is unable to live up to increasingly narrow standards of female beauty and sex appeal that are normatively required' (Gill, 2008: 44). Certainly, many media representations of women in action sports continue to celebrate a young, white, heterosexual, athletic femininity, with 'other' women remaining largely invisible. In other words, the media tends to focus on those women who demonstrate physical prowess and a risk-taking attitude while simultaneously maintaining a heterosexual femininity, and who can thus be positioned as a 'sexy' commodity for male consumption.

Yet the selective incorporation of female action sports athletes during the late 1990s and early 2000s was significant in altering the perception that women were less capable than their male counterparts, and in so doing helped shore up new space for (primarily young, white, heterosexual) women in both the mass and niche media and the broader action-sports cultures and industries. As a result of the increasing visibility of female role models (such as Dakides), combined with the expanding female niche market and opportunities for female-only lessons, camps and competitions, the female action sport demographic has grown over the past two decades (Thorpe, 2007). Snowboarding, kayaking and skateboarding, for example, were among the fastest growing sports engaged in by American women in the early 2000s (NGSA, 2005). In 2004, female skateboarders constituted approximately 25.3 per cent (or 2.6 million) of the 10.3 million skateboarders in the United States, up from just 7.5 per cent in 2001 (McLaughlin, 2004), and the number of American women who surf every day grew by 280 per cent between 1999 and 2003 (Women in Focus at ASR, 2003). The athleticism of committed female participants is now highly visible on the mountains, in the waves, rivers and lakes and in some media, and there is some evidence to suggest that boys and men are adjusting and, in some cases, radically altering their perceptions of women's abilities and capabilities (Olive, 2013a, b; Thorpe, 2007; Wheaton and Tomlinson, 1998). In part due to these changes, action sports are increasingly attracting female participants from varying age groups, sexualities, abilities and levels of commitment, and from different cultures and ethnicities (Comer, 2010; Roy, 2013; Wheaton, 2013).

In the remainder of this chapter I draw upon my previously published Foucauldian analysis of the mediated discourses of female snowboarders (Thorpe, 2008) and my ongoing research into the mass, niche and social media portrayals of women in action-sports cultures more broadly, to illustrate some of the diverse media representations of sex, sexuality and the sexual identities of women in action sports. I conclude with a brief examination of how women are making meaning of, and responding to, such representations in a new feminist context.

Representations of action sportswomen in mass and niche media

Despite their early and continuing presence in action sports cultures, women have long been subjected to what Foucault (1981) terms the processes of exclusion in relation to media coverage (see Thorpe, 2008). 'In the 1980s', US professional snowboarder Michele Taggart, has noted, 'women were only included in the magazines because of their cuteness and their beautiful hair flowing down the mountain' (cited in Howe, 1998: 64). Henderson has made similar observations, arguing that the *Tracks* surfing magazine celebrates the 'pleasure[s], dreams and nostaliga' of 'patriarchal ideology and masculine symbolic identities' while simultaneously creating a 'necessary illusion of some openness to women's advancement in surfing' (2001: 320). Contextualising changes in the representations of female surfers over a 30-year period, Henderson observes contemporary female surfers 'experiencing the most extreme forms of objectification' (2001: 329). Rinehart (2005) also observed the explicit sexualisation of women in skateboarding magazines, with very little space given to female skateboarders as competent cultural participants.

Following many years of exclusion from the media, today a plethora of media forms cover women's participation in action sports. Yet mass media (i.e. television, newspapers, mainstream magazines), niche media (i.e. action sports magazines, films, websites) and social media (i.e. Facebook, Instagram, YouTube) cater for different audiences and have different consequences and 'markedly different cultural connotations' (Thornton, 1996: 122) for women in action sport cultures. Mass media tends to be produced by non-participant journalists and producers for a mass audience often with little knowledge of action sports cultures, whereas niche media tend to be created by journalists, editors, photographers and film-makers who are, or have been, active participants. Action sports participants are also active consumers *and* producers – or 'prosumers' – of new digital and social media (see Thorpe, 2014, 2016). In this, they are often critical consumers of mass media products, and enjoy the social activities of responding to existing cultural products as well as co-producing their own. Typically, peers (in local and international contexts) regulate each other's practices via comments, 'like' buttons and various other 'linking' or 'liking' options. A number of sport and physical cultural scholars have critically discussed mass and niche media representations of women in action sport cultures (Bruce, Falcous and Thorpe, 2007; Frohlick, 2005; Henderson, 2001; Rinehart, 2005; Thorpe, 2011; Wheaton, 2003; Wheaton and Beal, 2003), and a growing number are considering representations of gender, sex and sexuality in social media (MacKay and Dallaire, 2012; Olive, 2015; Thorpe, 2014).

As various sport scholars have explained, the sports mass media and associated commercial interests occasionally seize images of female athletes and place them at the 'center of cultural discourse, at least temporarily' (Messner, 2002: 109). As Messner explains, the media 'seem most likely to do so when there is high profit potential (and this usually means that the women can be neatly packaged as heterosexually attractive)' (ibid.: 109). American snowboarder Gretchen Bleiler is a good example of such selective incorporation. After winning a silver medal in the 2006 winter Olympic half-pipe event, Bleiler featured for the second time in *FHM* and *Maxim* magazines. In such photographs, action sportswomen often combine action sports-specific objects (e.g. surfboard, snowboard) with symbols of traditional femininity (e.g. bikini, passive and sexually suggestive poses). Arguably, mass media representations that emphasise women athletes' physical appearances promote responses that position female action sport participants as sex symbols for male consumption, rather than as serious participants.

In contrast to the mass media, which typically portrays women's participation in action sports as a hetero-sexy style of activity to be consumed, the discourses of women in the niche media are diverse. Discursive constructions of sexuality and femininity in the action sport niche media range from women as respected athletes and cultural participants to women as models in sexually suggestive poses. Indeed, the niche media is not a homogenous category; various forms of niche media exist within and across action sports cultures. While the majority target young 'core' male and female participants committed to the action sports lifestyle (e.g. *Transworld Surfing, Skateboarder* magazine), others cater to smaller niches, including young male enthusiasts (e.g. *Stab*; see Thorpe, 2007; Wheaton, 2000), female participants (e.g. *Curl, Sunshine Surf Girls*, www.longboardgirlscrew.com; see Thorpe, 2006) or more mature audiences (e.g. *Snowboard Life, Surfer's Journal*). The representations of women vary considerably across (and within) such niche media. For example, while many niche magazines are increasingly covering (some) women and are offering an alternative discourse of femininity based on active participation and cultural commitment, the same sources also reinforce traditional discourses of heterosexual femininity by including advertisements that feature female models (as distinct from female athletes) in sexually suggestive poses (also see Rinehart, 2005; Wheaton, 2003). In contrast, the sexual status of men or male action sports participants is almost never compromised.

Female athletes using sex to sell: second-wave, third-wave and neoliberal feminisms

While hyper-sexual images of female models have always been a feature of niche magazines, the appearance of professional female action sports athletes in male magazines such as *Maxim*, *Sports Illustrated* and *FHM* is a more recent phenomenon. Like many other contemporary female athletes (e.g. Amanda Beard, Danica Patrick, Gabrielle Reece, Maria Sharapova), these women proclaim their awareness of their commodity value and have no qualms about marketing their sexuality to boost their public profile and image, and reaping the financial benefits (see Thorpe, 2006, 2008; also see Heywood and Dworkin, 2003). Images that promote athletes' heterosexual femininity, however, tend to be interpreted differently by women (and men) from different social and cultural backgrounds and in different historical contexts. The distinctions between second-wave, third-wave and neoliberal feminism are insightful here.

Developing in the 1960s, second-wave feminism focused on the radical reconstruction or elimination of traditional sex roles and the struggle for equal rights. Second-wave feminists built feminist organisations and fought for legislative changes regarding the family, sexual relations, reproduction, employment and education. Women who view overtly sexualised images of female athletes through a second-wave discursive lens typically interpret them as diminishing women's power, trivialising their strength and putting them in their sexual place (Burstyn, 1999). Donna Lopiano, the executive director of the US-based Women's Sports Foundation, for example, proclaims that 'any exposure in a sports magazine that minimizes athletic achievement and skill and emphasizes the female athlete as a sex object is insulting and degrading' (cited in Drape, 2004). Women born in the last quarter of the twentieth century, however, have different experiences from those of previous generations. Many contemporary young women, and particularly middle-class women, for example, have access to opportunities, time and support unknown to their mothers and grandmothers.

Hence, it should come as no surprise that their feminist questions and strategies, and indeed interpretations of the media, differ from those of earlier generations.

Acknowledging that the material conditions that facilitate women's agency – space, encouragement and legislation – have changed considerably since second-wave feminism, younger feminists developed a new strand of gender politics often referred to as 'third-wave feminism' (Baumgardner and Richards, 2000; Heywood and Drake, 1997; Heywood and Dworkin, 2003). While a detailed discussion of third-wave feminism is beyond the scope of this chapter (see Thorpe, 2008), a notable difference between second- and third-wave feminists is that the latter feel at ease with contradiction. Third-wave feminism, which began speaking for itself in the early 1990s, is a product of the contradiction between ongoing sexism and greater opportunities for women. 'We are the daughters of privilege', claims Joan Morgan, a black feminist speaking on behalf of the younger generation; 'we walk through the world with a sense of entitlement that women of our mothers' generation could not begin to fathom' (Morgan, 1999, cited in Heywood and Dworkin, 2003: 41). Although 'sexism may be a very real part of my life', Morgan says, 'so is the unwavering belief that there is no dream I can't pursue and achieve simply because "I'm a woman"' (ibid.). The new social context fostered a third-wave feminism that explicitly embraces contradiction, hybridity and multiple identities. Heywood and Drake, for example, define feminism's third wave as 'a movement that contains elements of the second-wave critique of beauty culture, sexual abuse and power structures' while also acknowledging and making use of 'the pleasure, danger and defining power of those structures' (1997: 3). From the third-wave feminist perspective, binaries like masculine/feminine, active/passive, strong/weak, violent/peaceful and competitive/co-operative belong to essentialist gender natures that have long ceased to have relevance (Heywood and Dworkin, 2003). Indeed, among many young women, displays of 'feminine physical attractiveness and empowerment' are not viewed as mutually exclusive or necessarily opposed realities but as 'lived aspects of the same reality' (Messner, 2002: 17–18). Thus, in contrast to second-wave feminists, many contemporary young women applaud hyper-feminine images of female athletes as a celebration of women's sexuality. According to third-wave feminists, bodies coded as athletic 'can redeem female sexuality and make it visible as an assertion of female presence' (Heywood and Dworkin, 2003: 83).

While young women (and men) are not united in their readings of sexual representations of professional action sportswomen, it is clear that some are interpreting these images through third-wave rather than second-wave feminist discourses; when combined with female athleticism, they are embracing rather than shunning women's sexuality. For example, semi-professional New Zealand snowboarder Hana believes that images promoting female boarders as 'hot' are 'good for the sport'; they promote snowboarding as 'cool for chicks' and could even 'encourage young girls to try snowboarding' (personal communication, 2006). Continuing, Hana proclaims: 'If the magazines include a sexy shot of a pro woman snowboarder, then it's fine because it shows that she's a talented snowboarder – and cute too – so, one up on the boys I say.' South African snowboarder Robyn also adopted a strong third-wave perspective in her reading of these sexual displays, asserting: 'women's sexuality is a tool that gives us power over men ... so go girls!' She applauded female snowboarders who 'make money off males' but admitted, 'it's a pity they have to take their clothes off. If they could do it while keeping their clothes on it would be *even better*' (personal communication, 2005, emphasis added). Robyn supports women who capitalise upon the financial opportunities available in a new economic and cultural system, and she understands these women's actions as the result of strategic decisions, rather than exploitation or manipulation. Her comments, however, are contradictory, in that she celebrates women's sexuality as a 'tool' for power in one breath and then advocates them 'keeping their clothes on' in another. Such contradictions are characteristic of many young third-wave feminists and, indeed, many of the female boarders interviewed for my research (Thorpe, 2008). Nonetheless, as the following comment from Pamela illustrates, some women are cautious of discourses that caricature one form of heterosexual femininity in both mainstream women's magazines and core snowboarding magazines:

> Models constantly reinforce a thin image, which we all carry around in our heads, but we all learn to deal with it in different ways. Self-confidence is key and this comes from age, independence, and finding something in life where you can excel and feel proud – for some girls, like me, this is snowboarding.
>
> There is a media image of the 'ideal' female snowboarder, but it is definitely different from the models in most women's magazines. In snowboarding magazines, there is a media image of a freestyle chick with long hair out of a beanie, matching snowboard outfit, a bit grungy, and riding hard with all the boys etc. I always felt like I was just doing my own thing, but heaps of young girls appear to feel the need to conform to this snowboarder 'image' to fit in.
>
> *(personal communication, October 2006)*

Indeed, some female action sports participants have become aware of the limitations of discursive femininity in society and action sports cultures more specifically, and consciously negotiate their own subjectivity within the existing power/discourses nexus (also see Olive, 2013a, b; Thorpe, 2009). However, while many of the snowboarders interviewed in my previous research articulated a critical awareness and problematisation of discourses that sexualise women, the majority simply adopted 'coping mechanisms' (Markula, 2003: 103). In order to preserve their enjoyment of core action sports magazines, they 'ignored' problematic advertisements (Thorpe, 2008).

Discourses of neoliberal feminism are also increasingly observable in action sports cultures, particularly with the growth of self-representational and self-sexualised social media portrayals of action sportswomen. For example, American professional surfer and model Alana Blanchard is a highly competent surfer, and although no longer competing on the World Surfing Tour, she remains the highest paid female surfer. Blanchard earned more than US$1.8 million in 2014 from her various sponsorships, including Rip Curl, Sony and T-Mobile ('The Stab List', 2014). Very aware of the economic potential of her hyper-sexualised blonde, tanned, toned 'surfer-girl' image in the current market, Blanchard uses an array of online and social media platforms in combination with various other media representations of her bikini-clad physique and surfing lifestyle, such that she is a regular feature on the 'world's hottest athletes' lists. Blanchard is a particularly prolific user of social media, with more than 1.4 million Instagram followers, almost 2 million Facebook 'likes' and 180,000 Twitter followers, who consume her daily self-promotional and hyper-sexualised images. Many other action sportswomen are following similar self-marketing strategies to Blanchard's. As such examples illustrate, we are increasingly seeing hegemonic discourses of individualism and entrepreneurialism being touted by many of those who opt to pose in these ways, often with the support and encouragement of their transnational sponsors (i.e. Roxy, Rip Curl), who encourage the use of social media for building the worth of the athlete's personal 'brand' (see Prügl, 2015; Rottenberg, 2014). Despite the arguments for their individual agency and empowerment, it seems that fewer of the women posing in such ways appear to do so with a critical consciousness of the broader impacts of their actions for the positions of women in action sports more broadly, or the ongoing lack of opportunities for women who do not meet such strict criteria of the heterosexual feminine ideal or do not want to use their bodies to make a profit in such ways. To paraphrase Prügl, the self-sexualisation of a growing number of sportswomen in action sports cultures might be considered yet another example of the 'way in which feminism has gone to bed with neoliberal capitalism' (2015: 614).

Not all women are passive to, or complicit in, such media portayals. For some, critique of hyper-sexualised representations of women in action sports media can prompt political responses: some women write to editors to express their concerns; others invest their energies in creating or contributing to media that offers alternative representations of female action sports participants, such as female-focused magazines, websites, videos and blogs (MacKay and Dallaire, 2013a, 2013b, 2014; Thorpe, 2008). Other women use social media, such as Facebook, Instagram, Twitter and their own personal blogs, to critique problematic media representations of women and/or create space for more positive images of women in action sports (see MacKay and Dallaire, 2013a, 2013b, 2014; Olive and Thorpe, 2011; Pavlidis and Fullagar, 2014, Thorpe and Olive, 2014). In their critical analysis of the all-female 'Skirtboarders' blog, for example, MacKay and Dallaire identify online niche media as an important space 'where crew members attempt to reflexively start a movement and, in so doing, construct and circulate a wider collective identity' (2012: 1). More recently, Olive (2015) has revealed how recreational female surfers use the photo-based social media platform of Instagram to offer their self-selected representations of particular lifestyles and relationships to place and people in Byron Bay, Australia. In so doing, such representations of their surfing selves both challenge and reinforce stereotypes: their photos emphasise women's active and committed participation in surfing and their positive relationships with other women surfers, while simultaneously emphasising the bikini-clad, slim, toned, bronzed, sun-bleached 'surf babe' stereotype. Female snowboarders have also been proactive in attempting to rectify the lack of female coverage in snowboarding films, via the production of 'all-female' snowboarding videos. As I have argued elsewhere, these films provide women with the opportunity to define their own criteria for inclusion, exhibit skills, create new meanings and values for women's snowboarding and challenge dominant gender discourses (see Thorpe, 2008). As the examples of female-produced social media and films illustrate, not all women are simply 'victims' of media discourses in action sports cultures. Rather, *some* women in action sports have engaged in the 'double act' of critique and self-stylisation (Markula and Pringle, 2006: 152), to shape and reshape sexual identities, cultural images and meanings of women's participation in action sports.

Conclusion

In sum, mass and niche media help to produce and reproduce numerous, often contradictory, discourses of gender, sex and sexual identities in action sports cultures. While niche media provides space for a range of discursive constructions, including women as respected athletes and cultural participants, mass media tends to focus on heterosexually attractive female athletes and promotes action sports as a fashion for consumption. The key point here is that the multiple discourses produced by the media systematically inform women's knowledge of action sports, and play a role in governing their statements and perceptions of gender, sexuality and physicality in action sports.

Drawing inspiration from Foucault's concepts of power, power/knowledge and discourse, this chapter has illustrated how the action sports media, as a social institution, helps to regulate the production and circulation of statements and perceptions of what it means to be a woman within action sports cultures. But the media is not simply a judicial mechanism that limits, obstructs, refuses, prohibits and censors knowledge about gender, sex and sexual identities. Rather, the media is only 'one terminal form power takes' (Foucault, 1978: 92) in action sports cultures. Adopting Foucault's unique conceptualisation of power reminds us to pay attention to the mundane and daily ways in which power is enacted and contested in sporting cultures and everyday society, and in so doing reveals sportswomen as both object and subject of media power relations.

Bibliography

Aitchison, C. C. (2007) (ed). *Sport and Gender Identities: Masculinities, Femininities and Sexualities*. London and New York: Routledge.
Baumgardner, J. and Richards, A. (2000). *Manifesta: Young Women, Feminism and the Future*. New York: Farrar, Straus and Giroux.
Beal, B. (1996). 'Alternative masculinity and its effects on gender relations in the subculture of skateboarding'. *Journal of Sport Behavior*. Volume 19: 204–221.
Bruce, T. (2008). 'Women, sport and the media: a complex terrain'. In C. Obel., T. Bruce and S. Thompson (eds) *Outstanding Research about Women in New Zealand*. Hamilton, NZ: Wilf Malcolm Institute of Educational Research.
Bruce, T. (2015). 'Assessing the sociology of sport: on media and representations of sportswomen'. *International Review for the Sociology of Sport*. Volume 50 (4–5): 380–384.
Bruce, T., Falcous, M. and Thorpe, H. (2007). 'The mass media and sport'. In C. Collins and S. Jackson (eds) *Sport in Aotearoa/New Zealand Society* (2nd edition). Melbourne: Thompson.
Burstyn, V. (1999). *The Rites of Men: Manhood, Politics, and the Culture of Sport*. Toronto: University of Toronto Press.
Cole, C. L. (1998). 'Addiction, exercise, and cyborgs: technologies of deviant bodies'. *Sport and Postmodern Times*: 261–275.
Comer, K. (2010). *Surfer Girls in the New World Order*. Durham, NC: Duke University Press.
Cooky, C., Messner, M. and Hextrum, R. (2013). 'Women play sport, but not on TV: a longitudinal study of televised news media'. *Communication and Sport*. Online First. DOI: dx.doi.org/10.1177/2167479513476947: 66–80.
Crouse, K. (2013). 'Why female athletes remain on sport's periphery'. *Communication and Sport*. Online First. DOI: dx.doi.org/10.1177/2167479513487722: 89–91.
Drape, J. (2004). 'Lots of skin but not much fuss as Olympians strike pinup pose'. *The New York Times*, 12 August. www.nytimes.com/2004/08/12/sports/olympics/12women.html (accessed 28 March 2017).
Duncan, M. C. (1994). 'The politics of women's body images and practices: Foucault, the panopticon and *Shape* magazine'. *Journal of Sport and Social Issues*. Volume 18: 48–65.
Duncan, M. C. and Messner, M. (1998). 'The media image of sport and gender'. In L. Wenner (ed) *Media Sport*. Routledge: London.
Elliot, J. (2001). 'The "It" girl: a knockout combo of skill, swagger and, yeah, sex appeal has turned Tara Dakides into snowboarding's brightest star'. 21 January. *SI Adventure*. www.si.com/vault/2002/01/21/317034/the-it-girl-a-knockout-combo-of-skill-swagger-and-yeah-sex-appeal-has-turned-tara-dakides-into-snowboardings-brightest-star (accessed 28 March 2017).
Foucault, M. (1978). *The History of Sexuality Volume 1: An Introduction*. London: Penguin Books.
Foucault, M. (1981). 'The order of discourse'. In R. Young (ed) *Untying the Text: A Post-Structuralist Reader*. London: Routledge Kegan Paul.
Frohlick, S. (2005). '"That playfulness of white masculinity": mediating masculinities and adventure at Mountain Film Festivals'. *Tourist Studies*. Volume 5 (2): 175–193.

Gill, R. (2008). 'Empowerment/sexism: figuring female sexual agency in contemporary advertising'. *Feminism and Psychology*. Volume 18 (1): 35–60.

Hardin, M. (2013). 'Want changes in content? Change the decision makers'. *Communication and Sport*. Online First. DOI: dx.doi.org/10.1177/2167479513486985: 92–94.

Henderson, M. (2001). 'A shifting line up: men, women, and *Tracks* surfing magazine'. *Continuum: Journal of Media and Cultural Studies*. Volume 15 (3): 319–332.

Heywood, L. and Drake, J. (1997). 'Introduction'. In L. Heywood and J. Drake (eds) *Third-Wave Agenda*. Minneapolis: University of Minnesota Press.

Heywood, L. and Dworkin, S. L. (2003). *Built to Win: The Female Athlete as Cultural Icon*. Minneapolis: University of Minnesota Press.

Howe, S. (1998). *(SICK) A Cultural History of Snowboarding*. New York: St. Martins Griffin.

Kane, M. J. (2013). 'The better sportswomen get, the more the media ignore them'. *Communication and Sport*. Online First. DOI: dx.doi.org/10.1177/2167479513484579: 95–98.

Kusz, K. (2007). *Revolt of the White Athlete: Race, Media and the Emergence of Extreme Athletes in America*. New York: Peter Lang Publishing.

MacKay, S. and Dallaire, C. (2012). 'Skateboarding women: building collective identity in cyberspace'. *Journal of Sport and Social Issues*. Online First. DOI: dx.doi.org/10.1177/0193723512467357: 548–566.

MacKay, S. and Dallaire, C. (2013a). 'Skirtboarder net-a-narratives: young women creating their own skateboarding (re)presentations'. *International Review for the Sociology of Sport*. Volume 48(2): 171–195.

MacKay, S. and Dallaire, C. (2013b). 'Skirtboarders.com: skateboarding women and self formation as ethical subjects'. *Sociology of Sport Journal*. Volume 30(2): 173–196.

MacKay, S. and Dallaire, C. (2014). 'Skateboarding women: building collective identity in cyberspace'. *Journal of Sport and Social Issues*. Volume 38(6): 548–566.

McLaughlin, L. (2004). 'The new roll model'. *Time Magazine*. Volume 164 (4): 74.

Markula, P. (1995). '"Firm but shapely, fit but sexy, strong but thin": the postmodern aerobicizing female body'. *Sociology of Sport Journal*. Volume 12: 424–453.

Markula, P. (2003). 'The technologies of the self: sport, feminism, and Foucault'. *Sociology of Sport Journal*. Volume 20: 87–107.

Markula, P. and Pringle, R. (2006). *Foucault, Sport and Exercise: Power, Knowledge and Transforming the Self*. London: Routledge.

Messner, M. (2002). *Taking the Field*. Minneapolis: University of Minnesota Press.

NGSA (2005). '2003 women's participation ranked by percent change'. www.nsga.org/public/pages/index.cfm?pageid=155 (accessed 12 September 2016).

Olive, R. (2013a). 'Blurred lines: women, subjectivities and surfing'. Unpublished PhD, University of Queensland.

Olive, R. (2013b). '"Making friends with the neighbours": blogging as a research method'. *International Journal of Cultural Studies*. Volume 16: 71–84.

Olive, R. (2015). 'Reframing surfing: physical culture in online spaces'. *Media International Australia, Incorporating Culture & Policy*. No. 155, June: 99–107.

Olive, R. and Thorpe, H. (2011). 'Negotiating the "F-word" in the field: doing feminist ethnography in action sport cultures'. *Sociology of Sport Journal*. Volume 28 (4): 421–440.

Owen, A. Stein, S. and Vande Berg, L. (2007). *Bad Girls: Cultural Politics and Media Representations of Transgressive Women*. Bern: Peter Lang Publishing.

Pavlidis, A. and Fullagar, S. (2014). *Sport, Gender and Power: The Rise of Roller Derby*. Farnham: Ashgate.

Pringle, R. (2005). 'Masculinities, sport, and power: a critical comparison of Gramscian and Foucauldian inspired theoretical tools'. *Journal of Sport and Social Issues*. Volume 29(3): 256–278.

Pringle, R. and Markula, P. (2005). 'No pain is sane after all: a Foucauldian analysis of masculinities and men's experiences in sport'. *Sociology of Sport Journal*. Volume 22: 472–497.

Prügl, E. (2015). 'Neoliberalising feminism'. *New Political Economy*. Volume 20 (4): 614–631.

Rinehart, R. (2005). '"Babes" and boards'. *Journal of Sport and Social Issues*. Volume 29 (3): 232–255.
Rottenberg, C. (2014). 'The rise of neoliberal feminism'. *Cultural Studies*. Volume 28 (3): 418–437.
Roy, G. (2013). 'Women in wetsuits: revolting bodies in lesbian surf culture'. *Journal of Lesbian Studies*. Volume 17 (3–4): 329–343.
The Stab Women's Rich List. (2014). *Stab Magazine*. 25 December. http://stabmag.com/news/the-2014-stab-womens-rich-list/ (accessed 28 March 2017).
Thornton, S. (1996). *Club Cultures: Music, Media and Subcultural Capital*. London: Wesleyan University Press.
Thorpe, H. (2006). 'Beyond "decorative sociology": contextualizing female surf, skate, and snow boarding'. *Sociology of Sport Journal*. Volume 23 (3): 205–228.
Thorpe, H. (2007). 'Extreme media: *Big Brother, Blunt, Jackass* and *Whiskey*'. In D. Booth and H. Thorpe (eds) *Berkshire Encyclopedia of Extreme Sport*. Great Barrington, MA: Berkshire.
Thorpe, H. (2008). 'Feminism for a new generation: a case study of women in snowboarding culture'. In S. Thompson, T. Bruce and C. Obel (eds) *Sporting Women's Success: Research about Women in Sport in New Zealand*. Waikato, NZ: Wilf Malcolm Institute.
Thorpe, H. (2009). 'Bourdieu, feminism and female physical culture: gender reflexivity and the habitus-field complex'. *Sociology of Sport Journal*. Volume 26: 491–516.
Thorpe, H. (2011). *Snowboarding Bodies in Theory and Practice*. Houndmills: Palgrave Macmillan.
Thorpe, H. (2013). 'Extreme media'. In D. Levinson and G. Pfister (eds) *Berkshire Encyclopedia of World Sport*. Great Barrington, MA: Berkshire Publishing Group.
Thorpe, H. (2014). *Transnational Mobilities in Action Sport Cultures*. Houndmills, UK: Palgrave Macmillan.
Thorpe, H. (2016). 'Action sports, social media, and new technologies: towards a research agenda'. *Communication and Sport*. DOI: 10.1177/2167479516638125.
Thorpe, H. and Olive, R. (2014). 'Gender politics in action sport cultures: the case of the Roxy promotional video'. Conference presentation at the *Sporting Females Conference* at University of Leeds, 4 September. www.youtube.com/watch?v=diePJQXsfEU (accessed 28 March 2017).
Wheaton, B. (2000). '"New lads?" Masculinities and the "new sport" participant'. *Men and Masculinities*. Volume 2: 434–456.
Wheaton, B. (2003). 'Lifestyle sport magazines and the discourses of sporting masculinity'. In B. Benwell (ed) *Masculinity and Men's Lifestyle Magazines*. Oxford: Blackwell Publishing.
Wheaton, B. (2013). *The Cultural Politics of Lifestyle Sports*. London: Routledge.
Wheaton, B. and Beal, B. (2003). '"Keeping it real": sub-cultural media and discourses of authenticity in alternative sport'. *International Review for the Sociology of Sport*. Volume 38: 155–176.
Wheaton, B. and Tomlinson, A. (1998). 'The changing gender order in sport? The case of windsurfing subcultures'. *Journal of Sport and Social Issues*. Volume 22: 251–272.
'Women a focus at ASR'. (2003). Press release, 3 September. Retrieved from www.expn.com

27
SEX AND HORROR

Steve Jones

The combination of sex and horror may be disquieting to many, but the two are natural (if perhaps gruesome) bedfellows. In fact, sex and horror coincide with such regularity in contemporary horror fiction that the two concepts appear to be at least partially intertwined. This is not to suggest that the sex-horror confluence is an exclusively contemporary phenomenon.[1] For instance, Hunter Gardner (2015) traces the lineage of contemporary psychosexual horror fiction back to antiquity. Brian Godaw (2002: 187–208) maps the relationship between sex and horrific violence in the Bible in order to anchor his exploration of modern horror cinema. Cathal Tohill and Pete Tombs (1995: 29) posit that the focus on violence and sex they find in Italian cinema is little more than 'a modern day version of the ancient Roman circus'; 'blood, passion . . . violence and sex were an integral part of these spectacles'.

It is unsurprising, then, that the horror genre boasts a bounty of sexual themes and sexually driven plots. The sex-horror relationship is sometimes connotative rather than overt; examples of this relationship range from the seduction overtones of *Nosferatu: Eine Symphonie des Grauens* (1922, dir. F.W. Murnau) and the juxtaposition of nudity and horror promised by European exploitation filmmakers (see Shipka, 2011: 5; Olney, 2013: 30), to *Hellraiser*'s (1987, dir. Clive Barker) sadomasochistic iconography. More overt explorations of sex are offered in horror films that are based around the porn industry, including *Zivot i Smrt Porno Bande/The Life and Death of a Porno Gang* (2009, dir. Mladen Djordjevic), *Muzan-e/Celluloid Nightmares* (1999, dir. Daisuke Yamanouchi) and *Quad X: The Porn Movie Massacre* (2015, dir. James Christopher). Many mainstream pornographic films have also explored horrific themes and utilised horror tropes. For instance, in *The Devil in Miss Jones* (1973, dir. Gerard Damiano), the eponymous protagonist is damned to a purgatory that is defined by her unfulfilled sexual desires; rape is a prevalent mode of sexual expression within violent Japanese *pinku eiga* (see Weisser and Weisser, 1998: 16; Wong and Yau, 2014: 33); and recent horror–porn crossover movies such as *The Walking Dead: A Hardcore Parody* (2013, dir. Joanna Angel) incorporate gore and archetypal horror characters (here, zombies) not just in the settings but also within pornographic sex sequences (see Marks, 2014).

In other cases, sex and horror are balanced in a manner that thoroughly blurs the distinction between porn and horror. For example, *Niku Daruma/Tumbling Doll of Flesh* (1998, dir. Tamakichi Anaru) is constituted by two lengthy sex sequences, followed by what is arguably the most horrific rape/mutilation sequence to be published in the Japanese micro-budget video market. The film's run-time is mainly composed of mundane pornography, yet its horrific crescendo is its most memorable segment. Although the film was marketed as gory horror – its finale dominates the video's packaging – its content is mainly focused on genitally explicit sex. Such subject-matter makes the film hard to classify in generic terms, but it also highlights that the two elements somehow fit together. In a more recent example, the 'dark-web' clip compilation film *MDPOPE: Most Disturbed Person on Planet Earth* (2013, dir. Thomas Extreme Cinemagore) juxtaposes real death footage with (mainly scatological) porn in a manner that blurs the boundaries between desire and disgust. *MDPOPE* thus implies that pornography can be both attractive and repulsive, while death footage can be simultaneously horrifying and titillating.

This sweeping overview is meant only to underline that the relationship between sex and horror – which I will refer to as 'sex-horror' to encompass the various combinations outlined above – is well established. The sustained presence of sex-horror in film suggests that these two elements fit together and the combination is a source of pleasure (entertainment, fascination, intellectual stimulation, and so forth) for many. Yet sex-horror is broadly perceived to be disturbing (see Hester, 2014: 119; Malone, 2011: 184). Where horror includes sex (or is presumed to include sex), moralistic critics have used labels such as 'gornography' and 'torture porn' to disparage those combinations (see Jones, 2013: 132). Despite the evident interest many individuals have in sex-horror, these negative reactions indicate that sex-horror is a source of trepidation, moral disdain or disgust for others. Thus, it appears that sex-horror inspires directly competing responses. One might conclude that sex-horror itself is paradoxical; that it holds two directly oppositional meanings simultaneously. However, as I will illustrate in this chapter, these dual responses are not as contradictory as they might first appear to be.

To begin, let us consider negative responses to sex-horror. In their bluntest form, these manifest as calls for censorship (see Hills, 2014; Petley, 2014). Sex-horror need not be explicit to incite censorship; even the juxtaposition (rather than merging) of sex and horror has been met with protest (see Caputi, 1992: 215; Ebert, 1981: 56; Russell, 1993: 155). Many such complaints have led to the outright banning of films that incorporate sex-horror. *A Serbian Film/Srpski Film* (2010, dir. Srdjan Spasojevic) is a notorious recent example; the film was banned in its uncut form in numerous countries (including Australia, Norway and Malaysia) because it contains: a) representations of consensual sex, rape and gory murder; b) juxtapositions of sex and horror; and c) scenes in which rape and murder are combined.

Routinely, such content is classified as 'obscene', and censorship is justified as a way of protecting the public from sex-horror. For instance, the landmark ruling *Miller v. California* (1973) evoked the public interest by positing that obscene materials contravene 'contemporary community standards'. The same sentiment is echoed in the UK Criminal Justice and Immigration Act 2008, which prohibits images that a 'reasonable person' – an average member of the populace – would find 'grossly offensive'. The British Board of Film Classification (BBFC) draws on that rhetoric in its guiding principles, one of which is to protect against 'retarding social and moral development, distorting a viewer's sense of right and wrong, and limiting their capacity for compassion' (BBFC, 2014). This same strategy for suppressing obscene images is echoed internationally. For instance, in 1977, Spain introduced the 'S' certificate to demarcate 'films that were likely to damage the sensibility of the viewer – in other words, sex and horror films' (Tohill and Tombs, 1995: 67). In another example, Section 3(1) of New Zealand's Films, Videos and Publications Classification Act

1993 defines an image as 'objectionable if it describes, depicts, expresses, or otherwise deals with matters such as *sex, horror*, crime, cruelty, or violence in such a manner that . . . is likely to be injurious to the *public good*' (emphasis added). More broadly, censorship groups typically posit that such materials will lead to 'moral decay'.[2]

Such complaints about moral and social deterioration are abstract in nature: it is not clear how representations of sex-horror have a corrosive impact on 'society' or 'morality' per se. The case is further confused by blurring the core elements of sex-horror as well as the line between fictional representation and reality. As Feona Attwood (2014: 1190) observes, within many anti-pornography arguments, 'reality and fantasy, sexual practices and representations, sex and violence have become so intertwined that they cannot be disentangled'. William Brown's claim (2013: 26) that the presence of 'sexually explicit' imagery in horror films 'makes it difficult to tell false from real' is underpinned by the same kind of conflation Attwood identifies. In this way of thinking, the sex-horror amalgamation confuses generic boundaries, but that confusion is made to stand in for an abstract problem regarding the distinction between reality and fantasy.

Those who seek to suppress sex-horror imagery typically garner support for their position by negating these complexities. The reality/fantasy 'problem' is re-configured into a proposal that exposure to sex-horror will have demonstrable negative impacts on its audience and society more broadly: that is, viewers who are exposed to sex-horror will be incited into committing acts of sexual violence. Although the media-effects model has been widely refuted (see Cameron and Frazer, 2000; Segal, 1993), the paradigm has numerous advantages for those who wish to suppress sex-horror. First, the complainant's inability to distinguish between fantasy and reality – which is intrinsic to the argument that fictional representations cause real crimes – is projected onto sex-horror's audience. Thus, the complainant need not justify their position because, they allege, it is sex-horror's *consumers* who fail to apprehend that fiction and reality are separate. Second, the vagueness about how sex-horror could cause social and moral deterioration is transmuted into a practical concern. According to this (flawed) logic, there is little need to engage with representations of sex-horror, or to understand why the combination is so disquieting to some; the problem is 'obvious', as is the 'solution' (censure).

This line of reasoning rose to prominence before the advent of horror or porn studies, both of which were ignited by scholars seeking alternatives to effects-based condemnation. Effects-based reasoning evidently influenced foundational work in these areas. For example, Linda Williams (1991) dubbed horror and porn 'body genres' based on their propensity to 'move' audiences. Although much more nuanced than the media-effects argument, Williams' paradigm begins from the premise that these films are significant because they have demonstrable affective impacts on viewers: horror scares or disgusts, while porn arouses.[3] Similar concerns are explored in Carol Clover's (1993) and Vera Dika's (1990) influential examinations of slasher movies. Both authors employ a psychoanalytic identification model to understand audience engagement,[4] suggesting that horror's antagonists achieve sexual gratification from killing, and that audiences vicariously attain voyeuristic sexual pleasure from watching horror.[5]

These early works did little to sway censorious complainants from the dual beliefs that sex-horror could cause an increase in real-world sexual violence,[6] and that sex-horror inculcates sadosexual pleasure.[7] In this view, sex-horror's target audience is an abnormal niche of people who do not share the majority's disdain for the sex-horror confluence (see, for instance, Jones, 2013: 47–51; also Hanich, 2010: 26). These presumptions are limited in two crucial ways. First, the target audience's responses are characterised as being homogeneous. However, given that sex-horror is presented as disturbing because the two elements supposedly do not belong together, one would expect to find evidence of multiple and/or conflicted responses within the target demographic, not just a divergence between the presumed audience's and the moral majority's views on sex-horror. Second, calls for censorship are frequently founded on (what are presumed to be) normative values, yet those values betray a set of 'moralistic assumptions about appropriate expressions of sexuality' (Carline, 2011: 326).

The ostensible sex-horror paradox stems from this unnecessarily limited vision of sexuality. Put bluntly, the moralistic position presents sex as being antithetical to horror, but this view fundamentally oversimplifies and misrepresents what sex is. Sex involves bodies (even if only imagined, or only one's own body). Bodies can be sources of disgust, and because sex commonly entails the exchange of various bodily fluids (such as saliva, sweat, vaginal juices, semen), sex can provoke fears about interpersonal pollution and pathogenic infection (see Chapman and Anderson, 2012: 63; Stevenson, Case and Oaten, 2011: 79; Tybur et al., 2011: 343). Genitals' proximity to excretory zones may also trigger related disgust responses (see McGinn, 2011: 193; Miller, 2009: 101–105). The moralistic characterisation of sex-horror severely underplays the importance of disgust to human sexuality. Acknowledging the affinities between sex and horror is imperative in developing sophisticated understandings of sex-horror.

The horrific side of sex has been considered in another of horror studies' foundational psychoanalytic works: Barbara Creed's *The Monstrous-Feminine* (1993). Creed focuses on genitals, gestation and castration within the horror-film context, acknowledging the connections between sex and corporeal horror. However, Creed's work suffers from the same flaw that plagues psychoanalytic textual analysis more generally: she focuses on symbolic content rather than on what is literally present onscreen. In fact, in the time that has elapsed since *The Monstrous-Feminine* was first published, many horror filmmakers have moved towards overt and literal depictions of sexual horror that render psychoanalytic interpretative methods redundant. Films such as *Teeth* (2007, dir. Mitchell Lichtenstein), *Bad Biology* (2008, dir. Frank Henenlotter), *Kiseichuu: Kiraa Pusshii/Sexual Parasite: Killer Pussy* (2004, dir. Takao Nakano), *She Kills* (2015, dir. Ron Bonk) and *One-Eyed Monster* (2008, dir. Adam Fields) present genitalia as a source of disgust and monstrosity, while *It Follows* (2014, dir. David Robert Mitchell), *Contracted* (2009, dir. Eric England), *Night of Something Strange* (2015, dir. Jonathan Straiton) and *Kannô Byôtô: Nureta Akai Kuchibiru/ The Slit-Mouthed Woman* (2005, dir. Takaaki Hashiguchi) are concerned with sexually transmitted infections.[8] These sex-horror films negotiate the complex terrain of pain, pleasure, disgust and attraction in an unambiguous fashion; psychoanalysis is not required to uncover repressed sexual horror in these cases.

Despite its shortcomings, Creed's work is notable for its serious engagement with psychosexual horror, and this area is worthy of greater scrutiny than it has received to date. Sex and horror overlap because they evoke some of the same phenomenal experiences and emotions (pleasure, disgust and so forth) to various degrees. Sex-horror is not an unholy union of opposites, in which horror is synonymous with harm and disgust while sex equates to pleasure and lust. Rather, their edges blur and merge. They are entangled, and so – at least sometimes – they belong together. Sex is not always a site of shared intimate pleasure; it is at least sometimes awkward, uncomfortable, painful, even traumatic. Simultaneously, horror is at least partially interlaced with drives regarding preservation of one's own life or the wellbeing of one's social grouping; horror narratives typically focus on displeasures (suffering, fear, anti-social behaviours, bodily damage, psychological anguish, and so forth) related to those impulses. Yet representations of such conditions do not exclude pleasure or preclude pleasurable responses.

The moralistic quest to censure representations of sex-horror entails denying these complexities in favour of over-simplified models such as the media-effects paradigm. In these suppressive discourses, horror and sex are presented as 'just bodily' matters (corporeally rather than cerebrally stimulating). Moreover, this connection with the physical is leveraged to characterise sex and horror as 'self-evident' (tangible, obvious) and unworthy of intellectual scrutiny (see Paasonen, 2012: 57; Williams, 1991: 4–5). Although sex-horror is condemned, the argument betrays an inability to sufficiently explain what is wrong with sex, horror or the sex-horror combination.

This gambit is indicative of what Haidt and Hersh term 'moral dumbfounding . . . the stubborn and puzzled maintenance of a moral judgment without supporting reasons', which 'seems to occur primarily when people have strong emotion-backed intuitions, as is often the case in matters involving sexuality' (2001: 194). Dumbfounding manifests as an 'inability to explain [moral "gut feelings"] verbally', leading towards the 'post hoc fabrication' of moral reasoning (Haidt, 2012: 25–26). It is precisely that form of dumbfounding that is evident in 'the inconsistencies, misunderstandings and deliberate legal manipulations of language and the interpretation of images' in obscenity cases involving sexual content (de Genevieve, 2007: 159).

Indeed, calls to censure sex-horror are typically marked by both conceptual confusion and a lack of detailed engagement with the films under scrutiny. For example, during the Minneapolis Public Hearings on Ordinances to Add Pornography as Discrimination Against Women in 1983, Ed Donnerstein referred to the infamous horror film *The Texas Chain Saw Massacre* (1974, dir. Tobe Hooper) as 'porn' in which 'women are killed in sexual ways' (Everywoman, 1988: 19–20). Yet the film contains no sex or nudity; the alleged 'sexual overtone' that makes *The Texas Chain Saw Massacre* a 'classic' example of sex-horror for Donnerstein (Everywoman, 1988: 20) is entirely of his own imagining. The same euphemistic projection of sex onto an asexual horror scenario is evident elsewhere in criticism of horror movies, and slasher films in particular. Critics commonly presume that for slasher-killers murder replaces sex (see Heba, 1995: 113);[9] as Cynthia Freeland has it, with 'orgiastic thrusting motions, the knife or other weapon obviously functions as phallus. *Everyone* knows (like the teenagers in *Scream*) what such violence "means"' (Freeland, 2000: 181, my emphasis). These proclamations reveal less about the film or the target audience than they do about the critic who perceives horror as sex and projects this evaluation onto 'everyone'.

Without a more nuanced understanding of the sex-horror confluence, the delegitimisation of such representations is nothing more than hollow rhetoric used to support taste judgements. It is particularly concerning that such insubstantial, subjective verdicts can become enshrined in law (see Carline, 2011: 327). Those who rally against sex-horror do not just limit the range of representations available; such censure also stigmatises sex-horror, and consequently territorialises even private contemplation of those perfectly natural elements. Perversely, suppression of sex-horror stifles our understanding not only of how complex representations of sex-horror are but also of how complex human sexuality is.

To illustrate, I will briefly consider a case study: *A Serbian Film*, a horror movie that has been widely censored as a result of flouting sexual taboos including necrophilia, paedophilia and rape.[10] The images that were (and were not) subject to censorship in this case reveal the dominant sexual norms of the moment. For instance, the most heavily censored sequence in the UK release involves a woman (Lejla) being suffocated by having a penis forced into her mouth, yet a scene in which a man (Tasa) is lobotomised by having a penis inserted into his eye-socket was left untouched. These parallel choices indicate that sexual violence perpetrated by men against women is less acceptable than male-on-male sexual violence. Indeed, by removing the former and not the latter, the BBFC perpetuates that norm.

A *Serbian Film* seeks to broaden the narrow vision of sex implied by such norms, demonstrating that sexual expression takes on a diverse array of non-normative forms. This enriched vision of sex adds depth to the characterisation, helping the audience to understand characters' motivations. For example, when Marko – brother of lead protagonist Milos – visits Milos's wife (Marija), Marko retires to the bathroom to masturbate both because he is aroused by being near her and in order to assuage (and thus gain control over) his desire for her. This sequence establishes Marko as a lonely, sexually frustrated character, and foreshadows the film's climactic sequence in which Marko rapes Marija as part of a pornographic production. Yet Marko's motivation is more fully explained in an intervening scene in which he receives oral sex from a prostitute while watching a video of Milos and Marija celebrating their son Petar's birthday. Footage of Petar being told to 'blow harder' to extinguish his birthday candles is intercut with Marko pushing the prostitute's head onto his penis in order to stimulate his failing erection (as she puts it, 'your animal is snoozing again'). The video then abruptly switches to a porn film starring Milos. Marko verbalises his jealousy over his brother's erection ('why isn't he fucking limp, like all the normal people?'). In the BBFC-certificated version of the film, the home-video footage of Petar's birthday (and the family's joy) is excised since it juxtaposes an image of a child with Marko's sexual activity. Yet that removal damages the audience's understanding of Marko's motivation. In the censored version, it appears that Marko is simply envious of his brother's sexual prowess. With the birthday footage in place, it is clear that Marko is jealous of Milos's familial happiness, and his envy is translated into a lament about Milos's prowess compared with his own impotence. That transference underscores how psychologically complex sexuality is. It also offers some explanation (but not *justification*) for why Marko rapes Marija in a scenario that pornographer Vukmir describes as a 'warm family home': Marko attempts to desecrate Milos's family because he feels excluded from their happiness. Consequently, the censored version portrays Marko as a one-dimensional monster; he is reduced only to the atrocity he commits because relevant information about his character is missing. Both cuts of the film condemn Marko's actions, but the uncut version offers a more psychologically nuanced account of Marko's sexual sadism, rather than abruptly revealing him to be an inhuman rapist as the censored version does.

Although many critics found the film's sex-horror irredeemably 'repulsive' even in its censored form (see Tookey, 2011), A *Serbian Film* does not eroticise sexual violence.[11] Indeed, the film could be interpreted as being highly critical of representations that eroticise degradation, particularly those found in extreme pornography. Within A *Serbian Film*, various behaviours that are characteristically found in extreme pornography are rendered as horrific acts of murder; for instance, Leija's and Tasa's deaths (detailed above) evoke the practices of cock-gagging and skull-fucking, respectively. Indeed, given that Milos's involvement with extreme porn leads to his own rape, that of his wife and child, and their subsequent suicides, the plot appears to vilify extreme pornography.

Even so, the film does not shy away from depicting behaviours that contravene sexual norms. In fact, A *Serbian Film* is also overtly critical of eschewing sex-horror to protect one's sensibilities. For example, when Milos is told to have sex with a child (Jeca), he holds his penis hostage by pressing a knife to his shaft, then launches himself out of a window. The absurd slapstick of his response pokes fun at the reactionary desire to forcibly distance oneself from taboo rather than negotiating one's offence in a more sensible fashion. Thus, A Serbian Film confronts its viewer with graphic displays of sex-horror, challenging audiences to manage their reactions to sexual taboo. The filmmakers do not simply seek to offend; they dare viewers to reflect on why sex-horror is offensive and how one reacts to sex-horror. As Schubert observes, A Serbian Film's 'challenging themes . . . provid[e] adults with a space where these issues can safely be explored' (2012: 146).

Furthermore, the film thrusts sex-horror into the limelight of public discourse. The film garnered attention for 'show[ing] unshowable things' (Spasojevic in Carey, 2011); that is, for portraying sex-horror in a public arena where that combination is typically eschewed. Consequently, journalists were challenged with finding ways of discussing that material and, as Scott (2011) notes in his review of the film, 'newspaper-friendly euphemisms do not really exist for the images Mr. Spasojevic conjures up'. Although the impetus to report on A Serbian Film demonstrates that sex-horror is of public interest, Scott's reflection indicates that the prevailing discourse is ill equipped to cope with sex-horror. That inadequacy reveals the need to openly address sex-horror, since eschewing and censuring it impoverishes the discourse. Confronting and being able to articulate the disgust, anger and disturbance that sex can generate is imperative to enriching our understanding of human sexuality. Sex-horror has the capacity to embody those aspects of sexuality, and to provoke precisely those forms of discussion.

Notes

1 My focus on horror film does not indicate that the sex-horror confluence is unique to film or to horror; rather, horror film is used as a sustained case study in order to illustrate the conceptual implications that follow from the handling of sex-horror within scholarly and legislative contexts.
2 See Strub, 2006: 258. For examples of how this plays out in public discourse regarding horror film, see Jones, 2013: 37.
3 The latter is echoed in the BBFC's classification of 'sex works' based on the assumption that their 'primary purpose is sexual arousal or stimulation' (BBFC, 2014: 6). Williams compares horror and porn, making direct reference to sex-horror as generically excessive (1991: 2), yet she does not explain precisely what responses or pleasures sex-horror combinations might elicit.
4 Far more nuanced and sophisticated models regarding audience reaction to horror film have been advanced in recent years. See, for example, Hanich, 2010; Plantinga, 2009; Strohl, 2012.
5 On the dominance of this model, see Dyer, 2002: 116; Hutchings, 2004: 195–196; Jenkins, 1994: 102.
6 Indeed, Clover and Dika's logic is echoed within censorial discourses; Martin Barker (2009: 58–60) has expressed concerns over the BBFC's unreflective appeal to identification-based media-effects models, for example.
7 This connection may have been fuelled by criminological literature suggesting that serial killers often have a history of being sexually abused, and are reputedly heavy users of porn (see Douglas, Burgess and Ressler, 1992: 25–26).
8 A bounty of recent horror films have also focused on pregnancy; on this trend, see Jones, 2015.
9 One defence for this position is that sex scenes and murder sequences are sometimes juxtaposed in slasher films. However, detailed engagement with the films themselves reveals that these juxtapositions are not as commonplace as is often presumed. Barry Sapolsky and Fred Molitor (1996: 46) demonstrate that juxtapositions of sex and murder are relatively rare in slasher films. They propose that slasher movies' reputation for combining sex and murder stems from misperception; when juxtapositions do occur, they are remembered more vividly than other incidents because they are more likely to offend audience members' sensibilities. Thus, sex-horror will be most prominent in an offended audience member's memory of the film *in toto* (see also Cowan and O'Brien, 1990: 187). For a discussion of the same dynamic in relation to more recent horror films, see Jones, 2013: 137.

10 For a detailed itinerary of countries that have rejected the film and cuts made to the UK release, see Kimber, 2014: 114–116.
11 Some critics, such as Brady (2010), acknowledge this. Others condemned the film without seeing it (see Johnston in Pascoe, 2011).

Bibliography

Attwood, F. (2014) 'Immersion: "Extreme" Texts, Animated Bodies and the Media'. *Media, Culture and Society*. Volume 36 (8): 1186–1195.
Barker, M. (2009) 'The Challenge of Censorship: "Figuring" out the Audience'. *The Velvet Light Trap*. Volume 63 (1): 58–60.
BBFC (2014) *BBFC Classification Guidelines 2014*. London: BBFC.
Brady, T. (2010) 'It Is Hell. It Is Not an Entertainment'. *The Irish Times*, 9 December. www.irishtimes.com/culture/film/it-is-hell-it-is-not-an-entertainment-1.686188 (accessed 28 March 2017).
Brown, W. (2013) 'Violence in Extreme Cinema and the Ethics of Spectatorship'. *Projections*. Volume 7 (1): 25–42.
Cameron, D. and Frazer, E. (2000) 'On the Question of Pornography and Sexual Violence: Moving Beyond Cause and Effect'. In D. Cornell (ed) *Feminism and Pornography*. Oxford: Oxford University Press.
Caputi, J. (1992) 'Advertising Femicide: Lethal Violence Against Women in Pornography and Gorenography'. In J. Radford and D.E.H. Russell (eds) *Femicide: The Politics of Woman Killing*. Buckingham: Open University Press.
Carey, A. (2011) 'Political Parable or Perversion?' *The Age* (Australia), 2 July. www.smh.com.au/entertainment/movies/political-parable-or-perversion-20110701-1gv0n.html (accessed 28 March 2017).
Carline, A. (2011) 'Criminal Justice, Extreme Pornography and Prostitution: Protecting Women or Promoting Morality?' *Sexualities*. Volume 14 (3): 312–333.
Chapman, H.A. and Anderson, A.K. (2012) 'Understanding Disgust'. *Annals of the New York Academy of Sciences*. Volume 1251 (1): 62–76.
Clover, C. (1993) *Men, Women and Chainsaws*. London: BFI.
Cowan, G. and O'Brien, M. (1990) 'Gender and Survival vs. Death in Slasher Films: A Content Analysis'. *Sex Roles*. Volume 23 (3–4): 187–196.
Creed, B. (1993) *The Monstrous Feminine: Film, Feminism, Psychoanalysis*. London and New York: Routledge.
de Genevieve, B. (2007) 'Censorship in the US or Fear and Loathing of the Arts'. *Social Identities*. Volume 13 (2): 159–173.
Dika, V. (1990) *Games of Terror: Halloween, Friday the 13th and the Films of the Stalker Cycle*. London and Toronto: Associated University Presses.
Douglas, J.E., Burgess, A.W. and Ressler, R.K. (1992) *Sexual Homicide: Patterns and Motives*. New York: The Free Press.
Dyer, R. (2002) *The Matter of Images: Essays on Representations* (2nd ed). London and New York: Routledge.
Ebert, R. (1981) 'Why Movie Audiences Aren't Safe Anymore'. *American Film*, March: 54–56.
Everywoman (1988) *Pornography and Sexual Violence: Evidence of the Links*. London: Everywoman.
Freeland, C.A. (2000) *The Naked and the Undead: Evil and the Appeal of Horror*. Oxford: West View Press.
Gardner, H.H. (2015) 'Curiosutas, Horror and the Monstrous-Feminine in Apuleius' Metamorphoses'. In M. Masterson, N.S. Rabinowitz and J. Robson (eds) *Sex in Antiquity: Exploring Gender and Sexuality in the Ancient World*. New York: Routledge.
Godaw, B. (2002) *Hollywood Worldviews: Watching Films with Wisdom and Discernment*. Madison: InterVarsity Press.
Haidt, J. (2012) *The Righteous Mind: Why Good People Are Divided by Politics and Religion*. New York: Pantheon Books.

Haidt, J. and Hersh, M.A. (2001) 'Sexual Morality: The Cultures and Emotions of Conservatives and Liberals'. *Journal of Applied Social Psychology*. Volume 31 (1): 191–221.

Hanich, J. (2010) *Cinematic Emotions in Horror Films and Thrillers: The Aesthetic Paradox of Pleasurable Fear*. New York: Routledge.

Heba, G. (1995) 'Everyday Nightmares: The Rhetoric of Social Horror in the *Nightmare on Elm Street* Series'. *Journal of Popular Film and Television*. Volume 23 (3): 106–115.

Hester, H. (2014) *Beyond Explicit: Pornography and the Displacement of Sex*. New York: SUNY Press.

Hills, M. (2014) 'Horror Reception/Audiences'. In H.M. Benshoff (ed) *The Companion to Horror Film*. Oxford: Wiley-Blackwell.

Hutchings, P. (2004) *The Horror Film*. Harlow: Pearson.

Jenkins, P. (1994) *Using Murder: The Social Construction of Serial Homicide*. New York: Aldine De Gruyter.

Jones, S. (2013) *Torture Porn: Popular Horror After Saw*. London: Palgrave-Macmillan.

Jones, S. (2015) 'Torture Born: Representing Pregnancy and Abortion in Contemporary Survival-Horror'. *Sexuality and Culture*. Volume 19 (3): 426–443.

Kimber, S. (2014) 'Transgressive Edge Play and *Srpski Film/A Serbian Film*'. *Horror Studies*. Volume 5 (1): 107–125.

McGinn, C. (2011) *The Meaning of Disgust*. Oxford: Oxford University Press.

Malone, A. (2011) *Censoring Hollywood: Sex and Violence in Film and on the Cutting Room Floor*. Jefferson: McFarland.

Marks, L.H. (2014) '"I Eat Brains . . . or Dick": Sexual Subjectivity and the Hierarchy of the Undead in Hardcore Film'. In S. McGlotten and S. Jones (eds) *Zombies and Sexuality: Essays on Desire and the Living Dead*. Jefferson: McFarland.

Miller, W.I. (2009) *The Anatomy of Disgust*. Harvard: Harvard University Press.

Olney, I. (2013) *Euro Horror: Classic European Horror Cinema in Contemporary American Culture*. Bloomington: Indiana University Press.

Paasonen, S. (2012) *Carnal Resonance: Affect and Online Pornography*. Cambridge: MIT Press.

Pascoe, A. (2011) 'Row over Violent Film'. Sunday Herald Sun (Australia), 21 August. www.heraldsun.com.au/ipad/row-over-disturbing-violent-film/news-story/b61d335fd771434b5b6e7c3d32b23727 (accessed 28 March 2017).

Petley, J. (2014) 'Horror and the Censors'. In H.M. Benshoff (ed) *The Companion to Horror Film*. Oxford: Wiley-Blackwell.

Plantinga, C. (2009) *Moving Viewers: American Film and the Spectator's Experience*. Berkeley: University of California Press.

Russell, D.E.H. (1993) 'The Experts Cop Out'. In D.E.H. Russell (ed) *Making Violence Sexy*. Milton Keynes: Open University Press.

Sapolsky, B.S. and Molitor, F. (1996) 'Content Trends in Contemporary Horror Films'. In J.B. Weaver and R. Tamorini (eds) *Horror Films: Current Research on Audience Preferences and Reactions*. New Jersey: Lawrence Erlbaum.

Schubert, C. (2012) 'Film Classification and Censorship'. *Alternative Law Journal*. Volume 37 (2): 145–146.

Scott, A.O. (2011) 'Torture or Porn? No Need to Choose'. *The New York Times*, 13 May. https://mobile.nytimes.com/2011/05/13/movies/a-serbian-film-directed-by-srdjan-spasojevic-review.html (accessed 28 March 2017).

Segal, L. (1993) 'Does Pornography Cause Violence? The Search for Evidence'. In P. Church-Gibson and R. Gibson (eds) *Dirty Looks: Women, Pornography, Power*. London: BFI Publishing.

Shipka, D. (2011) *Perverse Titillation: The Exploitation Cinema of Italy, Spain and France 1960–1980*. Jefferson: McFarland.

Stevenson, R.J., Case, T.I. and Oaten, M.J. (2011) 'Effect of Self-Reported Sexual Arousal on Responses to Sex-Related and Non-Sex-Related Disgust Cues'. *Archives of Sexual Behavior*. Volume 40 (1): 79–85.

Strohl, M. (2012) 'Horror and Hedonic Ambivalence'. *The Journal of Aesthetics and Art Criticism*. Volume 70 (2): 203–212.

Strub, W. (2006) 'Perversion for Profit: Citizens for Decent Literature and the Arousal of an Antiporn Public in the 1960s'. *Journal of the History of Sexuality*. Volume 15 (2): 258–291.

Tohill, C. and Tombs, P. (1995) *Immoral Tales: European Sex and Horror Movies 1956–1984*. New York: St. Martin's Griffin.

Tookey, C. (2011) 'It's Not Just the Internet That's Full of Violent Porn – So Are the Cinemas'. *Daily Mail*, 1 November. www.dailymail.co.uk/news/article-2055937/Christopher-Tookey-Its-just-internet-thats-violent-porn–cinemas.html (accessed 28 March 2017).

Tybur, J.M., Bryan, A.D., Lieberman, D., Caldwell Hooper, A.E. and Merriman, L.A. (2011) 'Sex Differences and Sex Similarities in Disgust Sensitivity'. *Personality and Individual Differences*. Volume 51 (3): 343–348.

Weisser, T. and Weisser, Y.M. (1998) *Japanese Cinema Encyclopedia: The Sex Films*. Miami: Vital Books.

Williams, L. (1991) 'Film Bodies: Gender, Genre, and Excess'. *Film Quarterly*. Volume 44 (4): 2–13.

Wong, H. and Yau, H. (2014) *Japanese Adult Videos in Taiwan*. London: Routledge.

Media

A Serbian Film/Srpski Film (2010) Directed by Srdjan Spasojevic [Film]. Serbia: Jinga Films.

Bad Biology (2008) Directed by Frank Henenlotter [Film]. USA: Media Blasters.

Contracted (2009) Directed by Eric England [Film]. USA: IFC.

The Devil in Miss Jones (1973) Directed by Gerard Damiano [Film]. USA: MB Productions.

Hellraiser (1987) Directed by Clive Barker [Film]. UK: Entertainment Film.

It Follows (2014) Directed by David Robert Mitchell [Film]. USA: Radius TWC.

Kannô Byôtô: Nureta Akai Kuchibiru/The Slit-Mouthed Woman (2005) Directed by Takaaki Hashiguchi [Film]. Japan: Kokuei Company.

Kiseichuu: Kiraa Pusshii/Sexual Parasite: Killer Pussy (2004) Directed by Takao Nakano [Film]. Japan: Total Media Corporation.

MDPOPE: Most Disturbed Person on Planet Earth (2013) Directed by Thomas Extreme Cinemagore [Film/Doc]. USA: MDPOPE.

Muzan-e/Celluloid Nightmares (1999) Directed by Daisuke Yamanouchi [Film]. Japan: Japan Video Distribution.

Night of Something Strange (2015) Directed by Jonathan Straiton [Film]. USA: Duke.

Niku Daruma/Tumbling Doll of Flesh (1998) Directed by Tamakichi Anaru [Film]. Japan.

Nosferatu: Eine Symphonie des Grauens (1922) Directed by F.W. Murnau [Film]. Germany.

One-Eyed Monster (2008) Directed by Adam Fields [Film]. USA: Liberation Entertainment.

Quad X: The Porn Movie Massacre (2015) Directed by James Christopher [Film]. USA: Twitchy Dolphin.

She Kills (2015) Directed by Ron Bonk [Film]. USA: SRS Cinema.

Teeth (2007) Directed by Mitchell Lichtenstein [Film]. USA: Lionsgate.

The Texas Chain Saw Massacre (1974) Directed by Tobe Hooper [Film]. USA: Bryanston Distribution.

The Walking Dead: A Hardcore Parody (2013) Directed by Joanna Angel [Film]. USA: Wicked.

Zivot i Smrt Porno Bande/The Life and Death of a Porno Gang (2009) Directed by Mladen Djordjevic [Film]. Serbia: Synapse Films.

28
SEX IN SITCOMS
Unravelling the discourses on sex in *Friends*

Frederik Dhaenens and Sofie Van Bauwel

Introduction

Chandler: Alright. I'll sleep with my girlfriend . . . But I'm just doing it for you guys.
(season 4, episode 11)

The sitcom – essentially a prime-time family genre, and one whose conventions are generally determined by a 'comic impetus' (Mills 2009: 5) – has long dealt with sex and sexuality. Elana Levine (2007: 169–207) points out how sexually suggestive humour and sexual themes such as homosexuality and promiscuity were present in 1970s American television sitcoms such as M*A*S*H (1972–83), Happy Days (1974–84), Soap (1977–81) and Three's Company (1977–84). The fascination with sex and sexuality in sitcoms has not faded. To this day, it is considered a key characteristic of many sitcoms – especially those labelled as 'sexcoms', such as Ally McBeal (1997–2002) and Sex and the City (1998–2004) (Ross, 2005; Scodari, 2005), as many of the conversations and episode themes deal with sex. However, since sitcoms are predominantly commercial and family-friendly products, they tend to suggest or insinuate sex instead of explicitly depicting it.

Scholars have produced contradictory readings of the ways in which sitcoms represent sex and sexuality. Some argue that sitcoms adhere to a conservative societal view. Attalah (1984), for instance, stresses that sexuality in sitcoms is domesticated by articulating sex to marriage and monogamy. Kim et al. (2007) confirm this while demonstrating that American sitcoms represent heterosexual scripts more often than is the case in drama. They argue that this could be partly explained by the prevalence of masculinised representations of sex, which resonates with Brett Mills' observation that both heterosexuality and masculinity are represented as the norm in sitcoms (2005). Similarly, Christine Scodari (2005) points out that sitcoms represent feminine topics (including sexuality) in a trivial, shallow and hegemonic way, and thereby reinforce binary gender relations and fixed gender identities. Others point out the genre dynamics of exaggerating and extrapolating traditional views on sex in order to mock and parody them. Frederik Dhaenens and Sofie Van Bauwel (2012) demonstrate how the adult animated sitcom succeeds in using postmodern representational strategies to subvert the sitcom genre conventions, including heteronormative conceptions of gender and sexuality, from within. Alexander Doty (1993), on the other hand, argues that sitcoms enable audiences to read the shows against the grain and uncover queer desires even though the main characters are represented as heterosexual. Joanne Morreale (2003: xii) reminds us of sitcom's ambiguity regarding social change, which is underscored by the genre's integration of multiple contradictory discourses to attract as many audiences as possible. However, Mills (2009: 5) warns that too often the interpretation of these multiple discourses ignores or downplays the genre's use of humour. Agreeing that the genre's comic impetus needs to be taken into account, this chapter aims to map and interpret the multiple discourses on sex that circulate within a single sitcom, namely the 'classic' sitcom *Friends*, which ran from 1994 to 2004.

Even though the final episode aired more than ten years ago, this long-lasting popular sitcom is still profiting from ongoing international distribution and broadcasting (e.g. Blu-Ray and DVD sale, re-runs) and merchandise (e.g. coffee mugs, t-shirts), and is considered a landmark television show and a point of reference for many. For the six central characters – three white heterosexual women and three white heterosexual men in their twenties and thirties – sex is an essential part of life. We aim to focus on how the series tackles sex practices, activities and desires, rather than taking a broad approach to sexuality or sexual identity. We inquire into how *Friends* represents sex practices, to what discourses these practices are articulated and what these articulations signify.

Situating the study of sitcoms and *Friends*

To interpret discourses on sex in sitcoms, we need to take genre conventions into account. Jason Mittell (2004: 8–11) has considered genres as discursive formations, shared notions that come out of a complex relation between texts, industries and audiences. Nonetheless, due to the genre's many differentiations, it is impossible to speak in general terms about its ideological dimensions. We agree with Jane Feuer (1992: 146) that sitcoms rely on stereotypes, a half-hour format, situations that unsettle and which are (mostly) resolved at the end of the episode and, most importantly, humour. For Mills, humour is the key characteristic of the genre (2009: 5). This humour can be read in different ways, leading for example to discussions about whether representations of racial, ethnic, gender or sexual identities are harmful stereotypes or critical representations that mock the process of stereotyping (Gray, 2006; Dhaenens and Van Bauwel, 2012). For Feuer (2008: 83), this investment in depicting ideological conflicts in an entertaining fashion typifies the genre and explains its longevity. The genre has ideological flexibility, because some hegemonic ideas within a sitcom might be challenged and reversed over the course of seasons. Hence, an inquiry into the meanings of a single sitcom starts from an acknowledgement of its own particularities and conventions in relation to the interpretive community in which it is produced and consumed. That is why we do not map what different scholars have argued about the representation of sex in sitcoms, but instead narrow our scope to the series at stake in this study.

Media scholars have described *Friends* as reinforcing hegemonic discourses with regard to class, gender, ethnicity and race. Phil Chidester (2008: 160) focuses on how the series privileges whiteness, portraying the white main characters as comprising a closed and mono-ethnic group that goes to great lengths to limit the relations it has with racialised and ethnic others. Race is never explicitly broached, thereby rendering whiteness as the only normative reference point. Naomi R. Rockler (2006b: 454) argues that the series treats identity issues as 'problems of the past that have been eradicated and replaced with equality'. These post-identity politics obscure and minimise sociocultural inequalities while implying that emerging identity conflicts are personal and depoliticised problems. Rockler (2006a) considers the series a typical postfeminist product: the political dimension of gender is rendered invisible, and female empowerment can only be successful if perceived as an individual and self-fulfilling endeavour. Jillian Sandell (1998), however, stresses the discursive ambiguities of the text when it comes to gender. Based on a reading of the first four seasons, she argues that the series is engaged in challenging heteronormative accounts of family by focusing on the failures of traditional heterosexual coupling and favouring alternative ways of cohabitation and family formation. Yet the series fails to challenge gender roles, demonstrating that 'men and women *are* fundamentally different, even hip urban young men and women of the 1990s, and that gender divisions should be respected and maintained' (Sandell, 1998: 149, emphasis in original). This interpretation is confirmed by Margo Miller (2006), who points out that the men in particular aspire to hegemonic masculinity and 'correct' one another when failing to live up to the masculine norm or when expressing same-sex intimacy. This is often articulated by means of an ironic dismissal, a strategy that allows the intimate bond between heterosexual men to be desexualised, and reinforces strict sex and gender binaries.

The few scholars who deal with sex in *Friends* point to similar dynamics. Mills (2005), agreeing that the sitcom reiterates masculinity and heterosexuality as the norm, stresses that sex is strongly linked to the male characters, whereas the female characters serve as bodies that can be (sexually) objectified: 'successful masculinity – or, at least, masculinity which isn't mocked – is one which treats women as sex object[s] and denies any emotional core' (Mills, 2005: 113). Mills (2005: 114) and Rockler (2006a: 258) agree that Phoebe, one of the three main female characters, is allowed to express her sexuality, but both stress that she is represented as the goofy outsider, whose sexuality is often used as part of the comedy. Finally, Sandell (1998) looks at the sitcom's representation of sex as something that is always traumatic – potential 'love' interests are seldom accepted by the friends, while romantic and sexual desires for one another are presented as inappropriate or bound to fail (clearly, this account was produced when the sitcom was still running).

This chapter explores whether these critical readings still hold up when taking all seasons into account. To this end, we conducted a thematic textual analysis of 25 episodes, selected from across all ten seasons.[1]

Depicting sex: messing with metaphors

Our discussion of the series' representations of sex starts with an inquiry into the ways in which sex is depicted in the sitcom. Many of the selected episodes deal with sex practices in a straightforward manner, albeit predominantly as a topic of conversation. Sex is represented as something that needs to be scrutinised, and as such, it turns up in plenty of conversations. Yet the series also makes fun of how to speak about sex acts. Some conversations refer explicitly to sex but just as many use metaphors and in-jokes, a characteristic of sitcom genre. However, *Friends* often has its characters deconstruct the in-joke or mock the prudish metaphor. For instance, 'The one with Phoebe's uterus' (season 4, episode 11) begins with a conversation in which Chandler confides that he has not yet had sex with his new girlfriend, Kathy, who used to date Joey. A sniggering Ross assumes that Chandler is afraid that he 'won't be able to fill [Joey's] shoes'. Chandler, visibly annoyed, rephrases Ross's words, saying that he fears he will not be able to make love like Joey. The scene reveals that Chandler shows little concern about masking his insecurity regarding sex, and Ross becomes the butt of the joke instead.

Besides talking about it, sex is insinuated by means of before and/or after scenes. Even though these scenes are often accompanied by hesitant discussions about how to have sex with one another for the first time and evaluations of the sex just had, they remain implicit. Nonetheless, the series does push boundaries in a few scenes by having characters mimic sex. A prime example can be found in 'The one with the chicken pox' (season 2, episode 23). This features the return of Ryan, a Navy soldier who hooks up with Phoebe every two years for a short but passionate period. Phoebe and Ryan, however, contract chicken pox. Two scenes depict the couple in particularly ambiguous situations. In the first scene, the couple are playing Monopoly; in the second, they are at dinner. In both scenes, they initially fight the urge to scratch themselves and each other, but they eventually give in to the desire. The screams, gasps and moans are intended to mimic the sounds of sexual activity. For instance, Phoebe shouts: 'You know you want it. You know you want it too. Let's just be bad. It feels so good.' 'The one with Phoebe's uterus' features a representation of an orgasm in a scene where Monica and Rachel teach Chandler how to please a woman. Monica draws the body of a naked woman and points out seven erogenous zones. While demonstrating these she gets more and more aroused, eventually orgasming on the couch, unable to pronounce the number of the final zone.

Discursive meanings of sex practices

Our reading of *Friends* began by pointing out the various ways in which the series represents sex. This section will look closely at the discursive meanings embedded in these representations. Without claiming to be exhaustive, our analysis demonstrates that the show articulates its sex practices to four sets of discourses.

Discourse of feelings

First of all, sex is represented as something that needs to be frequently discussed and scrutinised. Sex is considered a key element of the fabric of the series and connected to all sorts of emotions and thoughts. In other words, many of the conversations and discussions that reflect on sex rely on a *discourse of feelings*. In particular, the episodes deal with expectations and evaluations of sex. All of the main characters discuss with their friends the sex they have had or might soon be having. Like the in-jokes that mock prudishness, these scenes defy the puritan attitude that sex is a strictly private matter and that conversations about it should not be held between members of both sexes. Even though the battle of the sexes often resurfaces, it is not used as a means to fortify the idea that men and women are essentially different, as Sandell (1998) reads into the series. Our analysis showed that all characters tap into a discourse of feelings when it comes to speaking about sex and often connect with one another, regardless of gender. For instance, Phoebe seeks advice from Joey (season 2, episode 7); Chandler asks Monica and Rachel how to please a woman (season 4, episode 11; discussed above); and Ross goes to Joey for suggestions on how to seduce a woman (season 8, episode 4). Even Joey, the most self-assured character when it comes to lovemaking, doubts his skills from time to time. In 'The one with the sharks' (season 9, episode 4), for example, Joey expresses insecurity about his sexual performance because of a girl who seems unable to remember having sex with him.

This example also illustrates that expectations and evaluations go hand in hand with doubts, frustrations or shame. From a genre perspective, it seems logical to represent sex as a source of conflict. 'The one with the videotape' (season 8, episode 4), for instance, features a closing scene in which Ross and Rachel watch a videotape of themselves having sex. Remembering the night as great, they settle down into a chair and start watching the video. The video is initially experienced as entertaining. However, when they witness themselves having actual sex, they are repulsed and run to the television set to turn it off, reiterating the common trope that sex is deeply problematic. The episode represents sex as something that should be privately experienced, not 'publicly' watched, even if the person you are watching with was your sexual partner. Having two characters who used to be intimate with one another express shame and disgust over their own sexual bodies can also be read as a rejection of the realness of sex in favour of beautified porn imagery, which is often consumed by the male characters throughout the series. It confirms what Mills (2005) identified as articulations to trauma in *Friends*, even though this does not apply to all the sitcom's representations of sex.

Discourse of desires and fantasies

A second significant discourse is the *discourse of desires and fantasies*. Even though the characters may experience doubts and insecurities, they seldom mask their desires. When Phoebe, who works as a masseuse, desires the body of a male client in 'The one with the ballroom dancing' (season 4, episode 4), she repeatedly shares her desires with her friends. Even though she knows she is not allowed to engage with clients sexually, she fails to abstain, in one instance 'innocently' biting his buttocks, which she was initially busy massaging. She is caught and finds out the client is married.

This episode is no exception to the rule. Episodes that broach the topic of sexual fantasies also articulate the discourse of desires and fantasies to a discourse of norms and values. The most common sexual fantasy presented is role-playing, especially between Ross and Rachel. Nonetheless, the implied fantasies remain gender-normative and relatively tame: to please Rachel, Ross dresses up as a Navy soldier to re-enact the final scene of *An Officer and a Gentleman* (season 2, episode 23), while Rachel wears a gold bikini to impersonate Princess Leia (season 3, episode 1) and a naughty cave woman (season 9, episode 4). The fantasies are also unsatisfactory, designed to evoke laughter because of their failure or awkwardness. Throughout the series, it seems that the best sex is the vanilla kind.

From this perspective, it is interesting to see how the double 'what if' episode of the sixth season, 'The one that could have been, parts one and two' (season 6, episode 15 and episode 16), is used to explore sexual desires and fantasies. This hypothetical setup is used to exaggerate certain personal traits or rewrite personal histories: Ross has not yet discovered that his wife Carol is a lesbian; Rachel did not leave her husband-to-be at the altar; Phoebe is a successful stockbroker; and 'fat' Monica is still a virgin. The most transgressive moment comes from Phoebe suggesting to Ross how to spice up his sex life:

> You could tie her up, she could tie you up. You could eat stuff off each other. Dirty talk, ménage à trois, toys. Role-playing, you could be the warden, she could be the prisoner. You could be the pirate, she could be the wench . . . you could be two stockbrokers, and you're rolling around naked on the trading floor and everybody's watching.

While Phoebe is generally represented as sexually progressive, she is allowed to acknowledge that explicitly in this episode. Ross discusses several of Phoebe's suggestions with his wife and they engage in a threesome with Susan, whom regular viewers will recognise as the woman who becomes Carol's wife. Yet, because of the episode's special status, this transgression remains part of a safe and controlled fantasy space within the series.

Discourse of norms and values

The series articulates various sexual practices to a discourse of norms and values, illustrating the argument that Laurent Berlant and Michael Warner (1998) make about sex in contemporary societies – that sex is not a private issue, since both the private and public expressions and experiences of all sorts of intimacies are governed by heteronormativity. In *Friends*, the expression of desires is often overshadowed or controlled by norms and values, with a heavy reliance on humour to do so. Comedy genres are able to tackle transgressive topics more bluntly than drama, but humour is also a means that is able to depoliticise, defuse or ridicule sensitive themes. Mills (2005) argues that to understand the sitcom's ideological position, the type of humour used in relation to the series or episode's narrative needs to be considered when scrutinising the series' norms and values. For the most part, *Friends* remains consistent throughout its ten seasons in reiterating certain norms and values. One of these is that sex is pleasure. Aligning itself with the sex-positive message of postfeminist television culture (Adriaens and Van Bauwel, 2014), the show emphasises the fun and pleasurable aspects of sex. However, the need to be good at sex is also a pressure. In 'The one with Phoebe's uterus', Chandler is afraid to fail at sex because it has to be good, and his fears are confirmed in the episode; his first night with Kathy only qualifies as mediocre, and Monica and Rachel try to make him understand that the female sexual body is complex.

This episode also articulates a second norm: romance without (good) sex is not possible. In each episode in which a character confesses that s/he has not yet had sex with a new partner, they are asked if there is something wrong. Chandler is insecure about whether he will be good enough in bed for his girlfriend (season 4, episode 11); Phoebe wonders if she is not sexy enough (season 2, episode 7); and in the 'what if' double episode, Monica – who is still a virgin in this universe – is considered a fool for waiting to have sex with her partner: 'Oh, my God. Do it! Honey, you've waited long enough' (season 6, episode 15). The inability to have sex is also the reason why relationships fail: Rachel and Joey split up after they fail to make love (season 10, episode 3). 'The one with Rachel's inadvertent kiss' (season 5, episode 17) features a storyline in which otherwise confident Monica panics over not having enough sex in her relationship with Chandler, accentuating the importance of sex in the everyday lives of young adults. This is equally apparent in the representation of single characters. Frequently, jokes focus on the length of time a character has been going through a 'dry spell' (e.g. Ross in season 8, episode 4).

Yet *Friends* favours a monogamous relationship as the ideal setting for sex. Even though this is largely unspoken, a few episodes do explore alternatives to monogamy. In 'The one with the butt' (season 1, episode 6), Chandler is dating a woman who is polyamorous. The male characters see this as a great opportunity for Chandler, but later he ends the relationship because he wants his girlfriend all for himself. While it is possible for characters to have sex without engaging in a relationship, serial monogamy is the norm.

However, the series does not assume a clear position in all matters that relate to sex. The ambiguity that typifies many popular culture products (Hall, 2005) manifests in *Friends* through the representation of contesting norms without favouring one or the other.

Mills (2005) considers the series as engaged in representing a hegemonic masculinity in which sex should be disarticulated from emotion, referring to how Chandler and Ross fail to adhere to this norm and how this is continuously mocked. Yet Chandler also learns that good skills and attentiveness to the female body are more efficient for good sex than simply being in love (season 4, episode 11), and Phoebe tells Joey that 'sex can be just about two people right there in the moment' (season 2, episode 7).

Friends also raises questions about 'good' and 'bad' sexual practices. Rubin has argued that sexuality is hierarchically organised in terms of good, normal or natural sex (e.g. heterosexual, married, monogamous, reproductive, at home) and bad, abnormal or unnatural sex (e.g. homosexual, unmarried, promiscuous, non-procreative, in public). Depending upon the specific sexual behaviour, individuals and activities can be either rewarded, tolerated, suppressed or punished (Rubin, 1993: 12–14, 34). As Rubin acknowledges, mores can change. In *Friends*, public sex is far from frowned upon; several characters have had sex in public or considered it. In 'The one with Rachel's inadvertent kiss', Phoebe and her boyfriend Gary casually mention to Monica that they had sex in the park and state with smiles that they thus 'violated section 12 paragraph 7 of the criminal code'. Monica rushes to the men's room to try to convince Chandler to have sex in there. Sex in public is presented here as adventurous and exciting. Some practices, however, put characters in hazardous or compromising situations. For instance, in 'The one with the cuffs' (season 4, episode 3), Chandler ends up being cuffed to a chair with his pants down in the office of Rachel's boss, Joanna, and is caught by Rachel. In 'The one with the ick factor' (season 1, episode 22), Monica pretends to be younger to have sex with a man who, in turn, is pretending to be older. When Monica discovers, after having sex with him, that he is a high-school student, she expresses her repulsion, although the sex was good. By explicitly telling the student that what they did is considered a criminal act in certain states, she renegotiates the experience as 'bad' sex.

A final example of ambiguity concerns the way the series treats same-sex desire. Miller (2006) argues that *Friends* falls back on ironic dismissal when male characters express some form of same-sex desire. Although the show features few lesbian or gay characters (e.g. the occasional appearance of Ross's ex-wife Carol and her partner Susan), many jokes depend on the misinterpretation of a certain gesture or look as an expression of homosexuality. Yet the show does not resolve all ambiguity. In 'The one with Ross's tan' (season 10, episode 3), Joey tells Chandler about the moves he makes during foreplay. Joey says that he looks a woman in the eyes, kisses her and continues by gently grazing her thigh. To demonstrate, he grazes Chandler's thigh, and Chandler responds by saying: 'I see what you mean. That's quite nice.' Joey nods with a complacent smile, but when they look up into each other's eyes they jump back to their feet and exclaim that they need to play foosball and drink beer. Two other scenes in the episode recall the homosexual moment. The first time, when his move fails to get Rachel in the mood, Joey refers to how 'Chandler loved it'. The second time, Chandler cannot understand how Rachel was unable to get turned on by that move. Though such moments are brief, they nonetheless return throughout the series – each time, homosexual intimacy is dismissed but not forgotten.

Discourse of power

Related to the discourse of norms and values is the discourse of power. Even though any discursive practice is always concerned with power, certain instances in *Friends* explicitly articulate sex practices to power. This is apparent in episodes where Joey uses sex to further his acting career. After being offered the role of a recurring character, he sleeps with the casting lady (season 2, episode 10), and he later sleeps with a female journalist in order to censor an opinion he expressed during an interview that could harm his career (season 8, episode 18). In this way, the series represents sex as having exchange value; however, rather than seeing this as exclusively linked to the female sexual body (Pateman, 1988), the show represents male sexuality as a means for upward mobility.

These examples also illustrate a second aspect of the discourse of power, namely the representation of sex in a hierarchical relation. What is remarkable is how the series features plenty of moments in which the male characters assume a subordinate role in a sexual relationship. In 'The one with the cuffs', Chandler confides that he likes sleeping with a woman who is in a powerful professional position and who also claims that role in the bedroom. The female characters, on the other hand, are sometimes represented as sexually interested in men who are, from a societal perspective, in a more fragile position: Monica has sex with a minor (season 1, episode 22); Rachel begins a relationship with her younger male assistant (season 7, episode 9); and Phoebe seduces her male massage client (season 4, episode 4). The clichéd storyline of a man with power seducing a powerless woman is thus repeatedly inverted. Yet ambiguity reigns here as well. For example, the female characters often learn that occupying a superior position does not lead to a relationship, which remains their main concern.

Conclusion

Despite its comic impetus and carefree setting, the sitcom should not be treated lightly. For Mills (2005), sitcoms are popular products that are able to reach large audiences and, as *Friends* shows, may become a point of reference for many men and women in contemporary Western societies. As our analysis of the show reveals, next to friendship and love, sex is a key trope throughout all seasons. While sex is not depicted explicitly, it is a topic of conversation and talk, mostly disguised in metaphors or insinuated by means of before/after sex scenes.

In contrast to earlier readings of the series by Mills (2005), Rockler (2006a) and Sandell (1998), our analysis of the ways in which *Friends* represents sex reveals much more ambiguity. In the four types of recurring discourses (discourse of feelings, discourse of desires and fantasies, discourse of norms and values, discourse of power) that are articulated to sex-related practices, many instances stress different ideological perspectives. The series reiterates heteronormative ideas about sex (e.g. monogamy), while deconstructing them in other instances. Both men and women express their feelings when it comes to sex and some transgressive sex acts are considered pleasurable and possible options. Key within this process is humour, which works to highlight and mock the ambiguity discovered. As Feuer (2008) argued, sitcoms have an ideological flexibility which, with regard to the representation of sex, is present even within single episodes. The ways in which *Friends* uses this to show different perspectives on sex without expressing value judgements challenges the expected ways in which sex has been articulated in sitcoms.

Note

1 To delineate our sample of episodes, we only selected episodes in which sex formed a pivotal theme. To ensure all seasons were included, three episodes were selected out of each of the first five seasons and two episodes out of each of the last five seasons. Since sex was a more dominant theme in the first five seasons, we chose to include more episodes from these to ensure a more thorough overview of the different kinds of discourses used in the series.

Bibliography

Adriaens, F. and Van Bauwel, S. (2014) '*Sex and the City:* A postfeminist point of view? Or how popular culture functions as a channel for feminist discourses', *Journal of Popular Culture*, 47(1): 174–95.

Attalah, P. (1984) 'The unworthy discourse. Situation comedy in television' in W.D. Rowland and B. Watkins (eds) *Interpreting television: Current research perspectives*, Beverly Hills: Sage.

Berlant, L. and Warner, M. (1998) 'Sex in public', *Critical Inquiry*, 24(2): 547–66.

Chidester, P. (2008) 'May the circle stay unbroken: *Friends*, the presence of absence, and the rhetorical reinforcement of whiteness', *Critical Studies in Media Communication*, 25(2): 157–74.

Dhaenens, F. and Van Bauwel S. (2012) 'Queer resistances in the adult animated sitcom', *Television & New Media*, 13(2): 124–38.

Doty, A. (1993) *Making things perfectly queer: Interpreting mass culture*, Minneapolis: University of Minnesota Press.

Feuer, J. (1992) 'Genre study and television', in R.C. Allen (ed) *Channels of discourse, reassembled. Television and contemporary criticism* (2nd ed), Chapel Hill and London: University of North Carolina Press.

Feuer, J. (2008) 'Situation comedy, part 2', in G. Creeber (ed) *The television genre book* (2nd ed). London: British Film Institute.

Gray, J. (2006) *Watching with the Simpsons: Television, parody, and intertextuality*, New York: Routledge.

Hall, S. (2005) 'Notes on deconstructing "the popular"' in R. Guins and O.Z. Cruz (eds) *Popular culture: A reader*, London: Sage.

Kim, J.L., Sorsoli, C.L., Collins, K., Zylbergold, B.A., Schooler, D. and Tolman, D.L. (2007) 'From sex to sexuality: Exposing the heterosexual script on primetime network television', *Journal for Sex Research* 44(2): 145–57.

Levine, E. (2007) *Wallowing in sex: The new sexual culture of 1970s American television*, Durham and London: Duke University Press.

Miller, M. (2006) 'Masculinity and male intimacy in nineties sitcoms: *Seinfeld* and the ironic dismissal' in J.R. Keller and L. Stratyner (eds) *The new queer aesthetic on television: Essays on recent programming*. Jefferson, NC: McFarland & Company.

Mills, B. (2005) *Television sitcom*, London: British Film Institute.

Mills, B. (2009) *The sitcom*, Edinburgh: Edinburgh University Press.

Mittell, J. (2004) *Genre and television*, New York: Routledge.

Morreale, J. (2003) *Critiquing the sitcom: A reader*, New York: Syracuse University Press.

Pateman, C. (1988) *The sexual contract*, Stanford: Stanford University Press.

Rockler, N. (2006a) '"Be your own windkeeper": *Friends*, feminism, and rhetorical strategies of depoliticization', *Women's Studies in Communication*, 29(2): 244–64.

Rockler, N. (2006b) '*Friends,* Judaism and the holiday armadillo: Mapping a rhetoric of postidentity politics', *Communication Theory*, 16(4): 453–73.

Ross, S. (2005) 'Talking sex: Comparison shopping through female conversation in HBO's *Sex and the City*', in M. Dalton and L. Linder (eds) *The sitcom reader: America viewed and skewed*, Albany: State University of New York Press.

Rubin, G.S. (1993) 'Thinking sex: Notes for a radical theory of the politics of sexuality', in H. Abelove, M.A. Barale and D.M. Halperin (eds) *The lesbian and gay studies reader*, London: Routledge.

Sandell, J. (1998) 'I'll be there for you: *Friends* and the fantasy of alternative families', *American Studies*, 39(2): 141–55.

Scodari, C. (2005) 'Sex and the sitcom: Gender and genre in millennial television', in M. Dalton and L. Linder (eds) *The sitcom reader: America viewed and skewed*, Albany: State University of New York Press.

29
SEX AND REALITY TV
The pornography of intimate exposure

Misha Kavka

Whether as an explicit accusation, a sidelong swipe or a coy implication, reality TV has long been associated with pornography. From the moment that Endemol, the Dutch production company behind *Big Brother*, launched its 'social experiment' in 1999 to see what would happen when 12 ordinary people were confined together in a house under the watchful eye of mounted and manned television cameras, many commentators reached for the rhetoric and logic of pornography to express their fascinated revulsion. As a term that encompasses the simultaneously transgressive, shocking and enticing, pornography has been repeatedly used as a fitting analogy for reality TV's own transgressions of staged visualisation, the word seeming to click effortlessly into place to describe the graphic exposure of intimate contact between real bodies that is common to both genres. But is this simply a metaphor, or does the modality of pornography offer insight into, rather than just condemnation of, the purpose and function of reality TV? The answer requires coming to terms not only with the definitional limits of pornography but also with its ambivalent metaphoricity, especially as it enters the mainstream and its reach extends to zones where mediation and pleasure overlap – and where 'porn' may well connote libidinally charged acts of looking at images that strictly speaking have nothing to do with sex, such as 'food porn' or 'real-estate porn'.[1] At the same time, it is important to acknowledge that there is also a literal applicability of the term 'porn' to reality TV, given the numerous moments when cameras capture non-simulated sexual encounters in reality TV settings, even though such depictions 'feel' quite different from hardcore pornography. As I shall examine, this difference of feeling results from the way in which reality TV has reframed the definition and production of intimacy, which in turn has exerted considerable influence on the ways in which recent pornographic forms index realness (Patterson, 2004; Longstaff, 2013).

There is also more at stake here, however, for the iterative relation between reality TV and pornography points to the way in which the mention of sexuality and sexual practice seems almost inevitably to lead back to questions of reality, while attempts to probe the depths of reality, conceived as the 'truth' of the subject, often discover sexuality at its kernel. On the one hand, this can be historicised in terms of Michel Foucault's claim (1990) that the nineteenth-century emphasis on confession, or speaking the 'truth' of the self, required confession specifically of and about sex – a historical condition from which we have certainly not yet been freed. On the other hand, in the specific context of reality TV, this alone does not explain why the 'proof' of its reality appears to rely so strongly on sexual revelation, or why the mediation of intimate reality-events should tease us with the possibility, even the (disavowed) hope, that we will see porn. As Jon Dovey astutely notes in his study of camcorder culture, 'Domestic video cameras have a habit of finding their way into the bedroom at some point' (2000: 69) – a point echoed in Susanna Paasonen's coining of the phrase 'domestic pornotopia' (2011: 105–9) to describe the abundance of amateur videos that depict 'domestic spaces (living rooms and bedrooms) as sites of both porn consumption and production' (2011: 83). What is revealed here is the interdependence of reality and pornography *as an effect of domesticised mediation*, which promises both to document truth and to stimulate fantasy. In order to gauge the role of television in this constellation, reality TV must be addressed not as a debased genre of popular culture that sits one rung above porn, but rather, like pornography itself, as a visualisation of erstwhile private domains that exposes, often to viewers' distaste, the simultaneously fantasmatic and socially regulated relation between sexuality, reality and intimacy.

Under the covers

The connection between pornography and reality TV has been made in a variety of critical contexts, albeit usually in a metaphorical vein. Sam Brenton and Reuben Cohen, in one of the first books on the provenance of reality television, blithely refer to 'the pornography of the performing self' (2003: 53) in their discussion of reality game shows such as *Survivor*, thereby implying indecent – presumably both excessive and eroticised – self-exhibition. More consistently, the term 'pornography' has been used to reference the socially transgressive exposure of emotion on reality TV, not only by critics but also by industry insiders. Anita Biressi and Heather Nunn, for instance, quote British television producer Victoria Mapplebeck's approving use of the term 'hardcore' for reality shows that expose raw emotion (2005: 30). Influenced by Laura Grindstaff's argument that moments of heightened emotion on talk shows operate like 'money shots' in pornography because they offer 'external, visible proof of a guest's inner emotional state' (1997: 169), scholars such as Aslama and Pantti (2006) and Rachel Dubrofsky (2009) have used the money-shot analogy to draw attention to the displacement of the graphically climactic sex acts of porn onto the graphically climactic emotional acts of reality TV. According to Dubrofsky, moreover, the pornographic analogy highlights the patriarchal resonances between the two genres, since both require the hyper-expressive face and body of a woman – whether in the throes of orgasm or despair – in order for the climax to become visible, as is particularly evident in dating and marriage shows such as *The Bachelor*. As Biressi and Nunn point out, the framing of reality TV as emotional pornography also draws out generic similarities in the provision of 'extensive "access" and the opportunity to "look" at their subjects unchallenged' in both genres (2005: 30). June Deery takes the argument one step further by noting that, in reality TV and pornography, not only do viewers pay 'to see the conscious performance of something usually private and intimate', but both often involve performers 'agreeing to exposure for money' (2015: 46), which in turn highlights not only the commercial nature of these genres but also the morally uncomfortable exchange of privacy for profit.

Interestingly, the argument about an emotional pornography of reality TV obscures a key contradictory valence of the relationship between porn and reality TV, since emotion (as opposed to sexual arousal) is precisely what is closed out of classical pornography. With minimal narrative and characterisation – just enough to bring two or more bodies together and support the viewer's entry into the fantasy – pornography tends not to delve into the complications of emotional states or connections. 'Intimacy' in pornography is purely a matter of physical proximity and private acts, whereas on reality TV, as the scholars above have noted, intimacy is first and foremost an emotional condition. The same distinction functions in reverse, for while emotion appears front and centre in the diegesis of reality TV shows, sex – not to mention signs of sexual arousal – has largely been hidden under the covers, quite literally, in a negotiation between domestic video cameras' 'habit of finding their way into the bedroom' and the social norms, as well as media regulatory systems, that deem public sex indecent and even perverse.

Take, for instance, the following composite image: a camera mounted in a shared bedroom frames a mounded-up duvet on a bed, at a distance and angle common to surveillance cameras. The room is dark but the camera is equipped with night vision: the image is gritty, low-contrast, black-and-white – perhaps with a green tinge – and altogether difficult to make out, and hence difficult to treat as a representation. In the semiological terminology of Charles Peirce, indexicality overwhelms symbolism here. For the viewer, straining to make sense of this image so closely indexed to the reality TV setting, the only signs of people in the frame are the movements and possibly noises occurring under the duvet, from initial fumblings to the up-and-down rhythm that signals sex, all awkwardly carried out by bodies attempting to stay hidden under bedclothes. This opaque, moving mound captured in the uncanny grey wash of night-vision technology is iconic of the 'sex under a blanket' scenes that have graced reality TV screens from *Big Brother* to *Geordie Shore* and beyond, causing titillated outrage in countless ancillary media outlets.[2] The low visibility and surveillance-camera technology means that this kind of scene is hardly sexy in any softcore sense, but the camera does record actual – or, in the words of the pundits, 'live' – sex. So is it pornography?

Simon Hardy, surveying the development of pornographic subgenres such as gonzo, amateur and cyberporn,[3] argues that 'we are entering the era of reality porn', as pornographic producers strive for ever greater authenticity. This 'decisive shift in the pornographer's longstanding goal of greater realism', amounting to a change 'in the qualitative nature' of pornography (Hardy 2008: 60), has been largely driven by the availability of domestic recording technologies, supplemented by the development of online distribution platforms. From the 1980s onward, the entry of amateurs and pseudo-amateurs into porn production through home video, camcorder and digital technologies has caused a change in the style and content of pornography that goes hand in hand with a significant recalibration, if not outright blurring, of the distinction between the public and the private, as well as between fantasy (e.g. the idealised bodies and production values of professional pornography) and authenticity (bound to 'ordinary' bodies and 'amateur' camera techniques). Although this recalibration in favour of behind-the-scenes authenticity is part of a global media trend that can be traced back to the deregulation and tabloidisation of media culture in the 1980s/90s, for our purposes it is worth noting that by the early 2000s pornography was moving 'toward' reality at the same time as reality TV was moving 'toward' dramas of intimate encounter (Kavka, 2012), with both genres co-opting documentary strategies of immediacy in the service of intimacy.

This is not to say, however, that 'reality porn' is equivalent to sex on reality TV, especially if measured against a more literal definition of pornography. Following Linda Williams in her now-classic book *Hard Core: Power, Pleasure, and the 'Frenzy of the Visible'* (1989), we might argue that hardcore pornography encompasses (a) the event of real sex, (b) recorded in explicit detail, (c) framed and edited according to generic conventions, with the aim of (d) producing sexual arousal in the viewer and (e) generating profit from its distribution. Measured against these key components, reality TV's iconic 'sex under a blanket' scenes fall short: they are not shot in explicit detail, they do not follow the aesthetic conventions of hardcore porn and their primary intent is not to arouse viewers (although it should be pointed out that PornHub sports a number of 'reality TV sex' categories, which indicates the ease with which media objects can be repurposed for pornography). These divergences can be summarised as a radical reduction of visibility on reality TV, and hence in Williams' terms a reduction of visible evidence for the sexual act, since there are no close-ups of genitalia, no framed faces experiencing sexual pleasure, no cum shots and rarely any bodies to be seen. The sex act itself has to be assumed, derived from movements and noises that connote rather than confirm its 'real' status; indeed, the question of whether someone actually had sex on reality TV is usually a point of avid discussion after the fact, often by the ancillary media on the morning after or by participants themselves once they leave the show.

Rather than depending on a representational 'frenzy' of visible evidence, in Williams' phrase, the night-vision capture of bodies moving under bedclothes offers *indexical* evidence of sexual encounter. As Dovey has noted, the low-definition image signals authenticity by bearing the traces of a domestic or surveillance camera filming in a particular place and time; the technological mode of production, in other words, does not erase itself but is indexically materialised in the footage. By the late 1990s, argues Dovey, 'the low grade video image ha[d] become *the* privileged form of TV "truth telling", signifying authenticity and an indexical reproduction of the real world' (2000: 55; original emphasis). The night-vision lens of iconic reality TV sex scenes enhances this 'quality of indexical accuracy' (ibid: 65), since the footage bears the technical imprint of the conditions under which sex occurred, including the participants' unwillingness to appear *in flagrante*. In failing to adopt the key visual conventions of pornography, then, reality TV sidesteps representation and instead provides 'proof' of sexual encounter through an affective indexicality. Rather than visible evidence, the fact that two (or more) people dare to have sex on camera – even, or especially, under the covers – delivers an affective charge, a thrill arising from the broken norms of what TV has previously allowed us to see, that serves as both the stamp of authenticity and the *ersatz* for sexual arousal. In fact, the less visible the sexual act, the greater the participants' implicit acknowledgement of social transgression and thus the greater the affective charge, precisely because something must be extracted from the visual field as the condition for showing 'real' sex – rather than pornography – on television.

Instead of simply showing sex, the night-vision scenes on reality TV show an index of sex while shrouding the act itself. This technical shrouding of sex moves beyond the 'truth telling' associated with televised low-gauge video of the 1990s to night vision as a technology of intimacy that indexes both proximity and relationality between the participants. The indexicality of sex on TV thus does not push towards realism, but rather towards a relational affectivity that secures the authenticity of the intimate encounter. The mistaken assumption about such night visions is that viewers want to *see more* sex than is on offer; rather, 'sex under a blanket' scenes work because viewers want to *feel* the authenticity of these relationships whose erotic pull is so great, even if momentarily, that the participants must seek a porous privacy under covers. Indexicality in these night visions has suspended its referent; the reference becomes the affect of its absence, since without meat shots, viewers do not know whether actual sex has occurred or not. At the same time, indexicality produces an affect which is real whether or not the event is there. Pornography cannot produce this because it remains caught in the relay between representation and reality, whereby the latter is always undermined by the mediation and performance required to achieve the former. Reality TV, precisely because it shows less, breaks out of the representational circuit into the zone of affective authenticity, which itself induces relationality. For the iconic reality TV scenes of night-vision sex, where the duvet slips but never falls, the fascination is not with the pornographic act, which is missing from the visual field, but with everything surrounding the sex: the talk before and after, the foreplay, the will-they-or-won't-they suspense, as well as the have-they-or-haven't-they debates. It is in the emotional minutiae of intimate encounters that real(ity) sex on TV distinguishes itself from pornography.

Full-frontal, full-blown on *Showtime*

I have yet to make the obvious point, namely that the screening of graphic sexual acts on mainstream television is heavily regulated, if not outright banned, in most countries, and hence television (unlike, say, cinema) is an anti-pornographic medium. This results not only from censorship laws which aim to protect children as well as anyone offended by such images, but more largely from television's own history as a domestic medium whose programming works in the service of the family – itself configured, at least in the West, as an ideological formation which polices and regulates sexuality. In recent years, however, this has not prevented nudity from appearing on mainstream channels, where 'mainstream' means accessible to anyone with a digital TV subscription in the UK and Europe[4] or a basic-cable digital subscription in the US. In fact, in a volte-face from 'sex under a blanket' scenes on cohabitation programmes, American broadcasters began experimenting with nudity-based reality TV in 2013 in shows such as *Naked and Afraid* (June 2013–), a hetero-survivalist series on the Discovery Channel ('they have no clothes, no food, no water – only their skins, and their will to survive!') and *Buying Naked* (TLC, November 2013–), a real-estate show with nudists searching for homes in 'clothing optional' communities. These programmes were followed in 2014 by the seemingly inevitable yoking of dating formats with nudity, which first appeared on Dutch television (RTL5, March 2014) as *Adam Zkt. Eva* (*Adam Seeking Eve*), an Edenic-parable format that was quickly adopted by other European countries and substantially overhauled for US television as the aptly titled *Dating Naked* (VH1, July 2014–).

Notably, though, before reality TV went naked on mainstream channels, it had already gone pornographic on particular US premium-cable channels. By 'pornographic' here I simply mean programmes that include graphic footage of sexual activity, such as the genre-bending *Gigolos* on Showtime, which premiered in April 2011, followed by *Polyamory: Married and Dating*, also on Showtime, premiering in July 2012. Both of these shows are notable for their multi-camera, full-visibility coverage of unsimulated sex acts; moreover, rather than the sex being incidental, as on cohabitation programmes, sex acts are thematically central to these programmes' narrative arcs, visual rhythms and confessional interviews. This certainly blurs the line between reality TV and pornography, but it does not actually overturn television's status as an anti-pornographic medium, since, as I will argue, these programmes set strict conditions on overt sexual display. Even behind a premium pay wall, the modes of screening sexual activity remind us that there are socially derived televisual norms, media regulations and, especially, genre conventions at play which limit what and how sex appears.

Prior to 2011 there had been precursors to putting real sex on TV for premium-cable subscribers short of the outright 'adult' channels. In June 1990 HBO launched what would become its long-running, if sporadically scheduled, magazine-style programme *Real Sex* (1990–2009), which borrowed the multiple short-segment format popularised by *60 Minutes* to focus on a mix of racy sexual topics (e.g. striptease), niche sexual sites and performances (e.g. sex shops) and sex education (e.g. 'How to please a penis', ep. 24). Moving in the other direction, the Playboy channel began diversifying its offerings by dabbling in reality formats, with dating shows such as *Foursome* (Playboy TV, 2006–11), in which four singles spent 24 hours in a house together engaged in sexually oriented play, as well as the reality talent show *Jenna's American Sex Star* (Playboy TV, 2005–6), hosted by porn queen Jenna Jameson, in which porn-industry hopefuls competed in sexual performances in front of an expert panel before being voted out by viewers. There has also long been a traversable line between the reality TV and porn industries when it comes to casting participants, with porn performers seeking mainstream visibility (and paycheques) on reality TV (e.g. *Survivor Thailand*, *Flavor of Love*: see Clark-Flory, 2011) while some reality TV contestants have leveraged their popularity into a centrefold or even a porn career (cf. Longstaff, 2013). But none of these various forays – which tend to signal pornographic content through programme title, subscription channel and named performers – have resulted in the 'jarring dissonance' that Tracy Clark-Flory ascribes to *Gigolos*, whose first episode apparently made the *Salon.com* writer squirm so much that she broke her office chair (2011). The 'dissonance' generated by the appearance of graphic sex in *Gigolos* and *Polyamory* arises from the fact that these shows are both porn *and* 'ordinary' reality TV. Rather than pornography borrowing from reality TV formats in order to increase authenticity effects, *Gigolos* and *Polyamory* embrace their status as reality TV, making the 'sex' part of 'sexual intimacy' secondary to, and a quotidian component of, intimacy *per se*.

In an article on early amateur porn websites, 'ranging from camgirls who show a little skin periodically to professional produced shots of . . . airbrushed and implanted women', Zabet Patterson argues that consumers on these sites purchase 'a fantasy of private access to a person', of which the specifically pornographic element is only a small part (2004: 111, 112). Rather, consumers engage in 'a "relationship" based on and created through the purchase of intimacy' (112), which extends beyond outright sexual activity to the 'secondary activities' such as 'eating sushi, baking cookies and buying pizza' that are included in online amateur porn (119). Reversing the conventional argument about the purpose of pornography being sexual arousal, Patterson radically claims that

> the sexual activities [on these amateur sties] are somehow less important than the other activities. It suggests the possibility that even the graphic sexuality within amateur porn exists mainly as an incitement for subjective identification with the performer, for this ever-fuller sense of participation with that performer's life, and that it is this ever elusive relationship, in effect, that itself becomes the obscure object of desire.
>
> (Patterson, 2004: 119)

Writing in 2004, Patterson is not discussing reality TV, and yet within a decade she easily could be. In fact, given that by the mid-2010s camgirls had become highly professionalised YouTube vloggers with promotional contracts while amateur porn videos had morphed into sex tapes promoting brand personas, it is reality TV which now carries the legacy Patterson describes of 'secondary activities becom[ing] primary' in the construction of mediated intimacy as an obscure object of (pornographic) desire. On reality TV, even graphic sex ultimately works in the service of relationality, rather than vice versa, as in pornography. This means that, while sex scenes in reality shows may receive the most critical attention and PVR replay, it is the footage of participants reflecting on the meaning of sex for their relationships – whether talking endlessly with one another or to camera, in a mundane kitchen, living room or bar – that generates both the purpose and the appeal of these shows.

Showtime has unashamedly led the field in the graphic sexualisation of reality TV intimacy, with its entertainment president, David Nivens, stating in January 2011 that the network aimed to incorporate 'late-night adult shows featuring sex' as 'part of what we offer' (Maerz, 2011). Although one can only speculate about the boardroom discussions leading to this strategic shift, it seems possible to trace it back to the impact of a memorable sexual encounter in Season 1 of *The Real L Word* (Showtime, 2010–12), when two cast members, Romi Klinger and Whitney Mixter,

> distinguished themselves [through] . . . their willingness to cross the 'porn' line by granting [producer Ilene] Chaiken permission to use graphic footage of them having wild, drunken sex with a reportedly unwashed strap-on dildo at a 'white trash' theme party.
>
> (Heller, 2013: 11)

As Tara Shea Burke notes of her shock at seeing a scene such as this on reality TV, rather than the usual 'dark rooms, subtitles and blankets covering the action', '[s]urely this was the first time for American television in general, let alone lesbians' (2013: 216). Given that only Klinger and Mixter were recast for Season 2 of *The Real L Word* and that *Gigolos* began its six-season run a year later, it seems that a connection can be drawn from the unanticipated strap-on encounter to a formal, if experimental, strategy adopted by Showtime. While the participants on these shows do not strictly have sex for a living (the men on *Gigolos* are technically escorts, we learn, not prostitutes), they do willingly have sex for the camera, but largely as a form of *affective* labour.

An analysis of *Gigolos* makes it clear that the show differentiates itself from the representational conventions of porn, despite the central scenes of graphic sex. On this programme, which follows five men who work for the 'elite' Las Vegas-based escort agency Cowboys4Angels, sex scenes usually occur at least three times per episode. In terms of framing and editing, though, producers are careful to excise the visible signifier of sexual arousal, the erect penis (and, indeed, most penis shots, despite many shots of nudity and *in medias* sexual intercourse), as well as any signifiers of sexual climax, with the possible exception of women's moans and gasps – but these, as Linda Williams has noted, are notoriously difficult to pin down as signifying climax, hence the central function of the cum shot in hardcore porn. This is a scopic regime beyond the phallus, which shifts attention to a different affective purpose than bodily arousal. Notably, in the first episode to Season 2, a sex session with Brace, the mature buck of the agency, includes numerous shots that would not have been out of place in hardcore domestic porn (e.g. kitchen-counter sex that starts with a close-up of the woman's hands gripping the edge of the counter before reframing to the man hard at work behind her), but the scene fast-forwards to the sexual denouement of two bodies happily depleted on a couch, erasing the climactic moment. Rather, any suggestion of a pornographic climax is displaced onto a later segment involving Brace at home watching porn on his laptop, of which viewers can only hear the audio track, and explaining to his visitor, fellow gigolo Nick, that he is doing 'research' because 'just straight-up fucking is no good anymore'. The distinction is clear: porn is the wild stuff that can be accessed on a laptop, while reality is the normal fare that can be accessed on TV. On the porn-laptop, men 'face-fuck these women until they vomit', while on reality TV Brace assures us, in a to-camera interview between graphic sex sequences, 'For me it's not all about sex. I'm more into maybe trying to connect with somebody and getting to know them so they know me as a person'. This is echoed in the selection of sex scenes in the last episode of Season 2, two of which involve gigolos with their girlfriends rather than clients. When Brace talks about connecting with somebody rather than being 'all about sex', he could be – and in effect is – talking about the pleasure of reality TV itself.

This pleasure, even when drawn from sexually graphic reality shows, turns out to have political potential, especially in the reminder that non-heteronormative sexuality operates in the larger context of relationships bound by community, family and – as these shows reiterate like a mantra – love. Writing about *Polyamory*, whose first two seasons intercut between a foursome (of two married hetero-couples) and a trio (of one married hetero-couple and their girlfriend), *Gawker*'s Rich Juzwiak notes that 'it works not just as the freak show that we've come to expect from reality TV, but also on a political level' because it tests viewers' belief in 'the fundamental principle of sexual equality' (2012). He argues, moreover, that the complicated intimacy of polyamorous groups is perfectly suited to reality TV, since both require ongoing self-reflection on and negotiation of the rules that allow these forms of relational play to persist: 'with or without cameras pointed at them, [t]he show was already going on.' In between lengthy reflections on the tension between polyamorous love practices and jealousy, the show adds generous helpings of sexual activity in couples, trios and groups, with a particular emphasis in Season 1 on sex between women. These sex scenes include hardcore elements of oral and penetrative sex, but are presented through softcore aesthetic conventions, such as a close-up of a hand on a breast and closely framed faces whose smiles telegraph loving pleasure rather than the pouts or grimaces of pornographic passion. Even among these softcore conventions of representation, reality TV indexicality comes into play, as there is little attempt to hide the multiple cameras, from a ceiling-mounted cam to hand-held shots at different vantage points, elegantly (and self-consciously) edited together into a triple split-screen effect that dissolves one shot position into another.

This is meant to be beautiful rather than gritty sex, in a paean to the programme's central emphasis on 'amory', which translates into love equality. As trio member Anthony says, 'You should never be telling people how to live their private lives, tell them what kind of family [they] should have. And it's amazing that most people accept this but can't make the connection with poly' (cited in Juzwiak, 2012). Of course, having sex before reality TV cameras is not the traditional interpretation of living 'private lives' – a point of discomfort for many viewers, whether politically progressive or conservative; Dana Heller summarises this difficulty as 'the controversial question of whether [graphic on-camera sex is] grossly and unnecessarily exploitative or socially revolutionary in its depiction of . . . sexual agency and pleasure, or an unsettling combination of both' (2013: 10). For Juzwiak, *Polyamory* 'is at once a cautionary tale and an argument for the freedom to participate in these kinds of living/loving situations' (2012). Just as Juzwiak is caught between the framings of a cautionary tale and an argument for freedom, so the jury remains out on the controversial question framed by Heller. And yet, while the affective labour of the participants on these shows is framed by discomfiting reminders that they are involved in the material practices of sex work, the shows themselves are doing another kind of full-frontal work for viewers, to do with the exposure not (just) of bodies but of contradictory yet highly restrictive social norms.

Reality TV is easily connected to pornography because it is a frontalising medium, which gives affront because it brings to the fore that which had been behind the scenes, in putatively private spaces which have historically never been beyond the reach of social and juridical law. The lure of reality TV lies precisely in the fantasy on offer that we viewers will see 'behind' the scenes, will always see *more* – but in fact we never do see the 'real'. What are instead exposed, through feeling, are our own standards of judgement, splayed out on the bed for discussion and dissection of whether this is a grossly exploitative or socially progressive visibility. This brings its own buzz, suggesting that the reality quotient of pornography – and the pornographic quotient of reality – has to do with our confrontation with our own standards, themselves constructed through the libidinal labour of belonging that Christina von Braun has called 'sex with the group' (2000). Reality TV may adopt the content of pornography, but it gives to pornographic activity a sense of emotional intimacy that positions it firmly within the 'ordinary', indeed the real, space of sex – even if you're a gigolo.

Notes

1 The distinction between metaphorical and literal uses of 'porn' is so slippery that one of the few scholarly articles to directly address 'food porn', a term used predominantly in the context of beautifully shot TV cooking programmes, argues for its terminological mis-application (McBride, 2010), while 'real estate porn', used colloquially to describe the practice of trawling through online photos of high-end properties one cannot afford to buy, is at the same time a thriving gonzo subgenre on online porn sites (e.g. a man goes to see a property, holding a camera because his partner supposedly can't be there, and finds an attractive, young real estate agent on-site with whom he strikes a sex-for-sale deal).
2 Examples of such titillation range from Kerstin and Alex, who 'wrote their way into *Big Brother* history' (FocusOnline, 2010) by having sex under a blanket in the first season of German *Big Brother* in 2000 (when asked about the event ten years later by the FocusOnline interviewer, Alex admitted to being surprised by how 'good the night camera was'); through *Teen Big Brother: The Experiment* (Channel 4, 2003), which is credited with showing the first 'live' sexual act on British television; to the regular tabloid discussions of which couple has had or will have the now proverbial 'first sex in house' on *Celebrity Big Brother* in the UK.
3 'Gonzo' porn is a subgenre characterised by the pornographer's participant–observer status, usually signalled by point-of-view shots and hand-held cameras. 'Amateur' denotes homemade porn or pornography made to look homemade, while cyberporn refers broadly to pornography available online.
4 In the UK and continental Europe, a digital subscription usually consists of all free-to-air channels plus a selection of homegrown digital-only and imported basic-cable broadcasters.

Bibliography

Aslama, M. and Pantti, M. (2006) 'Talking alone: reality TV, emotions and authenticity'. *European Journal of Cultural Studies*. Volume 9 (2): 167–84.

Biressi, A. and Nunn, H. (2005) *Reality TV: Realism and Revelation*. London and New York: Wallflower Press.

Brenton, S. and Cohen, R. (2003) *Shooting People: Adventures in Reality TV*. London: Verso.

Burke, T.S. (2013) 'Why *The Real L Word* matters: community and lesbian sex, in the flesh'. In D. Heller (ed) *Loving the L Word: The Complete Series in Focus*. New York: I.B. Tauris.

Clark-Flory, T. (2011) 'How reality TV ruined porn'. *Salon*. 10 April. Online. www.salon.com/2011/04/10/gigolos_2/ (accessed 15 May 2016).

Deery, J. (2015) *Reality TV*. Cambridge, UK and Malden, MA: Polity Press.

Dovey, J. (2000) *Freakshow: First Person Media and Factual Television*. London: Pluto Press.

Dubrofsky, R. (2009) 'Fallen women in reality TV: a pornography of emotion'. *Feminist Media Studies*. Volume 9 (3): 353–68.

FocusOnline (2010) 'Big Brother: eine Bettdecke und null Ahnung'. 1 March. www.youtube.com/watch?v=jLrFl2v4p24 (accessed 15 May 2016).

Foucault, M. (1990) *The History of Sexuality*, vol. 1, trans. Robert Hurley. London: Vintage Books.
Grindstaff, L. (1997) 'Producing trash, class, and the money shot: a behind-the-scenes account of daytime TV talk shows'. In J. Lull and S. Hineman (eds) *Media Scandals*. Cambridge: Polity Press.
Hardy, S. (2008) 'The pornography of reality'. *Sexualities*. Volume 11 (1–2): 60–4.
Heller, D. (2013) 'Introduction: loving and losing: from *The L Word* to the "R" word'. In D. Heller (ed) *Loving the L Word: The Complete Series in Focus*. New York: I.B. Tauris.
Juzwiak, R. (2012) 'Showtime's *Polyamory* is trashy, profound and the best reality show on TV'. *Gawker*. 26 July. http://gawker.com/5929318/showtimes-polyamory-is-trashy-profound-and-the-best-reality-show-on-tv (accessed 15 May 2016).
Kavka, M. (2012) *Reality TV*. Edinburgh: Edinburgh University Press.
Longstaff, G. (2013) 'From reality to fantasy: celebrity, reality TV and pornography'. *Celebrity Studies*. Volume 4 (1): 71–80.
McBride, A.E. (2010) 'Food porn'. *Gastronomica* Volume 10 (1): 38–46.
Maerz, M. (2011) 'Sex and more sex: *Gigolos* on Showtime in April'. *Los Angeles Times*, 16 March. http://latimesblogs.latimes.com/showtracker/2011/03/las-vegas-gigolos-coming-to-late-night-on-showtime.html (accessed 14 April 2016).
Paasonen, S. (2011) *Carnal Resonance: Affect and Online Pornography*. Boston: MIT Press.
Patterson, Z. (2004) 'Going online: consuming pornography in the digital era'. In L. Williams (ed) *Porn Studies*. Durham and London: Duke University Press.
Von Braun, C. (2000) 'Big Brother, oder der frei zirkulierende Eros'. *Tages-Anzeiger* (Switzerland), 5 December: 57.
Williams, L. (1989) *Hard Core: Power, Pleasure and the 'Frenzy of the Visible'*. Berkeley and Los Angeles: University of California Press.

Media

Adam Zkt. Eva/Adam Seeking Eve (2014) [TV Series]. Netherlands: RTL5.
Big Brother (1999–) [TV Series]. Netherlands: Veronica.
Buying Naked (2013–) [TV Series]. USA: TLC.
Dating Naked (2014–) [TV Series]. USA: VH1.
Flavor of Love (2006–8) [TV Series]. USA: VH1.
Foursome (2006–11) [TV Series]. USA: Playboy TV.
Geordie Shore (2011–) [TV Series]. UK: MTV.
Gigolos (2011–) [TV Series]. US: Showtime.
Jenna's American Sex Star (2005–6) [TV Series]. USA: Playboy TV.
Naked and Afraid (June 2013–) [TV Series]. USA: Discovery Channel.
Polyamory: Married and Dating (2012–) [TV Series]. USA: Showtime.
Real Sex (1990–2009) [TV Series]. USA: HBO.
Survivor (2000–) [TV Series]. USA: CBS.
Survivor Thailand (2002) [TV Special]. 19 September–19 December. USA: CBS.
The Bachelor (2002–) [TV Special]. USA: ABC.
The Real L Word (2010–12) [TV Series]. USA: Showtime.

30
IT'S ALL ABOUT YOUR SEX APPEAL

Deconstructing the sexual content in women's magazines

Claire Moran

Women's magazines

Women's magazines have a long history, dating back to the first publication of *Ladies Mercury* in the UK in 1693 and *Lady's Magazine* in the United States in 1792 (Ballaster et al., 1991). Much of the early content focused solely on domestic issues, and outlined ideal domestic female behaviour. It wasn't until the very late 1800s that magazines began to move beyond household tips to the inclusion of topics such as sexuality and employment for women (Albisetti, 1986; Zuckerman, 1998). This reflected the changing role of women – from one governed by the domestic sphere to one that included broader social issues such as suffrage and women's inclusion in public life (ibid.).

The early presence of sexual content was typically indirect and moralistic, valorising women's virginity, with sex positioned as only occurring in marriage. Sex was a husband's right and a wife's duty, with women themselves represented as having little interest in it (Zuckerman, 1998; Dias et al., 2012). Not until the 1960s and 1970s was there a shift in how sex was represented – from something shameful and negative to a source of pleasure. This was reflective of broader social changes around the role of women – a resurgence of feminism, a push for greater equality and a challenge to the subordination of women and their traditional positioning as homemaker to the exclusion of other possibilities (Weinberg et al., 1983). This challenge was reflected in women's magazines of the time, such as the revamped *Cosmopolitan* launched in 1965 (Zuckerman, 1998).

Sex was central to this, and was to become a core feature of women's magazines. This marked a significant shift in representations of women as sexual beings, and sexual content has increased in recent decades (Winship, 1987; Kim and Ward, 2004; McRobbie, 2009). Some researchers have argued that this cultural shift represents liberation and greater freedom, allowing women greater ownership over their sexuality (e.g. McNair, 2013; Paglia, 2011). Others are more critical of the *ways* in which women's sexuality is represented, arguing that this is defined by a masculine model and in terms of the male gaze (e.g. Farvid and Braun, 2006; Gill, 2012). They have highlighted magazines' focus on sex and monogamous heterosexual relationships, where relationships with men are depicted as women's primary preoccupation in life and primary source of identity (e.g. Batchelor et al., 2004; Farvid and Braun, 2006; Gill, 2009; Saywell and Pittam, 1996). 'Great sex' is positioned as something that can only occur in monogamous heterosexual relationships (e.g. Farvid and Braun, 2006; Ménard and Kleinplatz, 2008). Contemporary women are presented as being independent, but the overarching imperative is to find a man (Durham, 1996; Raynaud, 2014).

Many researchers have noted the polysemic and contradictory nature of women's lifestyle magazines as they 'perform ideological juggling acts', with contradictory representations of femininity coexisting within their pages (Winship, 1987; Gill, 2009; Machin and Thornborrow, 2003). In an analysis of *Cosmopolitan* magazine, Machin and Thornborrow (2003: 465) noted that while the 'fun fearless female' is constructed as having agency, power and the confidence to get what she wants, she is elsewhere positioned as 'naïve, in need of basic instruction and driven by the need to please a man'. Further, her power is represented as being derived from her appearance and from her sexual ability, rather than any intellectual or practical abilities, or other interests or aspects of her life.

Research has demonstrated that there is considerable variability in depictions of sex, depending on the genre of a magazine. For example, despite the extensive content in women's lifestyle magazines that relates to sex, there is conspicuously little focus – textually or visually – on male appearance. Clarissa Smith provides a clear contrast to this in her book *One for the Girls!* (2007), in which she examines women's consumption of soft-core pornography. Focusing on the British magazine *For Women*, Smith's research explores a genre of women's magazine where sex and being sexy is about women enjoying erotica, male pin-ups and the male body, rather than a preoccupation with the female body.

In an analysis comparing magazine advertisements in heterosexual and lesbian magazines, Mililo (2008) also highlighted some stark contrasts. These included the absence of beauty advertisements in lesbian magazines and women being depicted in defined contexts, such as doing sport, and as more varied in age and body size. In contrast, the women in heterosexual magazines were typically more conventionally beautiful, wore more make-up and revealing clothes and were depicted against decontextualised backgrounds. In heterosexual lifestyle magazines, power and identity is defined primarily by appearance and sexual appeal to men.

Contrasts are also evident between women's and men's lifestyle magazines, in a number of regards. For example, while the focus on women's bodies and bodily improvement in women's magazines is typically vis-à-vis a male gaze, where male bodies are depicted or discussed in men's magazines there is no corresponding female gaze. Further, there is a disjuncture in how sex is represented in each – as the work of femininity and relational issues in women's magazines, with sex going hand in hand with relationships, romantic love and intimacy, but as hedonistic, episodic and recreational in men's magazines, with sex a marker of individualism. Interestingly, women's bodies are used to represent sex in both men's and women's magazines, and there is largely an absence of male bodies in both genres (Attwood, 2005; Benwell, 2003).

The sociocultural context

The weight of importance placed on these aspects of women's lives, and the narrow and proscriptive ways in which 'great sex' and looking good are presented, can be interpreted as aspects of postfeminist media culture, with its focus on individualism, choice and empowerment largely achieved through commodification and consumerism, as well as on heterosexuality and hyperfemininity (Gill, 2008). Women are required to engage in an extensive range of bodily maintenance and modification practices in order 'to produce a sexually desirable – or just apparently normal – feminine body' (Braun et al., 2013: 3). Looking a certain way and appearing sexy are positioned as significant modes by which women can enact power and agency (e.g. Gill, 2007; Gill, 2009; Moran and Lee, 2013; Machin and Thornborrow, 2006).

In what follows I draw on a thematic analysis of all articles related to sex and sexuality in six consecutive monthly issues of the Australian editions of *Cosmopolitan* and *Cleo* (April–September 2009: see Moran and Lee, 2011). For this chapter, I return to these two magazines, revisiting the original analysis of the 2009 issues and examining six more recent issues of both magazines (September 2013–March 2014) with particular focus on the ways in which women's sexuality is constructed. All direct quotes used from the magazines are from the 2013–2014 editions.

Images of slim, white, young, able-bodied, attractive women; articles mostly geared towards solving problems (mostly related to appearance and relationships with men); and advertisements for an extensive range of products indicate that readers should follow the advice, master the tricks and purchase the products featured in order to be successful women in today's world. Successful femininity requires extensive work and is linked to having a hetero-monogamous relationship, as well as to looking and behaving 'correctly' in order to either achieve or maintain that relationship.

Consistent with the findings of previous research (e.g. Dias et al., 2012; Farvid and Braun, 2006), women in *Cosmopolitan* and *Cleo* are represented overwhelmingly as being in, or wanting to be in, monogamous heterosexual relationships, with constant references to 'your partner', 'your boyfriend' or 'your man'. Positioning such relationships as central to women's identity and well-being is at odds with the reality of the majority of their readers' lived experience. There is also frequent reference to 'the One', with the unquestioning assumption that women want to get married:

> The right man for you is out there but . . . chances are you won't recognise Mr happily ever after without a few Mr 'WTF was I thinking?'s to compare him to.
> (*Cleo*, October 2013)

The focus on relationships is reflected in the sheer volume of material dedicated to this topic, with headlines such as 'Where is my Prince Charming?' (*Cleo*, October 2013), 'What guys really want' (*Cleo*, January 2014) and 'Save your relationship in seven minutes' (*Cosmo*, March 2014).

A defining characteristic of postfeminism is the resurgence of the belief in the 'naturalness' of gender difference (Gill, 2007). Despite research that demonstrates women have varied preferences for relationship types, including casual sex (e.g. Moran and Lee, 2012a; 2012b), a hetero-monogamous relationship is presented as something which women 'naturally' yearn for and need:

> We're just not as good at casual sex as men. We're wired differently, we haven't been put on earth to spread our seed. Biologically, dames are meant to menstruate, get pregnant to the best possible suitor, have a baby and our job is done.
> (*Cosmo*, March 2014)

Simultaneously, this is positioned as something that men do not want:

> Every guy is challenged about the idea of being with one woman forever . . . some guys will just never get their head around marriage no matter how many ways and times you try to sell it to them.
>
> (Cosmo, November 2013)

But gender differences are also presented as culturally learnt, with single readers tutored on how to behave in dating and sexual matters in order to maximise their chances of obtaining the desired heterosexual relationship. One example, from an article entitled 'It's time to man up', attempts to help women navigate the fine line between making the first move and engaging in the pretence that the man has the agency and power:

> It is a balancing act between approaching a guy but still giving him room to pursue and chase you . . . this is a subtle way of giving him the opportunity to take the lead, but in reality, you've done all the groundwork.
>
> (Cleo, January 2014)

Women are encouraged to make decisions about whether or not to have sex on the first date based on how they would then be perceived by the man (thus affecting the likelihood that he would enter into a relationship with her), not on their own desire. According to one 'real man' in an article from Cleo (November, 2013), 'I've had mates who've said their opinions of a chick changes if she sleeps with them on the first date'.

It probably comes as no surprise to find that men are not positioned as having any equivalent dilemmas.

The conflation of physical appearance with sexuality in women's magazines has been well documented (e.g. Farvid and Braun, 2006; Travis et al., 2000). Researchers have shown that magazines focus relentlessly on physical appearance, with a significant portion of each edition dedicated to beauty advice, and front-cover headlines such as 'tone and tighten in a hurry' (Cosmo, November 2013), 'style, sex, beauty – own it' (Cleo, October 2013) and '50+ ways to wear your wardrobe differently' (Cosmo, March 2014). Women's appearance is constructed as their primary source of identity, and going to great lengths to appear sexually desirable is positioned as not just normative but also an important source of personal satisfaction for women (Stuart and Donaghue, 2011). This highlights the positioning of women's bodies as commodities for male consumption; however, contemporary post-feminist ideology has shifted the focus on how and why this happens, from something that is done to women to something that women freely choose to do to themselves. Women are no longer positioned as simply being objectified, but are now positioned as subjects who choose to present themselves in an objectified way (Gill, 2007). Appearing sexy and desirable to men is what counts, but readers are encouraged not to be too obvious:

> Dear Boyfriend. . . . . . be wowed by my 'oops I wasn't even trying to look sexy' perfect pony and let's not mention how I looked twenty minutes before you arrived.
>
> (Cleo, March 2014)

There is also an imperative to 'love your body' (Gill and Elias, 2014). 'Feel-good' interviews with celebrities inform readers that they are on their 'way to body confidence' (Cleo, November 2013) and there is encouragement to '[learn] to love the body you were born with' (*Cosmo*, March 2014). Ironically, in another issue, the reader is told the 'best advice for rocking a bikini with confidence' is 'Don't put too much pressure on yourself' (*Cleo*, November 2013).

Great sex

A substantial focus in the magazines is on achieving great sex, and a plethora of advice for doing so is offered. Consistent with previous research (e.g. Farvid and Braun, 2006; Ménard and Kleinplatz, 2008; Carpenter, 1998), sex is overwhelmingly positioned as occurring in hetero-monogamous relationships and as a vital component of relationship success, with no consideration that sex might *not* occur in a relationship. A number of other assumptions are also made around sex.

First, penetrative sex is positioned as 'real' sex, with no exploration beyond the coital imperative, that is, the normative sexual script of foreplay leading to penetrative sex. For example, in situations such as the woman getting her period, the advice is either to stop, lie on a towel or move to the shower (*Cleo*, November 2013). The presumption here is that if the vagina is not available for penetration, sexual activity might as well be abandoned. Second, women are depicted as being responsible for every aspect of the sexual experience, including being sufficiently lubricated for penetration, with advice given by a woman who has 'always had a little trouble getting really wet'. Here the 'trouble' is positioned as the woman's, with no mention of the man or his role. Rather than expecting the man to get her sufficiently aroused, the woman takes responsibility to remedy the situation:

> I make sure I've got some lube in my bedside table . . . I don't make a big deal about it – I just put some on my fingers and touch myself.
>
> (*Cleo, November 2013*)

There is an alarming absence of information about sexual health across the entire data set, but where it is discussed, it is positioned as the woman's responsibility. For example, in the case of having difficulty putting on condoms, a reader was advised to learn 'how to put it on with your mouth' (*Cleo*, November 2013).

Feminist researchers regard modern constructions of 'normal' heterosexuality as a 'masculine model' of sexuality (Dias et al., 2012; Jackson, 1984) centred on sexual ability, performance and competence (Tiefer, 2004), with female sexuality constructed as more passive, vulnerable and less desiring (Allen, 2003). There is a pervasive assumption that men are always interested in sex and will go to any lengths to get it, and this is reflected in the magazines:

> If there is the faintest hope it will get us into your bed, an unscrupulous guy can 'fake' chemistry.
>
> (*Cleo, March 2014*)

In contrast, women are frequently depicted as needing to engage in sex to keep men happy or stop them from straying. This concern was expressed regarding only wanting sex once a week:

> I need to find my libido again, quickly before he finds someone else.
>
> (*Cosmo, March 2014*)

This works to position men and women in competing terms: sex is positioned as the priority for the man, while the woman needs to 'find her libido' because it may result in her losing the thing that is most important to her – her relationship. Men are also positioned as naturally more sexually adventurous than women:

> When it comes to anal, a huge 96% of guys say bring it on (surprise, surprise). 61% of girls say they want to tick this off their list too – didn't see that one coming.
>
> (Cleo, *January 2014*)

These depictions of men as more 'naturally sexual' allow sexuality to be positioned as the man's domain (Moran and Lee, 2012b). Women are encouraged to engage in sexuality on male terms, not to explore their own desires.

A number of scholars of women's magazines have noted the conspicuous absence of alternative sexualities (Batchelor *et al.*, 2004; Gupta *et al.*, 2008; McRobbie, 1997), and this was also the case here. There is very limited consideration of alternative relationship models such as non-monogamy, which, when discussed, are typically framed in negative terms:

> There is an increase in open relationships because Gen Y are exposed to a greater lapse in sexual judgement.
>
> (Cleo, *February 2014*)

The imperative for monogamy is also reinforced by linking sex to emotion, with emotional connection positioned as vital to having satisfying sex:

> If you can't feel emotionally intimate, you're not going to have good sex.
>
> (Cosmo, *January 2014*)

The quest for sexual pleasure was frequently overshadowed by a preoccupation with appearance, with women choosing sexual positions based on what will make them look better for their male partners:

> My go to position with a new guy is girl on top, leaning back, grabbing his ankles behind my back. It's flattering-flat abs, perky boobs – so I can relax and enjoy myself and not get obsessed about my flaws.
>
> (Cosmo, *October 2013*)

This focus on a woman's appearance during sex positions the body as a source of anxiety and shame rather than pleasure, and thus serves to turn attention away from the woman's own sexual feelings and desires. On the whole, the construction of women's role in sex encapsulates a 'technology of sexiness' (Radner, 1999), whereby sexual knowledge, practice and agency have become part of the toolkit of the modern woman. While on the surface this may appear to signal an acknowledgement of women's sexual desire, on closer inspection it signals 'the *performance* of sexual desire rather than the *experience* of it' (McClelland and Fine, 2008: 234; emphasis in original). However, it is also clear that any demonstration of sexual agency or performance of desire is only acceptable within the confines of a hetero-monogamous relationship.

Occasional representations of sexualities outside the heterosexual norm are accompanied at times with an acknowledgement of sexual fluidity, an example being a discussion of the benefits of 'label-free relationships' in an article entitled 'The new free love' (*Cleo*, March 2014). However, this article positions lesbianism and/or bisexuality as matters of youthful experimentation. There are occasional challenges:

> We are obsessed to comparing ourselves with others, but when you're talking about sex, there is no such thing as normal.
> (*Cleo*, October 2013)

But these are tokenistic offerings, given the repeated implicit and explicit reinforcement of heteronormativity.

The magazines also contained a smattering of articles on global and political issues such as asylum seekers (*Cosmo*, March 2014) and child soldiers in Uganda (*Cosmo*, October 2013). There were also articles on sexism, including one related to sexist search-engine terms (*Cosmo*, March 2014) and another on the lack of female ministers in the Australian cabinet (*Cleo*, November 2013). These articles certainly make for a refreshing change from the majority of content, which by and large fails to place topics that affect women in a larger social context, or – as also noted by Machin and Thornborrow (2006) – to challenge the construction of sex as being women's primary source of power.

Conclusion

Women's magazines continue to construct women's primary preoccupations as their appearance and their ability to be desirable and sexually pleasing to men. Content is overwhelmingly dedicated to these areas. A significant shift has taken place in the ways in which sex for women is represented in contemporary magazines – a move away from a morality-based discourse and one of sex for the purpose of procreation. Despite this, the way in which sex is constructed remains limiting for women.

The woman who inhabits the pages of these magazines exists in a world where there are seemingly no structural or cultural constraints, only free choice and empowerment achieved through consumerism, a beautiful appearance and a hetero-monogamous relationship. The version of femininity presented even in contemporary magazines remains one where a woman's identity and success are defined primarily vis-à-vis her appeal to men.

Bibliography

Albisetti, J. C. (1986). 'Women and the professions in Imperial Germany'. In R.-E. B. Joeres and M. J. Maynes (ed) *German women in the eighteenth and nineteenth centuries: A social and literary history*. Bloomington: Indiana University Press.

Allen, L. (2003). 'Girls want sex, boys want love: Resisting dominant discourses of (hetero) sexuality'. *Sexualities*. Volume 6 (2): 215–236.

Attwood, F. (2005). '"Tits and ass and porn and fighting": Male heterosexuality in magazines for men'. *International Journal of Cultural Studies*. Volume 8 (1): 83–100.

Ballaster, R., Beetham, M., Frazer, E. and Hebron, S. (1991). *Women's worlds: Ideology, femininity and the woman's magazine*. Houndmills: Macmillian.

Batchelor, S. A., Kitzinger, J. and Burtney, E. (2004). 'Representing young people's sexuality in the "youth" media'. *Health Education Research*. Volume 19 (6): 669–676.

Benwell, B. (2003). *Masculinity and men's lifestyle magazines*. Oxford: Blackwell Publishers.

Braun, V., Tricklebank, G. and Clarke, V. (2013). '"It shouldn't stick out from your bikini at the beach": Meaning, gender, and the hairy/hairless body'. *Psychology of Women Quarterly*. Volume 37 (4): 478–493.

Carpenter, L. M. (1998). 'From girls into women: Scripts for sexuality and romance in *Seventeen* magazine, 1974–1994'. *Journal of Sex Research*. Volume 35 (2): 158–168.

Dias, A. R. C., Machado, C. and Goncalves, M. (2012). 'From "chastity as a gift" to "doing it as a sign of love": A longitudinal analysis of the discourses on female sexuality in popular magazines in Portugal'. *SAGE Open*. Volume 2 (4): 1–13.

Durham, G. (1996). 'The taming of the shrew: Women's magazines and the regulation of desire'. *The Journal of Communication Inquiry*. Volume 20 (1): 18–31.

Farvid, P. and Braun, V. (2006). '"Most of us guys are raring to go anytime, anyplace, anywhere": Male and female sexuality in *Cleo* and *Cosmo*'. *Sex Roles*. Volume 55 (5–6): 295–310.

Gill, R. (2007). 'Postfeminist media culture'. *European Journal of Cultural Studies*. Volume 10 (2): 147–166.

Gill, R. (2008). 'Culture and subjectivity in neoliberal and postfeminist times'. *Subjectivity*. Volume 25 (1): 432–445.

Gill, R. (2009). 'Mediated intimacy and postfeminism: A discourse analytic examination of sex and relationships advice in a women's magazine'. *Discourse & Communication*. Volume 3 (4): 345–369.

Gill, R. (2012). 'Media, empowerment and the "sexualization of culture" debates'. *Sex Roles*. Volume 66 (11–12): 736–745.

Gill, R. and Elias, A. S. (2014). '"Awaken your incredible": Love your body discourses and postfeminist contradictions'. *International Journal of Media and Cultural Politics*. Volume 10 (2): 179–188.

Gill, R. and Scharff, C. (2011). *New femininities: Postfeminism, neoliberalism, and subjectivity*. Basingstoke: Palgrave Macmillan.

Gupta, A. E., Zimmerman, T. S. and Fruhauf, C. A. (2008). 'Relationship advice in the top selling women's magazine, *Cosmopolitan*: A content analysis'. *Journal of Couple & Relationship Therapy: Innovations in Clinical and Educational Interventions*. Volume 7 (3): 248–266.

Jackson, M. (1984). 'Sex research and the construction of sexuality: A tool of male supremacy?' *Women's Studies International Forum*. Volume 7 (1): 43–51.

Kim, J. L. and Ward, L. M. (2004). 'Pleasure reading: Associations between young women's sexual attitudes and their reading of contemporary women's magazines'. *Psychology of Women Quarterly*. Volume 28 (1): 48–58.

McClelland, S. I. and Fine, M. (2008). 'Writing on cellophane: Studying teen women's sexual desires, inventing methodological release points'. In K. Gallagher (ed) *The methodological dilemma: Creative, critical and collaborative approaches to qualitative research*. London: Routledge.

Machin, D. and Thornborrow, J. (2003). 'Branding and discourse: The case of *Cosmopolitan*'. *Discourse & Society*. Volume 14 (4): 453–471.

Machin, D. and Thornborrow, J. (2006). 'Lifestyle and the depoliticisation of agency: Sex as power in women's magazines'. *Social Semiotics*. Volume 16 (1): 173–188.

McNair, B. (2013). *Porno? Chic! How pornography changed the world and made it a better place*. London: Routledge.

McRobbie, A. (1997). '*More!* New sexualities in girls' and women's magazines'. In J. Curran, D. Morley and V. Walkerdine (eds) *Cultural studies and communications*. London: Arnold.

McRobbie, A. (2009). *The aftermath of feminism: Gender, culture and social change*. London: Sage.

Ménard, A. and Kleinplatz, P. (2008). 'Twenty-one moves guaranteed to make his thighs go up in flames: Depictions of "great sex" in popular magazines'. *Sexuality & Culture*. Volume 12 (1): 1–20.

Milillo, D. (2008). 'Sexuality sells: A content analysis of lesbian and heterosexual women's bodies in magazine advertisements'. *Journal of Lesbian Studies*. Volume 12 (4): 381–392.

Moran, C. and Lee, C. (2011). 'On his terms: Representations of sexuality in women's magazines and the implications for negotiating safe sex'. *Psychology & Sexuality*. Volume 2 (2): 159–180.

Moran, C. and Lee, C. (2012a). 'Australian women talk about non-romantic sex'. *Psychology & Sexuality*. Volume 5 (3): 210–231.

Moran, C. and Lee, C. (2012b). 'Women's constructions of heterosexual non-romantic sex and the implications for sexual health'. *Psychology & Sexuality*. Volume 5 (2): 161–182.

Moran, C. and Lee, C. (2013). 'Selling genital cosmetic surgery to healthy women: A multimodal discourse analysis of Australian surgical websites'. *Critical Discourse Studies*. Volume 10 (4): 1–19.

Paglia, C. (2011). *Vamps & tramps: New essays*. London: Vintage.

Radner, H. (1999). 'Introduction: Queering the girl'. In H. Radner and M. Luckett (eds) *Swinging single: Representing sexuality in the 1960s*. Minneapolis: University of Minnesota Press.

Raynaud, J. (2014). 'How to construct your sexuality according to French magazines'. *Social Semiotics*. Volume 24 (2): 243–258.

Saywell, C. and Pittam, J. (1996). 'The discourses of HIV and AIDS in women's magazines: Feature articles in Australian *Cleo* and *Cosmopolitan*'. *Australian Journal of Communication*. Volume 23 (1): 46–63.

Smith, C. (2007). *One for the girls! The pleasures and practices of reading women's porn*. Bristol: Intellect Books.

Stuart, A. and Donaghue, N. (2011). 'Choosing to conform: The discursive complexities of choice in relation to feminine beauty practices'. *Feminism & Psychology*. Volume 22 (1): 98–121.

Tiefer, L. (2004). *Sex is not a natural act & other essays*. Boulder, CO: Westview.

Travis, C. B., Meginnis, K. L. and Bardari, K. M. (2000). 'Beauty, sexuality, and identity: The social control of women'. In C. B. Travis and J. W. White (eds) *Sexuality, society, and feminism*. Washington, DC: American Psychological Association.

Weinberg, M. S., Swensson, R. G. and Hammersmith, S. K. (1983). 'Sexual autonomy and the status of women: Models of female sexuality in US sex manuals from 1950 to 1980'. *Social Problems*. Volume 30 (3): 312–324.

Winship, J. (1987). *Inside women's magazines*. London: Pandora.

Zuckerman, M. E. (1998). *A history of popular women's magazines in the United States, 1792–1995*. Westport, CT: Greenwood Press.

31
THE INVISIBLES
Disability, sexuality and new strategies of enfreakment

Niall Richardson

Popular media has a long history of representing disabled bodies as asexual – neither sexually desiring nor desirable. Throughout popular culture, disabled characters have operated as a defining other and have either been coded as monsters, who are often psychotic because of their disability, or else have occupied the position of the politics of pity and reminded the viewer of the need for compassion for those who are less fortunate (see Zola, 1985; Nelson, 1994; Norden, 1994; Whittington-Walsh, 2002).

Not until relatively recently did the media begin to represent disabled bodies as having any form of sexual desire or sexual desirability. This is hardly surprising when we consider that, for the past 50 years, disability activism has been concerned – quite understandably – with addressing disability discrimination in the workplace rather than in the area of personal relationships. Disability rights have been underpinned by the social model of disability which reads disability as a social construct – the result of legal and social oppression. The body may have an impairment but it is the workplace's failure to take account of this impairment which dis-ables the body. For example, a wheelchair-using professor would only be dis-abled if the university did not make allowance for his wheelchair and asked him to teach in a room that was not wheelchair-accessible. In other words, disability is not an essential attribute but the result of social discrimination and oppression (Oliver, 1990; Davis, 1995; Hughes, 2002; Barnes and Mercer, 2003). As Tom Shakespeare has argued (2000), it is hardly surprising that disability rights have focused on legal and social issues rather than debates about sexual identification, as 'ending poverty and social exclusion comes higher up the list of needs than campaigning for a good fuck' (see also Gerschick, 2006).

Therefore, one of the subjects to have been raised in recent disability activism is the lack of media representation of sexual (and sexualised) disabled bodies. Given that the media helps to shape discourses of romantic courtship and introduce wide-eyed teenagers to the perils and pleasures of falling in love, it is a political problem that so few media representations ever address the issue of sexual and romantic relationships for disabled bodies. Leonore Tiefer uses an apt metaphor to describe the sexually ableist agenda of contemporary media:

> Imagine how you would feel if playing gin rummy, and playing it well, was considered a major component of happiness and a major sign of maturity, but no

one told you how to play, you never saw anybody else play, and everything you ever read implied that normal and healthy people just somehow 'know' how to play and really enjoy playing the very first time they try!

(Tiefer, 1995: 12)

Recently, however, contemporary film and media have started to consider the intersection of disability, sexuality and romantic relationships. Recent film texts that have made this the subject of their narratives have included *Theory of Flight* (1999, dir: Paul Greengrass), *Inside I'm Dancing* (2004, dir: Damien O'Donnell), *Intouchables* (2011, dirs: Olivier Nakache and Eric Touledano), *The Sessions* (2012, dir: Ben Lewin) and, most recently, *The Theory of Everything* (2014, dir: James Marsh). These films are remarkable in that the issue of workplace discrimination and disablement is rarely even considered or, if it is addressed, is secondary to the main theme of finding emotional and sexual love. Indeed, *Intouchables* could be criticised for its focus on a financially privileged hero whose wealth makes the everyday problems which may be faced by other less affluent quadraplegics seem irrelevant. The hero's main anxiety is whether he should meet up in person with Eléonore, the woman with whom he has been having an epistolary relationship.

Similarly, recent media discourses that have sought to de-essentialise the sexual act – in other words, represent something beyond the penis–vagina model of sexual expression – have, arguably, helped to broaden cultural awareness that sexual pleasures can be multiple and may move in excess of traditional erotic performances by normatively abled bodies. Brian McNair aptly describes this as the 'democratisation of desire' (2002). For example, the mainstreaming of BDSM has raised awareness that sexual pleasure may not be related exclusively to the genitals (Richardson, Smith and Werndly, 2013: 141–153). The same could be argued for the identification of alternative sexual activities such as muscle worship and feederism (see Richardson, 2008; 2010; 2016). Similarly, the growing pornographication of culture, in which amateur porn is two mouse-clicks away, has raised awareness that bodies of all shapes and sizes can engage in a variety of sexual expressions, as opposed to the pneumatic bodies of earlier porn iconography or the 'heavenly bodies' (Dyer, 2003) of Hollywood (see McNair, 2002; Smith, 2007; Attwood, 2009; McNair, 2013). As Tom Shakespeare points out, this growing realisation that sexual pleasures are multiple, and enacted by a variety of bodies in different ways, is very welcome knowledge for people who may be deemed incapable of normative sexual coitus:

> We can perhaps challenge a whole lot of ideas that predominate in the sexual realm, and enable others – not just disabled people – to reassess what is important and what is possible. Why should men be dominant? Why should sex revolve around penetration? Why should sex only involve two people? Why can't disabled people be assisted to have sex by third parties? What is normal sex?
>
> (Shakespeare, 2000)

Indeed, it is the questions of what 'normal' sex and a 'normal' relationship actually are that have been the most powerful for contemporary activism in the field of disability and sexuality.

This chapter will consider a recent media text, *The Undateables*, which has made the subject of relationships and dating for disabled bodies its main focus. Now into its sixth series, *The Undateables* first appeared in the UK on Channel 4 in 2012, and each yearly series has contained four 60-minute episodes. Each season has featured a variety of participants who have identified as having a different disability. These have included facial disfigurement, physical mobility issues and a broad spectrum of identifications classed as 'learning difficulties', such as autism and Asperger syndrome.

Reviewers have continued to debate how *The Undateables* should be interpreted, with the majority of commentators eventually deciding that the show treads a very fine line between raising public awareness of disability issues and unashamed exploitation (see, for example, Denham, 2014). Recent academic criticism has argued that *The Undateables* can be read as offering simply 'the spectacularization of disability', which, although it claims to 'bring disabled people's romantic and sexual needs into the mainstream', actually only succeeds in 'setting the disabled participants apart from the non-disabled society' (Soorenian, 2014: 48).

However, it is the hyper-ironic coding of *The Undateables* that makes it an extremely problematic show to critique via textual analysis. The title itself exemplifies the highly controversial irony of the series as, arguably, it is drawing attention to society's prejudiced view of disability and asserting that these people are *not* undateable. Yet, it can only be speculated how many viewers are aware of the irony. Many people who saw the initial billboard posters may well have interpreted the series as a patronising show which asks the viewer to pity these unfortunate people who, because of their disability, actually *are* undateable.

This double-signification of the series' semiotics continues in the way the show vacillates between documentary genres. *The Undateables* is reality television but at times borrows from the generic conventions of the participatory documentary (in which the participants are very obviously aware of the presence of the film-maker) and on other occasions draws on the codes of the reflexive documentary, which foregrounds the obvious constructed-ness of the situations and the performance of the participants.

Although, on one level, the show is certainly attempting to break down prejudice and make the viewer aware that everyone – whether identifying as disabled or able-bodied – experiences problems in contemporary dating, *The Undateables* can also be seen to draw upon many of the codes and conventions of the archaic spectacle of the 'freak' show. This chapter will first discuss the history of the representation of disabled bodies, before considering if earlier 'freak' show strategies can be seen to be functioning in *The Undateables*. The question the chapter will ask is whether *The Undateables* is raising awareness of disability and sexuality, or merely bringing new strategies of enfreakment to the television screen.

Strategies of representation: from 'monsters' to 'freaks' to disabled people

Within all the great civilisations (from Greco-Roman to Christian), there have been stories of 'monsters' and mythical creatures who have been read as godly forecasts – either showing the power of God/gods or warning of things to come. Ambroise Paré's sixteenth-century text read 'monsters' as direct signals from God (trans. Pallister, 1982); they either represented the wrath of God (often a warning of divine punishment) or, paradoxically, could also be read as a celebration of the power and glory of God.

However, Rosemarie Garland Thomson argues that many of our mythical 'monsters' can be viewed as explanations for unusual or different bodies that have startled people from different cultures (1996: 1). Bodies that strayed too far from what is considered to be the acceptable or predictable would have been classed as 'monsters' and explained by recourse to religious doctrine. Until the nineteenth century, it was common for surgeons to take the Biblical examples as a precedent and diagnose 'monstrous' births as punishment from God (see Spinks, 2006). Conjoined twins, for example, were either an omen of an angry God or, paradoxically, could be interpreted as celebrating the glory of God (see Shildrick, 2002: 12).

It wasn't until the early nineteenth century that teratology (the study of 'monsters') was actually established within medical discourses. A greater understanding of the processes of reproduction and embryology allowed scientists to point out that unusual births were not the result of divine intervention but rather of atypical foetal development. Professor Étienne Geoffroy Saint-Hilaire, a key figure in these debates, published an influential thesis in 1822, arguing that 'monstrous' births could be traced to unusual influences on the foetus while in development.

One of the key advancements made by teratology was that it changed the position of the 'monster' from something unfathomable to something that was *almost* human. As a result of this, identification with 'monstrous' bodies became possible and the same/other dichotomy, which had been supported by myth, was broken down. It was from this period onwards that medical science began exhibiting unusual bodies – 'monsters' – for the (supposed) purpose of education. These medical exhibits were intended to educate the people, informing them that 'monstrous' births or unusual bodies were not the result of the wrath of God, but rather of a variety of scientific factors that had contributed to unusual foetal development.

However, when it became apparent that many spectators at the medical exhibits were more interested in marvelling at the unusual bodies than learning of the medical and scientific issues behind them, the 'freak' show was born. Robert Bogdan (1988) argues that the genesis of the 'freak' show can be traced back to 1850, when showman P. T. Barnum started exhibiting human curiosities in the American Museum in New York. Within a few years, this museum had attained unprecedented popularity and had set the template for what we now term the 'freak' show – soon to be thriving on both sides of the Atlantic.

One of the key points about the 'freak' show was that it was a platform which turned unusual bodies into 'freaks'. The term 'enfreakment' was coined by the critic David Hevey (1992: 53) to describe the mechanism through which bodies that were different or strange were re-presented in a variety of media as 'freaks'. Underpinning this thesis is the assertion that nobody *is* a 'freak'. The body may be different or even strange, but it is the strategy of re-presentation which renders this unusual body a 'freak' (Garland Thomson 1996; Bogdan, 1988: 10). In 'freak' shows, all the bodies exhibited were mis-represented to the viewer. For example, the exhibit 'The World's Fattest Lady' was undoubtedly a very fat body, but the publicity blurb would add some extra pounds to her weight, she would have padding under her clothes to increase her overall bulk and she would be exhibited on an undersized mise-en-scène in order to increase the illusion of size.

Robert Bogdan (1988) has argued that there were two main strategies of representation within the 'freak' show: the aggrandised mode and the exoticised mode. The aggrandised mode stressed that the 'freak' body was a normative member of society despite his/her physical difference (1988: 108). Very often this type of performance stressed that the 'freak' body had a particular talent or ability, such as a beautiful singing voice, and so was either heroicised as someone overcoming his/her disadvantages or else presented as being trapped as a victim of circumstance.

The other mode of representing the 'freak' body was the exoticised mode, in which the viewer was invited to marvel at the sensationalised difference of the body on the stage (Bogdan, 1988: 105). This could either be an orientalised delight (the sexuality of the Asian snake charmer) or a subtle erotic delectation at the differences of the body's proportions. 'The World's Fattest Lady', for example, would be displaying considerably more flesh than would have been deemed culturally acceptable, and so this 'freak' offered a covert eroticism not available in any other representations.

Arguably, one of the pleasures of the 'freak' show was that it allowed the viewers to define their well-managed and 'proper' bodies against the 'freak' bodies on display (Shildrick, 2002: 24). 'Freak' shows had their heyday after the Industrial Revolution when the nature of factory work dictated that society offer a workforce of regular, uniform-sized bodies, who could work like automatons (see Marks, 1999: 80). The unusual bodies displayed on the stage made the viewers feel more secure in their identification with a community of well-managed, working bodies.

Related to this idea of a proper, working community is the development of the idea of the norm, which, Lennard Davis argues, came into existence around 1840–1860 (1997: 10). Although there have always been representations of the ideal human form (paintings and statuary of ideal bodies have existed since the Greco-Roman empires), the concept of the ideal as something *attainable* for humans was not considered until the mid-nineteenth century. Prior to this, the ideal was the realm of the divine and not the flawed, earthly body. However, as Davis points out, the ever increasing need to account for people in terms of workforce statistics moved from being simply a way of documenting the state to become a way of describing and quantifying average men and women (1997: 11–13). By formulating an idea of the average man, based on his physical characteristics and potential contribution to the workforce, the idea of the well-managed body came into existence. As a result, the norm became linked to the ideal. No longer simply the dream of artists and sculptors, the ideal body became the one that could contribute to the development of socio-economics. The 'freak' show exhibit functioned as a very reassuring spectacle to its visitors in that it reminded them that they were part of the collective norm of society and not like those marginalised on the stage.

This, of course, raises the other key dynamic in enfreakment strategies, in that the 'freak' body can, like 'monsters' before it, act as a sponge for all the anxieties of the period. Different 'freaks' have had greater popularity in different contexts and cultures. In contemporary culture, for example, we are now terrified of the – so-called – obesity epidemic (Monaghan, 2008; 2014), and fatness is one of the main anxieties of Western society (Orbach, 1979; Bordo, 1993; Hesse-Biber, 1996; Braziel and Lebesco, 2001). Therefore, contemporary Anglophone media continually delight in documentaries and reality shows that demonstrate the 'horror' of fat. If viewers are worried about their weight then it is, arguably, a great relief to watch such extremely fat bodies on the screen, as it reassures the viewer that he/she may be a little overweight but is at least not as fat as the bodies on display.

However, there has always been an ambivalent response to the body of the 'freak' being represented on the stage or in contemporary media. On one level this is the exoticised mode, in which there is a curious mixture of horror and covert eroticism regarding the extraordinary body, but there is also the flutter of anxiety that the 'freak' body on display is not really all that different from the viewer's own body. Arguably, the dynamic power of the 'freak' on display is that it may force the viewer to reconsider his/her own politics of the normative. Watching an unusual body may make the viewer question what is normative, what is beautiful, what is acceptable and, most importantly, what is an 'appropriate' body. In this respect, it is possible to argue that 'freak' shows were not *necessarily* exploitations of poor, unfortunate people, but a celebration of their unusual quality – a chance for marginalised bodies to gain recognition and a voice and, in doing so, to challenge our preconceptions and prejudices (see Gamson, 1998; Stephens, 2006; Richardson, 2010).

Rosemarie Garland Thomson, on the other hand, cautions against a naïve celebration of the dynamic of enfreakment. Garland Thomson, one of the most respected critics within disability studies, argues that a key problem with Victorian 'freak' shows was that they conflated all unusual or different bodies under the label of 'freak' and therefore eradicated any particularity or specificity of difference (1996). Politically, is it correct to align the identity of 'The Giant' – a body who is exceptionally tall – with the exhibit known as 'The Frog Man' – a body who has unusually formed legs (which, arguably, resembled those of a frog's) but who, most importantly, is unable to walk? In other words, one of the problems with excusing enfreakment narratives and representational strategies is that they did not acknowledge the identification which we now label disability – a term which only attained cultural currency in the 1970s. Indeed, until the birth of 'identity studies' (Garland Thomson, 2002: 1) in the academy in the 1960s, in which identifications were argued to be social constructs rather than inherent characteristics, the disabled body could be identified only as a medical problem or 'freak' of nature. Constructionist ideology underpinned the social model of disability, which drew a distinction between the physical impairment of the body and its identification as 'disabled'. The Union of the Physically Impaired Against Segregation (UPIAS) outlines the distinction as follows:

> Impairment: lacking part or all of a limb, or having a defective limb, organism or mechanism of the body.
>
> Disability: the disadvantages or restriction of activity caused by a contemporary social organisation which takes little or no account of people who have physical impairments, and thus excludes them from the mainstream of social activities.
>
> (1976: 3–4)

Therefore, the social model argued that dis-ability was how society and culture responded to the body's physical difference. A body is only dis-abled if society fails to take any account of the body's impairment (see Barnes and Mercer, 2003).

The question that this chapter will now consider is whether or not *The Undateables* can be read as trying to make viewers aware that the social model should be considered in the area of romantic relationships as well as work environments, or if, on the other hand, the programme can be seen as a new variation on the 'freak' show formula. Is *The Undateables* progressing the social model or returning us to strategies of enfreakment?

New strategies of enfreakment?

Although *The Undateables* is certainly raising disability awareness, it is possible to read the show as a textual sponge which, like earlier 'freak' shows, absorbs one of the main anxieties of contemporary culture: being single. Given the rise of mediated forms of dating in a variety of dating apps, it could be speculated that there is an ever increasing expectation that someone need *not* be single. Although some media texts from the late 1990s exalted a particular type of single-ness – for example, critics lauded the television drama *Sex and the City* (1998–2004) for the way it synthesised elements of queer culture with postfeminism so that the friendship between the female characters was their support network while they had a range of transitory sexual partners (Gerhard, 2005; Jermyn, 2009; Richardson *et al.*, 2013) – it should be noted that the more recent *Sex and the City* movies (2008 and 2010, dir: Michael Patrick King) represented nearly all the characters as married (Richardson, 2012). It does seem as if the traditional Hollywood rom-com formula still exalts a monogamous union as the ultimate goal in anyone's life. Similarly, the recent legalisation of same-sex marriage in the USA and most of Western Europe has, arguably, instilled a sense of the importance of monogamy in queer cultures. In short, there seems to be an overwhelming importance placed upon coupling in contemporary culture.

The Undateables can be read as trying to appease viewers' anxieties: we may find contemporary dating culture to be difficult, but at least it's not as difficult for 'us' as it is for the bodies represented in the series. While the early 'freak' shows were appeasing the viewers' anxieties about their bodies' abilities to contribute successfully to a community's workforce, The Undateables may be read as an attempt to soothe concerns about incapacities to perform in the social world of dating. Although it is possible to interpret The Undateables as attempting to foreground the importance of mobilising the social model in the dating world as well as the work environment (a person's impairment is only a disability in the dating world if his/her date is not prepared to make some accommodation of the difference), it is the text's use of comedy, particularly the coding of the specific participants' actions *as comic*, that moves the show into the questionable territory of enfreakment.

Disability and comedy have moved through three main stages of evolution (Albrecht, 1999; Shakespeare, 1999). First, there was the coding of people with disability as 'freaks', in which viewers were invited to laugh or tremble at the 'others'. Second, there was the development of disability humour, in which the witticism or pun became the joke. In this type of comedy, the participant is not laughing at the disability itself, but at the innuendo or 'mind trap' created by the joke. For many years, a lot of quadriplegic jokes were in place which followed this agenda. (Example: I went to see a quadriplegic juggler last night. He wasn't very good – he kept dropping the quadraplegics.) Finally, and most recently, we have the tradition of disabled people making fun of themselves, in which people with disabilities have used comedy as a way of making society aware of its prejudices. For example, a wheelchair user might tell the story: 'After my flight landed in the airport, the air hostess said "Will those who require wheelchair assistance please remain seated".'

On one level, The Undateables mobilises this trajectory of disability comedy, in that the participants' disability is acknowledged so that viewers can consider the prejudices that are normally in place in relation to disability and dating. These disabled bodies are just like everyone else struggling with the highly complex world of dating in contemporary, technology-dependent culture.

However, while every participant's representation in The Undateables features a voice-over narration that acknowledges the specificity of the disability, the sequence then invites the viewer to laugh at the complications *which result from* this person's disability. This strategy has been repeated throughout all the episodes that have featured participants with learning difficulties, Tourette's syndrome and speech impediments. For example, series 1, episode 2 featured one of the most popular participants of the series, a very charming poet called Shaine. Shaine is identified from the start of the episode as having 'learning difficulties' and as liking to write poetry. Shaine has met Jackie while speed-dating and is now preparing to go on a first serious date with her. In a direct-to-camera interview, Shaine tells the interviewer that his feelings for Jackie are 'magical', that she has made his 'heart flutter' and that he is actually in love with her – despite the fact that he's only met her for a couple of minutes on a speed-date. Obviously, the viewer is invited to smile affectionately at Shaine's naïvety for believing that he has fallen in love so quickly. However, after Shaine has announced his feelings of love for Jackie, there is an edit to a shot of the iron that

Shaine has been using to prepare his clothes for the date. The juxtaposition of Shaine's proclamations of intense romantic love with the shot of the everyday item that is the iron emphasises Shaine's inability to gauge levels of *genuine* emotional involvement with people and his naïve interpretation of being in love. Shaine then proceeds to announce that he's actually told Jackie that he loves her. When the interviewer asks Shaine how he told Jackie of his love for her, Shaine replies that he texted the information to her. Shaine's revelation of texting 'I love you' to Jackie (whom he'd only met for a few minutes) is the 'punch line' of the sequence and is certainly an invitation to the viewer to laugh (albeit affectionately) at his childlike naïvety.

However, irrespective of how the viewer interprets the dynamics of comedy in the sequence, what the scene is doing is clearly absolving the viewer of any guilt should he/she laugh at Shaine's impetuous SMS declaration of love. Disability is openly identified at the start of the sequence in order to excuse any subsequent laughter at the issues which occur because of the disability. Acknowledgement of difference is a standard trope within comedy. Many stand-up comedians openly identify as part of a stigmatised minority (such as gay or Muslim or Jewish or fat) in order to make the audience aware that it is now acceptable to laugh at this identification. A gay stand-up comedian, for example, might openly acknowledge his homosexuality in order to make jokes about gay men acceptable. However, there are two key differences between stand-up comedy routines and *The Undateables*. First, Shaine *may* not be complicit in this act of identification. Even though the voice-over narration and the participant may identify the disability at the start of the sequence, it's not always obvious that the participant himself fully appreciates the signification of terms such as 'autism' or 'learning difficulties'. Second, the viewer is not being invited to laugh at the disability itself but at other issues, such as Shaine's lack of understanding of love or his impetuous SMS declarations. Yet these misunderstandings have only occurred *due* to Shaine's disability. Therefore, *The Undateables* is excusing any laughter at a disabled person because, arguably, the viewer is not giggling at disability itself but at the issues that have occurred because of the specific identification.

Indeed, *The Undateables* develops this strategy even further by often identifying a disability but then proceeding to ignore it and representing the participant as merely eccentric or, sometimes, downright foolish. In series 1, episode 1, the viewer is introduced to 23-year-old Penny. Penny has a condition that makes her bones extremely brittle and as a result is only 3ft (91cm) tall. Nevertheless, Penny will not allow her impairment to dis-able her activities, and she is first represented as engaging in aerial acrobatics – performing gymnastics in a suspended trapeze ring. Obviously, it's not difficult to read Penny as coded in accordance with the aggrandised mode of enfreakment, in that she is a heroic figure who should be lauded for not letting her condition limit her activities. More worrying, however, is the fact that Penny's disability is identified in the scene only to be superseded by an emphasis on her eccentric desires. Penny announces that, even though she is only 3ft tall, she is attracted to *extremely* tall men and would only consider dating a guy who is well over 6ft (182cm) in height. As one YouTube commentator stated: 'Another woman with physical limitations not prepared to consider men who are not taller than average – regardless of personality – *it's pretty funny really*' (www.youtube.com/watch?v=WoC9oHFKmNQ, link no longer available; accessed 27 January 2015, emphasis added). Although most YouTube commentators do tend to be rather misanthropic, it is fair to say that this particular critic has a valid point. Is it sensible to desire a sexual partner who is more than twice your size? Therefore, this representation of Penny is, arguably, not only an example of a body that is coded in the aggrandised mode of enfreakment strategies but also, more worryingly, a representation in which the disability is superseded by an invitation to giggle at Penny's eccentricity and illogical fancies.

Of course, it would be possible to argue that *The Undateables*' representation of Shaine and Penny is attempting to challenge the 'them'/'us' binary by suggesting that *everyone* – irrespective of physical and mental ability – finds the dating world to be a challenge. Any viewer who has ever attempted dating will recognise the anxiety, awkwardness and naïvety of desire demonstrated by Penny and Shaine and, in that respect, the series may be read as asking the viewers to consider if they are really all that different from the bodies on the screen.

However, one of the key problems with the series is the issue that Garland Thomson raised about naïve celebrations of the transgressive potential of earlier enfreakment spectacles: the conflation of different bodies and disabilities into the same identification. This is a particular issue in *The Undateables* when, in each series, a body is featured which, in accordance with the social model, may not even be identified as dis-abled at all. For example, series 4, episode 1 features 31-year-old Matthew: a very handsome, muscular African-Caribbean man who makes a living from working as a life model. The introductory sequence represents Matthew posing for an art class and the camera offers various medium close-up shots of parts of his sculpted body, such as his muscular chest and shoulders and his pert buttocks. This fetishistic editing, usually employed to objectify the female body on the screen (though in more recent years also used to eroticise masculinity), codes Matthew as an object of the gaze and, by this point, the viewer should probably be wondering why Matthew is even being identified as undateable. The next scene reveals that Matthew has an extreme stammer and is struggling to utter the word 'love' in his interview.

Matthew's inclusion in *The Undateables* is obviously intended to demonstrate that the social model of disability fails to take account of the importance of romantic relationships through its exclusive focus on the workplace. Matthew's stammer is no dis-ability when he is modelling, but is certainly a concern when it comes to chatting up a date. Yet the problem remains that the series has included a classically proportioned male model alongside people who have facial disfigurements and identified them all under the banner of undateable. Like the representation of 'The Snake Charmer' alongside 'The Frog Man' in the Victorian 'freak' show, the inclusion of a male model alongside many of the other participants can be read as trivialising the very identification of dis-ability itself. While it is never politically effective to engage in an Olympics of oppression in which bodies are ranked in order of societal difficulties, it is a definite problem that the show glosses over the specificities of the identifications in order to mobilise the placard of 'undateable'.

However, although Matthew may be read in accordance with the exoticised mode of 'freak' show spectacle (the sequence at the start offers the viewer the illicit pleasure of gazing upon the eroticised racial other), the sequence is most worrying for the way it forces the strategy of enfreakment through the revelation of personal issues. Given that the combination of Matthew's physical beauty and stammer may not qualify him as dis-abled in the eyes of many viewers, the sequence then proceeds to emphasise another aspect of Matthew's performativity which may be read as 'freakish'. In a direct-to-camera interview (and again in the next scene with the administrators of the dating agency), Matthew reveals that he has an unusual fetish, in that he likes his sexual partners to have a shoulder-width measurement in excess of 16 inches. Indeed, Matthew is so specific about this that he even likes to bring a tape-measure to check the diameter. The revelation of this unusual fetish corresponds with the key dynamic of enfreakment, in that it is not the person who is a 'freak' but the mechanism of narrative representation which codes him/her as freakish. Matthew is interested in bodybuilding, and it is actually not unusual for someone who devotes much of his life to labouring under the tyranny of the tape-measure to fetishise specific body measurements. ('How big is your bicep?' is almost an everyday greeting in bodybuilding gyms.) Yet *The Undateables* does not reveal this issue to the viewer but instead is simply using this unusual sexual taste (which should normally be reserved as a personal, intimate matter) to code the body as a 'freak'.

In this respect, *The Undateables* may represent a return (although in a very sophisticated and ironic fashion) to earlier strategies of enfreakment. Not only is disability being acknowledged in order to excuse any laughter at the actions which result from this sociocultural identification but also, as in the earlier 'freak' shows, the physical difference is merely used as a springboard in order to code the body in a narrative of freakishness. The viewer is not marvelling at Penny's height but at her freakish desire to date a man who is twice her size. Matthew's stammer is not an issue, but his strange fetish for a specific shoulder width is coded as freaky. Shaine's 'learning difficulties' are not coded as a source of humour, but his reckless SMS proclamations of love are.

Conclusion

This chapter has considered a highly controversial show which, like many contemporary media texts, is shrewdly ironic and open to a variety of interpretations. Indeed, *The Undateables* operates on a similar brand of irony as that which can be found in 'new racism' or, more recently, 'new sexism'. For example, when Gok Wan manhandles a woman in the make-over show *How to Look Good Naked* (2006–2008), cupping her breasts and referring to them as 'bangers', this is deemed acceptable because Gok is openly gay-identified (see Richardson and Wearing, 2014: 92). Yet, as with *The Undateables*, we are still seeing an offensive representation excused on the screen because it has been qualified by an explanation at the start.

While textual analysis can interrogate the codes and conventions at work within the mediation, it cannot identify with any certainty how these codes will be read by audiences. In order to fully appreciate how *The Undateables* is being interpreted by viewers who identify as both disabled and non-disabled, audience research would be required. There is still considerable work to be done in this area. Are we watching a series that is actually breaking down prejudice, raising awareness of disability and sexual relationships and asking for a reconsideration of the social model as applicable to personal as well as work relations, or are we merely viewing new strategies of enfreakment?

Bibliography

Albrecht, G. L. (1999) 'Disability Humour: What's in a Joke?' *Body and Society*. Volume 5 (4): 67–74.
Attwood, F. (ed) (2009) *Mainstreaming Sex: The Sexualization of Culture*. London: I.B. Tauris.
Barnes, C. and Mercer, G. (2003) *Disability*. Cambridge: Polity Press.
Bogdan, R. (1988) *Freak Show: Presenting Human Oddities for Amusement and Profit*. Chicago: University of Chicago Press.
Bordo, S. (1993) *Unbearable Weight: Feminism, Western Culture, and the Body*. Berkeley: University of California Press.
Braziel, J. E. and LeBesco, K. (eds) (2001) *Bodies Out of Bounds: Fatness and Transgression*. Berkeley: University of California Press.
Davis, L. J. (1995) *Enforcing Normalcy: Disability, Deafness, and the Body*. New York: Verso.

Davis, L. J. (1997) 'Constructing Normalcy: The Bell Curve, the Novel and the Invention of the Disabled Body in the Nineteenth Century'. In L. J. Davis (ed) *The Disability Studies Reader*. New York and London: Routledge.

Denham, J. (2014) 'The Undateables to Return for Fourth Series'. 12 February. *The Independent*. www.independent.co.uk/arts-entertainment/tv/news/the-undateables-to-return-for-fourth-series-9124282.html (accessed 2 February 2015).

Dyer, R. (2003) *Heavenly Bodies: Film Stars and Society*. London: Routledge.

Gamson, J. (1998) *Freaks Talk Back: Tabloid Talk Shows and Sexual Nonconformity*. Chicago: University of Chicago Press.

Garland Thomson, R. (1996) 'Introduction: From Wonder to Error – A Genealogy of Freak Discourse in Modernity'. In R. Garland Thomson (ed) *Freakery: Cultural Spectacles of the Extraordinary Body*. New York: New York University Press.

Garland Thomson, R. (2002) 'Integrating Disability, Transforming Feminist Theory'. *National Women's Studies Association Journal*. Volume 14 (2): 1–32.

Gerhard, J. (2005) '*Sex and the City*: Carrie Bradshaw's Queer Postfeminism'. *Feminist Media Studies*. Volume 5 (1): 37–49.

Gerschick, T. J. (2006) 'The Body, Disability, and Sexuality'. In S. Seidman, N. Fischer and C. Meeks (eds) *Introducing the New Sexuality Studies*. London: Routledge.

Hesse-Biber, S. (1996) *Am I Thin Enough Yet? The Cult of Thinness and the Commercialization of Identity*. Oxford: Oxford University Press.

Hevey, D. (1992) *The Creatures that Time Forgot: Photography and Disability Imagery*. London: Routledge.

Hughes, B. (2002) 'Disability and the Body'. In C. Barnes, M. Oliver and L. Barton (eds) *Disability Studies Today*. Cambridge: Polity Press.

Jermyn, D. (2009) *Sex and the City*. Detroit: Wayne State University Press.

McNair, B. (2002) *Striptease Culture: Sex, Media and the Democratization of Desire*. London: Routledge.

McNair, B. (2013) *Porno? Chic! How Pornography Changed the World and Made It a Better Place*. London: Routledge.

Marks, D. (1999) *Disability: Controversial Debates and Psycho-Social Perspectives*. London: Routledge.

Monaghan, L. F. (2008). *Men and the War on Obesity: A Sociological Study*. London: Routledge.

Monaghan, L. F. (2014). 'Civilising Recalcitrant Boys' Bodies: Pursuing Social Fitness through the Anti-Obesity Offensive'. *Sport, Education and Society*. Volume 19 (6): 691–711.

Nelson, J. (1994) 'Broken Images: Portrayals of Those with Disabilities in American Media'. In J. Nelson (ed) *People with Disabilities, the Media, and the Information Age*. Westport: Greenwood Press.

Norden, M. F. (1994) *The Cinema of Isolation: A History of Physical Disability in the Movies*. New Brunswick: Rutgers University Press.

Oliver, M. (1990) *The Politics of Disablement*. Basingstoke: Macmillan.

Orbach, S. (1979) *Fat Is a Feminist Issue: A Self-Help Guide for Compulsive Eaters*. New York: Berkley Books.

Paré, A. (1982) *On Monsters and Marvels* (trans. J. L. Pallister). Chicago: University of Chicago Press.

Richardson, N. (2008) 'Flex Rated! Female Bodybuilding: Feminist Resistance or Erotic Spectacle'. *Journal of Gender Studies*. Volume 17 (4): 289–301.

Richardson, N. (2010) *Transgressive Bodies: Representations in Film and Popular Culture*. Farnham: Ashgate.

Richardson, N. (2012) 'Fashionable "Fags" and Stylish "Sissies": The Representation of Stanford in *Sex and the City* and Nigel in *The Devil Wears Prada*'. *Film, Fashion & Consumption*. Volume 1 (2): 137–157.

Richardson, N. (2016) 'Feed: A Representation of Feederism or Fatsploitation?' In J. Gwynne (ed) *Transgression in Anglo-American Cinema: Gender, Sex and the Deviant Body*. London: Wallflower Press.

Richardson, N., Smith, C. and Werndly, A. (2013) *Studying Sexualities: Theories, Representations, Practices*. Basingstoke: Palgrave Macmillan.

Richardson, N. and Wearing, S. (2014) *Gender in the Media*. Basingstoke: Palgrave Macmillan.
Saint-Hilaire, É. G. (1822) *Philosophie Anatomique: Des Monstruités Humaines, Ouvrage Contenant une Classification des Monsters*. Oxford: Oxford University Press.
Shakespeare, T. (1999) 'Joking a Part'. *Body and Society*. Volume 5 (4): 47–52.
Shakespeare, T. (2000) 'Disabled Sexuality: Towards Rights and Recognition'. (No date) *Bent Voices*. www.bentvoices.org/culturecrash/shakespeare.htm (accessed 20 August 2009).
Shildrick, M. (2002) *Embodying the Monster: Encounters with the Vulnerable Self*. London: Sage.
Smith, C. (2007) *One for the Girls! The Pleasures and Practices of Pornography for Women*. Bristol: Intellect.
Soorenian, A. (2014) 'Media, Disability, and Human Rights'. In M. Gill and C. J. Schlund-Vials (eds) *Disability, Human Rights and the Limits of Humanitarianism*. Farnham: Ashgate.
Spinks, J. (2006) 'Wondrous Monsters: Representing Conjoined Twins in Early Sixteenth Century German Broadsheets'. *Parergon*. Volume 22 (2): 7–112.
Stephens, E. (2006) 'Cultural Fictions of the Freak Body: Coney Island and the Postmodern Sideshow'. *Continuum: Journal of Media and Cultural Studies*. Volume 20 (4): 485–498.
Tiefer, L. (1995) *Sex is Not a Natural Act*. Boulder: Westview Press.
UPIAS (1976) *Fundamental Principles of Disability*. London: UPIAS.
Whittington-Walsh, F. (2002) 'From Freaks to Savants: Disability and Hegemony from *The Hunchback of Notre Dame* (1939) to *Sling Blade* (1997)'. *Disability and Society*. Volume 17 (6): 695–707.
Zola, I. (1985) 'Depictions of Disability: Metaphor Message and Medium in the Media: A Research and Political Agenda'. *Social Science Journal*. Volume 22 (4): 5–17.

Media

The scenes from *The Undateables* analysed in the chapter can be found on the Channel 4 website: www.channel4.com/programmes/the-undateables (accessed 10 February 2016).
The Undateables (2012) Series 1, episode 1. Channel 4, 3 April.
The Undateables (2012) Series 1, episode 2. Channel 4, 10 April.
The Undateables (2015) Series 4, episode 1. Channel 4, 5 January.

How to Look Good Naked (2006–2008) [TV Series]. UK: Channel 4.
Inside I'm Dancing (2004) Directed by D. O'Donnell [Film]. Ireland: WT2 Productions.
Intouchables (2011) Directed by O. Nakache and E. Touledano [Film]. France: Quad Productions.
The Sessions (2012) Directed by B. Lewin [Film]. USA: Fox Searchlight Pictures.
Sex and the City (1998–2004) [TV Series]. USA: HBO.
Sex and the City: The Movie (2008) Directed by M. P. King [Film]. USA: New Line Cinema.
Sex and the City 2 (2010) Directed by M. P. King [Film]. USA: New Line Cinema.
The Theory of Everything (2014) Directed by J. Marsh [Film]. UK: Working Title Films.
Theory of Flight (1999) Directed by P. Greengrass [Film]. UK: Distant Horizon.

PART IV
Deconstructing key figures

32
THE METROSEXUAL

John Mercer and Feona Attwood

Figures of masculinity

The media have frequently played an important role in presenting new models of gender and sexuality, often attracting attention because of the androgynous, macho, queer, 'girly' or highly sexual figures they offer their audiences, and sometimes calling into question 'received notions of "masculine" and "feminine", straight and gay, girl and woman, boy and man' (Garber, 1997: 354). While it is often regarded as commonsensical to identify the central role of the media in the cultural construction of femininity in its many guises, it is equally important to note that the media have played an equally vital role in identifying and extoling masculine archetypes, values and their variants, or by calling the same values into question. Indeed, the 'crisis of masculinity' – a term that has been used routinely to describe everything from representations of male angst in 1950s Hollywood cinema to the plight of working-class youth in contemporary urban settings – was first coined by the political commentator Arthur Schlessinger Jr in an article of the same name in *Esquire* magazine in 1958. It is in this process of identifying what it means to be a man and consequently giving a name to new iterations of masculinity that the media can be seen as being in the business of 'producing' masculinity, and this is an activity that has gathered pace in recent years.

In this chapter we focus in particular on one of these media-generated models of masculinity: the figure of the metrosexual, and his place in a succession of figures of masculinity and male sexuality. The 'metrosexual' – a term coined by journalist and cultural commentator Mark Simpson (1994, 2002, 2005) – can be seen as a contemporary development related to the earlier figure of the 'sensitive, nurturing, caring' 'new man', alongside fashion and grooming-related representations of men which use a 'vocabulary of "style"' to present the male body as an object of desire and looking (Nixon, 1996: 164). The metrosexual, therefore, is not without precedent. Indeed, the construction of media and commercial spaces for 'the display of masculine sensuality' (Nixon, 1996: 202) and the sexualisation of men's bodies have been the subjects of a degree of academic attention since the 1990s (MacKinnon, 1997; Bordo, 1999). While a different kind of figure – the 'new lad' of the 1990s – was characterised by 'naughtiness', 'schoolboy vulgarity' (Whelehan, 2000: 65–66), 'drinking to excess, adopting a predatory attitude towards women and obsessive forms of independence' (Jackson *et al.*, 2001: 78), the more recent emergence of the metrosexual has referred to a vocabulary of style to represent 'a straight man with some stereotypically feminine traits, such as taste in grooming and culture' (Ervin, 2011: 58), as well as a figure whose sexual identity depends on mediation, consumerism and lifestyle, rather than sexual preference or practice.

According to Hall, metrosexuality is 'a more liberal and equitable identity' (2014a: 329) which embraces some traditionally feminine appearance-related practices and characteristics that are often also stereotypically associated with gay men, such as the use of cosmetics and an interest in fashion and leisure retail more generally (2014b). Notably, in both of the accounts of metrosexuality just given, Hall and Ervin tend – albeit unintentionally – to present 'straightness' and heterosexuality as ostensibly known, transparent and unproblematic categories; both also, to a greater or lesser degree, draw attention to a stereotypical and now rather arcane connection between femininity, effeminacy and homosexuality. This tends to flatten out the complexity of the masculinity that metrosexuality evidences and also perhaps the ways in which modern men make sense of their own identities within a contemporary consumer culture. This rather conflicted construction of the discourse of metrosexuality is one of its most prominent features.

While media representations often present the metrosexual as a 'stylish heterosexual man', the term can also be seen in use in popular discourse, often pejoratively, to denote homosexuality or effeminacy (Hall, 2014a: 329), making a connection between an over-investment in grooming and appearance and compromised masculinity, or at least illustrating a rather ambivalent attitude to modern masculinities. This is often evidenced in media reportage on the growth of the male grooming consumer sector, a development that is more often than not directly linked to the emergence of the metrosexual. For example, a relatively typical article in *The Independent* in January 2016 about the 'multi-billion pound' men's grooming business mixes hyperbole with a picture of insecure modern men, uncertain about making informed consumer choices, who look to role-model figures from the world of entertainment and high fashion for 'relatability'. The rather improbable example of 'relatability' chosen in the article is the designer Tom Ford, a gay man whose 'male-friendly' branding has featured the designer as a model in his own right. Ford, we are advised, 'is groomed to within an inch of his life, stubble perfectly contoured across his chin, tanned and moisturised and, generally, perspiration-free' (Fury, 2016).[1] Ford's public persona is that of an openly gay man and, furthermore, a man who invests (professionally, artistically and aesthetically) in his appearance, as the figurehead and in large part the brand ambassador for his company. This epitome of the impeccably groomed and successful professional man is scrupulously marketed and constructed as simultaneously, and resolutely, *not* effeminate, and perhaps also as representative of a masculinity that transcends (or makes irrelevant) rather more arcane notions of 'real men' in opposition to effeminate 'sissies' who are superficially concerned with their appearance. Indeed, to mitigate against the uncertainties and ambiguities that the metrosexual seems to generate – in media reportage at least – in terms of those figures in the public eye that have been associated with metrosexuality, it is often the case that their non-traditional gender practices are framed by 'masculine markers such as heterosexual prowess, heroism, career progression, sporting endeavor and individuality', suggesting a masculinity that is 'reworked for a contemporary consumer-driven lifestyle' (Hall, 2014a: 329).

The most vivid example of this reworking is perhaps offered by the footballer, model and personality David Beckham, who, in reportage on the subject, is posited as the metrosexual *sine qua non*.[2] Indeed, in Mark Simpson's 2002 article for *Salon* in which the characteristics of the metrosexual are the most clearly enumerated, Beckham is not just an arbitrary example; instead, he is identified in terms that draw ironic attention to the ambiguities of the assignation as a 'shrieking, screaming, flaming, freaking metrosexual'.

The emergence of David Beckham as a celebrity, and the Beckham celebrity brand, goes hand in hand with the development of metrosexuality as a category of masculinity that was to gain purchase within popular culture at the very same time that Beckham's star status was being established. Beckham's marriage to the style arbiter Victoria Beckham, his investment in his appearance as part of a scrupulously managed PR strategy designed to establish his celebrity persona and his transition from professional sportsman to the world of fashion/celebrity point to a cultural moment in which the so-called celebrity culture was in the ascendant, where fashion and beauty marketing was targeted at male consumers in an increasingly aggressive fashion and where normative models of masculinity were being rethought. Beckham's emergence within and contribution to this new cultural context has largely ensured his continued popularity as a celebrity, and also his relevance as a figure through which to consider modern masculinities. When, in 2004, artist Sam Taylor Wood was commissioned to produce a video portrait of Beckham for the National Gallery, she chose to represent him in the manner of a modern-day Sleeping Beauty. Beckham's physical beauty in repose was unambiguously situated as a passive spectacle for consumption by both men and women, and onto which any number of fantasies of intimacy could be projected. The artwork attracted a storm of international press and large audiences, for whom the chance to voyeuristically gaze at the sleeping beauty in repose was irresistible, but also in part at least because it seemed to problematise, in a subtle but profound move, the dynamics of spectatorship of the male body.[3]

While his profile and prominence can scarcely be questioned, it would not, however, be accurate to regard Beckham as unique – instead he is representative of a generation of men, often in the public eye, who perform their masculinity in ways that have been described as metrosexual or as indicative of metrosexuality. Like previous models of masculinity, especially those connected to and expressed through fashion and style, metrosexuality is both generational and temporally bounded, in that it is a term used to describe and reflect the manner through which specific groups of men, usually within a specific age bracket, at a specific cultural and historical moment, articulate and express their masculinity, and the ways in which they are represented through culture. So the fashion model David Gandy, longstanding face of Dolce and Gabbana fragrances, fronts an underwear line for Marks and Spencer that trades on his muscular physique and physical beauty, appealing to both male and female consumers. Reality TV stars such as Mark Wright and Joey Essex, both of whom found fame in *The Only Way is Essex*, have a celebrity status founded on their notoriously exaggerated interest in their physical appearance. The straight-identified actor, writer and director James Franco flirts with gay sexuality both in his creative work such as *Interior: Leather Bar* (2013) and in a more self-parodic form through his comedy collaborations with Seth Rogen. Mainstream TV presenters and personalities such as Dermot O'Leary and James Corden flirt in a more direct fashion with their guests, both male and female; this performance of a liberated and unrestricted sexual and gender identity that need not disavow homosexuality at all costs demonstrates a level of comfort with homosexuality that Eric Anderson, as we will note later, has elsewhere regarded as indicative both of an 'inclusive masculinity' (2009) and perhaps more contentiously, writing with Mark McCormack (2010), as evidence of declining homophobia in Western society.

Evidence of the 'generational' nature of these models of masculinity is offered by the proliferation of 'new' masculinities that have followed in the wake of the metrosexual. Notably, we have recently seen the emergence of the 'lumbersexual', a figure with an iconography drawing on hyper-macho signifiers including beards, tattoos and a uniform of plaid shirts and outdoors attire that seems, in part at least, to be a stylistic reaction to the scrupulous grooming associated with metrosexuality, but is nonetheless equally self-conscious and contrived in its post-modern conflation of the stylistic tropes of American ruralism, urban hipsterism, the affectations of folk culture devotees and the dress style of the 1970s gay macho culture. More recently still, Mark Simpson has announced the arrival of the 'spornosexual', marked out by

> painstakingly pumped and chiselled bodies, muscle-enhancing tattoos, piercings, adorable beards and plunging necklines . . . Eagerly self-objectifying, [and] *totally tarty*. Their own bodies (more than clobber and product) have become the ultimate accessories, fashioning them at the gym into a hot commodity – one that they share and compare in an online marketplace.
>
> *(Simpson, 2014)*

As in the cases of the 'new man' in the late 1980s and the metrosexual in the early 2000s, the spornosexual has gained popular purchase and become an object of scholarly attention with relative ease and speed. In all cases, these models of masculinity provoke ambivalent and conflicted responses from commentators and scholars just as easily as they generate attention-grabbing feature opportunities replete with the scope to publish seductive images of sexually attractive (and, more often than not, scantily clad) male bodies in magazines, newspaper supplements and websites. Some writers have related the emergence of these figures to contemporary fears about masculinity and shifts in the social position of men. Rather prosaically, for example, Miller (2005) has noted that the metrosexual can be connected to a growing pressure on men to look young and fit, and Sender (2006: 146) has argued that this version of masculinity demonstrates that 'straight white guys have to work harder', most particularly by becoming consumers.

However, as we have already observed, the practice of connecting changes in manifestations of masculinity in (and through) popular culture to wider social and cultural anxieties is not new. Indeed, this debate, in its contemporary sense, is at least as old as 1958, when Schlessinger argued that the crisis of 1950s masculinity was in fact to be attributed to the growing emancipation of women, and has been a fairly constant way in which reportage has tended to account for the evolution or shift in masculinities – and especially masculine representations – ever since. So when Mark Simpson (2002) writes, with a witty and altogether knowingly polemical turn, that the metrosexual represents the 'emasculation' of straight men, his argument, designed to provoke, is referencing a popular journalistic tradition of writing about masculinity as a site not of fixity and stability but instead of flux and uncertainty, which, at the time he wrote those words, was already half a century old.

Moving forward and developing ways in which to think about modern masculinities, Jamie Hakim adopts Simpson's formulation of the spornosexual to write in reflexive and sophisticated terms identifying, like Simpson, that the spornosexual is a 'second generation' metrosexual focused less on fashion and more on the body – a figure associated with a substantial increase in young men attending gyms in order to work on their bodies (2015: 85). In the context of austerity in the UK, this kind of body work can be seen as a development of self-branding strategies (see Banet-Weiser, 2012) in order to create social and cultural value (Hakim, 2015: 86). It may also represent the increasing kinds of men's participation in contemporary performances of masculinity. While precursors to the metrosexual were 'only to be found inside fashion magazines such as GQ, in television advertisements for Levi's jeans or in gay bars' in the 1980s, by the arrival of the 1990s they were 'everywhere' and 'going shopping' (Simpson, 1996: 225), and through spornosexual practices in the contemporary moment they are now actively self-fashioning their bodies – 'direct practitioners rather than aspiring consumers' (Hakim, 2015: 87).

Sex, sexualisation and metrosexuality

One of the key ways in which new models of gender and sexuality and their depictions in the media have been discussed is as part of a 'sexualisation of culture'. For the most part, these discussions have focused on young women and girls and an emerging construction of a discourse of female sexuality as 'something requiring constant attention, discipline, self-surveillance and emotional labour', set up in contrast to more traditional representations of male sexuality as a form of 'youthful, unselfconscious pleasure-seeking' (Gill, 2007: 257). This is not the externally imposed 'objectification' described in earlier feminist writings, but 'sexual subjectification' – a form of self-policing (in Gill, 2007: 258) 'organized around notions of choice, empowerment, self-surveillance, and sexual difference (Gill, 2007: 271). The truncated, binaristic nature of this kind of argument, which is highly visible across media reportage and academic writing, presents a seductively if superficially simple position that erases the very complexity and ambiguity that is perhaps the most prominent characteristic of contemporary Western lives, identities and sexualities.

For example, metrosexuality itself, while a term usually applied to a specifically masculine set of practices, can be seen as existing within a broader sphere of contemporary sexual identities. Carrie Bradshaw, the central figure of the TV and film series *Sex and the City*, has been seen as emblematic of a model of 'postfeminist' femininity which emphasises the importance of self-making through image, consumption and lifestyle. It is part of a broader shift in which female sexuality is increasingly represented as 'active, recreational, material, independent, consumerist and consumed' (Evans, 1993: 41). Simpson (2002) has described this kind of character as a 'female metrosexual', highlighting the way in which narcissism, a key feature of metrosexual identity for Simpson, has become 'a survival strategy' for both men and women.

Some writers have also seen this kind of development as part of the changing history of sexual communities and the identities they offer. Alan Sinfield has noted that in a 'post-gay' era (1998: 5), a singular model of homosexuality is replaced by multiple homosexualities. While Sinfield sees this as a largely progressive trend, the term 'post-gay' has become attached to a set of politics and cultural developments that for some are regarded as indicators of the erasure of a gay identity. Stephen Maddison argues, for instance, that what the post-gay context allows for is an assimilation of gay identities, in which gay men disappear 'culturally and politically' and also 'aesthetically and stylistically' (2012: 97). As Mark Simpson noted as early as 1996, metrosexuality is, demonstrably, in part the adoption of a 'gay lifestyle' by straight men (1996: 227), and in this sense 'there is nothing "straight" about metrosexuality' (Simpson, 2004). Metrosexuality, then, as a contemporary model of masculinity, can perhaps be regarded as illustrative of both of these trajectories, simultaneously providing evidence of both the utopian post-gay society that Sinfield predicts and a rather more ambivalent post-gay society in which gay identities have become assimilated into the mainstream.

In the twenty-first century, this appropriation and assimilation of gay lifestyles and practices into the vocabulary and behaviours of what we will describe for the sake of simplicity, if not accuracy, as heterosexual culture leads sociologists such as Eric Anderson to argue that there is evidence of a new 'inclusive masculinity' that allows men to 'act in ways once associated with homosexuality, with less threat to their public identity as heterosexual' (2009: 7). According to Anderson, young straight men are able to connect emotionally and be physically or even sexually intimate with each other, without feeling that their masculinity or their sexuality is compromised (Anderson, 2014). Once again, the optimism of Anderson's theorisation is challenged by others, who argue instead that this shift is primarily a process in which 'sexual tastes and sexual ideologies that police gender are increasingly driven by the needs of capital' (Maddison, 2012: 97). In this sense, a 'liberated' sexuality is part of consumer capitalism and its promotion of 'pleasure as a duty' (Bourdieu, 1984: 365–371). In this 'neosexual revolution' (Sigusch, 1998: 331–359), sexuality is 'fragmented again and again in order to ascribe new desires and meanings to it, to implant new urges and new fields of experience, to market new practices and services' (Sigusch, 2014: 138). Social, cultural and sexual categories and identities that were once clearly marked are constantly updated, refined, revised and added to in this neoliberal setting, in which the logic of the market is the principle determinant of social and cultural practices. This extends beyond the metrosexual, to a wide range of other 'diverse eroticisms' (Bristow, 1997: 219) that range from the relatively clearly defined practices of bisexuality to the more fluid categories of bi-curiosity or 'heteroflexibility' (Diamond, 2008).

Plastic sexuality

While remaining mindful of the connections that Bourdieu, Sigusch or Maddison rightly make between capitalism and sexual identities, it would nonetheless be inaccurate to describe the shifts that have been identified in this chapter as merely part of a process of sexual commodification. They are instead, we would argue, part of a much broader and yet more profound shift in the relations between sexuality and identities. Whereas nineteenth-century ideas about sexuality focused on sexual preference and orientation, 'identity and personality . . . are instead based on lifestyle choices, consumption patterns, brands, social circles' (Simpson, 2004) in a contemporary context in which sexual identity increasingly becomes less about a sense of having a stable sexual core and more a question of performance and appearance. This is a twenty-first-century sexuality that is not fixed and constant, but rather 'plastic' (Giddens, 1992: 58) and 'precarious' (Woltersdorff, 2011: 167).

This model of sexuality disrupts the idea of a 'real' sexual self that can be categorised. It is part of a broader preoccupation with people's individual experiences, desires and aspirations and an idea of the self *'for itself'* rather than for other people (Simon, 1996: 13). In some ways it is less about sex as something we *are* and more as something we *do*, with a variety of goals and outcomes, for example as a form of self-pleasure, a route to personal development and fulfilment (Plummer, 1995: 124–125) or a means of becoming part of a community. This model of sexuality has become more and more prominent because of the growing centrality of occupations concerned with presentation and representation (Jancovich, 2001) and of the cultural intermediaries who are 'involved in the provision of symbolic goods and services', such as journalists, designers, PR practitioners, advertisers, sex therapists, marriage counsellors and dieticians (Nixon and du Gay, 2002: 496). Furthermore, sexual discourse is increasingly organised by new cultural intermediaries – in particular, by 'sexperts'.

Sex is a central theme in much visual culture (Poynor, 2006: 7–8) and is increasingly entrenched within media forms (Plummer, 2003a: 275). Within the media, sex and sexuality are perennial subjects of debate, and sexually explicit materials are more and more widely accessible, alongside representations of diverse and often complex presentations of genders and sexualities. As media have become more interactive and participatory, they have also become vehicles for sexual expression, part of what Brian McNair describes with intentional flippancy as a 'striptease culture' for 'self-revelation . . . exposure' (2002: 81) and for creating a paradoxical 'public intimacy' (2002: 98).

In *Liquid Modernity*, Bauman describes our late-modern period as 'multiple, complex and fast moving' (2000: 117), a time in which identity appears to be fluid and constantly in flux. In a similar vein, the social psychologist Kenneth Gergen (1991), in *The Saturated Self*, has argued that we are so overwhelmed with opportunities for self-expression in contemporary societies that we demonstrate a condition he calls 'multiphrenia' (1991: 73–80) – that our sense of self becomes fractured, 'saturated' and overwhelmed by the variety and choices that are the consequence of technologically developed modern societies. This metaphor can be extended to analysis of the contemporary construction of gender and sexuality, and in particular, we would argue, to the cultural construction of masculinities. It's important to note here, though, that while we might contrast these new models to 'traditional' ideas about gender, masculinities have always been 'hybrid' and 'always formed by tension and conflict' (Aboim, 2010: 3). Earlier figures of masculinity such as the nineteenth-century 'dandy' bear this out – the dandy also embodied a masculinity focused on the pursuit of individual style, distinctions of taste and the importance of aesthetics, culture and lifestyle (see Sontag, 1990; Featherstone, 1991; Chaney, 1996). Nonetheless, the contemporary cultural context of the mass media, internet and social media provides conditions in which models of gender and sexuality proliferate at an exponential rate. This in turn has produced a condition that we would describe as 'saturated masculinity' (Mercer, 2017), in which there are such a multitude of differing and sometimes contradictory or competing representations of masculinities that the meaning of masculinity becomes ever more elastic and fluid. In this contemporary setting, then, the idea of a 'dominant' or 'hegemonic' model of masculinity (Connell, 1995) is no longer tenable. In this context the metrosexual, his progenitor the 'new man' and his predecessor the 'new lad', as well as the panoply of variants and new masculinities that have followed in his wake, can all be regarded as manifestations of a fluid and multifarious saturated masculinity.

Notes

1 For further examples of articles about the boom of the male grooming industry and the connections to the figure of the metrosexual, see www.telegraph.co.uk/finance/businessclub/sales/11459654/Rise-of-style-conscious-men-boosts-UK-hair-and-beauty-industry.html and www.cnbc.com/2014/12/05/real-men-dont-cry-but-they-are-exfoliating.html (both accessed 12 November 2016).
2 See www.nytimes.com/2003/06/22/style/metrosexuals-come-out.html?pagewanted=all, http://edition.cnn.com/2013/05/17/opinion/beckham-metro-symbol/ and www.vice.com/en_uk/read/whatever-happened-to-the-metrosexuals-324 (all accessed 12 November 2016).
3 www.telegraph.co.uk/culture/art/3616013/Beckham-the-sleeping-beauty.html (accessed 12 November 2016).

Bibliography

Aboim, S. (2010) *Plural Masculinities: The Remaking of the Self in Private Life*. Farnham: Ashgate.
Anderson, E. (2005) 'Orthodox and Inclusive Masculinity: Competing Masculinities among Heterosexual Men in Feminized Terrain'. *Sociological Perspectives*. Volume 48 (3): 337–355.
Anderson, E. (2009) *Inclusive Masculinity: The Changing Face of Masculinities*. New York: Routledge.

Anderson, E. (2014) *21st Century Jocks: Sporting Men and Contemporary Masculinity*. London: Palgrave.

Arthurs, Jane (2003) 'Sex and the City and Consumer Culture: Remediating Postfeminist Drama', *Feminist Media Studies*. Volume 3 (1): 83–98.

Attwood, F. (2011) 'Sex and the Citizens: Erotic Play and the New Leisure Culture'. In P. Bramham and S. Wagg (eds) *The New Politics of Leisure and Pleasure*. London: Palgrave Macmillan.

Banet-Weiser, S. (2012). *AuthenticTM: The Politics of Ambivalence in a Brand Culture*. New York: NYU Press.

Bauman, S. (2003) *Liquid Love*. Cambridge: Polity.

Bauman, Z. (2000) *Liquid Modernity*. Cambridge: Polity.

Bernstein, E. (2007) *Temporarily Yours: Intimacy, Authenticity, and the Commerce of Sex*. Chicago: University of Chicago Press.

Bethan, B. (2003) *Masculinity and Men's Lifestyle Magazines*. Oxford: Blackwell.

Bordo, S. (1999) *The Male Body: A New Look at Men in Public and in Private*. London: Macmillan.

Bourdieu, P. (1984) *Distinction: A Social Critique of the Judgement of Taste*. London: Routledge.

Bristow, J. (1997) *Sexuality*. London: Routledge.

Cashmore, E. (2004) *Beckham*. Cambridge: Polity.

Chaney, D. (1996) *Lifestyles*. London: Routledge.

Coad, D. (2008) *The Metrosexual: Gender, Sexuality, and Sport*. New York: State University of New York Press.

Connell, R. (1995) *Masculinities*. Cambridge: Polity.

Diamond, L. M. (2008) *Sexual Fluidity*. Cambridge, MA: Harvard University Press.

Ervin, M. C. (2011) 'The Might of the Metrosexual: How a Mere Marketing Tool Challenges Hegemonic Masculinity'. In E. Watson (ed) *Performing American Masculinities: The 21st Century Man in Popular Culture*. Bloomington, IN: Indiana University Press.

Evans, D. (1993) *Sexual Citizenship: The Material Construction of Sexualities*. London: Routledge.

Featherstone, M. (1991) *Consumer Culture and Postmodernism*. London: Sage.

Fury, A. (2016) 'Men's Grooming is Now a Multi-billion Pound Worldwide Industry'. *The Independent*. 14 January. www.independent.co.uk/life-style/fashion/features/mens-grooming-is-now-a-multi-billion-pound-worldwide-industry-a6813196.html (accessed 23 March 2016).

Garber, M. B. (1997). *Vested Interests: Cross-Dressing and Cultural Anxiety*. London: Psychology Press.

Gergen, K. J. (1991) *The Saturated Self: Dilemmas of Identity in Contemporary Life*. New York: Basic Books.

Gerhard, J. (2005) 'Carrie Bradshaw's Queer Postfeminism'. *Feminist Media Studies*. Volume 5 (1): 37–49.

Giddens, A. (1992) *The Transformation of Intimacy: Sexuality, Love and Eroticism in Modern Societies*. Cambridge: Polity.

Gill, R. (2003). 'Power and the Production of Subjects: A Genealogy of the New Man and the New Lad'. *The Sociological Review*. Volume 51 (S1): 34–56.

Gill, R. (2007) *Gender and the Media*. Cambridge: Polity.

Hakim, J. (2015) '"Fit is the New Rich": Male Embodiment in the Age of Austerity'. *Soundings: A Journal of Politics and Culture*. Volume 61 (Winter): 84–94.

Hall, M. (2014a) '"It's a Metrosexual Thing": A Discourse Analytical Examination of Masculinities'. *Body Image Dissertation Abstracts and Summaries*. Volume 11 (3): 329.

Hall, M. (2014b) *Metrosexual Masculinities*. Basingstoke: Palgrave Macmillan.

Jackson, P., Stevenson, N. and Brooks, K. (2001) *Making Sense of Men's Magazines*. London: Polity.

Jancovich, M. (2001) 'Naked Ambition: Pornography, Taste and the Problem of the Middlebrow'. *Scope*. June. www.nottingham.ac.uk/scope/documents/2001/june-2001/jancovich.pdf (accessed 28 March 2017).

McCormack, M. and Anderson, E. (2010) '"It's just not acceptable any more": The Erosion of Homophobia and the Softening of Masculinity at an English Sixth Form'. *Sociology*. Volume 44 (5): 843–859.

MacKinnon, K. (1997) *Uneasy Pleasures: The Male as Erotic Object*. London: Cygnus Arts.
McNair, B. (2002) *Striptease Culture: Sex, Media and the Democratization of Desire*. London: Routledge.
Maddison, S. (2012) 'Is the Rectum *Still* a Grave? Anal Sex, Pornography and Transgression'. In T. Gournelos and David J. Gunkel (eds) *Transgression 2.0: Media, Culture and the Politics of a Digital Age*. New York: Continuum Books.
Mercer, J (2017) *Gay Pornography: Representations of Sexuality and Masculinity*. London: I.B. Tauris.
Miller, T. (2005) 'A Metrosexual Eye on Queer Guy'. *GLQ: A Journal of Lesbian and Gay Studies*. Volume 11 (1): 112–117.
Nixon, S. (1996) *Hard Looks: Masculinities, Spectatorship and Contemporary Consumption*. London: St. Martin's Press.
Nixon, S. and du Gay, P. (2002) 'Who Needs Cultural Intermediaries?' *Cultural Studies*. Volume 16 (4): 495–500.
Plummer, K. (1995) *Telling Sexual Stories*. London: Routledge.
Plummer, K. (2003) *Intimate Citizenship: Private Decisions and Public Dialogues*. Washington: University of Washington Press.
Poynor, R. (2006) *Designing Pornotopia: Travels in Visual Culture*. New York: Princeton Architectural Press.
Richardson, H. (2003) '*Sex and the City*: A Visible Flaneuse for the Postmodern Era?' *Continuum: Journal of Media and Cultural Studies*. Volume 17 (2): 147–157.
Schlesinger, A. Jr (1958) 'The Crisis of American Masculinity'. *Esquire*. Volume 51 (November): 64–66.
Sender, K. (2006) 'Queens for a Day: *Queer Eye for the Straight Guy* and the Neoliberal Project'. *Critical Studies in Media Communication*. Volume 23 (2): 131–151.
Sigusch, V. (1998) 'The Neosexual Revolution'. *Archives of Sexual Behaviour*. Volume 27 (4): 331–359.
Sigusch, V. (2000) 'Social Transformation of Sexuality in the Past Decades. An Overview'. *Fortschritte der Neurologie, Psychiatrie, und ihrer Grenzgebiete*. Volume 68 (3): 97–106.
Sigusch, V. (2014). 'Neosexualities and Self-Sex: On Cultural Transformations of Sexuality and Gender in Western Societies'. In C. Schmidt, M. Mack and A. German (eds) *Post Subjectivity*. Newcastle on Tyne: Cambridge Scholars Publishing.
Simon, W. (1996) *Postmodern Sexualities*. London and New York: Routledge.
Simpson, M. (1994) *Male Impersonators: Men Performing Masculinity*. London: Cassell.
Simpson, M. (1996) *It's a Queer World*. London: Vintage.
Simpson, M. (2002) 'Meet the Metrosexual'. *Salon*. 22 July. www.salon.com/2002/07/22/metrosexual/ (accessed 28 November 2016).
Simpson, M. (2004) 'MetroDaddy Speaks!' *Salon*. 5 January. www.salon.com/2004/01/05/metrosexual_ii/ (accessed 28 November 2016).
Simpson, M. (2005) 'Metrodaddy V. Ubermummy'. *3am Magazine*. www.3ammagazine.com/litarchives/2005/dec/interview_mark_simpson.shtml (accessed 28 November 2016).
Simpson, M. (2014) 'The Metrosexual Is Dead. Long Live the "Spornosexual"'. *The Telegraph*. 10 June. Www.telegraph.co.uk/Men/fashion-and-style/10881682/The-metrosexual-is-dead.-Long-live-the-spornosexual.html (accessed 28 November 2016).
Sinfield, A. (1998) *Gay and After*. London: Serpent's Tail.
Sinfield, A. (2004) *On Sexuality and Power*. New York: Columbia University Press.
Smith, C. (2010) 'Pornographication: A Discourse for All Seasons'. *International Journal of Media and Cultural Politics*. Volume 6 (1): 103–108.
Sontag, S. ([1966] 1990) *Against Interpretation and Other Essays*. New York: Anchor Books/Doubleday.
Whelehan, I. (2000) *Overloaded Popular Culture and the Future of Feminism*. London: The Women's Press.
Woltersdorff, V. (2011) 'Paradoxes of Precarious Sexualities: Sexual Subcultures Under Neo-Liberalism'. *Cultural Studies*. Volume 25 (2): 164–182.

33
THE SEX ADDICT

Barry Reay

The sex addict did not exist before the late twentieth century. Now the concept is a cultural commonplace. In 1972 the notion of out-of-control sexual behaviour was described as 'a rare phenomenon' (Salzman, 1972: 49), but by 2011 the cover story in that gauge of the US cultural mainstream, *Newsweek*, was 'The Sex Addiction Epidemic' (Lee, 2011). The disorder of sex addiction, and its sufferer the sex addict, are recent inventions.[1]

Helen Keane once wrote of the work that has gone into constructing the syndrome of sexual addiction, 'of producing a recognizable disease entity through epistemological labour' (Keane, 2001: 14). The labour that went into this birth was multilayered. The concept began as a product of late twentieth-century cultural anxieties and has remained responsive to those tensions, including in its most recent iterations, 'hypersexual disorder' and addiction to cybersex (Irvine, 1995; Kafka, 2013; Ley, Prause and Finn, 2014). Although sex addiction is a spurious ailment – with diagnostic imprecision and confusion, and with little or no scientific, peer-reviewed evidence that any of its supposed treatments have been effective – it has to be taken seriously as a phenomenon. Rarely has a socio-psychological discourse taken such a hold on the public imagination. Its success and unquestioning acceptance at the academic level is also remarkable (Reay, Attwood and Gooder, 2015). That the concept is so marked by an essential social conservatism and has become a convenient descriptor of disapproved sex – what Jerome Wakefield has termed a confusion of 'social disapproval and morality with issues of health and disorder' (Wakefield, 2012: 215) – makes its short history all the more intriguing.

Sex addiction's success as a purported malady lay with its medicalisation, both as a self-help movement in terms of self-diagnosis and as a rapidly growing industry of therapists on hand to deal with the new disease. The crucial setting for the early history of sex addiction was the combined rise of a wider addiction discourse – what Frank Furedi has called therapy culture – where addiction became a fetish, with all the powerlessness, vulnerability and passivity associated with that state (Furedi, 2004: 120–4). 'In common parlance we now extend addiction to relate to almost any substance, activity or interaction', Lawrence Hatterer wrote in 1982. 'People now refer to themselves as being addicted to food, smoking, gambling, buying, forms of work, play and sex' (Hatterer, 1982: 149). By the end of the 1980s, Stanton Peele, a specialist in the area of alcohol and drug abuse, was warning against what he termed the addiction treatment industry: 'It is hard to escape the conclusion that ownership of an emotional-behavioral-appetitive disease is the norm in America' (Peele, 1989: 140–1).

Sociologists and cultural historians of medicine and psychiatry have outlined the ingredients for the expansion of a syndrome, which, with modifications here and there, can be applied to the development of the sex addict. First, the illness was named. Then it needed the drugs and the pharmaceutical companies to market both the ailment and its supposed cure. Then there was the role of patient advocacy (consumers who already thought they knew what their ailment was) and self-help groups. Then it required therapists of various sorts: psychologists and psychiatrists; the primary-care physicians with prescribing powers (and far more numerous than psychiatrists); but also the other agents with access to possible sufferers, including an army of specialist clinicians of uncertain qualifications and with untested therapies. There were open-ended tests to locate the complaint, celebrity confessions, sufferers' memoirs and self-help guides. We need also to include the research institutes and projects, and new specialist journals (the academic impact mentioned earlier). And finally there was the constant promotion by a less-than-critical media and new media (Horwitz, 2002; Conrad, 2007; Horwitz and Wakefield, 2007; Lane, 2007; Frances, 2013; Pierre, 2013; Sadler, 2013). If health policy researchers were to claim in 2005 that in the course of their lives nearly half of all Americans would meet the criteria for a recognised psychiatric disorder, it is scarcely surprising that sex was part of this national inclusion (Kessler *et al.*, 2005).

The 'sex' in the sex addict and sex addiction is obviously important. The sex addict is situated in a culture in which sex has become central to everyday discourse and representation (Williams, 2004; Paasonen, Nikunen and Saarenmaa, 2007; Attwood, 2010). Feona Attwood has nicely captured this cultural shift as 'the proliferation of sexual texts', and we will see that sexual addiction is very much one of those texts (2006: 78).

As already hinted at, the media has played a role in this history, first with TV, the tabloids and the case histories of claimed celebrity victims all helping to popularise the concept, and then with the impact of the internet. The technological sexual temptations faced by the sex addict in 1990 were the VCR and phone sex. By the 2010s the addictionology timeline of sexual access had expanded to include chat rooms, porn sites, sexting, Craigslist, Facebook, Twitter, Grindr and many other sites and applications. Smartphones had replaced laptops (Weiss and Samenow, 2010). A critic of the diagnostic value of sexual addiction, the Denver family therapist Tracy Todd, wrote that

> [m]ore and more people are showing up at my door with it branded on their foreheads. 'I learned it from a talk show', one man told me . . . Clients arrive with a wealth of information obtained from the Internet.
>
> (Todd, 2004: 68)

Todd was clearly impressed, though concerned, at the speed with which the label was 'gaining popular attention and acceptance' (ibid.). And this was a decade ago.

My concern in this chapter, then, is with the role of the media in the making of the sex addict. As Janice Irvine observed, 'The power of sex addiction lay not in the number of sufferers but in the expansion of this particular narrative of sexual disease' (Irvine, 1995: 440). I want to explore some of the elements of this narrative through case studies: *Time* magazine's (cross-media) feature 'Sex Addiction: A Disease or a Convenient Excuse?'; the talk shows *Rikki Lake* and *Dr. Phil*; and Reality TV's *Sex Rehab with Dr. Drew*.

It is worth first summarising the dynamics of the media's role in this, where hardcopy combined with digital delivery and printed stories were reinforced by the moving image.

Television, newspapers, magazines and the internet converged in what became, in effect, the marketing of a concept. News blurred with entertainment in the form of reality TV, chat shows, celebrity culture, documentary and film, while the sex-addiction industry itself made impressive use of these myriad forms and genres of media delivery. It is interesting that the Clinton/Lewinsky affair of 1998 (when the US House of Representatives impeached President Bill Clinton for perjury and obstruction of justice in respect to his relationship with a White House intern, Monica Lewinsky) was pivotal in this media merging and that sex addiction featured in the discourse surrounding that scandal. However, we are concerned here with the public's acquaintance with a term – a relatively un-interrogated concept with an appeal that resided in its simplicity. What is notable is the ease with which 'sex addiction' became part of what Fedwa Malti-Douglas has dubbed (in another, not unrelated, context) the 'American imaginary' (Malti-Douglas, 2009: 162). This process did not have the dramatic intensity of 1998, when, as it has been observed, 'One could literally spend 24 hours a day watching, listening to, and reading about the Clinton scandal' (Williams and Delli Carpini, 2000: 75). Sex addiction's media legitimation has been a protracted affair. But it did share some of the characteristics of that late-1990s moment, including the unlimited number of sources with rather limited perspectives and the folding of the distinctions between hard news and entertainment and producer and consumer (Williams and Delli Carpini, 2000). Though its genesis preceded such developments, the rise of sex addictionology was arguably facilitated by what has been called the 'collapse of media gatekeeping' (Williams and Delli Carpini, 2000). Over time it would become, like addiction culture generally, 'a matter of common sense, a concept so familiar that it seemed to evade – or perhaps not even require – definition' (Travis, 2009: 3).

Newsweek's cover story, we have seen, was an iconic instance. However, a better example of the phenomenon is *Time* magazine's 2011 feature 'Sex Addiction: A Disease or a Convenient Excuse?' and its follow-up piece on NBC's daily US morning TV programme, *The Today Show*, and then on the internet on *Today.com*. The *Time* feature was by no means uncritical of its subject, but the general tone was noncommittal:

> they are still trying to address very basic questions. Should we regard out-of-control sexual behavior as an extreme version of normal sexuality, or is it an illness completely separate from it? That question lies at the heart of the sex-addiction field, but right now it's unanswerable.
>
> (Cloud, 2011)

The video follow-up on NBC and *Today.com* was less guarded. 'This disease, this particular affliction is so misunderstood', declared a 'sex addict' as he outlined marital infidelities that, in his opinion, became life-threatening. John Cloud, the *Time* journalist, seemed less circumspect when in front of the camera, as the segment cut to his explanation of his subject's almost hallucinatory sexual needs: 'The urges were so strong that he was powerless to overcome them.' The item used the words of a widely known media medical expert, psychologist Jeff Gardere ('Dr. Jeff'): 'For someone who has a real sexual addiction to the point of their being destructive in their lives there is a major treatment option available and that's checking yourself into an in-patient program that's based on a 12-step system.' The video was, in other words, sex-addiction 101. The addict explained that his recovery was 'a process that will last a lifetime ... it just envelops you, it takes your being ... it's a very dark place'. Dr Gail Saltz, a psychiatrist and another well-known TV commentator, clarified that she saw the problem more as compulsion than addiction – 'a compulsive, incredibly overwhelming urge'. And the programme ended with her words: 'you keep doing it and you cannot stop' (*Today*, 2011). The likelihood was that viewers of this item would have been left with the opinion that sex addiction was real, characterised by overwhelming, uncontrollable sexual impulses, and was best conceived and treated as an addiction, like alcoholism. The original *Time* article, while hesitant about aspects of the diagnosis, never really questioned its ontology and, like NBC's *Today*, helped to popularise the concept. An article in the *Columbia Journalism Review* has referred to the manner in which such uncritical journalism has effectively fetishised sex addiction (Brainard, 2011).

From its beginnings, sex addiction seemed perfectly suited to the issue-oriented format of what has been termed the 'first generation of daytime talk shows' (Shattuc, 1997: 3; see also Gamson, 1998). Indeed, their beginnings coincided: Patrick Carnes, sex addiction's early guru, was appearing on *Donahue* in 1985 (Vatz, Weinberg and Szasz, 1985). The baseball star Wade Boggs claimed that he first realised he was a sex addict when he watched an episode of *Geraldo* (1989) that dealt with the subject (Kornheiser, 1989). Marion Barry, the disgraced mayor of the District of Columbia, was a guest on the *Sally Jessy Raphael* show in 1991, presented along with other supposed sex addicts (Specter, 1991). Sex addiction was an ideal topic for a genre that thrived through exploring topical social-interest problems at a personal level: combining audience participation, in fact performance, with guest expertise and facilitating such interaction – almost a mirror image of the conceptual success of sex addiction in wider American society and culture. Sex addiction dealt with sexual excess, of course, another characteristic of the talk shows. And it was therapy. Jane Shattuc estimated in 1997 that about two-thirds of talk shows were devoted to psychological matters (Shattuc, 1997).

The topic was still appearing in the later generation of more confrontational talk shows. *Ricki Lake* featured female sex addicts in 2004 – an interesting programme because three of the four admitted to being sex addicts but were defiant about it: 'Yes, I am a sex addict . . . Hi Ricki, I love your show . . . I don't think I have a problem.' One woman, with more than 700 claimed sexual partners, responded that her only problem was that she did not 'get enough'. Another, aged 23 and with more than 150 male contacts, said: 'Yes, I am addicted to sex . . . I've done it with ten guys [in a day], but usually it's five!' Only the fourth admitted to being in any kind of quandary about the issue and needing help (*Ricki Lake*, 2004). Though the first women interviewed remained unrepentant in a loudly subversive manner, the programme was structured so it finished with the addict who was willing to enter therapy (Hutchby, 2001). The other principal participants – an 'expert', Catherine Burton (a Texas family and marriage therapist), and a recovered sex addict and memoirist, Sue William Silverman – were there to reinforce the problematic nature of sex addiction, to emphasise that the recalcitrant three were in denial, to advocate therapy and to ensure a master theme of disapproval – reinforced by Ricki Lake's wrinkled nose as she commented: 'Clearly she has a problem' (see Figure 33.1).

Furthermore, the sex engaged in was presented as addictive, a message that was never challenged: 'I love sex, it's like a drug to me'; 'I have to have it'; 'She likes sex all the time . . . She eats it, sleeps it, dreams it'; 'My friend Lynette is a very big sex addict. She says that sex is like coffee in the morning for her' (*Ricki Lake*, 2004). All the tropes of sex addiction were present: the ubiquity of the malady, even in women ('Yes, it's very common . . . it's not at all unusual'); acknowledging (or not acknowledging) the problem; shame ('You have a lot of shame'); seeking self-worth from men, then feeling bad and immediately requiring another man to provide that sense of identity again; and sexual melodrama ('A road to death') (*Ricki Lake*, 2004).

Figure 33.1 Ricki Lake (2004): female sex addicts.

Phil McGraw's talk show *Dr. Phil* has also included discussion of sex addiction. The 'Suburban Dramas' episode in 2011 featured McGraw's trademark polygraph test:

> Brett says he's addicted to sex, online pornography and talking dirty to other women . . . Brett insists he's never had a sexual relationship with anyone other than his fiancée. Mandy says she doesn't believe him and wants to know if he's lying.
> (Dr. Phil, 2011)

The 'Secret Life of a Sex Addict' episode in 2013, which featured both the critic David Ley and the advocate Doug Weiss as guests, actually came out against sex addiction as the prime explanation of the subjects' woes. Marcos had had more than 3,000 sexual partners (both male and female) in only 17 years. His wife of nine years, Yvette ('I didn't know he was a sex addict'), was unfaithful too: 'I'm obsessed with hooking up with other men. I cannot maintain monogamy in a relationship with one guy. I have a wandering eye' (*Dr. Phil*, 2013). However, the experts concluded that sex addiction was the least of their problems. Dr Phil himself listed a range of possibilities – narcissism, borderline personality disorder, antisocial personality disorder – that might have contributed to what he termed a 'highly dysfunctional family', stating that 'Sex addiction might wind up on the list but it wouldn't be near the top.' Yet the banner headline was 'Secret Life of a Sex Addict' (*Dr. Phil*, 2013). The side-bars on the website for the shows included links to sex-addiction tests and advice and support centres.

Sex Rehab with Dr. Drew (2009), which involves three weeks in the Pasadena Recovery Center under the care of Dr Drew Pinsky, is perhaps the best example of the media's uncritical familiarisation of the concepts of sex addiction and the sex addict. Despite the show's name, it is entertainment rather than treatment, with its format, editing, casting and much else determined by the parameters of reality TV, the genre that combines documentary and soap opera, reality and unreality; where viewers look for glimpses of authenticity amid all the acknowledged, staged fakery (Holmes and Jermyn, 2004; Kavka, 2012; Edwards, 2013; Weber, 2014). Reality TV, Brenda Weber has observed, 'is anything but real' (2014: 4). Significantly, *Sex Rehab with Dr. Drew* was a spinoff from *Celebrity Rehab with Dr. Drew* (2008–12). The cast of porn stars and ex-porn stars, models and ex-models, a (minor) rock star and a pro-surfer were hardly randomly selected: the women had the same agent and the surfer was allegedly paid for product endorsement (which may explain the frequent clothing changes, his mismatching sneakers – 'Interesting shoes' – and the fact that he brought his surfboard with him to the treatment centre!), and all were either self-declared non-addicts (the sex with 3,000 women reported by the rock star was a potential aspect of any performer's CV) or were multiply addicted (sex being just one of their worries). Amber Smith was addicted to alcohol and opiates. Kari Ann Peniche was a methamphetamine addict. Drummer Phil Varone had a cocaine dependency, as did Nicole Narain, a former Playboy Playmate. Several became almost professional celebrity addicts: Jennifer Ketcham, Peniche and Kendra Jade Rossi would also appear in Season 2 of *Sober House* (2010), and Peniche (again) in Season 3 of *Celebrity Rehab* (2010); Smith had already featured in Season 2 of *Celebrity Rehab* (2008) and Season 1 of *Sober House* (2009).

One of those 'treated' – Duncan Roy, a gay English film director who had some knowledge of production – wrote later of blatant playing to the camera, and that he was concerned that some 'might not be on the show for the same reasons as I was. That they might not have any desire for sexual sobriety. That I might be part of a huge pantomime' (Roy, 2009). Rossi blogged that when she signed up for the show it was for the money, and she did not know what sex addiction was (Rossi, 2009). Varone recalled that his agent phoned and said:

> 'OK, we have a supermodel, we have a porn star, we have a Playboy Playmate, we need a rock star.' They need this cast. Do you want to do it? And I said, 'Well to be on television I guess I will.' That's the decision. Those shows are scripted out a certain way.
>
> (McCombs, 2012)

He did not consider himself a sex addict; he just had access to a lot of groupies and took advantage of it (ibid.). After the show he produced his own sex DVD, *The Secret Sex Stash*, and commercially manufactured a dildo replica of his penis called the 'phildo' (Bauman, 2011).

The programme's mise-en-scène is sexualised in ways totally incongruent with the declared aims of detox. The publicised three weeks of celibacy (including a ban on masturbation), the very public confiscation of sex toys, the ban on digital contact with outside temptations (cell phones, laptops, tablets) only serve to heighten the flirting, sexual innuendo, flaunted cleavages, and the very sexualised avoidance of sex by participants, who include porn stars whom the viewer may well have seen elsewhere engaged in very explicit activity – why else would the producers want such actors.[2] Gareth Longstaff has argued that when the former reality TV celebrity Steven Daigle became a porn star, the visual techniques of reality TV merged with those of pornography:

> the mixture of intimacy, liveliness, extreme-close-up, amateur and hand-held camera work, and surveillance imagery associated with the visual rhetoric of both Reality TV and pornography were reworked and repositioned as dual markers of both reality and fantasy.
>
> (Longstaff, 2013: 71)

With the female porn stars in *Sex Rehab* the movement is in the opposite direction, a fascinating example of the intertextual relationship between pornography and sex addiction. Unsurprisingly too, given the presence of those porn stars, there are many emotional 'money shots', those moments of raw feeling – crying, rage – integral to the talk show and reality TV, named by Laura Grindstaff after pornography's famed ejaculatory money shots: visible signs of pleasure rather than grief (Grindstaff, 2002) (see Figure 33.2).

Figure 33.2 Sex Rehab with Dr. Drew (2009): the money shot.

But it is theatre based on the scripts of sex addiction. James Lovett, the surfer – 'I love sex, ah, ha, ha' – claims that his sex addiction is hurting his career. His friends have abandoned him because he slept with their wives, and he has lost all his money: 'Sucked me into a hole that ruined my life.' In his consultation with Pinsky and the therapist Jill Vermeire, who sometimes finishes his sentences for him, he refers to staying home masturbating instead of checking the waves. Diagnosis: 'James clearly has severe addiction where sex is the dominating factor in his life.' The porn actress and director Ketcham (Penny Flame) has lots of sex on camera and is indifferent to her partners. Dr Drew: 'You know that sexual addiction, for the most part, is an intimacy problem?' Ketcham: 'Oh yeaah.' Varone, who admitted later that he was not a sex addict, appears a little bemused by the programme, but seizes eagerly on the suggestion that the death of his mother was pivotal. Diagnosis: 'Although Phil claims he didn't suffer childhood abuse, his grief over his mother's death has certainly affected his addiction' (*Sex Rehab with Dr. Drew*, 2009) (see Figure 33.3).

The message that intervention was required, as already intimated, was reinforced by talk shows, explicitly so in the case of both *Oprah* and *The Tyra Show* in 2009. Oprah Winfrey provided a conduit for Pinsky, a promotion of his show with an epilogue by Winfrey that included a homily about the importance of spirituality in the healing process – 'Because you know that you are carrying God's body. You're God's body' (*Oprah.com*, 2009). *The Tyra Show* combined marketing of *Sex Rehab* and a guest spot for Pinsky with interviews with a 15-year-old supposed sex addict (whose mother later sued the programme) and a man who had purportedly spent 48 hours masturbating to porn. Misleadingly, *Sex Rehab* was presented as a genuine look inside a sex addiction clinic: 'We're taking you inside sex rehab for the very first time'; 'We're going to go behind the scenes of a sex addiction clinic.' This is, in a sense, 'reality' within 'reality': reality TV meets the older talk-show format. Sex addiction is simply assumed in its dramatic presentation. 'You're a baby, you're 15 years old, so you're in high school . . . what does it feel like to be an addict?' 'So imagine this . . . you get up in the morning and you masturbate, you get in the shower and you are masturbating, in the bathroom . . . at the computer masturbating, um' (Tyra Banks's words). Sex addiction is rampant, with a claimed 24 million American sex addicts. It is shocking, as we see in the facial expressions of the open-mouthed studio audience (*The Tyra Show*, 2009).

The sex addict

Figure 33.3 Sex Rehab with Dr. Drew (2009): the concerned doctor.

It is perhaps appropriate that reality TV, a media form that Misha Kavka and Amy West (2004) have characterised as standing outside history to achieve emotional intensity and immediacy, should, in this case, have been promoting a disorder (sex addiction) whose proponents have been so lacking in historical awareness. But the point with this, and other such television, is that it was publicising the concept. As a blog for the show put it: 'I think after watching this show, a lot of people are going to think, "Am I a sex addict?"' (Juzwiak, 2009).

Although there were moments of critique, of questioning, amid all the unthinking valorisation – the defiant young women on *Ricki Lake*, Ricki's wrinkled nose and Dr Phil's incredulity – the examples above illustrate the dynamics of an ultimately uncritical media familiarisation with the shorthand sexual diagnostic term 'sex addiction' and its protagonist the sex addict. Even when coverage was less than complimentary, it was still advancing habituation: the addictionologist Patrick Carnes himself noted that the fact 'that pop culture is making jokes about sex addicts is a sign that awareness of the condition is percolating in mass consciousness' (Salkin, 2008). We can wonder at the reductive powers of these concepts as they became convenient, one might say facile, terms to describe what was once termed promiscuous sex. Sex and addiction lose any analytical complexity once the two words are combined in those limiting designators 'sex addiction' and 'sex addict'.

Notes

1 This chapter draws on material from my contribution to Reay, Attwood and Gooder (2015).
2 For Rossi's work as a porn actress, see *Kendra Jade Rossi The Extreme Squirt*, Scene 1, www.tube8.com/hardcore/kendra-jade-rossi-the-extreme-squirt-scene-1/1166781/ (accessed 15 November 2014) and *Kendra Jade Fucked Up*, www.tube8.com/hardcore/kendra-jade-fucked-up/357272/ (accessed 15 November 2014).

Bibliography

Attwood, F. (2006) 'Sexed Up: Theorizing the Sexualization of Culture'. *Sexualities*. Volume 9 (1): 77–94.
Attwood, F. (ed) (2010) *Mainstreaming Sex: The Sexualization of Western Culture*. London: I.B. Tauris.

Bauman, W. (2011) 'Exclusive Interview: Phil Varone Talks Sex Tapes, Politics and Rock n Roll', *Disarray Magazine*, 23 July: www.disarraymagazine.com/2011/07/exclusive-interview-sex-tapes-politics.html (accessed 16 November 2011).

Brainard, C. (2011) '*Newsweek* Fetishizes an "Epidemic"', *Columbia Journalism Review*, 15 December: www.cjr.org/the_observatory/newsweek_fetishizes_an_epidemi.php?page=all (accessed 13 November 2013).

Cloud, J. (2011) 'Sex Addiction: A Disease or a Convenient Excuse?' *Time*, 28 February: http://content.time.com/time/magazine/article/0,9171,2050027,00.html (accessed 29 August 2013).

Conrad, P. (2007) *The Medicalization of Society: On the Transformation of Human Conditions into Treatable Disorders*. Baltimore: Johns Hopkins University Press.

Dr. Phil (2011) 'Suburban Dramas', 2 March. See also *Dr.Phil.com*: www.drphil.com/shows/show/1612 (accessed 12 December 2013).

Dr. Phil (2013) 'Secret Life of a Sex Addict', 9 September. See also www.drphil.com/shows/show/2062 (accessed 12 December 2013).

Edwards, L.E. (2013) *The Triumph of Reality TV: The Revolution in American Television*. Santa Barbara: Praeger.

Fiske, J. (1996) *Media Matters: Race and Gender in U.S. Politics* (revised edition). Minneapolis: University of Minnesota Press.

Frances, A. (2013) *Saving Normal*. New York: William Morrow.

Furedi, F. (2004) *Therapy Culture: Cultivating Vulnerability in an Uncertain Age*. London: Routledge.

Gamson, J. (1998) *Freaks Talk Back: Tabloid Talk Shows and Sexual Nonconformity*. Chicago: University of Chicago Press.

Grindstaff, L. (2002) *The Money Shot: Trash, Class, and the Making of TV Talk Shows*. Chicago: University of Chicago Press.

Hatterer, L.J. (1982) 'The Addictive Process'. *Psychiatric Quarterly*. Volume 54 (3): 149–56.

Holmes, S. and Jermyn, D. (eds) (2004) *Understanding Reality Television*. London: Routledge.

Horwitz, A.V. (2002) *Creating Mental Illness*. Chicago: University of Chicago Press.

Horwitz, A.V. and Wakefield, J.C. (2007) *The Loss of Sadness: How Psychiatry Transformed Normal Sorrow into Depressive Disorder*. Oxford: Oxford University Press.

Hutchby, I. (2001) 'Confrontation as a Spectacle: The Argumentative Frame of the *Ricki Lake Show*'. In A. Tolson (ed) *Television Talk Shows: Discourse, Performance, Spectacle*. Mahwah, NJ: Erlbaum.

Irvine, J.M. (1995) 'Reinventing Perversion: Sex Addiction and Cultural Anxieties'. *Journal of the History of Sexuality*. Volume 5 (3): 429–50.

Juzwiak, R. (2009) 'A Sex Rehab Primer With Jill Vermeire'. *VH1+ Shows*, 30 October. http://blog.vh1.com/2009-10-30/a-sex-rehab-primer-with-jill-vermeire/ (accessed 17 November 2013).

Kafka, M.P. (2013) 'The Development and Evolution of the Criteria for a Newly Proposed Diagnosis for DSM-5: Hypersexual Disorder'. *Sexual Addiction & Compulsivity*. Volume 20 (1–2): 19–26.

Kavka, M. (2012) *Reality TV*. Edinburgh: Edinburgh University Press.

Kavka, M. and West, A. (2004) 'Temporalities of the Real: Conceptualising Time in Reality TV'. In S. Holmes and D. Jermyn (eds) *Understanding Reality Television*. London: Routledge.

Keane, H. (2001) 'Taxonomies of Desire: Sex Addiction and the Ethics of Intimacy'. *International Journal of Critical Psychology*. Volume 1 (3): 9–28.

Kessler, R.C., Berglund, P., Demler, O., Jin, R., Merikangas, K.R. and Walters, E.E. (2005) 'Lifetime Prevalence and Age-of-Onset Distributions of DSM-IV Disorders in the National Comorbidity Survey Replication'. *Archives of General Psychiatry*. Volume 62: 593–602.

Kornheiser, T. (1989) 'For Your Sins and Mine, Let Me Say I'm Sorry'. *The Washington Post*. 24 February. www.washingtonpost.com/archive/sports/1989/02/24/for-your-sins-and-mine-let-me-say-im-sorry/39a6ee0f-00de-4a94-bb2f-7971e0d00a97/ (accessed 29 March 2017).

Lane, C. (2007) *Shyness: How Normal Behavior Became a Sickness*. New Haven: Yale University Press.

Lee, C. (2011) 'The Sex Addiction Epidemic'. Newsweek. 5 December. www.newsweek.com/sex-addiction-epidemic-66289 (accessed 29 March 2017).

Ley, D., Prause, N. and Finn, P. (2014) 'The Emperor Has No Clothes: A Review of the "Pornography Addiction" Model'. *Current Sexual Health Reports.* Volume 6 (2): 94–105.

Longstaff, G. (2013) 'From Reality to Fantasy: Celebrity, Reality TV and Pornography'. *Celebrity Studies.* Volume 4 (1): 71–80.

McCombs, E. (2012) 'The Only Interview That Ever Made Me Blush', *xoJane*, 24 January: www.xojane.com/sex/sex-rehab-phil-varone-sex-addict (accessed 16 November 2013).

Malti-Douglas, F. (2009) *Partisan Sex: Bodies, Politics, and the Law in the Clinton Era.* New York: P. Lang.

Oprah.com (2009) 'Struggling With Sex Addiction', 23 November: www.oprah.com/relationships/Inside-Sex-Addiction-Rehab-with-Dr-Drew-Pinsky (accessed 12 August 2013).

Paasonen, S., Nikunen, K. and Saarenmaa, L. (eds) (2007) *Pornification: Sex and Sexuality in Media Culture.* Oxford: Berg.

Peele, S. ([1989] 1995) *Diseasing of America.* San Francisco: Jossey-Bass Publishers.

Pierre, J.M. (2013) 'Overdiagnosis, Underdiagnosis, Synthesis: A Dialectic for Psychiatry and the DSM'. In J. Paris and J. Phillips (eds) *Making the DSM-5, 2013: Concepts and Controversies.* New York: Springer.

Reay, B., Attwood, N. and Gooder, C. (2015) *Sex Addiction: A Critical History.* Cambridge: Polity.

Ricki Lake (2004) 'Exposed: Female Sex Addicts!', 3 March.

Rossi, K.J. (2009) 'Just a Girl . . . Sex Rehab', 13 December. http://kendrajaderossi.blogspot.co.nz/2009/12/sex-rehab.html (accessed 17 November 2013).

Roy, D. (2009) 'Is Dr. Drew a Phony?' *Daily Beast*, 17 December: www.thedailybeast.com/articles/2009/12/17/i-am-a-sex-addict-and-i-play-one-on-tv.html (accessed 15 November 2014).

Sadler, J.Z. (2013) 'Considering the Economy of DSM Alternatives'. In J. Paris and J. Phillips (eds) *Making the DSM-5, 2013: Concepts and Controversies.* New York: Springer.

Salkin, A. (2008) 'No Sympathy for the Sex Addict. *New York Times.* 7 September. www.nytimes.com/2008/09/07/fashion/07sex.html (accessed 28 March 2017).

Salzman, L. (1972) 'The Highly Sexed Man'. *Medical Aspects of Human Sexuality.* Volume 6 (1): 36–49.

Sex Rehab with Dr. Drew (2009). Television. VH1 Netwok. Originally TX. 1 November–20 December 2009.

Shattuc, J.M. (1997) *The Talking Cure: TV Talk Shows and Women.* New York: Routledge.

Specter, M. (1991) 'Marion Barry Airing His Vices: On Sally Jessy Raphael, the Ex-Mayor Tells of Sex Addiction'. *The Washington Post.* 14 May. www.washingtonpost.com/archive/lifestyle/1991/05/14/marion-barry-airing-his-vices/5fc15d55-2cd6-45e9-9aa8-3d4df295911d/?utm_term=.57b39d8b60f2 (accessed 29 March 2017).

Today (2011) 'Sex Addiction: An Illness or an Excuse?' 18 February: www.today.com/video/today/41662640#41662640 (accessed 15 November 2014).

Todd, T. (2004) 'Premature Ejaculation of "Sexual Addiction" Diagnoses'. In S. Green and D. Flemons (eds) *Quickies: The Handbook of Brief Sex Therapy.* New York: W.W. Norton & Company, Inc.

Travis, T. (2009) *The Language of the Heart: A Cultural History of the Recovery Movement from Alcoholics Anonymous to Oprah Winfrey.* Chapel Hill: University of North Carolina Press.

Vatz, R.E., Weinberg, L.S. and Szasz, T.S. (1985) 'Why Does Television Grovel At the Altar of Psychiatry?' *The Washington Post.* 15 September.

Wakefield, J.C. (2012) 'The DSM-5's Proposed New Categories of Sexual Disorder: The Problem of False Positives in Sexual Diagnosis'. *Clinical Social Work Journal.* Volume 40 (2): 213–23.

Weber, B.R. (ed) (2014) *Reality Gendervision: Sexuality & Gender on Transatlantic Reality Television.* Durham: Duke University Press.

Weiss, R. and Samenow, C.P. (2010) 'Smart Phones, Social Networking, Sexting and Problematic Sexual Behaviors – A Call for Research'. *Sexual Addiction & Compulsivity.* Volume 17 (4): 241–6.

Williams, B.A. and Delli Carpini, M.X. (2000) 'Unchained Reaction: The Collapse of Media Gatekeeping and the Clinton–Lewinsky Scandal'. *Journalism.* Volume 1 (1): 61–85.

Williams, L. (2004) 'Porn Studies: Proliferating Pornographies On/Scene: An Introduction'. In L. Williams (ed) *Porn Studies.* Durham: Duke University Press.

34

THE STRIPPER

Alison J. Carr

The rapid fire of images around us on billboards and television, in film and social media, can make it feel as though the most prevalent of them are of sexualised bodies on display. Amid them, the stripper, with her skill at bodily performance, stands out. The resonance of her image is perhaps in part because what she represents also reveals something about the conditions of our late-capitalist context.

As an avatar of our culture, her image relies on compliance with the demand for sexualised self-presentation. The variety of representations of the stripper in popular culture varies from the clichéd to the audacious. The stripper often appears in media representations as something like an outlaw – on the one hand, she is conflated with the degradation of societal values, the decay of morality; on the other, she can be used as a way of instantly rejuvenating an ageing celebrity's image. A Google News search for 'stripper' finds such links as: 'Stripper accuses city's public defender of hitting her'; '18 most scandalous confessions by strippers'; 'Man gets life in prison for turning 15-year-old into stripper'; 'Hollywood's sexiest celebrity stripper scenes!' Stripping as represented by the news is variously titillating, contentious, taboo, seedy, corrupting and linked with violence. Underpinning these headlines are wider fears and prejudices of sexualisation and exploitation.

In this chapter I will unpack a wide range of representations of strippers, demonstrating the differing attitudes and biases at work in them. I am interested in asking what kind of understanding we have of the stripper, in spite or because of the excess of her image. This is a practical as well as a scholarly question – if we only have access to narrow, superficial representations of strippers, what impact does this have on the lived experiences of women who work in striptease? If we do not see her represented with multiple dimensions, with personhood, how does this affect how we describe her and how we treat her?

Striptease in popular culture

A defining aspect of the stripper is her sexy dancing. She pole-dances, twerks and grinds in laps. This makes her ideal for featuring in pop-music videos. In 50 Cent's *Disco Inferno* (2004), stripper bodies are ass-shaking objects that surround the rapper. He is at liberty to slap their buttocks and rap about them. In Frank Ocean's *Pyramids* (2012) they pole-dance in slow motion, with their faces shown in close-up and tassels on their nipples.

Here, the stripper adds cachet to the image of the male artist, who appears wealthy enough to be able to pay for and enjoy her.

Videos for female artists use the figure of the stripper to underscore or denote their own sexiness. They embody the stripper to signify they are sexy while simultaneously emphasising that they are not strippers – their status is higher. Examples include Toni Braxton's *Hands Tied* (2010) or Ke$ha's *Dirty Love* (2012). Mya's *My Love Is Like. . .Wo* (2003) stands out among these as she dances through a range of outfits and dance styles, with a climactic pole-dancing into tap-dancing section. Another approach shows the female singer mirroring the male artist's approach, with strippers in the background. In *Pour It Up* (2013), where Rihanna dominates the video, sitting on a throne in a showgirl-style open diamante bra, strippers pole-dance as anonymous decorations. There is a purposeful lack of clarity in the video: is Rihanna one with these strippers, or, like the male artists, is she demonstrating she can afford their bodies?

Hole's *Violet* (1994) adopts a different style: a visual medley of child-pageant smiles, ballet dancers *en pointe*, life models, music-boxes, burlesque dancers and Courtney Love sliding down a pole, with an old-style film grainy texture. Amid this montage of performance and presentation, the strippers represent exuberant rebellion, a joyful way to play with one's own body.[1]

Within films, another set of standard tropes is applied to strippers. The classic film *Gilda* (1946) sets up a number of these. Two overbearing men control Rita Hayworth, the eponymous character, until she rebels by performing a song-and-dance routine. As the song ends she peels off her long gloves and necklace, tossing them into the crowd, and asks for help unzipping her tight black column dress. Briskly ushered away from the floorshow, she argues with her husband, Johnny Farrell: 'Now they all know what I am', she says; 'now they all know that the mighty Johnny Farrell got taken in and that he married a. . .'. Johnny slaps Gilda across the face so we do not hear the final word. Did she mean to say stripper or whore? The narrative implies: yes, Gilda is beautiful and exudes charisma, but she is sullied too.

In the cult film *Showgirls* (1995), a misanthropic re-telling of *42nd Street* (1933), we see the familiar narrative of Nomi, the young performer who lands the role of star-of-the-show because the current star fell downstairs – though here, Nomi purposefully causes the accident. We see the down-on-her-luck arrival to Las Vegas work her way through dancer jobs, from lap-dancer, through chorus girl, up to star. In the dance scenes, the suggestion is that Nomi learned her sexy dancing moves not from dance class but as a sex worker. A notorious scene involves Nomi giving a flamboyant high-energy lap-dance.

Even the more recent art-house film *Afternoon Delight* (2013) reproduces the implication that strippers are prostitutes who dance. Rachel, a bored wife and mother, receives a lap-dance from McKenna in a strip club. This encounter piques her curiosity and Rachel gives McKenna a room in her family's home. Rachel incorporates McKenna into the daily routine, until it's revealed in casual conversation that McKenna also sleeps with her customers. The polite connection is broken: McKenna is the wrong sort of girl to rescue.

Compare the representations of female strippers in films to those of male strippers. In *The Full Monty* (1997), a group of out-of-work men are explored in detail to expose who they are and why they strip – in a sense, to show the audience why making the decision to 'degrade' themselves in this way can be seen as a powerful and defiant act.[2]

Anecdotes from real strippers fill popular stripper memoirs. Detailing the mundane and salacious aspects of the life of a stripper, the memoirs describe the appeal of stripping and the realities of being a stripper and offer accounts of unsavoury strip clubs and punters.

A particular insight is the constant rejection that strippers feel while circulating the club, offering dances: 'The rules of attraction were reversed at a strip club. Girls that could halt midday traffic', writes Diablo Cody, 'were rejected'. The customer's power to reject strippers has an emotional effect on the women, who, 'regardless of how loved they were by husbands or paramours or infants at home, would feel worthless for an instant' (2006: 197).

The writers tend to place themselves on a spectrum of strippers, differentiating themselves against 'the stripper who went too far', and end with reflections tinged with sadness and regret. A lively example of the genre is *Strip City*, by Lily Burana. In her vivid and lyrical description of watching another stripper perform, she defends the magic of stripping, nonetheless bemused by her defence:

> There is nothing in the club that can compete with what's happening onstage. A bomb could drop in the parking lot and no one would move a muscle. She has single-handedly brought the entire audience to its knees, this common genius, this protean hottie. And here is the heart of striptease: You can analyze and deconstruct the act all you want – you will never totally demystify it. You can't break the spell. Nothing can fully explain why some people take to strip clubs – sometimes to the point of addiction, why some find the very idea offensive, and why others just don't get it and shrug. What I like best about stripping is this, the arbitrariness. The mystery. The fact that you can't definitively state what makes one woman stand out from the next. That some tiny part of every dancer's soul spills out when she performs, whether she means it to or not. That you can see a woman totally nude before you, and there's still so much about her that you don't, and can't, know. And that you can never predict that singular instance, like right now, when the world falls away and the only thing that matters is the light falling on the stage and the dancer unfurling herself against the music the way a singer wraps her breath around a note.
>
> (Burana 2001: 180)[3]

The feminist critique of stripping

Strippers appear in different types of media, from the marginal to the mainstream, from headlines and brief ass-shaking images to full monograph memoirs. However, the majority of stripper images tend to show young, female, taut, often white bodies on display. This particular congealing of factors, along with a gendered dynamic of female stripper and male patron, invites feminist analysis and critique. Indeed, stripper bodies pose a number of questions that feminists have sought to negotiate: for example, what are the implications of performing at a price – as bodies for hire – for the general population of women? Does stripping exacerbate what we might consider to be the wider issues of objectification and sexualisation?

Ariel Levy writes of women's collusion in 'raunch culture', pointing out ways in which women casually incorporate into their own dress and vocabulary traits and trends from stripping and porn without pausing to reflect, becoming what she terms 'female chauvinist pigs' (Levy, 2006: 3–4). Natasha Walter writes about the lack of agency in the lives of women. Her chapter 'Pole-dancers and prostitutes' opens with a description of Ellie, whom she describes as privately educated and with a degree from a 'respected university', who worked as a lap-dancer for six months (2010: 39). The chapter's argument is that lap dancing has become so mainstream that Ellie can drift into it as a way of making money.

This tells us something 'of the way that lap dancing has become an unremarkable part of British urban life in an incredibly short space of time' (2010: 40). From their emergence in the mid-1990s, lap-dancers have shifted from peripheral and sleazy to cheeky mainstream entertainment. Walter offers some valuable observations on the realities of strip clubs: 'The women didn't get paid unless they made money directly from the customers, and they would pay to be there, so there were nights when Ellie actually went home with less money than she started with' (2010: 45). However, her argument relies on her own biases and the emphasis of her chapter is on disproving any claims that sex work is empowering; she concludes it is always exploitative, without convincingly presenting data or anecdotes to back up these insights.

In *How to Be a Woman*, Caitlyn Moran scrutinises episodes in her life, pronouncing them feminist and not-feminist. In her chapter 'I Go Lap-Dancing!', she concludes that strip clubs are not-feminist, but rather 'the bastard child of misogyny and commerce'; cold, shameful places, reflecting badly on the men who go and the women who perform in them (2011: 172–173). She writes, 'One doesn't want to be as blunt as to say, "Girls, get the fuck off the podium – you're letting us all down," but: "Girls, get the fuck off the podium – you're letting us all down"' (2011: 172). Although this line packs a humorous punch, her style of writing makes it difficult to see her argument clearly. I am left wondering: what exactly is it about strip clubs that are cold and shameful? The décor? The ambience? The drinks' prices? The clientele? Her line urging strippers to get off the podium, repeated, *is* hilarious. But why? In what way are strippers letting us down, and who is *us* anyway?

In differing ways, Levy, Walters and Moran are all deriving meaning from stripping, strippers and strip clubs without thoroughly engaging the environments or people. This means their arguments emerge mainly from their own prejudices. Together with the rise and the visibility of these books and others like them, there has been a resurgence of vocal feminist activism leading campaigns against stripping. The 'Stripping the Illusion' campaign in 2008 saw two groups unite: high-profile feminist campaign group the Fawcett Society joined forces with activist group Object! to oppose legislation around the regulation of strip clubs. They produced the document 'Stripping the Illusion: Countering Lap Dancing Industry Claims' and successfully pressured the government to reclassify strip clubs as Sex Encounter Venues as part of its Policing and Crime Act 2009, while ignoring any opposition and debate from strippers themselves. Teela Sanders and Kate Hardy (2014; see also Sanders, Hardy and Campbell, 2015) investigate the implications of this change in the law and also bring in the voices of the strippers trying to oppose the campaign.

In her summary of the academic research into stripping, Katherine Frank (2007: 502) observes that the same dichotomy between stripping as exploitation and as empowerment is reproduced again and again, and asks: 'Why does this question of empowerment versus exploitation arise so regularly and repetitively?'

This re-circulation of the exploitation/empowerment bipolarity, in spite of the breadth of studies that have investigated stripping, in effect decreases the visibility of the research material that *has* been created, particularly that which seeks to reframe the terrain. In her summary of the findings of the numerous articles and papers she has collated, Frank concludes: 'The most frequently recurring answer, across decade, discipline and type of club, has been that stripping is neither wholly liberating nor wholly oppressive and that power and resistance come in different forms' (2007: 505). Focusing on empowerment/exploitation within stripping deflects from other more pressing questions, and isolating stripping to consider empowerment/exploitation is divisively partial – empowerment/exploitation are part of the experience of any worker in our capitalist context.

Seeking to resist either moralising or championing, Frank (2002) produced an ethnographic study examining a range of strip clubs, immersing herself in the environment as a stripper. She lap-danced, talked to patrons, interviewed regulars and chatted to other dancers in the dressing room. Interspersed in the study are first-person fictional interludes that voice the experiences of dancers, giving them presence in the text. From physical preparations to internal reflections, the reader is shown the women's experiences and feelings, bringing the complex, multi-faceted subjects to life. More recently, R. Danielle Egan (2003, 2006) and Rachela Colosi (2010) have conducted their own ethnographic studies of strip clubs, speaking back to repetitive dismissals that emerge from biases rather than rigorous study.

The stripper as art

Visual art has played a part in the over-emphasis of the exteriors of beautiful naked women, while neglecting to consider their interiority. The canon of Western art presents an excess of naked women. 'The nude' is a category of art that typically depicts women, often reclining, with an allusion to a mythological figure. But, as John Berger (1972) writes, the nude's idealised and passive bodies are presented to be enjoyed by the person standing in front of the painting: the viewer, who is assumed to be male. The nude's passivity contrasts with the contemporary stripper's body: self-owned, confidently presenting herself. Only when Impressionist painters and others at the end of the nineteenth century started to use theatre performers and prostitutes as their muses and models did the female subject become active and confront the viewer, for example in the straight-on stare of Édouard Manet's *Olympia* (1863) – an update on Titian's *Venus of Urbino* (1538) – as well as in his famous *A Bar at the Folies-Bergère* (1882), in Henri de Toulouse-Lautrec's paintings at the Moulin Rouge in the 1890s and in Walter Sickert's music-hall scenes at the turn of the century.

The painting *Girlie Show* (1941) by Edward Hopper depicts a naked burlesque dancer strutting onstage. She confidently presents herself, stepping out in blue heels, her calf muscles defined. With her chin tilted upwards, she has a defiant insouciance. This is not an idealised or passive goddess-body but a woman working onstage. Similarly, the photographic series *Lucky 13* (2004) by Philip-Lorca Di Corca shows pole-dancers suspended in athletic poses on the pole. The backgrounds are in darkness, with the strong lighting highlighting the bodies as they athletically push out into dynamic geometric shapes on the pole, displaying the physical honing of these professional performers. In both artworks there is an attention to detail, to faithfully representing the skills, the ready-for-scrutiny body and the confidence of the performer. These artworks show a curiosity about their subjects: I detect neither disrespect nor judgement; rather, they empathetically pay tribute to the women they depict.

A development of this type of curiosity-representation is the use of the stripper as an aesthetic element in an artwork supporting a larger idea or theme. In Francis Alÿs's video *The Politics of Rehearsal* (2005), we see a stripper performing in an empty bar, accompanied by a pianist and singer as they rehearse. Her strip is frequently halted by their breaks; she re-arranges her clothes and then carries on when they recommence. We hear a voiceover of a male speaking in Spanish, transcribed onscreen – he tells us that the faltering development of Latin America is like a stripper. Here she is both metaphor and embodiment. The musicians ignore her repeating her craft over and over again, and she has no audience to tease; yet the video bears witness to her, and her labours are given meaning.

Silhouetted figures, mainly female but male too, pole-dance in *Abstraction Licking* (2013) by Cristina Lucas. Here they are a rhythmic component against a background of geometric animation based on Piet Mondrian paintings – a playful intervention in which we see the strong bold stripes become dancing poles. With both of these video works, the figure of the stripper is a component of the whole artwork and the meanings we attach to the stripper add to our understanding of the piece. In the latter piece, there are clear parallels with the pop videos I mention earlier, in terms of energy and pace. Crucially, the bodies here are not represented as being in the service of a pop singer. In fact, they are given the privilege of Mondrian paintings to perform on.

Artists have and continue to embody the stripper in their own artwork – finding permission to do and act beyond conventional strictures. In a sense, this is where the figure of the stripper is understood, contradicted, developed and problematised with a productive ambivalence.

Female artists in particular have taken on the role of the stripper as a way to investigate what actively stripping and presenting their own body means. In the seventies, Cosey Fanni Tutti made collages using soft-porn glamour magazines, and it occurred to her that she could insert herself into the work by posing as a glamour model herself, producing *Piccadilly International Vol. 10, No. 10* (1976). Tutti modelled and started to work as a stripper in pubs in parallel to using her naked body in gallery-based art performances. Looking back on her magazine spreads and documentation of strip and art shows, she realised they were 'all about how people perceive what you're doing in different places' (Singer, 2014). Teasing apart the three kinds of performance, she says:

> Stripping is very different to modeling because, with modeling, you are there to provide your body to produce a product for sale. With stripping you're there live, you're the one who's producing and creating. Although it's prescriptive, like modeling, the prescriptive element of modeling is down to the photographer and then the editor and the magazine owners, who are working to a particular formula that works for their readers. *I* was in that position when I was stripping, I knew that a particular formula worked with striptease and I had to express myself within that, in order to let myself feel that I was getting anything out of it. And then when you have pieces like at the Hayward, where I was naked and doing performance work, that's different altogether because I was totally expressing myself, it was *me* coming through there and communicating with people about things that interested *me*. The others things were very much a job that I was doing, I was working my way through them. That is what really interested me, and that fed into my art action – and into the music, as well. I had a full-on, first hand experience of what it was like to produce sexual product; both live as a stripper and in magazines. And I didn't go into those things as anyone other as a stripper or a model – I never went in as 'Cosey Fanni Tutti, the artist', it just wouldn't work in that situation.
>
> (Singer, 2014)

Jemima Stehli adopted the position of the stripper in her photographic series *Strip* (1999–2000), in which she questioned the designation of power in the art world. We see Stehli with her back to the viewer, in different states of undress, in the act of removing her clothes. In front of her is a seated male, clearly visible to the viewer, with a long cable-release in his hand – he controls the moment at which the photograph is taken. The power of the male is emphasised by including his job in the title: 'Critic', 'Writer', 'Curator' or 'Dealer'.

The curiosity of each photograph is in seeing the male's facial expressions, which range from amusement to laughter, intimidation and indifference, registering his level of complicity or discomfort. Art-world power is depicted and subverted as Stehli embraces the parallels between nude, model, stripper and subject.

Kate Spence creates durational live pole-dancing performances, dressed in stripper-wear and working with the physical vocabularies of stripping to demonstrate the strength and power used in pole-dancing, as well as the prowess, confidence and vulnerability needed to be on display. *Strike a Pose* (2015) lasts for 30 minutes and 30 poses: a minute each, with a photograph projected behind Spence of herself executing each pose. The exertion required to hold the perfect image wanes over the minute; her muscles shake; her body slides down the pole. Reality fails to live up to the image.

Sister (2014) is a performance by sisters Rosana Cade and Amy Cade. I walk into the small theatre space to see a pole, with two chairs in front of it. As the audience choose their seats, Rosana and Amy find audience members to sit on the chairs, and perform lap-dances for those audience members. Both performers wear small black PVC bikinis, long red wigs, glitter make-up and stripper heels. As the show gets going they strip down, and they stay naked for the majority of the show. They start to speak, to recollect memories – vignettes and anecdotes paired with periodic projections of home footage behind them. They introduce each other at the same time, so it's difficult to hear: 'she's my sister and she's a sex worker' and 'she's my sister and she's a lesbian'. The performance is electric, with touching moments of self-awareness and the deep insight that comes from confronting one's own prejudices through empathy, in this case, learning from your sister. Both of them unflinchingly detail the ways in which they have made choices. Amy reads out a letter to her mother about her choice to become a sex worker in Berlin and what this means to her, emphasising that she is not being exploited, but acknowledging that that does happen and it is abhorrent. Rosana lists many things she did not choose and the few places where she does have choice, and how she seizes those – for example, she starts, 'I'm choosing to do this' and 'I'm choosing to perform – to show you my body'. She continues: 'I didn't choose my body. I didn't choose my family. I didn't choose where I was born. I didn't choose my name.' Powerful, affirmative statements continue: 'I am choosing to show you my naked body. I am not choosing whether it turns you on or disgusts you. I'm choosing not to care.' During the performance, I had the opportunity to look at naked female bodies and think about how these bodies have agency and how they produce pleasure, for themselves and for others, as well as when and how they refuse that pleasure.

By displacing stripping from the strip club, the art approaches I have detailed allow us to reflect more deeply on the stripper. These artworks offer us space to reflect on how we feel about performing naked female bodies. Without strip clubs in the frame, it's easier to see these bodies on their own terms. So, what of strip clubs – are they permissive, productive sites? Cosey Fanni Tutti identifies strip clubs as a place to perform away from oneself, a practice or think space. But they can be exploitative, unregulated places. Sadly, San Francisco's pioneering *The Lusty Lady*, a unionised, collectively run feminist peep show that opened in the 1970s, shut its doors in 2013. A haven for politically active strippers, its singularity and its unsustainability pose questions for what a strip club might be if it were more orientated towards strippers.

Internet environments are offering new possibilities for stripper community-building. For example, the resource website *Dancers Information* is the result of extensive research conducted by Teela Sanders, Kate Hardy and Rosie Campbell and was created in consultation with strippers to create practical resources, from suggestions about personal safety to tips on tax and self-employment. East London Strippers Collective describe themselves on their Twitter account as 'a collective of strippers who challenge stereotypes, attack stigma and demand better working conditions in the UK industry. And strip. Obvs'. Using social media tools, the collective stage events and showcases for their stripping that bring their skills – their ability to strip and pole-dance – to new audiences. By doing what they do away from the strip-club context they are able to powerfully demonstrate that they strip because they want to, not out of coercion, and by forming new sites of performance – online and off – they are also able to challenge the exploitative practices of strip clubs, reach out to new allies and supporters and demystify who they are and what they do.[4]

Throughout this chapter, my intention has been to complicate assumptions around mediations of the stripper. Superficial representations appear to work in tandem with the repetitive reductions that position strippers along the lines of either exploitation or empowerment, obfuscating more nuanced insights and representations. These reductions are gifts to the venues that do not adequately value the labour of their stripper employees, as well as to critics who want to force strip clubs to close and strippers to abandon their work.

The work of Frank (2002, 2007), Egan (2003, 2006) and Sanders, Hardy and Campbell (2015 and the *Dancers Information* website) demonstrates that there are other possible approaches to thinking critically and supportively around stripping – more ways in which we can listen to the testimonies of strippers. Collectives such as East London Strippers Collective lead the way in articulating how they wish to be understood and supported. Artists adopt different ways of presenting strippers in formats outside the strip-club environment. By engaging with these, we can resist the temptation to see stripping only through the lens of fears and headline-grabbing accounts, and find space to reflect on meanings, power dynamics and politics in ways that can bear different fruit. I draw this chapter to a close certain that naked performing bodies have a kind of potency: the task is to support rather than diminish it.

Notes

1 Other pop videos featuring strippers include Jentina, *Bad Ass Strippa* (2004); Beyoncé, *Suga Mama* (2006); Britney Spears, *Gimme More* (2007); Enrique Iglesias, *Tonight (I'm Lovin' You)* (2010); Diplo, *Set It Off* (2012); Iggy Azalea, *Work* (2013); and Kool Keith, *Strip Club Husband* (2014).
2 Films with strippers as a crucial component of the film include *Flashdance* (1983), *Showgirls* (1995), *Striptease* (1996), *Dancing at the Blue Iguana* (2000), *Closer* (2004), *Powder Blue* (2009) and *Magic Mike* (2012).
3 Biographies include Heidi Mattson, *Ivy League Stripper* (1995); Lily Burana, *Strip City: A Stripper's Farewell Journey Across America* (2001); Elisabeth Eaves, *Bare: On Women, Dancing, Sex, and Power* (2002); Lara Clifton, Sarah Ainslie and Julie Cook, *Baby Oil and Ice: Striptease in East London* (2002); Diablo Cody, *Candy Girl: A Year in the Life of an Unlikely Stripper* (2006); Ruth Fowler, *No Man's Land* (2008); Jennifer Hayashi Danns and Sandrine Leveque, *Stripped: The Bare Reality of Lap Dancing* (2011); Samantha Bailey, *Stripped: A Life of Strip and Tease in Clubland* (2012); Sheila Hageman, *Stripping Down* (2012); and Laila Lucent, *The Yoga Stripper* (2013).
4 Blogs by strippers include *Tits and Sass*, http://titsandsass.com/; *London Lapdancer*, www.londonlapdancer.com/; and *Stripping the Illusion*, http://strippingtheillusion.blogspot.co.uk/.

Bibliography

Barnett, J. (2016). *Porn Panic!* Winchester, UK: Zero Books.
Barton, B. (2006). *Stripped: Inside the Lives of Exotic Dancers*. New York: New York University Press.
Berger, J. (1972). *Ways of Seeing*. London: British Broadcasting Corporation and Penguin Books.

Burana, L. (2001). *Strip City: A Stripper's Farewell Journey Across America*. New York: Miramax Books.
Cody, D. (2006). *Candy Girl: A Year in the Life of an Unlikely Stripper*. New York: Gotham Books.
Colosi, R. (2010). *Dirty Dancing? An Ethnography of Lap Dancing*. Abingdon: Willan Publishing.
Dancers Information, www.dancersinfo.co.uk (accessed 24 August 2015).
East London Stripper Collective, www.ethicalstripper.com/ (accessed 19 January 2016); https://twitter.com/ethicalstripper and www.facebook.com/pages/East-London-Strippers-Collective/335178040020752 (accessed 24 August 2015).
Egan, R. D. (2003). 'I'll Be Your Fantasy Girl, If You'll Be My Money Man: Mapping Desire, Fantasy and Power in Two Exotic Dance Clubs'. *Journal for the Psychoanalysis of Culture and Society*, vol. 8, no. 1, pp. 109–120.
Egan, R. D. (2006). *Dancing for Dollars and Paying for Love: The Relationships Between Exotic Dancers and their Regulars*. New York: Palgrave Macmillan.
Frank, K. (2002). *G-Strings and Sympathy: Strip Club Regulars and Male Desire*. Durham: Duke University Press.
Frank, K. (2007) 'Thinking Critically about Strip Club Research'. *Sexualities*, vol. 10, no. 4, pp. 501–517.
Levy, A. (2006). *Female Chauvinist Pigs: Women and the Rise of Raunch Culture*. London: Pocket Books.
Moran, C. (2011). *How to Be a Woman*. London: Ebury Press.
Object (2008) 'Stripping the Illusion: Countering Lap Dancing Industry Claims'. London: Object. www.yumpu.com/en/document/view/24876923/stripping-the-illusion-countering-lap-dancing-industry-claims-object (accessed 28 March 2017).
Sanders, T. and Hardy, K. (2014). *Flexible Workers: Labour, Regulation and the Political Economy of the Stripping Industry*. New York: Routledge.
Sanders, T., Hardy, K. and Campbell, R. (2015). 'Regulating Strip-Based Entertainment: Sexual Entertainment Venue Policy and the Ex/Inclusion of Dancers' Perspectives and Needs'. *Social Policy and Society*, no. 14, pp. 83–92. doi: dx.doi.org/10.1017/S1474746414000323 (accessed 19 January 2016).
Singer, O. (2014). 'Stream Cosey Fanni Tutti's Experimental Decade-Hopping Mix'. *Dazed*. www.dazeddigital.com/music/article/21671/1/stream-cosey-fanni-tuttis-experimental-decade-hopping-mix (accessed 23 January 2015).
Walter, N. (2010). *Living Dolls: The Return of Sexism*. London: Virago.

Films

Afternoon Delight. 2013. Directed by Jill Soloway [film]. USA: Cinedigm.
The Full Monty. 1997. Directed by Peter Cattaneo [film]. USA: Fox Searchlight Pictures.
Gilda. 1946. Directed by Charles Vidor [film]. USA: Columbia Pictures.
Showgirls. 1995. Directed by Paul Verhoeven [film]. USA: MGM Home Entertainment/France: Pathé.

35
THE PEN IS MIGHTIER THAN THE WHORE

Victorian newspapers and the sex-work saviour complex

Kate Lister

The media's fascination for the figure of the sex worker has been well documented, and interest in her shows no signs of abating (McCracken, 2013; Li, 2009); in fact, numerous scholars have noted a recent increase in that fascination (Negra, 2008; Boyle, 2008; Arthurs, 2004; Gunter, 2002). Of course, sex work has been written about and debated in print for as long as there have been sex workers and the means to write. Using an analysis of the British Newspaper Archive and the 1,375,810 newspapers published from 1800 to 1900 held in the archive, this chapter explores how British Victorian journalistic narratives established the discourse of the sex worker as a social victim in need of rescue by her moral superiors which continues to frame modern journalistic debate concerning sex work to this day.

Rudyard Kipling first coined the phrase 'the world's oldest profession' in his short story *On the City Wall* (1898). The tale opens with the immortal line 'Lalun is a member of the most ancient profession in the world'; that expression has since become common parlance as a historical truth. But perhaps what Kipling wrote after those words offers even more insight into what is, at least, a very ancient profession: 'In the West, people say rude things about Lalun's profession, and write lectures about it, and distribute the lectures to young persons in order that Morality may be preserved' (Kipling, 1898: 1). As Kipling notes, attitudes towards sex work are not fixed, but are culturally and historically determined. Particularly pertinent to this chapter is his observation that people 'write' about sex work, and that such writing is undertaken as an effort to police social morality. When Kipling wrote those words, perhaps nowhere was the sex worker more widely and intensely debated than within British newspapers.

The term 'sex-work saviour complex' is used here to identify those media narratives that seek to 'save' the sex worker by constructing her as a social victim in need of rescue. This narrative operates within similar dynamics to the so-called 'white saviour complex' – a term widely used in cultural and colonial/post-colonial studies to recognise the often well-meaning, but ultimately damaging and egotistical, narrative of the white, privileged Westerner rescuing the uneducated, grateful non-whites from their primitive ways (Straubhaar, 2014; Bell, 2013; Hughey, 2010). While those works are concerned with race and nationality, a similar process of cultural othering, insistence on rescue and narratives of 'privilege' which assume the voice of those they wish to save is at work within modern media constructs of the sex worker. Paulo Freire identified the dangers of the saviour-and-victim narrative in 1970, going on to observe that rescuers often privilege their own voice above that of the group they mean to help, rather than allowing space for constructive dialogue among equals (Freire, 1973). As I will show, the same process of subtle disempowerment has been at work within media constructs of the sex worker since the advent of mass media in the nineteenth century. Culturally, we take a certain amount of satisfaction in 'othering' the Victorians as repressive, prudish and draconian, especially in matters of sexuality (Sweet, 2001), preferring to think of modern times as sexually liberated. However, far from having shaken free the shackles of Victorian sexual morality, many modern journalistic narratives surrounding sex work are firmly rooted in discourses of Victorian moralising rather than progressive reform. Victorian sexual scripts continue to exert a powerful influence in present-day accounts of sex work.

The causal effects of media narratives are of central concern to sex worker-rights activists precisely because of their power to shape public opinion (Hunt and Hubbard, 2015; Grant, 2014; Mendes *et al.*, 2009). Press interest in the sex worker operates, in a Foucauldian sense, not only to propagate discourses of sexuality but also to gain knowledge of, and therefore power over, the sex worker (Foucault, 1986). Media narratives around the sex worker exert powerful influence upon sex-worker rights and the experiences of those within the industry. The media can, and does, construct viewpoints and ways of understanding various subjects for specific audiences (Happer and Philo, 2013; Hallgrimsdottir, Phillips and Benoit, 2006; Philo and Berry, 2004). Of course, media do not dictate public opinion, nor are the public unquestioning of media messages, but, historically, media have set the agenda of public debate around sex work. The bias of reporting focuses public attention upon specific scripts, such as the sex worker as a victim, in need of management, or as a subject of titillation. Not only do the media control the angle of reporting, but they also ultimately control and stifle voices that might challenge this or offer a different perspective. In 2000, John Lowman identified a 'discourse of disposability' in media reports on sex workers: analysing media descriptions of efforts by politicians, police and local residents to get rid of street prostitution; Lowman went on to trace links to a sharp increase in the murders of street sex workers in British Columbia after 1980. Lowman argued that 'It appears that the discourse on prostitution of the early 1980s was dominated by demands to get rid of prostitutes from the streets, creating a social milieu in which violence against prostitutes could flourish' (Lowman, 2000: 1003).

Once the public understand the sex worker as disposable – a message formed, shaped and reflected as truth within the media – this discourse then permeates policy and practice (Lowman, 2000; see Kinnell, 2008).

Significantly, much debate around sex work focuses on street sex workers, despite their constituting a minority (around 20 per cent) of the sex industry (Scoular and Carline, 2014). Street sex work tends to dominate policy debates and interventions and becomes the standard narrative of the sex-worker experience (Soothill and Sanders, 2005). Despite excellent work done by sex worker-rights groups (such as the Global Network of Sex Work Projects (NSWP) and the Sex Workers Project), the sex-work saviour complex continues to dominate and shape most modern media narratives surrounding sex workers, drawing on discourses of disposability, victimhood, rescue and contagion as anti-sex work moralists assume the role of rescuer and set about constructing and othering the sex worker as a victim in need of their help. An example can be found in recent UK media coverage of the 'managed approach' for sex workers in the UK city of Leeds.[1]

The murder of sex worker Daria Pionko in December 2015, within the managed area, led to intense media focus on street sex workers and the city's efforts to introduce new initiatives to address sex work more effectively. It might be noted that Pionko herself actually features very little in these reports; rather, her death offers a springboard from which to launch into familiar and well-established narratives around the sex worker: victim, degenerate, disposable or in need of rescue. The themes of victimhood are picked up on in numerous reports, statistics, expert opinions, etc. which are then crowded together and used to reinforce the 'reality' of sex work across all contexts. In her 2016 article for *The Guardian*, Catherine Bennett employs discourses of victimhood in her description of the Leeds managed zone as a 'pimp's paradise', constructing sex workers as victims not only of pimps, 'kindly traffickers' and customers but also of the local authorities, which Bennett paints as the architects of the failing system from which Pionko was 'benefiting'. Throughout the piece, Bennett adopts a sarcastic, mocking tone and belittles the very women she wishes to 'rescue'. Bennett establishes an aggressive dialectic between decent, normal women (presumably like herself) and those who 'consider supplying oral and anal sex on demand could make a nice change from waitressing'. If there were any doubt as to how Bennett understands sex work, she finishes the piece by comparing it directly to slavery: 'the trade is "as old as time". So, of course, was slavery' (Bennett, 2016).

Stanley Cohen argued that the media operate as 'agents of public indignation', and can 'generate concern, anxiety, indignation or panic' in their reporting of the 'facts' (Cohen, 1987). This is certainly the media's role in the typification of the Leeds managed approach: the moral objection to the selling and buying of sex is palpable, and frames the 'facts' presented. Sarah Rainy, writing about the Leeds zone for the *Daily Mail*, focuses less on the discourse of victimhood than on what Lynn Comella calls 'depictions of sex workers as social outcasts and dirty whores' (Comella, 2009: 497) in order to 'other' the sex worker in her piece, 'Devastating truth about Britain's first "legal" red light district' (2016). Yet this is just as rooted in the sex-work saviour complex as Bennett's article. Again, a powerful distinction is established between decent, normal people and the sex worker. Rainey characterises sex work as 'squalid activities', 'awful' and 'rock bottom'. The sex workers about whom she writes are described as 'weary', 'sallow' and 'disturbingly vulnerable', but, more than that, as 'undesirable people' who use 'gardens as a toilet' (Rainey, 2016). It is easy to see Lowman's discourse of disposability in full force here.

Though most of the newspaper articles concerning Leeds are written from the perspective of wanting to rescue the sex worker, such narratives of victimhood are drawn together and present a 'truth' of all sex workers. By constructing the sex worker as a victim, she is subtly disempowered, stripped of her own agency and tacitly presented as inferior. Thus the sex-work saviour complex has impact: allowing the saviour space to validate their own moral agenda, it reinforces social hierarchy and stigmatises the 'rescued'. Sarah Ditum's *New Statesman* article 'The death of Daria Pionko shows there is no "safe" way to manage prostitution' (2016) gives some space to considering the managed area's 'genuine potential to do good', but ultimately concludes that prostitution is an 'obscenity'. Ditum's critique (like Bennett's and Rainey's) is grounded in heteronormative assumptions that sex workers are heterosexual women and their clients are heterosexual men, stating that 'the problem with prostitution always comes from one thing without which it could not exist at all: the men' (Ditum, 2016).[2] Ditum links violence against sex workers to a process of dehumanisation, asking the question: 'how much easier to be violent to someone you already see as inferior?' Of course, the answer is 'much easier'. It is far easier to be violent towards someone who is understood to be part of a drug-addicted, degenerate underclass of women upsetting locals with their 'obscene' behaviour. However, what these articles neglect to address is what part media narratives might play in this process. As Lowman argued, the process of dehumanising sex workers starts in the media discourses of disposability: the sex worker is dehumanised long before any violence takes place; she is dehumanised in well-meaning articles that write of her work as 'obscene' and 'degraded'.

Although the media debate surrounding the Leeds managed zone and Pionko's death is a reaction to contemporary events, the narratives that structure such debates are not. The sex-work saviour complex has been formative in media narratives since the mid-nineteenth century. The narrative of the sex worker as in need of rescue is entrenched in wider scripts of disease, moral pollution, addiction and social responsibility, all of which merge together to emphasise the horror from which the sex worker needs saving. Such debates have a reliance on historically established discourse surrounding sex work; the same narratives are recycled time and again, serving to stunt rather than open space for progressive debate surrounding sex work. The sex worker-as-victim discourse supersedes empirical evidence or subjective experience, operating as a cultural meme.[3] By analysing Victorian print media we can see that the narrative of the sex-worker victim has a long history and continues to shape modern media debate.

Going back to the archive

Digitisation of millions of newspapers in repositories such as the British Newspaper Archive has made it possible to chart the frequency with which certain words and phrases appear in print. *The British Newspaper Archive* has (to date) digitised some 802 titles published throughout the nineteenth century, running to 1,375,810 issues, including local and national prints, and this archive is the basis for what follows in the rest of this chapter. Rather than focusing on one run of newspapers or series of articles, it is now possible to use digitised archives to gauge the mood and interests of the nation on a daily, and even regional, basis. Bob Nicholson writes that 'no other form of Victorian print culture allows us to explore the period with such precision' (Nicholson, 2012: 242).

Newspapers have been in circulation since the sixteenth and seventeenth centuries, but it was in the nineteenth century that the modern mass media became established, with regular daily newspapers, columnists, editors and, crucially, the expression of opinion and voice in editorials and letters (Williams, 2010). The abolition of newspaper advertising duty in 1853, stamp duty in 1855 and paper duty in 1861, combined with an increase in literacy rates, a drop in production costs and increased leisure time, saw an explosion in the number of British newspapers circulating in the second half of the nineteenth century (Hewitt, 2013; Lake and Frost, 1984). The surge in popularity and circulation is seen in the print runs recorded in the British Newspaper Archive. Of course, the archive is not exhaustive, but it does clearly show the spike in newspaper publications in the middle of the nineteenth century (see Figure 35.1).

When Kipling wrote of the 'oldest profession' in 1898, sex work (described in the press as 'the great social evil') was indeed a subject of acute concern for Victorian moralists. The sex worker loomed large in the Victorian conscience and newspapers offered space to attempt to rationalise and understand her, as well as those who sought sexual services and, by extension, those that did not. Wendelin has explored how Victorian newspapers operated as a moral surveillance authority or 'public eye', arguing that 'for Victorian London, there could not have been a better police force' than the media (2010: 56). That newspapers saw themselves as the moral guardians of the nation drives much of the coverage on sex

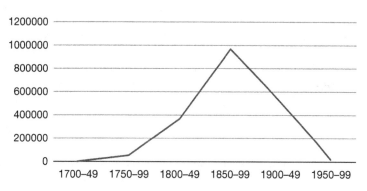

Figure 35.1 Nineteenth-century newspapers in circulation.

work. Foucault wrote of a Victorian 'need to take sex "into account", to pronounce a discourse on sex that would not derive from morality alone but from rationality as well' (Foucault, 1986: 24), and newspapers gave voice to numerous discourses around the sex worker. She was discussed, analysed, held up for inspection; her body was medicalised, legalised and politicised. But more than this, newspapers did not simply record public concerns regarding sex work; they also played a role in shaping them.

Historians have long noted that debates around sex work intensified significantly in the middle of the nineteenth century, and that there was a distinctive softening of public attitudes towards women working in the sex trade (Wendelin, 2010; Fisher, 1997; Walkowitz, 1982). The *Oxford University and City Herald* reported on a surge of media interest in sex workers, hoping it was not merely a trend: 'We trust that the attention which in London and throughout the country is being given to the painful and important subject of prostitution will not prove a mere transitory outbreak of popular enthusiasm and indignation' ('The great social evil', 1858). *The Saturday Review* noted that the mid-nineteenth century witnessed a 'great ripping up of the skirts of society, and a very appalling exposure of the filth concealed under an outward show of purity' ('The sin in scarlet', 1863). Walkowitz and Fisher link this intensification of debate to the religious revival and 'puritan polemics' of the 1840s and 1850s, while Wendelin (2010) attributes a shift in media focus to the passing of the first Contagious Diseases Act in 1864 (Wendelin, 2010; Fisher, 1997; Walkowitz, 1982). But, given the demonstrable swell in the numbers of printed newspapers at this time, it seems likely that newspapers, then as now, played a significant role in inflaming and driving public concern over sex work. The shift in public attitudes was, in no small part, dictated by the media's construction of the sex worker as an exploited victim in need of rescue and management. Rather than condemning her as the lustful whore, newspapers mobilised a national rescue effort. Journalists themselves acknowledged the role of the press in shaping the public debate around sex work. The *East London Observer* certainly felt that the press was instrumental in changing public opinion about sex workers:

> The press is no longer ashamed to discuss the subject of prostitution. We believe we should not be beside the truth if we were to say that there is scarcely an English newspaper which has not directed public attention within the last twelve months. This is an incalculable blessing. The people of England are generally slow to move. To them, beyond all others, the French proverb applies, *c'est le premier pas qui coute*. But after our fellow-countrymen have had full time to digest and understand its

nature – they seldom fail to do what is honest, just, virtuous and right. And the committee of the Associate Institution feel it due to themselves, and those friends by whose liberality they have been enabled to carry on their operations, to state their conviction that those operations have been mainly instrumental in producing a very wholesome change in the minds of the English people on the subject of prostitution.

('*The great social evil*', 1859)

Using digitised archives, we can see how widely, and in what terms, sex work was discussed throughout the nineteenth century. It is important to note the sharp spike in newspaper titles in circulation from the middle of the nineteenth century, as it is reflected in the number of papers carrying key terms. If there are more newspapers in circulation in the 1850s then the number of raw hits for terms such as 'prostitute' will increase as well. Certain words and phrases also need to be treated with caution: for example, the word 'whore' is also used as an adjective and can potentially skew data. Certain phrases, such as 'the great social evil', can (rarely) refer to 'evils' other than sex work. It is far more useful to understand raw hits in terms of a percentage of newspapers in circulation, and this can show us key shifts in the nature of early media debates. By far the most widely used terms for sex workers and sex work throughout the nineteenth century were 'prostitute' and 'prostitution', which remain fairly consistent throughout nineteenth-century newspaper runs. Of the 372,894 newspapers printed from 1800 to 1849 held in the British Library Newspaper Archive, 11 per cent carry the terms 'prostitute' or 'prostitution'. This increases slightly to 12 per cent in the years 1850–1900, drops to 2 per cent in the years 1900–1950 and falls further to 1.6 per cent of newspapers in the years 1950–1999. That the terms 'prostitute' and 'prostitution' were consistently used in at least 11 per cent of Victorian newspapers shows us that this was, indeed, a very prominent subject for media scrutiny, as seen in Figure 35.2.

Moreover, we can trace noticeable trends in language that reflect shifting social attitudes. The phrase 'the great social evil' is found in less than 1 per cent of all newspaper articles, though it was used widely as a headline. We can see that the term 'great social evil' is only in use from the 1850s up to 1900, when it disappears altogether. Similarly, other Victorian euphemisms for sex workers, such as 'unfortunate woman' and 'fallen woman', have brief, but sharp, peaks in the 1850s–1900s. This language is thus uniquely Victorian.

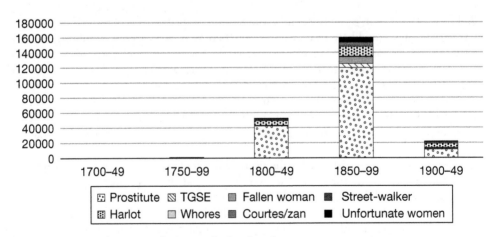

Figure 35.2 Use of synonyms for 'sex worker' in British newspapers.

The language used to describe sex work is revealing in itself. It is tempting to read the term 'great social evil' as a reflection of Victorian prudishness and outright condemnation of sex workers, but the term is largely employed in similar fashion to Catherine Bennett's description of sex work as 'evil' in 2015: it's not the sex workers themselves who are 'evil', but the wider sex trade. The phrases 'unfortunate woman' and 'fallen woman' also speak of sympathy for the sex worker and work to codify her as a victim; more than that, however, she is the victim of a great *social* evil and, therefore, it must be society's responsibility to save her. Sympathy for the plight of the sex worker and a need to save her were endemic in Victorian newspapers. In 1857, *The Times* wrote that 'in common with the rest of the world, we are glad to see anything done to relieve these poor creatures'; 'The evil is a terrible one, and we welcome anything like a remedy' ('We insert in another column a letter on the', 1857). The debate was thrashed out in parliament and reported in the press as lawmakers sought to save sex workers from themselves: 'There was a principle of the law which recognised the duty of protecting those who needed protection from the arts of those who sought to make a profit of their unwariness and simplicity' (Debate on the Bill for the Protection of Females, second reading, 5 June 1848). *The Birmingham Daily Gazette* asked: 'The great social evil: how should it be dealt with and who is responsible for its abasement?' ('The great social evil', 1863a). The *Dundee, Perth, and Cupar Advertiser* described the management of prostitution as 'the great question of the day' ('The great social evil', 1863b). In *The Prostitute's Body: Rewriting Prostitution in Victorian Britain*, Nina Attwood (2010: 10) describes the narrative of the Victorian sex worker in need of rescue as a 'firmly established mythology', and one that would dominate all future debates around sex work. Significantly, newspapers focus almost exclusively on 'street prostitutes' or 'common prostitutes'. The *Times* wrote:

> [In] No capital city in Europe is there daily and nightly such a shameless display of prostitution as in London. At Paris, at Vienna, at Berlin, as everyone knows, there is plenty of vice; but, at least, it is not allowed to parade the streets.
> ('Prostitution in London', 1858)

Just as today, the effect of reporting almost exclusively on the most destitute of the sex-work demographic feeds the narrative of *all* sex workers being in need of rescue and reform (Soothill and Sanders, 2005).

Widespread media coverage was mirrored by the hundreds of charitable organisations established to rescue and reform fallen women. The Cardiff Female Refuge Society, the London Society for the Rescue of Fallen Women, the Portsmouth Social Purity Organisation, the Glasgow Midnight Rescue Brigade, the Staffordshire County Refuge for Discharged Prisoners and Fallen Women and the Liverpool House of the Ford are but a handful of the many such rescue charities; and, of course, there is the Salvation Army, which is recorded as having opened rescue homes for fallen women in 'London, Glasgow, Plymouth, Reading and the Australian colonies' ('The Salvation Army', 1885). When William T. Stead published his sensational week-long expose on British children forced into prostitution, 'The maiden tribute of modern Babylon', in the *Pall Mall Gazette* in 1885, a media frenzy ensued. *The Worcestershire Chronicle* commented: 'Conversations in clubs, in railway carriages, in workshops and even schools, has suddenly been drawn into impure and prurient veins . . . If revelations of this kind became a common feature of English journalism, Fleet-street would out-rival Holywell-street' ('The bitter cry', 1885).

The idea that young British girls were being sold into 'modern slavery' took hold in newspapers, creating something of a national panic. Although the articles focused on minors, concern shifted to adults and sex work, again discussed in terms of slavery: numerous articles were published under the heading of 'The white slave trade' detailing the trafficking of women and children in and out of Britain. Newspapers throughout the country discussed the credibility of Stead's claims, debated what was to be done and set about further exposing the 'virgin trade', albeit with limited success. The *Sunderland Daily Echo and Shipping Gazette* ran a brief but sensational column titled 'The maiden tribute' that reported cases of child sexual exploitation; however, owing to a distinct lack of reported cases of sexual slavery in the Sunderland area, the column was short-lived and eventually resorted to reporting on suspected cases in America, before finally disappearing after a month.

It is important to note that the narrative of the sex-worker victim was not unchallenged in the Victorian media: many journalists commented on the power of this myth and its distortion of the truth. The *Leeds Mercury* was one of several papers that cautioned many reports were misleading:

> Ever since the outpouring of loathsome details regarding a great social evil which took place a few weeks ago, our newspapers have been filled with stories of abduction and outrages upon young females. It would be well for the public to take the majority of these statements with a great deal of caution.
> (Leeds Mercury, 1885)

Sex-worker voices are noticeably absent in much of this journalism, but when they are heard they frequently offer a very different perspective. In a series of letters written to *The Times* in 1858, an anonymous sex worker, referring to herself as 'Another Unfortunate', openly challenges an earlier letter from a woman known only as 'An Unfortunate' who claimed to speak for 'that abandoned sisterhood' (1858a). The tone of 'Another Unfortunate' is defiant, proud and succinctly identifies the sex-work saviour complex in the moralists who wish to save her.

> You railers for the Society for the Suppression of Vice, you the pious, the moral, the respectable, as you call yourselves, who stand on your smooth and pleasant side of the great gulf you have dug and keep between yourselves and the dregs, why don't you bridge it over, or fill it up, and by some humane and generous process absorb us into your leavened mass, until we become interpenetrated with goodness like yourselves?
> ('Another Unfortunate', 1858b)

The frustration 'Another Unfortunate' feels at being shamed by those trying to save her is palpable throughout. The letter caused something of an embarrassment for Charles Dickens (the patron of Urania Cottage, a home for fallen women), who, having not read the article in full, wrote to the editor of *The Times*, John Thadeus Delane, to ask for the name of 'Another Unfortunate' 'with the view of doing good to someone' (Dickens, 1858a). Upon reading the article for himself and finding 'Another Unfortunate' to be quite resistant to efforts to save her 'class', Dickens quickly wrote again retracting his enquiry, explaining that Angela Burdett-Coutts (the owner of Urania Cottage) had informed him of the article but, having read it in full, was now 'immensely staggered and disconcerted by the latter part of it', and 'even troubled by its being seen by the people in her household' (Dickens, 1858b). In this brief exchange of letters, we can see the level of disconnect between the sex workers, the rescuers and the media that characterises Victorian debates: the rescuers are trying to rescue a media fiction and that fictitious character, standing in for the authentic voice, shames and alienates the very women it purports to want to save. Rather than engage with the experience of 'Another Unfortunate', Dickens distances himself from her lest it disturb the narrative of the sex-work victim that he prioritises.

Though much of the moralising language used to construct the sex worker in the nineteenth-century media seems dated to our twenty-first-century ears (the great social evil, the Contagious Diseases Acts, the white slave trade, the fallen women, purity organisations and the Glasgow Midnight Rescue Brigade), modern media discourse might be considered to be firmly embedded within similar cultural scripts to those which framed the earliest media discourse of the sex worker. As the recent media reports surrounding the death of Daria Pionko demonstrate, the urge to rescue the sex worker from her terrible life is still with us. The portrayal of sex workers as addicted, diseased, exploited and abused, and as 'slaves', continues to set the agenda for media debate. There have been subtle shifts in the media mythology of the sex worker – the disease of concern is now HIV rather than syphilis, and she is addicted to heroin and crack rather than gin and opium – but the underlying emphases on contagion and addiction are still in force. Of course, there are sex workers who are abused, addicted, etc., but victim narratives do little to explore the complexities of those who choose sex work, and whose experiences and voices continue to be subsumed beneath the constant focus on moral delinquency, contagion and exploitation. The Victorian media discourse focused less on genuine experience of the sex worker and more on the moral agenda of those who wished to save her. Yet we are still turning to Victorian cultural scripts to discuss sex work, which, though often well-meaning, exclude and disempower the very group that is the focus of the rescue effort. 'Another Unfortunate' succinctly understood the power inherent in casting a group as composed of victims in need of help when she wrote:

> the difficulty of dealing with the evil is not so great as society considers it. Setting aside 'the sin' we are not so bad as we are thought to be. The difficulty is for society to set itself with the necessary earnestness, self-humiliation and self-denial of the work.
>
> (1858b)

This sentiment is as true now as it was in 1858.

Notes

1 The 'managed approach' was introduced in Leeds in 2014 as a pilot scheme between the police, the local council, residents and various outreach organisations. Sex may be sold and bought, within a specified zone of the Holbeck area of Leeds, between the hours of 7pm and 7am, without fear of police sanctions. Extra CCTV has been installed, police regularly patrol the area in marked vehicles and a sex-work liaison officer is available for sex workers to talk to. Due to the changes in Leeds, the proportion of sex workers reporting incidents to National Ugly Mugs (NUM) who were also willing to report to West Yorkshire Police increased from 15 per cent in 2013 to among the highest in the UK, at over 52 per cent, in 2015.
2 According to recent research, 33 per cent of people advertising as escorts in the UK self-identified as male, with 68 per cent of those identifying as straight and advertising to female clients (Smith and Kingston, 2015).
3 Richard Dawkins famously defined a meme as conveying 'the idea of a unit of cultural transmission, or a unit of imitation' (Dawkins, 1989: 192).

Bibliography

An Unfortunate (1858a). 'The delicate question'. *The Times*. 4 February: 12.
Anon. (1857). 'Medical annotations'. *The London Lancet*: 2.
Another Unfortunate (1858b). 'The great social evil'. *The Times*. 24 February: 12.
Archives, T.N. (1887). *Records of the National Vigilance Association*. 15 June.
Arthurs, J. (2004) *Television and sexuality*. London: McGraw-Hill Education.
Attwood, N. (2010). *The prostitute's body: Rewriting prostitution in Victorian Britain*. London: Pickering & Chatto.
Bell, K.M. (2013). 'Raising Africa? Celebrity and the rhetoric of the white saviour'. *Journal of Multidisciplinary International Studies*. Volume 10 (1): 1–24.
Bennett, C. (2015). 'Why do so many men still think the sex trade is fine?' *The Guardian*. www.theguardian.com/commentisfree/2008/jan/20/comment.society (accessed 22 April 2016).
Bennett, C. (2016). 'Criminalise the sex buyers, not the prostitutes'. *The Guardian*. www.theguardian.com/commentisfree/2016/feb/21/sex-trade-prostitution-criminalise-sex-buyers (accessed 12 April 2016).
Beusch, D. (2006). 'Book review: Television and sexuality: regulation and the politics of taste'. *Media, Culture & Society*. Volume 28 (3): 473–474.
Bindel, J. (2016). 'Jeremy Corbyn's views on the sex trade sum up the male left's betrayal of women'. *The Guardian*. www.theguardian.com/society/commentisfree/2016/mar/04/jeremy-corbyn-sex-trade-left-women-exploitation (accessed 15 April 2016).
Boyle, K. (2008). 'Courting consumers and legitimating exploitation'. *Feminist Media Studies*. Volume 8 (1): 35–50.
Brunschot, E.G.V., Sydie, R.A. and Krull, C. (2000). 'Images of prostitution'. *Women & Criminal Justice*. Volume 10 (4): 47–72.
Cohen, S. (1987). *Folk devils and moral panics: The creation of the mods and rockers*. Oxford: Blackwell Publishers.
Comella, L. (2009). 'Representing sex work in Sin City'. In Mendes, K., Silva, K., Ray, A., Baldwin, D., Orchard, T., Weissmann, E., Thornham, H. and Long, J. (eds) 'Commentary and criticism'. *Feminist Media Studies*. Volume 9 (4): 493–515.
Dawkins, R. (1989). *The selfish gene*. New York: Oxford University Press.
Dickens, C. (1858a). *To John Thadeus Delane*. 25 February.
Dickens, C. (1858b). *To John Thadeus Delane*. 28 February.
Ditum, S. (2016). 'The death of Daria Pionko shows there is no "safe" way to manage prostitution'. *New Statesman*. www.newstatesman.com/politics/feminism/2016/01/death-daria-pionko-shows-there-no-safe-way-manage-prostitution (accessed 13 April 2016).
Fisher, T. (1997). *Prostitution and the Victorians*. New York: St. Martin's Press.
Foucault, M., trans R. Hurley (1986). *The history of sexuality*. New York: Pantheon Books.
Freire, P. (1973). *Pedagogy of the oppressed*. 11th edn. New York: Herder and Herder.
Grant, M.G. (2014). *Playing the whore: The work of sex work*. London: Verso Books.
Gunter, B. (2002) *Media Sex*. Mahwah: Lawrence Erlbaum.
Hallgrimsdottir, H.K., Phillips, R. and Benoit, C. (2006). 'Fallen women and rescued girls: Social stigma and media narratives of the sex industry in Victoria, B.C., from 1980 to 2005'. *Canadian Review of Sociology/Revue canadienne de sociologie*. Volume 43 (3): 265–280.
Happer, C. and Philo, G. (2013). 'The role of the media in the construction of public belief and social change'. *Journal of Social and Political Psychology*. Volume 1 (1): 321–336.
Henderson, T. and Henderson, A. (1999). *Disorderly women in eighteenth-century London: Prostitution and the metropolis, 1730–1830*. London: Longman.
Hewitt, M. (2013). *The dawn of the cheap press in Victorian Britain: The end of the 'taxes on knowledge', 1849–1869*. London: Bloomsbury Academic.
Hughey, M.W. (2010). 'The white savior film and reviewers' reception'. *Symbolic Interaction*. Volume 33 (3): 475–496.

Hunt, S. and Hubbard, B. (2015). 'The representation of sex workers in south African media: Danger, morals and human rights'. *Stellenbosch Papers in Linguistics Plus*. Volume 46 (0): 19–43.

Kammerer, C., Klein Hutheesing, O., Manneeprassert, R. and Symonds, P.V. (1995). 'Vulnerability to HIV infection among three hill tribes in Northern Thailand'. In H.T. Brummelhuis and G. Herdt (eds) *Culture and sexual risk: Anthropological perspectives on AIDS*. London: Routledge.

Kinnell, H. (2008). *Violence and sex work in Britain*. United Kingdom: Intl Specialized Book Service.

Kipling, R. 1898. *On the city wall*. Philadelphia: Henry Altemus.

Lake, B. and Frost, J. (1984). *British newspapers: A history and guide for collectors*. London: Sheppard Press.

Leeds Mercury (1885). 12 August.

Li, L. (2009). 'Media salience and the process of framing: coverage of the professor prostitution'. *Asian Social Science*. Volume 4 (10).

Lowman, J. (2000). 'Violence and the outlaw status of (street) prostitution in Canada'. *Violence Against Women*. Volume 6 (9): 987–1011.

McCracken, J. (2013). *Street sex workers' discourse: Realizing material change through agential choice*. London: Taylor & Francis.

Mendes, K., Silva, K., Comella, L., Ray, A., Baldwin, D., Orchard, T., Weissmann, E., Thornham, H. and Long, J. (2009). 'Commentary and criticism'. *Feminist Media Studies*. Volume 9 (4): 493–515.

Michel, J., Shen, Y.K., Aiden, A.P., Veres, A., Gray, M.K., Pickett, J.P., Hoiberg, D., Clancy, D., Norvig, P., Orwant, J., Pinker, S., Nowak, M.A. and Aiden, E.L. (2010). 'Quantitative analysis of culture using millions of digitized books'. *Science*. Volume 331 (6014): 176–182.

'Milliners and dress-makers assistants' (1959). *The Manchester Guardian*. 4 February: 4.

Murdock, G.P. (1952). 'Anthropology and its contribution to public health'. *American Journal of Public Health and the Nation's Health*. Volume 42 (1): 7–11.

Negra, D. (2008). *What a girl wants? Fantasizing the reclamation of self in postfeminism*. New York: Routledge.

Nicholson, B. (2012). 'Counting culture; or, how to read Victorian newspapers from a distance'. *Journal of Victorian Culture*. Volume 17 (2): 238–246.

Pajnik, M. (2013). 'Reconciling paradigms of prostitution through narration'. *Drustvena istrazivanja*. Volume 22 (2): 257–276.

Philo, G. (2008). 'Active audiences and the construction of public knowledge'. *Journalism Studies*. Volume 9 (4): 535–544.

Philo, G. and Berry, M. (2004). *Bad news from Israel*. London: Pluto Press.

Proceedings of the Old Bailey (2003). *The demography of urban growth*. www.oldbaileyonline.org/static/Population-history-of-london.jsp (accessed 15 April 2016).

'Prostitution in London' (1858). *The Times*. 8 January.

Rainey, S. (2016). 'Devastating truth about Britain's first "legal" red light district'. www.dailymail.co.uk/news/article-3402023/Devastating-truth-Britain-s-legal-red-light-district-police-council-insist-s-city-safer-reality-Intimidation-murder-locals-scared-out.html#ixzz45WtXhQYq (accessed 11 April 2016).

Ruuskanen, D.D.K. (1993). 'There is no word for adultery in Hawaiian: The translation of non-existent concepts'. *The Competent Intercultural Communicator*. Volume 51. 235–244.

Sanders, T., O'Neill, M. and Pitcher, J. (2009). *Prostitution: Sex work, policy and politics*. Thousand Oaks, CA: SAGE Publications.

Sanger, W.W. (1859). *The history of prostitution: Its extent, causes, and effects throughout the world*. New York: Harper & Brothers.

Scoular, J. and Carline, A. (2014). 'A critical account of a "creeping neo-abolitionism": regulating prostitution in England and Wales'. *Criminology and Criminal Justice*. Volume 14 (5): 608–626.

Smith, N. and Kingston, S. (2015). *Policy-relevant report: Statistics on sex work in the UK*. www.academia.edu/17096231/Statistics_on_sex_work_in_the_UK (accessed 30 March 2017).

Soothill, K. and Sanders, T. (2005). 'The geographical mobility, preferences and pleasures of prolific punters: A demonstration study of the activities of prostitutes' clients'. *Sociological Research Online*, Volume 10 (1).

Straubhaar, R. (2014). 'The stark reality of the "white saviour" complex and the need for critical consciousness: A document analysis of the early journals of a Freirean educator'. *Compare: A Journal of Comparative and International Education*, Volume 45 (3): 381–400.

Sweet, M. (2001) *Inventing the Victorians*. London: Faber and Faber.

'The bitter cry' (1885). *Worcestershire Chronicle*. 18 July: 4.

'The great social evil' (1858). *Oxford University and City Herald*. 6 February: 10.

'The great social evil' (1859). *East London Observer*. 2 October: 4.

'The great social evil' (1863a). *Birmingham Daily Gazette*. 23 February: n.p.

'The great social evil' (1863b). *Dundee, Perth, and Cupar Advertiser*. 15 September: 5.

'The Salvation Army' (1885). *Yorkshire Post and Leeds Intelligencer*. 12 December: 9.

'The sin in scarlet' (1863). *Saturday Review*. 12 September.

Walkowitz, J.R. (1982). *Prostitution and Victorian society: Women, class, and the state*. Cambridge: Cambridge University Press.

'We insert in another column a letter on the' (1857). *The Times*. 6 May: 8.

Wendelin, G. (2010). 'The prostitute's voice in the public eye: police tactics of security and discipline within Victorian journalism'. *Communication and Critical/Cultural Studies*. Volume 7 (1): 53–69.

Williams, K. (2010). *Get me a murder a day! A history of media and communication in Britain*. 2nd edn. London: Bloomsbury USA Academic.

36
THE PORNOGRAPHY CONSUMER AS OTHER

Alan McKee

Introduction

It might be thought to be self-evident that, if we want to understand pornography consumption, we should include the perspectives of the people who actually consume pornography. However, in a 2011 book chapter, the Australian academic Helen Pringle argues strongly that we should not: 'after all, we do not consult racists in formulating laws against hate speech on the basis that they are involved in and know a lot about racism' (Pringle, 2011: 127). Pringle's position is merely the radical expression of what is a curious characteristic of research into pornography: that in trying to understand pornography, the people who consume it are consistently silenced – or, to put it another way (as I explain below), 'Othered'.

In order to understand how this came to be the case – and why it matters – we need to understand how the consumption of pornography and the ways in which this consumption has been represented have changed over the years.

A history of pornography consumers

Historian Walter Kendrick has shown that, although sexually explicit representations have existed throughout human history, it is only in the nineteenth century in Western countries that 'pornography' emerged as a distinct category of human culture. The English word itself was used in print for the first time in 1850, to describe the sexually explicit artefacts uncovered at Pompeii, and Kendrick shows how in the first decades of its use art historians and museum curators struggled to ensure that only properly educated white gentlemen were allowed to see it. As one of these curators wrote in 1877:

> We have taken all the prudential measures applicable to such a collection of engravings and text. We have endeavoured to make its reading inaccessible, so to speak, to poorly educated persons, as well as those whose sex and age forbid any exception to the laws of decency and modesty.
>
> (Barré, quoted in Kendrick, 1996: 15)

So long as pornography could be kept private, only available for the edification of well-educated people, and so long as the pornography consumer was a connoisseur rather than a pleb, pornography consumption was not a problem. But as Kendrick notes, 'books being sluttish as they are' (1996: 15), over the succeeding decades pornography escaped from the 'secret museum' and circulated freely among the 'wrong types' of people – particularly the working classes. The problematic 'pornography consumer' (the 'wrong kind' of consumer) was born. And at the same moment were born campaigns against pornography.

In the first half of the twentieth century, these campaigns tended to be organised in terms of morality – 'decency' and 'family values' (Strub, 2006). The 1960s and 70s, however, saw radical changes in social organisation in Western countries. The rise of feminism, the civil rights movement and gay liberation saw public attacks on conventional structures of authority. Condemnations of pornography that relied on appeals to a shared religious conviction grew increasingly unconvincing. Conservatives who wished to attack pornography needed a new approach to 'proving' the harms done by pornography.

In this history, 1970 is an important year: the year that the US President's Commission on Obscenity and Pornography released its report on the place of pornography in American life and emphatically placed social-scientific research methods at the heart of understanding the people who consume pornography. The Commission had been formed in 1967 as part of the progressive 'Great Society' social programme of President Lyndon Johnson (Lewis, 2008: 8), and tasked to

> analyse obscenity law and recommend a useful legal definition for obscenity . . . explore the nature and volume of traffic in pornographic materials . . . study the effect of such materials on the public . . . [and] recommend legislation to regulate such volume and traffic.
>
> (Lewis, 2008: 10)

As the first major review of pornographic materials by a government body, it commissioned numerous empirical studies on the effects of pornography, which comprised the bulk of the final report.

The research and publication of this report marks a turning point for academic research on pornography. Before 1970 it is difficult to find any academic journal articles that investigate the relationship between pornography and violence; after 1970, a small flood of social-science research in this area appears – and it has never stopped.

The findings presented in the Commission's report are not in themselves particularly important. Based on these studies, the report concluded that there was no reliable evidence of negative effects from the consumption of pornography, and recommended its decriminalisation (Lewis, 2008: 13). More important than this finding was the fact that the report made the relationship between pornography and violence the central concern when thinking about the government's role in managing sexually explicit material – more so than questions of morality or decency. In particular, it suggested that psychology was the most suitable academic discipline for addressing this concern. Rather than humanities methods studying the different ways in which people might use pornography, or sociological approaches that would explore the cultures within which pornography circulated, psychology would now be the most authoritative source of evidence about pornography consumers.

The main research methods that psychology has applied to the study of pornography have been quantitative. For the first decades of this research, experimental work had a central place. For example, researchers exposed subjects in the laboratory to (usually violent) pornography and then measured changes in their levels of aggression and attitudes towards women. The results of this research were contradictory. There was general consensus that viewing non-violent pornography does not produce any significant effects. In terms of violent pornography, the results were more variable. Some researchers managed to produce significant negative effects in consumers from viewing violent pornography in laboratory experiments. These included increased tendencies to aggression against women (Donnerstein and Berkowitz, 1981), an acceptance of rape myths (Malamuth and Check, 1981) and decreased support for women's rights (Zillmann and Bryant, 1984). However, other researchers were unable to replicate these results (Barak and Fisher, 1997; Linz, Donnerstein and Penrod, 1988). The fact that in some laboratory studies a link was found between the consumption of violent pornography and negative attitudes conflicts with studies of actual sex offenders which refuse such a correlation (Fisher and Grenier, 1994: 25).

For the purposes of this chapter, a key element of laboratory experiments into pornography is that they do not recruit people who use pornography in their everyday lives. Rather, they tend to recruit college students, many of whom are not consumers of pornography. These cohorts are then shown material that many find upsetting or distasteful (violent pornography), in public settings where they are not allowed to masturbate (most consumers of pornography masturbate while consuming the genre) (Potter, 1996: 111). In short, we can say that laboratory experiments tell us little about consumers of pornography in the world beyond the laboratory. They tell us, rather, about the effects of pornography on people who may or may not be pornography consumers, who are exposed involuntarily to pornography that they may find upsetting, in unfamiliar, non-sexual surroundings. Such studies do not explore the ways in which people who regularly use pornography make sense of its place in their lives. Indeed, not only do we not hear actual porn consumers' voices in these statistical analyses, but subjects are also – as is common in psychological testing – deliberately misled as to the purpose of the experiments so that they do not know that their attitudes towards pornography are of interest (see, for example, Donnerstein and Berkowitz, 1981).

More recently the survey has emerged as the main method for gathering data about pornography and its effects. One might think that this would allow the voices of consumers to be heard – but this turns out not to be the case. Surveys are often quantitative in nature, which does not allow consumers to explain the meanings that pornography consumption holds for them, or to draw attention to what, for them, are the most important aspects of the genre. Rather, surveys decide ahead of time what are the most important questions to ask about pornography use. Psychological approaches tend to assume that the most powerful effects of pornography are negative, rather than considering the wide range of ways – some pro-social, some undesirable – in which consumers might engage with the texts (Brannigan, 2004: 95). They often assume that pornography is the most important variable in producing a variety of negative social outcomes, defending this premise by reference to previous researchers who have made the same assumption, rather than to measurements of the relative impact of parents, schooling, peers, religion, and so on (see, for example, Collins et al., 2004: e280). Studies from a psychological perspective have paid surprisingly little attention to obvious confounding variables in the relationship between the consumption of sexualised entertainment and sexual behaviours, particularly class, sexual development and sexual adventurousness (Mort, 2000). They consistently confuse correlation with causality (see, for example, Collins et al., 2004: e288). Further, psychological approaches tend to homogenise pornography, treating every text as communicating the same message (Smith, 2007: 19). These approaches assume that the 'effects' of exposure to pornography are the same for everybody, ignoring the multiple ways in which media texts can be used by different consumers in different situations (see, for example, Bragg, 2006). Psychological approaches also tend to automatically assume that parents and schools provide a positive 'corrective' (Fisher and Barak, 1989) to pornography's assumed negative teachings about sex – an assumption that much research into those sources of information finds to be unwarranted (see, for example, McKee, Dore and Watson, 2014).

Perhaps the most disturbing aspect of psychological approaches to pornography has been the consistent strand of heteronormativity that has run through them. In study after study the vision of desirable sexual development has been one in which young people accept conservative sexual ideals of committed lifelong monogamy. The concept of 'risk' is used in these studies in order to condemn sexualised entertainment for sending 'permissive' (Eyal and Kunkel, 2008: 162) messages to young people, such as the acceptability of sex outside of committed relationships (Brown and Bobkowski, 2011: 102). Researchers taking these approaches assume that respect for 'remaining a virgin' before marriage is a positive sexual ideal (Kunkel, Cope and Biely, 1999: 230). They condemn 'casual sex' or 'sexual behaviors with two or more partners in the past 12 months' (Eyal and Kunkel, 2008: 161). At its most extreme, this conservative approach to sexuality in psychology remains committed to the idea that sex should only occur within marriage, naming 'engagement in premarital sexual intercourse' as a negative practice (ibid.: 162), and even explicitly saying that sexualised entertainment is dangerous because it affects young people's 'moral attitudes' towards sex (ibid.: 165). Some articles in this tradition even imply that the ideal situation for young people is complete ignorance about sex, judging even any 'talk' about sex as having dangerous negative effects for young people (Kunkel et al., 1999: 231). This research is not interested in how the consumers of pornography understand their own experiences of consumption: it begins with a conservative model of sexuality and forces survey respondents to answer questions within that paradigm.

In short, the dominant modes of academic research into pornography consumption have neglected the voices or experiences of people who actually consume pornography.

Journalistic coverage of pornography consumption

The situation is similar in journalistic coverage of pornography consumption. Consumers of pornography are the objects of much controversy in the news media. We see ongoing debates about the kinds of people who consume pornography and the effects this has on their attitudes towards relationships, violence and crime. There has been concern that pornography can 'damage' people (Hamilton, quoted in Symons, 2004: 4) – particularly young people. Commentators worry that pornography 'plays on the confusion and ultimate emotional sterility of those who use it' (Shanahan, 2004: 13). There is an ongoing concern that 'exposure to pornography' can turn people into sex offenders (Fewster, 2004), including paedophiles and gang rapists (Hamilton, 2004). Some argue that it can create unrealistic expectations of sex, and put people off the reality of sexual relationships (Hamilton, 2004). Other commentators assert that pornography is contributing to a general increase in violent crime in our society (Pell, 2004), and that it is addictive and is turning people into 'junkies' (Anon., 2004). The voices most commonly heard in these news stories are those of opinion columnists, politicians, church leaders and academic researchers. The thoughts of pornography consumers themselves are rarely published. Indeed, the only consumers of pornography regularly heard to speak in news stories are those who name themselves as 'addicts' and are seeking to stop watching the genre (see, for example, Taylor, 2005).[1]

In both psychological research and journalistic coverage, pornography consumers are seen but not heard. They are represented, and spoken for, by others. They are not allowed to represent themselves.

What is Othering?

In her germinal 1949 book *The Second Sex*, Simone de Beauvoir argued that in patriarchal cultures the woman is 'the Other': 'She is defined and differentiated with reference to man and not he with reference to her; she is the incidental, the inessential as opposed to the essential. He is the Subject, he is the Absolute – she is the Other' (de Beauvoir, 2014 [1949]: 16). In his 1978 book *Orientalism*, Edward Said (1995 [1978]) expanded this argument to address explicitly the ways in which representation contributes to this process. He argued that throughout recorded history Western representations of 'the Orient' (the 'Middle East' and 'Far East') have been linked by the fact that they have not involved self-representations by the people who live in this geographical area. Westerners have created their own versions of 'the Orient' that make sense according to Western logics, that create a unified vision that claims that it is sensible to discuss 'the Orient' as a whole and in which everyone who lives there can be described as having similar characteristics: 'there is no question of an exchange between [their] views and an outsider's: no dialogue, no discussion, no mutual recognition. There is a flat assertion of quality' (Said, 1985: 8).

In short, Said argues, the 'Orient' has been Europe's 'silent Other' (ibid.: 5). For Said, the important point is not whether or not these representations are 'accurate' or 'stereotypes' – as he notes, there is no such thing as a single accurate representation that would cover every person who lives in all of these countries. Rather, his point is that these representations are created solely by outsiders. The peoples of the 'Orient' 'cannot represent themselves, they must therefore be represented by others' (ibid.: 7).

Said goes on to argue that there are political implications in such forms of representation: 'this, I submit, is neither science, nor knowledge, nor understanding: it is a statement of power and a claim for absolute authority' (ibid.: 8). He calls 'such a relation between Western writing ... and Oriental silence the result of and the sign of the West's great cultural strength, its will to power over the Orient' (Said, 1995 [1978]: 94).

The concept of the 'Other' has proven productive for cultural theory. From its initial applications to gender and colonial relations between national, ethnic and racial groups, the term has been expanded to include, for example, queer groups (Essig, 1999) and the working classes (Lawler, 2005). In each case the argument has been made that by excluding a group from the production of their own representation a power relationship is being played out. An analysis of academic and journalistic representations of pornography consumers demonstrates the same play of power in the ways in which they are represented.

The effects of Othering pornography consumers

Despina Chronaki has shown that young people learn about sex from journalism, among other sources, and the version of sex they learn about from the news is not a positive one: newspapers are determined to protect young people from the 'perversity of their own sexuality' (Chronaki, 2017: 423). We have evidence that, at least since the 1950s, significant numbers of adolescents have sought out sexually explicit material as part of their sexual learning – a recent survey of pornography consumers found that of those growing up in the period before the end of the 1950s, 36.7 per cent had first seen pornography before the age of 16 (McKee, Albury and Lumby, 2008: 37). A 2008 study suggested that, while pre-adolescent exposure (prior to age 13) remains 'relatively uncommon', more than 90 per cent of boys under 18, and more than 60 per cent of girls, had seen sexually explicit material (Sabina, Wolak and Finkelhor, 2008). These young people find themselves in the strange situation where they are part of a large group that engages in a certain behaviour (viewing sexually explicit images), but the public discourses that explain the meaning of that behaviour exclude the voices of anyone who actually does it. It is the non-consumers (or, at least, people who present themselves publicly as non-consumers) in academia and journalism who get to set the agenda on how this behaviour should be understood.

The example of Professor Gail Dines' publicity tour for her book *Pornland: How Porn Has Hijacked Our Culture* (Dines, 2010b) is typical of this 'Othering'. Dines travelled the world, receiving extensive news coverage for her argument that everyone who consumes porn is necessarily damaged by it – and becomes damaging to other people: 'Boys and men don't realize the power they're giving away to pornography. They don't understand the power it has to shape who they are, their sexuality, and their sexual identity' (Dines, quoted in Avard, 2010).

She talks about the damage that young people are doing to themselves by consuming porn:

> Children who are 11½ years old are now looking at pornography because it comes straight into the home. There's no limit on how much you can access . . . So what happens is that desensitization sets in that much quicker and that much earlier. In order to keep the consumer base going, the pornographers have to keep upping the ante. They make it more violent, body-punishing, or abusive as a way to keep men interested. When you think about it, if you're exposed to it at age 11 or 12, you're jaded by 20.
>
> *(Dines, quoted in Avard, 2010)*

There is no space for the voices of porn consumers in Dines' account. Rather, using a classic Othering strategy, Dines speaks for them and on behalf of them:

> What I've found with my interviews with men is the more they watch, the more they want porn sex, because they become habituated to that kind of industrial-strength sex. Once you become habituated to that, anything else looks boring or uninteresting. What I find is that some men lose interest in their partners altogether and use more pornography. Other men nag and cajole their girlfriends to perform porn sex, or they use prostitutes because that's who they think they can play this porn sex out on.
>
> *(Dines, quoted in Avard, 2010)*

Porn consumers, for Dines, cannot be permitted to represent themselves. They must be represented – by people who will explain to them how harmful their behaviour is. Dines' tour received extensive coverage as she travelled across the world, bringing her academic message through journalistic channels (Bindel, 2010; Dines, 2010a; 2011). A generation of young people were told that they are dangerous, damaged and damaging.

I would like to propose one way of understanding the effects of this Othering, based on personal experience. I recognise the combination of being powerfully drawn to a behaviour, while at the same time being told that the practice is disgusting, wrong, damaged and damaging. This was my experience of being a young gay man in the 1970s and 80s in Scotland. As an adolescent I spent several years as a Christian, desperately struggling to fight off the demon of homosexuality through the power of prayer. Many nights I would lie in the dark, sorely tempted to masturbate, thinking about handsome men – but knowing that these thoughts came directly from Satan, who was tempting me in order to draw me away from my heavenly father. Leaders in my church prayed for me, attempting to cast out the demon of homosexuality. They never succeeded. Too many evenings I would fall into sin, masturbating and then immediately spiralling into depression and self-loathing. I knew that being gay was disgusting and perverse, but I just couldn't help myself. This continued for many years until finally one night, at the age of 19, I decided to give up belief in God. It was a blessed relief.

Thus, when I see the discourses of the damaging effects of porn – rejecting the voices of consumers in order to create a clear picture of their awful despair – I hear an echo of what I went through. As with Christian attempts to stamp out homosexuality, the academic and journalistic Othering of porn consumers says: 'We can't stop them from doing it – but at least we can make them hate themselves'. I propose that we can call this the inculcation of self-loathing as strategy. Anti-pornography voices tell young people that even though 'we' may not have the authority to force 'you', the Other, to stop looking at pornography, we can ensure that you are fucked up about it. We can ensure that there are few voices in academia or the news to contradict the assertion of Clive Hamilton, currently a professor of public ethics, who states with confidence in a newspaper story that '[n]o man who regularly uses pornography can have a healthy sexual relationship with a woman' (Symons, 2004: 4).

What do porn consumers say?

The situation is changing. Certainly in academic writing, and occasionally in journalistic news, the voices of consumers are starting to be heard. And when this happens, the picture they paint is far from the sexually damaged portrait painted by psychology, or the desperate addict who appears in journalism. One of the few pieces of academic writing in which porn consumers speak for and about themselves is Clarissa Smith's account of interviews with 16 female consumers of the British pornographic magazine *For Women*. She notes that 'the motivations of porn readers are rarely examined' (Smith, 2002: 1) and that theorists have tended to imagine that ordinary consumers of pornography are unable to have any response beyond sexual excitement: 'Only academic, radical feminist or moralist viewers seem able to experience responses other than the "purely" sexual: *they* can talk of their boredom. "Ordinary" porn users are never disappointed, embarrassed, put off, worried, or appalled' (ibid.: 6).

Smith found from speaking to the 16 consumers that in fact responses to pornography were highly differentiated, and these women consumed pornography for a variety of reasons. She gives the example of one reader whose husband was not interested in her sexually. This woman says that the effect of her use of sexually explicit materials was that 'it gave me strength . . . I didn't feel like my husband was the norm, thank god . . . there were blokes out there that did enjoy making love' (ibid.: 9).

Another mixed-methods study, which combined a large-scale survey with in-depth interviews with 46 consumers of pornography (26 men and 20 women), found a diverse range of views among them about how pornography represents sex (McKee, 2005). Some consumers worried that pornography presents a phallocentric view that places the penis at the centre of sexual acts; others were concerned that it fails to show the complexity of sexual negotiations. Several used the word 'education' to discuss their experience of consuming pornography, learning about new practices and positions. Related to this issue, other interviewees suggested that pornography, by showing them forms of sexuality that they could relate to but hadn't seen represented before, had the positive effect of reassuring them about their identity and their right to practise their own sexuality. Other consumers made the point that it doesn't make sense to talk about the 'effect' of pornography on ideas about sexuality without looking at the wider cultural context – at the effect that other media and institutions such as church, family and education have on attitudes towards sexuality.

The most ambitious attempt to date to allow pornography consumers to represent themselves is contained not in an academic publication but in a book by journalist David Loftus. In *Watching Sex*, he reports on interviews with more than 140 male consumers of pornography. His findings are surprising when compared with the data generated within psychological research: these male pornography consumers

> would like to see more plot and romance in pornography ... they do not particularly enjoy close ups of genitals ... they not only do NOT find violence against women or domination of women sexy, they are specifically turned off by such behaviour on the rare occasions they see it in pornography, and most haven't even seen any ... they have not sought ever more vivid, kinky and violent pornography, but have either stuck with what they liked from the first, investigated wilder content and returned to what they preferred, or lost interest altogether ... they don't like the way men are portrayed in pornography ... [and] they are against making it available to children, even though many of them were exposed to pornographic stories and images before the age of 12 and don't feel the worse for it.
> (Loftus, 2002: xii)

These stories remain on the periphery of the debate, not represented in the dominant discourses around pornography in journalism. And in academia it was still possible in 2011 for researchers to write in a peer-reviewed article that 'It is difficult to find a methodologically sound study that shows a lack of some kind of harm when men view pornography' (Foubert, Brosi and Bannon, 2011: 213–214) (in an article that – of course – involves no voices of actual consumers).

Conclusion

To conclude, I return to the quotation that opened this chapter: 'we do not consult racists in formulating laws against hate speech on the basis that they are involved in and know a lot about racism' (Pringle, 2011: 127). But it could be argued, on the contrary, that anyone who is interested in reducing racism in a society could find talking to racists a valuable source of information that could help understand why people do what they do – and thus to find ways to address the problem. There is a tradition of academic research that has spoken to sex offenders, for example, in order to understand the reasons for their abuse (see, for example, Beauregard et al., 2008; Driemeyer et al., 2013). There is no suggestion that these researchers support sexual abuse or approve of sexual offenders. Rather, they accept that listening to the offenders helps them to understand the problem. In this context, the insistent Othering of porn consumers, the refusal even to countenance the possibility of listening to what they say, looks like something quite different from a genuine commitment to understanding the issue. This Othering of pornography consumers by academics and journalists is – as Said puts it in relation to Orientalism – 'neither science, nor knowledge, nor understanding: it is a statement of power and a claim for absolute authority' (1985: 8). Said calls for 'an exchange between [their] views and an outsider's ... dialogue ... discussion [and] mutual recognition'. In understanding the consumers of pornography, such forms of engagement look like the obvious way forward.

Note

1 Karen Boyle has suggested that the situation is different for fictional representations (Boyle, 2010), although it should be noted that fictional representations do not present the voices of actual people as does journalism.

Bibliography

Anon. (2004). 'Lust junkies flooding cyberspace'. *Gold Coast Bulletin*. 31 July: B68.
Avard, C. (2010). 'Interview with Christian Avard'. *Pulse*. http://gaildines.com/2010/07/pulse-media/ (accessed 16 March 2016).
Barak, A. and Fisher, W. A. (1997). 'Effects of interactive computer erotica on men's attitudes and behavior toward women: an experimental study'. *Computers in Human Behavior*. Volume 13 (3): 353–369.
Beauregard, E., Stone, M. R., Proulx, J. and Michaud, P. (2008). 'Sexual murderers of children: developmental, precrime and postcrime factors'. *International Journal of Offender Therapy and Comparative Criminology*. Volume 52 (3): 253–269.
Bindel, J. (2010). 'The truth about the porn industry'. *The Guardian*. www.theguardian.com/lifeandstyle/2010/jul/02/gail-dines-pornography (accessed 16 March 2016).
Boyle, K. (2010). 'Porn consumers' public faces: mainstream media, address and representations'. In K. Boyle (ed), *Everyday Pornography*. London and New York: Routledge.
Bragg, S. (2006). '"Having a real debate": using media as a resource in sex education'. *Sex Education: Sexuality, Society and Learning*. Volume 6 (4): 317–331.
Brannigan, A. (2004). *The Rise and Fall of Social Psychology: The Use and Misuse of the Experimental Method*. New York: Aldine de Gruyter.
Brown, J. D. and Bobkowski, P. S. (2011). 'Older and newer media: patterns of use and effects on adolescents' health and well-being'. *Journal of Research on Adolescence*. Volume 21 (1): 95–113.
Chronaki, D. (2017). 'What does news teach about sex? Young people's understandings of the media framing of sexuality'. In L. Allen amd M. L. Rasmussen (eds), *The Routledge Handbook of Sexuality Education*. London: Routledge: 423–437.
Collins, R. L., Elliott, M. N., Berry, S. H., Kanouse, D. E., Kunkel, D., Hunter, S. B. and Miu, A. (2004). 'Watching sex on television predicts adolescent initiation of sexual behavior'. *Pediatrics*. Volume 114 (3): e280–e289.
Davies, K. A. (1997). 'Voluntary exposure to pornography and men's attitudes toward feminism and rape'. *The Journal of Sex Research*. Volume 34 (2): 131–137.
de Beauvoir, S. ([1949] 2014). *The Second Sex*. Women and Marxism Archive. www.marxists.org/reference/subject/ethics/de-beauvoir/2nd-sex/introduction.htm (accessed 22 December 2014).
Dines, G. (2010a). *New York Post*. http://gaildines.com/2010/07/new-york-post/ (accessed 29 September 2012).
Dines, G. (2010b). *Pornland: How Porn Has Hijacked Our Culture*. Boston, MA: Beacon Press.
Dines, G. (2011). 'How the hardcore porn industry is ruining young men's lives'. *The Courier*. 17 May. www.thecourier.com.au/story/89041/how-the-hardcore-porn-industry-is-ruining-young-mens-lives/ (accessed 1 April 2017).

Donnerstein, E. and Berkowitz, L. (1981). 'Victim reactions in aggressive erotic films as a factor in violence against women'. *Journal of Personality and Social Psychology*. Volume 41 (4): 710–724.

Driemeyer, W., Spehr, A., Yoon, D., RichterAppelt, H. and Briken, P. (2013). 'Comparing sexuality, aggressiveness, and antisocial behavior of alleged juvenile sexual and violent offenders'. *Journal of Forensic Sciences*. Volume 58 (3): 711–718.

Essig, L. (1999). *Queer in Russia: A Story of Sex, Self and the Other*. Dunham, NC: Duke University Press.

Eyal, K. and Kunkel, D. (2008). 'The effects of sex in television drama shows on emerging adults' sexual attitudes and moral judgments'. *Journal of Broadcasting and Electronic Media*. Volume 52 (2): 161–181.

Fewster, S. (2004). 'Guilty pedophile sobs as judge revokes bail'. *Adelaide Advertiser*. 27 August: 17.

Fisher, W. A. and Barak, A. (1989). 'Sex education as a corrective: immunizing against possible effects of pornography'. In D. Zillmann and J. Bryant (eds), *Pornography: Research Advances and Policy Considerations*. New Jersey: Lawrence Erlbaum Associates, Inc., Publishers.

Fisher, W. A. and Grenier, G. (1994). 'Violent pornography, antiwoman thoughts, and antiwoman acts: in search of reliable effects'. *The Journal of Sex Research*. Volume 31 (1): 23–38.

Foubert, J. D., Brosi, M. W. and Bannon, R. S. (2011). 'Pornography viewing among fraternity men: effects on bystander intervention, rape myth acceptance and behavioral intent to commit sexual assault'. *Sexual Addiction & Compulsivity*. Volume 18 (4): 212–231.

Hamilton, C. (2004). 'Guarding our kids from a perverse twist'. *The Australian*. 17 August: 11.

Kendrick, W. (1996). *The Secret Museum: Pornography in Modern Culture*. Berkeley/Los Angeles/London: University of California Press.

Kunkel, D., Cope, K. M. and Biely, E. (1999). 'Sexual messages on television: comparing findings from three studies'. *The Journal of Sex Research*. Volume 36 (3): 230–236.

Lawler, S. (2005). 'Disgusted subjects: the making of middle-class identities'. *The Sociological Review*. Volume 53 (3): 429–446.

Lewis, J. (2008). 'Presumed effects of erotica: some notes on the report of the commission on obscenity and pornography'. *Film International*. Volume 6 (36): 7–16.

Linz, D. G., Donnerstein, E. I. and Penrod, S. (1988). 'Effects of long-term exposure to violent and sexually degrading depictions of women'. *Journal of Personality and Social Psychology*. Volume 55 (5): 758–768.

Loftus, D. (2002). *Watching Sex: How Men Really Respond to Pornography*. New York: Thunder's Mouth Press.

McKee, A. (2005). 'The need to bring the voices of pornography consumers into debates about the genre and its effects'. *Australian Journal of Communication*. Volume 32 (2): 71–94.

McKee, A., Albury, K. and Lumby, C. (2008). *The Porn Report*. Melbourne: Melbourne University Press.

McKee, A., Dore, J. and Watson, A.-F. (2014). '"It's all scientific to me": focus group insights into why young people don't apply safe sex knowledge'. *Sex Education*. Online First publication: 1–14.

Malamuth, N. M. and Check, J. V. P. (1981). 'The effects of mass media exposure on acceptance of violence against women: a field experiment'. *Journal of Research in Personality*. Volume 15: 436–446.

Mort, F. (2000). *Dangerous Sexualities: Medico-moral Politics in England since 1830* (2nd ed). London: Routledge.

Padgett, V. R., Brislin-Slütz, J. A. and Neal, J. A. (1989). 'Pornography, erotica, and attitudes toward women: the effects of repeated exposure'. *The Journal of Sex Research*. Volume 26 (4): 479–491.

Pell, G. (2004). 'Crime figures prove we live in an age of violence'. *Sunday Telegraph*, 8 August: 83.

Potter, H. (1996). *Pornography: Group Pressures and Individual Rights*. Sydney: Federation Press.

Pringle, H. (2011). 'A studied indifference to harm: defending pornography in The Porn Report'. In M. Tankard Reist and A. Bray (eds), *Big Porn Inc: Exposing the Harms of the Global Pornography Industry*. North Melbourne, Victoria: Spinifex Press.

Richters, J., Grulich, A., de Visser, R. O., Smith, A. M. A. and Rissel, C. E. (2003). 'Autoerotic, esoteric and other sexual practices engaged in by a representative sample of adults'. *Australian and New Zealand Journal of Public Health*. Volume 27 (2): 180–190.

Sabina, C., Wolak, J. and Finkelhor, D. (2008). 'The nature and dynamics of internet pornography exposure for youth'. *CyberPsychology & Behavior*. Volume 11 (6): 691–693.

Said, E. (1985). 'Orientalism reconsidered'. *Race and Class*. Volume 27 (2): 1–15.

Said, E. ([1978] 1995). *Orientalism* (2nd ed). London: Penguin.

Shanahan, A. (2004). 'Memo to the gender police: sex is not a morality-free zone'. *The Australian*. 8 August: 13.

Smith, C. (2002). '"They're ordinary people, not aliens from the planet Sex!" The mundane excitements of pornography for women'. *Journal of Mundane Behavior*. Volume 3 (1): http://mundanebehavior.org/theyre-ordinary-people-not-aliens-from-the-planet-sex-the-mundane-excitements-of-pornography-for-women (accessed 20 September 2016).

Smith, C. (2007). *One for the Girls! The Pleasures and Practices of Reading Women's Porn*. Bristol: Intellect Books.

Strub, W. (2006). 'Perversion for profit: Citizens for Decent Literature and the arousal of an anti-porn public in the 1960s'. *Journal of the History of Sexuality*. Volume 15 (2): 258–291.

Symons, E. K. (2004). 'Torn on porn's net effects'. *The Australian*. 17 August: 4.

Taylor, P. (2005). 'Child porn "addict" jailed for three years'. *The Australian*. 14 April. n.p.

Zillmann, D. and Bryant, J. (1984). 'Effects of massive exposure to pornography'. In N. M. Malamuth and E. Donnerstein (eds), *Pornography and Sexual Aggression*. Orlando: Academic Press.

37
THE PORN PERFORMER

Angela Gabrielle White

Pornographic becomings: beyond the victim/agent divide

Within the media, as well as in the academy and in feminist debates, one image looms large as a powerful symbol of victimisation or agency: the female porn performer. Three decades after the 'porn wars' began, the victim/agent divide persists as the dominant framework within which the discussion of pornography takes place. Too often female porn performers are either described as having been forced by male pimps into a life of sexual degradation and abuse or regarded as sexual freedom fighters, empowered by their transgression of outdated social norms and paving the way to a future of authentically female sexual agency (Corsianos, 2007; Coy and Garner, 2010; Dworkin, 1981; Hardy, 1998). A focus on the female performer as either victim or agent has limited how performers and their work are represented (Smith, 2012) and impeded research into other aspects of their lives as sex workers.

This chapter moves beyond the victim/agent divide by engaging directly with female performers in the Australian pornography industry. Direct engagement with the views of performers offers a far more nuanced understanding of the experiences and motivations of the female porn performer than has been possible in the majority of previous research – work which has made little or no reference to their voices. Rather than focus on well-trodden yet irreconcilable arguments, this chapter uses qualitative research to identify a theme within the personal narratives of six female performers: that pornography offers possibilities for female performers to explore creative sexual expression, exploration, exhibitionism and same-sex sexual pleasures, and that performing in pornography has challenged these women's understandings of their own sexual identities. Drawing on the work of Michel Foucault and queer theory, the article positions pornography as a queer space that subverts heteronorms, destabilises sexual identity categories and can enable new sexual possibilities, or, as I will characterise them here, *becomings*.

Performers as experts on their own lives

This chapter draws on research I undertook into female experiences in the Australian pornography industry. Six female volunteers aged 20–25 were invited to write a personal narrative about their experiences working in the porn industry. The small sample size reflects a focus on depth rather than breadth, and means that the findings cannot be generalised or applied to all women who perform in pornography. Nor can the findings tell us anything about how men or intersex or transgender people experience performing in porn. However, the evidence gathered in these personal narratives enables a perspective beyond the victim/agent divide presented in most previous work on this topic. Through writing their own narratives, participants in the research became active contributors to the production of knowledge about their lives, challenging the consensus both of anti-porn feminists and of moral guardians about the motivations and justifications of female porn performers. It proceeds from a respect for performers as 'experts on their own lives' (Wahab, 2003: 640). Sex workers are frequently denied self-representation, and without reference to their voices, studies on sex workers do not reflect their realities (ibid.: 626). Allowing sex workers to tell their own stories is necessary to put 'a real face on the mythological creatures that are the subject of so much fantasizing and demonizing' (Oakley, 2007: 11).

The groundbreaking anthologies *Sex Work* (1987) and *Whores and Other Feminists* (1997) created an opportunity for women in other areas of sex work, such as escorts and exotic dancers, to speak for themselves about their experiences. However, porn performers were largely absent from these texts. The recent publication of *The Feminist Porn Book* (2013) and the 2014 launch of the peer-reviewed journal *Porn Studies* have begun to address this gap in the existing literature by publishing the writings of porn performers alongside work written by academics. Over the past two decades there have been numerous calls for a greater amount of research on sex workers to be carried out by sex workers themselves (Agustín, 2010; Pyett, 1998; Wahab and Sloan, 2004). Laura Agustín draws attention to the way in which most of the research on sex workers has been conducted by people outside of the industry, often by those who tend to approach the subject from a position of moral or political disapproval. Agustín argues that:

> [W]e need a lot more research undertaken by people who are very close to sex workers' lives, or who are sex workers themselves . . . who will above all commit themselves to recording honestly all the different and conflicting points of view and stories they run into during research.
>
> (2010: 26)

This chapter presents a contribution to that goal. A notable advantage of being personally involved in the pornography industry as a performer, director and producer is the access I have had to other performers, both through working directly with them and by being part of a sex-worker community. Sex workers are often stigmatised and pathologised by research and thus can be wary of researchers. Being a performer myself meant I was granted considerable trust in pursuing the research presented in this chapter.

At the same time, my proximity to the industry could be conceived as disadvantageous to the process of data analysis. Some observers may argue that I have a vested interest in polishing the image of pornography in order to recuperate a possibly tarnished sense of self (given that sex work in general, and performing in pornography in particular, are perceived as either shameful, even disloyal to women as a class, or imposed by exploitative men on women deemed damaged in some way). But qualitative researchers have consistently argued that qualitative data and research findings are always the product of the unique relationship between the 'researcher' and the 'researched', and the different social positions that frame their subjectivities (Warren and Karner, 2010: 245). Part of the ongoing feminist epistemological project has been to critique the idea that objective 'truth-claims' are even possible, and to emphasise the ways in which research and knowledge are enriched through acknowledging the social position of the researcher (Wilton, 2004: 37). This chapter, written from within the community which forms its research object, expands scholarly knowledge of the porn industry and women's place within it.

Pleasure has no passport

In modern Western societies, sexuality is commonly understood as a natural force. Before the 1970s, this was also the widely held view within academia. Many anthropologists, psychoanalysts, sociologists and sexologists pointed to the cultural diversity of sexual practices but continued to understand sexuality as a natural force subject to different kinds of social organisation and varying degrees of repression (Garton, 2004: 1–2; Hall, 2003: 21–22; Weeks, 2003: 18–19). But the work of French philosopher Michel Foucault argued instead that sexuality was *invented* in the nineteenth century (1978: 42–43). Foucault insisted:

> Sexuality must not be thought of as a kind of natural given which power tries to hold in check, or as an obscure domain which knowledge tries gradually to uncover. It is the name that can be given to a historical construct.
>
> *(Foucault, 1978: 105)*

In his seminal work *The History of Sexuality* (1978), Foucault argues that sexuality is not a pre-discursive, natural phenomenon that culture attempts to repress or liberate. Rather, he asserts, sexuality is a regulatory system that only exists through its social organisation (Weeks, 2003: 18). Foucault argues that sexuality is 'an especially dense transfer point for relations of power' (1978: 103). Sexuality is a regulatory system founded upon an artificial unity of disparate practices, sensations, pleasures, impulses, biological functions, hormones, muscular activities, wishes, hopes and desires, and this regulatory system functions most powerfully and effectively through categories of sexual identity (1978: 154; Angelides, 2001: 144; Grosz, 1994: 154; Grosz, 2005: 198).

Foucault's work challenged the connection between sexual practices and sexual identity that had long been taken for granted. He points out that in the West, prior to the emergence of sexuality as a discourse in the nineteenth century, same-sex sexual practices (referred to as 'sodomy') were considered unnatural but were not understood to be a defining aspect of a person's identity. However, beginning in the nineteenth century, same-sex sexual practices were transformed from a fleeting transgression of (hetero)sexual norms into a 'sexual identity': the homosexual. Quoting Foucault:

> As defined by the ancient civil or canonical codes, sodomy was a category of forbidden acts; their perpetrator was nothing more than the juridical subject of them. The nineteenth-century homosexual became a personage, a past, a case history, and a childhood, in addition to being a type of life, a life form and a morphology, with an indiscreet anatomy and possibly a mysterious physiology . . . The sodomite had been a temporary aberration; the homosexual was now a species.
>
> *(1978: 43)*

Likewise, opposite-sex sexual practices have come to be understood as the representation of an innate heterosexual identity. Foucault's work demonstrates that the statements 'I am homosexual' or 'I am heterosexual' have only become possible, and subsequently mandated, relatively recently in the West. These assertions are only intelligible in a society where sexual desires and practices are understood as having 'an identity-determining capacity' (Hall 2003: 23). In other words, through the deployment of sexuality as a regulatory system, sexual practices have come to be understood as a reflection of an essential, stable and inherent core.

Following Foucault, many queer theorists have pointed out that categories of sexual identity are fundamentally limiting and exclusionary (Hall, 2003; Kirsch, 2000; Sullivan, 2003). However, the identification of sexuality as a discursive, social construct also enables us to imagine the possibility for change. Foucault argues that '[t]he rallying point for the counterattack against the deployment of sexuality ought not to be sex-desire, but bodies and pleasures' (1978: 157). The meaning of this enigmatic suggestion has been the subject of significant debate (Butler, 1999; Grosz, 1994; Jagose, 2010). What does it mean to separate sex-desire (that is, desire as it has been organised into sexual identity categories) from bodies and pleasures? Elizabeth Grosz (1994: 155) wonders: 'is it that bodies and pleasures are somehow outside the deployment of sexuality?' Or is it more the case, as Ladelle McWhorter (1999: 184) suggests, that 'normalizing discourses have not colonized pleasure as they have colonized desire[?]'. Indeed, perhaps pleasure cannot be colonised, because it is unruly, reckless and chaotic.

The six personal narratives explored here provide strong grounds for arguing that pleasures are capable of exceeding the regulatory power of sexuality insofar as it is possible to experience pleasures without recourse to desire or categories of sexual identity. And in doing so, the narratives illustrate how the pleasures of pornographic performance are capable of destabilising desire and sexual identity.

Annamarie Jagose suggests that intense pleasures may have transformative potential since they are capable of detaching us, at least momentarily, from the regulatory deployment of sex-desire:

> Where desire is concerned with psychologisation and the deep attachment of an interiorised sexual subjectivity to the classificatory categories of sexology, pleasure is concerned with intensification and the temporary dissolution of the subject. As Foucault puts it 'Pleasure has no passport, no identification papers'. For Foucault, intense sexual pleasure, particularly that which reorganises the body's erogeneity, is productively impersonal in so far as it has the capacity to reorder momentarily the subject's sense of self, to detach the individual from the stable, coherent identity through which modern sexuality is administered and regulated.
>
> (2010: 523)

In other words, intense and unpredictable pleasures have the potential to challenge our sense of sexual identity as fixed, and at these moments we are most susceptible to new sexual becomings.

Foucault's work and his invocation of bodies and pleasures have been influential in queer projects that challenge the regulatory and normalising functions of categories of sexual identity. Queer theorists promote the creation of new sexual economies based not on static identities but on permanently fluid becomings (Grosz, 2005: 213). One of the reasons why categories of sexual identity are so limiting is that they tabulate past and present sexual practices in an attempt to regulate future sexual encounters (ibid.). In contrast, thinking of sexuality as an evolving set of becomings points towards indeterminable futures. Becomings are never fixed or static, and are queer in the sense that, as David Halperin argues, '[queer] describes a horizon of possibility whose precise extent and heterogeneous scope cannot in principle be delimited in advance' (cited in Sullivan, 2003: 43). Similarly, Mandy Merck suggests that 'queer is not what has gone before but what has yet to come'. Queer is a permanent becoming and an unimaginable future (Merck, 2005: 187).

The personal narratives explored below illustrate the ways in which pornography functions as a queer space that opens performers up to new sexual possibilities (or becomings). To begin with, all sex work is always already queer. Selling sex queers the heterosexual economy because women involved in selling sexual services step beyond the bounds of acceptable female sexuality and femininity and put a price (often high) on sexual services which patriarchy requires that they give away for free (preferably only to one man, to whom they are married) (Pendleton, 1997: 76). However, the narratives also reveal that the intense and unpredictable pleasures experienced while performing in pornography can challenge regulatory notions of sexual identity as fixed and inherent. Pornography emerges from these narratives as a queer space that subverts heteronorms, destabilises categories of sexual identity and is capable of opening performers up to new sexual possibilities.

Pornography as a queer space

As a work environment, pornography creates a unique opportunity for performers to experience sexual pleasures disinvested from sexual desire and what they take to be their own sexual identity. For example, a female performer who identifies as heterosexual and monogamous may believe she can perform in a girl–girl scene outside of her relationship without having this impact on what she takes to be her own sexual identity. After all, the same-sex encounter can be conceptualised as a requirement of a job rather than a representation of desire. This logic is not uncommon in the pornography industry, and is typified by the popular expression 'gay-for-pay'. However, the intense and unexpected pleasures arising from such a performance can lead to a dissonance between what one believes oneself to be and what one feels – a dissonance between a heavily invested-in heterosexual identity and the intense pleasures experienced through same-sex sexual relations. The chaos, disorder and confusion brought about through the dissolution of the self in sexual pleasure have the potential to undermine a presumed stable sexual identity. Porn is unique in that sexual relations can occur without recourse to desire or sexual identity, which are socially mandated in normative sexual encounters. Thus, a frequent theme in the narratives which follow is that pornography places performers in sexual situations that would have been very unlikely under other circumstances. These excerpts highlight the unique capacity of pornography to create opportunities for sexual creativity, expression, encounters and pleasures that may not otherwise have been possible.[1]

> **Jackie**: I find pornography an exciting, creative and financially fulfilling career option, which has opened me up to sexual, artistic and financial possibilities that I never would have otherwise had the opportunity to experience.
>
> **Belinda**: I have enjoyed every single woman I have 'modelled' with. The experience in itself, the places and situations you couldn't possibly have been in without

the help of the industry, the creativity of the shoots, the sexual freedom and liberation you feel after your accomplishments and the feeling of being proud.

The creative elements of pornographic performance place the participants in unlikely sexual situations where they are encouraged to experiment with different sexual personas and characters:

Natalie: I love performing, dressing up and flirting with the camera. It's so much fun! We get to be very creative with different themes, backgrounds, poses, outfits and scenarios. In pornography I have been able to explore being sexual in many different ways.

Jackie: I've had lush sexual exchanges on camera with spontaneous, exciting womyn who I've experienced chemistry with. I've had the pleasure of being creatively involved in the process, whether contributing to shoot concepts or, with more artistic erotica sites, being sole creative contributor as well as performer. I love the process of crafting new personas to fit the sites I work with.

Pornography encourages sexual exploration and experimentation, and the active fashioning of new personae sets performers up to think outside the restrictions of what they take to be their own sexual identity. The presence of a camera during these sexual encounters and the active sexual engagement with the non-human (through 'flirting' with technology) already begin to queer heterosexual norms. These norms are queered further when Sarah, who identifies as heterosexual and monogamous and who is engaged to be married, employs pornography as a space to express herself sexually outside the confines of her relationship:

Sarah: A latent exhibitionism seemed as good a reason as any to take the plunge into amateur pornography. I felt like I had a split personality in terms of sex; the outwardly shy and nervous side hiding the very sexually active, curious and explorative side. Sexual attention was both terrifying and completely addictive. However by the time I'd realised how strong the sexual side of me was, I was in a very committed relationship with the man I now have a child with. He's a completely brilliant guy, and matches me perfectly, but meeting at 19 years of age meant that it cut out any possibilities for sexual exploration with anyone else, which, if I'm honest, I really wanted . . . I think I spent the majority of my earnings [from pornography] on [my partner]. I think this was because I was trying to say thank you for allowing me to express myself sexually without him and for supporting me.

Pornography functions as a space in which Sarah is able to indulge her sexual curiosity through exploration, expression and exhibitionism. Despite Sarah's fiancé supporting her career choice, Sarah's involvement in pornography queers monogamy and facilitates her desired sexual exploration outside of the bounds of their engagement.

Laura, also in a monogamous heterosexual relationship, had her first same-sex sexual experience through her pornography work:

Laura: To say I was nervous was an understatement – I was terrified! Nearly 19, here I was in front of this gorgeous woman (who I later found out was also her first lesbian experience too) thinking a million thoughts all at once. Does my breath smell? What if she's not attracted to me? Is she disappointed with the pairing? What if I say something really stupid that puts her off? What if I fart and she's near there? Of course these were all worst-case scenarios, none of which actually happened. It was in fact one of the most beautiful sexual experiences of my life, which simply cannot be replicated. Not only did I kiss a girl and enjoy it, I wanted to do more.

Pornographic performance not only opened Laura up to sexual experiences with other women but also opened her up to the possibility of exploring these pleasures further.

Pornographic becomings

The requirements of work in pornography open performers up not only to new sexual possibilities and creative sexual expression but also to new becomings. Pornography creates a queer space in which performers can experience pleasures disinvested from desire and what they take to be their own sexual identity. In the following excerpt, Natalie describes the effect that unpredictable sexual pleasures had on her sense of sexual identity.

> **Natalie**: My favourites have been the girl–girl lesbian shoots. They are so much fun because you get to interact more [compared with solo modelling]. I was so nervous on my first lesbian shoot, I had never been with a girl before, although I had thought girls were pretty and wouldn't mind kissing them. Geez, I had no idea what I was doing. But it was so much fun. I felt so many different sensations, it was so lustful and carnal. I was so nervous my whole body was shaking from fear but also from pleasure. I don't know if I ever would have been with another girl in that capacity otherwise but pornography opened me up to that possibility . . . I don't know how to explain my sexuality now because I have a boyfriend but I love to have sex with girls. Although I haven't had sex with a girl except on camera. Maybe that makes it different, like it's just playing around, but I get so horny and we really get to have sex and orgasm. I guess I am bisexual.

The pleasures that Natalie experienced in performing for pornography challenged her sense of her sexual identity as stable and fixed. Similarly, Tyler's sense of identity was challenged through her experience of same-sex pleasures in pornographic work.

> **Tyler**: The more girls I had sex with [in pornography] the more I realised how much I loved it, and I slowly found that I was losing interest in having sex with my [male] partner. Sex with him started to become a chore. I mean I loved my partner more than anything, but soon it got to the stage where I just lost complete interest in having sex with him! I started to change slowly, and this has been going on for a while. I guess when you spend so much time around women, beautiful women, things can change, and they did for me. Soon I found myself having no sexual attraction to males whatsoever and that sadly included my partner. I tried to pretend it wasn't happening, but one day I realised that I couldn't fight it anymore – I was gay. I still loved my boyfriend more than anything, but I had changed, I had become a different person . . . I became a person

that couldn't be with him. We broke up and it was one of the hardest things I ever had to do, but I really had no choice. It wasn't fair on him, and maybe it's a phase I'm going through, I don't know, but I have realised that I just love women too much and that's where my life needs to go right now! Do I think the porn industry contributed to my change in sexuality? Definitely in some way! I spent so much time around attractive and confident women, it was only natural for me to go down that path.

Tyler first suggests that her work helped her to discover her pre-existing lesbian identity (she could no longer 'fight' the fact that she had been gay all along). However, later she asserts that she 'had changed' and 'had become a different person'. Later still, Tyler questions whether 'it's a phase'. In any case, her sense of self has been rearranged due to her experiences of same-sex pleasures through her performances, and she has been opened up to the possibility of new becomings.

Belinda's narrative describes a similar evolution:

Belinda: Being involved in pornography has definitely affected my sexuality. I started at a young age and have been drastically influenced by it. I have found myself sexually more from the industry then any other vice because the industry is revolved around sexuality. I wouldn't say affected, though. It has made me question myself in more ways. It has made me open-minded, more so than I could have ever imagined. The advantages of being involved in such an industry are more so than the disadvantages – if any. I have always been confused about my sexuality. I think for the most part of my life I will be. I have at some stages desired to be a man. Bisexual, lesbian, omni-sexual, they are all terms. I have always been sexual and with an industry such as this, it lets me express myself in a comfortable, controlled situation whereby the people I'm surrounded by, I feel, will protect me and let me make my own decisions without pressure.

While there is a sense of confusion in parts of Belinda's narrative, she makes it clear that her involvement has made her question herself in ways that would not have been possible outside of her involvement in the porn industry. As a result of her porn performances she has rejected rigid categories of sexual identity, and come to identify as simply sexual.

The radical potential of pleasure in pornographic performance that is highlighted by these narratives is not unique to the Australian porn industry. Many contributors to *The Feminist Porn Book* touched on similar themes when discussing their experiences of being involved in the US industry, and observations by performers Sinnamon Love, Jiz Lee and April Flores echo those of my Australian respondents:

Sinnamon Love: I wrote my sexual story, one chapter at a time, in each and every video I've made. I've used my work in porn to explore many firsts and share those experiences with my fans: sex with a woman, double penetration, group sex, double anal, a blowbang, a gangbang or my first time with a Japanese woman who didn't speak English. I've let them watch me make love with a real-life partner and fuck complete strangers I had just met moments before the cameras rolled. I've even allowed my fans to watch me pregnant.

(*Taormino* et al., 2013: 102)

Jiz Lee: People often ask me, 'What made you decide you wanted to do porn?' and I tell them the truth: I want to share my sexual expression with others. I like it, it feels liberating, and I know that it helps others feel free too.

(Taormino et al., 2013: 274)

April Flores: I feel very lucky that I have had the chance to explore and expand my own sexuality through my work in pornography. I have lived out my own fantasies by having sex on a stage with an audience watching me, and participating in a scene in the middle of the forest in front of a huge waterfall. I've been able to experience many scenarios – group sex, dominance and submission, sex with other women and transgender men and women. These opportunities have led me from identifying as a straight woman to understanding that my sexuality is fluid and not dictated by the gender of my partner. These powerful, consensual experiences took place in safe, controlled environments, and everything was fully discussed before the shoots.

(Taormino et al., 2013: 281)

In particular, Flores' experience in pornography, and of moving from identifying as heterosexual to an understanding of her sexuality as fluid, points to the radical potential for pleasure gained through work in pornography to destabilise desire and normative categories of sexual identity.

Conclusion

The personal narratives of Belinda, Jackie, Laura, Natalie, Sarah and Tyler illustrate the ways in which a direct engagement with female performers can assist in breaking with the victim/agent divide in examinations of pornography. They demonstrate that the experiences of female porn performers can expose the volatility of categories of sexual identity and subvert heteronormative understandings of identity, pleasure and the experiences of sex work. If these accounts are not necessarily applicable to all female performers, neither can it be argued that all pornography is oppressive or exploitative of the women who perform in it. The narratives set out by these women illustrate the power of intense sexual pleasure to be experienced as a dispossession and an undoing of the self, opening up the individual to new sexual possibilities. The French refer to orgasm as *la petite mort* – the little death – and the potential to be reborn, and reborn differently, makes pleasure a powerful rallying point for the counterattack against restrictive categories of sexual identity, as well as for the unfolding of queer futures.

Note

1 Pseudonyms have been used for all performers.

Bibliography

Agustín, L. (2010) 'The (Crying) Need For Different Kinds of Research'. In M. Ditmore, A. Levy and A. Willman (eds) *Sex Work Matters: Exploring Money, Power and Intimacy in the Sex Industry*. London: Zed Books.

Angelides, S. (2001) *A History of Bisexuality*. Chicago: University of Chicago Press.

Butler, J. (1999) 'Revisiting Bodies and Pleasures'. *Theory, Culture & Society*. Volume 16 (19): 11–20.
Corsianos, M. (2007) 'Mainstream Pornography and "Women": Questioning Sexual Agency'. *Critical Sociology*. Volume 33 (5–6): 863–885.
Coy, M. and Garner, M. (2010) 'Glamour Modelling and the Marketing of Self-Sexualization: Critical Reflections'. *International Journal of Cultural Studies*. Volume 13 (6): 657–675.
Delacoste, F. and Alexander, P. (eds) ([1987] 1998) *Sex Work: Writings by Women in the Sex Industry*. San Francisco: Cleis Press.
Dworkin, A. (1981) *Pornography: Men Possessing Women*. London: Women's Press.
Flores, A. (2013) 'Being Fatty D: Size, Beauty, and Embodiment in the Adult Industry'. In T. Taormino, C. Shimizu, C. Penley and M. Miller-Young (eds) *The Feminist Porn Book: The Politics of Producing Pleasure*. New York: Feminist Press.
Foucault, M. ([1978] 1990) *The History of Sexuality: Volume 1, An Introduction*, trans. R. Hurley. New York: Vintage Books.
Gamson, J. and Moon, D. (2004) 'The Sociology of Sexualities: Queer and Beyond'. *Annual Review of Sociology*. Volume 30: 47–64.
Garton, S. (2004) *Histories of Sexuality: Antiquity to Sexual Revolution*. London: Equinox.
Grosz, E. (1994) *Volatile Bodies: Toward a Corporeal Feminism*. Bloomington: Indiana University Press.
Grosz, E. (2005) *Time Travels: Feminism, Nature, Power*. Durham: Duke University Press.
Hardy, S. (1998) *The Reader, The Author, His Woman & Her Lover: Soft Core Pornography and Heterosexual Men*. London: Cassell.
Lee, J. (2013) 'Uncategorized: Genderqueer Identity and Performance in Independent and Mainstream Porn'. In T. Taormino, C. Shimizu, C. Penley and M. Miller-Young (eds) *The Feminist Porn Book: The Politics of Producing Pleasure*. New York: Feminist Press.
Love, S. (2013) 'A Question of Feminism'. In T. Taormino, C. Shimizu, C. Penley and M. Miller-Young (eds) *The Feminist Porn Book: The Politics of Producing Pleasure*. New York: Feminist Press.
Hall, D. (2003) *Queer Theories*. Basingstoke: Palgrave Macmillan.
Jagose, A. (2010) 'Counterfeit Pleasures: Fake Orgasm and Queer Agency'. *Textual Practice*. Volume 24 (3): 517–539.
Kirsch, M. (2000) *Queer Theory and Social Change*. New York: Routledge.
McWhorter, L. (1999) *Bodies and Pleasures: Foucault and the Politics of Sexual Normalization*. Bloomington: Indiana University Press.
Merck, M. 2005. 'Afterword'. In I. Morland and A. Willox (eds) *Queer Theory*. Basingstoke: Palgrave Macmillan.
Mills, S. (2003) *Michel Foucault*. New York: Routledge.
Milne, C. (ed) (2005) *Naked Ambition: Women Who Are Changing Pornography*. New York: Carroll & Graf Publishers.
Nagle, J. (ed) (1997) *Whores and Other Feminists*. New York: Routledge.
Oakley, A. (2007) 'Introduction'. In A. Oakley (ed) *Working Sex: Sex Workers Write About a Changing Industry*. Berkeley: Seal Press.
Pendleton, E. (1997) 'Love for Sale. Queering Heterosexuality'. In J. Nagle (ed) *Whores and Other Feminists*. New York: Routledge.
Pyett, P. (1998) 'Doing It Together: Sex Workers and Researchers'. *Research for Sex Work*. Volume 1: 11–13.
Smith, C. (2012) 'Reel Intercourse: Doing Sex on Camera'. In C. Hines and D. Kerr (eds) *Hard to Swallow: Hard-Core Pornography on Screen*. West Sussex: Columbia University Press.
Sullivan, N. (2003) *A Critical Introduction to Queer Theory*. New York: New York University Press.
Taormino, T., Shimizu, C., Penley, C. and Miller-Young, M. (eds) (2013) *The Feminist Porn Book: The Politics of Producing Pleasure*. New York: Feminist Press.
Wahab, S. (2003) 'Creating Knowledge Collaboratively with Female Sex Workers: Insights From a Qualitative, Feminist, and Participatory Study'. *Qualitative Inquiry*. Volume 9 (4): 625–642.

Wahab, S. and Sloan, L. (2004) 'Ethical Dilemmas in Sex Work Research'. *Research for Sex Work*. Volume 7: 3–5.
Warren, C.A.B. and Karner, T.X. (2010) *Discovering Qualitative Methods: Field Research, Interviews, and Analysis*. Oxford: Oxford University Press.
Weeks, J. (2003) *Sexuality*. London: Routledge.
Wilton, T. (2004). *Sexual (Dis)Orientation*. Basingstoke: Palgrave Macmillan.

38
THE DOMINATRIX

Danielle J. Lindemann

Introduction

Sometimes it seems as though the Dominatrix is everywhere. She permeates popular culture and media, brandishing her whip in music videos and finding her way into advertisements for even mundane products like snacks and hair spray. The popular television shows *CSI* (2000–2015), *Law and Order: SVU* (1999–), *Private Practice* (2007–2013) and *House* (2004–2012) have all included dominatrices as characters. Facebook even has a 'dominate' option on its SuperPoke application, personified by a corset-clad, whip-wielding cartoon avatar.

Yet the public maintains a paradoxical relationship with the Dominatrix, despite her ostensible ubiquity. While dominatrices have historically been stigmatised and pathologised, in other cases they are shrugged off as amusing and even embraced. Treated as simultaneously unpalatable and tantalising, the Dominatrix is the subject of a dialectic that in some ways reflects broader attitudes towards sexuality but in others is unique to this particular cultural figure. In this chapter, I explore this duality by drawing upon theoretical work and popular media.

I also draw upon empirical data from in-depth, semi-structured interviews I conducted with 52 female professional dominatrices ('pro-Dommes') in the New York City metropolitan area and 14 in the San Francisco Bay Area. For the interviews, which I conducted between 2007 and 2008, I primarily located respondents through their internet advertisements and then through snowball sampling, although I found nine through personal connections. The average interview time was about one hour. My interviewees ranged in age from 20 to 58, with an average age of 37. A majority (62 per cent) self-identified as White, and all had at least a high-school diploma. Only one respondent's highest level of education was high school; in fact, 39 per cent had undertaken postgraduate training.

I use the term 'Dominatrix' throughout this chapter to refer to a woman who acts as the 'dominant' partner in erotically charged practices of BDSM ('bondage, discipline, sadism and masochism'). The other partners in these interactions are known as 'submissives', 'subs', 'slaves' or – in the case of paid interactions – 'clients'. 'Sadomasochism' refers to erotic pleasure experienced through giving and/or receiving physical or psychological pain.

Nineteenth-century sex researcher Richard Krafft-Ebing is typically credited with coining the term, which derives from the surnames of the Marquis de Sade and Austrian writer Leopold von Sacher-Masoch, who penned the 1870 erotic novel *Venus in Furs*. Dommes and subs engage in a variety of sadomasochistic practices, including spanking, paddling, flogging, whipping, 'electric play' (using shocks) and genital piercing.

The most salient cultural image of the Dominatrix – emblematised by the Facebook SuperPoke avatar – is a whip-clutching woman wrapped in a tight leather bodice and shiny black boots. However, in reality, BDSM practices are diverse (Kamel and Weinberg, 1983). Dominatrices also participate in activities that do not involve whipping or even pain; these include, for instance, bondage (tying up the submissive), 'golden showers' (urinating on the submissive) and 'foot worship' ('forcing' the submissive to hold, kiss and massage her feet). Dominatrices also dress in a variety of costumes, such as police or nurse uniforms, to play out various fantasy scenarios.

I use the term 'pro-Dommes' to describe women who, like my research subjects, receive money for these acts. The places where pro-Dommes perform their sessions with clients are known as 'dungeons'. Finally, when I use the terms 'BDSM' and 'sadomasochism', I mean them to refer only to *consensual* erotic activity (Beckmann, 2001).

'The bad guy in the movie is always wearing a leather hood': the stigmatisation of BDSM

Dominatrices and other BDSM practitioners have historically been subject to reproach, stemming from a variety of different sources, including the psychiatric community and the law. Krafft-Ebing, for instance, reflected early psychiatric attitudes towards these practices when he characterised sadomasochism as both a 'perversion' and an 'affliction' (1965: 53) – a view that Freud (1938: 569) shared. Psychologist Wilhelm Stekel felt similarly, describing the sadomasochistically oriented individual as 'a criminal' (1929: 410). Feminist theorist Gayle Rubin alludes to the legal challenges faced by individuals who engage in these types of non-normative sexual practices when she writes, wryly:

> In Western culture, sex is taken all too seriously. A person is not considered immoral, is not sent to prison, and is not expelled from her or his family, for enjoying spicy cuisine. But an individual may go through all this and more for enjoying shoe leather. Ultimately, of what possible social significance is it if a person likes to masturbate over a shoe? It may even be non-consensual, but since we do not ask permission of our shoes to wear them, it hardly seems necessary to obtain dispensation to come on them.
>
> (1992: 171)

The stigmatising attitude towards BDSM practitioners that is evidenced by Krafft-Ebing and Stekel and described by Rubin is also reflected in popular media. For example, one 1976 *Time* magazine cover story, 'The porno plague', cautions its readers about the increasing representation of sadomasochism in popular culture. More recently, in 2008, the British tabloid *News of the World* broke a story in which Max Mosley, head of Formula One's governing body, was 'today exposed as a secret sado-masochist sex pervert',[1] having been caught in a Nazi-themed sadomasochistic orgy. Mosley has since successfully sued the now-defunct tabloid.

A 2008 ABC News article, 'Love hurts: sadomasochism's dangers', begins by describing the case of a man who ended up in a coma after visiting a Dominatrix's dungeon in New York City. While the article acknowledges that, to some extent, BDSM practices have become normalised in popular culture, it also points to the 'deadly' turn they can take (Goldman, 2008). 'Hangy spanky', reads the title of a *New York Post* article covering the same news story (Wilner, Celona and Alpert, 2008). The *Post* article also describes a 2006 incident in which a British national suffocated to death while wrapped in heavy plastic and bound with duct tape in the closet of a Rhode Island man he had met over the internet. The Rhode Island man later committed suicide. A *Daily Mail* piece from 2010 similarly describes a BDSM session gone awry – in this case, resulting in the death of British motor-racing chief Robin Mortimer. 'Dominated to death in a "dungeon"', the title explains, adding: 'Body of motor racing boss found after session with S&M torturer' (Schlesinger, 2010).

As these articles suggest, the Dominatrix – and sadomasochism more broadly – is often catapulted into the public eye at times when extreme injury has occurred. And the portrayal of BDSM practices as perverted, criminal, unhealthy, dangerous and even deadly is not lost on pro-Dommes themselves. In my interviews, many of these women discussed their perceived stigmatisation. Some explicitly mentioned that they had agreed to speak with a researcher in order to help reverse the negative perception of dominatrices. One woman told me, for instance, 'You know, the portrayal of Dommes and the portrayal of BDSM in general is [as a] very sociopathic kinda thing. A very mean thing. [But] it's not mean. It's a *decadent* thing. It's really self-indulgence'. Another pro-Domme explained: 'The bad guy in the movie is always wearing a leather hood and has a dungeon. So people either take the fetish out of context or assume that we're all sociopaths.' In fact, many of these women were highly critical of fellow pro-Dommes who engaged in unsafe or unhealthy practices – in part because they felt that these women were contributing to the negative public perception of BDSM (Lindemann, 2011).

Accepting BDSM with a casual shrug: from tolerance to 'tolerant bemusedness'

While the Dominatrix has been the subject of rebuke and alarm, at the same time – somewhat paradoxically – she has received relative acceptance from unexpected corners. In recent years, scholars have challenged the contention that participation in BDSM is incompatible with a healthy psyche. One study of sadomasochistically oriented males, for instance, found that these individuals were largely 'well-adjusted' and that 'sadomasochistic behavior was merely a facilitative aspect of their sexual lives' (Sandnabba, Santtila and Nordling, 1999: 273). Some authors have explored the contention that BDSM practices may be healing in some ways (Califia, 1988; Barker, Gupta and Iantaffi, 2007) or that these activities may even involve mystical or spiritual properties (Comfort, 1978; Norman, 2004; Rubin, 2004). In fact, while the fourth edition of the *Diagnostic and Statistical Manual of Mental Disorders* (*DSM-IV-TR*) still classified both 'sexual masochism' and 'sexual sadism' as 'disorders', the text only recognised certain manifestations as problematic: 'The diagnosis is made if the person has acted on these urges with a nonconsenting person or the urges, sexual fantasies, or behaviors cause marked distress or interpersonal difficulty' (American Psychiatric Association, 2000: 566).

Moreover, in both scholarly literature and popular media, Dommes and other BDSM practitioners have been treated not just as acceptable but as sources of benign entertainment and even titillation. This ambivalent dialectic was at work as early as the 1980s, when researchers Chris Gosselin and Glenn Wilson explained:

> Somehow, most of the general public seem to have treated these excesses with some irreverence: although they have reacted strongly against those who would legalise sex with children, and even now have a considerable ambivalence towards homosexuality, they have made sadomasochism the subject of jokes, accepted it with a casual shrug, treated those who enjoy its practices with the sort of tolerant bemusedness reserved for the slightly mad or simply ignored it.
> (Gosselin and Wilson, 1980: 11)

This 'tolerant bemusedness' continues to infuse public representations of the Dominatrix today. For example, a 2015 article, 'Women's prison mass jail break after inmates in Dominatrix gear handcuff male guards expecting "mass orgy"', treats the incident with the equivalent of a shrug and a smile. The article, which characterises the plot as a 'daring plan', explains, 'Last night photos of one the naked wardens, believed to have been leaked by amused police officers who found him, had been shared thousands of times on social network sites' (Roper, 2015).

The police officers' 'amused' reaction to the BDSM aspect of the jailbreak is in line with other popular cultural representations that have found comedic value in these practices. On a 1997 episode of the sit-com *Frasier* ('Halloween'), for instance, the character of Roz attends a Halloween party in a leather BDSM costume. When Roz worries that she might be pregnant, Frasier quips, 'Well, I don't think discipline will be a problem'. One cartoon published in the *New Yorker* in 1998 shows a Dominatrix writing a letter in her dungeon; the caption reads: 'Dear Mom and Dad: Just a quick note to thank you for the very lovely desk set' (Cheney, 1998: 68). Another *New Yorker* cartoon depicts a woman outfitted as a Domme speaking to a man who lies in bed. It is captioned, 'Please listen carefully, as my menu options have changed' (Duffy, 1999: 66).

The advertising world, too, has capitalised on the humorous dimensions of the Dominatrix. In one commercial for Wonderful Pistachios, for example, a voiceover explains 'Dominatrices do it', as a Domme cracks open a pistachio with her whip. Another advertisement (for Sunsilk hair products) shows a whip wrapped around a stiletto boot and the caption 'My frizz is so wild even a dominatrix couldn't tame it'. As these examples – and numerous others like them – suggest, the Dominatrix pervades popular media in a multiplicity of ways. She is in the television we watch, the magazines we read, the food we eat. She is literally 'in our hair'.

Fifty shades of popularity: BDSM is everywhere

Perhaps the most notable recent popular representation of BDSM has been E.L. James's book *Fifty Shades of Grey* (2011a) – which spent more than 100 weeks on the *New York Times* best-seller list – and its two sequels, *Fifty Shades Darker* (James, 2011b) and *Fifty Shades Freed* (James, 2012). The trilogy, which has spawned more than one major motion picture, has sold over 100 million copies worldwide, placing it in the ranks of series such as *Harry Potter* (1997–2007), *Twilight* (2005–2008) and the *Nancy Drew* books (1930–) (Bosman, 2014). In the book, the protagonist, Anastasia Steele, falls in love with the multi-millionaire Christian Grey, who is obsessed with BDSM. While the plot does not specifically involve a Dominatrix, the *Fifty Shades* series is crucial to this discussion in that it is perhaps the most visible contemporary example of the mainstreaming of sadomasochistic imagery. These books have reached a vast audience and are sold everywhere, from sex-toy stores to airport kiosks. They have been translated into 52 languages, and in 2012 they outpaced *Harry Potter* to become the UK's fastest-selling paperbacks of all time (Bentley, 2012).

The overwhelming popularity of this series is a salient example of contemporary public consumption of BDSM. In fact, many critiques of the *Fifty Shades of Grey* film (2015, dir: Sam Taylor-Johnson) have suggested *not* that its subject matter is unpalatable but nearly the opposite: that the film fails because it portrays sexual sadomasochism too tamely. In a humorous review in the *New Yorker*, for instance, film critic Anthony Lane writes:

> And there you have the problem with this film. It is gray with good taste – shade upon shade of muted naughtiness, daubed within the limits of the R rating. Think of it as the 'Downton Abbey' of bondage, designed neither to menace nor to offend but purely to cosset the fatigued imagination. You get dirtier talk in most action movies, and more genitalia in a TED talk on Renaissance sculpture.
>
> (Lane, 2015)

One review in *Newsday* similarly explains that 'You might be . . . agog at how an R-rated film full of kinky sex and dirty talk could be so painfully dull' (Guzman, 2015), while a piece in *Rolling Stone* opines that 'The true audiences for *Fifty Shades of Grey* are gluttons for punishment – by boredom' (Travers, 2015). This type of critique has become so widespread that these reviews are now something of a cultural meme. For example, there is an entire round-up devoted to 'The best worst *Fifty Shades of Grey* reviews' (Rickman, 2015). These reactions to the film, which interpret its primary sin not as depravity but as mundanity, suggest that, in the public eye, at least some media portrayals of BDSM have now veered past 'acceptable' and careened into 'pedestrian'.

A second critique has been that the film fails because it unsuccessfully represents 'real' BDSM. One element of the books and film that some – particularly those in the BDSM community – find objectionable is the ambiguity around the issue of consent (Green, 2015). For example, there is some tension in the first book over whether Anastasia will sign a legal contract agreeing to be Christian's submissive – essentially, signing away her right to consent or not consent to their sadomasochistic practices in the future. Yet consent is a crucial element of the interactions that take place within the BDSM community. For example, participants in these activities regularly set 'safe words'. A safe word can be any term (such as 'red') that, when called out by the submissive, indicates that he or she does not wish to continue and ensures the termination of the activity (Lindemann, 2012). Indeed, most of the pro-Dommes I interviewed subscribed to a credo known as 'SSC': the expectation that their activities would be 'safe, sane and consensual'.

Other critics have pointed out that the relationship that unfolds in the film has more in common with abuse than with consensual BDSM. For example, one content analysis of the first novel published in *The Journal of Women's Health* found that emotional abuse – ranging from stalking and intimidation to isolation and violence – was present in 'nearly every interaction' in the book (Bonomi, Altenburger and Walton, 2013). In sum, the major critiques of this franchise – which tend to focus on either the quality of the writing or acting, the dullness of the representations or the skewed portrayal of consensual BDSM activities, and *not* on the kinky sex itself – are revealing of contemporary attitudes towards BDSM.

As one *Huffington Post* headline states succinctly, '"Fifty Shades of Grey" isn't a movie about BDSM, and that's a problem' (Marcus, 2015).

'They see it on TV and think they can make a quick buck': the Dominatrix is everywhere

While the explosive popularity of the *Fifty Shades* franchise has certainly contributed to the high cultural visibility of BDSM, these practices were already in the spotlight prior to the book's release. As early as the 1950s, American pinup girl Bettie Page had made a career out of modelling fetish clothing. The mainstream fashion industry has embraced BDSM themes as well; Gianni Versace's early-1990s collection is one notable example. In 2007, Dolce and Gabbana also put out a BDSM-inspired collection, complete with metallic whips, causing the *New York Times* Style section to proclaim: 'Dominatrix and Gabbana!' (Menkes, 2007). And the sadomasochistic themes that pervade popular media are not limited to clothing design. Music superstars such as Madonna, Lady Gaga and Rihanna have incorporated BDSM themes in their work, the latter crooning 'Sticks and stones may break my bones but chains and whips excite me' in the 2011 music video for her song 'S&M' (dir: Melina Matsoukas). Television shows have incorporated such imagery as well; for example, the cartoon characters on *Family Guy* (1998–) often dress in BDSM regalia. The central plot of the 2002 movie *Secretary* (dir: Steven Shainberg) involved a sadomasochistic relationship, and characters have dressed as dominatrices in a number of other films – *American Reunion* (2012, dirs: Jon Hurwitz and Hayden Schlossberg), *Frat Party* (2009, dir: Robert Bennett) and *Mr. and Mrs. Smith* (2005, dir: Doug Liman), to name a few.

In one sense, the Dominatrix has become so integrated in popular culture that she has become almost normalised. Dominatrices write how-to books – for instance, *Sex Tips from a Dominatrix* (Payne, 1999) and *Whip Your Life into Shape! The Dominatrix Principle* (Dubberley, 2006) – and find their way into other mainstream publications. The 'Apartments' sections of a 2007 issue of *Time Out New York*, for instance, featured a dungeon among the other real estate items. The piece explained that the 'lair', 'located in the depths of a two-bedroom Financial District duplex, looks as if it sprang from the pages of *Martha Stewart Living* rather than the stories of the Marquis de Sade' (Yun, 2007). Examples like these suggest that while on one level BDSM practices continue to be framed as subversive, on another level they are also highly culturally visible, somewhat normalised and even embraced.

In fact, while the pro-Dommes I interviewed emphasised the stigmas faced by the BDSM community, they also spoke about the mainstreaming of these practices. 'I think it would be kinda fun to be a consultant for movies and TV shows and stuff like that', one New York-based Dominatrix told me. 'I know people who've done that. I think it would be fun because I see stuff and I'm like, "That's so wrong. That doesn't happen."' Another pro-Domme, speaking about the influx of young women into the industry, explained, 'They see it on TV and think they can make a quick buck'. Comments such as these reflect the fact that, as in the case of the *Fifty Shades* controversy, dominatrices are often critical of these mainstream influences and representations of their work.

Subversive pleasure: a dualistic approach to sexuality

As suggested by the examples above, media constructions of BDSM in general, and the Dominatrix in particular, fall into two broad categories that exist in tension. These kinky practices are portrayed as perverse, pathological and even deadly. However, they are also treated as a source of benign amusement, or even of salacious fascination. This paradox reflects a broader dichotomy in how sexuality is publicly viewed, as well as two facets of the Domme/sub interaction – overtly recreational sexuality and female dominance – that render this interaction particularly provocative.

The public's paradoxical 'love/hate' relationship with the Dominatrix – and the fact that she is simultaneously decried as deviant and yet seemingly ubiquitous – is not something unique to this particular cultural figure. In fact, the more 'taboo' the realm of sexuality, the more we relish bringing it out into public discourse. Foucault writes that in the postmodern age:

> We have at least invented a different kind of pleasure: pleasure in the truth of pleasure, the pleasure of knowing the truth, of discovering and exposing it, the fascination of seeing it and telling it, of captivating and capturing others by it, of confiding it in secret, of luring it out into the open – the specific pleasure of the true discourse on pleasure.
>
> (Foucault, 1990: 71)

For Foucault, the salient question is not why we are sexually repressed – rather, it is why we constantly feel the need to speak about our own repression. This theory that there is pleasure in speaking about the repressed would explain why BDSM has been such a prime target of media discourse.

Moreover, there are also aspects of the Dominatrix that make her particularly subversive and, thus, particularly apt for this type of representation. One of these is the recreational 'play' element of sadomasochistic sexuality. If we think of modern Western societies' acceptability of sexual practices as looking like a pyramid, 'Marital, reproductive heterosexuals are alone at the top of the erotic pyramid', while sadomasochists are one of the 'most despised' categories, towards the bottom (Rubin, 1992: 279). While relationships between Dommes and subs can conceivably involve procreative sex, the trappings of BDSM are an overt reminder that sexuality, in actuality, is composed of many elements that are not there for a procreative purpose.

Other scholars have previously made related points about BDSM. For example, John Alan Lee has pointed out the importance of the fact that sadomasochism, like homosexuality, is divorced from the function of procreation. Lee explains:

> Gay sex has long been playful sex (probably one of the reasons for the intense disapproval of it by those who valued only procreational sex). So it is not surprising to find a greater evidence of S/M sex among contemporary homosexuals than among heterosexuals. *S/M sex is the epitome of recreational sex.*
>
> (Lee, 1979: 92; emphasis in original)

Following from Foucault and Rubin, the fact that BDSM interactions are overtly separated from the procreative function may contribute to their subversiveness and, paradoxically, to their cultural salience. Accordingly, the vast majority of pro-Dommes I interviewed did *not* have intercourse with their clients. Furthermore, my interviewees often emphasised that their encounters with clients were a form of recreation. One woman, for example, mentioned that both she and her clients greatly enjoyed enacting erotic cross-dressing scenarios, 'like, taking a guy and really, completely changing the way that he looks and then playing with personas. Seeing if I can bring the female persona out, which gives him a break from his regular life'.

The concept of BDSM as a kind of 'break' from reality was a theme that emerged commonly in interviews. In fact, most pro-Dommes described their sessions as 'playing' or 'play'.

In addition to being an overtly non-procreative erotic exchange, the Domme/sub interaction is subversive in that it inverts gender roles. My interviewees often argued that, for their clients, the pleasure in these exchanges lay in overturning the standard arrangement of power and not only gender but also race and economic privilege. Pro-Dommes generally described their clients as white men in positions of relative power who were paying to have the burden of that power temporarily removed. 'They have to make decisions every day', one woman told me. 'Million-dollar decisions. And they're always in control. Every once in a while they just wanna let go of everything and have somebody else do decisions, even if it is for an hour.' Another interviewee explained, similarly, 'It's a white privilege thing. The more power you have, the more you wanna give it up. That's how it works. If you don't have any power, you don't wanna give it up.' It is a short logical step to argue that, just as they stimulate erotic excitement in BDSM participants themselves, these inversions also contribute to the broad appeal of salacious media representations of these participants.

Conclusion

In public discourse, the Dominatrix is at once nowhere and everywhere. She is rebuked, pathologised, criminalised and interpreted as dangerous. At the same time, as previous scholars have pointed out (Weiss, 2006; Barrett, 2009; Khan, 2009; Wilkinson, 2009; Allen, 2013), sadomasochistic imagery – which constructs dominatrices and other BDSM participants as benignly entertaining and even exhilarating – has made its way into various forms of popular culture. This seemingly paradoxical dualism reflects a broader postmodern Western handling of sexuality, in which pleasure derives from speaking about that which is putatively deviant and repressed. Furthermore, specific features of the Domme/sub interaction – overtly recreational eroticism and female dominance – render it particularly 'deviant' and, thus, particularly tantalising.

However, if her appeal is intimately bound up in her subversiveness, then, looking ahead, there could come a time when the Dominatrix begins to lose her cultural power, as popular culture becomes increasingly saturated with these representations and BDSM practices become more normalised than deviant. The fact that many critics reacted to the *Fifty Shades* film with a yawn is perhaps a signal that we are moving in this direction. The Dominatrix is a powerful woman, but if her power is dependent on her ostensible overturning of the norms of gender and erotic pleasure, it will be fascinating to watch how her media presence evolves in the future.

Note

1 The tabloid is now defunct and no longer accessible, but Gorman (2008) provides a summary of the content.

Bibliography

Allen, S. (2013) *Cinema, Pain and Pleasure: Consent and the Controlled Body*. Basingstoke: Palgrave Macmillan.

American Psychiatric Association (2000) *Diagnostic and Statistical Manual of Mental Disorders (DSM-IV-TR)*. Washington, DC: American Psychiatric Association.

Barker, M., Gupta, C. and Iantaffi. A. (2007). 'The power of play: the potentials and pitfalls in healing narratives of BDSM'. In D. Langdridge and M. Barker (eds) *Safe, Sane, and Consensual: Contemporary Perspectives on Sadomasochism*. Basingstoke: Palgrave Macmillan.

Barrett, J. (2009) '"You've made mistress very, very angry": displeasure and pleasure in media representations of BDSM'. *Particip@tions* 4. www.participations.org/Volume%204/Issue%201/Articles%20in%20Word/Barrett_Checked.doc (accessed 4 February 2016).

Beckmann, A. (2001) 'Deconstructing myths: the social construction of "sadomasochism" versus "subjugated knowledges" of practitioners of consensual "SM"'. *Journal of Criminal Justice and Popular Culture*. Volume 8 (2): 66–95.

Bentley, P. (2012) 'Fifty Shades of Grey outstrips Harry Potter to become fastest selling paperback of all time'. *Daily Mail*. 18 June. www.dailymail.co.uk/news/article-2160862/Fifty-Shades-Of-Grey-book-outstrips-Harry-Potter-fastest-selling-paperback-time.html#ixzz1y9SHlzQU (accessed 30 March 2015).

Bonomi, A.E., Altenburger, L.E. and Walton, N.L. (2013) '"Double crap!" Abused and harmed identity in *Fifty Shades of Grey*'. *Journal of Women's Health*. Volume 22 (9): 733–744.

Bosman, J. (2014) 'For *Fifty Shades of Grey*, more than 100 million sold'. *The New York Times*. 27 February. www.nytimes.com/2014/02/27/business/media/for-fifty-shades-of-grey-more-than-100-million-sold.html?_r=0 (accessed 30 March 2015).

Califia, P. (1988) *Public Sex: The Culture of Radical Sex*. San Francisco, CA: Cleiss Press.

Cheney, T. (1998) 'Dear Mom and Dad: just a quick note to thank you for the very lovely desk set'. Cartoon. *New Yorker*. 11 May.

Comfort, A. (1978) 'Sexual idiosyncrasies: deviation or magic?' *Journal of Psychiatry*. Volume 9: 11–16.

Dubberley, E. (2006) *Whip Your Life into Shape! The Dominatrix Principle*. Riverside, NJ: Andrews McMeel Publishing.

Duffy, J. C. (1999) 'Please listen carefully, as my menu options have changed'. Cartoon. *New Yorker*. 15 November.

Foucault, M. (1990). *The History of Sexuality: An Introduction, Volume 1*. New York: Vintage Books.

Freud, S. (1938) *The Basic Writings of Sigmund Freud*, trans. and ed. A.A. Brill. New York: Modern Library.

Goldman, R. (2008) 'Love hurts: sadomasochism's dangers'. *ABC News*. 14 February. http://abcnews.go.com/Health/story?id=4285958andpage=1 (accessed 30 March 2015).

Gorman, E. (2008) 'FIA president refuses to resign over Nazi-inspired orgy'. *Huffington Post*. 16 April. www.huffingtonpost.com/2008/04/08/fia-president-refuses-to_n_95578.html (accessed 23 March 2015).

Gosselin, C. and Wilson, G. (1980) *Sexual Variations: Fetishism, Sadomasochism and Transvestism*. New York: Simon and Schuster.

Green, E. (2015) 'Consent isn't enough: the troubling sex of *Fifty Shades*'. *The Atlantic*. 10 February. www.theatlantic.com/features/archive/2015/02/consent-isnt-enough-in-fifty-shades-ofgrey/385267/ (accessed 30 March 2015).

Guzman, R. (2015) '"Fifty Shades of Grey" review: highly unsatisfying'. *Newsday*. 10 February. www.newsday.com/entertainment/movies/fifty-shades-of-grey-review-highly-unsatisfying-1.9924557 (accessed 30 March 2015).

James, E.L. (2011a) *Fifty Shades of Grey*. London: Vintage Books.

James, E.L. (2011b) *Fifty Shades Darker*. London: Vintage Books.

James, E.L. (2012) *Fifty Shades Freed*. London: Vintage Books.

Kamel, G.W.L. and Weinberg, T.S. (1983) 'Diversity in sadomasochism: four S&M careers'. In T. Weinberg and G.W.L. Kamel (eds) *S and M: Studies in Sadomasochism*. Buffalo, NY: Prometheus Books.

Khan, U. (2009) 'Putting a dominatrix in her place: the representation and regulation of female Dom/male sub sexuality'. *Canadian Journal of Women and the Law*. Volume 21 (1): 143–175.

Krafft-Ebing, R.F. (1965) *Psychopathia Sexualis*, trans. Franklin S. Klaf. New York: Stein and Day.

Lane, A. (2015) 'No pain, no gain: *Fifty Shades of Grey*', *New Yorker*. 23 February. www.newyorker.com/magazine/2015/02/23/pain-gain (accessed 30 March 2015).

Lee, J.A. (1979) 'The social organization of sexual risk'. *Journal of Family and Economic Issues*. Volume 2: 69–100.

Lindemann, D.J. (2011) 'BDSM as therapy?' *Sexualities*. Volume 14 (2): 151–172.

Lindemann, D.J. (2012) *Dominatrix: Gender, Eroticism, and Control in the Dungeon*. Chicago, IL: University of Chicago Press.

Marcus, S. (2015) '"Fifty Shades of Grey" isn't a movie about BDSM, and that's a problem'. *Huffington Post*. 23 February. www.huffingtonpost.com/2015/02/16/fifty-shades-of-grey-isnt-bdsm_n_6684808.html (accessed 30 March 2015).

Menkes, S. (2007) 'Dominatrix and Gabbana! Fendi is refined'. *The New York Times*. 22 February. www.nytimes.com/2007/02/22/style/22iht-Rmilan23.4691446.html?_r=0 (accessed 30 March 2015).

Norman, S. (2004) 'I am the leatherfaerie shaman'. In M. Thompson (ed) *Leatherfolk*. Los Angeles, CA: Daedalus Books.

Payne, P. (1999) *Sex Tips from a Dominatrix*. New York: Regan Books.

Rickman, D. (2015) 'The best worst *Fifty Shades of Grey* reviews'. www.indy100.com/article/the-best-worst-fifty-shades-of-grey-reviews–gkimbyJ82e (accessed 30 March 2015).

Roper, M. (2015) 'Women's prison mass jail break after inmates in dominatrix gear handcuff male guards expecting "mass orgy"'. *The Mirror*. 7 February. www.mirror.co.uk/news/world-news/womens-prison-mass-jail-break-5120591 (accessed 1 April 2017).

Rubin, G. (1992) 'Thinking sex: notes for a radical theory of the politics of sexuality'. In C. Vance (ed) *Pleasure and Danger: Exploring Female Sexuality*. London: Pandora Books.

Rubin, G. (2004) 'The Catacombs: a temple of the butthole'. In M. Thompson (ed) *Leatherfolk*. Los Angeles, CA: Daedalus Books.

Sacher-Masoch, L. ([1870] 1977) *Venus in Furs*, trans. John Glassco. Burnaby: Blackfish.

Sandnabba, N.K., Santtila, P. and Nordling, N. (1999) 'Sexual behavior and social adaptation among sadomasochistically-oriented males'. *Journal of Sex Research*. Volume 36 (3): 273–282.

Schlesinger, F. (2010) 'Dominated to death in a "dungeon": body of motor racing boss found after session with S&M torturer'. *Daily Mail*. 25 June. www.dailymail.co.uk/news/article-1289216/Racing-boss-Robin-Mortimer-dies-sadisticsex-session-perverted-dominatrix.html (accessed 30 March 2015).

Stekel, W. (1929). *Sadism and Masochism: The Psychology of Hatred and Cruelty, Volume 2*. Authorised English version by Louise Brink. New York: Liveright.

Travers, P. (2015) 'Fifty Shades of Grey'. *Rolling Stone*. February 11. www.rollingstone.com/movies/reviews/fifty-shades-of-grey-20150211 (accessed 30 March 2015).

Weiss, M.D. (2006) 'Mainstreaming kink: the politics of BDSM representation in US popular media'. *Journal of Homosexuality*. Volume 50 (2–3): 103–132.

Wilkinson, E. (2009) 'Perverting visual pleasure: representing sadomasochism'. *Sexualities*. Volume 12 (2): 181–198.

Wilner, R., Celona, L. and Alpert, L.I. (2008) 'Hangy spanky: kinky clubgoer is choked near death'. *New York Post*. 9 February. www.nypost.com/seven/02092008/news/regionalnews/hangy_spanky_414490.htm (accessed 30 March 2015).

Yun, H. (2007) 'House call: Dominatrix dungeon'. *Time Out New York*. October 4–10. www.timeout.com/newyork/style-design/house-call-dominatrix-dungeon (accessed 1 April 2017).

Media

American Reunion (2012) Directed by J. Hurwitz and H. Schlossberg [Film]. USA: Universal Pictures.
CSI (2000–2015) [TV Series]. USA: CBS.
Family Guy (1998–) [TV Series]. USA: Fox.
Fifty Shades of Grey (2015) Directed by S. Taylor-Johnson [Film]. USA: Universal.

Frat Party (2009) Directed by R. Bennett [Film]. USA: SuperMassive Films.
Harry Potter (1997–2007) [Fantasy Novel Series]. UK: Bloomsbury Publishing.
'Halloween' (1997, 28 October), Season 5, Episode 3, *Frasier* [TV Series]. USA: NBC.
House (2004–2012) [TV Series]. USA: Fox.
Law and Order: SVU (1999–) [TV Series]. USA: NBC.
Mr. and Mrs. Smith (2005) Directed by D. Liman [Film]. USA: Regency Enterprises.
Nancy Drew (1930–) [Mystery Fiction Series]. USA: Edward Stratemeyer.
Private Practice (2007–2013) [TV Series]. USA: ABC.
Secretary (2002) Directed by S. Shainberg [Film]. USA: Slough Pond.
'S&M' (2011) Directed by M. Matsoukas [Music Video]. USA.
Twilight (2005–2008) [Novel Series]. USA: Little, Brown and Company.

39
THE PERVERT

Lauren Rosewarne

The word *pervert* has a long history of use as a diagnosis, a slur and a way to marginalise and condemn those with sexual interests deviating from the norm. To be classified as a pervert is to be inextricably linked to the darker, dirtier and more commonly repressed aspects of sexuality. That the word still carries such negative connotations in a culture where fringe sexual practices and deviant sexualities are mainstreamed, and notably even *commodified*, is a paradox.

In my book *Part-Time Perverts: Sex, Pop Culture and Kink Management* (2011), I proposed that participation in sexual perversion is near-universal: that a spectrum of engagement exists spanning vicarious enjoyment through to full immersion, in turn positioning each of us as perverts. Drawing from the participation taxonomy presented in that book, here I focus on the middle part of the spectrum and the terrain where engagement is most common: the market, and more specifically cultural consumption.

I begin with a discussion of definitions, identifying the varying uses of the word and explaining how it is used in this chapter. Pornification and the mainstreaming of porn are then outlined as key – but not sole – drivers of universal perversion. Finally, the widespread integration of the perverse into daily life is examined through reference to consumer products including clothing, cosmetics and popular media.

To claim, as I do in this chapter, that we are all perverts is to go beyond simply contending that the increased presence of porn in the public sphere means that we are each exposed to kinkiness. While this is of course true, deliberately choosing to see a film with perverse themes or wearing an item of apparel with obvious perverse allusions moves a person beyond being held captive to, for example, hypersexual street advertising (Rosewarne, 2007), and instead demonstrates perverse initiative. While such initiative can be demonstrated through actual participation in perverse sex, in this chapter I focus on the more passive forms where perversion is expressed through consumer purchases.

Definitions: from pathology to pride

Given the widespread use of *perversion* to mean anything from a diagnosis through to a badge of honour, the term is not effortlessly defined. The Macquarie dictionary provides a useful overview of the gamut of popular deployments:

> 1. to turn away from the right course. 2. to lead astray morally. 3. to lead into mental error or false judgment. 4. to bring over to a religious belief regarded as false

or wrong. 5. to turn to an improper use; misapply. 6. to distort. 7. to bring to a less excellent state, vitiate, or debase. 8. Pathol. to change to what is unnatural or abnormal. 9. Psychol. to affect with perversion.

(2006: 905)

Words such as *right*, *astray* and *error* spotlight uses of the word at the negative end of the spectrum, where the range of perversions – homosexuality, sadism, masochism, exhibitionism, cross-dressing and fetishism, among many discussed in academic literature – are considered not merely as something that makes a person different, but as desires which make them sick, repellent or criminal: as psychologist Richard J. Stoller argued in his book *Perversion: The Erotic Form of Hatred*, there is a well-established 'moral taint' surrounding the word (1986: 111). The psychoanalyst Louise Kaplan provided a definition reflecting this negativity and othering:

[T]he sexual pervert behaves very differently from the countless men and women who evoke erotic fantasies, and sometimes enact them to heighten their sexual pleasure. *The pervert is not making love; he is making hate.* The pervert has no choice. His sexual performance is obligatory, compulsive, fixated and rigid . . .

(Kaplan, 1992: 40)

The psychiatrist Mervin Glasser takes a similar approach, contending that 'when the sexual deviance is a persistent, constantly preferred form of sexual behaviour which reflects a global structure involving the individual's whole personality, I consider it appropriate to use the term "perversion", despite its pejorative overtones' (1996: 279). These authors not only subscribe to a definition that pathologises and demonises but also favour use only in circumstances where – in the context of the taxonomy presented in *Part-Time Perverts* – full immersion has transpired: where perversion is placed at the forefront of identity (Rosewarne, 2011).

While Stoller, Kaplan and Glasser propose definitions skewed towards diagnosis, others focus less on value judgements – on inferences that certain fantasies or practices are wrong, bad or immoral – and instead place emphasis on the *distort* aspect of the Macquarie definition (distort as associated with the unconventional rather than the aberrant). The philosopher Alan Goldman offers a definition along such lines:

Perversion does not represent a deviation from the reproductive function (or kissing would be perverted), from a loving relationship (or most sexual desire and many heterosexual acts would be perverted) . . . It is a deviation from a norm, but the norm in question is merely statistical.

(2008: 69)

The psychoanalyst Joyce McDougall similarly alludes to statistical norms, proposing simply that 'a pervert is someone who does not make love like everyone else' (1991: 243). Goldman and McDougall provide the basis for how *perversion* is used in this chapter: it is about sex that is *different* from what is popularly considered normal or *vanilla*.[1] I am not concerned here with the championing of the label as a way to reclaim a traditional slur or celebrate sexual marginalisation; rather, I simply use it to describe sexual behaviour that deviates from the mainstream. While 'the mainstream' is a highly contested concept, in simple terms it describes values and practices participated in, and ascribed to, by *most* people. Sex that exists outside of the so-called mainstream is, therefore, considered – with varying degrees of fervour – not only as marginal but as deviant, as perverted. This situation is, of course, paradoxical, because the supposedly atypical sex that constitutes the 'pervert' label is actually represented and marketed widely throughout the mainstream and, in turn, experienced by many people within it (Rosewarne, 2011; 2013). While some theorists focus on perversion as describing different ways of having sex, in line with theorists such as Kaplan – who identify the label as appropriate even for those who only fantasise – I am concerned here with the *interest* in perverse sex. Be it manifesting in practice or more commonly, as is the focus of this chapter, voyeuristically, vicariously and via allusion; we are all perverts to the extent that we each share at least some interest in the sexually different.

Perversion and the queer question

In the 'Love Plus One' episode of the sitcom *Will and Grace* (2000), Grace (Debra Messing) admits to her friend Will (Eric McCormack) that she has bailed from a threesome:

Grace: I guess I always thought of myself as a little kinky.
Will: Come on, Grace. It's okay. I've never been in a three-way.
Grace: Yeah, but you're gay. You have the kinky built in.
Will: Oh, sure. That's why I joined.

I reference this comic exchange both to introduce the topic of non-heterosexuality to this discussion and to spotlight the default inclusion of non-heterosexual practice in a definition of perversion. I noted earlier that homosexuality – along with behaviours such as sadism, masochism, exhibitionism, cross-dressing and fetishism – is widely considered perverse. While homosexuals have a long history of classification as perverts in academic literature (and, equally, the term has long been used as a slur against them), the inclusion of homosexuality in the definition used in this chapter centres simply on statistics. Regardless of the degrees of monogamy or vanilla-ness with which a homosexual might practice their sexuality, the simple premise that same-sex attraction is not the statistical norm means that non-heterosexual practice has tended to be rendered as outside of the mainstream and, in turn, perverse. This situation is, however, in flux: research indicates that tolerance towards homosexuality has been increasing over time (Bobo and Licari, 1989; Loftus, 2001; Andersen and Fetner, 2008; Haider-Markel and Joslyn, 2008; McNair, 2013), and thus gay sex no longer retains the stigma it did prior to the 1970s, when it was considered – and treated – as a crime and/or mental illness. That said, while the extent to which gay sex is rendered deviant or perverted will likely continue to decrease over time, the minority status of the act nonetheless continues to position it outside of the norm.

Perversion and pornification

The internet has made porn easy to access and distribute, and in turn has overhauled the image of porn consumption from something centred on creepy old men in raincoats and teenage boys with tattered *Playboys* to behaviour that anyone, regardless of age, gender, sexual preference or favoured kinks, may be involved with. The nature of smartphone technology specifically means that most people are scarcely an arm's length away from porn at any given moment (Rosewarne, 2016). The drama *Don Jon* (2013, dir: Joseph Gordon-Levitt) illustrated this well – the porn-addicted title character took heed of any opportunity to access porn, in one scene doing so on his smartphone while driving his car, in another while attending a lecture.

Continued calls to regulate internet content and the persistent condemnation of its proliferation and production from Christians, conservatives and radical feminists (MacKinnon, 1993; Paul, 2005; Dines, 2010) indicate that the place of porn in society is neither uncontested nor fully embraced. The politics of proliferation aside, however, the increase in porn's availability underpins two important factors driving the changing role of perversion in our culture: mainstreaming and pornification – or *pornographication*, as coined by media theorist Brian McNair (2002; 2013). Both terms are loaded and extensively discussed, and both have led to a variety of positive *and* negative consequences, but suffice it to say here that they have both been key in creating an environment in which expressions of perverse desire are more accepted than at any other time in history.

While it would be hyperbolic to claim that pornography is mainstreamed to the extent that *everyone* is exposed to it nowadays – avoiding it is still relatively easy – the concept of mainstreaming is slightly more complicated than this. Mainstreaming describes the process whereby porn moves out of websites and magazines and appears in new guises in the public sphere – a process sometimes described as *porn creep* (Glöckner, 2009; Ferguson, 2010). In his book *Striptease Culture*, McNair termed this mainstreaming 'porno chic', identifying it as 'the *representation* of porn in non-pornographic art and culture; the pastiche and parody of, the homage to and investigation of porn; the postmodern transformation of porn into mainstream cultural artefact for a variety of purposes' (2002: 61). Media theorist Feona Attwood discussed the same phenomena in her contribution to the *Mainstreaming Sex* anthology:

> Porn stars are entering the world of mainstream celebrity, writing bestselling books, acting as sex advisors in lifestyle magazines and becoming the stars of lads mags. Porn has turned chic and become an object of fascination in art, film, television and the press. Porn *style* is also now commonplace especially in music video and advertising, and a scantily clad, surgically enhanced 'porn look' is evident, not only in the media, but on the streets.
>
> (Attwood, 2009: xiv)

While – like the content of porn itself – the so-called *pornification* of the public sphere has been extensively criticised (Levy, 2005; Walter, 2010), it is also at the heart of the mainstreaming of perversion. Pornification, akin to mainstreaming, refers to the idea of porn 'creeping' out of the private sphere and merging with the mainstream, but the word also has specific use as a verb. Pamela Paul's book *Pornified* (2005) is an examination of the mainstreaming of porn, but the more general idea of something being 'pornified' has great relevance to this discussion. Pornified can describe the process whereby something is made to be *like* porn: where something is hypersexualised and becomes infused with the values and images of porn. *Porn* in this context serves as shorthand for the sexually explicit, and while, of course, actual porn undoubtedly helps to make perversions visible, porn itself didn't create them.

One area of the market that illustrates the involvement of ordinary people in perversion – as well as highlighting the ideas of mainstreaming and pornification – is fashion.

Perversion and fashion

In their research on gender and sexuality, psychologists Cheryl de la Rey and Michelle Friedman connected non-vanilla practice to fashion: '[it is] what trendy people do and it involves experimenting with sex toys, experimenting with all sort of things, including perhaps power relations' (1996: 43–44). While the authors' discussion is by no means celebratory, they nevertheless point to the idea that perversion – be it in practice, fantasy or apparel – is not merely a way to mark a person as sexually different (which might, of course, have appeal itself), but can help shape a person as liberal, as progressive and, notably, as *fashionable*.

While neither singular nor homogenous, perversion certainly has an aesthetic whereby items of apparel are inextricably linked to sexual practices. In their discussion of BDSM venues, for example, urban planning theorists Christine Steinmetz and Paul Maginn discuss fashion:

> The material culture associated with BDSM gives it its aesthetic strength and visibility as a minority sexual interest. There are certain items of clothing and props made from leather, PVC, or chainmail that may be directly associated with the symbolic material of BDSM.
>
> *(Steinmetz and Maginn, 2015: 120–121)*

While the existence of BDSM and sadomasochistic aesthetics outside of physical practice has been widely analysed (Steele, 1996; Rosewarne, 2011; Call, 2012; Byrne, 2013), other sexual perversions are also known to have an aesthetic and a life outside of sexual practice. In *Part-Time Perverts*, for example, I discussed the 'handkerchief code' popular in the 1970s, whereby homosexual men would position handkerchiefs of certain colours in their back pockets to connote their favoured sexual practices. The image on the cover of Bruce Springsteen's *Born in the USA* album, released in 1983, is a rear view of the singer with a red baseball cap sticking out of his back pocket – a cap that looks strikingly like a handkerchief. The image has been widely identified as homoerotic in style (Marsh, 2004; Ferguson, 2005). In later years rock stars such as Slash from Guns N' Roses and James Hetfield from Metallica would display real handkerchiefs in their back pockets, quite possibly making a similar allusion. The Springsteen album image exists as an example of the aesthetics of a perversion being subtly appropriated by someone both from the mainstream and, more specifically, outside of the sexual subculture being hinted to.

Sex work is another perversion identifiable in fashion, whereby the aesthetics of those working in this industry have come to influence those with no connection to it. The curator Richard Harrison Martin, for example, discussed how the style of street sex workers long influenced the fashion designer, Gianni Versace, and thus eventually came to alter what people wore in the mainstream:

> Versace located the prostitute as the last unexamined figure in fashion's twenty-year sociology of the street ... No one had taken the prostitute into fashion as Versace did. In a feat worthy of literature, Versace seized the streetwalker's bravado and conspicuous wardrobe, along with her blatant, brandished sexuality, and introduced them into high fashion.
>
> *(Martin, 1998: 11–12)*

On one hand, fetishwear having a life outside of sexual practice is nothing new: fashion theorist Valerie Steele (1985; 1996) dates the presence of fetish garments worn outside of perverse sex play back to the 1920s. Equally, the visibility of anything sexual can, at least in part, be explained by contemporary mainstreaming: as literary theorist Romana Byrne explains in *Aesthetic Sexuality*, 'Fetish fashion is also known for its tendency to "bubble-up" into *haute couture* design, which is then "knocked off" by mass-market clothing manufacturers' (2013: 161). Some people will end up wearing perversion-inspired fashion simply because the aesthetic has been absorbed and sold by mass-market fashion retailers. For others, however, I propose that something more deliberate is going on. To return to *Born in the USA*, a number of theorists have identified Springsteen's flirtations with homoeroticism in his stage presence and branding (Smith, 1992; Garman, 2000; Guterman, 2005). As cultural theorist Bryan Garman noted, 'Springsteen was so secure in his heterosexuality, whiteness, and enormous popularity that he could engage in homoerotic displays without having to face the political realities of gay male identity and without suffering any consequences' (2000: 225). Politics aside, Springsteen was making an allusion to a perverse sexuality that he was not physically practising: via this aesthetic he presented himself as sexually interesting and chic and, in turn, potentially expanded his fan base, with the kinkier allusion being detected by those in the know and missed by others. Celebrities in fact often use this subtle device to frame themselves as cutting-edge or gossip-worthy. In a 2006 appearance on the American chat show *The View*, for example, when asked how he would react if his daughter Ivanka posed for *Playboy*, Donald Trump responded: 'I don't think Ivanka would do that, although she does have a very nice figure . . . I've said if Ivanka weren't my daughter, perhaps I'd be dating her' (see Withnall, 2016). In 2008, celebrity Victoria Beckham made a seemingly random quip in claiming 'You have to go to a sex shop to buy the polish for my high-heel shoes' (*Mirror*, 2008). In 2010, *Sex and the City* star Kim Cattrall commented to the press that she never wears underpants (Heilbron, 2010). On the surface such comments, which appear commonly in the media, seem simply like the personal trivia often included in celebrity interviews; however, they can equally be viewed as conscious attempts to make a person seem more intriguing, and thus function as a deliberate effort at titillation. Such comments are invariably successful in this capacity because many people are intrigued, if not *aroused*, by the sexually renegade. Alluding to a life more interesting/sexy/controversial may similarly explain why ordinary people wear apparel with origins in perverted sexual practice: doing so makes them feel unique and at the vanguard of culture, even if such displays exist completely independently from sexual practice. Wearing a perverse item of clothing enables a person to play at a perversion without the burden, danger, embarrassment or identity conflict that actual participation might pose. This can also be achieved through intimate purchases such as fragrances and cosmetics, whereby a foray into the kinky becomes an extension of private life.

Nearly all aspects of the perfume and cosmetics industry can be connected to the promotion of sexual attraction, and it is thus unsurprising that elements of perversion are easily detected there. While this can of course be construed as an example of the mainstreaming of porn – for example, the use of pinup-style images on the packaging of Benefit cosmetics is a good illustration of this (Rosewarne, 2007) – in many examples such products have little to do with the visual medium of porn and substantially more so with the tropes of perverse sex. In 2007, French fragrance house Etat Libre d'Orange launched a collection of controversial fragrances. One scent, 'Sécrétions Magnifiques' (Magnificent Secretions), was marketed to smell like milk, blood, sweat, sperm and saliva; the image on the front of the bottle showed a cartoon of an ejaculating penis. The same company's 'Putain des Palaces' (Hotel Slut) fragrance was marketed to smell like a well-utilised boudoir, the label showing a cartoon of a vagina being penetrated by a key. The Fragrance Library of American company Demeter includes a perfume called 'Riding Crop'. Cosmetics company Nars has blushes in shades named 'Orgasm' and 'Deep Throat' and Benefit has a face powder called 'Thrrrob'. Nail-polish manufacturer Chi has a shade named 'Double-Fisted Fuchsia' and Urban Decay has a mascara called 'Perversion'. On one hand, these products are simply exemplifiers of the 'sex sells' principle: to achieve cut-through in a saturated beauty market, salacious names are used as a mark of distinction. Another explanation, however, is that they each give the user the tiniest experience of a sex life that they might not have – that they might not even *want* to have – but which piques their interest nevertheless. Through such purchases, people wanting to feel a little naughtier can integrate some ever-so-slightly perverse products into their daily lives.

Perversion and the screen

While wearing perverse apparel and embodying a visually risqué aesthetic is one way in which perversion is engaged with by the mainstream, another is through voyeurism.

Voyeurism – as manifested in 'peeping Tom' activity, for example – is commonly categorised as a perversion in academic discussions. In this section I propose that through the display of perverse sex in popular culture, audiences become perverts themselves by vicariously experiencing kinky sex via voyeurism. While vicarious access can be obtained through a number of sources – spending time with kinkier people, for example, or conducting research into sexual topics (Rosewarne, 2011) – this section focuses on pleasures that might be visual, cerebral or even masturbatory, and which are experienced through perverse media content.

As discussed earlier in reference to the work of McNair and Attwood, a sign of the mainstreaming of porn is its inclusion as a theme in popular media. Another aspect is explicit displays of sexuality which once were only found in porn but are now readily located in mainstream film and television. A variant of this is not just pornographic sexual displays but also presentations – be they explicit or not – of perverse sexualities that were once considered too taboo for general consumption, such as 'S&M chic'. While presentations of sadomasochism in films such as *Secretary* (2002, dir: Steven Shainberg), *Nymphomaniac* (2013, dir: Lars von Trier) and *Fifty Shades of Grey* (2015, dir: Sam Taylor-Wood) or television shows such as *The Sopranos* (1999–2008) can be viewed as indicative of the mainstreaming of perversion, numerous other perversions – and ones not considered to be standard porn inclusions – are also identifiable in film and television and are, therefore, less a matter of porn creep and more about the widespread commercial appeal of sexual taboos (Rosewarne, 2013). In this section I discuss incest and bestiality – two perversions in which, for innumerable reasons, physical participation is commonly avoided. Both are, however, often considered titillating, and while pornographic displays of such content are illegal in many countries, fictional representations within mainstream narratives provide an arm's-length opportunity to experience their thrill without audiences putting themselves in jeopardy.

Incest

In 1997, writing for the *New York Times*, Karen De Witt claimed that incest is now 'plat du jour in the 90's marketplace'. The author referenced the release of three incest-themed films, including *The House of Yes* (dir: Mark Waters), *The Locusts* (dir: John Patrick Kelley) and *This World, Then the Fireworks* (dir: Michael Oblowitz), and two incest-themed books, including Kathryn Harrison's *The Kiss: A Memoir* and Linda Katherine Cutting's *Memory*

Slips: A Memoir of Music and Healing. While incest might have been *plat du jour* in the 1990s, it was of course part of popular culture long before 1997 – Roman Polanski's *Chinatown* (1974) being an obvious example – and has remained an inclusion within the decades since.

In 2003, *Rolling Stone* magazine titled an article about celebrity twins Mary-Kate and Ashley Olsen 'America's Favorite Fantasy' and documented the lead-up to the twins' upcoming 18th birthday. Given the title and the sexy poses of the twins, the article explicitly hinted at fantasies centring on twins *and* incest. In her study of the British soft-core magazine *For Women*, cultural theorist Clarissa Smith identified that many of the female readers sourced pleasure from 'imagining sex – other people having sex rather than imagining the self engaged in sexual activity' (2007: 136). Whereas much porn research has assumed that audiences place themselves in the material – that is, pretend that it is them having sex – as Smith identified, for some the pleasure is very much about voyeuristically watching others. In the context of incest, this idea was illustrated well in the 'Swimming from Cambodia' episode of *Will and Grace* (1998–2003) when Grace commented about a novel: 'By the way, I read that book. And there's a double flip at the end that proves that he is her brother. But it's still pretty hot.' Although many of us recoil in horror at the thought of sexual relations with our own family members, the screen depiction of familial couplings reminds us that incest can be 'pretty hot' if participation is restricted to spectatorship.

While overt incest plots are identifiable in DeWitt's list, in *Chinatown* and in a wide variety of other mainstream examples (Rosewarne, 2011), another common way in which perversion is integrated into a film or television story is via the 'incest possibility' storyline. In *The Judge* (2014, dir: David Dobkin) and *My Old Lady* (2014, dir: Israel Horowitz), couples make a post-intimacy discovery that they might be related, in turn creating an incest speculation. Such storylines provide an are-they-or-aren't-they thrill, but do so within films which would otherwise be considered completely innocuous and in turn draw a very wide audience (Rosewarne, 2014a).

Bestiality

Film theorist Tanya Krzywinska has discussed bestiality on screen and noted that it is routinely presented tacitly, allegorically or metonymically, 'but never explicitly' (2006: 140). This isn't entirely true – a decent handful of films have presented human/beast sexual relations: Nagisa Ôshima's film *Max mon amour* (*Max My Love*) (1986) centres on a woman's relationship with a chimpanzee and in Woody Allen's *Everything You Always Wanted to Know About Sex* (1972), a man is in love with a sheep. In the Canadian drama *Léolo* (1992, dir: Jean-Claude Lauzon) a boy rapes a cat and in John Waters' film *Pink Flamingos* (1972) a man rapes a woman with a chicken. In my work on screen depictions of masturbation (Rosewarne, 2014b), I discuss a number of scenes in which animals aid in self-stimulation: in the Spanish mystery *Caniche* (*Poodle*) (1979, dir: Bigas Luna), a woman spreads honey on her genitals for her dog to lick off; in the French period-drama *Les héroïnes du mal* (*Heroines of Evil*) (1979, dir: Walerian Borowczyk), Marceline's (Gaëlle Legrand) genitals are attended to by rabbits. A dog assists in autoeroticism in the Spanish drama *La mosquitera* (*The Mosquito Net*) (2010, dir: Agusti Vila), and in the French thriller *Sitcom* (1998, dir: Francois Ozon), Sophie (Marina de Van) reaps erotic pleasure from having a mouse run over her breasts and genitals. In *Another Gay Movie* (2006, dir: Todd Stephens), Andy masturbates with a gerbil inserted into his rectum.

But bestiality – particularly in the mainstream – is much more commonly presented subtly. The film *Snakes on a Plane* (2006, dir: David R. Ellis) presents some typical examples of this: in one scene, a snake slides up the skirt of a woman sleeping in her seat; in another, as a couple have sex in the plane's toilet, a snake slithers out of the ceiling and bites an exposed breast. These images function as bestiality only in the minds of viewers who want to see something titillating and to experience the ensuing arousal. Similar subtle presentations are detectable widely in pop culture. In the 'Homer vs. Dignity' episode of the animated series *The Simpsons* (2000), Homer – dressed as a panda – is dragged off by a real panda into a cave; he later complains that he reeks of 'panda love'. In the episode 'A Fish Called Selma' (1996), the career demise of the actor Troy McClure is attributed to his sexual fetish involving fish. In the episode 'The Mansion Family' (2000), the old sea captain marries a cow in international waters. In *The Simpsons Movie* (2007), Homer flirts with a pig, teasing it with 'Don't you get any ideas', and eventually asks: 'Should we just kiss to break the tension?' In the 'We Love You, Conrad' episode of the cartoon series *Family Guy* (2009), Brian, the family dog, is in bed with reality TV star Lauren Conrad. The 1988 cartoon film *Who Framed Roger Rabbit?* (dir: Robert Zemeckis) centres on a rabbit married to a human. In the 'Truly, Madly, Deeply' episode of *Boston Legal* (2005), the team represent a client whose wife wants an annulment because her husband had sex with their cow.

Fictional displays of incest and bestiality provide audiences the opportunity to voyeuristically – perhaps even *vicariously* – experience their favoured perversions, or to be titillated by new ones. Most notably, media representations of perversions provide audiences the opportunity to participate in a manner that doesn't put them at risk. Returning to the 'Love Plus One' episode of *Will and Grace* discussed earlier, Grace articulates her rationale for not going through with the threesome:

> This isn't me, okay? I'm a good girl from Schenectady. I went to Sunday school for ten years. I was sixteen before I let Bobby Kay go to second, so for me to come here and participate, this is a big deal. Too big a deal.

In the episode of the sitcom *Seinfeld* entitled 'The Switch' (1995), the title character (Jerry Seinfeld) offers a similar explanation for not getting involved with a threesome:

> Don't you know what it means to become an orgy guy? It changes everything. I'd have to dress different. I'd have to act different. I'd have to grow a moustache and get all kinds of robes and lotions and I'd need a new bedspread and new curtains. I'd have to get thick carpeting and weirdo lighting. I'd have to get new friends. I'd have to get orgy friends . . . Nah, I'm not ready for it.

In both examples, the characters do not want to make a corporeal commitment to their perversion: the vague idea of a threesome arouses them, but actual engagement creates a number of anxieties. There are a variety of reasons – for example, identity, illegality, mess – that might deter a person from participating in certain sexual acts. Popular culture, however, gives such a person a way to do so from a distance: they can still reap the arousal without having to deal with the consequences. In biologist Midas Dekkers' book *Dearest Pet*, he identifies that 'More bestiality takes place in our heads than in any hand or vagina' (1992: 151). While gauging participation figures for perversions – particularly those that are illegal – is near impossible, Dekkers' assumption certainly seems feasible in the context of many perversions: thinking about one – even *masturbating* to thoughts of one – is surely more likely to transpire in a world where such behaviour is still considered verboten.

Conclusion

Regardless of their favoured kinks, the reality is that not everyone will want to physically participate in perverse activity. Being a pervert is, of course, still possible – is still, as I have argued above, in fact *highly likely* – without physical engagement: the cultural marketplace provides a variety of options whereby kinky sex can be experienced voyeuristically, vicariously and, in turn, safely.

Given that the vast majority of us buy clothing and consume pop culture that is mass-produced, it is no surprise that we are each participating in a culture that has been shaped by a number of factors, including the mainstreaming of pornography. While this trend has facilitated sexually explicit displays, it has also enabled a comfortable and accepted presence of perversion in the public sphere and the marketplace, in turn rendering each of its consumers a tacit pervert.

Note

1 Queer theorist Gayle Rubin proposes that it is only vanilla sex that society considers as acceptable: 'heterosexual, married, monogamous, procreative, noncommercial, paired, relationship-oriented, between persons of the same generation, private, pornography-free, uses only bodies (no toys)' (Rubin, 1993: 13). In turn, sex that exists outside of this summary – sex that Rubin identifies as 'bad sex' – helps not only to illustrate *non-vanilla*, but to define *perverse sex* for the purposes of this discussion: 'Bad sex may be homosexual, unmarried, promiscuous, non-procreative, or commercial. It may be masturbatory or take place at orgies, may be casual, may cross generational lines, and may take place in "public" or at least in the bushes or the baths. It may involve the use of pornography, fetish objects, sex toys or unusual roles' (Rubin, 1993: 16). More than 20 years on, and while some sexual liberalisation has transpired, the 'bad sex' that Rubin describes still remains outside of the mainstream.

Bibliography

Andersen, R. and Fetner, T. (2008) 'Cohort Differences in Tolerance of Homosexuality Attitudinal Change in Canada and the United States, 1981–2000'. *Public Opinion Quarterly*, Volume 72 (2): 311–330.

Attwood, F. (2009) 'The Sexualization of Culture'. In F. Attwood (ed) *Mainstreaming Sex: The Sexualization of Western Culture*. London: I.B. Tauris.

Bobo, L. and Licari, F.C. (1989) 'Education and Political Tolerance: Testing the Effects of Cognitive Sophistication and Target Group Affect'. *The Public Opinion Quarterly*, Volume 53: 285–308.

Byrne, R. (2013) *Aesthetic Sexuality: A Literary History of Sadomasochism*. New York: Bloomsbury.

Call, L. (2012) *BDSM in American Science Fiction and Fantasy*. New York: Palgrave Macmillan.

Cutting, L.K. (1997) *Memory Slips: A Memoir of Music and Healing*. New York: Harpercollins.

de la Rey, C. and Friedman, M. (1996) 'Sex, Sexuality and Gender: Let's Talk About It'. *Agenda*, Volume 28: 39–47.

De Witt, K. (1997) 'Incest as a Selling Point'. *New York Times*. 30 March. www.nytimes.com/1997/03/30/weekinreview/incest-as-a-selling-point.html (accessed 26 January 2015).

Dekkers, M. (1992) *Dearest Pet: On Bestiality*. Trans. P. Vincent. London: Verso.

Dines, G. (2010) *Pornland: How Porn Has Hijacked Our Sexuality*. Boston, MA: Beacon Press.

Ferguson, A. (2010) *The Sex Doll: A History*. Jefferson, NC: McFarland and Co.

Ferguson, M. (2005) *Idol Worship: A Shameless Celebration of Male Beauty in the Movies*. Sarasota, FL: STARbooks Press.

Fiorina, M.P., Abrams, S.J. and Pope, J.C. (2006) *Culture War? The Myth of a Polarized America*. New York: Pearson/Longman.

Garman, B.K. (2000) *A Race of Singers: Whitman's Working-class Hero from Guthrie to Springsteen*. Chapel Hill, NC: University of North Carolina Press.

Glasser, M. (1996) 'Aggression and Sadism in the Perversions'. In I. Rosen (ed) *Sexual Deviation*. Oxford: Oxford University Press.

Glöckner, C. (2009) *Sex 2.0: Pornography and Prostitution Influenced by the Internet Feminist Views on Pornography and Prostitution*. Munich: Verlag.

Goldman, A. (2008) 'Plain Sex'. In A. Soble and N.P. Power (eds) *The Philosophy of Sex: Contemporary Readings*. Lanham, MD: Rowman and Littlefield.

Guterman, J. (2005) *Runaway American Dream: Listening to Bruce Springsteen*. Cambridge, MA: Da Capo Press.

Haider-Markel, D.P. and Joslyn, M.R. (2008) 'Beliefs about the Origins of Homosexuality and Support for Gay Rights: An Empirical Test of Attribution Theory'. *Public Opinion Quarterly*, Volume 72 (2): 291–310.

Harrison, K. (1997) *The Kiss: A Memoir*. New York: Random House.

Heilbron, A. (2010) 'Kim Cattrall Doesn't Wear Underwear' *Tribute.ca*. 12 May. www.tribute.ca/news/kim-cattrall-doesnt-wear-underwear/2010/05/12/ (accessed 28 March 2017).

Kaplan, L.J. (1992) *Female Perversions: The Temptation of Madame Bovary*. New York: Doubleday.

Krzywinska, T. (2006) *Sex and the Cinema*. London: Wallflower Press.

Levy, A. (2005) *Female Chauvinist Pigs: Women and the Rise of Raunch Culture*. New York: Free Press.

Loftus, J. (2001) 'America's Liberalization in Attitudes toward Homosexuality, 1973 to 1998'. *American Sociological Review*, Volume 66 (5): 762–782.

McDougall. J. (1991) *Theaters of the Mind: Illusion and Truth on the Psychoanalytic Stage*. New York: Brunner-Routledge.

MacKinnon, C.A. (1993) *Only Words*. Cambridge, MA: Harvard University Press.

McNair, B. (2002) *Striptease Culture: Sex, Media and the Democratisation of Desire*. New York: Routledge.

McNair, B. (2013) *Porno? Chic! How Pornography Changed the World and Made it a Better Place*. New York: Routledge.

Macquarie Concise Dictionary. (2006) 4th edition. Sydney: University of Sydney.

Marsh, D. (2004) *Bruce Springsteen: Two Hearts, the Story*. New York: Routledge.

Martin, R.H. (1998) *Gianni Versace*. New York: Metropolitan Museum of Art.

Mirror (2008) 'Victoria Beckham Learning How to Smile'. 7 December. www.mirror.co.uk/3am/celebrity-news/victoria-beckham-learning-how-to-smile-364344 (accessed 26 January 2015).

Paul, P. (2005) *Pornified: How Pornography Is Transforming Our Lives, Our Relationships, and Our Families*. New York: Times Books.

Rosewarne, L. (2007) *Sex in Public: Women, Outdoor Advertising and Public Policy*. Newcastle: Cambridge Scholars Publishing.

Rosewarne, L. (2011) *Part-Time Perverts: Sex, Pop Culture and Kink Management*. Santa Barbara, CA: Praeger.

Rosewarne, L. (2013) *American Taboo: The Forbidden Words, Unspoken Rules, and Secret Morality of Popular Culture*. Santa Barbara, CA: Praeger.

Rosewarne, L. (2014a) 'The Judge, the Old Lady and the Incest Spectre'. *The Conversation*. 13 October. http://theconversation.com/the-judge-the-old-lady-and-the-incest-spectre-32856 (accessed 28 March 2017).

Rosewarne, L. (2014b) *Masturbation in Pop Culture: Screen, Society, Self*. Lanham, MD: Lexington Books.

Rosewarne, L. (2016) *Intimacy on the Internet: Media Representations of Online Connections*. New York: Routledge.

Rubin, G. (1993) 'Thinking Sex: Notes for a Radical Theory of the Politics of Sexuality'. In H. Abelove (ed) *The Lesbian and Gay Studies Reader*. New York: Routledge.

Smith, C. (2007) *One For The Girls! The Pleasures and Practices of Reading Women's Porn*. Bristol: Intellect.

Smith, M.N. (1992) 'Sexuality Mobilities in Bruce Springsteen: Performance as Commentary'. In A. DeCurtis (ed) *Present Tense: Rock and Roll and Culture*. Durham, NC: Duke University Press.
Steele, V. (1985) *Fashion and Eroticism: Ideals of Feminine Beauty from the Victorian Era to the Jazz Age*. New York: Oxford University Press.
Steele, V. (1996) *Fetish, Sex and Power*. New York: Oxford University Press.
Steinmetz, C. and Maginn, P.J. (2015) 'The Landscape of BDSM Venues: A View from Down Under'. In P.J. Maginn and C. Steinmetz (eds) *(Sub)Urban Sexscapes: Geographies and Regulation of the Sex Industry*. New York: Routledge.
Stoller, R.J. (1986) *Perversion: The Erotic Form of Hatred*. London: H. Karnac Books Ltd.
Walter, N. (2010) *Living Dolls: The Return of Sexism*. London: Virago.
Withnall, A. (2016) 'Donald Trump's unsettling record of comments about his daughter, Ivanka'. *Independent*. 10 October. www.independent.co.uk/news/world/americas/us-elections/donald-trump-ivanka-trump-creepiest-most-unsettling-comments-a-roundup-a7353876.html (accessed 10 October 2016).

Media

'A Fish Called Selma' (1996, March 24) Season 7, Episode 19, *The Simpsons* [TV Series]. USA: Fox.
Another Gay Movie (2006) Directed by T. Stephens [Film]. USA: Luna Pictures.
Born in the USA (1984) Image by A. Liebowitz [Album Cover]. USA: Columbia Records.
Caniche (Poodle) (1979) Directed by B. Luna [Film]. Spain: Figaro Films.
Chinatown (1974) Directed by R. Polanski [Film]. USA: Paramount Pictures.
Don Jon (2013) Directed by J. Gordon-Levitt [Film]. USA: Voltage Pictures.
Everything You Always Wanted to Know About Sex (1972) Directed by W. Allen [Film]. USA: Rollins-Joffe Productions.
Fifty Shades of Grey (2015) Directed by S. Taylor-Wood [Film]. USA: Universal Pictures.
Les héroïnes du mal (1979) Directed by W. Borowczyk [Film]. France: Argos Films.
'Homer vs. Dignity' (2000, November 26) Season 12, Episode 5, *The Simpsons* [TV Series]. USA: Fox.
The House of Yes (1997) Directed by M. Waters [Film]. USA: Bandeira Entertainments.
The Judge (2014) Directed by D. Dobkin [Film]. USA: Warner Bros.
Léolo (1992) Directed by J.-C. Lauzon [Film]. Canada: Alliance Films Corporation.
The Locusts (1997) Directed by J.P. Kelley [Film]. USA: Motion Picture Corporation of America.
'Love Plus One' (2000, November 9) Season 3, Episode 6, *Will and Grace* [TV Series]. USA: NBC.
'The Mansion Family' (2000, January 23) Season 11, Episode 12, *The Simpsons* [TV Series]. USA: Fox.
Max mon Amour (1986) Directed by N. Ôshima [Film]. France: Serge Silberman.
La mosquitera (2010) Directed by A. Vila [Film]. Spain: Eddie Saeta S.A.
My Old Lady (2014) Directed by I. Horowitz [Film]. USA: BBC Films.
Nymphomaniac (2013) Directed by L. von Trier [Film]. Denmark: Zentropa Entertainments.
Pink Flamingos (1972) Directed by J. Waters [Film]. USA: Dreamland.
Secretary (2002) Directed by S. Shainberg [Film]. USA: Slough Pond.
The Simpsons Movie (2007) Directed by D. Silverman [Film]. USA: Twentieth Century Fox Film Corporation.
Sitcom (1998) Directed by F. Ozon [Film]. France: Fidélité Productions.
Snakes on a Plane (2006) Directed by D.R. Ellis [Film]. USA: New Line Cinema.
The Sopranos (1999–2008) [TV Series]. USA: HBO.
'Swimming from Cambodia' (2003, November 20) Season 6, Episode 8, *Will and Grace* [TV Series]. USA: NBC.
'The Switch' (1995, January 5), Season 6, Episode 11, *Seinfeld* [TV Series]. USA: NBC.
This World, Then the Fireworks (1997) Directed by M. Oblowitz [Film]. USA: Balzac's Shirt.
'Truly, Madly, Deeply' (2005, November 8) Season 2, Episode 7, *Boston Legal* [TV Series]. USA: ABC.
The View (2006, March 6) [TV Series]. USA: ABC.
'We Love You, Conrad' (2009, May 3) Season 7, Episode 14, *Family Guy* [TV Series]. USA: Fox.
Who Framed Roger Rabbit? (1998) Directed by R. Zemeckis [Film]. USA: Touchstone Productions.

40
THE PORNOGRAPHER

Neil Jackson

The pornographer as transgressive figure

Whether operating in the soft or hardcore realm, the socio-cultural profile of individuals labelled 'pornographer' has been informed by representations in fictional and non-fictional media, and moralists, regulatory bodies and oppositional feminists have usually deployed the term pejoratively. That 'official' label has been joined by an array of colourful but none-too-polite designations such as 'smut peddler', 'sleaze merchant' or 'porn baron' which suggest that the conventions of language compartmentalise sexual entrepreneurs outside the realm of 'respectability', consigning them to the abject status of social pariah. However, despite their low cultural standing, pornographers have embraced technological change and operated across the social scale in networks of national and global business.

The alignment of the word 'pornographer' with sex-industry jargon such as 'pimp' and 'prostitute' fuels further assumptions regarding exploitation, criminality and moral degeneration, obliging practitioners to remain outside mainstream media spheres (although there are notable exceptions). Laura Kipnis argued there has been 'zero discussion of pornography as an expressive medium in the positive sense' (1999: 119), which has further diminished its cultural value. Any notion of artistic achievement has been subsumed by matters of morality or legal concerns about free speech and personal liberty. As exciters of sensory rather than intellectual activity, pornographers generally work within well-defined formulae according to specific realms of desire. Customer demand overrides claims to personal expression, restricting content creators to only occasional authorial interventions. Historically, the pornographer's predominant socio-cultural and ideological role has been to satisfy heteronormative masturbatory requirements through a privileging of the male gaze; however, post-feminist and queer interventions have at least partly challenged this assumption. The identity of the pornographer as a secure unitary figure is further destabilised by the blurring boundaries of the roles of writers, photographers, directors, models, actors and performers in the internet age, as well as the economic practicalities of publishers, agents, distributors, retailers, exhibitors, collectors and curators.

Widespread institutional – indeed, *constitutional* – resistance marks the pornographer as a transgressive figure. The contentious definitions of obscenity initiated by the UK's 1857 Obscene Publications Act resulted in legal actions that ensnared figures as diverse as

D.H. Lawrence, Henry Miller, Hubert Selby, William Burroughs and Robert Mapplethorpe. Authored pornographic texts and images pre-dating Victorian manners scandalised and satirised the societal conventions of their respective epochs. Marcantonio Raimondi and Pietro Aretino's *I Modi* (aka *The 16 Pleasures*) combined erotic text and image and outraged the sixteenth-century Catholic hierarchy; John Cleland's *Memoirs of a Woman of Pleasure* (aka *Fanny Hill*, 1748), generally regarded as the first novelistic work of pornography, was subjected to obscenity charges well into the mid-twentieth century; and Thomas Rowlandson's late eighteenth-century caricatures established a comic mode of English sexual expression which was later reflected in the 'saucy' seaside postcard and the cinematic sex comedies which flourished and withered in the 1970s.

For better or worse, one figure has been identified as the embodiment of the post-Renaissance, pre-Victorian pornographer: the Marquis de Sade. Writing largely during a lengthy period of incarceration in post-revolutionary France, Sade's elitist and secular libertarianism reveals a complex dialectic of instinct and intellect. His anarchic attacks upon the tenets of morality, church and state revelled in defiance of a new institutional order that had removed his title and possessions. Emphasising the scatological and the scabrous, his very name has passed into language as the definition of violent, coercive sexuality, influencing fields as diverse as psychoanalysis and surrealism and setting the parameters of any pornographer's expressive freedoms. *The 120 Days of Sodom* (1789), *Justine* (1791), *Philosophy in the Boudoir* (1795) and *Juliette* (1799) were widely suppressed for decades, but his ideas have been appropriated by filmmakers as diverse as Pier Paolo Pasolini and Jesus Franco and a literary tradition that runs from Pauline Reage to E.L. James, the latter pair transforming Sade's seemingly unpalatable imaginings into both objective and subjective expressions of female desire.

Building porn empires

By 1887, Eedweard Muybridge's photographic explorations of anatomical motion were indicating that technical experimentation in photography perhaps functioned unconsciously in erotic contemplation of the human body. Photography's realistic dimensions, and the shift into mass production, ensured that *visual* rendition became the pornographer's primary mode of expression, while rapid industrialisation expedited global distribution through newly established modes of transportation and delivery. Eric Schlosser has argued that 'the modern American sex industry began on the kitchen table of a small Chicago apartment, where Hugh Hefner pasted together the first issue of *Playboy* in 1953' (2003: 116). Schlosser identifies Hefner and Cleveland entrepreneur Reuben Sturman as the men who capitalised most comprehensively upon the early steps of the skin trade's publishing wing. Emerging amid America's 1950s consumer boom, their respective profiles and business practices were radically different. *Playboy* was forged in realisation of its proprietor's lifestyle fantasies, where women became one more commodity object within a swirl of socio-economic ambition. Hefner achieved fame, wealth and a certain legitimacy, while ensuring the global proliferation and recognition of a brand that sought to make sexual imagery respectable. This required a strictly softcore vision and careful adherence to state and federal law, trading upon diluted examples of erotic images that had circulated underground for decades. Figures such as Bob Guccione would adapt the *Playboy* ethos as a gradual liberalisation took hold, with Guccione launching *Penthouse* magazine in 1965 to develop his own commercially and legally viable glamour images, exploring body parts resolutely hidden in the *Playboy* universe.

Alternatively, Reuben Sturman personified the pornographer's transition into global criminal capitalist, the true extent of his personal wealth unknowable to this day. Largely unknown to the public until his 1992 imprisonment, the former comic-book salesman established a vertically integrated business empire in the early 1950s spanning several continents, popularising the so-called peep machine in porn establishments. Secreting profits in offshore accounts and making enemies of both J. Edgar Hoover and President Richard Nixon, the success of Sturman was instrumental in the federal instigation of the 1970 Presidential Commission on pornography. Sturman harboured no creative or artistic ambitions – his (usually successful) defence in multiple obscenity cases sought solely to protect his vast fortune. Sturman's eventual incarceration was a consequence of his steadfast refusal to pay federal dues: Schlosser notes he was possibly the single greatest tax evader in US history (ibid.: 196).

Larry Flynt's trials and tribulations shifted debates on the pornographer's status into the realm of rights enshrined in the First Amendment. As publisher of *Hustler* magazine from 1974 up to the present day, Flynt combined disregard for conventional standards of taste with an absolute dedication to attacking both liberal and conservative ideologies in his publication, hence the charges against him of obscenity, libel and blasphemy. Such were the extremes of Flynt's provocations that, when Hollywood told his story in *The People vs Larry Flynt* (dir. Milos Forman, 1996), the film was severely hamstrung by its inability (or unwillingness) to show the material upon which his legal battles were predicated. Dismissive of notions of cultural value, Flynt commented that, unlike Hefner and Guccione, 'I never tried to justify what I was doing by wrapping it in art . . . Hustler is about sex. [It's] an entertainment magazine' (quoted in O'Toole, 1998: 12).

Flynt's defence of expressive freedoms bears similarities to the experiences of Al Goldstein, whose *Screw* magazine provided, from 1968, a street-level view of New York's sex industry. Goldstein was even more forthright than Flynt in his disdain for conventional morality, expressing nominally base desires in celebration of his own lifestyle choices. This expanded into Midnight Blue, an independent cable television station which broadcast from 1974 until 2003; however, trying to juggle the varied demands of his costly legal fights and libertarian instincts brought Goldstein to bankruptcy in 2004, followed by poverty in the years leading to his death in 2013.

These US producers are paralleled by British figures such as Paul Raymond and David Sullivan, who built corporate empires (encompassing property and football-club ownership) with profits from the often criminalised UK sex industry (Tomkinson, 1982). Navigation of British legal constraints enabled their diversification into business areas whose profits surpassed those of porn. Raymond's ventures included the noted Revue Bar in London's Soho, which opened in 1958, and later the long-running magazine titles *Men Only*, *Mayfair* and *Razzle*. Until his death in 2008 he was one of the UK's richest individuals (a position also attained by Sullivan), with the investment of his fortune in West London real estate earning him the sobriquet 'The King of Soho'.

These individuals embody concepts of the pornographer capitalist, their contrasting fates as businessmen, spokesmen and cultural icons determined amid constantly shifting cultural values and market forces. Their economic aspirations intersected with the limits of their legal and constitutional rights. Their successes shaped the contours of the sex industry, defining the pornographer's social function while challenging the moral constraints that rejected their images, but more importantly, might impede their wealth. The progressive rhetoric that has informed the public image of figures such as Hefner, Flynt and Goldstein was thoroughly refuted by Andrea Dworkin, who dismissed them as the 'the boys of the sixties' grown into the 'pimps of pornography' (1981: 208). Along with attorney and fellow activist Catherine MacKinnon, Dworkin drafted the Indianapolis and Minneapolis ordinances in the 1980s, designed to prosecute pornographers on the grounds that their work was a causal factor in sexual harassment and assault. Although these moves were largely unsuccessful, pornographers were now embroiled in legal activity that highlighted their status as not just purveyors of obscenity or paragons of free speech but also violators of the freedom and safety of women everywhere.

Porn auteurs

Amid this debate, the emergence of particular photographers and filmmakers also moulded the image of the pornographer as an unabashed, professional voyeur. Susan Gubar has argued that the pornographer trades in images of women that are 'portraits of the male artist's fears about himself' (1989: 61), a position which certainly informs any assessment of the work of Russ Meyer. As a glamour photographer, Meyer idealised and fetishised the voluptuous, large-breasted female form in a string of prestigious *Playboy* spreads in the 1950s, before making a series of highly idiosyncratic independent feature films (e.g. 1965's *Faster, Pussycat! Kill! Kill!* and 1968's *Vixen*) and having a brief flirtation with the Hollywood studios with *Beyond the Valley of the Dolls* (1970). Resolute adherence to softcore formulae, characterised by a distinctive montage aesthetic, allowed his films to be exhibited widely and profitably, establishing him as a master of the soft-porn aesthetic.

By the 1970s, hardcore filmmakers were navigating new intersections of aesthetics and economics, with developments into feature-length filmmaking accommodating a new potential for the pornographer as auteur. American filmmakers such as Bob Chinn, Shaun Costello, Gerard Damiano, Alex De Renzy, Radley Metzger, Jim and Artie Mitchell, Carter Stevens and Chuck Vincent produced work that exhibited shape and form, and sometimes contained meanings beyond the singular aim of satisfying masturbatory urges. Damiano's films, particularly *Deep Throat* (1972) and *The Devil in Miss Jones* (1973), drew on both mainstream popular culture and progressive feminist ideas to represent female sexual agency within pornography's supposedly masculinist narrative structures. However, the principal economic beneficiaries of *Deep Throat* (and many other films besides) were Damiano's Mafia paymasters; thus reclamation of these films is beset by the dilemma of how to reconcile the cinematic exploration of female desire with a rigidly phallocentric artistic and economic base. This conception of the porn filmmaker as unable to satisfy women is self-reflexively embedded in the denouement of *The Devil in Miss Jones*, in which Damiano himself appears onscreen as an abject figure locked for eternity in a room with the title character (Georgina Spelvin) and utterly indifferent to her demands for sexual pleasure. Damiano also incorporated a wry self-critique in *Skin Flicks* (1978), casting himself as a Mafia investor harassing a young filmmaker, whose creative inertia also threatens his latest production. The final sequence suggests that the filmmaker has retreated into fantasy to escape the pressures of his occupation.

However, it is the softcore and hardcore work of Radley Metzger which best represents the pornographer's potential for cultural commentary. Often dazzlingly cinematic, there are stylistic and thematic continuities across Metzger's *Camille 2000* (1969) and *The Lickerish Quartet* (1970) – as well as his acknowledged hardcore masterworks, *The Opening of Misty Beethoven* (1976) and *Barbara Broadcast* (1977), released under the *nom de porn* 'Henry Paris'. Metzger was keenly attuned to debates around sexual identity and orientation, giving them elaborate expression in the sado-erotica of *The Image* (1975) and the polymorphous mind-games of *Score* (1974). The latter was based upon the stage work of key gay-porn pioneer and innovator Jerry Douglas, whose presence on set ensured a physical, emotional and psychological authenticity in the film's delirious identity-switch climax.

Even at this phase of development, the cultural identity of the pornographic filmmaker was sufficiently advanced to allow for satirical, even self-reflexive, renditions. Terry Southern's 1970 absurdist novel *Blue Movie* imagines the consequences of a fêted Hollywood director's decision to shoot a big-budget hardcore movie starring the world's top female actress and funded by the government of Lichtenstein in order to boost tourism to the principality. Southern contrasts the venality and corruption of the Hollywood players (whose predilections and perversions extend to incest and necrophilia) with the ambitions and pretensions of the creative talent.

Some films actually had the benefit of industry insider experience. The barely released *Loops* (dir. Shaun Costello, 1973) combined fictional and insider documentary elements in its outline of the sex filmmaker's travails. Bob Chinn was executive producer on *Blue Money* (dir. Alain Patrick, 1972), which made several references to the pornographer's lot after the 1970 President's Commission on pornography. Its protagonist is a filmmaker (played by the director himself) beset by creative, legal, marital and economic obstacles, and dealing with an assortment of flakes, kooks and unscrupulous investors. Societal constraints prevent him from leaving the porn business to establish a yearned-for quasi-hippie lifestyle with his young family. Alternatively, John Lindsay, the UK's premier film pornographer of the era, outlined his own philosophy and working methods in his documentary *The Porn Brokers* (1972), a direct riposte to the 1972 anti-pornography Longford Report. Featuring interviews with European contemporaries such as Lasse Braun, Berth Milton and Joop Wilhelmus, *The Porn Brokers* celebrates and justifies scenarios of not only straight sexual activity but also gang rape, bondage, flagellation, bestiality and (simulated) paedophilia (Wilhelmus would soon serve prison time for the latter offence). If anything, the film stands as a lasting testament to Lindsay's commitment to '100% action. Sucking, licking, fucking, screwing, you name it. I want it and I want it good' (quoted in Thompson, 2007: 230).

Women and gay men as pornographers

Gubar notes that the majority of historical accounts of pornography have tended to neglect the 'feminine fictional perspective [or] female voyeurism or fetishism'. She points to the importance of 'obscene fiction' by figures such as Marguerite de Navarre, Edith Wharton, Anais Nin, Ayn Rand and Gael Greene (1989: 64). However, women's creative or economic contributions to the production of porn films in the 1970s, while ostensibly defined as trail-blazing purely through their relative scarcity or perhaps even their novelty value, vary wildly in terms of challenging the dominant structures and iconography of the form. Roberta Findlay's work as a director, producer, writer and cinematographer in both softcore sexploitation and hardcore (often in collaboration with her husband, Michael Findlay) has become a key example of nihilistic tendencies in the sex film. In print, Suze Randell's photographic output for publications as varied as *Playboy*, *Hustler* and the British tabloid newspaper *The Sun* eschewed the ethos of hardcore, bringing a soft-focus sensibility more appropriate for general consumption.

Despite criticisms of objectification and commodification, performers such as Annie Sprinkle, Jane Hamilton (aka Veronica Hart), Gloria Leonard, Sharon Mitchell, Candida Royalle and Nina Hartley parlayed star images into pursuits as diverse as performance art, journalism, sex-industry activism, directorial work, education and healthcare. Nevertheless, their contributions have often been met with bemusement, with culture still, seemingly, unwilling to accept unabashed and uncompromising female expressions of sexuality. Hartley has stressed that a combination of political and libidinous needs drove her career, feeling it essential to 'speak about sex, sexuality and sexual expression from a place of practice and not just theory' (Hartley, 2013: 228). Royalle, on the other hand, confronted the inherent sexism of the porn film's form and structure through her Femme Productions brand, developing work which eschewed staple conventions of visible male pleasure (primarily the cumshot), even de-emphasising genital close-ups to open up other iconographic possibilities. Royalle argued that 'it's not showing genitals that is exploitive; it's the philosophy behind it, and the acts and images that philosophy fosters' (Royalle, 2000: 549). These women's contributions laid the groundwork for alternative, sex-positive gender perspectives which can be found in the directorial efforts of Stormy Daniels, Belladona, Shine Louise Houston, Nica Noelle, Courtney Trouble and Jacky St James, whose work has collectively expanded the parameters of more inclusive, and perhaps even progressive, discourses of representation with regard to sexual orientation, identities and ethnicities.

The gay softcore photographic works of Bob Mizer, Dick Fontaine and Pat Rocco, and the hardcore films of figures such as Peter De Rome, Wakefield Poole, Fred Halsted, Joe Gage and Bill Higgins, are perhaps even more radical in intent and purpose through their appropriation of hyper-masculine iconography to confront the mincing, effeminate stereotyping of mainstream gay representation. These directors voiced desires subdued by the inherent homophobia of the cultures in which they were produced and mirrored homoerotic expressions in the underground and avant-garde films by Kenneth Anger and Andy Warhol, thus forging links between underground queer cultures and those with wider public acceptance (Escoffier, 2014).

After the 'golden age' of porn

Notwithstanding the individualism of such creative output, the American porn industry has also been notable for the collaborative community in front of as well as behind the cameras (McNeil and Osbourne, 2006). This camaraderie was evident in *Boogie Nights* (dir. Paul Thomas Anderson, 1997) through its presentation of a largely imagined 1970s LA scene populated by a surrogate family of wayward miscreants and damaged dreamers. Jack Horner (Burt Reynolds), the film's porn auteur, is shown to be deluded about the artistic value of his work, while committed to fulfilling his role and responsibilities to the various misfits in his charge. Central to the film is the significance, for the pornographer, of the switch from celluloid to video tape as the industry progressed into the 1980s (Alilunas, 2016). If affordable and accessible video technology further enabled mass production and distribution, its low technical status also contributed to the impression that porn production required very little creativity. Now, *everybody* had the potential to become a pornographer. Gerard Damiano has ruefully observed that 'with the advent of the video camera . . . it was over. You didn't need filmmakers anymore' (Paasonen and Saarenmaa, 2007: 28).

Adoption of, and adaption to, video technology encouraged alternative approaches. On the one hand, textual control passed into the hands of consumers, whose ordering of experience was facilitated by the remote-control button. On the other, video enabled a closer, less obviously professional aesthetic, as seen in the early gonzo work of Ugly George (on his public-access cable TV show established in the 1970s) and Jamie Gillis (in his *On The Prowl* video series initiated in 1989). These quasi-documentary experiments were refined, popularised and monetised by John Stagliano in the guise of his 'Buttman' character, an enterprise which saw him (successfully) fighting federal obscenity charges as recently as 2010. The gonzo sensibility features in Ben Dover's productions – his peculiar take on the British porn film is informed as much by national traditions of farcical comedy as by sexual desire.

The sense of a community steeped in a counter-cultural zest gave way in the 1980s to a new corporatisation, fine-tuned during the relative stability of the industry in the latter part of the decade. Some leading male performers, such as John Leslie and Paul Thomas, were able to draw upon their extensive experience to sustain careers as directors, working within a new legitimate business model in the wake of the 1986 Meese Commission. Joseph Slade noted that 'the effect of legal action . . . has been to diminish the role of organised crime and to open pornographic industries to standard business and accounting practices' (2000: 200). The successes of VCA, Vivid Video and Evil Angel suggest that it was as much company branding (embodied by the stars who adorned product packaging) as any aspiration to individual creative legitimacy that defined the identity of the video-age pornographer. The work of Andrew Blake and Michael Ninn has infused the porn film with a post-MTV sheen and gloss, revealing new levels of technical competence that emphasise dazzling surfaces over exploration of sexual freedoms. Even so, the spectre of moral backlash still haunts the industry – in 2009, Rob Black and Lizzie Borden (working under their Extreme Associates brand) were not only imprisoned on obscenity charges but also found themselves effectively ostracised by leading business figures who did not want their legitimate markets tainted by association.

The pornographer in film

The figure of the pornographer has sporadically aroused the curiosity of mainstream cinema, with several films locating him amid explorations of moral, spiritual, artistic and psychological decline. *Inserts* (dir. John Byrum, 1975) looked back to the stag era, its protagonist (Richard Dreyfuss) identified only as 'Boy Wonder' and describing himself as a 'pioneer in the neoplastic arts'. A contemporary (and equal) of De Mille, Griffith and Von Stroheim, he is now housebound, alcoholic and impotent, cynically shooting rape-porn films with a coterie of deluded wannabes and has-beens in his decaying Hollywood villa. As talkies blossom, he is mocked by his paymaster (Bob Hoskins) for the uselessness of his creative abilities. His misanthropy is leavened only slightly by self-loathing, and his failure is embodied in contrasting relationships with two women (Veronica Cartwright and Jessica Harper) who serve very different purposes in his personal trajectory.

In *Hardcore* (dir. Paul Schrader, 1979), events take place in the urban squalor of contemporary Los Angeles and San Francisco, where pornographers are sleazy opportunists amid an array of pimps, whores, hustlers, motel owners, publishers, producers, directors and performers – a chain that leads to a ruthless kingpin trading in snuff movies. This is the flipside of the life led by a devoutly religious Michigan businessman (George C. Scott), whose daughter's disappearance leads him on a gradual descent into the maelstrom. The process of pornographic dehumanisation is summed up by the private detective (Peter Boyle) who assists Scott in his quest – 'Nobody makes it. Nobody shows it. Nobody sees it' – an assertion that suggests a silent collusion between pornographers and their consumers.

The alleged dangers of this sinister underground world are also explored in films as disparate as *The Last House on Dead End Street* (dir. Roger Watkins, 1977), *8MM* (dir. Joel Schumacher, 1999) and *A Serbian Film* (dir. Srdan Spasojevic, 2010), which characterise pornographers as rapists and murderers through their creation of snuff movies (see Jackson, 2016 for discussion). Fascination with the pornographer's evolution in the 1970s has also surfaced in bio-pics such as *Rated X* (dir. Emilio Estevez, 2000) and *Lovelace* (dir. Rob Epstein/Jeffrey Friedman, 2013), the former outlining the career of Jim and Artie Mitchell and the latter tackling the issue of Linda Lovelace's mistreatment and exploitation by Gerard Damiano, her husband Chuck Traynor and the Mafia before, during and after the production of *Deep Throat*.

Cinematic renditions of the video-age pornographer have been sporadic and uneven, veering wildly between gross-out comedy, earnest introspection and hysterical condemnation. *Orgazmo* (dir. Trey Parker, 1997) foregoes serious interrogation in favour of a satire on the relationship between organised religion and the sex industry. Its venal porn mogul/gangster capitalises on the innocence and naivety of a young Mormon missionary, who unwittingly becomes not only a crossover sex superstar but also half of a crime-fighting duo! On the other hand, *The Pornographer* (dir. Doug Atchison, 1999) suggests that enthusiasm for, and creative participation in, pornography is both a conduit and a symptom of emotional disconnection and addiction, making the film a precursor to *Shame* (dir. Steve McQueen, 2011). Its titular figure is an awkward, disenchanted paralegal (Michael DeGood), connecting sexually only with a series of strippers and prostitutes. Moved to create his own pornography, he is confronted with the stark 'increase the sex, decrease the lead-in' philosophy of a reptilian producer (Craig Wasson) and veteran female star (Monique Parent), the latter harbouring ambitions for productions that are 'pussy-owned and pussy-run'. While this reflects the tension between traditional and progressive movements within the industry, each mentor is cynical and manipulative. The protagonist's ambitions are complicated by his attachment to a small-town innocent (Katheryn Cain) whose vulnerabilities make her ideal for his particular mode of objectification.

The titular character of *Le Pornographe* (dir. Bertrand Bonello, 2001) is a veteran film-maker who returns to the industry through financial necessity, his creative vision now undermined by a young producer intent on mining every porno cliché. The film harks back to a golden age by casting Jean-Pierre Léaud in the title role, thus alluding to his status as Francois Truffaut's frequent onscreen surrogate and the heady 1960s pomp of *les politique des auteurs*. While Laurent's (Léaud) youthful idealisation of cinematic sex was founded in the revolutionary zeal of 1968 Paris, the move into the professional field illuminates profound contrasts between the supposed political charge of shooting 'nude women in front of factories' and the well-worn sight of semen streaming onto his leading lady's face, the stuff that supposedly feeds the desires of his 'audience of truck drivers'.

This notion of an educated bourgeois sating the demands of a weary working-class audience is inverted in *Zack and Miri Make a Porno* (dir. Kevin Smith, 2008). Here, economic necessity also drives the title characters to embark upon porn production, but their attempt at a *Star Wars* parody ('Star Whores') becomes a string of riotous porn vignettes shot clandestinely in a Starbucks-like coffee shop. Amid jokes which run the gamut from the profane to the scatological, the film comments upon the cultural and economic gulf between low-end sex-video subcultures and the more legitimate business that porn has now become. Unusual in its emphasis on porn as a unisex, shame-free creative enterprise, *Zack and Miri* defines no-budget amateurism as a viable means of sex-positive (even romantic) expression, underlined by an ironic mid-credits coda in which the couple's (Seth Rogen and Elizabeth Banks) shambolic venture has blossomed into a successful commercial exercise. This intersection of pornographic creation and inter-personal bonding is pursued further in *Humpday* (dir. Lynn Shelton, 2009), which comically interrogates the conventions of male friendship, sexuality, marriage and commitment so crucial to the buddy movie. The film highlights men's refusal to confront their needs for physical and emotional intimacy. In it, the protagonists (Mark Duplass and Joshua Leonard) re-assess their relationship after an encounter with a commune of neo-hippie swingers compels them to produce a low-budget, experimental art-porn video production in which they are the participants.

Boogie Nights, *Orgazmo* and *Zack and Miri* make direct contact with pornographic heritage through casting renowned porn professionals from the past and present (respectively Jane Hamilton, Ron Jeremy and Traci Lords). The forthcoming (2017) HBO television series *The Deuce*, set in New York's urban sprawl and tracing the industry's development in the 1970s, also makes use of industry professionals.

As is discussed in the chapters in Part II of this volume, the digital age saw the return of enthusiastic amateurs, as corporate bodies struggled to adapt to technological and market transformations. The creative pornographer's work has been overshadowed by the functional, fragmented, short-form content on websites such as Pornhub, X Video and X Hamster. Moreover, the internet has fostered a breakdown in distinctions between the private and the public, unleashing an unprecedented level of voyeuristic abandon. Private sexual adventures of figures such as Kim Kardashian and Colin Farrell are now available for instant perusal, providing celebrity endorsement to the notion of the DIY pornographer. This locates the twenty-first-century pornographer in a space where the potentials and pitfalls of mediated sexuality are informed by technological democratisation, ensuring proliferation at the expense (perhaps) of the creative and expressive progress once pursued by some of the more radically minded purveyors of sexual sounds and images.

Bibliography

Alilunas, P. (2016) *Smutty Little Movies: The Creation and Regulation of Adult Video*. Berkeley: University of California Press.
Dworkin, A. (1981) *Pornography: Men Possessing Women*. London: The Women's Press Ltd.
Escoffier, J. (2014) 'Beefcake to Hardcore: Gay Pornography and the Sexual Revolution'. In E. Schaefer (ed) *Sex Scene: Media and the Sexual Revolution*. Durham/London: Duke University Press.
Gubar, S. (1989) 'Representing Pornography: Feminism, Criticism, and Depictions of Female Violation'. In S. Gubar and J. Hoff (eds) *For Adult Users Only: The Dilemma of Violent Pornography*. Bloomington, IN: Indiana University Press.
Hartley, N. (2013) 'Porn: An Effective Vehicle for Sexual Role Modelling and Education'. In T. Taormino, C.P. Shimizu, C. Penley and M. Miller Young (eds) *The Feminist Porn Book: The Politics of Producing Pleasure*. New York: The Feminist Press at the City University of New York.
Jackson, N. (2016) 'Wild Eyes, Dead Ladies: The Snuff Filmmaker in Realist Horror'. In N. Jackson, S. Kimber, J. Walker and T. Watson (eds) *Snuff: Real Death and Screen Media*, New York/London: Bloomsbury.
Kipnis, L. (1999) 'How to Look at Pornography'. In P. Lehman (ed) *Pornography Film and Culture*. New Brunswick/New Jersey/London: Rutgers University Press.
McNeil, L. and Osbourne, J. (2006) *The Other Hollywood: The Uncensored Oral History of the Porn Film History*. New York: Regan Books.
O'Toole, L. (1998) *Pornocopia: Porn, Sex, Technology and Desire*. London: Serpent's Tail.
Paasonen, S. and Saarenmaa, L. (2007) 'The Golden Age of Porn: Nostalgia and History in Cinema'. In S. Paasonen, K. Nikunen and L. Saarenmaa (eds) *Pornification: Sex and Sexuality in Media Culture*. Oxford, New York: Berg.
Royalle, C. (2000) 'Porn in the USA'. In D. Cornell (ed) *Feminism and Pornography*. Oxford: Oxford University Press.

Schlosser, E. (2004) *Reefer Madness and Other Tales From the American Underground*. London: Penguin.
Slade, J. (2000) *Pornography in America*. Santa Barbara/Denver/Oxford: ABC-Clio.
Thompson, D. (2007) *Black and White and Blue: Adult Cinema from the Victorian Age to the VCR*. Toronto: ECW Press.
Tomkinson, M. (1982) *The Pornbrokers: The Rise of the Soho Sex Barons*. London: Virgin Books.

Media

8MM (1999) Directed by Joel Schumacher [Film]. USA: Sony Pictures Entertainment.
A Serbian Film (2010) Directed by Srdan Spasojevic [Film]. Serbia: Jinga Films.
Barbara Broadcast (1977) Directed by Radley Metzger [Film]. USA: Audubon Films.
Beyond the Valley of the Dolls (1970) Directed by Russ Meyer [Film]. USA: Twentieth Century Fox Film Corporation.
Blue Money (1972) Directed by Alain Patrick (as Alain-Patrick Chappuis) [Film]. USA: Crown International.
Blue Movie (1970) Authored by Terry Southern [Novel]. New York: Grove Press.
Boogie Nights (1997) Directed by Paul Thomas Anderson [Film]. USA: New Line Cinema.
Camille 2000 (1969) Directed by Radley Metzger [Film]. Italy: Audubon Films.
Deep Throat (1972) Directed by Gerard Damiano [Film]. USA: Arrow Production.
The Deuce (forthcoming 2017) [TV Drama Series]. USA: HBO.
The Devil in Miss Jones (1973) Directed by Gerard Damiano [Film]. USA: Pierre Productions.
Faster, Pussycat! Kill! Kill! (1965) Directed by Russ Meyer [Film]. USA: Eve Productions.
Hardcore (1979) Directed by Paul Schrader [Film]. USA: Columbia.
Humpday (2009) Directed by Lynn Shelton [Film]. USA: Magnolia Pictures.
The Image (1975) Directed by Radley Metzger [Film]. USA: Synapse Films.
Inserts (1975) Directed by John Byrum [Film]. USA: United Artists Corporation.
The Last House on Dead End Street (1977) Directed by Roger Watkins [Film]. USA: Cinematic Releasing Corporation.
Le Pornographe (2001) Directed by Bertrand Bonello [Film]. France: Haut et Court.
The Lickerish Quartet (1970) Directed by Radley Metzger [Film]. Italy/USA: Audubon Films.
Loops (1973) Directed by Shaun Costello [Film]. USA: Sean S. Cunningham Films.
Lovelace (2013) Directed by Rob Epstein/Jeffrey Friedman [Film]. USA: Millenium Films.
On The Prowl (1989–) Directed by Jamie Gillis [Video Series]. USA: General Video of America.
The Opening of Misty Beethoven (1976) Directed by Radley Metzger (as Henry Paris) [Film]. USA: Catalyst.
Orgazmo (1997) Directed by Trey Parker [Film]. USA/Japan: October Films.
The People vs Larry Flynt (1996) Directed by Milos Forman [Film]. USA: Columbia Pictures.
The Porn Brokers (1972) Directed by John Lindsay [Documentary]. UK: Target.
The Pornographer (1999) Directed by Doug Atchison [Film]. USA: The Asylum.
Rated X (2000) Directed by Emilio Estevez [TV Documentary]. USA: Showtime.
Score (1974) Directed by Radley Metzger [Film]. US/Yugoslavia: First Run Pictures.
Shame (2011) Directed by Steve McQueen [Film]. UK: Momentum Pictures.
Skin Flicks (1978) Directed by Gerard Damiano [Film]. US: Adult Video Corportation.
Vixen! (1968) Directed by Russ Meyer [Film]. USA: Eve Productions.
Zack and Miri Make a Porno (2008) Directed by Kevin Smith [Film]. USA: The Weinstein Company.

INDEX

4Chan.org 189
9½ Weeks 61
20th Century Fox 156
50 Cent 362
'101 Ways to End Up in a Canadian Shack' 121

Abercrombie & Fitch 109
abstinence 193, 197, 198, 224; see also celibacy
Abstraction Licking 367
Academy Awards 46
ACARA (Australian Curriculum, Assessment and Reporting Authority) 232
action sports, women in: and femininity 279, 280–1, 282–4, 285–6; and feminism 282, 283–5, 285; mass and niche media representations 282–3, 286; power dynamics and male domination 279–80, 281, 283–5, 286, 287; 'sexy bad girl' representations 280–2; and social media 285, 286
Adam Zkt. Eva 313
advertising: and children 268–9, 270, 274–6; *Crazy Domains* advertisement 271–3; and fantasy 271–3; and objectification 268, 271, 274–5; and pornography 269, 270, 271, 272–3; and representations of sexuality 268, 269–74; and 'sexualisation' 268, 269, 274–6; *Zesty* advertisement 271, 273–4
aesthetic/formal debate (in art/porn) 164, 166–8
Aesthetic Sexuality 421
affirmative consent model 111, 198
Afternoon Delight 363
Aggleton, P. 224–5
Aguilera, Christina 255

Agustín, Laura 395
AHF (AIDS Healthcare Foundation) 218
Akhavan, Desiree 77–8
Akon 263
Alexandra 120
All About Eve 96
Allen, L. 224, 226, 231
Allen, Lilly 252
Allen, Woody 423
Ally McBeal 300
Almost Crying 136
alternative pornographies: authenticity of 152, 156, 157; digital revolution/websites 152–4; and feminism 152, 156–7; history and evolution of 151–4; identity politics and representation strategies 156–8; and independent movie industry 154–6; and 'subversive re-appropriation' 158
Altman, R. 144
altporn.net 154
Alÿ, Francis 366
amateur pornography: across media 177–80; appeal of amateur content 174–7; authenticity of 175–7, 178; celebrity sex tapes see celebrity sex tapes; comparison with professional pornography 176–7; and deviance 175–6; ephemerality and longevity 180; historical roots of 174–5; memory-work project 174, 175, 178–80; and reality TV 314
American Independent Cinema 154–5
American Museum of Natural History 7, 10, 11
American Pie 227

Index

Amis, Martin 141
'Anaconda' 265
anal fisting 163, 164, 170
'anal gaping' 145
Ancient Greece 50
Anderson, Eric 345, 347–8
Anderson, Judith 97
Anderson, Pamela 187, 249, 271–3
Angel, Buck 31
Angelides, S. 196
Angel, Joanna 155, 156, 157
Anger, Kenneth 433
anime 130, 133, 136, 137
Aniya, Yuiji 132
Another Gay Movie 423
'Another Unfortunate' 378–9
anthropology 10, 11, 12, 29, 92, 396
Anticlimax 87–8
APA (American Psychological Association) 228, 259, 274, 275
APAs (Amateur Press Associations) 118
Appropriate Behavior 77–8
Aretino, Pietro 429
Are You Being Served? 53
'Are you Norma, Typical Woman?' 12
Art and Pornography 164
Artifice 134
art/porn debate: aesthetic/formal argument 164, 166–8; and censorship 163–4, 165–4, 166–7, 171; disciplinary approaches to 164–5; and feminism 165–6, 168, 171; legal debate 165, 169–71; origin of pornography 165–6; philosophical debate 164–5, 168–9; and strippers 366–9
Art/Porn: Seeing and Touching 164
asexualities: asexual reading practices 20–4; 'compulsory sexuality' 19–20, 21, 22–5; and disabled people 23, 328; and erotica 110; and horror 294; and sex advice books 206
Aslama, M. 310
Attalah, P. 300
Attenberg 74
Attwood, Feona 171, 186, 209, 292, 353, 419
authenticity: and alternative pornographies 152, 156, 157; and amateur pornography 175–7, 178; and celebrity sex tapes 185–6, 187, 188, 190; and lesbian representation 38, 42–4; and reality TV 311, 312–13, 314
'autogynephilia' 28
AVEN (Asexual Visibility and Education Network) 19
AVN (Adult Video News) Magazine 31, 141, 152–3

Baby Boy 253
'Baby Face' 262–3, 264
Bachelor, The 310
Bad Influence 183, 184
Bailey Review 274, 275, 276
Banana Fish 133
Band Sluts 155
Bar at the Folies-Bergère, A 366
Barely Evil 153
Barker, Meg-John 88, 210, 276
Barnum, P. T. 331
Barounis, Cynthia 23–4
Barry, Marion 355
Basic Instinct 62, 64, 70, 249
Basic Instinct 2 65
Basingstoke 122
Bauman, Z. 349
Baym, N. K. 194
Bazin, André 158
BBFC (British Board of Film Classification) 51, 259–60, 291, 295
BBSs (Bulletin Board Systems) 175
BDSM (bondage/discipline/sadomasochism): and art/porn debate 167–8; and childhood trauma 63–4, 66; and consent 60, 62, 65, 66, 409; and 'deviance' 59, 61, 64, 65, 66–7; and disabled people 329; dominatrices *see* dominatrices; and erotic thrillers 60, 61–2, 64, 66; and fashion 420–1; female dominant portrayal 64–5, 66; *Fifty Shades* trilogy *see Fifty Shades* trilogy; male dominant portrayal 60, 61–2, 66; male submissive portrayal 65–6; rape and consent 61, 64, 112; and romantic dramas 59, 61, 65, 66; and slash stories 124–5, 126–7; stigmatisation of 60, 62–3, 405, 406–7, 410; and subversion 411–12; tolerance of 407–8
Beadle, Gaz 189
Beam, Lura 11
Beatles 260
Beauté 275
Becker, Ron 101
Beckham, David 344–5
Beckham, Victoria 345, 421
Belladonna's Strapped Dykes 158
Bellwether, Mira 29
Belskie, Abram 7, 9–10, 11
Beltran, M. C. 252
Benefit cosmetics 421, 422
Bennett, Catherine 373, 377
Bennett, Tony 7
Berger, John 366
Berlant, Laurent 305

Berlin PorYes Award 33
Bersani, Leo 111
bestiality 423–4
Bettcher, T. M. 30
Better Than Chocolate 42
Bevan, K. 207
Beyoncé 252–3, 264, 265–6
Beyond the Hills 74
Beyond the Valley of the Dolls 431
Biasin, Enrico 158
Bieber, Justin 248
Big Brother 185, 309, 311
Biodildo 157–8
Birdcage, The 99
Biressi, Anita 310
Birmingham Daily Gazette 377
Birthing Atlas, The 10
'Birthing Series' 9, 11
bisexualities: binary constructions of sexuality 71; and 'commodity bisexuality' 72; 'compulsory monogamy' and 'monosexuality' 71–2, 75, 78; and erotic perversion 73–4; as '(in)convenient truth' 74–5; as 'not just a phase' 75–6; and pathological mimicry 72–3; queer bisexualities 77–8, 93; representation of 70–1; and television serials 76–7
bishonen 132
BL (Boys' Love) 130–7
Black, Forrest 153
Black Lace 114
Black, Rob 434
Black Swan 73
Blains, Joss 32
Blake, Andrew 434
Blanchard, Alana 285
Blanchett, Cate 46
Bleakley, A. 227
Bleiler, Gretchen 282
Blood and Semen II 163
'Blue' 265
Blue Blood 153
Blued 217, 218
Blue Is the Warmest Color 43, 44–5, 72–3, 75
Blue Money 432
Blue Movie 169, 432
Blurred Lines 253, 264–5
'bodice ripper' fiction 111–13
Body of Evidence 62
Bogarde, Dirk 49, 51
Bogdan, Robert 331
Boggs, Wade 355
Bold Strokes Books 110

Bonds-Raacke, J. M. 39, 40, 41
Bone People, The 22–3
Boogie Nights 433, 436
Borden, Lizzie 434
Born in the USA 420, 421
Born on the Fourth of July 23
Bornstein, Kate 31
Born to Die 72
Boston Legal 424
Bound 2 248–9
boundary-drawing 207, 208
Boy Meets Girl 34
Boys Don't Cry 30
Boys in the Band, The 99
Boys Love Manga 137
Boys Love Manga and Beyond 137
Bragg, S. 276
Brathwaite, Brenda 243
Braxton, Toni 363
Breaking Bad 41
Breaking the Waves 23
Breathe 73
Breathing Lessons 23
Breck, S. E. 224
Brenton, Sam 310
British Newspaper Archive 374
Brokeback Mountain 1, 75
Bromwich, R. 63–4
Brown, Helen Gurley 86
Brown, William 292
Bryant, Chris 54
Buckingham, D. 276
Buckland, Warren 146
Buffalo Museum of Science 11
Buffy the Vampire Slayer 39
Bulletin Board Systems (BBSs)
Burana, Lily 364
Burchill, Julie 261
Burdett-Coutts, Angela 378
Bureau of Home Economics 7
Burke, Tara Shea 315
burningangel.com 154, 155
Burton, Catherine 355
Burton, Jeff 163
'butch' characters 40, 96, 97, 99, 101
Butler, Heather 273
Butler, Judith 32–3, 158
Buying Naked 313
Byrne, Romana 421

'Cabaret' 263
Cacchioni, T. 24, 204

Cade, Amy 368
Cade, Rosana 368
Cadeux 275
Café Flesh 169
Califia, Patrick 59, 66–7
Cameron, David 270
Campbell, Anna 112
Campbell, C. 224–5
Campbell, Rosie 368, 369
camp characterisations 52–3, 98
Caniche 423
Can't Get You Out of My Head 253
Captain Tsubasai 133
Cardiff Female Refuge Society 377
Carnes, Patrick 355, 359
Carol 45–6
Carter, Julian B. 8–9
Cassidy, E. M. 216
Castillo, Raul 101
casual sex (heterosexual): and class 81, 85, 86; and 'dating apocalypse' 81, 83–4; and feminism 81, 86–8; 'gamification' of dating 81, 83–5, 88; and marriage 81, 84, 85, 86; recent history of 85–8; Tinder dating app 81, 82–5, 88
Cattrall, Kim 421
celebrity media: and feminism/postfeminism 249, 251, 254, 255; Miley Cyrus 248, 249, 253–6; objectification of celebrity bodies 249, 251, 252; and race 251, 252–3; and reality TV 248; representing celebrity 249–51; and role models 255; sex tapes *see* celebrity sex tapes; 'sexy' bums/body parts 251–3; 'sexy' narratives 254–5; and social media 248, 249, 252, 253
Celebrity Rehab with Dr. Drew 356, 357
celebrity sex tapes: and authenticity 185–6, 187, 188, 190; consent, risk, regulation, pleasure and consequence 185; consumption and distribution of 186–7; on- and off-screen identities 185–6; as promotional tools 248–9; and 'revenge porn' 184, 187; Rob Lowe scandal 183–4, 186, 187; and self-representation 187–90; and social media 187–90; types and characteristics of 184–6
celibacy 20–1, 24, 206, 357; *see also* abstinence
Celluloid Closet, The 99
censorship: art/porn debate 163–4, 165–4, 166–7, 171; erotica 107–8, 109; horror 291–3, 294–5; reality TV 313; representing gay sexualities 51–3; trans representations 32; videogames 243
'C'est Si Bon' 263
Chaiken, Ilene 43
'charmed circle' model 81

Chasing Amy 70
'Cheap Sunglasses' 120–1
Chen, Edison 187
Chen, Jo 134
Chicago Blackhawks 125–6
Chicago, Judy 166
Chidester, Phil 301
childhood trauma 63–4, 66, 73
child pornography 135, 136–7, 170, 171, 194–5, 197–8
Child Pornography Prevention Act (US) 136
Children's Hour, The 38, 99
Chinatown 423
Chinn, Bob 432
Chisholm, Melanie 259
Chloe 73
Choisir 131
Cholodenko, Lisa 45, 78
choreographed dance performances 261–2, 263
Christmas Tree 170
Chronaki, Despina 387
Claiming the Courtesan 112
Clark-Flory, Tracy 314
Clark, L. S. 226
Clausen, B. C. 15
Clavo, Lola 33
Clayton, Jami 33
Cleland, John 429
Cleo 230, 321–5
Cleveland Museum of Health 7, 11, 12
Cleveland Plain Dealer 7, 12–14
Clift, Montgomery 49
Clinton, Bill 49, 354
cliteracy 111, 114
Closer 249
Cloud, John 354
Clover, Carol 292
Cody, Diablo 364
Cohen, Reuben 310
Cohen, Stanley 373
coital imperative 206
Cold War 96
Cole, Sheri Kathleen 259
Collins, R. L. 227
colonialism 50–1, 252
Colosi, Rachela 366
Columbia Journalism Review 355
Comella, Lynn 373
Comiket 130
'coming out' strategy 50
Commission on Obscenity and Pornography (US) 384

Index

'commodity bisexuality' 72
community outreach 217
'compulsory heterosexuality' 19
'compulsory monogamy' 71–2, 78
'compulsory monosexuality' 71–2, 75, 78
'compulsory sexuality' 19–20, 21, 22–5
'Compulsory sexuality and asexual/crip resistance in John Cameron Mitchell's *Shortbus*' 23–4
Connell, R.W. 86, 87, 88
Conrad, Lauren 424
consent: and amateur pornography 178; and BDSM 60, 62, 65, 66, 409; and celebrity sex tapes 185; and erotica 111–13, 114; and erotic Manga 135; and rape 111–13; and sexting 193, 195, 196, 197–8, 199
Contagious Diseases Act (UK) 375, 379
continuity editing 144–5
'Conversation, The' 223, 232
Cook, H. 225
Cooper, D. 20
Corden, James 345
Corn, L. 209
Coroners and Justice Act (UK) 137
Corporate Paedophilia 274
Cortese, A. J. 270
Cosmopolitan 86, 230, 319, 320, 321–5
Couch 169
Courbet, Gustave 165, 166
Couric, Katie 33
Cowboys4Angels 315
Cox, Laura 255
Cox, Laverne 33
Cox, Tracey 207
Craigslist 215
Cramer, F. 155
Crash Pad, The 156
crashpadseries.com 154, 155
Crazy Domains 271–3
Creadick, Anna 8, 9
Creed, Barbara 98, 293
Creedence Clearwater Revival 262
Criminal Justice and Immigration Act (UK) 170, 291
Criminal Minds 62
Crimp, Douglas 168
Crimson Spell 134
Crosby, Charlotte 189
'cross-coding' 168
Cruising 62
Crying Game, The 30
CSI 405
Cunt Grid #13 166

Cunt Is a Rose Is a Cunt, A 166
Cunt Painting #7 166
Cupid 112
Cutting, Linda Katherine 422
Cyrus, Miley 248, 249, 253–6

DADT (Don't Ask, Don't Tell) policy 49, 123
Daigle, Steven 357
Daily Mail 255, 373, 407
Dakides, Tara 280–1
Daley, Tom 190
Dallaire, C. 286
Dallas Buyers Club 75
Damiano, Gerard 431, 433, 435
Dancers Information 368–9
'Dance While You Can' 120
Dangerous Method, A 63
'dangers of wired love, The' 194
Danish Girl, The 28
Danto, Arthur C. 166, 167
Darling, James 33
'dating apocalypse' 81, 83–4
dating apps *see* online dating/dating apps
Dating Naked 313
Davenport, Charles 7
Davis, Lennard 332
Dearden, Basil 51
Dearest Pet 424
de Beauvoir, Simone 387
de Botton, A. 204, 208, 209
Deep Throat 164, 431, 435
Deery, June 310
Defense of Marriage Act (US) 123
DeGeneres, Ellen 41
DeGenevieve, Barbara 31
DeJong, M. M. 63–4
Dekkers, Midas 424
Delane, John Thadeus 378
de la Rey, Cheryl 420
'de-lesbianising' representations 42, 43
Deller, R. 60
Del Rey, Lana 72, 74
Demeter 421–2
'demotic turn' 186, 187
Dennis, Kelly 164, 165
de Sade, Marquis 406, 410, 429
desires and fantasies discourse (sitcom study) 304–5
Deuce, The 436
Deutsches Hygiene Museum 11
Deveaux, Drew 32

'deviance': and amateur pornography 175–6; and BDSM 59, 61, 64, 65, 66–7; and 'extreme pornography' 171; and lesbian representation in film and TV 45; and perverts 416, 417–18; and representing gay sexualities 49; and trans sexualities 27–8
Devil in Miss Jones, The 290, 431
De Voss, Danielle 153
DeWitt, Karen 422, 423
Dhaenens, Frederik 300
Diagnostic and Statistical Manual of Mental Disorders 28, 407
Diamond, Morty 31
Diaz, Cameron 184
Dickens, Charles 378–9
Dickinson, Robert Latou 7, 9–10, 11
Di Corca, Philip-Lorca 366
diegetic space 142
Dika, Vera 292
Dines, Gail 388
Dinner Party, The 166
Dirty Love 363
disabled people: and asexualities 23, 328; disability rights 328; and 'enfreakment' 331–7; and heterosexual normativity 23; and humour 334–6, 337; and 'monsters' 330–1, 332; representing disabled bodies 328–9, 330–3, 337; and *The Undateables* 329–30, 333–7
Disco Inferno 362
disgust 293
Dith, Sasha 265
Ditum, Sarah 373
doingitonline.com 33, 156
Doing It Ourselves 32–3
Dolan, Xavier 78
Dolly 230
dominatrices: acceptance/tolerance of 407–8; and dualistic approach to sexuality 410–12; prevalence/popularity of 405, 408–10, 412; 'pro-Dommes' 406, 407, 409, 410, 411–12; stigmatisation of 405, 406–7, 410; and subversion 411–12; terminology 405–6
Dominic and Elliot series 167
Domino 74–5
Donahue 355
Don Jon 419
Donnerstein, Ed 294
Doty, Alexander 300–1
'Douchebags of Grindr' 55
Douglas, Jerry 432
Douglas, Michael 65
Dover, Ben 434

Dover, K. J. 50
Dovey, J. 242, 310, 312
Dragon Age 241
Drag Race 33
Drake, J. 284
Draughtsman Drawing a Nude 165
Dreamers, The 73
Dr. Phil 356, 359
'Drunk in Love' 265
DuBois, Ellen Carol 86
Dubrofsky, Rachel 310
Due South 121, 122–3
Duguay, S. 83, 88
Dundee, Perth, and Cupar Advertiser 377
'dungeons' 406, 407, 408, 410
Durer, Albrecht 165
Durst, Fred 187
Duschinsky, R. 276
Dworkin, Andrea 430–1
Dyer, R. 52, 99
Dyer, Richard 92, 249–50, 254

Eaklor, Vicki L. 41
East London Observer 375–6
East London Strippers Collective 369
Edwards, T. 273
effects-based reasoning 292
Egan, R. Danielle 366, 369
Ehrenreich, Barbara 85, 260
Elastic Assholes 5 142–3, 145–6
Elbe, Lili 28, 33
Eler, Alicia 88
Ellis, Havelock 93
Ellora's Cave 114
Embracing Love 134
emergent play 241–2
Emin, Tracey 166
Emirain 134
Emperor of the Land of the Rising Sun 133
'enfreakment' 331–7
Epprecht, M. 51
Eros 108, 111, 112
erotica: and censorship 107–8, 109; and climax 111, 113–14; and consent 111–13, 114; defining 107, 108, 109, 110; and feminism 108, 109–10, 112, 114, 115; imagination and fantasy 110–11, 113, 114; liberating potential of 109–11, 113, 114–15; and pornography 107–8, 109, 114; and romance fiction 108–9, 111–13
'Erotica vs. pornography' 107
Erotic Fandom 153

erotic thrillers 60, 61–2, 64, 66
Esquire 343
ESRB (Entertainment Software Review Board) 241, 243, 244
Essex, Joey 345
Etat Libre d'Orange 421
eugenics 7, 10, 11, 15
'Eugenics in New Germany' 11
Everett, Rupert 100
EverQuest 242
Everything You Always Wanted to Know About Sex 423
Everything You Know about Sex is Wrong 208
Evil Angel network 154
'exhibitionary complex' 7
Exit to Eden 64–5, 66
'extreme pornography' 163, 170–1, 295

Facebook: and celebrity media 248, 252; and dominatrices 405, 406; and sexual health 214, 216, 218; and sexuality education 230; and Tinder dating app 81, 82; trans representations 27, 31; and women in action sports 285, 286
'face-pics' 54
Fake 134
Family Guy 410, 424
fan fiction 59, 117, 178, 241; *see also* slash stories
Fanlore.org 120
fantasy: and advertising 271–3; and BDSM 406, 407; and erotica 110–11, 113, 114; and horror 292; and reality TV 310–11, 314, 317; and sex advice books 206, 207; and sitcoms 304–5, 307; and slash stories 117
'Fappening' 188–9, 249
Farrell, Colin 436
Fassbender, Michael 73
Fatale Video 152
Fat Girl Fantasies 156
Fawcett Society 365
Fay, D. 84
feature pornography: comparison with gonzo 146–8; continuity editing 144–5; production of 143; storylines/narratives 141, 142, 143–4, 147; stylistic model of 141–2, 146; traits of 142, 148
Fedtke, Jana 22
feelings discourse (sitcom study) 303–4
Fein, Ellen 85
femininity: and BDSM representation 60; and bisexual representation 70; and celebrity media 249, 250, 253, 254; and lesbian representation in film and TV 42; and

metrosexuals 343, 344, 347; 'normal' 13, 14; and queer representation 96; and trans representations 29, 30, 31; and women in action sports 279, 280–1, 282–4, 285–6; and women's magazines 320, 321
feminism: and advertising 269–70, 276; and alternative pornographies 152, 156–7; and art/porn debate 165–6, 168, 171; and casual sex 81, 86–8; and celebrity media 249, 251, 254, 255; and erotica 108, 109–10, 112, 114, 115; and female pornographers 432–3; and metrosexuals 347; and porn performers 394, 395–6, 401; and sex advice books 203; and slash stories 118, 123, 124; and strippers 364–6, 368; and women in action sports 282, 283–5, 285; and women's magazines 319, 321–2, 323
feminist porn 31–2, 108, 110, 152, 395, 401
Feminist Porn Awards 32, 108, 110
Feminist Porn Book, The 108, 395, 401
'femme' characters 31, 62, 64, 65, 66, 72, 96, 98
Femme Productions 152, 433
femslash 117
Ferrer, Nino 263
Feuer, Jane 301, 307
FHM 282, 283
Fifty Shades trilogy: and childhood trauma 63–4, 66; and dominatrices 408–10, 412; and erotica 109, 112; and erotic thriller genre 60, 61–2, 64, 66; and fan fiction 59, 117, 178; and normalisation of BDSM 61, 66–7; and perverts 422; and plot/narrative 59, 60, 61–3; and romantic drama genre 59, 61, 65, 66; and stigma of BDSM 60, 62–3
Films, Videos and Publications Classification Act (New Zealand) 291–2
Finder Series 134
Findlay, Roberta 432
Fine, M. 226
Fingle 240, 244, 245, 246
Finnish Literature Society 174
Fisher, T. 375
Fitzgerald, F. Scott 75
Flamingo 120
Flesh and the Word 108
Flores, April 401, 402
Flynt, Larry 430
Forbes 83
Ford, Tom 344
Forever Amber 109
'Forget About the Dirty Looks' 125, 126–7
Forster, E. M. 52

For Women 320, 389, 423
Foster, Thomas 54
Foucault, Michel 92, 279, 280, 281, 282, 287, 309, 375, 394, 396–7, 411
Foursome 314
Fox Searchlight 156
'Fragment Out of Time, A' 119
Franco, James 345
Franco, Jesus 429
Frank, Katherine 365, 366, 369
Frasier 408
'freak' shows 331–2, 336
Freeland, Cynthia 294
Freeman, Elizabeth 118
Freire, Paulo 372
Frennea, M. 135, 136
Freud, S. 86
Frida 74–5
Friedman, Michelle 420
Friends 38–9, 300, 301–7
Frith, Simon 261
Fukutomi, M. 130
Full Monty, The 363
Furedi, Frank 352
furrygirl.com 153

Gagnon, J. H. 109
Gaï, Djeïnaba Diop 75
Galanos, Mike 196
Gallagher, Rob 243
Game, The 85
G, Amelia 153
Game of Thrones 76
'gamification' 81, 83–5, 88, 239
Gamma Entertainment 155
Gandy, David 345
Gardere, Jeff 354
Gardner, Hunter 290
Garland, Judy 249
Garland Thomson, Rosemarie 330–1, 332, 336
Garman, Bryan 421
Garnett, Gale 263
Garr, Teri 113
Garrity, J. 272
Gaydar 216, 217, 218
Gay Liberation Front 50
Gays and Film 99
Gebhard, Bruno 11, 12, 14–15
Geordie Shore 189, 311
Geraldo 355
Gergen, Kenneth 349
Getting Some 110

Gia Darling Entertainment 31
GID (Gender Identity Disorder) 28
Gielgud, John 52
Gigolos 313, 314, 315–16
Gilda 363
Gill, R. 269, 271, 272, 280, 281
Gillis, Jamie 433
Girlfriend 38, 230
Girlie Show 366
Girl Meets Boy 142, 143–5, 146
Girls' Comic Extra 132
'girl-to-girl relations' 271, 272–3
Girl with the Dragon Tattoo, The 70–1
Giuliano, Traci A. 39
GLAAD 33
Glasgow Midnight Rescue Brigade 377, 379
Glasser, Mervin 417
Glee 40, 44, 76
Glitterland 112
Godaw, Brian 290
Godson, S. 208
'golden age' of porn 433–4
Goldman, Alan 417
Goldman, Emma 86
Goldstein, Al 430
Gomillion, Sarah C. 39
gonzo pornography: comparison with feature pornography 146–8; and 'golden age' of porn 433–4; immediacy and hyperbole 145–6; production/editing of 143, 146, 147; stylistic model of 141–2, 146; traits of 142, 148
Goodger, Lauren 187
Good Wife, The 76–7
Gordon, Linda 86
Gosselin, Chris 408
Gothic Sluts 153
Grand Theft Auto 244
Gravitation 133
Grayson, Larry 53
Great Gatsby, The 75
'great sex' 205, 209, 320, 323–5
'great social evil' 374, 375–8, 379
'Great Society' social programme 384
'Green River' 262
Gregory, Tim 188
Grey's Anatomy 77
Grey, Sasha 148
Grindr 54, 55, 214, 215, 217, 218
Grindstaff, Laura 310, 357
Groff, Jonathan 101
Grosz, Elizabeth 397
Growlr 54

Guardian 83, 259, 260, 373
Gubar, Susan 431, 432
Guccione, Bob 429, 430
Guinness, Alec 49
Gupta, K. 19–20, 24, 204
gynaecology 165

Hagio, Moto 132
Haidt, J. 294
Hakim, Jamie 346
Hall, Alexis 112
Hall, M. 344
Hall, S. 53
Halperin, David 78, 398
Halsted, Fred 151
Hamilton, Clive 389
Hana 284
Hancock, J. 204–5
'handkerchief code' 420
Hands Tied 363
'Hanged Man' 122–3
Hannah Montana 254–5
Haraway, G. 165
Hardcore 434
Hard Core: Power, Pleasure, and the 'Frenzy of the Visible' 311–12
Hard Out Here 252
Hardy, Kate 365, 368, 369
Hardy, Simon 311
Harrington, Eve 96
Harris, Anne 131
Harris, Neil Patrick 31
Harrison, Kathryn 422
Harry Potter 408, 409
Hartley, N. 433
Hatterer, Lawrence 352
Hayward, P. 184–5
Hayworth, Rita 363
Heart of Thomas, The 132
Heart of Whiteness, The 8–9
Heavenly Bodies 249–50
Hefner, Hugh 244, 429, 430
Helenish 125
Heller, Dana 315, 316
Hellraiser 290
Helmut and Brooks 164, 166, 170
Henderson, M. 282
Henry, J. Hue 183
Hentai, Yaoi 134
Hersh, M. A. 294
Her Story 33–4
Herzog, Amy 262

Hesiod 108, 111
Hess, Amanda 84
'heteroflexibility' 39, 71, 348
heterosexuality: and alternative pornographies 157–8; and bisexual representation 71–2, 75, 77; casual sex *see* casual sex (heterosexual); 'compulsory' 19; and erotica 110, 113, 114; and erotic Manga 131; and lesbian representation in film and TV 39, 41, 42–3, 44–5, 46; and metrosexuals 343–4, 346, 347–8; and 'normal bodies' 8–9, 16; and sex advice books 205–6, 207, 208, 209, 210; and sexual identity 397, 402; and sitcoms 300, 301, 302, 305–6; and slash stories 117, 121, 123; and women in action sports 279, 280–1, 282–3, 285, 286; and women's magazines 319–20, 321–2, 323, 324–5
Hetfield, James 420
Hevey, David 331
Heywood, L. 284
Highsmith, Patricia 45
High Tension 38
Hill-Meyer, Tobi 30–1, 32, 33
Hillyer, M. 187
Hilton, Paris 187, 251
His Secret 74
History of Sex, The 170
History of Sexuality, The 92, 396
Hitchcock, Alfred 64, 97–8
HIV/AIDS: and bisexual representation 75; and queer representation 99; and representing gay sexualities 50; and sex advice books 203; and sexuality education 224; and slash stories 119, 120, 122; and social media 214, 215, 216–18
hobbyism 175
Hofer, Kristina Pia 177
Hole 363
Holmes, Steve 145, 146
Holmes, Su 185
Home, S. 155
homophobia 39, 46, 49–50, 51, 55, 98, 121, 122–3, 345
homosexuality: and art/porn debate 167–8; and celibacy 20–1; and disability 23; and erotica 110; and erotic Manga 130–4, 135; gay pornographers 433; and humour 335; and metrosexuals 344, 345, 347–8; and perverts 418, 420, 421; and pornography consumers 389; and porn performers 394, 397, 398–402; queer representation *see* queer representation; and religion 389; representing gay sexualities 49–55; and sex advice books 203, 204, 206,

208–9, 210; and sexual health 214, 215, 216–18, 219; and sexual identity 396–7, 398, 399, 400–1, 402; and sitcoms 300, 301, 306; slash stories *see* slash stories; trans representations in queer porn 30–3
'hook-ups' 82–5, 87, 214, 215, 217, 218
Hoover, J. Edgar 430
Hopper, Edward 366
horror: and censorship 291–3, 294–5; and 'freak' bodies 332; and pornography 290–1, 292, 294–5; and rape 290, 291, 294–5; sex–horror relationship 290–1, 292–4, 296
'Hot Coffee Mod' 244
'hot lesbians' figure 271, 272
House 21, 405
How to Be a Woman 365
How to Look Good Naked 337
Hudson, Rock 49
Huffington Post 410
Hulme, Keri 22
Human Sex Anatomy 10
humour 240, 244, 246, 300, 301, 304, 305, 307, 334–6, 337, 408
Humpday 435–6
Hunting, Kyra 124
Hustler magazine 430, 432
hypersexualisation: and advertising 268, 274–5; and BDSM 62, 64; and celebrity media 251, 252–3; and perverts 416, 419; and queer representation 93; and trans representation 28, 31; and video games 239–40, 242; and women in action sports 279, 283, 285–6; *see also* sexualisation

identification communication 147, 148
Identity 64
Illouz, Eva 112
I Modi 429
incest 63, 73, 178, 422–3
'inclusive masculinity' 345, 347
Independent 344
Indie Porn Revolution 156
Inman, John 53
Inserts 434
In Sickness and in Health 53
Inside I'm Dancing 329
'Instafamous' 188
Instagram 188, 253, 285, 286
Interior: Leather Bar 345
interpellation 146, 147, 148
In These Words 134
'In the Sun Room' 132

Intouchables 329
inversion model 93, 96
invisibility 30, 32, 34, 38, 44, 49, 50, 71, 91, 94
IRC (Internet Relay Chat) 175
Irvine, Janice 353
Ives, David 66
'I Wanna Love You' 263

Jackson, Sue 39
Jagose, Annamarie 397
James, E. L. 59, 67, 408, 429
Jameson, Jenna 314
J-Boy by Biblos 134
Jeffreys, Sheila 87–8
Jenkins, Henry 240
Jenkins, Tricia 40
Jenna's American Sex Star 314
Jesse McBride 170, 171
Jim and Tom, Sausalito 166
John, Mike 142
Johnson, Lyndon 384
Johnson, Paul 260
Jones, Quentin 256
Jones, Sara Gwenllian 121
Jong, Erica 86
Jorgensen, Christine 33
Journal of Graphic Novels and Comics 137
Journal of Women's Health, The 409
Judge, The 423
Juzwiak, Rich 101, 316

Kahan, Benjamin 20
Kakoudaki, D. 269
Kaleidescope 163
Kamise, Y. 130
Kane, Patrick 126
Kaplan, Louise 417
Kardashian, Kim 187, 249, 252, 436
Kardon, Janet 168
Karmen Geï 75
Katz, Jonathan Ned 85–6
Kaveney, Roz 32
Kavka, Misha 185, 359
Keane, Helen 352
Keesling, B. 209
Kendrick, Walter 383–4
Kennedy, H. 242
Kerner, I. 209
Kerrigan, Elliot 34
Ke$ha 363
Ketcham, Jennifer 357, 358
Kids Are All Right, The 45, 46, 76

'Kids Are All Right but the Lesbians Aren't, The' 41
Killing Me Softly 61, 62, 63
Killing of Sister George, The 99
Kim, Eunjung 23
Kim, J. L. 300
King, Geoff 154–5
King, Jaime 72
Kingsley, E. 209
Kink Bingo 125
Kink.com 154
Kinney, Nan 152
Kipling, Rudyard 371, 374
Kipnis, Laura 428
Kiss: A Memoir, The 422
Kizuna 134
Klein, N. A. 224
Klinger, Romi 315
Kodaka, Kazuma 134
Koons, Jeff 164–5, 169
Kouga, Yun 136
Krafft-Ebing, Richard 93, 406
Krzywinska, Tanya 242–3, 423–4
Kunkel, D. 227
Kurzbard, G. 269

Ladies Mercury 319
Lady Chatterley's Lover 107–8
Lady Gaga 248, 410
Lady's Magazine 319
Lake, Ricki 355–6, 359
Lambda Literary Award 112
La mosquitera 423
Lane, Anthony 409
LaNeuze, A. 274
'Lapdance' 264
lap dancing 363, 364–5, 366, 368
LA Pink – A XXX Porn Parody 157
L.A. Plays Itself 169
Larsson, Stieg 70
Last Exit to Brooklyn 52
'Lavender Scare' 49–50
Law and Order 405
Law Reform Committee (Victoria Parliament, Australia) 197–8
Lawrence, D. H. 107
Lawrence, Jennifer 189, 249
Léaud, Jean-Pierre 435
Leeds Mercury 378
Lee, Jiz 157, 401, 402
Lee, John Alan 411
Lee, Tommy 187, 249

legal debate (in art/porn) 165, 169–71
Lei, Keeani 145, 146
Leistner, C. E. 63
Léolo 423
Le Pornographe 435
lesbian representation: and advertising 271–3; authenticity 38, 42–4; dialogue, performance and costume 42–3; and femininity 42; and heterosexuality 39, 41, 42–3, 44–5, 46; pornography 43–4, 46; and queer representation 95–6; and sex advice books 203, 204, 206, 208–9; terminology and definition 39–42; and women's magazines 320; *see also* homosexuality
Leslie, John 187, 434
'Le Telefon' 263
Levande, Meredith 259
Levine, Elana 300
Levinson, Jerrold 168–9
Levy, Ariel 364, 365
Lewinsky, Monica 354
Lewis, Lisa 261
Ley, David 356
Life 74
'Lil Freak' 74
Lindsay, John 432
Liquid Modernity 349
Literotica 178
Little Britain 33
Little Mix 264
Liverpool House of the Ford 377
Loftus, David 390
Logue, Anna 153
London Society for the Rescue of Fallen Women 377
Longstaff, Gareth 357
Looking 101
Loops 432
Lopez, Jennifer 252
Lopiano, Donna 283
L'Origine de la guerre 166
L'Origine du monde 165–6
Lorre, Peter 95
Lost and Delirious 38
Lost Girl 41, 76
Lou, NYC 166–7
Love A La Carte! 136
Love, Albert G. 7
Love, Courtney 363
Love Crime 73
Love Island 189
Lovelace 435

Lovelace, Linda 435
Loveless 136
'Love Shack' 121
Love, Sinnamon 401
Lovett, James 358
Lowder, Brian 101
Lowe, Rob 183–4, 186, 187
Lowman, John 372, 374
Lucas, Cristina 367
Luckett, M. 86
Lucky 13 366
Ludacris 264
Luhrmann, Baz 75
'lumbersexual' figure 345–6
'luscious lesbian' figure 272
Lusty Lady, The 368
Luxuria Superbia 240, 244–5, 246
L Word, The 40, 41, 43, 100

McCall, Leena 164
MacCallum-Stewart, E. 242
McCarthy, Anna 76
McCarthy, Joseph 49
McCarthy, Paul 170
McConaughey, Matthew 75
McCormack, Mark 345
McDougall, Joyce 417
MacGowan, Sharon 42
McGraw, Phil 356, 359
Machin, D. 320, 325
Machinima 241–2
Macho Sluts 59, 67
McKai, Eon 156
MacKay, S. 286
McKee, A. 276
McKellen, Sir Ian 50
MacKinnon, Catherine 431
McNair, Brian 269, 270, 329, 349, 419, 422
McRobbie, Angela 261
McWhorter, Ladelle 397
Maddison, Stephen 347
Made in Heaven series 164–5, 169
Madoka, Aoi 136
Madonna 249, 250, 259, 261, 410
Maginn, Paul 420
Mainstreaming Sex 419
Maltese Falcon, The 95
Malti-Douglas, Fedwa 354
Manet, Édouard 366
Manga, erotic: Boys' Love 130–7; and child pornography 135, 136–7; female fans and authorship 130–1, 132–3, 134, 135; legal issues and controversy 130, 133, 135, 136–7; and pornography 134–5, 136–7; rape and consent 135; *shonen-ai* 130, 132–3, 136; *shotacon* (mxm) 130, 131, 133, 135–6; and slash stories 131–2; *yaoi* 130, 131, 133–5, 136
Manganello, J. 227
Mangold, James 64
Manhunt 217
Mansfield, Elizabeth 171
Mapplebeck, Victoria 310
Mapplethorpe, Robert 163, 164, 166–8, 170, 171
Mara, Rooney 46, 70
Marchant, Diana 119
Mark, K. P. 63
Marnie 64
marriage: and BDSM representation 60, 61, 65; and heterosexual casual sex 81, 84, 85, 86; and queer representation 102; same-sex 102, 123, 124, 334; and sex advice books 203, 205; and slash stories 123, 124; and women's magazines 319
Marriner, C. 228
Mars and Venus in the Bedroom 204
Martha Stewart Living 410
Martin, A. 67
Martin, Richard Harrison 420
Marwick, Alice 188
Marx, Karl 86
Mary Tyler Moore Show, The 86
Masaki, Satō 131
masculinity: and advertising 271, 273, 274–5; and bisexualities 70, 74, 77; and gay sexualities 52, 53, 55; and lesbian representation 39, 42, 43; and metrosexuals 343–7, 348, 349; and pornographers 431, 433; and queer representations 93, 98; and sitcoms 300, 302, 306; and trans representation 29, 30, 31; and women in action sports 279, 280, 282, 284; and women's magazines 319, 323
Massanari, Adrienne 189
masturbation: and beastiality 423; and celebrity media 249; and erotica 114; and horror 295; and pornography 145, 146; and pornography consumers 385, 389; and queer sexualities 92, 94; and sexuality education 226; and videogames 243, 244
Mating in Captivity 209
Matoh, Sanami 134
Maurice 52
Ma vie en Rose 30
Maxim 282, 283
Max mon amour 423

Maye, Marilyn 263
MDPOPE: Most Disturbed Person on Planet Earth 291
Meese Commission 434
Memoirs of a Woman of Pleasure 429
Memory Slips 422–3
memory-work project 174, 175, 178–80
Men of Tattoos 132
Men's Journal 24
Merck, Mandy 398
Messner, M. 282
metrosexuals: and advertising 271; and heterosexuality 343–4, 346, 347–8; and homosexuality 344, 345, 347–8; and masculinity 343–7, 348, 349; and plastic sexuality 348–9; sex and sexualisation 347–8
Metzger, Radley 431–2
Meyer, Richard 168
Meyer, Russ 431
Meyer, Stephanie 59
Mickalene Thomas 166
Middleton, Kate 249, 252
Middleton, Pippa 252
Mildred Pierce 73
Milillo, D. 320
Miller, Jody 264
Miller, Margo 302, 306
Miller, T. 346
Miller v. California (1973) 291
Mills, Brett 300, 302, 304, 305, 306, 307
Minaj, Nicki 74, 259, 265–6
Minami, Haruka 136
Ming-liang, Tsai 78
Minogue, Kylie 252, 253
Minotaur 122
Mintz, L. 205
Miramax 156
'Missing Piece, The' 33
Mitchell, Artie 435
Mitchell, Jim 435
Mittell, Jason 301
Mixter, Whitney 315
Mock, Janet 33
Mondrian, Piet 367
'Money Maker' 264
'money shots' 113–14, 155, 310, 357–8
monogamy: and bisexualities 71–2, 75, 78; and heterosexual casual sex 81, 86; and porn performers 398–9; and queer representations 100; and sex advice books 202, 205–6, 209; and sitcoms 300, 305–6, 307; and slash stories 123–4; and women's magazines 319–20, 321, 323, 324–5
Monroe, Marilyn 249, 250, 254
'monsters' 330–1, 332
monstrative episodes 142
Monstrous-Feminine, The 293
Montagu, Lord Edward 52
Montrose 125, 126
Moore, Alan 64
'moral dumbfounding' 294
Moran, Caitlyn 365
Morgan, Jane 263
Morgan, Joan 284
Morgan, Jonathan 142
Morreale, Joanne 301
Mortimer, Robin 407
Mosley, Max 406
Mowlabocus, Sharif 93, 217
MPAA (Motion Picture Association of America) 243
MPPDA (Motion Pictures Producers and Distributors Association) Code 94, 99
Murakami, Maki 133
music video: and choreographed dance performances 261–2, 263; and race 265–6; Scopitone films 260, 262–4, 265; sexualisation of female bodies 259–60, 262–5; and strippers 362–3, 367; women in music industry 260–1; *see also* celebrity media
Muybridge, Eedweard 429
mxm (*shotacon*) 130, 131, 133, 135–6
Mya 363
My Best Friend's Wedding 99, 100
My Big Fat Gypsy Wedding 251
My Chemical Romance 125–7
My Cunt Is Wet With Fear 166
My Love Is Like …Wo 363
My Old Lady 423
My Secret Life 165
My Summer of Love 72

Naked and Afraid 313
Narain, Nicole 357
National Crime Agency 198
Native American cultures 50
'native white' American 7, 9, 10, 12–13, 14, 16
Natural High Studio 136
Natural History Magazine 10
Nazism 11, 49–50
Neko, Kichiku 134
Nelson, Winona 134
neoliberal feminism 283, 285–6

Neophytou, Nadia 59
NERD 264
NerdPr0n 153–4
Netmums 259
'new iconoclasm' 170
'new lad' figure 343, 349
New Line 156
'new man' figure 271, 343, 346, 349
'New Queer Cinema' 99
Newsday 409
News of the World 406
newspaper problem pages 209–10
New Statesman 260, 373
Newsweek 87, 352, 354
New Yorker 408, 409
New York Post 84, 407
New York Times 410, 422
Ng, Dania 223, 232
Nicholson, Bob 374
Niku Daruma/Tumbling Doll of Flesh 290–1
Ninn, Michael 434
Nitta, Youka 134
Nivens, David 315
Nixon, Richard 430
NoFauxxx.com 154, 156
No More Heroes 243, 244
Norma (statue) 7–8, 9, 10–16
'normal bodies' 8–11, 12–16
Normman (statue) 7–8, 9, 10–12, 16
norms and values discourse (sitcom study) 305–6
Nosferatu: Eine Symphonie des Grauens 290
Nostalgia 157
Nothing Compares 2 U 254
November Gymnasium, The 132
Nunn, Heather 310
Nurse Jackie 76
Nurses 148
Nymphomaniac series 73, 74, 422

Oasis 23
Object! 365
'object choice' 92–4
objectification 31, 127, 164, 242, 264, 282, 302, 322, 336, 364; and advertising 268, 271, 274–5; and celebrity 186, 190, 249, 251, 252; and metrosexuals 346, 347; and pornographers 432, 435
Object of My Affection, The 99
Obscene Publications Act (UK) 428–9
Ocean, Frank 362
O'Connor, Sinead 248, 254
OkCupid 27

O'Keefe, Georgia 166
O'Leary, Dermot 345
Olive, R. 286
Olsen, Ashley 423
Olsen, Mary-Kate 423
Olympia 366
One for the Girls! 108, 320
One Night at McCool's 65
online dating/dating apps: and representing gay sexualities 54–5; and sexual health 214; Tinder dating app 81, 82–5, 88
Only Way is Essex, The 345
On the City Wall 371
Oprah 358
Orange Is the New Black 41, 77
orgasm: and asexualities 23–4; and erotica 111, 113–14; and pornography 144, 145, 146; and porn performers 402; and sex advice books 203, 206, 208
Orgazmo 435, 436
Orientalism 387, 391
Origin of the Universe 2 166
Orphan Black 76
Oscar Wilde 51
Ôshima, Nagisa 423
otaku 136
'others'/'othering' 280, 281, 334, 372, 373, 383, 387–9, 390–1
Out of the Woods 31
Owens, Scott 153
Oxford University and City Herald 375
Ozon, François 78

Paasonen, Susanna 310
Paddick, Hugh 52
Page, Bettie 410
Pall Mall Gazette 377
Pam and Tommy Lee 187
panopticism 279
Pan's People 262
'pansy'/'sissy' characters 52, 53, 95, 98, 100
Pantti, M. 310
Papadopoulos, Linda 274–5
Paré, Ambroise 330
'parodic repetition' 158
Parsler, J. 242
Parsons, Lena Jan 183
Part-Time Perverts 416, 417, 420
Party in the U.S.A. 253
Pasolini, Pier Paolo 429
Passion 73
pathological mimicry 72–3

Patterson, Z. 190, 314
Paul, Pamela 419
Pearce, S. 227
Peckham, Morse 164
Peele, Stanton 352–3
PEGI (Pan European Games Information) 241, 243
Peirce, Charles 311
Penal Code 377 (India) 51
Peniche, Kari Ann 357
People magazine 183
People vs Larry Flynt, The 430
Perel, E. 209
Perfectly Average 8, 9
Perfect Medium, The 170
Perfect Moment, The 167, 168, 170
Perry, Imani 259
Perversion: The Erotic Form of Hatred 417
perverts: bestiality 423–4; defining 416–18; and deviance 416, 417–18; and fashion 420–2, 425; and homosexuality 418, 420, 421; incest 422–3; perversion in popular media 422–4, 425; and pornography 416, 418–19, 421, 422–3, 425; and voyeurism 422–4, 425
Peyser, Eve 88
Peyton Place 86
Pfeffer, Carla A. 27
Philadelphia 99
philosophical debate (in art/porn) 164–5, 168–9
Philosophy and Literature 168
Piano Teacher, The 61, 63
Piccadilly International 367
Pico No Boku 136
Picture of Dorian Gray, The 93
Piercy, Marge 86
Piess, Kathy 86
Pieta 170
Pink and White Productions 154, 155, 157
Pink Flamingos 423
pinklabel.tv 155, 156
pinku eiga 290
Pinsky, Drew 356–9
Pionko, Daria 373, 374, 379
PIV (penis-in-vagina) intercourse 113, 114, 203, 206, 207, 208
plastic sexuality 348–9
Playboy magazine 250, 421, 429, 431, 432
Playboy: The Mansion 240, 241, 244
Playing with the Edge 167
Play School 45
Polanski, Roman 66, 423
pole-dancing 362, 363, 366, 367, 368

Politics of Rehearsal, The 366
Polyamory: Married and Dating 313, 314, 316
Poole, Wakefield 151
porn auteurs 431–2
Porn Brokers, The 432
'porn creep' 419, 422
porn empires 429–31
Porn Film Festival Berlin 108, 110
'pornification'/'pornographication' 1, 109, 177, 180, 189, 253, 270, 329, 416, 418–19
Pornified 419
Pornland: How Porn Has Hijacked Our Culture 388
'porno chic' 151, 255, 419
Pornographer, The 435
pornographers: building porn empires 429–31; female pornographers 432–3; in film 434–6; gay pornographers 433; 'golden age' of porn 433–4; porn auteurs 431–2; as transgressive figures 428–9
'pornographic art' 168–9, 171
pornography: and advertising 269, 270, 271, 272–3; alternative pornographies *see* alternative pornographies; amateur *see* amateur pornography; art/porn debate *see* art/porn debate; celebrity sex tapes *see* celebrity sex tapes; child pornography 135, 136–7, 170, 171, 194–5, 197–8; consumers of *see* pornography consumers; and disabled people 329; and erotica 107–8, 109, 114; and erotic Manga 134–5, 136–7; 'extreme pornography' 163, 170–1, 295; feature pornography *see* feature pornography; feminist porn 31–2, 108, 110, 152, 395, 401; 'golden age' of porn 433–4; gonzo pornography *see* gonzo pornography; and horror 290–1, 292, 294–5; lesbian representation in film and TV 43–4, 46; performers *see* porn performers; and perverts 416, 418–19, 421, 422–3, 425; pornographers *see* pornographers; and reality TV 309–15, 316–17; representing gay sexualities 53–4; revenge porn 176, 185, 187; and sex addicts 356–7; and sexuality education 228–9, 390; and trans representations 29, 30–3
pornography consumers: history of 383–6; journalistic coverage of pornography consumption 386–7; negative effects of pornography consumption 384–6; 'othering' of 383, 387–9, 390–1; and violence 384–5; voices of 389–90; young people 387–9
porn performers: as experts 394–6; and feminism 394, 395–6, 401; and homosexuality 394, 397, 398–402; pornographic becomings 400–2;

pornography as a queer space 398–400; and sexual identity 396–8, 399, 400–2; and sexual pleasure 394, 396, 397–8, 399, 400, 402; victim/agent divide 394, 395, 402
Porn Studies 395
Portrait of Ms Ruby Ray, Standing 164
'Portrait of the American People' 10, 12
Portsmouth Social Purity Organisation 377
'positive' characters/images 41, 99
Potts, A. 204, 206
Pour It Up 363
power discourse (sitcom study) 306–7
Pramaggiore, Maria 71
Preaching to the Perverted 65, 66
Preciado, Paul B. 157
Presley, Elvis 260
Preston, John 108
'Pretty Girls Everywhere!' 262, 263
Pretty Little Liars 40
Price, Katie ('Jordan') 187
Price of Salt, The 45
Prince Shoutoku 133
Prince William 252
Pringle, Helen 383
Private Practice 105
'pro-Dommes' 406, 407, 409, 410, 411–12
Production Code (US) 242–3
Professionals, The 119, 120
Prostitute's Body, The 377
PROTECT Act (US) 136–7
Prügl, E. 286
Przybylo, E. 20
Psycho 97, 98
PUAs (pick-up artists) 85
Puccini for Beginners 75–6
Pulp Fiction 62
Pyramids 362

Queer as Folk 39, 41, 100, 123–4, 125
Queer Eye for the Straight Guy 101
queerporn.tv 32, 156
queer representation: era of visibility 99–102; history of modern queerness 92–4; inversion model 93, 96; and invisibility 91, 94; screening queer sexualities 94–8; sexology 91–4, 95–6; slash stories *see* slash stories
queer space, pornography as 398–400
queer theory 20, 394, 397
Quinn, Marc 31

race: and BDSM representation 65; and bisexual representation 77–8; and celebrity media 251, 252–3; and music video 265–6; 'native white' Americans 7, 9, 10, 12–13, 14, 16; and 'normal bodies' 8–9, 12–13, 16; and racism 383, 390; and sexting 195; and 'sex-work saviour complex' 371–2; and sitcoms 301; and trans representations 33
Race, K. 84, 217
'Race Is On, The' 264
Radway, J. A. 60
Rahn, A. 184–5
Railton, D. 252–3
Raimondi, Marcantonio 429
Rainy, Sarah 373
Randell, Suze 432
Rapace, Noomi 70
rape 22, 23, 61, 64, 112, 111–13, 135, 290, 291, 294–5
Rated X 435
'raunch culture' 253, 364
Raver Porn 153
Raymond, Paul 430
Reage, Pauline 429
reality TV: and authenticity 311, 312–13, 314; and celebrity 185, 186, 187, 189–90, 248; and fantasy 310 11, 314, 317; and metrosexuals 345; nudity and real sex 313–16; and political progressiveness of 316, 317; and pornography 309–15, 316–17; 'under a blanket' scenes 310–13
Real L Word, The 315
Real Sex 313–14
Rebecca 97
Red Butt 169
Reddit 188
Redmond, Sean 186
referential communication 147
relationship normativity 205–6
religion 24, 51, 87, 109, 167, 290, 330–1, 389
'representation matters' 91, 94
'reveal' 29–30
revenge porn 176, 185, 187
Rice, Anne 131
Richard 167
Richards, Jen 34
Ricki Lake 355–6, 359
Rihanna 252, 259, 363, 410
Riley, Naomi Schafer 84, 88
Riptide Publishing 110
Roberts, Julia 100
Robertson, Josephine 12–14
Robeson, Paul 249
Robyn 284–5

Rock, Chris 46
Rockler, Naomi R. 301–2, 307
Rogen, Seth 345
Rojek, C. 250
role models 39, 53, 255, 260, 281, 344
Rolling Stone magazine 409, 423
romance fiction 108–9, 111–13
romantic dramas 59, 61, 65, 66
Ronsō, Yaoi 131
Root, Rebecca 34
Rope 97
Rossi, Kendra Jade 357
Rossi, L. -M. 269
'Round the Horne' 52–3
Rowe, Ken 31
Rowlandson, Thomas 429
Roy, Duncan 357
Royalle, Candida 152, 432–3
Rubber Dollies 153
Rubin, Gayle 81, 406, 411
Rubin, Lillian 85, 87
Rules, The 85
RuPaul 31, 33
Rush, E. 274
'Russian Girls' 265
Russ, Joanna 117, 119
Russo, Julie Levin 117, 157
Russo, V. 52, 99

'S&M' 410
Sacher-Masoch, Leopold von 406
sadomasochism *see* BDSM
'safe words' 60, 409
Said, Edward 387, 391
Saigado 136
Saint-Hilaire, Étienne Geoffroy 331
Saitō, T. 136
Sales, Nancy Jo 83, 84–5, 88
Sally Jessy Raphael 355
Salon 344
Saltz, Gail 354–5
'Salute' 264
Salvation Army 377
same-sex marriage 102, 123, 124, 334
Sandell, Jillian 302, 303, 307
Sanders, Teela 365, 368, 369
Sanger, Margaret 86
Sassbandit 125, 126–7
'saturated masculinity' 349
Saturated Self, The 349
Saturday Review, The 375
Savage, Dan 31

Savage Grace 73
Schechter, Brian 127
Schlessinger Jr, Arthur 343, 346
Schlosser, Eric 429
Schneider, Sherrie 85
Schodt, F. L. 130
Schubert, C. 296
'scissoring' 44
Scodari, Christine 300
Scopitone films 260, 262–4, 265
Scott, A. O. 296
Screw magazine 430
Scruff 54, 218
Seburt, Tara 183
Second Sex, The 387
second-wave feminism 283–4
Secretary 61, 63, 66, 410, 422
Secret Sex Stash, The 357
Sedgwick, Eve 93, 96
Seid, Danielle M. 29–30
Seinfeld 424
self-help industry 202–3, 210
'selfies' 54, 188–9
self-improvement 7, 11, 15, 16
Self-Portrait 166
self-representation 53–5, 187–90, 285, 395
Sell Your Sex Tape 177
semantic intensification 145
Sender, K. 346
Sense8 33
Sentinel, The 122
Serano, Julia 31
Serbian Film/Srpski Film, A 291, 294–6, 434
Serious Charge 51
Serrano, Andres 163, 170
Sex 250
sex addicts: diagnosis and 'treatment' of 352, 353, 355, 356–7; history of sex addiction 352–3, 354; and media 353–9; TV talk shows 354, 355–6, 357–9
sex advice books: authors of 204–5; contemporary books 203–4; and heterosexual casual sex 85; newspaper problem pages 209–10; 'problem' concept 202, 205–6, 209; resistance to 208–9; self-help industry 202–3, 210; and sexual improvement 24; 'solutions' 202–3, 204, 207–8, 209; and trans sexualities 29
Sex and the City 300, 333–4, 347, 421
Sex Education 276
'sex for health' discourse 24
Sex Myth, The 208

sexology 11, 27–8, 91–4, 95–6, 144, 147, 203, 397
Sex Rehab with Dr. Drew 356–9
Sex Tape 184
sexting: abstinence from 193, 197, 198; alternative responses to 197–8; and child pornography 194–5, 197–8; and consent 193, 195, 196, 197–8, 199; criminalisation of 193, 194–5, 198; and gender disparities 193, 195–6; media panic over 193–6, 198–9; and social media 188
Sex Tips from a Dominatrix 410
Sexual Behavior in the Human Female 96
Sexual Behaviour in the Human *Male 96
sexual health: HIV/AIDS *see* HIV/AIDS; and homosexuality 214, 215, 216–18, 219; public health promotions 214–15; and sexuality education 224–5, 228; and sex workers 375, 379; and social media 214–19; and women's magazines 323; and young people 215–16
sexual imperative 205, 209, 210
sexual improvement 24
Sexual Inversion 93
sexualisation: of children' 223, 228, 274–6; of culture 31, 114, 177, 249, 253, 269, 343, 347; of media 2, 109, 196, 268; of women 251–3, 253–4, 255, 259–60, 282, 286, 362, 364; *see also* hypersexualisation
Sexualisation of Young People Review 274
sexuality education: and advertising 276; history of 224–5; media effects 226–8, 231–2; pleasure and desire in 225–6, 227, 228, 231; and pornography 228–9, 390; and relationships 230–1; in schools 223–4, 225, 226, 227, 228, 230, 231–2; and sexual health 224–5, 228; and 'sexualisation of children' 223, 228; and social media 229–30
sexual scripts 109–10
Sex Work 395
sex workers: and childhood trauma 63–4, 66; contemporary media portrayal of 373–4, 379; and fashion 420; as 'great social evil' 374, 375–8, 379; porn performers *see* porn performers; 'sex-work saviour complex' 371–2, 373, 375–6, 377–9; and stigma 63–4, 66, 369, 395; and Victorian newspapers 371–2, 374–7
'sex-work saviour complex' 371–2, 373, 375–6, 377–9
'sexy bad girl' representations 280–2
Shakespeare, Tom 328, 329
Shame 73, 74
Shameless 41
Shapiro, Harry L. 10–11, 12, 14

Shattuc, Jane 355
Shi, L. 40
Shogakukan Manga Award 132
shojo 132
shonen-ai 130, 132–3, 136
Shortbus 23–4
shotacon (mxm) 130, 131, 133, 135–6
Showgirls 363
Showtime 313, 315
Shunga 164
Sickert, Walter 366
Side Effects 73
Silverman, Sue William 355
Simmons, Gene 187
Simon, W. 109
Simpson, Mark 271, 343, 344, 346, 347
Simpsons, The 424
Sinatra, Frank 260
Sinfield, Alan 347
Single Woman, The 11
'sissy'/'pansy' characters 52, 53, 95, 98, 100
Sister 368
Sitcom 423
sitcoms: depicting sex 302–3; *desires and fantasies discourse* 304–5; discursive meanings of sex practices 303–7; *feelings discourse* 303–4; heterosexuality and masculinity 300, 301, 302, 305–6; and homosexuality 300, 301, 306; and humour 300, 301, 304, 305, 307; *norms and values discourse* 305–6; *power discourse* 306–7; study of 300–2
Skidmore, Martha 14, 15
Skin Flicks 431
Skins 40
'Skirtboarders' blog 286
Slade, Joseph 434
Slash 420
slash stories: and BDSM 124–5, 126–7; and erotic Manga 131–2; and fantasy 117; female authorship of 117, 118, 119–20, 123, 124; and feminism 118, 123, 124; femslash 117; first-wave narratives 118–21, 127; and heterosexuality 117, 121, 123; and HIV/AIDS 119, 120, 122; and 'kink' 124–5; political and social issues 118, 119–20, 121–4, 125–8; second-wave narratives 121–4, 127; and self-identification 124; third-wave narratives 124–7; and videogames 241
Slate 76
Slavesen, Britt 170
'Small Potatoes' 263
Smith, Amber 357

Smith, Clarissa 60, 171, 320, 389, 423
Smith, Jack 151
Snakes on a Plane 423–4
Snapchat 188
Snoop Dogg 263
snuff movies 434
Sober House 357
social media: and celebrity media 248, 249, 252, 253; and celebrity sex tapes 187–90; and representing gay sexualities 54–5; and sexting 188; and sexual health 214–19; and sexuality education 229–30; and strippers 369; and Tinder dating app 81, 82, 84; trans representations 27, 31, 33; and women in action sports 285, 286
Socrates 194
Soley, L. 269
Solomon-Godeau, A. 165
Somers, C. L. 225
Song of the Wind and Trees 132
Sopranos, The 422
Sothern, M. 209
Southern, Terry 432
South of Nowhere 39, 40
Spears, Britney 251, 255
spectacular space 142
Spence, Kate 368
Speranza 119–20, 122
'spicing it up' 207–8
'spornosexual' figure 346–7
Sports Illustrated 281, 283
Springsteen, Bruce 420, 421
Staffordshire County Refuge for Discharged Prisoners and Fallen Women 377
Stagliano, John 433–4
Stanley Parable, The 240
Stanley, Richard T. 260
Stargate: Atlantis 125
Star Trek 118, 119, 131
Starr, Allanah 31
Starsky & Hutch 119, 120–1
Stead, William T. 377–8
Steele, J. R. 227
Steele, Valerie 420–1
Stehli, Jemima 367–8
Steinem, Gloria 107
Steinmetz, Christine 420
Stekel, Wilhelm 406
stigma: and asexuality 20; and BDSM 60, 62–3, 405, 406–7, 410; and disabled people 335; and erotica 110; and heterosexual casual sex 85; and homosexuality 53–4, 418; and horror 294; and sexting 198; and sexual health 216; and sex workers 63–4, 66, 369, 395; and trans sexualities 29, 31
STIs (sexually transmitted infection) 87, 214, 215, 216–18, 224, 225, 228; *see also* sexual health
Stokes, Peter 152
Stoller, Richard J. 417
Stone, Sharon 249
'straight panic' 101
Strauss, Neil 85
'Strawberry Pop Tarts' 122
Strike a Pose 368
Strip 367–8
Strip City 364
strippers: and art 366–9; and dancing 362–3, 364–5, 366, 367, 368; feminist critique 364–6; and music videos 362–3, 367; striptease in popular culture 362–4
'Stripping the Illusion' 365
Striptease Culture 419
Stryker, Susan 29
stud cultures 29
Sturman, Reuben 429, 430
'subjectification' 202, 271, 347
'subversive re-appropriation' 158
Sugar Rush 41
Suicide Girls 154
Sullivan, David 430
'Summertime Sadness' 72, 74
Sun 432
Sunderland Daily Echo and Shipping Gazette 378
Sunsilk 408
Surmann, A. T. 225
sur-porno 158
Survivor 310
SWA (Society for Women Artists) 164
Swift, Taylor 248
'Switch' 125, 126
syntactic deconstruction 145

Taggart, Michele 282
Takahashi, Mako 136
'Take Clothes off as Directed' 125
Takemiya, Keiko 132
Tan, C. 113
Tangerine 33
Taormino, T. 276
Taylor, T. L. 242
Teahouse 134
Teen Choice Awards 253
teen pregnancy 224, 225

teratology 331
Texas Chain Saw Massacre, The 294
Texas School Safety programme 196
That Girl 86
Theogony 108
Theophano, T. 44
Theory of Everything, The 329
Theory of Flight 329
'The women! They're using gadgets and having sex!' 84
Thicke, Robin 253, 264–5
Think Before You Post campaign 197
'Thinking sex' 81
third-wave feminism 283, 284–5
Thomas, Kamini 207
Thomas, Kirk 207
Thomas, Paul 434
Thornborrow, J. 320, 325
Three 169
Tibbals, Chauntelle Anne 141
Tiefer, Leonore 328–9
Time magazine 7, 33, 353, 354, 355, 406
Time Out New York 410
Times 377, 378
Tinder 81, 82–5, 88, 214, 218
'Tinder effect' 84, 85, 88
Titian 366
Today.com 354–5
Today Show, The 354–5
Todd, Tracy 353
Toews, Jonathan 126
Tohill, Cathal 290
Tombs, Pete 290
Tompkins, Betty 166
Tongue Tied 255–6
Tootsie 113
Top of the Pops 261–2, 264, 265
Toulouse-Lautrec, Henri de 366
Tracks 282
TrannyFags 31, 32
Trannywood Pictures 31, 32
Trans Bodies, Trans Selves 29
Trans Comedy Awards 34
transformative play 241–2
Trans Grrrls: Revolution Porn Style Now! 33
Trans Media Watch 33
trans-misogyny 31, 34
Transparent 77
trans sexualities: framing trans representation politics 27–8; genital epistemologies 29–30; and LGBT identities 28–9; and pornography 29, 30–3; proliferation of press coverage 33–4; and social media 27, 31, 33; trans activism 28
travesti cultures 29
Traynor, Chuck 435
Tredwell, Aaron 33
Trials of Oscar Wilde, The 51
Trouble, Courtney 32, 33, 156, 157
Trouble with Normal, The 124
Truffaut, Francois 435
Trump, Donald 421
TSQ: Transgender Studies Quarterly 29
Tulisa 187
Tumblr 55, 188, 189
Turner, Graeme 186, 187, 250
Turner, Ted 156
Turner, Tina 265
Tutti, Cosey Fanni 367, 368
'twerking' 253, 362
Twilight series 59, 117, 178
Twister 243, 245
Twitter 188, 248, 285, 286
'two-spirit' identities 50
Tyler, M. 206
Tyra Show, The 358

Ugly George 433
Ui, M. 130
Uidhir, Christy Mag 169
Undateables, The 329–30, 333–7
'under a blanket' scenes (reality TV) 310–13
Undertow 74
United States Armed Forces 49
Untitled #211 (Hand in Butt) 163
UPIAS (Union of the Physically Impaired Against Segregation) 333
'upskirting' 251
Usher 74, 187

Valentine, David 29
Van Bauwel, Sofie 300
van Doorn, Niels 176–7
van Hooff, J. 210
Vanity Fair 83–4
'variations' 207
Varone, Phil 357
VCA 156
Vee, Bobby 262–3, 264
Venus in Fur (film) 66
Venus in Furs (novel) 66, 406
Venus of Urbino 366
Vermeire, Jill 358
Versace, Gianni 410, 420

Victim 51
victim/agent divide 394, 395, 402
Victorian newspapers 371–2, 375–9
Victoria's Secret 109
videogames: comparisons with other media 239, 240–2, 246; games about sex 240, 243–5, 246; and 'gamification' of sex 239, 243; and humour 240, 244, 246; hypersexualised avatars 239–40, 242; representations of sex 239–40, 242–3, 244, 246
View, The 421
Violet 363
Violette 74–5
Vivid Alt 156
voyeurism 43, 124, 147, 269, 292, 345, 422–4, 425

Wakefield, Jerome 352
Walk All Over Me 65, 66
Walking Dead: A Hardcore Parody, The 290
Walkowitz, J. R. 375
Wallace, Sophia 114
Walt Disney Company 156
Walter, Natasha 364–5
Wan, Gok 337
Warhol, Andy 151, 169, 433
Warner, Michael 124, 305
War Workers 13–14
Watching Sex 390
Watchmen 64
Water Lilies 73
Waters, John 423
Watson, P. 252–3
Way, Gerard 127
webcomics 134
Weber, Brenda 356
Weiss, Doug 356
Well of Loneliness, The 52
Wells, C. 225
Wendelin, G. 374, 375
Wendell, S. 113
West, Amy 185, 359
West, Kanye 248–9
Whipping Girl 31
Whip Your Life into Shape! The Dominatrix Principle 410
WHO (World Health Organisation) 225
Who Framed Roger Rabbit? 424
Whores and Other Feminists 395
'Why Bisexual Women are TV's Hot New Thing' 76
'Why Pornography Can't Be Art' 169
Wicked Pictures 142
Wilde, Oscar 52, 93
Wild Search, The 157
Will and Grace 41, 418, 423, 424
Williams, Kenneth 52
Williams, Linda 30, 43, 44, 292, 311–12, 315
Williams, R. 268
Wilson, Glenn 408
Winfrey, Oprah 358
Winsor, Kathleen 109
women's magazines: and feminism and postfeminism 319, 321–2, 323; and 'great sex' 320, 323–5; and hetero-monogamous relationships 319–20, 321–2, 323, 324–5; history of 319; representations of sex 319, 320; sociocultural context 320–3; *see also* specific magazines
Women's Sports Foundation 283
Wonderful Pistachios 408
'Wonders of Life, The' 11
Wood, Sam Taylor 345
Woodiwiss, J. 210
Woodruff, Ron 75
Woods, Tiger 250
Woolfson, Alex 134
Worcestershire Chronicle 377
World, The 74
World of Warcraft 241–2
World's Fair (New York, 1939) 9, 11
Wrecking Ball 253, 254
Wright, Mark 345

X Portfolio 166–7, 170

Yamagishi, Ryouko 133
Yamane, Ayano 134
yaoi 130, 131, 133–5, 136
Yatabe, Katsuyoshi 136
Year 24 Group 132
'Yoncé' 264, 265
Yoshida, Akimi 133
Young, S. D. 217
YouPorn 176, 184
YouTube 248

Zack and Miri Make a Porno 435, 436
Zak, Laura 34
Zanghellini, A. 135
Zecca, Federico 158
Zesty 271, 273–4